It was a beautiful day. Blue sky, ... fleecy clouds. We rode ..... the East bank of the ..... Godesberg in which Chamberlain ..... We could see in the distance the Hotel ..... Chamberlain stayed. The lunch was ..... Hitler's bedroom. The Rhineland was ..... a suggestion of brown, with the Rhine ..... serene, powerful & majestic.

We left the bikes in a shed & walk..... Roland's Eck. Elsie was very beautif..... with her white blouse, her pink cheeks, and ..... from her forehead, very winsome & ne.....

We took lunch in the Roland's ..... (probably salted!), bread, and water (if ..... had to pay!). We talked — then we rode ..... twilight. That night we talked, an..... our position, especially the potential ..... disturbed us. ..... the shell was bro.....

An Eye for Eternity

AN EYE FOR ETERNITY

The life of Manning Clark

MARK McKENNA

For Fiona, Siobhan and Claire McKenna

THE MIEGUNYAH PRESS
An imprint of Melbourne University
Publishing Limited
187 Grattan Street, Carlton,
Victoria 3053, Australia
mup-info@unimelb.edu.au
www.mup.com.au

First published 2011
Reprinted 2011
Text © Mark McKenna, 2011
Design and typography © Melbourne
University Publishing Limited, 2011

Designed by Pfisterer + Freeman
Typeset by J&M Typesetting
Printed in China by Australian Book Connection

National Library of Australia
Cataloguing-in-Publication entry

McKenna, Mark, 1959–
Title: An Eye for Eternity: the life of Manning
Clark / Mark McKenna.
ISBN: 9780522856170 (hbk.)
Notes: Includes bibliographical references and index.

Clark, Manning, 1915–1991.
Historians—Australia—Biography.
Australia—Historiography.

Dewey Number: 994.007202

Come now, let us consider the generations of Man,

Compound of dust and clay, strengthless,

Tentative, passing away as leaves in autumn

Pass, shadows, wingless, forlorn,

Phantoms deathbound, a dream.

ARISTOPHANES, *The Birds*

CONTENTS

... 'Hoping ... and am very unhappy about it. ... to be leading a more disciplined ... an unhappier life to be ... well ... for yourself-conscious, and ... much by ... take over me ...

PART ONE

1: SONG OF HIMSELF

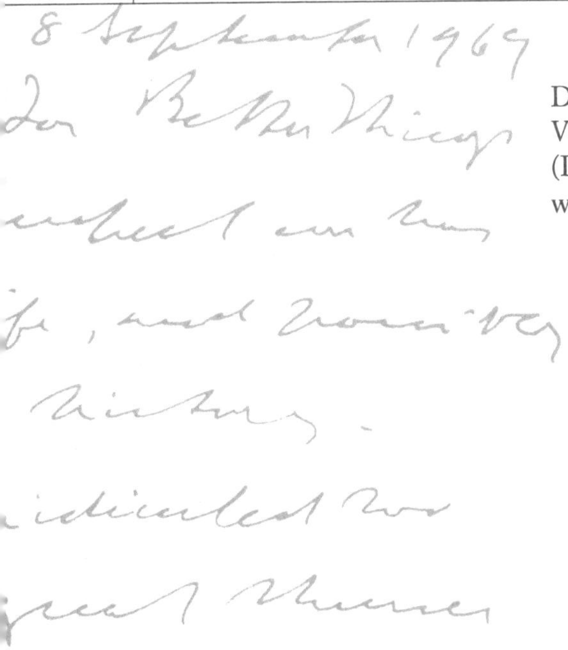
8 September 1969

> Do I contradict myself?
> Very well then I contradict myself,
> (I am large, I contain multitudes.)
>
> WALT WHITMAN, *Song of Myself*, 1855

His voice sounded the entire person. In its melodious timbre and infinite variation, it said everything there was about him.

On 15 November 1990, an old family friend wrote to him after seeing him interviewed on national television: 'your voice is the same as it was when you were about fourteen, staying with us at Rockwood'. He was then seventy-five. Throughout his life, even to his last years, his voice seemed to remain on the point of breaking, trembling slightly as it took flight. In sound recordings, one hears the voice of the mature and older man: soft, gravelly, vulnerable, a voice that seems always to be about to whisper the most intimate details in your ear, a voice that you must strain to hear yet cannot turn away from. It draws you in. Now and then, it is shot through with sudden gusts of laughter. It pauses often, as if to summon strength. The words are often heavy with melancholy, yet the sound of the voice embodies lightness, as if at any moment it might break into song. From his first years, he had an impressive singing voice. Friends describe his conversational voice as 'musical', 'tentative, even reluctant'; yet all the while its musicality 'made you want to listen'.

For those who knew him well, the memory of his voice still conjures the spirit of the man. Close friend Pat White, the partner of historian Don

Baker, recalls that it was 'the most memorable thing about him: you always had a sense that something was going on … His voice had this dancing pitch and tone to it. He loved to tell you things quietly, especially on the telephone. He was a lover of the secretive and the enigmatic.' Novelist Helen Garner remembers his long vowels, 'a light, teasing tone, and a kind of posh accent, but always a trickle of incipient laughter in his manner'. His voice would drop in mock seriousness, becoming almost inaudible before some light-heartedness, quickening slightly as the moment of delivery approached. The receiver would frequently be addressed formally, in hushed tone— 'Listen to this Miss Ford', 'Now Mr Hancock,' 'Tell me Mr Brown'—only heightening the comic effect. In tutorials, his voice was soft. 'If you wanted to hear him (and his jokes) you'd have to sit in the front row.' His voice could drop very low. His spoken voice possessed greater humility than his writing voice, perhaps because in the more fluid realm of conversation it floated, 'gentle, wavering, at times cracking to falsetto'.

Writing his obituary in 1991, historian Ken Inglis recalled 'a different voice for the prophet on the platform: hard, with much less variety than in ordinary speech, as he prompted himself from his black notebook', observing that 'the prophet who called on his people to declare themselves independent of Anglo–Australia did so in vowels of Anglo–Australian purity'.

Was he a simple boy from the Australian bush, as he so often claimed? His accent echoed the early twentieth century Australia in which it was formed—the educated Melbourne Protestant world of the 1930s—the very origins some would later accuse him of betraying.

Poet Alan Gould, a student in Canberra in the 1960s, remembers him as the first university lecturer heard to 'say fuck in the voice of the gentility'. From his first years as a schoolteacher in his early twenties until his emergence as a public figure in his sixties and seventies, he always held his audience. Some who saw him speak in public describe how he had them 'eating out of his hand'.

Sometimes he teetered on the edge of nervous collapse before shouting his way out. Addressing the Alice Springs Folk Festival in 1987, he began shakily, declaring 'I'm a historian, not a prophet', but by the time he read the words of Henry Lawson's 'Song of the Republic', he was sounding very much like a prophet, his voice exploding in fierce, declamatory bursts. Even on a public platform, he had an uncanny ability to cut through at a personal level, his voice retreating into confessional mode, wondering out loud; posing questions of faith and national direction in a quivering vernacular that managed to inspire a kind of love. From middle-age, on radio and television, he would occasionally stop talking mid-flight, as if pausing to signal an emotional impact so profound he could no longer speak. On TV, such moments would be accompanied by downcast eyes and bodily trembling, deeply felt performances, which, in retrospect, appear half-feigned. But this was part of his magic, you were never quite sure if he was having you on.[1]

His everyday speech, like his prose, was peppered with the voices of the canon—literary, historical and biblical phrases dredged from the classics, often without attribution. Every act of speech, even life itself, was transformed into an ongoing literary festival. He spoke through others, hiding himself behind the voices of writers past. His father, an Anglican clergyman, laced his speech with the language of the gospels, every experience and possibility in life drawing breath from the life of Christ. In this sense, the son mimicked the father's way of speaking, adding layers of erudition through his knowledge of literary apostles such as Dostoyevsky and Tolstoy. He loved nothing more than to test others. Conversing with him could be 'a very halting thing, a test to find out what you knew'. Books would be lent to gauge your sensitivity to 'the great questions in life'. He often spoke in riddles, quotations surfacing obliquely in conversation; when asked to explain he would remain silent, preferring to leave a trail of ambiguity, all the while cultivating the enigmatic character. Canberra poet Mark O'Connor speaks of his capacity to 'bewilder'—his 'shimmering uncertainty'. The philosopher Gwen Taylor remembers him 'searching for the *bon mot*, the grand aphorism or the wry remark, his way of speaking suggesting the pretence of greatness', adding: 'But this was more than game playing, he also thought he was great.'[2]

The musicality of his voice was matched in the playfulness of his light-blue eyes: they betrayed his vulnerability, shifting and darting continually in conversation. When stilled, they could be piercing; when caught by the camera, they sometimes suggested sorrow. Set deeply beneath black

eyebrows and a large forehead, his eyes softened his long, intense countenance. Portraits of the young man reveal his searching gaze, his lips rarely parted, his hair wavy as it receded hastily to the side of his scalp. By his thirties he was almost completely bald, which only accentuated the size of his forehead, his children teasing him about the island of hair that remained on the top of his head.

In his late thirties and early forties, the years of heavy drinking and smoking, the downward lines from the edge of his lips became more pronounced, his hair greying and retreating to bushy clumps at the side of his head before finally arriving at the wiry wisps that protruded from under his hat in old age. He always said that he needed a bank of life experience before he could write *A History of Australia*; and the photographs of the older man show that very experience etched onto his face. When caught off-guard, that person seemed capable of emanating a warmth and sympathetic air that the younger man had not learnt how to express—age brought resignation of a kind. Yet many of his former friends remark that, regardless of his age, he always tended to look older than he was. Perhaps it was a function of his dress. As fellow historian Bob Reece recalled, when describing their first meeting, in 1958:

> My first impression was of an austere and serious man with rimless spectacles who spoke very little but possessed an air of authority. Although he was only about forty at the time, his manner and appearance suggested a man in his sixties ... he was wearing a rusty old three piece suit which looked as if it came straight out of a St. Vincent de Paul's box. His shirt was one of those grey-striped working men's items that Oshkosh used to make. To set this off, he had a watch and chain in his waistcoat pocket and ankle boots just like my engine-driver grandpa from Broken Hill used to wear. Indeed, there was something of the respectable working class tradition about this quaint rig-out. But with his domed and shining forehead and goatee beard, [he] had more the manner of an eccentric Anglican clergyman or a Russian émigré.[3]

At no stage of his life was he described as dapper. His normal appearance was reliably dishevelled—trousers unpressed, shirts crumpled, bright red socks that clashed with his grey suit, hair unkempt, tie hastily knotted, and a wide-brimmed hat thrown over the top of it all, like a ragged bushman's crown. His clothes rarely appeared new or modish, usually because his wife, Dymphna, had picked them up second hand at the Salvation Army store.

Saturday was his day of rest, the day he would put on his old clothes and work in the garden, usually planting and mulching. Eldest son Sebastian remembers, as a young boy, watching him work in the garden, impressed by his physicality and strength. 'The stunning thing was how much he sweated. He sweated so much his shirt was completely soaked. Within half an hour his back would be completely smothered in flies.' In Croydon, east of Melbourne, in the mid-1940s, he would be outside many weekends, fencing and gardening, building the chook shed, performing odd carpentry tasks and cutting the grass of the one-and-a-half-acre property with a scythe, the children raking the grass into haystacks as he cut his way forward.[4]

In his demeanour there was always a slight hesitancy, which may have had its origins in his epilepsy. From his early teens, he suffered from *petit mal*. Dymphna remembered his hesitation in walking during the first years of their courtship—'I never said anything. I just waited for him.' His writing began in the shadow of his epilepsy, as did his bond with the writing of another epileptic—Fyodor Dostoyevsky—the Russian novelist whose mystical prose would become his lodestar. It was due to epilepsy that, in 1930, aged fifteen, he took one year off from his high school studies at Melbourne Grammar, dutifully following his teacher Richard Penrose Franklin's intimation that he was just the sort of person who would like Dostoyevsky. In 1935 he was again forced by epilepsy to take a year's leave from his studies at the University of Melbourne. At home, he filled several exercise books with his diary, 'Jottings of a Recluse', now lost. Attending a Rhodes scholarship interview two years later, he suffered an attack and was immediately deemed ineligible for the award. While the attacks decreased as he entered his thirties and forties, rumours that he 'fell down' persisted well into his time in Canberra in the 1950s.

Traces of nervous behaviour endured. His sister-in-law, Eirene, recalls his habit of getting up from the dinner table when she first met him in the 1940s—'he'd get up from the table, take a few steps forward, then a few back'. Sebastian recalls how he would break into a slight 'skip' every time he approached a gutter. Others remember his tendency, while walking, to stop suddenly, lift one foot from the ground, bend his leg and shake it vigorously before continuing. Long after the epileptic attacks had left him, in times of great agitation his brow would furrow, his face flush red in anger. As he grew older, his epilepsy became the one thing he preferred not to speak about in public. A mark of suffering and a mark of difference, its psychological impact was profound. Novelist David Malouf wonders whether the humiliation he experienced through the disease—being 'forced' uncontrollably to the ground—became his 'shameful secret'. Perhaps much of his ambition, Malouf thinks, was driven by a desire to prove that 'he was not still lying on the ground'.[5]

Painfully self-conscious and preposterously self-centred, he was propelled by a need to give expression to the tempest within him. His most intriguing character was himself. He was no narcissist. Egotistical and vain, yes; but he lacked the one crucial ingredient of the narcissus: self-love. Instead, he seemed haunted by self-doubt and consumed by self-loathing, his ego and vanity driven by a cry for admiration, by the desire to prove that he was indeed worthy of love.

He was always desperate to make his mark as a writer. When he first caught sight of his books in print, he wept. He craved reassurance and expressive demonstrations of love, and throughout his life he was acutely sensitive to criticism of any kind, whether a personal remark or what he called the 'hissing of the academic serpents'. Historian John Molony found him extremely touchy: 'the smallest sleight or slur would hurt him deeply and spark an immediate over reaction'. If he thought someone had slighted him, he simply cut the person off, refusing to speak or even acknowledge his presence. He nurtured grievances, and he could be extremely petulant and manipulative when he wanted to get his way, just as he could humour and charm nearly all those he encountered. To his children, he was affectionate without being overly physical in expressing his love. After their early childhood, he was not inclined to embrace them. But, as Sebastian has remarked, 'pretty much the whole of Australia was non-touching before the 1960s'.[6]

Many women found him sexist, largely because they saw what the men didn't see, especially if he'd been drinking. He was prone to kissing and touching women on impulse, particularly in his middle and old age. In the manner of some of the god professors of his time, he took liberties with women, sometimes meeting resistance, sometimes finding willing partners. With a sense of private schoolboy naughtiness and titillation, he loved to tease: 'she's a Catholic girl you know'. There were also women who found him disarming. Historian Ann Moyal, on first meeting him in the Mitchell Library in Sydney in 1947, was touched by 'his wonderful ability to say something moving'. 'So many Australian men weren't capable of that, he was very *simpatico* with women; he knew how to communicate with them.' His need for physical closeness could also be an expression of his natural warmth and tenderness. To feel 'in love' was his greatest need from women. His closest female friends seemed drawn to him by his heightened emotional awareness, spiritual frailty, incurable romanticism, and mischievous sense of humour. They were also attracted by his desire to talk and his great need for intimacy. Pat Gray, a colleague with whom he had a brief affair in 1955, saw him as 'quite an intuitive person', someone who had a 'great urge to talk about everything'. His daughter-in-law, Alison Clark, would also recognise these qualities: 'He was very seductive, he was always tuned in to the feelings of others.' His sensitivity drew him to people at times of great emotional crisis in their lives. He ministered to others, seeking out friends who were suffering or grieving, consoling and embracing them, offering comforting words and writing letters of condolence, summing up their lives in prose fit for kings.[7]

Although he grew quieter with age, he was, according to his friend Laurie O'Brien, that 'rare combination of intelligence and wit', someone who could be 'tremendously funny, entertainingly funny, and quite barmy in a way'. Former prime minister Bob Hawke, a student in Canberra in the mid-1950s, remembers him in his early forties as a 'garrulous' man, 'with a ribald sense of humour, a figure whom others talked about and gossiped about'. Playing the lark was one of his specialties. So many stories have survived from different periods of his life that reveal his talent for theatrical improvisation.

In his early thirties, lecturing in History and Politics at Melbourne University, he drank heavily and often, sometimes suffering memory loss. Drinking sessions with students, many of them ex-servicemen of a similar age, were common after lectures, sometimes beforehand. One former student and lifelong friend, diplomat and foreign policy analyst Bruce Grant, remembers how 'he would often be seen riding to Croydon Station on his Malvern Star bicycle with a shoulder bag containing books and the sandwiches Dymphna had cut for his lunch'.

In 1946 or 47, we had gone to the pub for a few drinks after his lecture from 5.15 to 6.15 pm. We got on the tram a little pissed. I remember him walking up and down the aisle of the tram several times. He opened his Malvern Star bag and pulled out some of Dymphna's now soggy beetroot sandwiches. Stopping in front of passengers, he peered intently into their eyes and said: 'You look like a victim of the class struggle—would you like a beetroot sandwich?'[8]

When he was not drinking he made sure that the glasses of his friends were full. If he couldn't be the source of entertainment himself, he learnt quickly to get the most enjoyment as a spectator, often pitting communists and Catholics against one another at dinner parties. As he aged, he acquired a droll, subtle wit. Attending dinner at his home some time in the 1980s, together with Sidney Nolan, the poet John Tranter recalled him telling the story of his visit to the Rimbaud Museum in France. With deadpan delivery, he told Tranter that in the margins of one of Rimbaud's books on display in the museum he saw that Rimbaud had written the words 'Wagga Wagga'. His musical voice, complemented by an ear for the music of speech, gave him a talent for mimicry, ventriloquism and role-play. To some extent, he was always playing games and posturing. Pat Gray described this aspect of his personality: 'in his personal life as much as in his public performances he was an actor, taking roles from grand opera (or perhaps rather an atmosphere and an ethos), impersonating characters from Heathcliff to Alyo'. She thought he tended to live in a world of fantasy more than reality.[9]

From his years as a student at Melbourne University, he was seen as eccentric and unconventional, a tale spinner extraordinaire. Noel Carroll, a former classmate, remembers him as 'a queer bloke'. 'He used to hold court in the

university library at night. He had a gaggle of girls from the law school and he'd entertain them with stories of the strange sexual exploits of the ancients. He had an extremely vivid imagination.' Some of the more evocative episodes of outlandish behaviour occurred in the early 1950s when, on trips down to Melbourne from Canberra, cut free from domestic and professional routine, he would stay with former colleagues from Melbourne and indulge in flamboyant drinking sprees. June Philipp was one who had the pleasure of his company:

He would arrive at my door usually after closing time at 6pm, looking like Tolstoy at the Railway Station, ready to die. He cultivated the appearance of a tramp; hand-me-down trousers, sandshoes without socks and an ancient felt hat. I knew it was going to be a long night ahead! I would often ring around to ask friends if they could help me save him from himself.

The late Creighton Burns, former editor of the *Age*, occasionally put him up during these years. Early one morning, Burns was standing over the kitchen stove, holding his six-month-old son, warming the milk for his bottle, when his guest entered the room clutching a Bible. Opening the book, he approached Burns's baby, cleared his throat mockingly, and whispered, 'Hmmm hmmm, I think we should have a reading from Isaiah.' A few mornings later he pulled one of his better-known pranks on Burns, opening his hand to reveal a coachbuilder's nail. 'It's from the left foot,' he whispered deadpan. Fifty years later, Burns was still unsure if he was sending himself up—'with someone like him, you could never be sure'.

Playing with religious imagery was one of his favourite sources of amusement, if only to stand back and watch the ripple effects. Staying with friends, he could sometimes be heard shouting 'Jesus, Jesus!' at the top of his voice while under the shower. During his first years in Canberra, in the early 1950s, he would cycle to the University College Library. One morning, university librarian Verna Coleman was greeted by the sight of a man in a large

straw hat, his bicycle clips still wrapped around the cuffs of his trousers. Invariably, he would approach the desk and proclaim in booming voice: 'The day of vengeance is upon us.' 'People thought he was God,' Verna recalls. 'He was one of the great eccentrics, we all liked him.'[10]

In retrospect, it is possible to see that much of his dramatising in his thirties and forties was a form of experimentation, a means of trying out various personas until he perfected his main character: the sage-like historian with the bushman's hat—a creative amalgam of all the characters he had admired throughout his life. Layers were added over time, drawn from personal experience, from the world of the novel and politics, from his father, from *The Brothers Karamazov* Alyosha and Ivan (the monk and the atheist), from Dostoyevsky himself and, finally, from Vladimir Lenin and the English historian Thomas Carlyle. After his visit to Russia in 1958, he grew a goatee beard, the first publicity shots for Volume I of *A History of Australia*, in 1962, portraying an eerie similarity to the leader of the Bolshevik revolution.

Hats had long been part of his rig-out—felt hats, straw hats, cricket hats and bush hats of all kinds. For most of his adult life, he lived in a culture in which nearly all men wore hats, but his baldness gave him added reason to protect his scalp from the sun. The one thing his hats all had in common was that they were always wide-brimmed. Bogarts were not his style. If the face wore the mask of the intellectual—the mark of learning and urban sophistication—it had to be offset by the mark of authenticity, the ordinary man of the land. One photograph, taken in Dublin in 1956, caught him at a moment middle-age can sometimes exhibit. It is possible to see in his face both the younger man that he was and the older man that he would become. Standing on a Dublin street wearing a loose-fitting linen jacket he had bought in India, he seems to exude the innocence of his country: the freshness of the colonial, a slight awkwardness and just a trace of the grave-faced public man of the future. The hat sits on his head like a bush canopy—a crown of difference and eccentricity.

Not long after this visit to England, a *Times* correspondent noted that he was 'so consciously an Australian that he very often wears a broad-brimmed hat and a rugged two-inch leather belt'. There were more hats to come. In 1980, in New Zealand, he showed off 'a wonderful Western hat, made to measure in Texas, in an establishment no romantic could resist, the owner proclaiming himself hatter to John Wayne'. Said the Duke's hatter to the Australian: 'You've got two feet of head up there.' The hat was a Stetson, and he wore it continuously in public—'people noticed it happening'. Other hats—Akubras and battered fishing hats—hung in the kitchen at home, waiting for different sides of his personality to flower.

In Edinburgh, The National Portrait Gallery of Scotland holds a portrait of the historian Thomas Carlyle, painted in 1879 by Walter Greaves. It is possible that he saw this painting of Carlyle (overleaf), one of his greatest sources of inspiration, on one of several visits there. Looking at the portrait of Carlyle next to photographs of himself at the same age, there is an uncanny similarity between the two men.

For teacher and editor Anne Gollan, someone who knew him most of his adult life, his hat was a theatrical prop that only added to his aura. 'When we lived at Bermagui [on the south coast of New South Wales], everybody

Walter Greaves.
1872

thought he was extraordinary. He had a presence—the hat—it made him look different from everyone else, and he had a sort of knack of just being important.' Other friends, like Helen Garner, saw a comic nature to his sage-like demeanour. 'I never felt he was doing this one hundred per cent seriously. He had a way of smiling sideways, when he put on his hat, that made you think it was all a sort of teasing joke.' Whatever his intentions, when added to his eccentric behaviour, the incongruous hat had the desired effect: it helped to make him a subject of intrigue and gossip, a figure people noticed and remembered, a figure others liked to talk about. He also had an exceptional talent for set-piece performance.[11]

Sheila Fitzpatrick, historian and the daughter of the late historian Brian Fitzpatrick, one of his former friends, would recall a visit he made to New Haven in the mid-1970s. As they strolled together on a cool, windy day by the water at Long Island Sound, he asked her if she knew Thomas Hardy's poems, written towards the end of his life. When Sheila replied in the positive, he slowed his pace slightly and recited word perfect, with tremendous feeling, Hardy's poem 'The Voice', written in December 1912. The poem begins, 'Woman much missed, how you call to me, call to me', and ends:

Thus I; faltering forward,
Leaves around me falling,
Wind oozing thin through the thorn from norward,
And the woman calling.

As he came to the end of the poem, Sheila recalled that he placed particular emphasis on these last lines, particularly the words 'faltering forward'. She saw that 'he was moved by Hardy's attempt to express the depth of difficulty in bearing the everyday difficulties of life, that we all stumble forward in a kind of half-light'. What Sheila recalled most of all was his 'feeling for performance and his sense of deep emotional communication'. She could see he needed to be reassured that he was not alone in the world.

He believed that there were some people who were intuitively spiritual—that there was, floating about in the world, 'a community of the spiritually elect'. He also knew full well that his performances would not be forgotten; in their improvised theatricality, they were immediately etched in the memories of all those who encountered them. His greatest trick was to know how to be remembered. As Heather Rusden, one of his closest friends, has said: 'He was always about creating moments, he loved the heroic aspect of existence. He'd sometimes ring and ask me to come over. His home was about a twenty-minute walk from mine.' As Heather walked down the drive, she could hear the sound of Satie's *Gymnopédies* drifting in the afternoon air, the sound of anticipation, the moment remembered. 'When I arrived, he would usually be sitting at the piano playing … "Ah you've arrived!" he'd exclaim as I walked through the door, but I was sure he'd only sat down five minutes before, timing the music for my arrival.' In this quite magical way, he lived his life as story, fashioning everyday experience into a transcendent narrative that managed the almost impossible feat of being both scripted and freewheeling. Life was never mundane. His romantic imagination strove constantly for a heightened sense of experience, in which every moment of existence carried the potential for significant revelation.[12]

That so much of this was contrived does not mean it was not 'felt'. Nor does it make him fraudulent. Historian Iain McCalman, a former student, remembered one address he gave to staff members in the History department at the Australian National University in Canberra, in the late 1960s. After regaling his audience with his predictable stock phrases, describing postwar Australia, for example, as 'the kingdom of nothingness', he finished his speech by telling his colleagues: 'Of course, some people say I'm a bullshit artist.' Just as he was capable of inhabiting the grand and slightly portentous character he'd created for the public stage, he was also capable of stepping outside that character and sending himself up. At the moment you had him pinned as a *poseur*, he shifted ground and indulged in self-mockery. In his letters, he would occasionally refer to himself impishly in the third person ('Australia's most unreliable historian') or imagine himself as a historical character (Robert Burke). He revelled in inhabiting different characters, yet it is precisely this talent for playful self-reinvention that makes him so bewitching.[13]

The invented worlds he encountered in the novel, in theatre, poetry, art and music were just as real for him as the reality of his everyday existence. His performances drew their inspiration from the stories he loved, even from particular scenes in novels or a memorable remark from one of Tolstoy's characters. Because of this, some friends thought he lacked a sense of 'spontaneous reality', as if he was 'not quite true to himself'. But he was searching for poetic truth as much as self-knowledge. His creative imagination animated his whole being, and it formed part of 'his powerful dominating charisma', which so many who knew him willingly fell for. As David Fitzpatrick, historian and brother of Sheila, explained:

> His charm was a semi-magical concatenation of gesture, expression, voice, playful intelligence, tolerance of failings on the part of the interlocutor, ability to pamper rather than flatter, generosity, hints of malice and naughtiness, hints of boundless knowledge and experience … leavened by rough edges and a sort of disarming naiveté—what does this all mean? He made one complicit in his games, forming mock alliances against whoever happened to be present or under discussion, then turned his charm with equal effect on somebody else so provoking jealousy or pique. In other words, he was a seducer but generally a benign one. One was always aware that the charm was a weapon as well as a magic cure, and that he was a very effective networker and manipulator of those whose help he needed … The charm was stronger when he was sober, as always in later years, because when drunk the merriment verged on madness and the rough edges became coarser. … [but] for me, as for countless academic or would-be-intellectual males who played only games of the mind and spirit with him, the charm is everlasting.[14]

The breadth of his intellectual interests also drew others to him. For outsiders, like the American historian Edmund Morgan, his patriotism was palpable. 'Everything about Australia engaged and excited him. He had a love of country and of his countrymen, whom he regarded with admiration and awe.' Armed with his passion for Australia, which was present from his early twenties, he slowly and painfully developed a talent for narrative history, which finally flowered in his forties. Setting out to

1947

*'He was an egoist and
he became more egotistical
as he got older.'*[16]

1967

*He was both
strong and weak.'*[15]

1983

*'Some people need heroes
and he certainly attracted
those people, he had a
messianic quality.'*[17]

1980s

'He was not self-aware
but he was self-conscious.
I felt that he always wanted
to be significant but he was
never quite sure what that
significance was—so
he experimented.'[18]

1985

'I could understand how
God loved him. The only
thing he didn't do was make
the world.'[19]

discover Australia—'Who are we? Where have we come from?'—he added a brilliant array of quotations and visionary moments trawled from European culture. A stalker of the profound and the profane, he gave the sense that all human experience was open to him. Yet in his constant spiritual questing, friends like David Malouf sensed 'a desperate need for certainty', and a 'huge desire for absolute truth'.[20]

He yearned for an *éternel*. He knew he was being asked to make a choice. Was he a communist? Did he believe in the resurrected Christ, the Son of God? Where did he stand? At the same time, his reading of history imbued him with an intuitive scepticism of any form of idealism. He prided himself on not being a 'joiner'. He danced with Catholicism from his middle-age, praying for the redemption of his soul but never being able to take the blind leap of faith. So he sat on the fence. Like a beggar outside the gates of heaven, he waited for someone to take him by the hand and lead him to the Promised Land his heart yearned to see.

The passing of time seemed to weigh more and more heavily on him with each year. If the younger man had met the older man on the street, they might have gazed at one another as strangers. With age, the lightness left him, he became less sanguine and more rueful, and as he grew older and became a national figure, his growing sense of self-importance emerged in photographs—as if, over time, he slowly came to inhabit his own myth.

At all times in his life his visual sense was keen. He believed it was possible to tell what someone was like by looking long and hard at portraits or photographs. In the final photograph overleaf, where we see both the man and his bust sculpted by Ninon Geier in 1985, the likeness seems to betray more than the man. While his eyes stare hard and intently at the camera, the eyes of the bust are strangely vacant, almost hollow. They gaze out at the world like the eyes of a blind man. At that time, he was one of Australia's few intellectual celebrities. By any measure, his work was an outstanding success; his multi-volume *A History of Australia*, together with his controversial public pronouncements, had made a significant impact on his country. Not long after this photograph was taken, on Christmas day 1987, aged seventy-two, he gave Dymphna a small address book. On the inside cover, he inscribed the following words:

My Dymphna,
From a man who never knows where or who he is
Yours Manning Xmas 1987[21]

Such is the life of Charles Manning Hope Clark (1915–91), historian, writer, teacher, public figure and father of six children—Australia's self-described lover and believer. From his youth until his final years, he asked that biographers view his life with the eye of pity.

Samuel Johnson, the first subject of modern biography, insisted that the only person who could write the story of another person's life was someone who had eaten and drunk and lived in social intercourse with them. Only the biographer who knew his subject intimately could stand any chance of capturing the life as it really was. I never met Manning Clark, although I have vague memories of passing the older man in a university corridor in the late 1980s, his eyes cast downwards, some books tucked under his arm, wearing what was then his uniform, a wide-brimmed hat and a three-piece suit. As I passed him, I said to myself: 'There goes Manning Clark.' I'm still not sure if the scene is a memory or a dream, but I am sure that when it comes to writing Clark's life, I'd rather him dead than alive. Clark's friends and family have brought the difficulty of writing his biography home to me. As Margaret Steven, his former colleague, told me: 'there was no consistency in him as a person and people like that are so difficult, it is so hard to get a sense of them—they keep shifting, keep moving—and they inhabit half a dozen virtual realities at any one time'. Anne Gollan reassured me that the last thing I would have wanted to deal with was a live subject: 'I think you really would have found it impossible to write about him when he was alive, he couldn't bear criticism. I couldn't imagine writing a biography of him because I see him in so many ways.' The comment that has probably stayed with me most of all came from his daughter-in-law, Alison Clark, 'I find I can't speak about Manning without contradicting myself.'[22]

Manning Clark lived and represented his life as one extended experiment, all the while riding a wave of hypnotic, inspired melancholy. He flaunted his flaws as much as his virtues, and he left behind a paper trail large enough to daunt the most persistent of biographers. He knew we would come to his life seeking to discover our own; that was what he wanted.

2: MANNING CLARK, MS7550

Life is not what one lived,
but what one remembers and
how one remembers it in
order to recount it.

—GABRIEL GARCIA MARQUEZ[1]

Manning Clark Papers,
National Library of
Australia, Canberra

Why do I write all this? Only so that I can
destroy it in time before I die? Or is it that
I desire that the world know all about me?

—THOMAS MANN, *Diary*, 25 AUGUST 1950

In October 1988, flying to the United States from Canberra, Manning
Clark was consumed by thoughts of his impending death. He complained
constantly of headaches, nausea, giddiness and leg pain. Doctors would
soon find two blockages in the artery of his left leg. Clark's heart was weak.
He had already undergone one heart bypass operation five years earlier.
Another bypass was thought too dangerous—medication was now his only
alternative. Thoughts of death were nothing new for Clark. Some time in
the 1980s, in the midst of one of his frequent bouts of illness and hypo-
chondriac gloom, Dymphna quipped to a close friend: 'Manning has been
dying since 1949.'[2]

Ever since his mid-twenties, as an earnest want-to-be writer, he had felt
that death should not exist. Only months after the birth of his first son,
Sebastian, in England in December 1939, he wrote in his diary that 'perhaps the saddest side of becoming a father is the realisation that life is
complete except for death … I can't find any answer to death.'[3] Clark would
go on searching for an answer for the remainder of his life—in love, in writing, in fame, and in Christ. Haunted by the ghost of death and racked by
feelings of guilt for past sins, he wandered the earth seeking redemption
through story—the stories he encountered in the old and new testaments,

25

in literature, in Australia's past, and those he wove from personal experience.

In Yale for a Commonwealth Literature conference in the autumn of 1988, his mood in the pages of his diary was characteristically dark, as it was for most of his final years. Clark was seventy-three. He felt unloved and deeply estranged from his wife, and was plagued by 'intimations' of death. Despite the fact that another conference delegate and friend, the novelist Thomas Keneally, had dubbed him 'Saint Manning' for his dignity under fire, he felt alone, weak and vulnerable. He mourned himself: his 'shrinking world', his declining physical strength and his fading memory. By the late 1980s, Australia's most lauded historian and its most controversial public intellectual during the last decades of the twentieth century was playing out the final act of his self-penned tragedy—the man who had been lionised in public but who lived in a private hell. 'I sit here bewildered, not afraid,' he wrote, 'wanting to be forgiven, to be remembered kindly by some, not by all, [still this] malaise which will never go away.' Landing in San Francisco a few days before, he had scribbled down a line from Philip Larkin's 1973 poem 'The Old Fools':

At death you break up: the bits that were you
Start speeding away from each other for ever
With no one to see.

Larkin's atheistic eye was too much for Clark. He was dumbstruck by the poet's image of a grim truth—'extinction'—a truth that his mind told him he should accept but his heart refused. It was not only that death brought the end of consciousness that unsettled him; death was the one journey he would have to make alone, and the closer he came to the end of his life, the more terrified he became of this final loneliness. Suffering angina attacks, he left Yale a few days later for New York, where he wandered 'weeping in the atrium of the Grand Central', exclaiming like Hamlet: 'if it is to be now, it will be now'. He turned for solace, as he'd done so many times since his forties, to Catholic rites. At Harvard, he attended Sunday mass, and was moved to tears by the sight of the 'broken down negroes' praying beside him, perhaps because he saw in their forlorn figures the image of his inner self. The solemn rituals of the mass—the consecration of the host, the customary greetings of peace, and the soaring voices of the choir—washed Clark's fear of death away, allowing him to feel 'tender towards everyone' and to believe that there might be 'mercy' and 'forgiveness' after all. But once outside the sanctuary of the church, his fear of oblivion soon returned.[4]

Clark's behaviour in the USA during the autumn of 1988 conformed to a pattern that had been established for well over thirty years, ever since his move from Melbourne to Canberra in 1949. Plagued by guilt for his past misdemeanours, fearing death and desperate to make his mark on the world, Clark constantly walked a tightrope between exaltation and despair. Every moment in his life seemed to be lived at fever-pitch intensity, every emotion cut to the core of his being, and every aspect of his acutely felt existence had to be recorded—in diaries, in correspondence, in fiction and in history. Much of his prose seemed to suggest a cry for help, a search for an audience that might be willing to hear his confession and grant absolution. His moods oscillated wildly, moving from feelings of extreme self-loathing and depression through endearing self-mockery and impish humour to moments when all sense of irony vanished and he appeared possessed by a portentous and slightly ridiculous sense of self-importance.

The 'death' anxiety Clark experienced in America in 1988 was one he had grappled with since adolescence. Underlying this anxiety was a deep-seated fear that the story of his life would be forgotten, that any trace of his existence would soon be wiped out. Over time, writing and public performance became his creative response to death, each word from his pen another layer of sediment deposited in defiance of the passage of time.

Returning home to Australia that year, convinced that his days were numbered, he began to transfer his personal archive to the National Library of Australia. The timing was perfect. As he laboured on his last major works—two volumes of autobiography, *The Puzzles of Childhood* and *The Quest for Grace*—he consulted his papers, churning over past files and documents. Some he had not set eyes on for years, having crawled under the house to pull out boxes of half-forgotten material. Other files were scattered in the bedrooms of his home—in cupboards, drawers and wardrobes, a precious few even filed methodically in cabinets in his study. Year by year, his house had come to resemble a dispersed library, books overtaking bedrooms, manila folders of documents squashed into every available bit of space. After fifty years of collecting and hoarding, the archive of his life was slowly burying his present and, as the future dissolved, everything about his life turned on the past. Only days before he died, in May 1991, he was still tending his archive.

Between 1988 and 1989, the National Library's chief manuscripts librarian, Graeme Powell, visited Clark's home to collect his papers. He sometimes waited while Clark read a document or letter, 'silently deliberated, and then added it to the library pile or pushed it into his coat pocket'. Powell noted that the archive was quite unusual, even for a historian, not only because it appeared so comprehensive but (ironically, given Clark's reputation for factual inaccuracy) because of its close attention to the detail of his public life. When it came to himself, Clark was a meticulous record keeper. Powell quickly realised that, while Clark had always filed crucial documents, it was only from the 1960s, with the publication of the first of his six-volume *A History of Australia*, when he was described in *The Times* as Australia's 'hit muse', that he started new files which revealed he was beginning to see himself 'as a future subject'. File headings such as 'comments on my work', 'public life' and 'my great friends' showed Clark sculpting the documentary monument of his own life. The man who loved nothing more than to stand at the foot of historical monuments spent much of his last years building his own.[5]

The strongest image of the biographer—cultivated largely by novelists—is that of the thief or the voyeur, 'the post-mortem exploiter' as Henry James put it. Janet Malcolm, an American writer known for her disdain for conventional biography, has described biography as 'the medium through which the remaining secrets of the famous dead are taken from them and dumped out in full view of the world'. The message is explicit: there is something inherently intrusive, even unethical, in the very idea of biography. Stories of writers burning their personal documents are celebrated as a triumph of the writer's right to privacy over the sinister motives of the biographer. Philip Larkin told Andrew Motion, his future biographer, '"When I see the Grim

An Eye for Eternity

Reaper coming up the path to my front door I'm going to the bottom of the garden, like Thomas Hardy, and I'll have a bonfire of all the things I don't want anyone to see".' Larkin might have seen the Grim Reaper coming, but when he did he was in no condition to build the bonfire. His lover, however, dutifully carried out his instructions.[6]

For Manning Clark, there were no bonfires. He kept everything, from theatre tickets to newspaper clippings, reviews, lecture notes, address books, pocket calendar diaries, mountains of correspondence, and fifty-three years of notebooks and personal diaries. In the National Library alone, there are 200 boxes of documents, much of the material barely legible, thanks to Clark's handwriting, an impenetrable script that was once compared to 'micro barbed wire'.[7] The collection is one of the largest individual archives in Australia—almost double the size of Clark's contemporaries such as the poets AD Hope and Judith Wright. Remarkably, the collection does not include the more private papers which are still held at Clark's home, now known as Manning Clark House, in Forrest; nor does it include Dymphna Clark's papers. If these collections were added, the boxes would number well over 300. Just inside the storeroom of the manuscript room's holdings in Canberra, Clark's papers are the first to greet the visitor. Stretching eight metres in length and climbing some four metres high, they almost touch the ceiling. En masse, this mountain of cardboard boxes appears like a memorial wall—the house that Manning Clark built. My recurring dream has been one of being buried under an avalanche of cardboard boxes, each with the label 'Manning Clark, MS7550'.

Richard Holmes has written evocatively of the romance of the biographer's craft. Tracking his subject's footsteps, getting inside their skins, Holmes becomes a midnight sleuth, craving identification with his subjects but at the same time keeping his distance as he shines the torch on hidden biographical gems. Manning Clark has not left footsteps so much as a freeway, complete with signposts and a detailed road map. Far from resisting the biographer, Clark courts the biographer at every turn. As I began working on his archive in 2005, I soon realised that Clark foresaw this book in his mind's eye. With every page turned, I could hear his voice calling to me—'Come hither, come hither!' In my case, the detective work lies in dismantling the archival

monument Clark has left behind and finding different tracks—the life outside the library as well as the life within the library walls.[8]

Archives possess a lure and a romance all their own. Many of us keep
them, boxes of letters, old diaries, photo albums, mementoes of different
stages of our lives—different marriages, loves, friendships—objects we have
kept because we associate them with times we cannot bear to forget. But
very few of us erect the kind of archive built by Manning Clark. Most lives
are lived and forgotten. After death, our presence lives on for a time in
the memories of those we have known and loved before being extinguished.
Our lives exist primarily in the act of living; they do not find another life
unless we record them for posterity. Recovering undocumented lives is
difficult. But understanding the life of a writer who leaves behind so many
documents can be just as difficult because the subject has practised so
much self-crafting.

More than most, Manning Clark wanted to transcend his own time. His
archive reveals his powerful sense of self-importance, just as his gathering
and hoarding was a plea that someone would listen, that his life, more than
most, might speak to subsequent generations. As an historian, he possessed
an instinctive skill for highlighting the turning points and major achievements in his life. The elderly man in Yale who pleaded to be remembered
was also making a plea to history, issuing an open invitation for biographers
to find in his life story truths that might reveal wider truths about the human
condition. Clark's archive also represents a handing over of his personal,
family, and professional life for public examination to a degree that few of us
would dare countenance.

Launching Clark's selected correspondence *Ever, Manning* in August
2008, the historian Bill Gammage, a former friend and colleague, wondered
whether some of the more personal letters should have been published, finding it difficult to accept that 'such things are fit for biographic attention'.[9]
The things Gammage was discreetly referring to were Clark's extramarital
relations and the depth of personal detail about his relationship with
Dymphna. Gammage was also being open about his own feelings, forced
now to confront things he had never known about Manning Clark. Like
many of Clark's friends and family, he was making the journey that Clark, by

An Eye for Eternity

leaving his personal diaries and correspondence in a public archive, had insisted that he make after his death. Clark wanted his personal life made public regardless of the cost to others; *his* story mattered above all else.

Clark understood the public's hunger for biography because he shared it—about other writers and about himself. His archive is extraordinary not only because of its scope and personal nature but because it is scattered throughout with notes to the biographer. As Clark worked his way through his papers towards the end of his life, he was conscious that historians and biographers would use them in the future—so conscious that he could not resist the temptation to direct the biographer.

In the five years I spent working on Clark's archive, rarely would a day pass when I would not find a note by Clark. When a correspondent's name is unclear, he writes the name in capitals, often assigning the person one of his own categories. From one correspondent's name, for example, Clark's black arrow leads to his summary of the person at the top of the page—'One of the Abusers'. Other correspondents are described as 'my great wound', 'my violator' or 'backstabber'. Over the top of a critical review of his work by historian AGL Shaw in 1967, he editorialises: 'he [was] at it for years after the book came out'. In 1979, after a *Labor History* editorial declared that Clark's supporters had not yet produced evidence for the significance of his work, he scrawled angrily on the photocopy: 'After reading this I decided to sever my association with the History Department at the A.N.U. 23 November 1979'.[10] He continually portrays himself as the innocent victim of unjust attacks. Some of his notes to the biographer are dated, some not, but it's clear that he was doctoring his papers from at least the 1970s. Often, it's impossible to be certain exactly when some of these notes were written, the only telltale sign of a later comment being a fresher, different coloured ink. This has the curious effect of merging the younger, the middle-aged and the older man. Clark senior edits his earlier self to conform to his later, more magnanimous view of himself—the national sage who craves praise and brooks no criticism.

In Clark's later diaries, he often scribbles notes for public lectures. When he refers to one of these lectures in a later passage in his diary, he writes '(see above)'. The diary at this stage is an extended letter to future biographers.

As a writer himself, Clark is aware of the need to offer the biographer editorial assistance. He leaves finding aids ('for notes of this speech see small blue-covered notebook "The Trip to the Gulf"') and makes sure that the biographer does not miss crucial information ('see also SMH 18/12/76'). More often than not, he cannot resist the temptation to slam an opponent or indulge in regret ('in the days when students wanted to listen to me'). He can also appear desperately insecure (on a flyer for a Noel Counihan exhibition in Canberra, 28 February 1982: 'Opened by ME').[11]

But the self-aggrandiser is not the only Clark on display. Among his papers are notes, sketches, and curios relating to his children's early years. These are touching, because they are things he kept for no reason other than for the family moment they captured. For example, there is a beautifully illustrated menu for Christmas Day lunch in 1952, handwritten by Axel and Katerina, then aged nine and eleven, which includes the caveat: 'guests wearing dentures are warned to exercise care when dealing with the ham'. Another note, written by seven-year-old Andrew to his parents some time in 1955, reads: 'Dear Family: Is Axel going to the milk bar? I think he is going for the Columbines. I am having a lovely time here. Love from Andrew'. However, weighed against the bulk of his papers, mementoes of this type are still rare.[12]

Clark was firmly convinced that every scrap of biographical detail, no matter how trivial, would eventually be put to use. From the early 1960s, he sees significance in his every utterance, action and thought. His last research assistant, Roslyn Russell, recalled Clark ringing to remind her to make a cutting of a mention he'd received in the local paper. If his name appeared in print, it had to be captured and filed. In September 1976, he dated a cutting from the *Adelaide Advertiser*. It was the daily crossword. Question 11 down asked: 'With which subject is professor and writer Manning Clark associated?' In the late 1970s and early 1980s, Clark began the habit of scribbling notes on scraps of paper and placing them in his papers. About to be interviewed on television he wrote: 'I am sitting in my room in Tasmania Circle—hoping this time the reception will be warm, 3rd September 1987 (When being televised for 7.30 Report)'. Another piece of paper in his papers contains a woman's name and address. Underneath the address, is Clark's explanation: 'Woman who told me on Sunday 16 August 1987 in Melbourne airport that reading my Henry Lawson book changed her husband's life'. Ten years earlier, after chairing an ANU Convocation lunch at which Stewart Harris, the staff correspondent of *The Times*, spoke on the topic of Aboriginal land rights, Clark wrote on his invitation '[I] took the chair—and kissed the Aborigines with tears in my eyes. 17 May 1978'. Here, Clark seems to be writing to the biographer, describing his feelings at particular moments in time, and immediately filing them away in his papers. These notes to the future are Clark's dance with time, written in the voice of a man who seems to court history's judgement at the same time as he cowers before it.[13]

There is something unsettling and strangely moving about the thought of the unsteady hand of the older Manning Clark, already a national celebrity, guiding his ink pen to record in capitals the source and date of his every mention in the press. It is not the cuttings themselves that I find unsettling so much as the sight of his handwriting. I see him sitting at his desk in his study, dating each cutting with trembling hand, busily compiling his life after death, a life lived with an extraordinary degree of self-consciousness, a life in which every action is observed by an inner eye that views the present from a future vantage point, the eye of history and the biographer. And in the minutes and hours Clark spent archiving the self, there lies an ocean of time devoted to proving that he *was* a great man.

Working late one evening in the National Library in Canberra on the box of documents relating to Clark's final volume of autobiography, *The Quest for Grace*, I came across a folder entitled 'List of Illustrations'. Thinking it was no more than what it claimed to be, I was about to place it straight back in the box. But on opening the folder, I found one piece of paper bearing a handwritten list of photographs Clark had chosen for the book. At the bottom of the page, in much darker ink, he had added the following comment, probably at a later moment in time: 'The photographs, like the book, say nothing—the book is a lie, as it says nothing of what I lived through.'[14]

Walking out of the library that evening, I knew I was dealing with a man who had laid the story of his life down as a riddle. It is true that when compared with his diaries, *The Quest for Grace* reads as spin—the glossed and censored reflections of a man more interested in inflating his ego than in self-criticism; and in this sense, Clark's comment is an honest admission of hypocrisy. But it is also more than that. Clark sets up a conversation with the biographer who he knows will come sniffing like a bloodhound to the archive he has constructed. He then plays with his own truth, giving prominence to earnest descriptions of his virtues, on the one hand, while on the other suggesting that the whole edifice of his self-invention is nothing but a charade. In part, this is probably because Clark revels in sowing doubt and ambiguity and in layering the lines of his life with mystery. Like James Joyce, who remarked that he had ensured his fame by writing in such a way that would keep the professors of literature busy for decades trying to decode *Ulysses*, Clark, the self-styled enigma, always had one playful eye on posterity.[15]

And it is not only Manning Clark who has left pleas to the future. Dymphna, reading his diaries after his death, has occasionally written comments in the margins, some of them revealing her hurt after reading particular entries. Therefore, to read the diaries is not merely to read Clark but also to read Dymphna's final comments on their tempestuous relationship of more than fifty years. She, too, has left her notes to the biographer. Among the more personal material that remains at the family home is a handwritten note signed 'Dymphna Clark 29/2/96'. It reads:

> The material in this drawer was found in another part of this house <u>after</u> the contents of these filing cabinets was delivered to the National Library of Australia. It has not been copied, nor has it been deliberately withheld from the National Library. Manning Clark himself must have removed it from his study before he died.[16]

Despite the fact that Clark had written on the front of one folder of letters, 'to be destroyed after my death', Dymphna chose not to destroy it. Nor did she destroy the rest of the material he had hidden in the house. On the contrary, she wrote a librarian's note, explaining with detachment how the material came to be in his study. She then left it there, tidily bundled, for those she knew would come looking. It is not difficult to see why she made this decision, because most of the material does not show Clark in a very

Immortalised in bronze: Manning Clark gazing at his bronze bust, sculpted by Ninon Geier in 1985

positive light. Dymphna was conscious of Clark's legacy, as well as her own. She wanted her story told too. Forced to confront Clark's frequently critical comments about her in the diaries, she made a conscious decision not to destroy evidence that might balance Clark's version of their relationship. Unlike Clark, Dymphna did not volunteer her inner feelings easily. But by preserving a few crucial documents, she was clearly willing to leave evidence that revealed at least something of what she experienced. The result is a richly layered archive, an individual past constantly being rewritten and fought over. First, the documents (selected and approved for donation to the National Library by Clark), followed by Clark's later notes on the documents, Dymphna's comments on what Clark has left behind and finally, the work of all writers who work on the papers. Each layer adds to the archive, ultimately becoming part of the life stories of both Manning and Dymphna Clark.

Biographers often save their thoughts on their sources until after their work is published, talking eagerly in interviews about the process of researching their subject and the many different emotions they experienced towards them. But excising the relationship between the biographer and the archive from the narrative can hide some very large truths about the lives of others. In my own encounter with Manning Clark's archive, I have become acutely aware of the limitations of documentary sources—correspondence, diaries, official documents—as keys to understanding a life. This was brought home to me in a most unexpected way in December 2007, while working in the Manuscripts Room of the National Library. While reading Clark's diaries, I was interrupted by a librarian after the arrival of two women from Ireland 'who had come', she said, to 'look at Manning's diaries'. I looked up to see two women dressed in pleated skirts and short-sleeved white shirts. They were in their late sixties, only recently arrived from a European winter, the waxen pallor of their skin aglow in Canberra's summer light. They had known both Manning and Dymphna in the early 1980s during the time the couple spent in England and Ireland. They had been especially close to Dymphna. Now on holiday in Australia, they had come to the library to see if they were mentioned in Clark's diaries. As I happened to be working on the box they wanted, would I mind, they asked, if they could take a look? For two hours or more, sitting together, they pored over the relevant diaries. When they had finished, one of the women sat down beside me to thank me. I couldn't resist asking her if she had found any mention of herself. 'No,' she replied, 'nothing at all, and the children aren't mentioned much either. Dymphna and I talked, you see, and I had the utmost respect for her.' Standing up to leave, she said goodbye then turned with an afterthought. 'And do you know what?' she whispered, 'the Manning I knew is not the Manning I see in those diaries.'

By 2007 I had been working on Clark's papers for more than two years. In the few minutes of this conversation, a whole edifice of assumptions about the reliability of documentary sources crumbled. As I watched them leave, and thought of the encounter afterwards, they appeared like messengers who had come from afar to reveal a hidden truth. Knowing that diaries and letters are sometimes written with an eye to the future and can often leave behind an image of a person that varies greatly from the person someone remembers is one thing, but having it brought home in such a graphic fashion was another; it cast everything in a much sharper light. One of the greatest dilemmas in grappling with Clark's life story is the chasm between the dark, despairing and often self-pitying man found in his diaries and the mischievous, affectionate, witty, theatrical stirrer that so many people recall. Given his talent for impersonation and role-playing, it is not that one version of the man is necessarily less contrived, more truthful or more real than another; there is more than one mask in Clark's wardrobe. But understanding his purpose in keeping a diary reveals as much about him as the diary's content. Louis Menand's thoughts on the relationship between the biographer and a subject's diaries are especially relevant to Clark:

> People lie in letters all the time, and they use diaries to moan and vent. These are rarely sites for balanced and considered reflection. They are sites for gossip, flattery and self-deception. But diaries and letters are the materials with which biographies are built, generally in the belief that the 'real' person is the private person, and the public person is mostly a performance.[17]

Manning Clark was steeped in literary models of representing the self. He was drawn to the literature of psychological and spiritual crisis—Dostoyevsky, Tolstoy and DH Lawrence. He understood writing as a tortured and angst-ridden process. His diary was where he confronted, tested and punished himself, a place for complaint, confession and 'woe be me' refrain. In a manner reminiscent of the Ancient Greek notion of catharsis, in which the emotions are purged through vicarious experience, especially through art or drama, Clark used his diary to exorcise his demons, almost as if, in writing down his negative thoughts and emotions, he was shedding a character. From the 1960s on, Clark's diaries were written increasingly for a public audience. And they contained the signature stylistic devices of all his prose: exaggeration for dramatic effect and constant striving for tragedy—a pen

'The Man in Black'

locked forever in a minor key. For any biographer, there is a danger in relying on diaries that are so clearly written for future publication. The biographer risks becoming a ventriloquist, someone who merely gives voice to the subject's rendering of his own life.

The man who lived his adult life reading and re-reading the classics, especially Russian literature of the late nineteenth century, knew how to portray his life as tragic narrative. Clark's use of melodramatic language to describe his states of mind is but one example. He is frequently 'tormented', 'weeps tears of joy', suffers from 'black despair', or is overcome by 'wild frenzy' or some 'madness of the heart'—language reminiscent of Dostoyevsky. By making himself the dramatis persona, subjecting himself to scrutiny, tearing himself apart, exposing his every fear and frailty and documenting every moment of anguish, Clark leaves for posterity 'the man in black'.

Reviewing Donald Horne's autobiography, *The Education of Young Donald*, in 1968, Clark seemed, as he so often did, to be writing about himself more than Horne:

> We have been told that one man in his life plays many parts. We know, too, that inside the one person there are many persons. Some have been born to the cruel fate of only being able to play on the stage of life a sonata of unaccompanied dullness, and some have been born to the complex fate of having inside them, as it were, all the instruments of a symphony orchestra.[18]

The tone is patronising, but Clark had no doubt that he was one of the chosen few born to that 'complex fate'. He saw himself as one of the elite souls, those born with an acute sensitivity and emotional intelligence, capable of reaching the peaks of human achievement but also destined to a life of inner 'torment'. Accentuating the drama of his emotional life, he occasionally dropped notes into his papers:

GOD GIVE ME STRENGTH AND CHARITY AND LOVE 28/1/69

GIVE ME STRENGTH AND FAITH IN MY COUNTRY,
MY PEOPLE MY POWERS 29/11/69[19]

These two notes appear to be dated in a colour that doesn't match that of the ink used to write the original statements. Written in shaky capitals, they look more like the writing of an old man than a man in his fifties. This raises the possibility that Clark wrote the comments and dates at different times. It also seems feasible that, in order to leave behind a paper trail of dramatic struggle surrounding the writing of *A History of Australia,* he wrote the notes not in the late 1960s but in the 1980s, when he was working his way through his papers. The struggle was real, but it was also a struggle he shaped. Regardless of the accuracy of the dates, the intention is clear—Clark wanted to present an image of a tortured soul striving to realise his creative vision *of* and *for* his country. The best way of questioning the image of the 'tortured' Clark is to quote from a letter Dymphna wrote in Canberra on 18 April 1985 to Clark in London. Clark's letters home had been mournful, complaining constantly of his loneliness and depression. But Dymphna had also received letters from Benedict, their youngest son, and her friend, historian Amirah Inglis, both of whom had had contact with Clark in the UK. In thinly disguised frustration with Clark's constant stream of gloom, she asked him bluntly: 'Why do your letters always tell me that you are sad and miserable when Amirah & Benedict both report to me that you are well, vigorous and happy?'[20]

Dymphna's letter points to a crucial question for the biographer: the self who writes—'the writer'—is not the person who interacts with family and friends, but to what extent should we as readers and writers trust the person within the written word? Manning Clark's life was not only lived on the page; like all our lives, it was lived in the day to day. The greater accessibility of diaries and correspondence in contrast to the elusive encounters of the subject's daily existence does not necessarily make them more truthful or more significant. Clark, for example, frequently uses correspondence in much the same way as he uses his diary: to convey inner turmoil, to arouse emotion, to appear in need and, by strumming the dark night of the soul, to elicit a sympathetic response from the reader. Poet and writer Mark O'Connor, who knew Clark well in the last decade of his life, the period when his diaries were bleak, told me he never saw the 'dark otherness' in the man he encountered. Interviewing Clark's nephew Philip Ingamells in

Melbourne in 2007, I asked him if he had seen the darkness in Manning that appears in his diaries and correspondence. He paused, before saying emphatically, 'No.' This was the same answer I had received from the majority of Clark's friends I'd spoken with. But Ingamells went further, reflecting on the process of biography: 'I mistrust people working only from written correspondence, because to do so is to create a likeness of the person that is woven in the image of the correspondence that is kept. Often the most important things about a person are the things that are unsaid.'[21]

To write biography is to wrestle with both the archive material and the person as flesh and blood; to grapple with the likeness of another human being, a likeness fixed in text, and the much more intangible likeness that remains in human memory, a likeness that constantly shifts, like shadows dancing, much as it did when the subject was alive. Doris Lessing, for example, was driven to write her autobiography because she feared that biographers would turn her 'fleeting' and 'evanescent' life into something 'fixed and therefore lifeless, without movement'. Biography thus involves an inherent contradiction. It attempts to render still something that was experienced as fluid.[22]

In writing the pages that follow, I try to remind myself that I met Manning Clark not as others met him. In meeting him through his personal diaries and correspondence and the memories of his family and friends, my encounter with him is quite unlike life. I see the different faces wheeled out for the different audiences. I see the public figure, the private fears and anxieties, the father, the husband and lover, the teacher, the prankster and the performer. But in life, it is not possible to see these different selves at once. We are sealed within our own time, locked within the here and now. We struggle to retrieve our past selves. Nor can we see our future selves, or detect sense, rhyme and reason. Only death can achieve this; death and the hand of the biographer. If there is an art to biography, it is the art of defying the stillness of death and retrieving life as movement, chance and unpredictability.

3: BOATS AGAINST THE CURRENT

The glamour
Of childish days is upon me,
my manhood is cast
Down in the flood of remembrance,
I weep like a child for the past

DH LAWRENCE, '*The Piano*' (1913)

Unknown child, from
Catherine Clark's
family album

So we beat on, boats against the current, borne
back ceaselessly into the past.

F SCOTT FITZGERALD, *The Great Gatsby*, 1926

On a mild, overcast winter's day in August 1987, Manning Clark visited Box
Hill Cemetery in the eastern suburbs of Melbourne, together with his two
youngest sons, Rowland and Benedict. It was there that Clark's parents,
Catherine Hope and the Reverend Charles Clark, were buried. Visiting
cemeteries was one of Clark's pleasures; strolling through the grounds with
a notebook and pen, he believed that the pithy inscriptions on gravestones
held the secret to unlocking the passions and beliefs of lives past. Perhaps if
he stood and gazed long enough at the words chosen by grieving loved ones
for inscription on the stones, the dead might speak. Like so many of his
previous visits to Box Hill, he carried a letter he had written to his mother
and father. Leaning over their grave, he pulled the letter from his inside
jacket pocket, taped it to the granite headstone and asked his sons to take a
photo of the occasion. Using a disposable Kodak camera, Rowland took the
photo of his father and brother standing next to his grandmother's grave.

In this image, its blurriness only seeming to accentuate the poignancy of
the moment, it is possible to make out Clark's letter on the headstone. On
the back of the photograph, Clark wrote the words 'Mum & Dad's grave
with my letter August 1987'. We do not know what the letter said, but that
month saw the anniversary of Clark's father's birth and the launch of the

final volume of *A History of Australia*. After the death of his mother in 1943, and his father in 1951, at every milestone in his life, his first thought was of his parents. Sitting in his study in 1974, just after being awarded an honorary doctorate by the University of Melbourne, he pressed a rose petal inside a letter, placed it carefully inside an envelope, and addressed it: 'Mum and Dad'. Down the side of the envelope he wrote: 'Hon D. Litt Melbourne, 21 December 1974'. His message read:

An Eye for Eternity

To Mum and Dad
For remembrance and with the old love on the
day when what you hoped for me came true.
Your loving son Manning.[1]

Shortly after being made Australian of the Year in 1981, he wrote to his former research assistant Ailsa Zainuddin: 'Of course, I missed Mum & Dad very much on the night of 26 January. They have been very close to me since that day—as pictures in the mind, and their past words of encouragement and recognition.'[2] Clark's letters to his parents—letters of love, devotion and longing—cry out defiantly across the gulf that separates the living from the dead. He stands before his parents, the man still a boy, glowing with pride, and calls out: 'Look Mum! Look Dad! See what I have done.' Reading the letters of the mature man, it is impossible not to be struck by the number of times he refers to himself, half-jesting, half-pleading, as 'the boy from the bush' or 'the boy from Cowes', where he lived on Phillip Island in his boyhood. The adult Clark embraces his childhood for its innocence and freedom, longing for the time when life stretched out endlessly before him and regret was impossible. Sometimes his notes to his parents were written in his diary or on scrap pieces of paper and placed in his files, while at other times they were delivered in person. In Melbourne he would often drive to the cemetery before returning to Canberra, placing letters on his parents' headstone, usually postcards inscribed in slanting capitals—'*GOODBYE MUM, GOODBYE DAD*'. When he couldn't be there on the anniversaries of his father's or mother's death, he would write to one of his children, asking them to make the pilgrimage to Box Hill on his behalf: 'Dear Axel … If you feel like it, please go out to Box Hill within the next ten days and place flowers on her grave for me. Put on them: "For Mum From Manning 31 March 1964".'[3]

His dedication to the memory of both parents was unstinting, but it was his relationship with his mother that bordered on the pathological, particularly after her death. The memory of her words haunted him ('Mann dear'), the spectre of her unhappiness weighed on him ('there are things in my life I dare not tell you') and the longing to speak with her distracted him. He carried her with him constantly. Only a few months before his visit in August

1987, he was again at Box Hill Cemetery, penning missives to those 'pictures in the mind'. 'My Dear Mum, I never forget, Your Loving Son, Manning'.[4]

He was true to his word. Some time that same year, Clark's nephew Tim, together with his wife Renate and daughter Anna, stayed with the Clarks in Canberra. The following morning, before they left on their way to Melbourne, they stood in the glass-framed entrance hall of his home, their figures lit by the morning sun, saying their goodbyes. Renate remembers Manning looking closely at Anna, who was then only five.

> He bent down, took her by the chin, and removed a photo from his wallet, exclaiming proudly 'You look just like my mother!' There was a gentleness about his manner, but it struck me then as quite unusual. After all, how many men at age seventy-two carry a photo of their mother in their wallet?

Little more than twelve months later, in April 1989, Clark was back at his parents' graveside.

> Am sitting on grave of Mum and Dad, which I had restored out of some of the royalties from the history. Not a cloud in the sky. When walking to the cemetery from Box Hill Station I suddenly realised there was now no one with whom I could share the experience. My exile from family, from the past, is complete. Was it all worthwhile? Did I flower in exile or become poisoned by regrets? To whom can a man speak? The words on Mum & Dad's grave do not come from the heart. They say nothing about them or my feeling for them. They are hollow words.[5]

The epitaph on Clark's mother's grave reads 'Always abiding in the work of the Lord'. For his father, there is no epitaph. Clark had more faith in words than most of us. And like many writers, the words he chose had to be the right ones. He couldn't bear the thought that the words on his parents' tombstones were hollow because he believed that epitaphs stood as a quiet testament to eternity. His gravestone epistles show a man trying to free himself from the silence imposed by his parents' deaths and his endless grieving for their absence, all the while fighting against his 'exile' from the past.

Superficially, his letters to the dead are laments that his parents are unable to see *him*. Visiting their grave to speak in thought or prayer alone was not enough. For Clark, what remained unwritten remained unsaid. He reached out to his parents in death, wherever he imagined their spirits might reside, as he reached out to his friends and family in life—through correspondence. On so many occasions in Clark's life, the deepest form of communication with another human being came when he was separated from them— whether by distance, time or death. [6]

The vision of him sitting on his parents' grave, taping his notes to the dead on the headstone, is a vision of a man performing a solemn ritual, like a Buddhist monk hanging a red lantern in a temple, or raising prayers for the dead on small pieces of coloured paper. Perhaps Clark's prayer was embodied in his ritual of writing, personal delivery and graveside recital. The old man who walked from Box Hill Station to the cemetery, still his parents' boy at heart, paced out the proof of his loyalty to all things past; from the moment he began to realise his dream to be a writer, he turned his eyes back to his childhood, raking over memories, looking for clues, searching for answers. Whatever emotion he felt—unhappiness, joy, guilt, remorse or despair—its most likely origin, he believed, was the long, dimly lit hall of childhood experience.

So many of the friends I interviewed remarked on how tenaciously Clark had clung to the past. Anne Fairbairn, widow of Clark's friend and former colleague Geoffrey Fairbairn, thought that 'there was some wounding early on in his childhood'. 'There was a lack of some sort of intrinsic confidence,' she said, 'a need to prove something.' Wendy Sutherland, who edited volumes V and VI of the *History* saw in *Puzzles of Childhood* the image of a 'sickly child, experiencing a dark and dreary childhood, fixated with his mother and constantly overcompensating for his feelings of guilt towards her'. Humphrey McQueen wrote to him from Japan after reading *Puzzles*, observing that the book was 'not gloomy or depressing but sad'. 'So many of the people you describe,' he told him, 'are unable to do what would make them less unhappy.' It was not only himself that Clark had trapped in a melancholy past, it was the whole world of his childhood experience. Helen Garner saw Clark's preoccupation with his childhood as a trait that was characteristic of the entire Clark family. In different ways, she said, 'they all betrayed an obsessive memory and faithfulness to the past'.[7]

One of the recurring themes in Clark's correspondence is his attention to the anniversaries of his parents' births, deaths and marriage. He imbues their memory not only with a kind of holiness but with the act of remembrance itself. His obsessive 'faithfulness to the past' can also be heard in his speech. In his public engagements, whenever he mentioned the year in which an historical event occurred, he always pronounced the year in full—'in the year nineteen hundred and fifty six'—each number enunciated with biblical gravitas. Listening to his recorded voice, with its sonorous recitation of things past, it is possible to feel his reverence for the lost world of his childhood.[8]

Historian Inga Clendinnen, delivering the National Biography Lecture in 2007, asked her Melbourne audience a series of questions concerning childhood and biography:

When does our self when young become a stranger to us? That happens deep in the shadows; if it happens. My beginning thought is that it happens at different stages for different people, and that possibly for some people it might not happen at all. What about those people who sentimentalise their childhoods and who re-enact them tirelessly? What about those who recall their youth with a kind of tender intoxication? What is the relationship between memory and creativity there?[9]

For Clark, a man who indeed recalled his youth with 'a kind of tender intoxication', there was little sense of strangeness between his adult and childhood self; instead of separating from his childhood self, he carried it within him, nurturing his childhood joys, fears and anxieties. He was like a man standing before a door that had been closed on him, unable to walk away, forever peering through the keyhole to catch a glimpse of his former life. It's not simply that the intensity of some childhood memories seemed to coexist in his mind with the same vividness as his present—we all experience this to some degree—it was more that he refused to let go, living much of his life in a land of infant nostalgia and heartache. Yet it was not always like this. The older man was plagued by tortured memories of his childhood. How did

Clark arrive at this point? How and why did his memory of childhood change over time? What was he looking for in his childhood? And what was the relationship between his memory of childhood and his creativity?

'THOSE TO WHOM I OWE SO MUCH': CATHERINE HOPE AND CHARLES CLARK

'When I try to explain why it was that I wanted to write things, I'm inclined to think that one thing that influenced me very early in life was the great gap between my father's world and my mother's world. My father [Charles Clark], was a clergyman, he was an intellectual, he was also partly Irish and [working class] … In imagination he had a very great wit, and he had a great charm. He was both lovable and greatly loved … My mother [Catherine Hope] came from a quite different world. On her father's side she was a direct descendant of the Reverend Samuel Marsden. Her own family … belonged to the old squatting and patrician classes of Sydney. [She] was also very Anglo-Saxon, very upright, a stern person, possibly a greater disciplinarian than my father.' —Manning Clark, 1967[10]

In 1884, Charles Clark arrived in the Sydney inner city suburb of St Peters with his parents, Thomas and Jane Clark, and his younger sister Alice. He was three years old. His parents' cottage in St Peters was named 'Plumstead'— after the working-class London suburb in which he and his sister had been born. Thomas Clark, a blacksmith by trade, turned his hand to building in Australia, while Jane, an Irish Protestant from Tipperary, taught at Sunday School, involved herself in church affairs and raised four children, her youngest two daughters, Ruby and Annie, being born soon after her arrival in Sydney. Like Plumstead, the streets of St Peters in the 1880s were the province of the working class. Driven by the expansion of the brickworks ('like hives of bees'), which supplied most of the bricks for Sydney's burgeoning suburbs, St Peters had been transformed from the semi-rural area subdivided by the merchant Robert Campbell in the early nineteenth century.

Driving along the Princes Highway through St Peters today, it's impossible not to be struck by the chimney stacks from the old brickworks which Thomas Clark helped build. Close by, at Cook's River, built from sun-dried bricks, lies the gothic revival St Peter's Anglican Church (1840). Inside, remnants of the Clarks' presence can still be found on the walls. To the right of the altar you can see the cedar panelling donated by the Clarks in memory of Charles's mother, together with a plaque bearing her name—'To the Glory of God: In loving Memory of Jane Ann Clark, Born 2nd March 1856 Died 7th May 1928'. Charles Clark would eventually see similar words inscribed on his wife's gravestone when she died in 1943.[11]

Spellbound by the oratory of St Peter's vicar, Reverend James Napoleon Manning (Manning Clark's namesake), the young Charles was inspired to join the ministry. He was educated at St Andrew's Cathedral Choir School and Moore Theological College in Sydney, posts which Reverend Manning had helped him attain, and later served as a curate at St John's Ashfield (1906–10), before becoming an assistant at St Andrew's Cathedral (1910–17), chaplain of Long Bay Gaol (1912–17), assistant priest at Kempsey, on the north coast of New South Wales (1920–21), and finally vicar at Phillip Island (1922–24), Belgrave, in Melbourne's south-east (1924–34) and Mentone, on Port Phillip Bay (1934–51). Reverend Manning's liberal Evangelicalism, 'tinged with optimism and social reform', made a far deeper impression on Charles Clark than the stern, 'introspective' and 'fiercely Protestant' world of Moore Theological College and the Sydney Anglican establishment. Charles's focus as a minister always remained on his parishioners, not on church affairs. The mainstays of his life were the Book of Common Prayer, the English Hymnal and the King James Bible. This was the world he would eventually pass on to his children—the world of prayer and solemn ritual—together with the grand tradition of Protestant choral music—Bach's passions and cantatas, Handel's anthems and oratorios and Stainer's Crucifixion. Embodied in the rituals of the Church of England's Sunday service—the call and response of the liturgy, the oration from the pulpit and the steady gathering of parishioners outside the church afterwards—was the sense of community and society that characterised so much of Australia in the early twentieth century—duty bound; puritanical; God-fearing; and proudly, defiantly British. God and the Empire were on the same mission. At the 1911 Commemoration Service for the Coronation in St Andrew's Cathedral, Charles Clark stood before a pulpit draped in the cross of St Andrew and surmounted by the Union Jack. One year later, when he assisted in the service for more than 1500 people who lost their lives in the sinking of the *Titanic*, he heard the Anglican Archbishop of Sydney exhort his congregation to turn their backs on the decadence of the leisure- and pleasure-seeking society: 'Let us have done with motoring Sundays, tennis Sundays and dinner party Sundays', he told them; these were mere chimeras of happiness and fulfilment; true fulfilment would only come when they were united with God in eternal life in heaven.[12]

When Charles Clark became smitten with Catherine Hope in 1908, he was a curate at St John's Ashfield, 10 kilometres west of Sydney, and extremely conscious that he was falling for someone of a higher social class. Charles had escaped the confines of working-class St Peters with the help of Reverend James Napoleon Manning. Now he was attempting to take yet another step up the social ladder by courting Catherine. When the young man from St Peters took Catherine home to Florence Street to meet his parents for the first time, his mother, Jane Clark, spent a small fortune on a new tea set for the occasion. The pouring of that first cup of tea, as the two lovers sat in the small living room in St Peters, was a tense moment.[13]

In his early twenties, Manning Clark had stumbled across his grandmother's family album and felt 'her fear and concern when her Charlie began to be interested in a girl who was above his station'. Catherine was twentynine when she met Charles, and she was proud of her family pedigree; born in Dunedin, New Zealand, in 1878, to the Scottish wool-trader Charles Hope, whose family had formed one of the leading pastoralist enterprises in colonial Australia, and Mary Kettle, the daughter of the Surveyor-General of New Zealand, Catherine was directly descended on her father's side from two of the most significant figures in the establishment of the Protestant Church in Australia: Reverend Samuel Marsden, the first Anglican minister in New South Wales, and the Reverend Thomas Hassall. Catherine's brother,

John Hope, became vicar at Christ Church St Laurence in Sydney. Aside from John's embrace of the Anglo-Catholic tradition, with its emphasis on the 'social gospel', her parents were nominally Presbyterian, their background more traditionally Protestant and conservative. Stories of her family history, of the wool trade, colonial days, church affairs and the saving of souls, circled the family dinner table as Manning Clark grew up. When Catherine married Charles in 1910, she was teaching Sunday school at Ashfield and four days short of her thirty-second birthday—a latecomer to marriage by the standards of the time. The qualities she saw as attractive in Charles—his position of social respectability as an Anglican minister, his convivial nature, and his talent for storytelling—would ultimately prove to be the very things that led her husband into the arms of other women. Choosing Catherine as his wife, Charles Clark married the image of his mother, a pious woman who taught at Sunday school and devoted her life to family and church.[14]

Charles and Catherine's first home was at Park Road, Burwood, a 'progressive suburb' in Sydney's inner west that sported large Victorian mansions built by well-to-do families in the 1860s. In the first six years of her marriage, Catherine gave birth to three children: Russell (1912), Charles Manning Hope (1915) and Hope (1916). Writing his autobiography in the 1980s, Manning Clark imagined his mother praying that her third child would be her last. When he was born on 3 March 1915, Burwood's streets were unpaved—nearby Parramatta Road was a dirt track traversed by trams and the occasional horse-drawn vehicle. The word *colony* still captured the spirit of the place; everything seemed to be in a process of formation. Within a few years of Clark's birth, electric streetlights replaced gas lanterns, Parramatta Road was tarred and cluttered with the first waves of motorised traffic, and the Californian bungalows that would dominate Australian suburbs between the wars were just starting to be built. Aged four, sitting in the backyard at Burwood, Clark saw a plane piloted by Sir Keith and Ross Smith. His apocryphal tale of an innocent child gazing up at the sky to see the arrival of the first flight from England to Australia placed the beginning of his life at the moment of the nation's birth. The giant bird in the sky—the portent of war waged from the air, of the coming age of technology and globalisation—brought with it the historical forces of modernity that would shape twentieth-century Australia.[15]

Like so many Australian families at the time, war defined the first years of Charles and Catherine's marriage. At the end of 1915, soldiers had already returned from Gallipoli with 'terrible stories'. By the time Clark was five, memorials to Australia's fallen soldiers in World War I had been erected in parks and gardens around the country. When Charles Clark volunteered and

Charles Clark and a
Ceylonese boy on board the
hospital ship, Karoola, *1917*

enlisted as a stretcher-bearer in the Australian Army Medical Corps on 5
May 1917 ('5 feet nine inches, complexion: fair; eyes: blue; hair: black turning grey') Catherine was left at home with three children under the age of
five. Charles left Sydney in September 1917 and would not return home
until October 1918, when he was discharged as medically unfit due to a nagging hernia. Back home, his relationship with Catherine would never find its
way back to the closeness they had shared in their first years of marriage.

An Eye for Eternity

Her world had remained confined by domesticity, while his had opened out with the brutal realities of war. In his year away from home, he travelled from Europe through South-East Asia aboard the hospital ship *Karoola*. His homecoming was difficult. Not only did he need to rebuild his relationship with Catherine and the children; he also resigned his position at St Andrew's Cathedral in protest after he failed to gain the promotion he thought he deserved, and took up the position of curate in the staid rural community of Kempsey in northern New South Wales in 1920. Like all those returning from war, he looked on Australia with that mixture of familiarity and strangeness, wondering if he would ever belong again as he had belonged before.

The move from Burwood to Kempsey was a jolt for the Clark family. Leaving Sydney's 'bible-belt' for this frontier town in northern New South Wales was a journey from genteel suburbia to a town ringed by Aboriginal reserves and shanties, the homes of the Dangaddi people who had been dispossessed of their land and suffered from the usual effects of the colonial encounter—disease, high mortality and alcoholism. Thomas Keneally's father would run the general store in Kempsey shortly after the Clarks had left. Keneally recalled Kempsey's 'subtropical climate', 'lush vegetation' and the Macleay River, which 'ran through a valley of magnificent and sacred hills'. Almost all of the town's population was either English or Irish, hence the 'vigorous sectarian divide', intolerance of Catholics being only marginally less intense than that towards Aborigines. In Kempsey, the couple's marriage quickly came under great strain—so much so that for more than six months in 1921, Catherine sent Manning, Russell and Hope to Darriwill, the Hope family property near Geelong, a bluestone mansion tended by servants who joined the family every morning for prayers. While the children were looked after at Darriwill, she stayed with her sisters in Burwood. Why had the children been sent away? Did Catherine have a nervous breakdown? Had Charles been dismissed by the Church authorities? What had happened in Kempsey? These were the questions that would trouble Manning for much of his adult life.[16]

When Charles Clark was reunited with Catherine in 1922, the family moved to Phillip Island, where he took up the position of vicar at Cowes.

Phillip Island coastline

This was where Manning Clark's childhood began. The two years he spent on Phillip Island (1922–24) between the age of seven and nine would later become his vision of paradise. When the Clark family arrived in the early 1920s, no bridge connected the island to the mainland; that would not be built until November 1940. Phillip Island's isolation 140 kilometres south-east of Melbourne was accentuated by its windswept landscape of bare hills covered in pigface and low-growing shrubs. Along the southern coast, outcrops of dark basalt sliced through the pink granite, the whole shoreline sculpted by the pounding waves of the Bass Strait; shrouded in mist and sea-spray, the island exuded a desolate, romantic air. Even when the horizon was clear, locals claimed it was a sign of rain.

As Clark rode with his father and brother in the jinker from Cowes to Pyramid Rock, a journey of several hours along dirt roads, he passed the chicory kilns, some of which were in use until World War II, and saw the old homesteads of the first wave of free selectors in the late nineteenth century. The very names of the streets on which he journeyed reflected the reason for his father's coming—Stradbroke Grove, Broughton Avenue, Perry Avenue—the names of English Governors and Anglican bishops. The island's small

An Eye for Eternity

community was almost completely Protestant, a tight-knit little England at the end of the earth. Out with his father, Clark set rabbit traps, hoping to sell the meat to local guesthouses. One former resident, Raymond Grayden, long remembered the eight-year-old Clark 'shooting rabbits with a small bore shotgun'. Years later, when he returned with his own children on summer holidays, Clark would take them on the same rabbit-shooting excursions he had made as a child, donating the kill to local clergymen.

Charles Clark's vicarage was a small house set well back off the road at Cowes, the island's main town. Beside the house, he kept his jinker and horse—the sole means of transport. Lifelong resident of Phillip Island Edith Jefferey attended Sunday School with the three Clark children. 'Everyone was spruced up,' she said, 'we all wore our patent leather shoes on Sundays'. The lessons began at 2 pm, with Mrs Williams taking the class through the Bible stories and the whole of the Clark family helping out. As Edith would explain, remembering the words of the popular hymns, 'we sang with all our hearts "There is a happy land, We are but little children weak, Ask the Saviour to help you, Shall we gather at the river? and When I survey the wondrous cross."'

As they did with Edith, the melodies and words of these hymns lodged in Clark's mind for the remainder of his life. Many years later, when Russell Clark turned fifty, Clark sent him a telegram quoting the words of a hymn they had sung together in Sunday school: 'Now the day is over, night is drawing nigh, shadows of the evening steal across the sky.' The sight and sound of the sea at his favourite place on the island, The Springs, east of Pyramid Rock, stayed with him too. In old age, he remembered how frightened he was by the noise of the waves dumping their 'huge load of brine and foam on the stones at the foot of the cliffs' below. He told the story of how a young boy, Charlie McGregor, who had been standing on the red flat rock at The Springs, was washed into the sea by a freak wave. In Clark's telling, McGregor was saved from drowning. But was it McGregor who was saved or Clark himself? Both Edith Jefferey and Raymond Grayden distinctly recall another resident, Jack McFee, telling them shortly before he died that Manning had once got into trouble at Pyramid Rock while fishing. McFee dived in to save him, rescuing him from almost certain death.[17]

Today, Phillip Island is a holiday resort, the home of the Australian Motorcycle Grand Prix, its roads combed by tourist buses disgorging thousands of visitors every year. They gather on the boardwalk on the south-west coast, keen to catch a glimpse of colonies of fairy penguins. For Clark, this commercialisation was a deflowering of the island's rustic, pre-industrial innocence. He always maintained that, as he stood on the deck of the ferry in 1924, just nine years old, looking back across the water to the island he was leaving behind, he knew then that childhood was over.

Adolescence beckoned as soon as he arrived at Belgrave, the south-eastern suburb of Melbourne at the foot of the Dandenong Ranges, where the Clark family resided for a decade from 1924. But he would still return to Phillip Island in his early teens. It was from this time that Russell's friend, David Brown, remembered the young Clark, on holidays at Phillip Island. 'Manning had a small crystal radio set, on which he'd listen to all kinds of programs, including foreign ones; wireless was only just coming in, but to see a young boy with one was very rare: it was an example of how unusual Manning was.' Clark had built the radio himself at Belgrave. Sitting in his bedroom, sheltered from the windswept hills and beaches of Phillip Island, he searched for the shortwave broadcasts from Europe and America. Although he loved the rawness of its beauty, he was also willing the island's disconnection from the outside world to be overcome. Phillip Island, Melbourne and Canberra were never enough for him; all his life, he longed to connect with the world beyond Australia's shores, his wanting to leave as strong as his desire to return. When he looked back to Phillip Island in his last years, he was investing his memory of one place with an impossible rapture. The island Clark remembered was so infused with romance and nostalgia that it was entirely cut loose from its bearings. Yet it was the one glimpse of light amidst the pall of darkness he cast when telling the story of his childhood.[18]

In *Puzzles of Childhood*, published in 1989, Clark painted a bleak portrait of Charles and Catherine's marriage. He wrote of a childhood in which 'one moment of terror succeeded another'. The young Clark was portrayed as the sensitive, innocent and unusually gifted soul cast into a world of hypocrisy and cruelty ('Mann dear, you are a very special boy'). He was the child with an adult's eye, tormented by shame and guilt. His particular intelligence and

curiosity disturbed his mother ('If you ask questions like that people are going to think you're mental'). His parents appear in *Puzzles* either as characters playing out his own inner conflicts or as mere precursors of his later self. Charles Clark is depicted as 'a divided man', a man 'who feared those who were hard of heart', who 'wanted praise not criticism', a man who 'brooded over even the mildest rebuke', the great orator from the pulpit who remained 'obsessed with death'. My father, myself. How different is Clark's haunted vision of Charles from the prosaic recollections of his father's friend, Bob Wallace: 'He could have been out of an English TV program, he didn't dress that carefully, he didn't wear a jacket, and he was usually in the garden: his main interest was growing potatoes!' David Brown recalled Charles Clark as a decent and kind man but not the most inspiring preacher. Brown remembered Catherine Clark, in the late 1930s, sitting in the pew, dutifully following every word of Charles's sermons as the smell of the roast beef cooking in the vicarage kitchen wafted through the open doors of the church.

'Reverend Clark always spoke too long,' recalled Brown. His memory of Clark's parents was of a largely happy couple.[19]

In *Puzzles*, Clark dramatised his parents' relationship, imagined his way into their minds and hearts, spoke for them and through them, invented thoughts and conversations, and recreated the experience of his early family life as tragedy. The boy's world was inhabited by two types of human beings: angels and devils. His memories behaved with uncanny poetic licence (the infant Clark is stung by a bee while burying his face in a white lily); or they conveniently served to explain what the old man had become ('my mother tells me one day I will be a famous man'). The whole narrative was infused with a moody, eternal melancholy, like a Hopper canvas or a Mahler *adagio*, descending on the reader like a heavy fog, saved only by the idyllic vision of Phillip Island, Clark's 'Swanee River', where his heart was turning ever. This was Clark's 'view', the view he insisted could not possibly be wrong. But the view taken by Russell and Hope was markedly different.[20]

Russell and Hope barely featured in Clark's telling of his childhood. Hope, said her son Philip Ingamells, was 'hurt' by the book—not because of her absence from the story but because 'Manning played up the extent of dissent in the marriage.' 'Hope continued to live at home. She attended Melbourne Girls' Grammar, taking the train from Belgrave each day, unlike Manning and Russell, who were boarders and only home on weekends. Hope saw her parents daily. She recalled a largely happy relationship. It was not the same marriage that Manning saw'. Russell Clark's widow, Eirene Clark, who was also close to Hope, remembers her stating bluntly when *Puzzles* was published: 'Mum and Dad slept in the double bed together. What's wrong with Manning? He's making most of it up.' As for Russell, he 'never accepted' the picture of Catherine and Charles painted by Clark, at least not in public. Writing Russell's obituary, Canon Evan Burge remarked on Russell and Hope's 'sunnier and less questioning outlook', so different from that of their 'sensitive' brother. While Clark's autobiography spoke of sibling rivalry, especially of Russell's jealousy of the attention Manning received from his mother, he failed to mention his own rivalry with Russell. David Brown often spent time with the Clark family in the late 1920s, and he spoke glowingly of Russell's talent for dancing—'he always had plenty of girls trailing him, that's one of the reasons I befriended him!' Manning envied his brother's success with the opposite sex. When Russell took a girl for a walk in the garden after Sunday lunch at the vicarage in Belgrave, Manning sat between them on the garden bench, arms folded.

After Clark's death, Dymphna refused to comment on the *Puzzles of Childhood* 'except to say that Manning's brother and sister were very troubled by the book'. When I asked Eirene Clark about her husband's reaction to *Puzzles*, she agreed that he did not see the darkness in his parents' relationship that Manning saw. Then, mid-sentence, she paused, startled that a memory could return so vividly: 'But now I remember, it has just come back to me,' she said. 'I remember Russell saying to me just after our wedding day, 'Mum and Dad weren't very happy together, I hope we will be.' Although Russell sensed the unhappiness of his parents' marriage, he preferred not to articulate his thoughts in detail. Nor did he write a memoir. Only Clark discovered the psychological and spiritual drama of his parents' lives. Only Clark looked to understand their lives as adults independent of their role as his parents, and in writing the story found a great tragedy.[21]

SEPARATION

As a young man in Oxford in 1938, where he began to keep a diary and correspond with his parents back home in Melbourne, Clark was keen to record his impressions of life in England. Then only twenty-three, he was concerned with his studies, the looming threat of war in Europe, and his burning love for Dymphna Lodewyckx. Initially, he wrote to his mother from Oxford with regular reports about the splendours of the English countryside, his dietary habits ('first I have porridge, or weeties, and then eggs (good ones too) and then toast and marmalade, and a good cup of tea'), the washing of his clothes and the darning of his socks.[22] It was his first time overseas, and although he sometimes sounded as if he was still his mother's boy, he also tried to explain to her his need for greater independence. In late November 1938, just before leaving Oxford for Bonn, where he was to meet

Catherine Clark

Dymphna, he wrote to his mother of his desire to 'strike out' for himself, reassuring her that 'the flame of the old love, the old ties, will never die'.

> I do think that life with another person outside the family is essential. One can't love both with the same intensity, and the old tie has to be put on a new basis … the trouble is that there may be conflict between parental love and the other love. It requires understanding on both sides, and a willingness to accept the new situation. So we must go forward courageously to a new relationship, because a son can't give to his mother the passionate love that is directed towards his wife, and if a man should look to his wife

only for passion, and keep the old spiritual love for his mother, then he is doomed to failure, to conflict and unrest. So I rejoice that you do love Dymphna, and that I can love her in both ways, and keep pure my love and affection for you. One always longs not to be forgotten—as a refuge from spiritual loneliness. We children will never forget you and Dad, nor will we ever forget each other—But, to renew our life with the world, we look for a mate: that life may go on.[23]

'And keep pure my love'. He knew Catherine was feeling his absence from her life and his new and all-consuming love for Dymphna. He was devoted to his mother and he didn't want to fail her, so much so that he broached the issue with her directly. Many young men might have left such things unsaid. He wrote often, asking her to remember him to his father and addressed his letters to her personally (not to both his parents), which points to the special relationship he shared with Catherine. She was the one to whom he confided his feelings, at least in correspondence. She was the one for whom he was most anxious, because he sensed her emotional frailty. He wrote to Catherine's sister, Gladys Hope, asking her to 'make Mum brighter'. In postcards to his elder brother, Russell, he asked if Catherine had 'complained of loneliness' while he was in England.[24]

David Brown remembered Clark's mother as a 'difficult person'. He found her 'anxious', 'a worrier', unusually 'fussy', and easily upset by her boys' behaviour. She was particularly fearful of anything being broken in the house, an anxiety that was transferred to Russell, who carried the same fear with him into adulthood. As a young woman she won prizes at school for her academic prowess, but as a married woman she withdrew into an extremely limited social world. The daily rhythms of her life at the vicarage, Mentone, a seaside suburb on Port Phillip Bay, where the Clarks had moved from Belgrave in 1934, were focused very much on domestic duties and the church 'circle' attached to Charles's ministry. At the very time when Clark left Australia to study in England, she was watching over his sister, Hope, who had contracted polio in late 1937 while working as a nurse at the Royal Children's Hospital in Melbourne. The 'infantile paralysis' epidemic of 1937–38 hit Victoria particularly hard, with more than two thousand cases reported, schools forced to close down and Victorian children who travelled interstate quarantined for twenty-one days by 'border police'. There was no cure. Hope was still making a slow recovery throughout 1938–39 but the experience had shaken Catherine.

While Clark was coping with his first European winter, Catherine was writing to him of the terrible heat in Melbourne. Victoria had experienced one of its harshest summers on record, with temperatures hovering over 44 degrees Celsius between Christmas 1938 and January 1939. On 13 January, fierce northerly winds fanned bushfires until almost every part of the state was ablaze. At least seventy people died in the Black Friday bushfires. From this furnace, with her daughter Hope still recuperating—she could barely manage to sit in a chair for more than half an hour each day—her second son seemed even further away. Just over two weeks later, when Clark married Dymphna hastily, in Oxford, in late January 1939, it was yet another blow. Catherine found this difficult to accept. Clark wrote her twice in less than a few days to explain the hastiness of their decision, acutely aware of her disappointment.[25]

> You don't need to worry about anything … I intended to write to you about it, and tell you our plans, but now it is all over, and you have to accept me as your first married son, and Dymphna as your first daughter in law. You always said that I would take you by surprise—and so I have. Mum, our only regret was that you could not be there.[26]

Few of Catherine's letters in reply have been found. But judging from the language and tone of the correspondence, it is clear the process of separation between mother and son was a difficult one. Reduced to communicating by post, Catherine suddenly felt even more removed from his life. She woke in the middle of the night, wondering where Clark was and worrying over his safety. As Clark's world expanded, the smallness of her world was laid bare. While he wrote to her of life in Oxford and European politics, she wrote to him about 'cleaning up the kitchen' and her 'pretty' garden—'quite gay with flowers'; explaining to Clark that 'there [was] no news in Mentone that [was] new or interesting'. Concerned for his wellbeing, she baked his favourite cakes and mailed them from Mentone, all the way to Oxford. In late 1938, when she heard that Manning and Dymphna were planning to visit Sweden, she fretted because she wasn't sure exactly where Sweden was. After ringing Dymphna's mother, Anna Lodewyckx, her fears were assuaged: 'she told me how near Sweden is to England'. When Clark pressed her to tell him something of her interior life, she seemed at a loss: 'you say I never say anything about myself—people all tell me I am looking better again'. Catherine was Clark's mother, she was not his friend, and her inability to understand many of her son's decisions continually frustrated Clark, who referred in one letter to the 'hopelessness of 1939' in his relationship with her, before stating his wish that 1940 would see their relationship grow closer.[27]

In late 1939, Dymphna had already given birth to their first son, Sebastian, and England was at war with Germany. Catherine was still finding it difficult to come to terms with the fact that her son's new family life was proceeding in her absence. Clark admonished her for not appreciating the tension the young couple had been subjected to while living in Europe: 'What you don't seem to realise is that we have lived through a time of perpetual crisis,' he told her, 'when we had to act before we could think.' While he was protective of her, he pinned much of her intractability on her limited outlook: 'sometimes I think your experience is even greater than your knowledge, a sad commentary on the life which you devoted so unselfishly to the welfare of your children'.

In the first years of both her sons' marriages Catherine continued to dote on them, displaying unusually protective behaviour. She even wrote Russell a letter on his honeymoon, a motherly intervention that Eirene continues to see as 'rather odd'. Although Hope still lived at home, Catherine struggled to let go of 'the boys' to whom she had devoted herself so unselfishly over more than twenty years.[28]

Half a century later, writing his autobiography in his early seventies, Clark idealised his mother, painting an image of a saintly, fey-like innocent who adored her second son. But the relationship they shared between Manning's birth in 1915 and Catherine's death twenty-eight years later, in 1943, was fraught. As Manning entered adolescence and approached adulthood, he saw her more clearly for the person she was—unworldly, cloying in her motherly love, and the bearer of a mystical, suffocating piety. Despite his devotion to her, as time passed they looked upon one another as strangers. Eirene remembers Clark's brother Russell remarking on several occasions, 'Mum would often say she couldn't understand Manning.' Thinking her second son was 'special' and unusually gifted (the image Clark perpetuated in his autobiography) is one thing, but understanding him is quite another. After Clark's death, Dymphna recalled with some amusement how his mother used to send him out with a billy to go and get more milk:

> he resented that she'd see that he was reading—in other words he wasn't doing anything and he might as well go and get the milk for her … that's long buried, but I can't help remembering that he once said that … his mother didn't understand and that she'd send him out for milk.

Manning, who loved reading so much that he could not be dragged away from his books, was the child Catherine looked on with bemusement. Yet she also placed him on a pedestal ('Mum's favourite' in Russell's eyes). Perhaps part of her leaning towards him lay in his *petit mal*, the intimation being that in the strange curse that struck like lightning there was also a spark of intellectual and creative insight given to few others.

By the time Dymphna met Catherine, in the late 1930s, she found her entirely detached from the wider world. She recalled a Sunday morning church service at St Augustine's Mentone, during which Clark, then in his early twenties, delivered the sermon:[29]

> On our way out from the church … she was just swelling with pride. I don't think she would have understood a word of what he said, really, but the more I think about it, at least when I knew his mother, she was just away. I'm not saying she was mad, I'm not saying that at all, but she was away, she was in another creation from my world, she lived only for her family and for the church and nothing else, nothing else.[30]

In later interviews, Dymphna revealed that '[Manning's] mother had many more reservations—[she] couldn't help identifying me with Germans … and she used to say to Manning, "The Germans are very clever you know, Mann!", thinking I had snared him I suppose.' Little wonder that Dymphna told her eldest son, Sebastian, that she 'could never see what Manning saw in his mother'. She knew all too well that the version of Catherine and Charles Clark painted in Clark's autobiography was packaged for a public audience, as she told Heather Rusden in 1997:[31]

His relations with both his parents were strained ... I think [as an adolescent] he thought his father was too inclined to gloss over all difficulties in life ... in theology ... in his relations with other people ... I've never said this to anybody before ... I remember when I first knew Manning he told me that he found life at the vicarage, at Belgrave ... full of contradictions ... occasionally he would say to his parents, 'I'm going to expose you in front of everybody' ... I think he felt that there was a lot of sham. Some of that is in *Quest for Grace*. But he doesn't say in *Quest For Grace* what he once told me: that he used to threaten his parents that he would expose them before everybody. Well, his father would have been included in that. I don't think he felt that his mother was ever in the slightest danger of being a hypocrite. She was just what she was, which was a very straight-laced but very good woman with very high principles. But his father ... loved to smoke and loved a drink, he loved the wrestling and the boxing ... on Monday nights he always listened to 'the big stoush', [as] he used to call it. [He also] loved fishing and cricket and wearing old clothes and loved his ducks ... [Manning] felt that his father ... covered up really ... he loved him ... but I think he probably looked down on him to the extent that he didn't think he was sufficiently principled.[32]

Catherine might have been sufficiently principled for her husband, but how content was she in her role as the dutiful vicar's wife at Mentone? In 1988, after hearing Clark interviewed by Caroline Jones on the ABC, a listener —'J.T.'—whose mother had worked as Catherine's washerwoman at Mentone wrote to tell him stories of his parents' lives. She remembered Charles Clark's gentle face, which 'crumpled like a spaniel's' when he smiled. She also told Clark of one comment her mother had made regarding Catherine: 'My mother said that your mother hated her life in Mentone.'[33]

Clark returned from England in August 1940 to the reality of his mother's declining health. In the months following the wedding, his mother, long troubled by kidney problems associated with diabetes, suffered a series of strokes. In October 1942, she had yet another relapse. Doctors told Clark for the first time that she would 'probably die'. After travelling from Geelong to Melbourne to see her in hospital, he was shocked by how weak she looked and 'almost cried'. Uncertain of his feelings, he was afraid of how he would cope with her death ('I am afraid of the scenes I may witness, & want to avoid them—I want … the sympathy without the suffering & the pain'). In later life, Clark told his close friend Don Baker that 'when [his mother] had the stroke … she came out of whatever state of unconsciousness she was in, sat up in the bed where she was lying and said: "Look at Manning over there he's just as sad as he ever was".' Looking back, Clark found this 'terribly painful'. At the time, he made no mention of it in his diary. Catherine clung to life for another six months, until, in late March 1943, Clark was informed that she had only days to live. He wrote that he felt calm—'almost unaffected'. The tone of his diary entry is stilted, even aloof: ('what sustains me is that no human events are worth fretting over'). His first emotions were of guilt and 'remorse'; immediately, he was plagued by regret for his 'past behaviour' towards her. He wrote not about her suffering, not about his father's feelings, but about his 'attitude' to her, his 'idea' of her—about the mother within him. At one point, he questioned the coolness of his response: 'Am I to infer that the loss of my mother is not disturbing? No! Rather—for five years I have repressed the affection felt for her. Will it recur in a great crisis: will the discipline of 5 yrs. withstand this test?'[34]

Catherine died two days later. Clark 'cried at first' but after listening to Beethoven's quartets he felt much 'better'. He drew up a table in his diary, mapping his response to the experience of viewing her body and attending the funeral, intending to use it as future source material; 'Mum's death: Life—its sordidness … The appearance of the dead—like wax dolls … Grief—painful … [I] cannot do justice to my experience. Why not write when the experience is still strong? Tonight I feel normal'. At twenty-eight, Clark appeared intent on controlling his emotion, passing the 'test' of his mother's death and getting his life back to 'normal'. 'Mourning', he thought, was simply 'showing off', 'a way to attract attention'. Maybe he had little alternative but to repress his grief. Dymphna gave birth to Axel, their third child, the day after Catherine's funeral.[35]

When Catherine died in 1943, Clark had seen little of her or his father over the previous five years. He had lived in England for almost two years and returned to take up his teaching position at Geelong Grammar, 65 kilometres south-west of central Melbourne. He saw his mother occasionally, on visits to Melbourne. Understandably, his life became more separate. This was one explanation for his feeling of guilt—not having spent sufficient time with her, not maintaining their 'special relationship'. As an adult, he never found the intimacy he shared with her as a child. His affection for her, which he claimed to repress after leaving for Europe with Dymphna in 1938, was a boy's love for his mother that never matured to find a new footing. Clark believed the 'rupture' of his departure from his family that year was one of the causes of his unhappiness in the years immediately preceding Catherine's death. For him 1943 had been a difficult year in other ways. He was deeply dissatisfied with his job at Geelong Grammar, beginning to feel estranged from his 'pregnant wife' and continually depressed at his failure to produce as a writer. 'I begin the year,' he wrote in his diary, 'without enthusiasm— angry—lonely—and discontented.'

Two months after Catherine's first major stroke, he noted how dependent he had become on the admiration of others: 'my mother, I suspect, made this indispensable for me'. Adore him she did, but with her early death, Clark was never granted the opportunity to prove her faith in him worthy. For much of the remainder of his adult life, he would become a pilgrim for her praise and adoration. In the years immediately after Catherine's death, he often seemed lost; he continued to indulge in bouts of self-flagellation, his diary and correspondence practically coming to a halt as he left Geelong Grammar and took up a tutorship in Political Science at Melbourne University in 1944. Yet in some ways, his mother's death had set him free.[36]

By 1949 he was the father of four children—Sebastian (born 1939), Katerina (1941), Axel (1943) and Andrew (1948). As he watched them grow, he began to reflect more and more upon his own childhood, seeing his own loneliness as a child mirrored in Axel's tendency to play alone, wondering how much each of his children's characters were 'innate' and how much shaped by their environment. Interacting with his children, he glimpsed echoes of his parents in his own parenting and caught stray bits of his own personality in their gestures and behaviour.[37] With Catherine gone, he began to dredge up the ghosts of his childhood, turning back to the past for answers to the dilemma that had plagued him for the last decade—how to write, what to write, why write? Since his early twenties, he had read Freud and Jung, adding an interest in their writings to his already long-standing devotion to Dostoyevsky, whose characters, perhaps more than any other novelist, were motivated by unconscious forces. Nearly thirty when he left Geelong Grammar for Melbourne University, Clark was coming to the point of believing, as did these three writers, that the source of his creativity lay buried in his childhood experience. Between 1946 and 1949, he devoted himself completely to teaching, reading voraciously, combing literature for the beacons that would shine a guiding light on his own path as a writer.

While he was lecturing in Political Science and Australian History at Melbourne during the five years from 1945 to 1949, Clark and Dymphna lived at Croydon, then a semi-rural outpost 30 kilometres south-east of the city. Upstairs, in the landing cupboard between the study and the bedroom, he kept the butterflies he had caught and pinned as a child, together with a handful of birds' eggs he collected as a boy on Phillip Island. These jewels of innocence he had kept boxed and wrapped in linen for over thirty years, but when it came time to leave the house in 1949, Dymphna refused to let him take them to Canberra. Perhaps she wanted him to sever his sentimental attachment to his childhood. Clark was annoyed and upset, but Dymphna prevailed. In other ways, too, Clark was making the final separation from his family and the physical environment of his childhood when he left Croydon for Canberra in October 1949. From now on, childhood would reside purely in the realm of memory and imagination. In the first weeks after his arrival in Canberra he wrote to Dymphna frequently (she remained in Melbourne with the children until January 1950), often late at night after bouts of reading had set his mind running. On 25 October 1949 he was reading DH Lawrence.

Late at night I have been reading some short stories by D.H. Lawrence. My impression now is that his relationship with his mother and 'Miriam' was the decisive thing in his life, and he was only a great writer when he used the material from that experience. There is an obvious comparison here with Henry Handel Richardson—I mean that her experiences as a child, her feeling for her father, were the creative sources for her.[38]

Next to Dostoyevsky, Lawrence had been one of Clark's most revered 'voices' since his late teens: he was taken by Lawrence's notion of spiritual love and his rejection of traditional Christianity. As with all of his favourite authors, Clark returned to Lawrence again and again throughout his life. Reading him in Canberra in 1949, together with Freud's *Outline of Psychoanalysis*, he began to see that the approach he should take as a writer was to try to understand his relationship with his mother and father. Separated from his family and home for the first time in more than a decade, he was able to use distance to help distil and shape his past. Scarcely six weeks after his arrival, he decided to resume his journal, surprised to find that the same problems that plagued him throughout 1941 to 1943 still lingered—'how to give up drinking … the desire to write a work—either of a literary or historical kind and the laziness which continually outstrips my ambitions'.[39]

Clark had only just settled in Canberra when his father died suddenly. In the summer of 1951, Charles Clark was holidaying at Sorrento on the Mornington Peninsula, together with Clark, Dymphna and their children. Sebastian was eleven at the time, and recalled sitting in the back seat of the car as his father drove back from the beach at Sorrento with his grandfather in the front passenger seat. On the way back home, Sebastian noticed that his grandfather was not speaking; he sat motionless in the car, his face frozen. Clark hurried back to the beach shack that the family were renting at Sorrento, jumped out of the car and called out to Dymphna: 'Dad's dying in the car.' Charles Clark, sixty-nine, had suffered a massive stroke. He died several days later, on 16 January 1951; on his bedside table a copy of Clark's first major publication, *Select Documents in Australian History, 1788–1850*, inscribed simply 'To Dad'.[40]

Clark had loved the joker and the raconteur in his father, loved his openness to life and celebrated Charles's mother's Irish ancestry. The obituaries in the Anglican press described 'Charlie' as someone renowned for his 'keen sense of fun' and 'skill at narrating stories'. This image was consistent with the image kept alive by Dymphna, who described Charles affectionately; he was the man who 'smoked and drank cups of tea with the parish ladies', the loving grandfather who dispensed sweets to her children from a large jar imprinted with the image of a bluebird, an absolute 'charmer' who had kept her in cigarettes when she and the children lived at the vicarage in 1944 while their house at Croydon was being built. She remembered the huge pile of unopened church journals (*The Anglican*) lying around the house, thinking then that he had little interest in the institutional affairs of the church.[41]

In the last years of his life, Charles had lived with his daughter, Hope. Clark saw his father occasionally during this time, usually during the family holidays each summer, when they returned to holiday on Phillip Island. But while Charles was alive, he never attempted to do what he longed to do so often after his death: to scratch beneath the surface of the everyday and talk to him about his emotional life. Even if he had tried, Charles may not have been very receptive. He'd always jokingly referred to Manning as 'the thoughtful customer', as much a pointer to Manning's introspective nature as it was to his own taciturn response when it came to talking about the big questions that preoccupied his son. With his father's death, Clark would embark on a lifelong quest for understanding: who was his father? What type of man was he? How had his father contributed to the person he had become?[42]

In 1954 he began sketching notes for a 'novel' based on his father's life story. He started to research various stages of Charles's life, noting the hymns he'd sung at St Peter's Church, digging for details about his time as a curate at St John's Ashfield. He kept asking himself why he had not been a success'—'what went wrong?' 'Was his soul seared and destroyed' by the Anglican hierarchy in Sydney? Inventing conversations between his parents, he tried to understand the friction between them. 'Did [Dad] flirt with the parishioners?' Clark would not let his parents rest. His narrative sketches based on his childhood memories were sparked by the literature in which he lived, blending with the words and images of the writers he held dear, until they seemed to coexist in one tumultuous present.[43]

He read the work of Henrik Ibsen repeatedly. One play, in particular, that resonated for him above all others was *Ghosts*, Ibsen's middle-class family drama that attacked some of society's most sacred conventions, particularly marriage, and shocked Scandinavian society when it was first published in December 1881. In the 1964 Penguin edition of the play on the shelves of Clark's study in Canberra, the passage that Clark quoted on numerous occasions throughout his life is marked clearly. The widowed Mrs Alving is speaking with the defender of faith and convention, Pastor Manders:

I'm haunted by ghosts ... [and] I'm inclined to think we are all ghosts Pastor Manders; it's not only the things that we've inherited from our fathers and mothers that live on in us, but all sorts of old dead ideas and old dead beliefs; and things of that sort. They're not actually alive in us, but they're rooted there all the same, and we can't rid ourselves of them ... And we are, all of us, so pitifully afraid of the light.

Ibsen's words would continue to serve as a torchlight for Clark who asked the same questions of his own life:

[I] have been thinking about the awareness of innocence and the awareness of evil in oneself ... the question is: who put these ... inside oneself? Are they inherited from a past, and if so from an unchanging and never to be changed past? Because it is important to know this, it is therefore important to know where one came from so that one might know what one is.[44]

Searching for the truth of Charles and Catherine's marriage, Clark was gripped by the mystery of fate. In 1964 he visited Ireland and sought out the stone monument for the Rose of Tralee; it was the song of that name that had been sung for his mother when the family left Belgrave for Mentone in 1934. 'There I stood,' he wrote, 'hatless, dumb, in front of the stone remembering things past which could never be undone.' The ghosts of his past continued to haunt him. Shortly after his fiftieth birthday in 1965, he marked a particular passage in Frieda Fordham's *An Introduction to Jung's Psychology*: 'Jung's dreams of mighty floods sweeping over Europe … destroying everything in their path'. He appeared to read Jung's image as a prophecy, sensing that he would soon be overwhelmed by a rising tide of 'unconscious material', the detritus of his past. Over the next two decades, he would slowly unearth one of the most extraordinary stories of his parents' lives.[45]

THE FALL FROM GRACE

The story unveiled its secrets gradually. Manning was five when the family moved to Kempsey in 1920, and his adult memory of the short time he spent there was hazy, to say the least. What he did recall, however, was how he, Russell and Hope were separated from their parents in 1921 and sent to live with Catherine's sister Gladys in Victoria. Growing up, he was told by his parents that Catherine had been 'unwell' and did not recover until 1922, when Charles took up the position as vicar on Phillip Island and the family was reunited. Clark always sensed there was more to the story; somehow the explanation he'd been given only fuelled his curiosity. Lurking beneath many of his diary entries in the wake of his parents' deaths was a conviction that a darker truth lay behind the sudden departure from Kempsey in 1921.

Catherine and Charles Clark's domestic help, Marjorie Thompson, had been a constant presence in Manning's childhood. Her first contact with the family was at Kempsey, where she was the housemaid at St George's Hostel, close by the church. She was then in her twenties. Later, she did housework for the Clarks at Phillip Island and Belgrave, but she also tended Catherine, assisting her during times of illness and supporting her as a friend. She wrote many years later to Clark, describing how 'fond' she was of his mother:

[On Phillip Island] I used to drive her about on the old horse and buggy … I taught your father to drive and to harness the horse, I used to drive down to the clergy rest home, and your Dad used to saw up all the old oak trees into foot blocks, I used to load them on to the buggy, it had a big tray in the back

An Eye for Eternity

and I would drive them home to the vicarage … your father used to play beautifully, so did his dear little mother, and his father played the violin.[46]

From 1922 until 1934, while she worked for the Clarks on Phillip Island and at the Belgrave vicarage, Marjorie, accompanied by Charles and Catherine, often visited her poverty-stricken mother, who lived in South Melbourne. The Clarks usually brought food and money with them. Hidden away somewhere in the house at South Melbourne, under strict instructions not to appear, was Marjorie's illegitimate daughter, Elizabeth, born in 1921, who was barely ten at the time. She had lived with her grandmother since her birth, having been brought up to believe that her grandmother ('Mrs Thompson') was her mother, and that Marjorie (her birth mother) was her sister. Somehow, for the first ten years of her daughter's life, Marjorie managed to maintain this fiction even when she visited her mother alone, usually once a month. Some time in the 1930s, in order to help support her mother and the daughter she longed to have as her own, Marjorie Thompson made the decision to leave the Clarks' employ and marry Reg Goulter, the grounds-man at the vicarage in Belgrave. It was an unfortunate decision. Goulter, a violent and abusive alcoholic, subjected Marjorie to repeated beatings, at one point forcing her onto the floor and kicking her unconscious. Within months he had drunk the family's meagre savings and terrorised Elizabeth who, in her teens, was forced to work as a hospital cleaner to support her family. Fifty years later, shortly after Clark published *Puzzles of Childhood*, Elizabeth, who by then had changed her name to Margaret Reynolds, wrote to him to reveal the tragedy of her story.

I, like yourself, lived a very puzzled childhood. I was told Mrs. Thompson was my mother [and Marjorie] was my sister. My father had been killed in the war. Until the age of 8, I was not allowed to mix with anyone … we lived in one small bug-infested, mice ridden room upstairs, directly above a gro-cer's shop … Eventually the authorities demanded I be sent to school. Now at the age of 8 years this proved really traumatic. Especially as Mrs. Thomp-son, now 68, insisted on escorting me on my way to and from … school … I suffered agony when the worldly-wise children of my class informed me of the impossibility of my "Mummy" being my mother. And of course her Scottish accent did not help ... It was not until my beloved Marjorie married Mr. Goulter that I discovered she was my mother. By then I was ten years old and had started secondary school. I was so shocked by it all that I lost all interest in my studies and at the age of 14 left for a job on a sheep station at Mansfield ... I had no one to turn to.[47]

Margaret Reynolds grew up believing 'she was a disgrace', the cause of a shame so great that she was not even allowed in full public view. Since 1961, when Clark found Margaret waiting outside his door after attending a meeting at the ANU, he had known that Reg Goulter was not Margaret's father. In his diary, Clark blamed himself, Russell and Hope, for not realising Marjorie Thompson's 'agony', 'as though she was of no account'. That day in October 1961, Margaret told Clark she had been so traumatised by her experience that she left home and eventually suffered a nervous breakdown. Desperate, she tried to visit Charles Clark at Mentone in 1951, only to find he had died three weeks earlier. Grief-stricken, she then attempted to commit suicide. If Clark's diary is to be believed, even after hearing Margaret's heart-rending story, he did not realise the whole truth for another twenty-six years. Charles Clark was Margaret's father. She was born to Marjorie Thompson in June 1921. Marjorie's affair with Charles, which was undoubtedly discovered by church authorities, was the cause of the family's sudden departure from Kempsey and the couple's separation in late 1921 and early 1922. One puzzle of Clark's childhood was now solved, but many other mysteries remained.[48]

On 22 June 1987, while writing his autobiography, Clark wrote in his diary that Margaret Reynolds had come to tell him the truth: 'my father was her father'.

She asked me: 'Manning, did you ever hear who was my father? Did you ever have a suspicion who he was?' I said 'No' (though a thought had crossed my mind). She then whispered in my ear—'Manning, I'm your sister ... Mum told me years ago.' We kissed passionately and wept. I did not tell Dymphna.

An Eye for Eternity

Clark's nephew, Philip Ingamells (Hope's son), who was close to Margaret during the last years of her life, thought that she revealed the true story to Clark not in the 1980s but 'sometime in the 1960s'. Margaret gave Ingamells a copy of the photograph of her standing with Manning, Dymphna, Andrew and Benedict in the garden of their house in Canberra.

This photograph was almost certainly taken at the time of Clark's diary entry in 1961. Even if Margaret had intended to tell Clark that day, and decided at the last minute only to tell him part of the story, it's surprising that Clark, after hearing of Margaret's last-minute attempt to see his father, and her suicidal impulses when she found out he had died only weeks earlier, did not draw the obvious conclusion. Other family members recalled hearing stories that Charles had been forced to leave Kempsey 'because of a sex scandal'. Clark himself referred frequently to his mother's great burden, making much of her oblique references to those 'things' in her life that were so painful she could not bring herself to speak about them. Other entries in his diary, even before Margaret's visit in 1961, suggest he had much more than a suspicion of his father's adultery. In 1960, Clark imagined what a 'relief' it must have been for his father when Catherine died. With her 'silent forever', he wrote, Charles's guilt for his 'un-atoneable act' would have been easier to bear. In 1983, Clark wrote to Russell that Hope had 'no idea of the tragedy of Dad's life' nor of their mother's struggle to survive her 'terrible ordeal'. It is possible that both Clark and Russell suspected that Margaret Reynolds was their half-sister long before 1987, when Clark became convinced that his mother knew of the existence both of his father's affair and of Margaret. Writing in his diary, he suddenly saw it as an explanation for so many of the ghosts that had haunted his memory of his parents' lives.[49]

> That explains the period at Darriwill in 1921–22 … Mum was not there. Dad was not there. They must have separated. How did Dad persuade the Archbishop of Melbourne to appoint him to Cowes? … that explains why Dad preached so passionately on [Nathaniel Hawthorne's] 'The Scarlet Letter'. That explains why Mum, in moments of distress said: There are things in my life, Mann dear, I hope you'll never hear anything about. Well, I was 72 when I found out why you said that Mum, but I have suspected something for forty years. I remember too [Marjorie] was often flirting with Dad & Mum's jealousy of all women who responded to Dad, the shoutings, the trapped man, did he go on tormenting himself till he died … did she ever trust him?[50]

If Clark was correct, and Catherine Clark did know about Charles's affair with Marjorie, it was remarkable that she allowed Marjorie to work as her domestic help for almost a decade afterwards, both at Cowes and at Belgrave. Was this her sense of Christian obligation and duty being lived out at her own expense? Did she know there was a child born of Charles and Marjorie's affair? If so, did she believe the child had been put up for adoption? Did she know about Margaret's existence at all? Marjorie Thompson effectively became part of the Clark family. Given the couple's separation and their hasty departure from Kempsey, Catherine surely knew about the affair.

How Marjorie's ongoing presence played out in the marriage of Catherine and Charles will never be known. But it is certainly possible that for the sake of the children and social propriety, Catherine swallowed her hurt and pride and accepted Charles's former affair with Marjorie. For Clark's siblings, it proved difficult knowledge to come to terms with. Hope did not find out until 1990, with the publication of Clark's second autobiographical volume *The Quest for Grace*. Initially, Clark arranged a meeting between Hope and Margaret at Melbourne's Treasury Gardens, telling Hope only that he wanted her to meet 'one of Dad's relatives'. Pointing Margaret out from the speakers' platform, Clark took no part in their conversation. As Hope later wrote to Dymphna, 'We did meet and chatted away but I just thought she was one of Dad's relatives who had come from Sydney and who were now living at Frankston. I did not hear any more or have any contact … [until I read the story] "In Search of Grace" [sic] which puzzled me'.[51]

Both Clark and Russell had obviously made hard work of telling their sister the truth, either denying the story in Russell's case, or in Clark's case by staging a meeting between Margaret and Hope in which he hoped the truth would spill. When she finally found out, Hope endured the opprobrium and malicious gossip of her fellow parishioners in Melbourne, many of whom were aware of the story through reading Clark's autobiography. Hope developed a friendship with Margaret, taking clothes for her two children and personally delivering cheques from Clark, who in the late 1980s, changed his will, leaving Margaret a considerable sum of money but nothing to Hope or Russell. Clark told Russell of their father's adultery in one of their 'whispering conversations' at family gatherings in the 1980s, conversations that Eirene Clark admits she was never privy too. 'I always knew Russell kept things from me,' she said. Both Hope and Eirene were 'protected' from the Clark brothers' private conversations. Nor could Clark simply tell the story. When Russell's son, Tim, visited Clark at his home in Canberra in 1989, Clark sent him upstairs to the study to 'read' the relevant pages from the manuscript of *The Quest for Grace*. 'I was in awe of him,' said Tim, 'and of course I went upstairs and read and it was all about Margaret but in fact it was less explicit than I expected and I was mystified until he finally explained the story to me.' Clark believed he had finally worked out one of the great mysteries of his life. Yet there is one crucial piece of evidence that suggests Clark was wrong in thinking his mother knew of Margaret's existence.[52]

In July 1991, two months after Clark's death, Margaret Reynolds wrote to Dymphna after being visited by Hope in hospital:

Poor Hope had no idea of my existence until she read [Manning's] book, and I fear it has been a very disturbing emotional experience for her. I, in turn, have discovered more of Mr Goulter's lies, as he always tortured me by saying I was the cause of violent quarrels between the Clark family, now this had always upset me, now I know it is not true, as I'm practically sure Mrs Clark was totally unaware of my existence.[53]

Margaret had never set eyes on Catherine (or Charles) and in all likelihood Catherine was indeed unaware of Margaret's existence. By hiding Margaret when the Clarks visited, Marjorie and her mother had no doubt conspired to ensure that Catherine would never know the full truth of her affair with Charles. When Margaret, aged thirty, travelled to Mentone in 1951 to see Charles Clark, she was attempting to speak to him for the first time in her life as her father. Charles's death stole her father away and Margaret, crushed by years of shame and abuse, must have felt rudderless, with no future in sight. Towards the end of her life she wrote almost apologetically to Clark, signing off philosophically but stoically: 'we were victims of uncontrollable circumstances, we can still see and walk so we must do our best with what is left'. For Clark, the mystery of his father's relationship with Marjorie Thompson, and what that had meant for his mother, was yet another lure drawing him back to the past. He wondered if Charles had ever shared his story with his family or friends, believing that it now explained his 'dismissal by the church', 'the contempt' of Catherine's sisters and 'the ostracism from his contemporaries'. Scribbling a note to himself as he made notes for his autobiography, he let his imagination fly: 'was that why he in part hated her, in part feared her ... had Mum rejected him in the bed? He was 38 and maddened by desire ... anger with Mum, the setting for disaster.'[54]

Would this become Clark's self-imposed fate, to stand before the past he exhumed, bemoaning all those things that could not be undone? His creativity was fuelled not so much by what he found there as by the emotional turmoil involved in the search, which welled inside him like a tidal force, feeding its way through to his prose. His search to understand Australia's past would be driven by the same underlying tensions. As Ibsen's Mrs Alving remarked, 'there are ghosts all over the country'. Every nation has its ghosts. From the publication of the first volume of *A History of Australia* in 1962, when Clark was asked to explain the motivation of his epic journey, he replied: 'to know where we have come from and to know who we are'. Occasionally, he sounded like Ibsen himself—exhorting his readers to study the 1840s because it would allow them to see that Australians were 'still haunted by certain ghosts, dead ideas and dead beliefs'; 'after all,' he declared, 'the whole point of knowing the past is to give men a chance to rid their minds of such ghosts'.

Throughout the 1960s, Clark continued to work on the short stories based on his childhood and adolescence. The ghosts of the past were indeed 'alive' within him, and his insistence on confronting them was slowly unleashing his creative imagination. The second volume of *A History of Australia* (1968) had already been released by the time the stories were published as *Disquiet* in 1969. Despite Clark's denials, the stories were transparently autobiographical. The opening story, 'Discovery', told the story of Tug Smith, 'night soil man', drunkard and social outcast on Phillip Island, whose mysterious death found only one minister willing to officiate at his funeral— the character who represented the Reverend Charles Clark. In all the stories, it's possible to sense Clark's regret that he didn't try harder to speak with his parents when they were alive. They portray his loneliness (the boy who is unable to speak about the things that matter to him); and explore the gulf between his mother (the woman of Christian principles and social propriety) and his father (life affirming and compassionate but deeply afraid of social censure). Like his hero Ibsen, Clark exposed the hypocrisy of religious and social conventions and the entrenched cruelty in institutions, which so often appeared convinced of their own benevolence; Melbourne Grammar, his alma mater, with its culture of bullying and intimidation, being a prime example. The collection was the fruit of nearly two decades of self-examination since his father's death in 1951. When he drafted the first ideas for the stories in 1954, he had not then started to write *A History of Australia*. By the time they were published in 1969 the stories already read like minor sidetracks and excursions to the main event. He'd now found the outlet for his creativity in historical writing. While the writing of fiction had helped him to attain that goal, he would pen very little fiction in the last twenty years of his life. Instead, he would find new reasons to dredge up the ghosts of his parents and childhood. For most of his adult life, Clark lived with the sense that the truth of his parents' emotional lives had been withheld, both from one another and from himself. The more aware he became of the sources of estrangement in their lives, the more convinced he was that his own success might atone for their unhappiness.[55]

THE PILGRIMAGE BEGINS

In 1969, with the first two volumes of the *History* behind him, Clark sat in the British Museum library 'working on Dickens'. Then fifty-four, he knew, perhaps for the first time in his life, that he had succeeded in the decision he had taken late in life—'to tell Australia's story'. As the writing of *A History of Australia* became something of a serialised drama in the national press in the 1970s, Clark was asked to reflect on the origins of his work. The context of his recollecting shifted, moving away from fiction and diary entries to a public stage. In oral history interviews, in media appearances, and in short essays for various publications, he began to draw on his childhood in order to explain 'the famous historian' he had become. By 1979, he had already developed the stock repertoire of stories that would be dramatised ten years later in *The Puzzles of Childhood*. Asked why he wanted to write history, he spoke first not of intellectual influences but of his family: the class differences between his parents—those 'two quite different visions of the world'; his mother's family dreaming (the Marsdens, the Hopes and the Hassalls); and the religious world of the vicar's son, a world that was already crumbling at the outset of the twentieth century, begging the question posed even earlier by Nietzsche— what would become of man in a world without God? As the controversy around his work raged and the accolades rained down for the *History* and his public activities, Clark dreamt increasingly of his parents standing beside him. Flying back from Harvard in 1979, he wrote to Russell, 'in tears': 'I would have loved Mum and Dad to know that Harvard was the greatest moment in my life. They would have known that all their love and faith had not been in vain'. More great moments were to follow.[56]

In December 1980, after being handed a letter that told him he had been nominated for Australian of the Year, he wrote in his diary: 'I thought of Mum and Dad, the two to whom I can no longer speak.' Clark was convinced that it was 'their faith and love' that had 'reaped such a rich harvest' in his life; that his 'modicum of worldly success and recognition' had been 'fashioned by them'. Yet his increasing longing for their approval also implied that their love could *only* be rewarded through his success. It was some time in the 1970s that he began to walk from Box Hill Station to his parents' graves, letters in pocket, determined to show them the glory of his achievement. The change was remarkable; Clark's pilgrimages to his parents' graves had begun in the 1950s but it was more than twenty years after their deaths, as his trophy cupboard overflowed, that he began to pen more elaborate notes to his parents, keeping some in his papers, pinning others on Catherine's and Charles's gravestones. As he entered his final years and attained a level of celebrity unheard-of for an Australian historian, his longing to stand before his parents became more desperate. How much of his longing was simply explained by his need to imagine himself basking in their pride? After reading Hardy's *Jude the Obscure* on a plane to Brisbane in 1977, awed by Hardy's ability to capture 'the spirit of place', he wrote of his mother as one of his 'admirers', 'for whom my success would compensate for all she had been through'. 'By the time I succeeded,' he lamented, 'she was lying in her grave.' Here, his longing for Catherine to see his success was driven as much by a desire to console her (a desire impossible to realise but real nonetheless) as it was by his wish for her to see his accomplishments. Success was changing his relationship with his past.[57]

Virginia Woolf, in the first pages of her autobiography, saw her past as 'an avenue lying behind ... a long ribbon of scenes [and] emotions'. 'One never realises an emotion at the time,' she reflected. 'It expands later, and thus we don't have complete emotions about the present, only about the past.' Time, ageing and the things that happen to us—either by chance or choice—are constantly changing the way we see and understand our past. We remember things we had forgotten and suppress things we would rather forget, we invest new meaning in events we once thought inconsequential, and whether we are writers or not, we strive to make sense of our lives in some way by telling stories.[58]

Clark's emotions associated with his memory of his parents took on a more tragic and elegiac hue as he aged, like drops of ink slowly clouding water. As he entered his forties and faced life without both his parents, he began to build a relationship with them in death that he was never able to in life, wanting to talk to them, wanting to understand their lives, wanting to express his love for them, almost as if he could only truly know his parents in death, when their silence left him free to create an image of them in his own likeness. In 1979, he tried to explain his affection for them:

> They made me feel that the only persons who would rejoice when something deeply pleasing happened were my mother and my father. They were the great source of my inspiration: they were the ones who had a never-ending faith in their prodigal son. I believe we are all children until our parents die. Then we are deprived of the opportunity to speak to the only people in the world who know what we are talking about.

Clark had managed to convince himself that the only people who could truly rejoice at his success were those who could no longer hear or speak. Wounded by criticism, he imagined an all-loving and divine image of his parents, a reverie that became his psychological refuge, a place where pain and criticism no longer existed. Asked to explain his motives in writing his autobiography, he replied that his parents were 'worthy of some immortality'. As he grew older, Charles and Catherine changed in his imagination; once mere mortals, they gradually became gods. As Clark himself became more revered, his image of his parents became more heroic. He described his mother's 'majestic face', how she appeared at times like a 'person transfigured', recalling a woman who was universally loved—'men and women in all walks of life revered her'—as if Catherine were a reincarnation of the Virgin Mary. His parents had become epic figures in the saga of his own life. As

Clark told Keith Dunstan in 1987, he was using memory to find a way of 'moving out of the darkness into the light', shaping his past through the prism of his needs as an older man. The final effect was to make the path he *chose* to follow appear as if it was his inevitable fate. Clark came to the end of his life believing that it had always been his destiny to become an historian; as if his life's course was predetermined. But Clark's 'fate' was never inevitable. He would make choices; he would try to change the course of his life; and he would always doubt if he had made the right choices.

Standing next to his parents' grave that winter's day in 1987, his note to Catherine and Charles taped to the headstone, Clark was like a man directing his own screenplay. He photographed the evidence of his defiant, romantic longing to conquer death and filed it away in his papers. Passersby might have seen him, an elderly man beside his parents' grave, cradling his notes to the dead.[59]

PART TWO

4: COMING TO HISTORY: THE MELBOURNE YEARS, 1928–38

Initiation ceremonies were usually held in the library, late in the evening. The surface of the old refectory table, dark from years of ink and French polish, was splashed with soapy water as the older boarders gathered around the perimeter, like baying spectators at a prizefight. One by one, the younger boys were forced up onto the table and compelled to recite a verse of poetry or song. Each time one faltered in his performance, he was pushed and pelted with a wet towel; each time he showed any sign of slipping, he was pushed from side to side with even greater force, the roar of the bullies' taunts and laughter rising and falling like some terrifying choir. The punishment was meted out by the 'self-appointed tyrants of the long dorm', the boys who 'instigated all sorts of petty persecutions' with which to greet the new arrivals. When new students failed to stay behind after school to cheer on cricket or rugby teams, they had their face and hair smeared in oil for extra encouragement. When young boarders arrived, they were forced to run naked through the Long Dorm as the older boys whipped them with wet towels, many of them 'scarred for life' by the experience. For Mervyn Austin, who at the age of twelve started at Melbourne Grammar in 1928 with Manning Clark, the 'barrack-like existence' of the senior boys in the boarding house made them 'in some respects like the Spartans, rather brutal, dumb and exclusive'.

Melbourne Grammar quadrangle, circa 1915

The dormitories were cold, with exposed beams, wide wooden floorboards and high windows—a dozen boys to each dorm and one prefect, appointed by the Housemaster, whose job it was to ensure that the boys were up, showered and dressed for breakfast at 7.30 am, followed by chapel. The drumbeat of the housemaster's shoes on the bare boards of the dorm was enough to strike fear into the heart of any boy who had not managed to prepare himself in time. After the school assembled for prayers at 9.15, the boys rushed to the lockers surrounding the main quadrangle before classes finally began. Sometimes, as the students settled and quiet descended, it was possible to hear 'the sound of savage lashings' drifting out into the stone-rimmed silence of the quad. When troublesome boys had accrued too much detention, they were permitted to 'sock off' their excess hours with the headmaster, Richard Penrose Franklin; the exchange rate—three strokes of the cane for each hour of detention. Years later, Mervyn Austin realised that so much of what passed for 'wholesome discipline' at the school was little more than 'pathological sadism'. Phil Harris was another of Clark's fellow students at Melbourne Grammar; together with Austin and Clark, he boarded his first year at Creswick House, only a short distance from the school, on Domain Road. The master of Creswick House was 'Dingo' Clarke—one of the English public school 'breed', then in his mid-forties, whom Harris

An Eye for Eternity

remembered as a 'sly old dog', 'brutal and nasty', a man who loved nothing more than to cane children. Harris hated the school so much that he ran away, only to be caught by police at Ballarat Railway Station before he could set out on the 48-kilometre trek to his hometown of Beaufort. Like so many boys who initially recoiled from the culture of violence and intimidation in the school, Harris returned and ended up enjoying his final years.[1]

In the late 1920s, Melbourne Grammar, set on 6 hectares adjoining Government House and the Botanic Gardens, appeared stark and forbidding, its sombre grey bluestone crowned by a clock tower and the school ensign flying from a turret mast. The only thing missing was a moat. To the east of the quadrangle, the chapel was positioned behind a solitary gaslight, the whole scene reminiscent of a bleak village square in the nether lands of Scotland. The bluestone buildings were matched by blue uniforms; the 1000-odd boys at the school wore a blue suit and blue cap, with a badge bearing a mitre and book; gold, silver and white badges indicating a boy's status in the school. Founded in 1858 in the 'grand' tradition of English public schools such as Rugby and Eton, the school exuded a distinctly militaristic air.

Manning Clark,
Melbourne Grammar, 1928

In Clark's time at the school (1928–33), many of the teaching staff had fought in World War I. The school's culture was exclusively male—upstanding gentlemen of the British variety—predominantly Protestant and proudly sport-obsessed. As Phil Harris described it: 'we had plenty of religion thumped into us. It was a muscular Christian type of outfit, chapel before school every morning and for the boarders, Matins and Evensong every Sunday and communion before breakfast. Captains and leaders were inevitably drawn from the sporty types.' For once, the school motto accurately summed up the ethos of the institution: *Ora et Labora*—Pray and Work. Outside the walls of the school, the rifle range, ovals, tennis courts, and boathouses on the Yarra River and Albert Park Lake added to the dominant impression. Well into the 1960s, ex-students joked about 'serving time' at Grammar. The school's imprint would remain with students for the rest of their lives—'he's a Grammar boy'—producing men of distinctive character, men who, in the words of Richard Penrose Franklin, had attained 'great mastery of self' and were capable of 'self-sacrifice of the individual for the whole' rather than simply giving free rein to 'self-expression'.[2]

MELBOURNE GRAMMAR 1928

In his seventies, when Manning Clark looked back on his years at Melbourne Grammar he saw a landscape of pain in which even the smallest acts of kindness appeared life-saving, remaining with him as nourishing mementos for life. Long afterwards, Clark claimed to see the face of Harold Hunt, the school's classics master, as he picked him up off the ground after his first seizure; Hunt's whispering voice chanting reassuringly: 'You'll be alright boy, you'll be alright.' He remembered how, as his shock at the brutality of the school's culture subsided, he had found a mentor in Richard Franklin, known as 'Lofty'—a giant of a man with a melancholy air and an eye for tragedy ('his eyes always terribly sad'), whom Manning 'adored' from the first meeting. Manning was by no means a victim of his parents' high hopes in being sent to Melbourne Grammar. Even before he won a scholarship to attend the school, he wrote personally to Franklin, requesting admission on the grounds that he was the son of an Anglican clergyman. As an adult, Clark tailored his memories of the school to the prejudices of his audience. In 1958, when he wrote for the *Age* on the occasion of Melbourne Grammar's centenary, he produced a standard historical overview that was entirely uncritical, reminding his readers that former Australian prime ministers Alfred Deakin and Stanley Bruce were ex-pupils, and that the school's role, after all, was 'to educate men for the professions, steeped in the tradition of classical scholarship, liberalism and Protestant Christianity'. Melbourne Grammar's elitism was a thing of the past, he argued; now it aimed to educate 'the many'. Perhaps this was a necessary show of loyalty, given that he had decided to send his sons to the same school. By the late 1970s and early 80s, however, he was shaping his memories to suit the nationalist bent of the last three volumes of *A History of Australia*, casting the school as the symbol of 'the apologists for British philistine culture in Australia', and likening his time as a student at Melbourne Grammar to that of a 'prisoner'. He grew fond of exaggerating class difference, telling the story of a boy from the 'genteel poor' who, on his first day, had suffered the ignominy of trundling up to the school gates in his father's single-seater Morris Oxford while all the other boys alighted like secondhand royalty from Packards and Buicks. In his final years, he wrote of being plagued by 'nightmares' and 'visions' of arrest and flogging. The boys who had bullied him at Melbourne Grammar transformed into 'the men in charge of the world', 'the men and women dressed in black', 'the ones to whom Australia belonged'. In short, they became stand-in caricatures for all who saw the world differently, the devils and oppressors in Clark's Old Testament world of partisan spirituality. In the midst of these memories, so often self-serving, lie shards of truth; part clues to one of the most intriguing questions of Clark's life—what was it that turned the mind of a young man in 1930s Melbourne towards the writing of history, and ultimately to write the history of his own country?[3]

From his early teens, Manning felt the compulsion to write; the act of writing had become instinctive, necessary, the only way he could become truly free—how he made experience real. In this sense, Manning Clark was a born writer; at an early age, he felt what he later described as his 'otherness', he saw himself as both of the world and separate from it, as someone who did not 'belong', an observer who carried a 'secret' creative life within him that no one else could possibly understand. If Clark the writer first emerged in early adolescence, he emerged in response to his experience, not because of it; his sensitivity, his musing and self-conscious self, his separateness, and his talent for expressing in words what others had only half-seen or half-felt, was, by the time of his adolescence, part of the mystery of his very being. Sitting the scholarships exam for Melbourne Grammar, a twelve-year-old Manning Clark experienced a 'sense of freedom' in writing his essay while many boys around him were no doubt fearful and apprehensive.

Once inside the bluestone walls, his extraordinary essay-writing drew him to Franklin's attention. In Clark's reckoning, Franklin was a key figure in his development as a writer and historian; the one teacher who recognised his talent for narrative history, turning his sights from medicine to history ('Clark, you have the gifts to be an historian, you can tell a story—only those who can tell a story should write history'). Franklin was the first man of letters to take Clark under his wing and glimpse something of his emotional life. Perhaps when he looked down at the fourteen-year-old Clark as he handed out the essays in Greek history, he saw something of himself as a young man, just as Clark saw in Franklin something of what he might become.

Searching for the spark that set his course in life as an historian, Clark did not recall events; instead he recited the poetics of his existence—insights, blinding realisations and epiphanies of body and soul. Many historians, when asked to pinpoint their turning towards history, isolate an historical event or site that captured their imagination, a moment or place in time they felt drawn to know, to understand and ultimately to explain. Clark's memory of his own coming to history painted an image of a lone creative artist emerging phoenix-like from the backblocks of Melbourne; where other historians saw a mere train of events, he would see pathos and tragedy.[4]

In late 1929, towards the end of Manning's second year at Melbourne Grammar, three of the school's students—Lindsay Cumming, Andrew Joshua and Richard Lewis—drowned in a boating accident. Only one boy, JG Brown, who swam ashore for help, survived. The funeral for all three boys was held in the school chapel. With the pews packed to overflowing, the sight of the three coffins in front of the altar, draped in the school colours, was a shattering blow for all who stood before them. Franklin was no exception. Clark never forgot the scene. 'Terribly upset', Franklin came forward and did what had to be done, telling the congregation in his 'beautiful, mellifluous voice' that there were two views of life, the Greek view and the Christian view, and that every human being was asked to decide which of them was true. Some days later, when Franklin penned the notice in the school magazine, he wrote that there was only 'one consolation': the three boys, he reflected, had 'met their deaths with a calmness and courage worthy of their school'. In this sentence, Franklin transformed the last moments of the boys' lives, which must surely have been horrifying and panic ridden, into a parable illustrating the school's stoic 'character'. Even in a boy's manner of dying, the mark of the school could apparently still be discerned. For Clark, the scene in the chapel, together with Franklin's eulogy, laid bare his own mortality; but it also showed him the importance to any community of 'a story-teller with a point of view', someone who could 'transcend all the pain and the suffering in the world', and 'lift us up'. The tragedy of the boys' drowning, and the rituals that accompanied their passing, stayed with Clark for decades before they finally flowered into his signature melancholy prose; but his talent for storytelling was there early on. Almost all those who remember Clark in his teenage years, recall his ability to hold an audience spellbound as he told a story.[5]

His first forays into print at Melbourne Grammar reveal a startling self-assurance—the voice of a sixteen-year-old that is at once determined, unwavering and prophetic. Clark, who as an adult would apologise to his readers for not having paid enough attention to Aborigines in *A History of Australia*, published his first piece of writing—'The Australian Aborigine'—in 1931, in the school magazine. After meeting the Aboriginal preacher and writer David Unaipon at the church in Belgrave, where he preached one Sunday that same year, and hearing his stories of hunting and food gathering as a boy, Clark was inspired to write on the topic. Praising the skill of Aboriginal hunting techniques, he lambasted unnamed 'historians' for failing to realise that 'the Australian Aborigine is not the idiot and brainless man [they] have made him out to be'. In other pieces of juvenilia, he drew parallels between the ancient and modern worlds (a conventional practice at the time), declaring that 'only a revolution' would 'save England from the diseases which grow out of democracy', and bemoaning the fact that, in Australia, there was 'no feeling of respect by the people for the gentility'. In his final year at the school, in 1933, he wrote Jeremiah-like on the 'world crisis', warning of a coming world war. 'In this war which I have predicted,' he proclaimed, 'all the great powers of Europe will be involved.' Clark's omnipotent eye was drawn to the past, to history as the story of the rise and fall of civilisations, and to history as a sourcebook for understanding the human condition. Franklin may have pointed the way, but he did little more than recognise what was clearly apparent by the time Clark reached his mid- to late teens—this 'history stuff' was Manning Clark's thing. Clark's first pieces of writing betrayed the emergence of the one attribute Franklin had hoped to suppress in his charges: a powerful urge for self-expression. Here was a young man who placed the solitary voice of the individual in an exalted position. Clark was already a historical writer of exceptional promise; that much was clear. What was not clear in the early 1930s was the focus his writing would adopt; this was something that would take decades to work through.[6]

Outside school, in the relatively few moments Clark spent at home after becoming a boarder at Grammar in 1928, his reading life and intellectual curiosity were sparked by a queue of 'characters' who in later life stood frozen in his imagination, like sculptures in a museum hall. There was Bluey Carter, who sat on a stool outside his service station at Belgrave, singing the praises of the Russian Revolution of 1917 and predicting the downfall of capitalist society; there was the Catholic aesthete Olaf Jorgensen, who lived nearby, beckoning the young Clark into the world of art; and there was his father's library, with its shelves of Dickens, Hawthorne and Austen which, after Charles's 'coaxing', Manning began to explore in his mid-teens, on his return trips home from Grammar.

Yet next to the world he encountered when he entered Melbourne University with a scholarship in 1934, these were minor influences. Clark's formative intellectual years were the late 1930s and early 1940s; reaching his twenties in 1935, he found himself in a world scarred by the Depression, in which a third of Melbourne's workforce had lost their jobs. Capitalist society had been brought to its knees and for many intellectuals and all those on the Left, there was a sense that an alternative path had to be found. As historian Stuart Macintyre explained: 'for many of the creative younger generation who came to adulthood during the decade, witnessed the collapse of old society and felt the dangers of fascism and war, communism seemed the only realistic alternative'. Disparities in wealth were wide and sectarianism was deeply entrenched. Melbourne, a fine imperial city that had served as the nation's capital until 1927, with its expansive boulevards and a population of just over a million, was still characterised by a pervasive insularity and prudish conservatism. Joyce's *Ulysses* was banned, as were 'dangerous' novels by Hemingway, Orwell and even Defoe. So too were various international journals, particularly communist publications. Freedom of expression could not be allowed to impede the cause of national unity. News of the outside world was limited to the small amount of cable news from London that found its way into daily newspapers. In 1934, Melbourne was a remote city orbiting on the outer reaches of the British Empire. Historian Janet McCalman has described 'the astonishingly culturally isolated world' of Australian universities between the wars.[7] For the few Australian students who had experienced life in Europe or the United States—and they were very few indeed—the silences in campus conversation were almost too much to bear. In her first years as an undergraduate, in the mid-1930s, Dymphna Lodewyckx, with her Flemish and Scandinavian family background, found Melbourne University stultifying:

How terribly painfully self-conscious Australian students were, how tongue-tied … they were all afraid of showing each other what they really were … conversation was rather limited and I think people coming from overseas still feel that about Australians, that they're rather withdrawn, they'll talk about the weather or sport but they won't talk about the things that really matter.[8]

Founded eighty years earlier, in 1853 (three years after the University of Sydney), the University of Melbourne carried a total enrolment of slightly

Clock tower, Old Arts, Melbourne University

over 3000 when Manning Clark arrived in 1934. In an environment of emotional repression and provincial gentility, female freshers wore gloves and most young men who had graduated from the parade grounds of the private schools nurtured a middle-class accent but had little or no idea how to talk to women, let alone basic knowledge of the facts of life. Nevertheless, for Clark, the transition from an earnest middle-class upbringing in the outer suburbs to the lecture theatres of Melbourne University was exhilarating. Alison Patrick, another former student, recalled that 'the shop', where you bought your degree and perhaps your spouse as well, was a lively place: 'people talked, they talked all the time … it was that kind of place … where one could sit in the Cafeteria all afternoon, from lunch until six o'clock arguing and seeing where the argument led.'[9]

Clark was relatively unaware of Melbourne's cultural isolation. Instead, from the moment he entered the university gates, he found his world opened out. He began to read more novels of Dostoyevsky and Lawrence and discovered the poetry of TS Eliot and the music of Beethoven. He won a scholarship to reside in Trinity College, enrolled in Latin, British History and Ancient History in his first year, and was slowly drawn into the intense political debates surrounding the rise of fascism in Europe and the impending 'threat' of communism, all of which found their way into public debate regarding the celebration of the Victorian centenary in 1934.

In his first three years as a student at Melbourne, Clark seemed more energised by events beyond the campus than within. Perhaps this is why he spent most Monday mornings playing billiards with Noel Carroll, instead of attending lectures. He found Jessie Webb, his lecturer in British History, aloof and uninspiring. Webb, whose chief interest was Mediterranean history, had lectured at Melbourne since 1908. In 1934, she was standing in for

Ernest Scott, who was on leave and would return the following year, offering Clark his first dose of Australian history. Easily distracted, Clark explored the streets of inner Melbourne alone for the first time, finding his way to the International Bookshop in Exhibition Street and the Communist Party bookshop across the road. There, he picked up his copies of *The Guardian* and *The Tribune* and began to understand the political environment from a communist perspective. One pamphlet in particular that had a major impact on his thinking was Joyce Manton's *The Centenary Prepares for War*, a communist tract that condemned the 1934 centenary of settlement in Victoria as imperialist propaganda, little more than a gigantic fireworks display designed to 'whip up patriotic fervour' for yet another war 'being organised by the capitalist class'. The stakes seemed high at the time. The Lyons government had tried unsuccessfully to deport Egon Kisch, the Czech socialist and leading anti-fascist, who had been invited by the anti-war movement (of which Manton was one of the prime movers), to speak at a rally organised for Armistice Day, 1934, on the banks of the Yarra River. Meanwhile, as if to make Manton's point, while Australian governments went to desperate measures to keep one man out, they did everything they could to keep another in: the Victorian Government and Clark's own college, Trinity, lavished welcome upon welcome on the Duke of Gloucester. In the cities, eminent historians such as Stephen Roberts, then Professor of History at Sydney, penned articles for historical supplements in major newspapers under the headline 'How England won the seas and Britain founded an Empire'. The political climate lurched from an overblown, asphyxiating loyalty to Empire to a blunt, reactionary conservatism, which, at least in the case of Kisch, had bordered on farce.

Two aspects of Manton's argument would reverberate in Clark's thinking in later years: her anti-imperialism and her condemnation of the British monarchy as a retardant to Australia's independence. Clark was beginning his long flirtation with communism. At the end of Manton's pamphlet there was an important reminder—'on Nov 7th [1934], the Victorian Council against War celebrates the 17th anniversary of the Soviet Union'. Since the Russian revolution of 1917, argued Manton, the Soviet Union had 'struggled for peace'. Stalin's purges would begin only eighteen months later. In 1935,

Clark enrolled in William Macmahon Ball's course in Modern Political Institutions and was introduced in a more formal way to Marxism, but his university studies were interrupted unexpectedly when, frighteningly, he suffered another bout of epilepsy early that year. Doctors insisted he take leave from his studies. For most of 1935, Clark lived not at Trinity but at the Mentone vicarage, no doubt doted on by Catherine, as he filled page after page of his first diary—flippantly entitled 'Jottings of a Recluse'. This outpouring of literary endeavour, which resulted in several large black exercise books of personal reflections, was his first major effort as a writer. Long before he became interested in Australian history or thought of himself as a professional historian, he wrote for and to himself, in response to the novels he read and to the first rush of intellectual life he experienced at Melbourne University. It was the beginning of an enduring affair: the need to write out his inner life.[10]

The self-styled 'recluse' spent the latter part of 1935 in domestic exile, immersed in Dostoyevsky's *The Brothers Karamazov*, Lawrence's *Sons and Lovers* and *The Rainbow*, Tolstoy's *Resurrection*, essays and letters, and Wilde's *De Profundis*. All of these works can still be found in his study in Canberra, heavily annotated, and inscribed simply 'M. Clark, The Vicarage Mentone'. Clark felt the rush of excitement that comes with the first discovery of literature, skipping lectures to sit in his 'oasis'—the reading room of the Melbourne Public Library—where, in 1934, he first read *The Brothers Karamazov*. Years later, Clark believed that he had bonded with the work of the Russian novelist as a young man because Dostoyevsky, he said, 'wanted what I wanted—"was there anyone who could forgive us all?"—he was a child of the age of unbelief but he had a thirst to believe'. Clark's 'thirst to believe' had suffered a crisis in his late teens, when he began to doubt his faith, but inhabiting the country of doubt also provided him with creative tension; art was not born of certainty. At the same time as his political antennae were pricked by the politics of the Victorian centenary, the visit of the English poet laureate John Masefield to Melbourne and Trinity College struck a chord with the young Clark's spiritual searching. Addressing a large student audience, Masefield suggested that art could lead humanity to 'the eternal city'. It was a message of salvation: great art could provide spiritual

An Eye for Eternity

nourishment. Similar ideas were coming to Clark from Lawrence. Reading *The Rainbow*, Clark saw that Lawrence, as he would tell a literary society audience only three years later, had filled the vacuum created by 'the breakdown of Catholic Christianity' not with socialism but with the promise of spiritual fulfilment through 'personal relationships', love, and 'communion with nature'. Inscribing his copy of *The Rainbow*, he dated it: '15/11/34 After the Death'; opposite, on the fly-leaf, he wrote:

Man that is born of woman
is full of sorrow.
For as in Adam all die even so
in Lawrence
Christ shall all be made alive.

The death Clark felt was the death of his belief in God. He was beginning to think that only art could offer him hope. At this very moment, he responded creatively to his doubt and began to write, a voice born in sorrow at his own mortality.[11]

Returning to Melbourne University in 1936, Clark won an array of prizes for his academic performance. Having enrolled in British History, he encountered Ernest Scott, then in his final year of teaching. Scott, an English-born autodidact and one-time journalist, was appointed to the Chair of History at Melbourne in 1913. Since that time, he had done more than any historian to write and popularise Australian history, then taught not as a separate subject but as part of British history. Former student Kathleen Fitzpatrick remembered him as a 'short, stocky man', always 'dapper', with bright, blue eyes, an historian who possessed 'a facile pen'; 'uncomplicated and direct', students often found him a 'stern disciplinarian', an impression reinforced by his relentless drive and work ethic. When Clark sat in Scott's lectures, he saw an elderly man in his academic gown who was then nearly seventy years of age, a man whose powers were waning and who longed to retire, his speech handicapped by a severe lisp, made even worse by ill-health and the quickening frailty of age. Writing in the afterglow of his own achievement, Clark recalled Scott derisively, making much of his idiosyncrasies—the rapid jerking of his right arm, 'like a railway signal which could not decide whether to stay up or down'—painting an image of an entertaining but cynical apologist for all things British. How much of this recollection was true to Clark's feelings in 1936 is difficult to tell. Zelman Cowen, who quipped that he did not have Clark's 'intensity of feeling', sat in Scott's honours course in 1936, and remembered him much more fondly, finding his lectures 'enjoyable' and stimulating. If Scott's 'distinctive mark as a teacher' was his ability to communicate 'his own love of the historical document', he might well have been more influential on the future direction of Clark's historical work than Clark was ever willing to admit.

Clark, however, wanted 'something more', and that person finally arrived in 1937 in the shape of Max Crawford. Now, in place of stalwarts like Webb and Scott, came the enthusiasm of youth. Clark was already taken with William Macmahon Ball, then in his mid-thirties, whose lectures had made a deep impression, but Crawford, the man whom he would later describe as one of the 'giants', exerted the most profound impact of all Clark's lecturers at Melbourne University.[12] Crawford was only thirty when he applied for the chair at Melbourne, sketching his plans for the new department in a sleepless night on the twelve-hour overnight train trip from Sydney to Melbourne. Raymond Priestley, Vice-Chancellor at Melbourne University, noted after the interview that Crawford would make 'a most stimulating head for our history school for the next thirty years with luck'. Crawford would not disappoint. Until he retired in 1970, he presided over what would become the most influential department of history in twentieth-century Australia. The scholars who emerged under his watch included Geoffrey Blainey, Graeme Davison, Ken Inglis, Stuart Macintyre, John Mulvaney, Hugh Stretton, Greg Dening and Inga Clendinnen. He would inspire great affection, not only for the depth of his scholarship—which ranged from the Italian Renaissance to British and Australian history—but because he was an enabler, someone who had a gift for empowering others. Possessed of a quiet, steely determination and a deep commitment to liberal notions of academic freedom, his journey from railwayman's son in Grenfell, New South Wales, through the University of Sydney to Balliol College and the Melbourne Chair was an astonishingly quick climb for such a young man. He came to

Max Crawford, circa 1940

Melbourne believing that the teaching of history had to speak to 'the problems of the day'. In his refined manner, in the sound of his voice—the steady, elongated vowels, which effortlessly oozed erudition—and in his ability to 'listen' to his students, especially the more promising ones, he had the knack of revealing their 'basic predilection for decency' and cultivating a 'moral sensitivity' within his department. This was a 'humanist conception of scholarship' that captured and inspired the young Clark's imagination.[13]

Writing about their peers, mentors and influences, historians are adept at making the activities of their own kind appear momentous. Clark's memories of Crawford are no different; the only thing that can be safely gleaned from them is that Crawford was, and remained, a figure of inspiration for

Clark throughout his life. Because Clark's recollections were written from the vantage point of his subsequent success, Crawford becomes another of the old man's gods, a Christ-like figure who took him up to 'a high mountain' and 'promised that Clio would help [him] to see "all the Kingdoms of the world"'. At times, Clark seems to remember Crawford merely as a vehicle for praising himself; but his most powerful memory, and the one he used repeatedly in later life, was of Crawford's first history lecture in 1937. When the lecture was over, Clark walked down the aisle of the theatre, a young student 'touched by magic' at what he had just heard. Crawford, barely ten years his senior, did not walk away in imperious silence like so many other lecturers. Instead, he stood at the lectern, tentative—almost shy—but still eager to converse with the students. Desperate for relief after his first appearance, he pulled a cigarette from his coat and asked if anyone had a light. Clark took a box of matches from his trouser pocket, but his fingers trembled so much that the matches fell to the floor. Picking one up, he struck a light and cupped the burning match in his shaking hands. Crawford bent down slowly, dipping his head like a man drinking from a fountain. Or so it seemed. As Clark told it, the story was one metaphor for the origin of his life's 'quest' as an historian as much as it was an illustration of Crawford's ability to provide intellectual inspiration. Whether it was true or not at the time, Clark felt it as truth at the end of his life; the melancholy he saw in the young Crawford struck a chord within him. For Clark, Crawford was the man who conveyed the potential of history, 'the excitement of the chase', the thrill of discovery, and the relevance of history—not only to the politics of the late 1930s but to the task of understanding humanity itself.[14]

In the same year that Crawford arrived, the political debate ignited by the Spanish Civil War entered Melbourne University with a ferocity remembered by all who experienced it. The war erupted in 1936, when General Franco's nationalists—predominantly Spain's conservative elite, the Catholic propertied classes and the military—challenged the leftist popular front that had come to power in the elections of February that year. With Hitler and Mussolini already in power in Germany and Italy, the war in Spain quickly became a 'symbol of the fight against fascism, and a desperate moment in resistance to the drive to world war'. In Europe and the United States, as in

Australia, the struggle captured the imaginations of writers, intellectuals, artists and a broad left–liberal coalition, all of whom were 'overwhelmingly on the side of the republic'. The isolated world of Australian universities would soon be shattered.

On Wednesday 17 March 1937, notice of a debate to be held in the Arts Building on the following Monday from 8 to 10 pm appeared in the University newspaper *Farrago*. The topic for debate: 'That the Spanish Government is the Ruin of Spain'. That evening, Manning Clark and Zelman Cowen were among more than a thousand people who crowded into the Public Lecture Theatre. Cowen described it as 'one of the most momentous events of [his] university career', recalling the tremendous 'shouting and disorder'. Clark remembered entering the theatre to find 'two howling mobs'. Inside, the atmosphere was stifling, the temperature was well over thirty degrees and there was little ventilation. Every seat was taken; even the aisles overflowed. All the floor space was occupied, with students 'suspended precariously from ventilators and skylights'. As the speakers began, men climbed on the roof, stomping wildly in the hope of drowning out the proceedings. More than half of the audience were from outside the university, mostly from the 'Catholic tribe', led by a brilliant young student for the affirmative side, who was making his first appearance on the political stage—BA Santamaria. Supporting him were Kevin Kelly, a public servant, and University Labour Society member Stan Ingwersen. Santamaria and Ingwersen were both members of the Campion Society, a Catholic Action group that rivalled the Masonic Lodge for secrecy—its members known only to one another. Leading the opposition was the cultural nationalist and socialist Nettie Palmer; then in her early fifties, Palmer had recently returned from Spain and was deeply committed to the republican cause. Supporting her were two members of the Communist Party, Gerry O'Day and a science student, Jack Legge.

What followed was not so much a debate, or 'an exercise in persuasion', as two political rallies in which the speakers held 'no assumptions in common'. Santamaria opened for the affirmative, raised his voice above the din of hecklers, and argued that 'the struggle in Spain was religious, insisting that the government must bear the responsibility for the revolt, in view of its bitter opposition to democracy and its organised intolerance'. Becoming more and more passionate as his supporters stirred him on, he declared that the republicans had denied freedom of the press, speech, and worship. You must be a Spaniard to understand, he exclaimed: 'the heart of my race has been torn'. With this, the audience exploded. At one point, open fights broke out in the aisles as men brought fire hoses into the building and flooded the corridors, only to be stopped from entering the lecture theatre at the last minute by police. Once decorum had returned, Palmer retorted that the republican government was democratically elected and 'had the support of the mass of Spanish people, many of whom were poor'. And so it went on, the audience shouting and interrupting the speakers, one side defending 'Christ the King' as it aggressively denounced the godless utopia promised by the communists, the other side defending the Spanish rural poor and urban proletariat, the last bulwark against the fascist tide sweeping across Europe.

Clark watched it all 'bewildered', unable to decide where to stand, his heart and mind wavering from one side to the other—achieve human perfectibility on earth or wait until the gates of heaven opened? At the time, he had little idea how much had changed that night in the Public Lecture Theatre. As Santamaria wrote many years later, 'the Spanish Civil War transformed the Catholic attitude to Communism in Australia from generalised opposition to passionate resistance'. In the content and tenor of the 1937 debate lay the seeds of the Cold War and the feverish paranoia of anti-communism that would pervade so much of Australian politics throughout the next twenty years, ultimately leading to the Petrov commission and the Labor Party split. What Clark could see, however, was the way the debate tore the university out of its cloistered isolation and graphically revealed the relevance of the study of history and politics to the world around him. From his first publications at Melbourne Grammar, he had wanted to speak to contemporary politics—to the rise of Nazism and to the spectre of war in Europe. As secretary of the debating society at Trinity College, he organised and took part in debates that cried out for an informed historical view: 'That the ideals of democracy are incompatible with modern capitalism', 'That the future of Australia lies with Tokyo rather than London' ... so many of these debates seemed to beg the question 'whither Britain? whither Australia?' After the Spanish Civil War debate, Clark could see even more clearly that history offered him the possibility of making his intellectual life relevant—it was no mere academic exercise. History would help him understand the rival political systems of his time and know their fate; it was as much about the future as the past. He watched as Crawford wrote publicly to defend the republican cause in Spain and as Raymond Priestley, the Vice-Chancellor, defended the university as a forum where political issues could be discussed openly. This was a vision of academic independence and engaged scholarship that Clark would carry with him for the remainder of his professional life. Nor would the political indecisiveness he felt that March night in 1937 ever leave him. History was leading him to a more ambiguous position.[15]

Clark was extremely impressed by Crawford's lectures 'on history', in which Crawford warned that, despite the value of Marxist theory, it risked merely 'equating the individual with his class', overlooking the 'variety of personality' in human beings. Sitting in Crawford's honours seminars on the Theory and Method of History, the first course of its kind at Melbourne, he sensed that his young lecturer did not believe that history was purely a science. Although Crawford argued that history needed to be clear about its methods of enquiry, process of selection and evidence, and the way its judgements were made, his view of history was far more holistic (or 'synoptic', as he later termed it). He saw history as transcending 'political activity' or 'economic structure'; history was the story of 'humanity on earth', and it included every aspect of human society—the individual, 'the family, class', religion and 'nation'. To deal with this vast panorama, the historian required not only 'critical alertness' but, more importantly, 'sympathetic insight'. Maybe this was the 'melancholy' Clark sensed in Crawford, his sensitivity to the immeasurable, the ambiguous, and the ultimately unknowable past, a profound literary sensibility.

Clark found something of the same sensibility in Thomas Carlyle, whom he read for the first time also in 1937, after finding Carlyle's three-volume history of the French revolution in a secondhand bookshop.[16] The beautiful edition, with its dark-brown cover and black floral imprint, published in London in 1837, still sits on the shelves of his study in Canberra. Clark

bought it on the spot and started reading immediately, scribbling notes and comments in the margins, marking particular passages; of these, two in particular, towards the end of the third volume, attracted his attention. For it was there that Carlyle exposed the folly of the revolutionaries' attempt to create a 'Fraternal Heaven on Earth' before which, he wrote, the world still 'gazes and shudders'. Rejecting any suggestion that 'cause and effect' might explain the course of the Revolution, Carlyle's concluding pages whipped up a kind of reverie that drew on a host of biblical allusions, seeing the descent into terror as 'a hubbub of voices in distraction' and calling on history, 'with just sympathy and just antipathy, with clear eye and open heart', to 'pity them all'. If all of the revolutionaries' insurrections and tribulations had come to nought, he asked, 'why was the Earth so beautiful, becrimsoned with dawn and twilight, if man's dealings with man were to make it a vale of scarcity, of tears, not even soft tears?' Clark admitted he didn't read 'every word' of the three volumes, but he surely read and re-read these passages he marked so heavily, drinking in Carlyle's mystic, seer-like prose, mesmerised by the voice of an historian who looked on the past with 'the eye of pity' and for whom the story of all human endeavour was tinged with sadness.[17]

An Eye for Eternity

When Clark wrote his BA Honours thesis at the end of 1937, it was as if he poured all he had learnt, both inside and outside the walls of the university, into his writing. Before submitting his thesis (titled 'The Victorian Electorate 1842–70: A Study in Democratic Conservatism'), he had studied Latin, Ancient, British, European and Economic history, the Constitutional and Legal History of Britain and Modern Political Institutions. At that point, he had read little Australian history, save the lectures offered by Ernest Scott in his British History course. That he should have chosen an Australian subject for his thesis is indicative of one thing: from the outset he was drawn to Australian history as a theatre in which the ideas of the old world were played out. His prose betrayed a remarkable self-confidence. Coming to his conclusion, he declared that he could not be bothered to restate his argument: 'it would be redundant,' he wrote, 'and certainly tedious, to recapitulate the whole argument advanced in this thesis'. At first he seemed to hanker for 'an empirical judgement', but in the end he came to the view that history had not shown whether the conflict between democracy and conservatism could ever be solved. Then, in the last sentence, came the shape of things to come:

> If there is a lesson to be drawn from the period, if there is one generalization which could be applied to the period, possibly it is this: that in that period, the conflict which developed does illustrate what Dostoyevsky once called 'all the humiliating absurdity of human contradictions'.[18]

Here was the Carlyle-like gaze, the eye that hovered above the past like a merciful God, dispensing pity to all below. Throwing Dostoyevsky over the history of Victorian democracy was part of Clark's gumption—he was looking to use the past as parable, as a window onto the whole human predicament. But he didn't stop at writing. Soon after submitting his thesis he addressed the Trinity College football club, reading the lads a paper on Dostoyevsky. Writing of Clark's speech to AD Lindsay, Master of Balliol College, Max Crawford referred to the footballers' 'great horror' when they slowly realised what they were in for. Clark was probably oblivious; as Crawford told Lindsay: 'Perhaps I can make the picture of Clark more complete by saying that he lives, just now, in Dostoevsky.'[19] At Trinity College, in 1938, Clark took several small tutorials in History and Politics, before teaching for one term at Trinity Grammar, Kew. Remembering his teaching, three of his former students—Jim Lemaire, Bill Brett and Bob Phillips—captured something of the young dreamer Clark, a man lost in literature and himself.

Lemaire recalled Clark sitting at High Table for the College evening meal, managing to look endearingly 'dishevelled', despite the fact his academic gown hid virtually everything he was wearing. Brett remembered Clark crossing the quadrangle in 'old flannel bags, an academic gown in tatters, his hands in his pockets'. With 'his looking nowhere at all countenance', said Brett, 'he had a very unworldly way to him'. 'Introverted' and 'lethargic', Clark's sense of humour always shone through. After Lemaire challenged him over his interpretation of Marxism in one tutorial, Clark, wearing a smile, put him in his place: 'You don't know anything about this subject and I do, so you'll have to accept my view.' They all found his teaching invigorating—he was 'enthusiastic about communist ideas' and possessed the air of a 'frustrated preacher'. Phillips, who had an injury to his right foot that prevented him from playing sport, carried Clark's words of encouragement with him for the rest of his life.

> Manning's effect on me, commencing in 1938, was to: encourage a hunger for literature and history; confirm my instinct that, if you have the will to achieve, you can overcome physical disabilities … and determine your own values. Later in life, I did not always agree with Manning's views but I respected them … and that did not alter, in any way … the deep respect I had for him as a teacher, a human being, and a friend.[20]

Clark identified with Phillips because he knew what it was like to deal with a physical impairment. Since his days at Melbourne Grammar, his epilepsy meant that he had needed a runner when batting for the First XI. Yet his outstanding ability on the cricket pitch was widely acknowledged. Years later, his skill with the bat was remembered in Homeric terms. Attending a Melbourne University dinner in 1958, Sebastian Clark spoke with Ian

An Eye for Eternity

Johnson, a former Wesley student who had then just retired as captain of the Australian cricket team. Sebastian asked Johnson if he could remember playing against Manning Clark, whereupon Johnson raised his arm in a salute to indicate the path of the balls that would so often fly over his head, one six even hitting the roof of an asylum across the road. The image of the red ball sailing high over Johnson's head, out into the blue, was something like Clark's promise at the end of 1938, his last year at Trinity College. References from his lecturers at Melbourne spoke of a young man 'of unusual calibre', 'a deep thinker ... with the power of communicating his enthusiasm to others', 'the best and most promising' of students, a gifted individual with a 'sensitive, poetic and imaginative mind'—one after another, the superlatives rained down. Max Crawford, writing to Lindsay at Balliol in support of Clark's application for 'advanced status', made it clear he was already thinking of Clark as a possible recruit to the History Department at Melbourne.

You have in Clark a very exceptional fellow. I expect to have a lectureship vacant here in five or six years time, and I am watching him as a possibility for that ... the only external sign of [his epilepsy] that I have seen is his habit of stopping short a step when he is walking with one. He is actually very tough, can work hard, and wrote a brilliant Finals Paper when his sister was in a bad way with infantile paralysis ... I know that Balliol can do a great deal for Clark; on the other side, I do not expect to be able to send you better material very often.[21]

When Clark visited Hope in the Melbourne Children's Hospital in 1938, he often asked his friend AGL Shaw to accompany him. Shaw went out of friendship, walking together with him the short distance from Trinity College, Clark 'stopping short a step' as always. Shaw sensed his fragility, going with him because he could see that 'he needed company'. Clark, who found being alone difficult to bear, would be driven to spend his days in the most solitary of all occupations—the writer's life. Like so many other Australians in the twentieth century, he sailed for England in August 1938, on the assumption that was what 'one did' if 'one' wanted a brilliant career, but he would not go alone.[22]

5: CORRESPONDING LOVES: MELBOURNE, OXFORD AND BONN, 1936–38

If we're to come to love a man,
the man himself should stay hidden, because
as soon as he shows his face—love vanishes.

DOSTOYEVSKY, *The Brothers Karamazov*[1]

Dymphna Lodewyckx, circa 1930

In the study of Manning Clark's family home in Canberra, there is one filing cabinet that contains the personal papers and possessions of Dymphna Clark. Manning's books and papers consume the remaining space, but the most precious keepsakes of Dymphna's life are interred there too. Opening the middle drawer of the cabinet, I was not prepared for what I found. Underneath several photographs, a pile of old financial statements and her last purse, which contained her hairbrush, address book, medical prescriptions and wallet, I could see a blue plastic bag, closed tight with a thick elastic band. I was intrigued by the suppleness of its contents so I untied the band. Looking inside I discovered two long tails of plaited hair with the same light brown lustre as the day they were cut. Tied around one of the tails was a note in Dymphna's handwriting: 'Hair of H.D. Lodewyckx, cut c.1931'.

I felt like an intruder, yet I also felt privileged to be allowed to come this close. After reading scores of documents relating to Dymphna's life, how strange was this physical intimacy. To touch her hair, cut when she was barely sixteen years of age, was to touch her longing for her own youth, and, momentarily, to sense the unspoken emotions she might have felt as an older woman, holding her hair in her hands—its very keeping, for nearly seventy years, the memory of a life before Manning Clark.

The woman I had known in the last four years of her life was warm, unsentimental and intensely private. Called on to speak because of her attachment to Manning, she rarely let down her guard, maintaining a stoic refusal to open a window onto her own feelings. As I read more and more of her correspondence, I began to see the life that she had hidden from almost everyone who knew her. I soon realised I was reading material that most of the Clarks' five surviving children had either not read or, at best, had only partly glimpsed. I could understand their reticence. Perhaps they preferred to leave their memories of Manning and Dymphna undisturbed. How many of us, after all, would rush to read our parents' personal correspondence? Would their death completely erase our respect for their privacy? Whenever Clark opened the wooden box that contained what remained of his own parents' correspondence, he could not read more than a few lines before he found himself turning away. The experience was too unsettling; rather than trespass, he preferred to leave his parents' private world locked in the past.

The letters between Clark and Dymphna, mostly written in the late 1930s, when they fell in love, or at times of separation and emotional turmoil over the next fifty years, can make for harrowing reading. Reading Manning and Dymphna's letters was no doubt easier for me than for their family and friends; I did not come burdened with the ties of blood. My initial enthusiasm was soon tempered by the realisation that, while I had been granted full access to the material, I had also been saddled with the responsibility of deciding what to publish. The ethical dilemma was now mine, at least initially. The decision was helped by the fact that the material had not been destroyed.

Clark's papers in the National Library tell his story but not Dymphna's story. In the papers of 'the great man' she appears as the 'long-suffering wife' or the loyal servant of a higher purpose; rarely does she emerge from behind Clark's shadow. The majority of her letters to Clark she kept from the National Library, preferring to leave them in Clark's study. During the last

Box of correspondence between Charles and Catherine Clark

eight years of her life, as she combed through all that remained in the house, she had ample opportunity to burn them. She did not, I believe, because she knew full well that her story of their relationship was contained in those letters and that, without her voice, the story of Clark's life would be not only incomplete but little more than a tissue of half-truths and lies.

Dymphna's letters, painful to read as so many of them are, are essential to understanding Clark's life. From the moment they fell in love in their early twenties, their lives became entangled; from now on, there would be no life entirely independent of one another—Clark's biography was Dymphna's biography.

MANNING AND DYMPHNA

Some time in late 1937, Eileen Gladys Martin looked out her kitchen window, across the backyard to the railway tracks beyond. It was early evening, and invariably, the 'stunning and beautiful young couple' crossed the railway line hand in hand on their way to walk in Churchill Gardens. They seemed 'so in love', so 'wonderfully happy', that she felt joyful just watching them pass by. Eileen did not know the young man with the tentative gait, but she knew that Dymphna Lodewyckx was the daughter of Augustin and Anna Lodewyckx, the 'European' family who lived on the other side of the tracks at Mont Albert, on Melbourne's south-eastern fringe. Like her father, Dymphna was 'a wiz' at languages; in fact, she spoke more languages than most people in Melbourne had heard in a lifetime. This was part of her attraction to the young Manning Clark. The man drawn to the grand themes of European history fell in love with a European woman, a woman who, at the age of little more than twenty, was fluent in Dutch, German, Italian, French, Swedish, Norwegian and Danish.[2]

In 1934, when she started at Melbourne University, Dymphna stood out from the other students: she was 'the mad girl without a hat', the weird one with 'flat walking shoes'. It was much the same at her secondary school, Presbyterian Ladies College, where she was seen as the eccentric girl who wore strange stockings or none at all. In the waspish den of 1930s Melbourne, Dymphna's Flemish and Scandinavian background leapt out as a suspicious mark of difference. Her schoolmates goaded her: 'Talk Belgian to us'. But, as she later joked, 'that was impossible'. Belgium's three major languages were Dutch, French and German. Although she won a scholarship to Janet Clarke Hall within Trinity College, she decided she was not much interested in 'playing ladies' and lived at home during her university years. Her father, Augustin Lodewyckx—a linguist and Flemish nationalist—was Associate Professor of German at Melbourne, while her mother, Anna Hansen, was the daughter of a gregarious Swede and a Norwegian sea captain. If this exotic background stamped her as odd to many who knew her, for Clark it was a powerful magnet.

Although the two had crossed paths in first-year Latin, Dymphna did not notice Clark until she saw him in the Melbourne University Library in 1936 where, together with Russell, he would flirt with the female students. At first, she had difficulty telling the brothers apart, until one day, towards the end of the year, while she was reading in the sun against the north wall of the Old Arts building, Clark 'engineered an introduction' and asked if she would partner him to the Arts Ball. She accepted, and a few weeks later, while on holidays, Clark was already penning his first letter to his beloved. She replied teasingly, telling him of her Sunday walk home with her mother, 'through a suburbia which looked and smelt positively glamorous after seeing *Desire* with Marlene Dietrich and Gary Cooper in the local fleahouse'. Their courtship would last well over a year, and throughout 1937 they would both have other partners. Clark was jealous of her contact with the European men she met at the German club and desperate to convince her that he, too, longed 'for the cosmopolitan—or rather the non-Australian element in life'. Dymphna already had a long-standing relationship with another fellow student, Noel Carroll, who later described their affair as typical of the classic 'shop couple': 'it was all pure and harmless'. Despite his affection for her, he thought she was probably 'better suited to Clark'. Besides, said Carroll, 'this Dutch–Norwegian family—they were not my people'.[3]

In late 1937, Clark handed Dymphna *The Brothers Karamazov*. He had already read the novel several times since 1934, when at nineteen, he pulled the Constance Garnett translation from the library shelves at Melbourne University and was 'swept away by the metaphysical discussion'. He was drawn to the tripartite struggle in the novel. Through the characters of the three brothers, Dostoyevsky revealed to Clark three different views of the world: Dimitri, the man of 'Dionysian frenzy', 'the man of action'—the 'heels up' man; Alyosha, the monk, the man of deep spiritual beliefs; and Ivan, the intellectual, the man racked by 'intellectual doubts'. For the remainder of his life, Clark would re-read the *Brothers* every five years. Like Tolstoy's *Anna Karenina* and the later poems of Thomas Hardy, it would become one of his spiritual and intellectual anchors. Now, in the first throes of love, the literature that meant so much to him became the gauge of his lover's sensitivity to the 'great questions in life', the possibilities of human love and happiness, and above all, the question of what would become of a world in which faith in God had evaporated.

Having travelled to Mentone to meet Clark's parents for the first time, Dymphna could see these same existential dilemmas writ large in Clark's mind: he was wrestling with his own doubts about the world of Protestant Christianity he had inherited from Charles and Catherine; as she watched him turn away from institutional religion she began to sense that he had found a new spiritual voice. To get close to Clark, she knew she had to understand his bond with Dostoyevsky. Dymphna devoured *Brothers* over the summer break of 1937–38, staying up until the early hours of the morning 'reading the last 600 pages'. When Clark received word that she too had loved the novel, he was ecstatic: 'the knowledge of it moving you pleased me', he wrote her, already looking forward to 'the very important discussion' they would have about Dostoyevsky when they next met. So deep was Clark's immersion in the world of the Russian novelist, it is impossible to imagine him accepting a woman who was not a fellow admirer. Dymphna hit the right note. In early 1938, *The Brothers Karamazov* became the lovers' libretto, the work of art through which they played out their feelings for one another.[4]

Clark's letters were also working their magic on Dymphna. By January 1938, she had fallen completely for him. Lying on her bedroom floor in her pyjamas, with her 'hair unkempt' and her 'belly full' she wrote him longing letters. 'With beating heart', she told him she had 'administered the death blow', telling Carroll in what she thought 'was the most suitable metaphor' at her disposal, that she was 'off the market'. Recoiling from the icy distance she saw in her parents' marriage, she turned to Clark to build something more meaningful and intimate: 'I miss you Manning in many ways and places, but perhaps most of all when I come home and find that dead kind of angry misery, that comes when people live at cross purposes.' Whenever he was away from her, he missed her badly, dreaming of their long walks together and the 'peace that passeth all understanding when we lie down in harmony'. Clark's sensitivity, and his yearning, ambitious spirit were already winning her over. That summer, he was staying with his favourite aunt, Gladys Hope, at Cronulla, on Sydney's southern beaches. He wrote to Dymphna of his walks along the beach, of how he would stand for hours moved by the sight of the 'roaring' Pacific Ocean—'so untamed, so relentless & so moody'. Against the drama and grandeur of nature, he placed the insipid landscape of a burgeoning Sydney suburbia.

The houses are dull, erected for profit. The general run of people too are most repulsive. They walk along in trunks with that smugness and self-satisfaction. They look too happy to be real. The failure of most people in Sydney to extend their vision beyond the material plane is at first fascinating, but later nauseating.[5]

For Dymphna, these were some of 'the most satisfying' letters she had received in her 'whole life'. As Clark drew her near with his romantic depictions of the tumultuous sea, he also appealed to her cultured European sensibility by rejecting the drab materialism of Australian cities. In a matter of weeks, Dymphna was making her own demands—insisting that Clark learn 'to understand spoken German as perfectly as possible'. 'For me,' she told him, 'to hear and sometimes speak [German] is what good historical writing must be to you.' She already knew Clark's love of history first-hand, having typed his honours thesis in the spring of 1937. Now she would teach him German; before long they were frequenting Tate's Coffee Lounge in the evenings, Dymphna taking Clark through an elementary German textbook as he had led her to Dostoyevsky.[6]

It said much about 1930s Melbourne that the major points of attraction for Clark and Dymphna lay outside Australia. When Dymphna sat the exam for her Mollison Travelling Scholarship in 1937, the question before her neatly captured the zeitgeist: 'What are the prospects for an Australian culture?' If Australia possessed a culture, it was nascent. Some even wondered if it would ever flower. To encounter a culture with depth it was necessary to travel to Europe. Melbourne newspapers regularly featured the smiling faces of those departing for England—professionals, members of parliament, government officials, and students bound for Oxford or Cambridge. Australians may have had two homes—Britain and Australia—but there was only one cultural heartland. Dymphna won the well-endowed (230 pounds) Mollison Scholarship in April 1937. Well before Clark sat his final exam later that same year, and completed his honours thesis, it was clear that she would travel to Germany to study for her doctorate. Throughout most of 1938, while Clark tutored at Trinity and read for his Bachelor of Education, Dymphna worked as a translator in the Postmaster General's Department in Melbourne's Treasury Gardens, 'clocking on at 8.20am, clocking off at 4.50pm, Monday–Friday'. Clark was determined to accompany her to

Europe. In April, the prize he longed for came nearer when he was awarded the 100 pounds Bartlett Travelling Scholarship and, shortly afterwards, free passage to England. Although Dymphna's financial position was much more secure than Clark's (she later won yet another scholarship), they could now plan their joint departure to Europe.

Some time in June 1938, they made love for the first time; less than four weeks later they were engaged. The word *fiancé* could now be applied in public. While they were both brilliant students, newspaper reports of their departure in August 1938 suggested that Dymphna was the star performer.

Romantic Students go Abroad: The Mollison scholarship winner, Miss Dymphna Lodewyckx, who is bound for the University of Munich to study for a doctorate of Philosophy, and her fiancé (Mr. CMH Clark) who is accompanying her, give romantic interest to the departure during the next fortnight of a number of Melbourne University graduates who are travelling abroad to continue their studies.[7]

More than fifty years later, in the last years of Clark's life, Dymphna was interviewed for the National Library's oral history unit. Whenever questions touched on the first years of her relationship with Clark, or their trip to Europe in 1938, she refused to answer, politely stating that she would 'rather not talk about it'. At that time, Clark had published *The Quest for Grace* and made countless media appearances in which he had told the story from his perspective. So long as he was alive he claimed Dymphna's story for himself; in his rendition, she became the silent accomplice to an artist's odyssey. Yet it was not only her modesty and natural instinct for privacy that made Dymphna decline to answer questions. She avoided telling her own story in public because she knew that she would have no choice but to contradict him. Even after his death, she held her silence.

When they sailed from Port Melbourne on the SS *Orama* on 16 August 1938, neither Clark nor Dymphna was setting out on an unexpected journey. He had followed the predictable path of the bright clergyman's son—Melbourne Grammar to Melbourne University and Trinity College to Balliol College, Oxford—while she was setting out to complete her father's long-

An Eye for Eternity

Hilma Dymphna Lodewyckx, March 1937, just before leaving for Europe

standing expectations of a brilliant academic career. It was not as if either had glimpsed an alternative life, or thought long of the road not taken. What seems remarkable now is just how clear they were about their life's future course. Clark had toyed with the idea of doing Law and, like Dymphna, imagined himself studying Medicine, but otherwise, they had little hesitation. They also lived at a time when the array of life choices was not what it is today; they expected less and were grateful for every opportunity.

On the eve of their departure Dymphna was twenty-one and Clark twenty-three. Like every couple lost in the heady rush of first love, they knew more of what they loved in one another than they did of their differences; from the moment they left Australia's shores, with her bound for

Germany and Clark for Oxford, Dymphna would have to grapple with Clark's voluminous outpouring of letters. She would begin to confront his highly wrought prose, a prose she was incapable of writing herself—much to his growing disappointment. He had already begun compiling their story, clipping the newspaper articles that reported on their departure, over which, years later, he would write his own cryptic comments ('the possibilities'). Yet in all of Clark's later recollections there was one thing he failed to reveal: the nature of the person who stood beside him on the deck of the *Orama*.[8]

If Clark's ancestral memory was a collage of working-class St Peters and the stern piety of colonial clergymen, Dymphna's was of distant European homelands, and family and friends scattered across the continent—from Norway and Sweden to Belgium and Germany. Her first memories were not of Australia but of the streets of Durban—of 'Malay rickshaw drivers … with their painted lace socks and great horn headdresses'. Her parents met in Capetown in 1909, where Augustin was Professor of German and French at Victoria College, and Anna was teaching physical education. Both were the children of empires; Anna's Norwegian father named their house in Durban 'Valhalla', flying the Norwegian flag from the rooftop; as a child she had lived an 'uneventful life in the lonely outposts of the South African veldt'. Dymphna remained haunted till the end of her life by her visit to Durban as a five-year-old, the old house surrounded by dense pine forests, run by black servants and under constant threat of robbery from 'poor coloured people'. One night, she was left alone in the house with her four-year-old cousin while her mother and grandmother went to 'the bioscope' nearby. She remembered their terror: 'we sang to each other all evening to keep our courage up'. Augustin and Anna left for Belgium in 1910, where Axel, their first child, was born, only to return to Africa when Augustin accepted the Belgian King's appointment as supervisor of the country's 'mission' at Katanga in the Congo. In South Africa, in the Congo, and in Australia, theirs was a colonial life. Leafing through the old Lodewyckx family albums, a series of photographs records the family's beginnings: 'Scandinavian picnics' in the African rainforest, white women in ankle-length dresses, shaded by parasols and fine mosquito net veils, colonial overlords in large cane chairs on wraparound verandahs, afternoon teas served

Augustin and Anna Lodewyckx (seated), Katanga, Congo, 1914

dutifully by Congolese servants. And now, as the old black-and-white photographs slowly disintegrate, their figures recede into oblivion, as though their lives were little more than an apparition.[9]

Anna's handwriting provides the labels for many of the photographs: 'our first colonial home', 'our second colonial home', 'our third colonial home', and so on. The house in which Dymphna grew up, at Beatty Street, Mont Albert, is there too. Mont Albert was the last in the line of a long run of 'colonial homes'. For the rest of their lives Augustin and Anna would adopt the Swahili names their servants had given them in Katanga—Kapo and Lala.

In 1914, Augustin left the Congo for Belgium via the United States and Australia, while Anna travelled with Axel to visit family in Scandinavia. In Melbourne, due to the outbreak of Word War I, the Belgian consul advised Augustin to remain in Australia. It would be more than a year before the family was reunited. On a hot December day in 1915, with 'the north wind howling and the chaff and manure flying', Anna's Swedish ship, loaded with Baltic pine, docked at Port Melbourne. As Anna leaned over the ship's railing and waved to Augustin on the wharf below, the Swedish sailors called out to her to 'come home', so certain were they that she was disembarking for life in some godforsaken furnace.

In December 1916, Dymphna was born the child of their reunion.

Beatty St., mont albert

Augustin, Anna and Dymphna, on the verandah at Mont Albert, early 1920s

Although she grew up in Australia, everything about the Lodewyckx family milieu was decidedly European. At Mont Albert, the house language was Flemish; but languages varied throughout the day—Dutch in the morning, German and French at night, or whenever visitors from either country arrived; and after Dymphna's Swedish grandmother (Hilma) came to live with the family, it was usually Swedish on Saturdays, while on Sundays, Hilma would read from the Norwegian Bible. Planting a garden became Kapo's way of recreating the lost landscape of Belgium—the bush at Mont Albert was to be replaced by 'the woods'. In anticipation, he named the house 'Huize Eikenbosch' (house of the oakwoods), planting hundreds of oaks of many different varieties. Standing in the garden in his wooden clogs, a rustic vision of the unyielding Flemish farmer, he cut the firewood with a large cross saw, making circular piles from the cut wood and placing the twigs carefully in the middle; a method which married the traditional wood-heap pattern of his ancestors with those he had discovered in the Congo and adapted them to Australian conditions. He worked his acre of land in the

An Eye for Eternity

suburbs of Melbourne as if it were Belgian farmland; digging trenches to drain the land and edging them with sods to form a wall. This he called 'the microcosmos'. So impatient was he to have a weeping exotic in the front garden that he tied bags of bricks, strung by rope, to the branches of a young ash—as if, by making the tree bend to his will, he might make the whole continent bend in unison.[10]

Over a period of more than forty years, Augustin held regular reading classes for his students at home, 'der Deutsche Leserverein' and the Icelandic reading group being among the most memorable. He perceived language not as a form of 'unreal celestial mathematics to be learned by rote, but rather as an exciting culture-bound human activity'. John Martin, linguist and fellow scholar, was one of 'the inner Lodewyckx circle'. He fondly recalls 'a liberal and humane man', deeply committed to the traditional values of scholarship and learning, someone who did not 'reject all things Australian' but perceived European culture as deeper, more sophisticated and superior to its colonial offshoots. He was also deeply committed to a European multicultural ideal in his new homeland. In 1932, he published *Die Deutschen in Australien*, the first scholarly examination of the experience of German immigrants in Australia. For the Melbourne press, he wrote many articles on his travels in Europe, combining culture, history and politics in a personal and accessible style. Over the next thirty years, he produced several books (primarily for a Dutch market), which argued convincingly for increased immigration to Australia; he was a 'populate or perish' man, sympathetic to cultural difference and resistant to aggressive assimilation. Despite the fact that he often felt the brunt of Australian xenophobia and discrimination, he remained an active and engaged citizen, seeking and gaining British–Australian citizenship in 1924. For John Martin, whose loyalty and affection for Lodewyckx remained undiminished, Augustin Lodewyckx exemplified Tennyson's dictum in 'Ulysses': 'I am a part of all that I have met'.

While Dymphna respected her father's scholarship, her memories of him tended to express respect more than love: standing on her tiptoes as a ten-year-old trying to read his newspaper, which was always placed on a stand, afraid of disturbing him ('you didn't interrupt my father while he was reading the paper'); placing her head in her arms as she listened to him in her

first lecture at Melbourne University, embarrassed because she found his method and manner dry and pedantic.[11] She was probably unaware at the time, but when she sailed with Clark for Europe to study German language and culture in Bonn, she was continuing a journey Augustin had begun as a young boy when, travelling to school by train in the 1880s, he had sat enthralled by the German families opposite him, many of them on their way to Antwerp and a berth to a new life in the United States. Dymphna's connection with German language and culture began at birth. She was christened 'Hilma Dymphna', after her maternal grandmother—Hilma being a shortened version of the old German 'Wilhelmina'—and from her first years she imbibed her father's passion for all things German. Whenever German friends visited the house, they would bring her gifts—usually German children's stories and fairytales; Augustin making her return the favour by writing thank you letters in German, despite the fact that she knew not a word of the language. By the time she reached her early teens, his draconian methods had paid dividends and she was fully fluent in a number of languages. At thirteen, she passed her Intermediate Certificate. Arriving home from school with her results late one afternoon, she ran down into the garden where her father was working to tell him of her achievement. Hearing the news, he turned towards her, rake in hand, and replied brusquely, 'A disgrace if you hadn't.'[12]

This fiercely reserved man, with an almost monastic need for solitude, headed the 'pathologically parsimonious and puritanical' household in which Dymphna's life's values were formed. Sebastian Clark remembered him as someone who was 'not very big on human feelings', a person who craved his study and books more than he needed the company of others and whose warmth and openness were more easily found in his written work than in

Anna and Dymphna Lodewyckx, (above) Mont Albert, early 1930s;
Augustin Lodewyckx (opposite), circa 1930

his daily interaction with others. In turning towards Clark, a man whose
emotions rippled on the surface of his personality, and who rejected academic life as poisonous and life denying, Dymphna chose the opposite of
her father. Perhaps a lifetime's emotional distance between Dymphna and
her father was encapsulated in his dying moments in 1964 when, as she
stood at his deathbed, he reverted to the rural Flemish dialect he'd spoken as
a boy, his daughter, the brilliant linguist, unable to understand him. The
'emotional colour' in Dymphna's life was provided by her mother, Anna,
who was more 'metaphysically inclined', and her grandmother, Hilma, the
uneducated daughter of a tailor who, together with the first mate Axel
Hansen, had jumped a Swedish ship in South Africa and stayed for forty
years. Hilma and Anna revelled in the dance parties held in the house in the
1920s, when the carpet in the drawing room was rolled up, the furniture
moved out, the floorboards waxed, and middle-aged couples danced the
Charleston, the Foxtrot and the Argentinean Tango (in wooden European
style) while Dymphna's brother, Axel, then in his mid-teens, changed the
blunt needles and records and maintained the delicate tension in the spring
mechanism on the gramophone.[13]

In her seventies, Dymphna looked back on her life and saw clearly for the first time many of the things that had shaped her. Contact with her grandchildren somehow cleared the mist that had settled over her own memories of childhood. Reading to her granddaughter, Anna, an abridged edition of Louisa May Alcott's *Little Women*—the book she had read countless times herself as a young girl—she suddenly saw how important the novel had been for her as a source of guidance. In its 'nineteenth century values' and 'puritan morality' she saw her own values—her frugality, her fierce independence, her pragmatism—but also something more confronting: her loneliness. Alcott's novel was based on her own experience growing up as one of four sisters, the sisters Dymphna wished she had as her own. Reading the novel late in life exhumed the feelings she had felt sixty years earlier, when she turned to reading as a refuge from boredom and isolation, lying in the sleepout, lost in *Little Women*. Six years younger than her brother Axel, she had always felt like an only child. From her school years, she made 'very few lasting friendships'. When she fell in love with Manning Clark in her early twenties, she was drawn to him in part because of his shared love of reading. Revealing their impressions of the literature they encountered became their way of revealing themselves to one another— year after year, page by page. She knew Clark would 'raise' her level of reading, taking her into the worlds she had shunned beforehand—the worlds of Russian literature, politics and history, but also closer to the country which she called home—Australia—the country that lay beyond the 'Oakwood' forest at Mont Albert.

The young woman who stood in Clark's arms on the deck of the *Orama* in August 1938 was still largely unknown to him. As time passed, the loneliness they had both felt in childhood would return to plague them, just as their different ways of expressing their love for one another would never cease to require translation. From the first moment, they were both lovers and strangers to one another. One thing, however, was clear as early as 1938. As Clark wrote to Catherine from the *Orama*: 'I have faith in my work and I have faith in Dymphna, in our life together … while she is alive I know that I can never be lonely'. Dymphna was earth to Clark's water; she was his only rock and safe harbour.[14]

EUROPE AT LAST

September 13, 1938: As the *Orama* passed through the Straits of Messina, Clark stood on the deck, looked out across the blue–green waters of the Mediterranean and caught his first sight of Europe. From a distance, the Calabrian town of Reggio, with its white houses 'ringed by olive groves' and red church steeple 'rising to the heavens' appeared 'unbelievably lovely'. Enraptured, he wrote immediately to his mother, Catherine. The Europe of all his intellectual and spiritual striving was now within reach; instantly he saw that, in Europe, despite the age of its civilisations and cultures, there was no 'sense of age in the land'. 'In Australia,' he reflected, 'you are always more aware of the split between the age of the country and the youth of its people.' So began a tussle that would continue for the rest of his life—the struggle between his longing for the deep, layered history of Europe, the lands of all his cultural dreaming, and his irrepressible love of the ancient emptiness of Australia. He left Australia believing that 'intellectual life' there was 'a back-water', knowing that he had little choice but to make the break. Yet it was only through leaving Australia that he was able to understand his attachment to his homeland. As he tried to explain to Catherine: 'at bottom, I belong to Australia … I love Australia passionately and know that my real work lies there'. Few students travelled to Oxford between the wars declaring such love for their country. Clark did not know his life's course in 1938, but he preferred to think of his life as the fulfilment of something pre-ordained, as if he were following the path of a power far greater than himself, a life intuited rather than a life planned.[15]

When the *Orama* moored at Naples, Clark's initial impressions were soon forgotten; he was repelled by the 'dirt and poverty' and disgusted by all 'the women over thirty', whom he found 'fat and ugly, and not very clean'. He rushed from the ship to buy a newspaper, pestering Dymphna all the way on the train up to Vesuvius to translate various paragraphs: 'What does this mean?—What does that say?' In September 1938, the British Government's policy of appeasement was being sorely tested by Hitler's insistence that Sudetenland, a region within Czechoslovakia inhabited predominantly by

Sudeten Germans, be ceded to the Reich. Hitler had delivered an ultimatum to the Czech government and Clark was extremely concerned that war was imminent. In Dymphna's recollection, he was 'agitated' and 'alarmed', incapable of putting his mind at rest. When they arrived in London a week later, his fears would only be exacerbated.[16] On 22 September, 'with the sun streaming down on the Thames', Clark and Dymphna alighted at Tilbury Docks. Clark's first reaction was awe: he felt dwarfed by 'the immensity' of London. Like a nineteenth-century man of letters, he made a beeline for the grave of Thomas Hardy in Westminster Abbey. There, at Poet's Corner, he stood, 'for a long time' gazing at Hardy's tombstone in solemn contemplation. It would be the first in a lifetime of literary pilgrimages.

Even before the couple arrived in London, Clark had made it plain to Dymphna that he believed England was unsafe, suggesting they leave immediately to stay with her cousins outside Stockholm. When he saw how tense the situation was in London—newspapers printing several daily editions, trenches being dug in city parks, gas masks being distributed to civilians and plans underway to transfer government offices from Whitehall to Oxford— his mind was made up. In a matter of days, they were on the train to Sweden, Clark writing Hope that he had been 'unable to sleep' in London due to exhaustion, so terrified was he by the thought of war. Europe, he told her, was 'a volcano' waiting to erupt. Once in Stockholm, 'everything simmered down'. Chamberlain signed the Munich agreement on 29 September and one day later announced the accord to a relieved British public. Convinced it was now safe to return to England, Clark and Dymphna took the train to Malmo, from where Dymphna travelled south to Germany and Clark continued on to Gothenburg and passage to England. Before he boarded the ferry, he wept uncontrollably, overcome by grief. As they parted, Dymphna knew he was concerned not only about the prospect of war but also about her safety in Nazi Germany. While Clark fretted, she remained calm, excited at the thought of experiencing life beyond the dull confines of suburban Melbourne. Nor was it the first time she had experienced life in Germany. As she sat on the train from Malmo to Berlin, she thought of her visit to Germany six years earlier, shortly after Hitler took power.[17] In early 1933, as 'a callow 16-year-old schoolgirl' accompanied by her mother, she had spent

Dymphna and Anna Lodewyckx, Belgium, 1933

Hilma Dymphna Lodewyckx
"Huize Eikenbosch"
1 Beatty St.
Mont. Albert
Melbourne E.10.
Australia

90

a pile of ~~ban~~ condemned books — by
Karl Marx, Kautzky, Remarque, Freud
Feuchtwanger, Emil Ludwig,
Glaser Kästner etc. The square was
crowded & the flickering torches
blazing books & glaring flares &
decorative students were very
awe-inspiring.

I have been back at school
now for almost 3 weeks. The teachers
are very mixed, both as to ability &
likeability, & the work decidedly hard,
nationalistic & not particularly interesting.
However I think I like it better than
before the holidays. This week I had
to write a six page essay in German
on "How can we German girls serve
our nation?" I actually accomplished
the Herculean task & am anxiously
awaiting the verdict of the teacher,

who is my pet aversion.

The Greek lessons also continue, with
me doing as little work as possible
which is all the same a fair bit.
The teacher (Prof Burghardt) & his wife
are very nice ... dley & she
particularly ...
temper...
At ...
be in ...
see ... a bit
some ...
may ...
the friends ...
will go a-walking somewhere.

This evening we are going to visit
old Dr. Anshauser. Mother goes to a lot
of the different lectures at the university
some of which are interesting & some not.
We are anxiously awaiting the answer

Dymphna's journal, 1933, with photo of Anna Lodewyckx

one year in Munich—'the cradle of the Nazi Party'—attending a German Gymnasium. She went to improve her German, Latin and Greek, and generally to 'please her father'. Remarkably, her journal from this time still survives, kept in the filing cabinet in Clark's study.

In mid-March 1933, Dymphna's and Anna's train left Venice, travelled through the Dolomites and crossed the German frontier near Rosenheim. As the train passed through the town, the passengers erupted with wild cheers and applause at the sight of the Nazi banners hung from the public buildings. Hitler had come to power only two months earlier. In Munich, Dymphna recorded the introduction of the boycotts of Jewish businesses, 'the stickers with "Jews forbidden" placed on shops and office plates'; in class, she complained of having to write 'nationalistic' essays—'How can German girls serve our nation?'—and she noted the day when the German salute became compulsory—'pupils & teachers have to raise a weary right arm before and after each lesson'. On 24 October—'Tag der Deutschen Kunst (Day of German Art)'—together with her schoolmates, she took part in the grand parade, the streets decorated with 'triumphal arches of fir twigs, golden swastikas and flags'. In the morning, she watched as 'the great man Hitler' laid the foundation stone of the 'Haus der Deutschen Kunst' [House of German Art], a model of which was carried in the procession. Later, Dymphna saw him and 'all the other Nazi leaders drive past slowly'. It was a great thrill, she thought, 'or [at least it] should have been. Hitler was slightly less repulsive than on his photos and portraits.' In May, mother and daughter witnessed the burning of the books in Munich. Dymphna's journal entry captured the attraction of the midnight spectacle: she described 'the lovely torchlight procession of gorgeously arrayed students parading through the illuminated city'. As the pile of condemned books was set alight, which included the works of Koestler, Marx and Freud, she stood 'awe inspired'— the square crowded with 'flickering torches, blazing books, glaring flares and decorative students'.

Without the knowledge of subsequent events, Dymphna's observations convey the magnetism of Nazi propaganda to the ordinary German—the solemn theatricality, the strength of conviction and the comfort of uniformity—and, most of all, the deft use of lurid spectacle to spellbind. Many years later, in her seventies, she wrote up her memories of the same events she had described in her journal in 1933. Describing the burning of the books she wrote: 'the torches were thrown into the cages, the flames licked around the books and then flared up into the night sky. Munich and its ancient backdrop of meadow, forest and Alps was as lovely as ever, but the air was full of menace'. How different from her journal entries in 1933. Writing long after the horror of the Nazi regime was fully known to her, her memory of her experience became the portent of what came to pass—'the air was full of menace'. The sense of 'awe' she felt as a sixteen-year-old was lost, replaced by a looming sense of terror. Reading her journal entries, which record her visit to Dachau, then a camp for 'political prisoners', and to Berchtesgaden, one of the many 'lovely places in the mountains', it is impossible not to feel the chill the mere mention of these place names brings today. But the chill is ours alone. It could not be felt in the same way in 1933. When Dymphna and Anna returned to Australia, Anna gave a press interview in 1934 in which she spoke of Hitler's 'brave' attempt to restore German morale. Like many in the early 1930s, both within and outside Germany, Anna believed Hitler had boosted German 'self-respect and self-confidence'. As late as 1938, Henry Gullett, who would become Minister for External Affairs in Robert Menzies' first ministry in April 1939, praised Hitler for restoring Germany's 'pride and power' and laying the groundwork for 'a future of great glory'. When Dymphna arrived as a graduate student it was not possible to view the regime so uncritically. As she travelled to Berlin in the spring of 1938, thinking of her visit to Germany five years earlier, her understanding of Nazi Germany was about to undergo a radical transformation.[18]

During her first days in Berlin, her mind was cast immediately back to 1933. Walking past a girls' secondary school in Potsdam she 'smiled' at the thought of herself five years earlier ('they are just the same!'). Writing her first letter to 'CMH Clark Esquire', at Oxford, she pleaded with him to be 'happy and cheerful'; it was only the thought of him being otherwise that could get her down. The difficulties of her new environment did not take long to surface. From the moment she read her father's first letter upon her arrival in Germany, any doubts she might have had about the seriousness of the situation were immediately dispelled. The tone of Augustin's letter was urgent and anxious; he had recently returned from Europe himself, but in the space of two or three months the prospects of war had increased significantly. He was concerned for her safety. Writing in Dutch, he gave her explicit directions:

> If war breaks out, offer your services to the British authorities as a translator ... if the present impasse continues go to Scandinavia or Iceland ... as long as the current tense situation between Great Britain and Germany continues there can of course be no possibility of study in Germany ... go to another Germanic country and continue your studies ... you could use [your] scholarship to write a dissertation on a Scandinavian or Icelandic subject ... but if amicable relations are restored between Germany and Great Britain, then you could also return to Germany, preferably to Bonn ... please answer this letter immediately by air-mail, and give us a permanent address in Europe to which we can write.[19]

Any sympathy Augustin and Anna might have had for Hitler in 1933 had now evaporated. Augustin's allegiance was to 'Germanic culture', not to Aryan supremacy or the Nazi Party. Given the tense situation in Europe, and with Clark in Oxford and with Dymphna still uncertain whether she would take up her first semester of study in Munich or in Bonn, the flurry of correspondence between Melbourne, Germany and England continued unabated. Anna's letters seemed more concerned about Clark's career than Dymphna's, while Augustin worried more for his daughter, asking her about her reading, advising her on the best course of action, and rarely mentioning Clark. Clark, meanwhile, wrote to everyone: at least once a week to Catherine, usually on Sundays after the morning service, then to Hope and to Dymphna's parents, and sometimes daily to Dymphna, while she wrote to him in Oxford, and to her mother and father in Melbourne. So much of the couple's first weeks in Europe were spent waiting, reading, writing and living from letters; like migratory birds flown too soon, they lived each day with the prospect that they might return home at any moment.[20]

Clark's letters to Anna Lodewyckx show him trying hard to endear himself to his future parents-in-law; reaching out to both Anna and Augustin, grateful for all their help, completely open about his love for Dymphna ('I don't mean to tell you how much I miss her, she is so sensible, balanced & stable') and keen to keep them informed of all his thoughts on the European situation ('England is played out ... her task, the self-imposed one of policeman, is over ... let us hope that the future will witness a rebirth, and not a holocaust'). Wrapped in the warmth of the sweater Anna had made for him, he wrote of his dreams for 'a genuine meal of beef steak, gravy, boiled potatoes and real Australian fruit salad' and of how he longed for escape from Oxford; 'we are foreigners here', he declared, 'strangers in a strange land ... Oh for the freedom of Australia, not this tension, with the sky bearing down on your shoulders, and the people empty shells—not living—"those barren leaves".' Often, as he reached the last paragraph of his letters, he tried to sweep Anna away with the same romantic air that had so beguiled her daughter:

> One more request—just look into the garden for me at twilight—with the dark shapes & the dim light in the sky. I wonder if the light in the bathroom needs attention, and if the cat still plays with the dog. We will have good talks in the future—when all is made clear.[21]

Arriving in Bonn in early October, Dymphna had much to deal with— her obligations to her scholarship; her father's expectations; a new and unpredictable environment; and the pressing needs of her lover in Oxford, who from the moment they parted in Malmo seemed incapable of surviving without her. She also had to cope with the prospect that she might be pregnant, writing to Clark of her 'relief' when she finally had her period. On the streets, it did not take long for the 'fierce grimness' of the Nazi regime to become visible. As a foreign student, she found herself isolated, 'ignored by German students and staff'. Visiting Beethoven House in Bonn, she was shocked to find a wall covered in 'a monster laurel wreath decked with swastikas and the name of Kulturminister Dr. Goebbels'. Her landlord, Frau Unger, a Catholic who was sceptical of the Nazis, often invited her up after dinner—'we'd gather with one bottle of wine, and ... smoke cigarettes'; occasionally, they attended dinner together at the home of Dr Busslei, who lived next door to Unger. When Dymphna first encountered Busslei, an art historian at the Rheinland Museum, she was so taken aback by his strident Nazi views that she translated slabs of his conversation in her letters to Clark. One of Busslei's comments in particular took her breath away: 'Mark my words, my English fräulein; in 1939 or 1940, will come the great war against Bolshevism, and in the course of this war, England and Russia will be wiped from the world map.' Busslei, whose house was filled with 'first class paintings and objets d'art', predicted the annihilation of these civilisations with the venom of a barbarian. While Dymphna dealt with the day-to-day reality of life in Nazi Germany, Clark in Oxford was still riven with angst over the possibility of war, writing Catherine only days after his arrival in London that Europe was ready to 'burst at any moment'. Although the Munich accord had resulted in a feeling of temporary relief in England, there was increasing division of opinion over Chamberlain's policy of appeasement. By the time Clark arrived in Oxford he would find that the earlier pacifist tendencies of college politics had given way to a new resolve: fascism had to be resisted at all cost.[22]

In London, he felt at sea. Feeling 'lost and lonely' in the city's vastness, he was drawn to its culture and history at the same time as he was 'revolted' by English snobbishness. Taking the train from London to Oxford, he read the copy of *The Idiot* he had bought in Stockholm, lifting his gaze occasionally from the pages of Dostoyevsky's novel to marvel at the English countryside—'the green fields, with their dark hedges and haystacks'. Once at Balliol, he poured out his anxieties and disappointments to Dymphna. He was 'not an Englishman' yet he was 'of English stock', and that made him even more a stranger. He felt lost between the 'loud-mouthed' American students and the prim English public school types. 'One may as well not exist,' he told her. Writing to his mother, or to her sister Gladys, both of whom he knew held an ideal image of England in their hearts, his refrain was somewhat different. To them he complained of Australia's materialism, its 'looseness and apathy', compared with England, where everything was 'very fine and serene' and there was such 'a deep-seated sense of unity and purpose'. Carried away by the architecture, church services and choral music, he could barely contain his enthusiasm: 'Tell Dad I have seen the spot where the Duke of Windsor used to sit for meals in Magdalen. [I] work in the same atmosphere as Newman, walk the same streets as Gladstone, and sit in the same library as Darwin. England is a beautiful place—almost intoxicating … the people here respect learning and culture.' 'This is the richest experience of my life,' he proclaimed. Taking a walk along the upper reaches of the River Isis, he wrote poetically to Catherine of the stillness of the landscape caught in 'the last protest of life against the death of winter', broken only 'by the lapping of the water against the banks of the river'. Writing to his sister, Hope, he had no one to please and no one to cajole, which is why his letters to her often seem more truthful to his experience because they betray his ambivalence. At first, he found it hard to believe he had made it to Oxford: 'Fancy, me a student at Oxford, the objective of every student in the English speaking world.' At the same time, he told Hope that Oxford made him feel like 'a schoolboy all over again' and reminded him of his 'state school' origins. 'I wonder what [people] would do if they knew how poor I was,' he said.[23]

For every audience, Clark gave a different recital, not because he was being selective about his true feelings, but because all these different responses were within him—the love of the English countryside, culture and history, the resentment of English condescension and class division, and the conviction that his 'first allegiance' would always remain 'with Australia and Australians'. He struggled to match the reality of what he found at Oxford with the landscape he carried in his imagination, the heartland of all the church services he had attended, the hymns he had sung, and so much of the literature and history he had studied. He was also reluctant to put his background in second place; his ego was so insecure that he took any suggestion of colonial inferiority as a personal slight. AGL Shaw, who was at Balliol with Clark, explained Clark's sensitivity to English superiority by telling the story of a dance he attended, organised by the Victoria League for the benefit of colonial students in England. As Shaw danced across the floor in the arms of a British General's daughter, the conversation turned to his undergraduate degree. 'So where did you do your degree?' she asked him. 'At Melbourne University,' he replied. She was surprised: 'Oh, you have universities in Australia do you?' Shaw saw her remark as 'funny', an example of ignorance as much as arrogance, whereas 'Manning', he said, 'would have been offended'. He was also keen to stress that Balliol College, which Clark encountered in 1938, was by no means unused to colonial students.[24]

In 1938, little more than 11 per cent of students at Oxford were from overseas, and within that percentage, imperial and Commonwealth student numbers easily outweighed those from Europe. The introduction of the Rhodes Scholarships in 1902 saw many students arrive in Oxford from India, Canada, New Zealand and Australia. Balliol, once the leading college, but by the late 1930s second to Queens College, was generally more liberal, and took significantly more overseas students than other colleges, so much so that the standard joke of 'white' students when they encountered a fellow-skinned student in the quadrangle was to exclaim, 'Dr Livingstone, I presume!' At Balliol, Clark entered a cloistered world in which undergraduates, known as 'men' (the college would not admit women until 1979), 'read' for their degrees with individual tutors, the rooms of the 'bachelor dons' serving as salons in the evenings. There were no prescribed lectures and essays were based on texts, hence the need for students' reading to be guided by their tutors. The only labour was intellectual. KC Bowen, a student at Balliol in 1937, recalled fondly that 'there were no domestic chores' for those in residence. 'Laundries were cheap and the scouts sent things out and checked them back in, shirts, collars, bedclothes, the lot.' Afternoon tea—'crumpets, cucumber sandwiches and toasted teacakes'—could also be couriered to private rooms.[25]

An Oxford education was one in which Greek and Latin were still considered the most prestigious subjects. At the core of the curriculum lay classical learning, in language, literature and philosophy, along with maths and theology. The university was a 'finishing school for the elite' in which men destined for the professions and public life cultivated the qualities necessary for English gentlemen—tolerance and leadership, oratorical eloquence, the ability to take one's drink, and an air of effortless, learned superiority. Released from what the English theatre critic Kenneth Tynan later called this 'gymnasium for the personality', in which men 'strutted their stuff' in preparation for the prominent life ahead of them, the Oxford man could slot into the ruling class virtually anywhere in the British Empire. For those who wanted to wear the label, one could be a 'Balliol man' for life, like the historians Arnold Toynbee, WK Hancock, John La Nauze and Max Crawford, or the novelist Graham Greene, whose time at Balliol was one long, alcohol-induced stupor.[26]

The costume drama was distinctive: 'Oxford undergraduates were instantly recognisable by their gowns, accents and clothing: grey flannel trousers, tweed jacket, collar and tie for ordinary occasions, white flannels and blazer for sporting functions.' At college dinners, the wearing of academic gowns was compulsory, official guests and college hierarchy were seated at 'High Table' while all others grubbed below, grace was said before and after meals, attendance at Chapel was encouraged, women were invisible, and as a form of compensation, hearty consumption of alcohol and lusty participation in sport were enthusiastically embraced. Fortunately, when Clark arrived in late 1938, he was not in residence within the college but renting a room nearby, and some of Balliol's insularity was breaking down; women had started to attend Labour club meetings and the introduction of radio, cinema and cars created more opportunity for men and women to socialise. Clark, however, still found the atmosphere restrictive, telling Dymphna that life at Balliol was too 'monastic', with 'no natural flow between the men and women'. Homosexuality was rife, he claimed, which led to 'deep complications'. The men at Oxford, he reflected, 'mix with men exclusively till they are 26, and so [they] can't make a spiritual association with a woman. They come to look to women for passion and nothing more.' As for the homosexuals, Clark found that they were 'not by nature perverse', but to his mind, they bore 'the burden of enforced penitence before women' because in loving one another they were 'sinning against women'.[27]

When Max Crawford wrote his letter of recommendation for Clark to AD Lindsay, the Master of Balliol, he warned that Clark was 'always apt to neglect the obvious for the remote'. Not long after his arrival in Oxford, Clark told Crawford he thought his finances would 'stand the strain', at least for his first year. But it quickly became clear that his meagre scholarship of 100 pounds was not sufficient, nor was he attracted to the relatively narrow research required to complete his doctorate. Initially, he wondered if he might have to abandon Oxford altogether, and during his first two months at Balliol oscillated between one scheme and the next, with Dymphna and Crawford as his sounding boards. In early November, he wrote to Crawford

An Eye for Eternity

of his plan to stay little more than a year before returning home and seeking a teaching post at Melbourne. His letter would have significant repercussions for the months ahead, with Dymphna worried it would mean the end of all chances for her own study, her parents concerned for Clark's future, and Crawford increasingly alarmed that Clark would not fulfil the obligations of his scholarship. Ultimately, Clark would be persuaded by his tutor, Humphrey Sumner, for whom he had quickly developed a great affection, to take on a wide reading course in the History of Nineteenth-century Europe. Eventually, by early 1939, this would lead him to focus on the French historian Alexis de Tocqueville. But in October and November 1938, before he left to join Dymphna in Bonn, none of this was clear. Clark was telling her not only of his loneliness in Oxford but also of his uncertainty about his academic future. At the centre of this was his determination to tie Dymphna's fate to his own. Because of Dymphna's later refusal to speak openly about the circumstances surrounding her marriage to Clark in January 1939, the conventional explanation for her departure from Germany has been accepted as the truthful one: that she simply fulfilled her promise to Clark and came to Oxford when the situation became untenable in Bonn, sacrificing her own career for a man whose talents she believed were superior to her own. The correspondence between Dymphna and Clark in late 1938 gives lie to this explanation. There was a great struggle between them; it began as soon as Clark arrived in Oxford and, while Dymphna was always devoted to him, she did everything she could to convince him they should continue their studies and avoid rushing headlong into marriage.[28]

LOVE BY CORRESPONDENCE

When they separated in Malmo in late September, they had been engaged for barely three months. Until now, the few letters Dymphna had seen from her fiancé were letters of warmth and longing affection. Clark's prose had revealed his delicacy of feeling, which only drew her closer to him. As soon as they parted, she discovered another side to Clark which would test her love for him and her own resolve. When Clark received her first letter from Berlin in the first week of October 1938, he berated her for the tone of her writing: 'don't write letters like that again. I can't understand how you can write so dispassionately about the spirit of Berlin … Darling, tell me more intimate details about yourself.' Her lack of emotion made him 'depressed' and he warned her that her 'intoxication with languages' could easily 'blur' her other feelings. With 'seven long weeks to go' until they were to meet in Germany in December, he doubted his ability to endure the time without her. When Dymphna received his letter she felt hurt, but still apologised, even penning a second note to her letter, apologising again. She wondered aloud: 'Oh Manning, my Manning, when will you & I, particularly you, come into our peace?'

In Bonn, which then had a population of little more than 90,000, she lived in Frau Unger's flat in Diezstrasse 4, in a square near the Romanesque Elizabeth Kirche, in a relatively new part of town. As she tried to come to terms with her own schedule of lectures and reading, throughout October, she received at least three letters a week from Clark. Cycling home after lectures she would often be greeted by the familiar sight of his tiny handwriting on the envelopes left on her doorstep. Within days of settling in to her new abode, she was already making it clear to Clark that she wanted to see through her time in Bonn. Her first letters show her straining to come to grips with the feverish intensity of his correspondence. On 6 October, she began by reassuring him that whatever he decided she would stand by him, but she reminded him of their plan. They had come, she told him, to study for two years 'with the help of money granted us for that purpose' and they now had the chance 'to see & do things which we would never be able to do again'. Yes, she felt lonely, but her experience in Germany was of 'tremendous interest', it was certainly not a 'waste'. He had reservations about Oxford, but he had his 'place there' which no one would begrudge him, and soon he would make friends. Concerned about his 'doubtfulness' over the doctorate, which she described as 'very unfortunate', she asked him to understand her position:

Manning, how lonely I would be if I could not write to you! And even so, I cannot write everything—it must wait till we meet. The letters to you are my only connection with the outer world—I haven't written to another soul except a letter of thanks to Stockholm & I haven't heard a word from the family since I left London. I am sorry if I sounded hard & impersonal— uninterested—in the beginning of this letter, but it was just that I felt as if the whole pack of cards were falling about my ears again when I read your letter last night.[29]

The cards still had some way to fall. During the course of the next week, Dymphna received one of the most extraordinary letters she would ever see from Clark. Although every letter from Clark aspired to be 'extraordinary'— he did not know how to be mundane—this letter was on a different plane. Written only a week after he heard of the death of his grandfather, Thomas Clark, on 27 September, Clark's sixteen-page screed arrived in Bonn some time in the second or third week of October 1938. Combing through his papers years later, Clark knew the significance of the letter, scribbling a note both to himself and his biographer: 'Vol. 1: there are volumes in this letter, the others are in a separate envelope.' He began with a declaration of love: '[you] are the only person in the world to whom I could write this letter.' Then came the bombshell: 'I have decided to apply for a job … there is no course here at Oxford for which I have the necessary money, which would be in any way valuable to me in my future career.' Worried that he would enter into significant debt if he borrowed money from Catherine to complete the doctorate, he argued he would place their financial future in jeopardy if he continued at Balliol. At times, he sounded as if he was searching for any excuse to opt out, complaining that he was unable to afford a 'sports coat' or any of the necessary 'gear' that would allow him to feel comfortable in 'a rich man's university'. He wanted to see Europe, not from his study, but in all its glory; he was a victim of the Australian anxiety—once in Europe see as much as you can lest you never return. He portrayed himself as the suffering one. He claimed he was going without meals to make ends meet. 'Every night I go to bed with pains of hunger in my stomach'. He insisted that he had put himself out to come to Oxford: 'I did not collect money to go to Oxford, but I did to come with you … I wanted you so much to go to Germany & have that life on your own … with the people you love, that I could not ask you to postpone your trip for my sake.' Even worse, he feared the onset of another epileptic attack: 'I can't guarantee that it won't triumph over me again & land me in the old 1930 or 1935 position.' In short, he appeared consumed by panic and fear, as if his very existence was now entirely dependent on hers.

> You have always shown me how well you understand my nervous condition … you are the only one who has never offended me in that way. Well, Oxford has a bad effect on me in that way & I feel very uncomfortable at social gatherings … I am getting back into the state of finding it hard to go to sleep at night & just lie there worrying, or staring blankly at the street lights playing on my pale, buff-coloured curtains … I only have that dreadful sense of spiritual isolation, of growing torment … as though the best part of me was being eaten up, or suppressed.

He then moved on to their sex life. 'Ever since June you have been subjected to a most nerve-wracking process with the double fear of exposure and pregnancy hanging over your head.' He regretted the secrecy of their lovemaking—pretending to others that they were not sleeping together—a game which seemed to make 'the whole thing very sordid and sneaking and furtive'. He was also consumed by jealousy, not only because Dymphna was asked out by other men in Bonn but also because of her past attractions, which he could not let rest. At the German club in Melbourne, Dymphna had had a brief flirtation with Erich Ventur, a friend of her brother Axel. Ventur was a man whose 'physical embraces' both she and Clark had not forgotten. Reading a 'scientific treatise' on sexuality and reproduction, Clark told her he 'now understood why this man's embraces had been so memorable'; he would explain why when they were reunited. Then came his pitch for immediate marriage.

> In return for the great gift, the sacrament which you make for me, I should assume the responsibility of protecting you & working for you. That is where I have fallen down and I feel so guilty about it … it is false and degrading … Don't you understand that that's my whole life, my core: loving someone

else & being dependent on them in some strange way & doing everything for them, in return for rescue of me from the abyss. And you say you love me. Ah, Kleinie, I walk round with that curse of [the] Irish in my head: 'Cursed be the man that is betrothed to woman & doth not take her in marriage.' It is not quite like that, but I do want to have done with the selfishness of the past. I lie awake at night remembering Russell's summing up of me: 'Manning you will always be unhappy if you are selfish like that' ... I have never loved you more deeply than at this very moment. The very words 'absolute separation' seem like ... an impossibility. The 'naughty girl' is still my woman, to whom 'all other women are shadows' ... I have just kissed your photo, a practice to which I may easily become addicted.

In the centre of his proposal for marriage, Clark placed his future career. He told Dymphna he would write to Crawford, 'setting out the reasons for his decision' and asking him if there 'was any chance of a job in Melbourne'. If need be, he would teach English in Germany before returning to Australia; this would give her 'a year at the University of Bonn' to fulfil her scholarship obligations and 'partly satisfy her father'. After writing through the afternoon, Clark stopped in the early evening to go to dinner with his friend and fellow student, the Rhodes Scholar Michael Thwaites, who, like Shaw, had started at Balliol at the same time. Returning to his flat after dinner, primed with a few drinks, he set forth again, in words exceptional for their certainty and vision, especially from a man who had only just turned twenty-three.

I feel that my real interests and my real talent (if there is any) can best be served in teaching. I do think that in academic work there must be a division of labour—between the teachers and the scholars. I am most certainly not a scholar—that is why the research here leaves me cold and angry—but I do feel genuine enthusiasm for teaching, and if possible at a University standard. This must be combined with something else, and I feel certain that I can write something one day on Australian history. I feel quite convinced that Australian history has been betrayed by Scott & Rusden & Giles [sic] Turner ... I believe quite passionately that Australia is a 'weird' country and that its weirdness has never been portrayed except in landscape painting.

Australia is virgin soil in this respect & I feel something can be done about it. My whole being is rooted in Australia, and I don't feel the temptation to betray her, to leave her. The other night, I was invited to dinner ... and held forth quite passionately on the 'weirdness' of Australia to an interested audience. I felt quite exhilarated afterwards ... What I do want you to realise is that two years here in Oxford would not help me at all in my career.

After barely one month in England, Clark's mind turned ever homewards, as if it was only through living in Oxford that he came to understand his life's calling. The link between his dependence on Dymphna and his future career was made explicit. In the same breath as he declared his love for her, and his desire to marry, he stated his intention to write Australian history; in his mind, the two were inseparable. Yet he was also declaring his love for Australia—'my whole being is rooted in Australia'. Few Australian intellectuals in the late 1930s could have made such an unequivocal declaration of patriotism. In 1937, together with Dymphna, Clark read Percy Stephensen's *Foundations of Australian Culture*, published in 1936, and imbibed Stephensen's fierce independence and nationalism. But it was not Stephensen who opened his eyes to the spirit of place in Australia. This is the astonishing aspect of his determination to write Australian history: it was grounded in place—in the land, sea and sky of his faraway home. As soon as he departed Australia, his letters spoke repeatedly of the 'weirdness' of Australia. Now that he had seen the English landscape, with its tight-knit beauty, layered by centuries of human sculpting, he could sense the strange beauty of the country he had left behind. Drawing on Marcus Clarke's 'weird melancholy', and DH Lawrence's *Kangaroo*, a novel that overflowed with depictions of the Australian landscape as weird and unearthly, Clark turned to history like an artist, rejecting 'scholarship' as arid. At one more with painters than historians, he renounced class-ridden English society and followed his creative instinct: the deepest antiquity lay not in England but in Australia. This was the mystery that lay at the heart of his ambition, and which would ultimately drive so much of his life's work. That evening, he continued writing his letter to Dymphna, well into the early hours, pulled along by his fear of losing her, and his own irrepressible ardour. When he finished the letter, it was so long that he might even have needed two envelopes to mail it the next morning. His last words were little short of an ultimatum.

all my weaknesses are being nourished in your absence … I fight against them … but it can't go forever … Life for me is life with you … I feel that it is like this: I must make a decision here & now, and that, to put it off is only to prolong the agony … I am going to have done with this place—with your consent. Perhaps I am wrong. I don't know. All the week I have had to fight against the temptation to go to see you in Bonn … I want to start a new life just now … but Kleinie, I am a weak, degraded person … I will make you happy one day, yes, really happy. I can do things for you—but I don't want to ask you 'to forsake all and follow me'. I am not worthy of that, and I know it.[30]

When Dymphna read the letter in Bonn, she was crestfallen: 'I have just read your letter, and it has made me very, very sad & hopeless. Why must you always be beaten by things, why must you always play the underdog to life, when you know yourself that you have un-sounded wells of strength to call upon?' She felt a mixture of disbelief, anger and disappointment—Clark seemed to be pulling out of his studies. She was also distressed because he saw himself as 'so inwardly wretched', and warned him not to think so much about her: 'the cure will not come through me' she told him. Her remedy for his depression—work harder— was reminiscent of the medicine her father might have meted out and she reminded him to get out of his flat: 'you have access to all the other normal means of solace—friends, music, natural beauty, art, exercise, society, writing, religion, drink & women too, although I won't insult you by mentioning it except as a joke'. When he suggested she read a passage from Lawrence's *Love Among the Haystacks* because he thought it analogous to her own situation, alone in Germany, she found it made her 'sick at heart' and tried to explain to him that she did not live in the novel's reality but her own—she had different motivations from Lawrence's characters. Well into early November, she wondered if he would ever 'come to rest', and then it quickly dawned on her that if the last few weeks were a glimpse of her future, she would not come to rest either.

Her love for him could be shaken, but it never faltered. Faced with Clark's demand for more passionate letters, she tried so hard to be the woman he wanted her to be. Reading her letters from this period, it is possible to feel her frustration: 'Why can't I write differently?' she pleaded, 'I <u>feel</u> strongly enough about it, & warmly enough to you. Why?' She struggled to get the things down on paper she had collected in her mind throughout the day, the things she told herself to 'tell Manning'. When it came to writing them down, the things that had only hours earlier seemed to carry so much weight somehow lost their significance. For Dymphna, her feelings of love and affection for Clark always welled larger in her heart than she could ever express them on paper; whereas for Clark, it was the reverse, he discovered his feelings through writing. In this way, they were like lovers who spoke different languages; their ways of expressing their love for one another rarely understood by the other; he needing unending reassurance that he was loved, she never able to reach the lofty heights he asked her to ascend. When all else failed, she tried humour, joking that his letters nearly drove her 'blind in the reading'—such thin paper, and [such] close handwriting on both sides'— and coping with his possessiveness by teasing him:

> Manning dear, have I said enough nice things? I always seem to let them be crowded out, don't I? … you should hear me talk to people about 'mein Verlobter'. Why it must be all over the town by now, because I haven't been approached by a single storm trooper yet![31]

Dymphna's unease with the shrill political propaganda grew stronger the more she walked the streets of Bonn. She described the daily aural attack to Clark: 'raucous political speeches issuing from cheap radios through the windows of 16th century farmhouses, almost wilting the geraniums on the window-sill & blasting the pious inscription over the door'. Every time Clark read letters such as these, it only increased his anxiety. In early November, the flood of correspondence from Oxford to Bonn began to arrive daily; each missive another canon in Clark's arsenal of literary persuasion. On 1 November, All Souls Day, Dymphna tried to hold her ground, urging him again to do all he could to fulfil his scholarship obligations and even offering to lend him money to buy a sports coat. She told him bluntly that marriage could wait until they abandoned their studies and employment was a reality:

> Don't forget that this is our last chance as independent free agents in Europe, if we marry. I expect it will be much better for us both together, but it is never the same again—particularly for a man … remember that bachelordom is a state not to be abandoned too lightly by a serious person. Spinsterhood is no good for a woman—widowhood is preferable I think! I too feel that it is an enormous waste to look at Europe through a library window, but remember that if we had not undertaken to do that, neither of us would have left Australia at all.[32]

Two days later, she wrote to Clark again, stating that she wanted to delay her passage home for as long as possible, preferably until February 1940. In Oxford, Clark already had his mind on something quite the opposite. He had written to her on the same day, asking her to make enquiries about 'being fitted with a contraceptive', and their letters crossed. 'You might find it easier to speak to a woman chemist,' he told her, before offering some words of advice: 'the actual fitting [and] measurements etc will be embarrassing, but it is the only thing to do. I can't do it myself, because it's not for me.' He was afraid that his whole being would 'crash' from the 'incompleteness and isolation' caused by their separation; at night, he stood in front of her photograph, 'wagged' his finger, and said in 'baby talk': 'you're such a naughty little girl'. He discovered that gazing at her face in 'pure love' was actually like being with her. 'Here, in the twilight, with the buildings outlined against the softly radiant sky, I feel the awareness of your love, and then I don't feel incomplete … I may not be great, or clever, or witty, but I do feel someone through you.' This was reminiscent of other protestations of love he'd made to her since they parted in Malmo—'I always live through another person'—declarations of his dependence.

The following morning, after mailing his letter, he returned to his flat near Balliol to find her letter warning against an unnecessarily hasty marriage. He was immediately thrown into despair; he felt 'torn up by the roots', convinced now that she did not want to marry him. Unable to bear the thought that she could be 'content' in Bonn without him, he believed his love for her was not reciprocated. While he could endure Oxford only if he had 'the prospect of marriage at the end of it', she obviously felt differently. By suggesting he preserve his freedom for a little longer before marrying, she had 'mocked' him. How could he be 'free' when she was not there by his side? There was clearly a 'great gulf' between them, it appeared that they had a 'different scale of values', a different way of being in the world; from this point, the future appeared bleak.

> I don't know what to do. I just feel that I have got myself in an awful mess, and am struggling to extricate myself. It is when I realise how finely balanced my whole system is, how the least upset can drive me immediately to the most extreme thoughts & actions, then I know the depths of despair, agony & remorse ... You seemed to be drifting away from me, no longer looking forward to seeing me—as though my suggestions had left a nasty taste in your mouth ... We must learn to accept each other for what we are. There will always be stresses because that is my nature ... with me there is always the seething cauldron—the peace and harmony never last for long. But I want you to stay with me—if you want to. Tell me, darling, if you forgive me and tell me if you still love me and want to marry me despite my faults ... I am glad that you are not lonely. You will be faithful to me, won't you? You see, that is where we are so different. You still take pleasure from going out to see other men and going out to talk with them. I don't notice other women these days. You will always live in the flow of men and I must accept that fact. It is not unfaithfulness on your part just a fulfilment of your being ... you have a natural sympathy for men, a natural flow towards them ... I do wish you would reveal yourself more to women.[33]

The struggle between them was now coming to a head. When Dymphna read his letter in Bonn, she had had to cope with one letter arriving each day for a week. She felt overwhelmed by the deluge of correspondence, as if she was slowly being enveloped in Clark's melancholy fog and could no longer respond rationally. His letters were so intense, so maudlin and so long that she couldn't 'hope to answer them all properly'. She sat down with the week's correspondence in front of her, 'too mentally tired and muddled to write', yet determined to 'say something'. If Clark was distraught, she was exasperated. Everything she wrote to him led to 'misunderstandings', so much so that it made her afraid to say anything. Since her arrival in Germany one month earlier, she had hardly had a moment free from his demands. There seemed to be little time or space for her own life. Nor was she impressed by Clark's instructions on lovemaking and contraception, and her reply was unflinching in its honesty.

> You may come to any conclusion about me you like—but by the time I had read through the <u>third</u> consecutive letter telling me about 'holding private parts' 'half undressing' 'it tickles'; muttering 'any chemist will tell you', 'pausing on the brink', private conduct 'quite simple', 'do it every night' 'you won't notice it' I was ready to scream. Don't worry I will do it all to the best of my ability, & I am sure it will not be nearly as bad as I instinctively imagine it to be, but I think your insistence on it in letters was rather a mistake. I never thought anything could look so horrible in your handwriting, and I never want to see anything like that in your handwriting again. That's not a command—it simply expresses my aversion. There![34]

The gulf that Clark spoke of was becoming palpable. He could not bear to be without her and yet he seemed deaf to her needs; she kept asking for breathing space, for time to complete her studies; he kept pleading for marriage, threatening total collapse if she failed to oblige or dared to suggest even a small delay. With the threat of war growing all the while in the background, the pressure on both of them was immense. She asked him again to wait at least another eight months before they were married. She tried refreshing his memory; she was the one who had kept on applying for scholarships to enable him to accompany her to Europe. She thought he 'would want to stay for a while'. Now he was pulling out. If Clark left Oxford and they returned to Australia as man and wife, both of them without 'definite prospects', it would 'only aggravate the situation'. She could see this clearly, whereas all he seemed capable of seeing was that she was 'unwilling to throw in [her] lot unconditionally with [him]'.[35] As she continued, her will seemed to tire. The stream of communication between them only ended in confusion and disappointment. Despite all his pleading and self-pity, and all his suffocating love, she still gave herself completely to him. Torn as she felt, worried as she was about their future, her love for him was still greater than her fear.

> I do love you Manning. I don't know how happy or unhappy we will be together, but I only know that you are the only one who can hold me, the only one I want to mean anything to. I often have horrible fears for our future, but I couldn't do anything but go on with you, if I tried—until of course you finish with me & then of course I will pick up the meaningless pieces & make some kind of meaningless design out of them. I don't love you in the same way as you do me—it's quite true … [but] I know that on the few occasions men have tried to stage a 'pick up' with me, however nice they have seemed, however much I would have liked to talk to them, my inside has turned right round & before I knew where I was, I had sent them packing as politely as I could & never felt the slightest twinge of regret.[36]

The intensity of their correspondence had exhausted both of them—'Ach it's no use talking!' Dymphna exclaimed. The next morning she was full of remorse for what she had written, describing her letter as 'foolish'. 'What's the use of fighting by post?' she asked him. 'We've had enough of that in person, heaven only knows.' Then she offered him her devotion. 'Of course, I will do everything you say, and gladly, because I love you and because I know you have thought about everything.' When Clark read her words of reassurance, he wandered the streets of Oxford 'humming music—as happy as a king'. They now had only a little over three weeks until they would be reunited in Bonn. Although Clark's worries did not disappear—he continued to find Oxford's social life lacking in warmth and geniality, and he suffered nightly from insomnia, taking aspirin or sleeping tablets to get through the night—now that Dymphna had committed herself, he calmed down. Suddenly, her 'dispassionate' letters became a source of strength to him. 'One can rely on you,' he told her. His outpouring of angst-ridden prose—obsessive and frenzied in its sudden flights of fancy and bouts of depression—had

had the desired effect. She was 'his woman'—completely. Dymphna admitted she was afraid of his anger, but she was also fearful for his mental health, particularly his 'nervous condition', the potential return of which seemed to be exacerbated every time she had clung to her independence.

At the height of these disagreements, some time in late October and early November, Clark made several 'helpful' appointments with a 'psychiatrist'. He did not describe the sessions in any detail, but they proved effective in managing his anxiety. His letters to Catherine in mid-November show his earlier tension subsiding (so much so that it might easily be another person writing), describing the small pleasures of his daily routine—breakfast in his study, reading until lunch ('Australian cheese' sandwiches followed by a cup of tea made by his landlady), then a walk or bicycle ride, home for afternoon tea and more study, dinner at 7.15, after which he went to a play, attended a concert, or took part in the activities of the two clubs he had joined, the Stubbs Historical Society and the Balliol Music Club, before returning to his flat for a reading from the gospels and bed—the Circadian rhythms of the young Australian student in Oxford. He even described his new 'polish' in his manners and social graces, not to mention the change in his accent— he was taking greater care with 'pronunciation and enunciation'—such were the benefits of living in a more 'refined' culture. At the same time, his academic program had finally gained some sense of direction. He had decided to make the nineteenth century 'his period', beginning his reading with the novels of Jane Austen and the Brontë sisters.[37]

As Clark counted down the days to his arrival in Bonn, relative quiet descended within him. But for Dymphna, the political and social upheaval was having the opposite effect. On the night of 9 November and around the early morning of 10 November, allegedly in response to the assassination in Paris of a German diplomat, Ernst vom Rath, by the Polish Jew Herschel Grynszpan, Nazi Storm Troopers and mobs of party activists unleashed a wave of violence against Jews across Germany. Dymphna saw the aftermath of 'Kristallnacht' on the streets of Bonn, walking past the Jewish shops with their windows smashed, watching the smoke rise from the burning synagogues in the distance, her mind haunted by the demeanour of the crowds as they moved through the scene—mute and numb—shuffling through the streets, now eerily silent, like spectators from another country. About to take a photograph of the devastation, she hesitated, afraid of being arrested. When she arrived back at her flat, she was confronted by a German student who was so consumed with panic and fear that she wanted only to get out of the country, preferably to England.

Predictably, when Clark read of the violence, it increased his fears for Dymphna's safety. 'Is Dostoyevsky any help?' he asked her. Visiting AGL Shaw in his rooms at Balliol, he told him of his concerns. There, late into the evening, they shared long conversations over 'endless cups of tea', Clark seeking endorsement of his plans to bring Dymphna to England, Shaw refusing to oblige. 'He wanted reassurance,' said Shaw, 'but I couldn't give it to him. I thought he was over-reacting and I told him quite plainly that Dymphna should be allowed to finish her studies, at least until war intervened, but he wouldn't take it, in fact, he would hear none of it.' Kristallnacht had given Clark a pretext to step up his campaign to bring Dymphna to England. As he told Hope, she had been shocked by the 'recent purges and the release of animal instincts against the Jews ... I feel quite anxious for her personal safety.'[38]

In Bonn, in the weeks before and after Kristallnacht, Dymphna received regular letters from her mother and father, both of whom were just as concerned as Clark. Within a day or two of the pogrom, she read Anna's warning: 'Your letters are most probably opened and read, and you must take care not to antagonize the people there; they can make it very uncomfortable for you.' In Melbourne, when Anna heard of the events on the night of 9 November, she offered Dymphna a demonstration of how to remain silent: 'What else will I tell you? I could tell you a few things about the local mood—that is, with regard to the persecution of the Jews, but perhaps it is better that I don't speak about these things.'

Despite the worsening situation in Europe, Augustin had not relinquished his hopes for a brilliant academic career for his daughter. Knowing this, Clark wrote telling Dymphna her father was wrong: if she pursued an academic career, he said, she would need to 'deny her very being'—she didn't have 'that type of mind'. Her life lay in a different direction, and if she made the mistake of chasing an academic career, he would 'scream' to the world that she would no longer be '[his] woman'. Dymphna would later agree: insisting that her father 'misread' her. She had never wanted to be an academic. How certain she was of this decision in 1938 is difficult to tell. When all the correspondence that Dymphna received in Bonn is laid on the table, it is possible to appreciate how much pressure she was under—from Clark, from her parents and from the increasingly volatile situation in Germany. In the face of so much advice from others, the mounting violence on the streets around her and the inferior quality of some of the teaching she received at the university—so many of the better teachers, many of them Jews, had already fled the country—it seems remarkable that she continued to hold fast to her original plan. Kristallnacht had certainly shocked her, but Clark was probably overstating her shock. Less than one week before Clark left England for Germany, she explained to him that she had not told Bonn University that she might leave at the end of 1938.

> But of course I mean to retire gracefully as soon as we decide the time has come for me to do so. In the meantime I will work more or less in tune with the course & read as widely as I can about general things ... My only personal aim is a successful compromise between getting what I (& I hope we) call the best value out of my stay here, in view of my intended career, and fulfilling my other obligations, at least so as not to cause too much criticism. Do you understand? Is that right?[39]

In Oxford, Clark had his mind on only one thing—their reunion. As he told Anna Lodewyckx, he was 'in the depth of excitement'. On the morning of Thursday 24 November, with Bonn's late autumn skies unusually 'clear and blue' above her, Dymphna opened his letter to find that he had brought forward his date of arrival. Would she meet him on Saturday in Cologne? 'Look for best dressed man on the station,' he said, or 'at least the happiest.' She told him she would wait at Cologne's main station even if it meant 'sitting up all night'. Bring 'your sports coat and the 12/6 trousers,' she reminded him, and don't forget 'an old pair greys for rough walks, your black ammunition boots, and maybe some dancing shoes.' Two months of separation had felt like two years. The waiting was finally over.[40]

6: WAR AND MARRIAGE, 1939–40

The front cover of Manning
Clark's first diary,
25 November 1938

On arrival in Bonn on the morning of Saturday 26 November 1938, Manning Clark bought a brown covered exercise book with a green cloth spine. Later that day, he wrote his first entry in his diary, describing his breakfast with Dymphna, his first walk through the streets of Bonn—'the sea of hostile, hard faces'—and their lunch in the university cafeteria, surrounded by soldiers and 'pictures of Hitler'. In the evening, on the small floor of the Konig's Hof hotel, they danced until midnight, then returned home, Clark falling asleep immediately in her arms, free at last from what he called 'the torture and agony of Oxford'.

During the eight weeks they had been apart, Clark had created an idealised image of Dymphna; standing before her photograph in his small room in Oxford, he imagined 'a radiant negation of eternity' and dwelt nightly on all 'the beauty' in her face, carried away by the 'purity and compassion' he saw in her eyes. Gazing intensely at her face, he hoped to experience 'a transfiguration'. In Bonn, Dymphna kept two framed photographs of Clark; each night, fearful of his oppressive melancholia, she would turn away from the 'stern and serious' face towards the 'smiling photograph' in the far corner of the room. To feel love, Clark needed to romanticise his beloved—to court a vision of perfection—living each day as if under a 'spell'. Yet with each vision

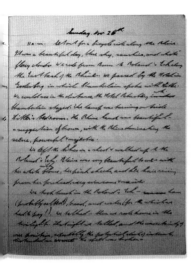

*The first page of Clark's
diary, Bonn, November 1938*

of his beloved he painted, the weight of his expectations only became greater, the fall from the great height he had climbed only more likely.[1]

In February 1934, when Dymphna returned to Australia after her first visit to Germany, her teenage beauty had inspired verse from one of the men she met on board the SS *Strathaven*. Before the ship docked at Port Melbourne, she opened a card to read the poem:

And then you came into my room;
You were the sun,
The dying garden & fading bloom
And I were one

In her journal, she copied out the poem and added her own preface: 'the first and—I hope—the last poem written to me by Harold Wenham!' Clark's literary skills were infinitely superior to Wenham's, but Dymphna's sensibility was not romantic. Her understanding of love was grounded not in fanciful visions of her beloved but in the unwritten rhythms of the everyday. While Clark's mind soared in search of divine epiphanies, her eyes remained focused on what was before her.[2]

In December 1938, the 'spell' was still cast. Until he returned to England in January 1939, Clark's diary entries recorded their daily activities—bike rides along the Rhine, visits to museums and galleries, concert and theatre attendances—and their many conversations with Jews and Nazis, some of which he found shocking. His diary began as a chronicle of *their* experience. So often, in fact, did he use the word 'we' instead of 'I', that it's possible to imagine Dymphna peering over his shoulder as he wrote. In these four weeks—their honeymoon before marriage —they were blissfully happy. For one of the few times in his life, Clark's recorded experience was at one with his lived experience; nothing seemed to jar, except for the environment around them, the brutality of Nazi racial hatred becoming more visible by the day.[3]

An Eye for Eternity

For any person in a close relationship, the act of keeping a diary is a statement that not everything in one's life can be shared. The diarist prizes his or her conversation with himself; the hours spent alone, writing soliloquies to an audience waiting in some darkened future. Once the diarist begins to write of his lover in the pages of his diary, and records those thoughts and feelings he dare not speak aloud, the keeping of a diary involves a necessary duplicity—or, more precisely, it leaves behind the evidence of duplicity. And it demands a double life—a fidelity to documentation, to the call of the diary, which coexists, but rarely coincides, with a fidelity to the person being written about. Evelyn Waugh managed to keep a diary without his wife ever knowing. In Clark's case, from the moment he first kept a diary in Germany, Dymphna knew of its existence, but it was nearly always on his person. Whenever she was by his side, the diary that contained Clark's frequently unforgiving judgements of her character lay within her hands' reach, in his bag, coat pocket or desk drawer. When the opportunity presented itself, she could easily have looked into the pages of his diary. In later years, as the diary became more of a notebook, a place to sketch out ideas, the exercise books of his early years gave way to small blue notebooks that fitted easily inside his jacket pocket. The diary lived with him constantly, almost becoming part of his anatomy. The only time he parted from it was at night, when he undressed before sleep.

December 1938 would be the last time Clark's diary entries were in unison with his everyday life with Dymphna. By the new year of 1939, back in Oxford, and for the next fifty-three years of diary keeping, his diary would document her shortcomings and her weaknesses and the 'spell' was quickly broken. What began to emerge in his Oxford diary was a one-dimensional image of both Dymphna and Clark. Of her, we see mostly Clark's complaints—the diary becomes a midden of his dissatisfaction with his wife—while of Clark, we see mostly his imperious, critical eye and self-pity. The vibrancy, colour and subtleties of both their personalities, and the texture of their everyday relationship, is largely lost; while we see Clark's internal monologue of woe, we share few of his joys, nor do we glimpse the infinite pleasures he shared with Dymphna. Fortunately, some of those pleasures can be found in their correspondence, which still retains the vividness and feel of a conversation.

As Dymphna walked with Clark through the streets of Bonn and Munich in December 1938, she had little idea of what Clark's diary-keeping would mean for their future. From the moment of their reunion in Bonn, when Clark left the bookshop with the mottled brown exercise book under his arm, his embrace of his diary was a recognition of his separateness, his need to give 'to the blank page' as great as his need to give to her. This was, after all, his greatest passion: to write, to communicate, to be heard and to be remembered. In this way, as he admitted to himself in his diary, 'they were poles apart'.

GERMANY: DECEMBER 1938

In November and December 1938, during the immediate aftermath of Kristallnacht in Germany, the Nazis turned from racial hatred towards genocide. In a matter of weeks 30,000 Jews were arrested and sent to labour camps at Dachau, Buchenwald and Sachsenhausen. Hitler's propaganda minister, Joseph Goebbels, described the events of Kristallnacht as the venting of the 'healthy instincts of the German people … [against] the parasites of the Jewish race'. On 12 November, the Nazi regime issued an edict that demanded that German Jews clean up and pay for the destruction that Goebbels himself had helped to orchestrate. Since the Nazis had come to power in 1933, more than half of Germany's Jewish population, one of the oldest and largest in Europe, had emigrated, many of them to the United States. In 1938, the Nazis had not yet devised the policy of exterminating Jews in death camps, but in the wake of Kristallnacht those Jews who remained in Germany tried desperately to find a way out of the country. Foreign embassies were flooded, borders rushed, and frantic pleas sent for help overseas as Jews found their remaining rights stripped from them on a daily basis. After Kristallnacht, no Jew was safe in Germany—every day was lived in constant fear of arrest and imprisonment.[4]

In a small village outside Dresden, on 15 December, the literary scholar Victor Klemperer described the atmosphere as suffocating: 'we continue in this simultaneously crushing and stupefying chaos, this empty and breathless busyness, this absolute uncertainty'. His diary, a record of one man's defiance in the face of tyranny, meticulously documented his journey from German citizen to virtual prisoner in his own home. In late November and December, as for nearly every Jew in Germany, Klemperer's freedom of movement was severely restricted; his right to drive withdrawn; his right to attend cinemas and places of entertainment denied; his right to use a library and attend university lectures retracted; even his ability to buy basic provisions was subject to curfews and exclusions. The German economy was steadily being 'Aryanised' and the Nazi state was closing in on every aspect of his daily existence. Klemperer wondered if he now inhabited 'the last circle of hell'. As he realised that it was only a matter of time before all his property would be confiscated and his pension stopped, he wrote letters of application for work in South America and Australia. But the response of the outside world to the plight of Germany's Jews in late 1938 was far from welcoming. Even if they succeeded in finding their way abroad, the Deutschmarks they carried with them were next to worthless once outside the country. Klemperer could not find any easy escape route. Many of his friends 'had been arrested and taken away'. He was free, he wrote, 'but for how long'? Like many Jews, he was 'tormented by the question … to go where we have nothing [or] to remain in this corruption?' As the persecution of Jews spread, Klemperer, under curfew from noon till 8 pm, felt that he 'could not bear it any more—I really felt as if I could not breathe.' Such was the environment Clark confronted in late November 1938.[5]

Together with Dymphna, he visited the homes of academics from Bonn University, many of them friends of Frau Unger's or contacts from Dymphna's visit in 1933. In the space of a few weeks he encountered almost every part of the political spectrum—aggressive Nazis, blind, unthinking supporters of Hitler, critics of the Party, as well as those who spouted a visceral hatred of the Jews. Everywhere he turned, the Jews were being hounded relentlessly. His record of some of the conversations he shared in Bonn and Munich captured the uncertainty of the moment; meeting a professor of Law in Bonn who described Poland and Russia as 'nations of dogs', he noted how in all other respects the professor was polite and 'not unpleasant'. Introduced to another retired professor from Bonn University who harangued him with 'scathing' and 'malicious' criticism of the Jews, Clark admitted that he found his criticisms 'so destructive' that it made his own position unclear; 'the Jewish question', he reflected, seemed 'quite complex'. Unable to fully grasp the course of events, many of his diary entries documented the 'chaos' to which Klemperer referred. No one seemed to know what would happen next—least of all the Jews. In Munich, Clark stood before the memorial to the Nazis who were killed in the abortive Beer Hall Putsch of 1923, impressed by the aesthetics of the memorial; 'the two sentries, very young ... in their blue uniforms & Nazi insignias, standing with bowed heads, and the six iron coffins with their wreaths of remembrance, & the snow resting on it—a beautiful scene, quite serene'. While he saw through the 'gloss' of Nazi propaganda and doubted the regime would last, he also appreciated the magnetism of the stark, rigid symmetry of Nazi choreography. In late 1938, there was no incarnation of evil to slay; rather, the atmosphere was one of creeping terror and disbelief as the drive to purge the Jews from Germany and 'ganz Europa' (all of Europe) became increasingly visible. All the while, the prejudice, intimidation and terror of the Nazi State existed beneath a veneer of selective civility and 'awe-inspiring' military theatre. Faithful to those Jews with whom he spoke, Clark recorded as much of their conversation as he could remember. Visiting the Munich home of Dymphna's school friend in 1933, Erika Wiener, who was then trying to escape to China with her Aryan husband, he documented the experience of her father, Otto, who, thanks to an earlier relationship with Hermann Goering, was released from Dachau only weeks earlier.

[Wiener] told us his experiences in the concentration camp at Dachau. They had to get up at 6 a.m., wear summer-weight pyjamas, and do exercises until 7 [am] in the open air. The temperature was 12°[Celsius] below zero. If they attempted to warm themselves they were thrashed from behind. The act of stepping off the path on to the grass was an invitation to be shot— this was an easy way of committing suicide. There were 16 sleeping in each room ... He emphasised the brutality & bestiality at the camp ... One S.S. man dangled a rope before a Jew's eyes & said maliciously: 'You Jewish pig—do you want to hang?'[6]

An Eye for Eternity

Wiener told Clark that his personal freedom had been taken away from him: 'I can't read what I want to read, I can't hear what I want to hear, and I can't say what I want to say.' Their situation, like that of so many other Jewish families, seemed hopeless. (In 1964, when Dymphna next returned to Munich, she could find no trace of the Wiener family.) After little more than three weeks in Germany, Clark saw that the Nazis had 'cleverly exploited the violent antipathy' of the 'lower orders of society', directing them into hero worship of Hitler and unleashing a wave of violence against Jews and communists. Everything he witnessed told him that despite the fact she was not Jewish, Dymphna's safety could not be ensured if she remained in Germany. Of course, this was also what he wanted to see. Dymphna, however, was still receiving contrary advice from home. During the month she was together with Clark in Bonn and Munich, she received regular letters from her parents. Clark had written to them more frequently than she had herself, sending them weekly updates from Oxford.

When Augustin and Anna first got wind of Clark's plans to leave Oxford after less than a year, aborting his plans for the doctorate, they were alarmed. Augustin went immediately to see Crawford in his office at Melbourne University, concerned that Dymphna had attached herself to an unreliable man who might make no more of himself than 'a serviceable librarian'. As Anna wrote to Dymphna: 'it would be unfortunate if [Manning] is not going to use this opportunity to prepare himself for something good ... Crawford seems to be surprised by what Manning told him, and I'm anxious that he will leave his studies simply because he doesn't feel comfortable in Oxford.' Anna had written to Clark herself, worried that he had become 'a victim of his feelings' and gently tried to get him out of 'his frame of mind', but she knew that even the most 'minor issues' caused him 'a great deal of unhappiness', so she asked Dymphna to intercede on her behalf. 'Manning,' she told her, 'finds the people cold and aloof, scornful of the Australians. You should not allow him to stay in this mood, since it will have an adverse effect on his work ... but it might be better if you approach him on this.' Dymphna knew that her parents were not pleased that Clark had left Oxford to visit her. On one occasion, Anna went so far as to suggest he should not have gone to Bonn. She sensed that Manning wanted

Dymphna to leave Germany and give up her studies, and she was determined to provide her daughter with a counter argument. 'Manning writes about your state of mind after the pogrom in Bonn,' she wrote. 'He sounds somewhat pessimistic about the European situation, and where you are, the situation appears to be really dark. On the other hand, nowhere is it really safe.' In one way, she was right; given the threat of a German invasion of England, Dymphna might have well been safer in Bonn than in Oxford. One thing she did not lack was advice. There was no shortage of people telling her what to do with her life.[7]

After Clark left Germany for England, on 5 January 1939, having received a promise from Dymphna that she would come to England immediately if the situation worsened, the frequent correspondence between him, Dymphna and Dymphna's parents continued as a six-way tussle for the remainder of the month. Clark asked Anna to 'trust' his judgement and that of the 'authorities' at Oxford should he be forced to 'take action' and bring Dymphna to England. Meanwhile, Augustin and Anna did all they could to persuade Dymphna not to place her future career in jeopardy. What her parents did not know at that point was that when Clark was in Bonn he had 'decided' that they 'ought to be married' in Germany. When Dymphna suggested to him that, as non-citizens, they would find marriage difficult under a Nazi regime, Clark told her they could easily find an Anglican clergyman who would perform the task. So they travelled on the Rheinuferbahn to Cologne, where the Anglican minister explained that his hands were tied. Dymphna was right; under German law, he could only marry couples of 'Aryan ancestry', and he required the necessary documents. Reluctantly, Clark was forced to abandon the idea, and their marriage was planned for England, early the following year.

In later life, Dymphna's memories of her 'promise' to Clark contain traces of disappointment and loss. In her written record of several visits she made to Germany in the course of her life, left to the National Library, she sounded flippant: 'he extracted a promise from me: If the oracles of Oxford declared the situation hopeless and dangerous he would send a telegram and I would pack my bags and come.' To Heather Rusden in 1991, she betrayed a hint of regret:

I had rather rashly given a promise to Manning when he was in Germany that if things were going to be really bad that I would come straight to England and of course it didn't take very long before the telegram arrived saying that things were going to be very bad, and so I had to fulfil my promise and just abandon everything in Germany, abandon my course, and go to England and we were married in Oxford.

To Clark's bibliographer Jan Nicholas, who became a close friend during the last decade of her life, Dymphna admitted she could have stayed longer:

I think in this I am right, that I would have had at least 6 months after war broke out to get out of Germany ... they didn't ... chop off your head straight away, lots of people trickled out for months after the war started ... but Manning was [worried] because he was that sort of type to be terribly apprehensive ... he was trying to give his life some security.

On more public occasions, she denied harbouring any misgivings about her decision to leave Germany in January 1939. As she told journalist Deborah Hope in 1995, '[My father] thought I'd be a glittering academic. But I was never in love with the idea. I have no regrets.' If Dymphna's later memories were inconsistent, what was the truth at the time?[8]

By the time Clark had crossed the Belgian border on his way back to England, wearing a huge black velour sealskin coat stuffed with gold watches and other treasures given to him by the Jews he met in Bonn for safe transport to England, Dymphna was already at her desk, writing how much she missed him. Now she was the one suffering insomnia. During the short time they had together, she had fallen more deeply in love with him: 'I am very quiet, very much in love,' she told him. From the flurry of letters in the month following Clark's departure—even the postman now recognised Clark's handwriting, shouting out 'Fräulein, Fräulein' as yet another letter arrived—it was clear that she had made the decision to abandon her course and follow Clark to England in late February. If war did not break out, then she might return to Bonn and Munich for further periods of study. Until Clark arrived in Germany, she was torn about her decision, but after his visit,

her letters spoke only of 'counting down the days' till the end of February—
'I love you all over the place Manning'. In the moments of intimacy they
must have shared in Germany, Dymphna's earlier hesitation subsided,
replaced now by almost total devotion. She had come back to the position
she declared to Clark when they first parted in Malmo: 'subconsciously I'm
not a complete entity and don't expect ever to be one again'. She was also
beginning to wilt under the pressure of living under a dictatorship, her longing letters written to the backdrop of battalions of marching soldiers singing
on the street below her window. The atmosphere in Bonn was heavy with
foreboding, as if Nazi Germany was hunting for war. One evening, Dymphna
came home to find Herr Unger cutting and numbering pieces of black paper
with which to cover every window in the house. Frau Unger refused to go
outside. People walked the streets carrying rolls of dark paper in preparation
for the blackouts ordered by the Nazis, practice for the air raids that would
eventually come. 'Some people find it terrifying,' Dymphna told Clark, 'the
city looks like the remnants of a lost civilization after dusk.' At night, she
suffered from dreams of arrest and deportation; one night, she dreamt her
brother Axel was with her in Bonn, had said something careless and was
immediately arrested. When she tried to intervene on his behalf, she was
'smilingly led off too'.[9]

In England, Clark arrived back to find that Kristallnacht and its aftermath were seen as a demonstration of the failure of Chamberlain's policy of
appeasement. With Franco close to victory in Spain, the fears of a fascist
alliance controlling Europe were widespread. He wrote quickly to Dymphna,
telling her that Chamberlain was now playing for time, merely trying to
raise British firepower before the inevitable war began. He remained uncertain as to whether or not 'defenders of the spirit' should 'advocate force
against Fascism'. He seemed unable to decide his position, and he was afraid
for the future. It was like the fear he had felt while walking in the German
Alps with Dymphna only days earlier: 'the snow covers the unknown', he
wrote, 'like the blue in the heavens'. In the last weeks of January, he let little
of his quandary filter through to her. Fearing Mussolini and Hitler would
issue an ultimatum to France at any moment, he warned her to get out
before the German frontier was closed and London was in flames. But

Dymphna was not the only one he had to convince, so he wrote to Anna as well, outlining the gravity of the situation:

> I can't be certain about the future in Germany. The penalty for disagreement is so terrible that one can understand their reluctance to oppose the rising tide of brutality, bestiality and barbarism. So they wait with their tongues tied, or close the doors and tell you nervously their fears for the future. If there is any explosion it would be hell on earth. There is no other alternative—the hopes for a peaceful change have gone, as they have also in Italy. So the German problem remains unsolved.

Writing on 21 January, he insisted that Dymphna have her bags packed in case of an emergency, suggesting that if things improved she could always return to Bonn for the second semester after they were married in England. Dymphna saw this advice as a change of their plans: 'Quite a lot of your letters are a riddle to me,' she complained. 'What makes you think I fail to see the urgency of marriage? Why the sudden change of front, advice that I should spend next semester at Bonn?' Three days later, after receiving another of his 'serious' letters—the ones Clark described as 'sad' with a 'demon' in them—she told him that she couldn't follow his train of thought, nor would she accept his view that she was 'indispensable' to him.

Whenever Dymphna's mood changed from undying love to critical confrontation, Clark reacted gloomily. Writing his diary after reading another of her letters, he overreacted, 'sad, bitter and angry' because she still appeared to hanker after her freedom; would she ever settle down, he wondered, or would she 'long for the roving restless life, always chafing against domesticity, and permanency?' His main worry seemed to be that she would 'interfere with [his] work'; yet he also knew that without her at his side, he could not work to his own satisfaction. Alone in his study, smoking, biting his nails, pushing the pen across the page, writing to every person dear to him, he often reached the point of nervous exhaustion. As he told Anna in late January, 'I have been writing letters for two days now, I feel too exhausted to continue.' Corresponding as frequently as he did, it seems astonishing that he managed to keep up his reading and social activities—the words flowed from him like water from a spring.[10]

OXFORD AND FRANCE: 1939

If anyone had expressed doubt about the couple's future in January 1939, it was not Dymphna but Clark. If she harboured even an inkling of regret about her decision to leave Germany, it remained largely unspoken and accrued slowly over decades, never surfacing, even towards the end, as more than a tinge of regret.

In the last week of January 1939 Clark sent the telegram Dymphna had always known would come. On 28 January, she arrived in Oxford. The following day, Clark wondered if it was merely his selfish concern for his 'own security' that had made him bring her to Oxford. He found 'her affectations' and 'her obvious attempts at originality' irritating, and worried about the loss of his 'independence'; yet he was also in awe of her beauty and determined his surrender to her would be 'complete'. Even before Dymphna arrived, he had made all the necessary preparations for the wedding, arranging the Balliol chaplain, the Reverend Malcolm Layng, an ex-Indian army officer, to marry them at St Michael's at the North Gate. Dymphna's abiding memory of Layng was the manner in which he referred to his wife: 'He used to call his wife "Wife"—"What are you doing now wife?" he'd say.'

There were fewer than a dozen people at the service on the morning of 31 January. AGL Shaw was Clark's best man, and George Kerferd, a fellow student from Melbourne, 'gave Dymphna away'. The small church was festooned with flowers courtesy of Kenneth Bell, Senior Fellow at Balliol, one of the college's more colourful figures, whom Graham Greene remembered as 'tolerant', beer swilling and 'aggressively heterosexual', much like the students who fell under his wing. After the service Bell shouted the wedding party to lunch at the Swan Inn in the tiny village of Minster Lovell. As Dymphna entered the pub, he called out at the top of his voice: 'Isn't she a corker!' In her eyes, Bell's unconventional behaviour helped to break the ice: many of those present, she said, 'thought we were getting married because I had a scone in the oven'.[11]

That evening they returned to Clark's rooms at 10 St Michael Street, on the old city wall, opposite the Oxford Union and less than a hundred metres

An Eye for Eternity

Oxford, circa 1940

away from the church where they had been married. The conditions were primitive and the rooms dark. Their bedroom was on the second floor, Clark's study in the basement, while a sixpenny spirit stove served as their kitchen. Clark still found time to write in his diary on his wedding night, yet when he sat down to write, he could barely muster the words to describe what had happened: 'At 10.30 a.m. I was married to Hilma Dymphna Lodewyckx … I can't write anything about it.' The following morning, 'as a gesture of devotion' to his mother, he was up early to take communion at St Michael's. When he returned home he found Dymphna 'despondent'— worried that she would now be forced to live as a 'parasite', with little chance of finding work. After giving up her travelling scholarship, she pooled her meagre savings together with his; their total weekly budget barely exceeded one pound per week. Clark thought that she was still 'hankering after her independence', 'unwilling to make the final surrender', reassuring himself that in time, she would adjust to her 'new future'.[12]

Dymphna caught a glimpse of one future on their honeymoon. Feeling sorry for the newlywed couple, Reverend Layng and his wife, Mabel, offered the use of their car for a honeymoon weekend. Dymphna couldn't drive and Clark didn't carry an English licence, so they asked AGL Shaw to drive them to Cambridge, together with another student–friend, Barbara Burton, who also attended their wedding. As Dymphna remembered, 'we went as "a party of four on our honeymoon"'. Arriving in Cambridge, Clark and Shaw were met by two Australians who immediately bore them off to their respective colleges. Dymphna and Barbara Burton were left behind to stay in a nearby boarding house. 'So this was our Cambridge honeymoon,' said Dymphna.

During the first two months of their marriage, she helped Clark in libraries and accompanied him to lectures, offering herself as a housekeeper to make some extra cash; but before the war, work was extremely hard to find. They both wrote home in an effort to reassure their parents that their marriage was not an 'impulsive' decision, Clark consistently making the point that he had acted on the 'advice' of his tutor, Humphrey Sumner, and Balliol's head, AD Lindsay. That was when he wrote affectionately to Catherine, 'Mum, our only regret was that you could not be there', asking her to accept him as her 'first married son'. Describing their cramped rooms, he reassured her that Dymphna always kept them tidy, cooking 'dainty' meals despite the 'limited' facilities. Dutifully, she penned addendums to Clark's letters, promising Catherine she would do her best to be the wife to Manning that Catherine wished for. Sometimes, in Dymphna's short notes to Catherine, there was a sting in the tail. Manning, she told her, had completely surprised his tutor by the amount of work he had managed to do on his 'honeymoon'. While Catherine needed little more than descriptions of domestic harmony to convince her that Clark's marriage was the right course of action, Clark knew from his sister Hope that Dymphna's parents had reacted less positively to news of the wedding and to Dymphna's abandonment of her studies. Like a defence attorney in a court of law, he set out immediately to 'clear

[his] name', marshalling his arguments in the language of a QC. His tone was slightly nervous and formal (he addressed Augustin as 'Sir') occasionally pleading ('may I end by expressing the hope that your confidence in me may be restored') and transparently fawning ('the morning was devoted, as it were, to singing your praises'). While his letters to Anna before their marriage reflected a natural warmth and openness, many of those written after January 1939 seem stilted, his discomfort palpable.[13]

So many of the circumstances surrounding Clark's marriage aroused in him feelings of guilt and indignation—guilt that his mother was not present, guilt that he had diverted Dymphna from her scholarship, and resentment that Dymphna's parents did not see him as worthy of their daughter, that he was somehow responsible for the end of the academic career for which her father had groomed her. At the same time, in the pages of his diary, he depicted Anna and Augustin as devils incarnate—'fiendish' parents-in-law who exposed his 'faults', jeered and laughed at his 'incompetence', and who tore him down from the pinnacle on which his mother had placed him. Transforming their doubts and reservations into a spiteful campaign to undermine his marriage, he created a psychological spur to his ambition: 'They will never shake my mother's faith,' he wrote, 'One day, I shall reply.' From the moment he was married, he was determined to 'prove' her parents wrong, to show them that he, Manning Clark, would not only provide for their daughter but, through his triumphant success, fulfil both Catherine's belief in his talent and justify Dymphna's sacrifice.

For Dymphna, their marriage would always be explained in the context of war; she had married away from home and family, with her parents' distant disapproval, in an academic compound for which she held little affection. While she gave herself completely to Clark at the time, succumbing to his insistence on immediate marriage and to what she always claimed as his 'more important work', she could never completely erase the yearning for independence she had felt on the first morning of her married life. It was not regret— she loved him completely; but as time passed, she saw how events and circumstance had conspired to deny her the chance of beginning their marriage as a more fully independent person, before children and domesticity swamped any possibility of performing more than her wifely obligation.[14]

Some of Dymphna's recollections about her marriage confided to her friend Jan Nicholas capture the sheer fun of the early months of their life together in Oxford, which is largely absent from Clark's diary and their correspondence with parents back in Australia. In his memoirs, Clark made much of his love of cricket and many who saw him play remembered his natural gifts as a batsman—both in Melbourne and in Oxford. Seventy years later, AGL Shaw could still picture Clark skylarking in his rooms at Balliol, delighting in giving him stand-up demonstrations of how to face the English bowlers. But cricket was also a test for Clark. He knew that, if he could perform well at the crease, he might gain entrée to the Oxford society from which he felt excluded. Whenever he was selected to play, he felt buoyed; when he was passed over, he wrote of his 'wounded pride'. In March 1939, he was selected for the University XI, only weeks before he and Dymphna left Oxford to live in East Woodhay, a small Hampshire village near Newbury, twenty-five miles away. Clark was there to tutor Dick Turner, the son of a wealthy shipping magnate. A 'congenial diabetic' who had never attended school, Turner was so well read that he required little assistance. For his efforts, Clark received the princely sum of 10 pounds per month. Eager to impress on the cricket pitch, he devoted his spare time to practising his stroke play in the garden of the governess's cottage. Dymphna told Jan Nicholas that, as the first game of the season approached, he was extremely concerned about his lack of batting practice. Unfortunately, there was no one around to bowl to him, so Dymphna filled the gap, bowling Clark a few overs in the backyard each afternoon.[15]

Within eight weeks of her wedding day, Dymphna was pregnant. Invited to the Balliol Ball in the summer of 1939 but too poor to pay the entrance fee, the couple was kindly paid for by AGL Shaw. By this time, 'I was already showing', said Dymphna. 'I was four months pregnant and I couldn't put anything on, so I bought a very cheap voile and made a dress. It was a drawstring waist, cotton, very simple, but it was all flared up and I had to cut the hem. Of course (laughing), I couldn't stand in the dress and cut the hem. So Manning put the dress on [and] stood on a chair and I cut round that.' If only Clark had insisted on a photograph for his archive! At the ball, after a lobster champagne supper and dancing till dawn, Kenneth Bell led the revellers through the halls of Balliol at 6 am, in a drunken crocodile trail, before taking the whole party to the Cherwell Arms for breakfast drinks. Dymphna and Clark were sitting on the terrace with the others, overlooking the river, when Bell appeared 'waving togs'. 'Who's going to swim across with me?' he shouted. 'So guess who swam across with Kenneth Bell,' said Dymphna. 'I'm not one for the crawl, I just do the side-stroke, but we swam over and back and then had bacon and eggs.' The following day, she was alarmed because she 'had a show of blood'. 'I was overcome with remorse,' she remembered, 'but all was OK.' She recalled Bell fondly because, unlike so many of the men at Oxford, he paid her attention: 'he didn't ignore me ... so many people everywhere ignored me, so when anyone did actually acknowledge my existence I found it delightful.' Bell's charm countered her feelings of isolation and her dependence on Clark—in Bell's company, she felt included.

Shortly after their marriage in January, Bell appeared unexpectedly at their doorstep the morning after they had over-indulged at a 'free sherry' party hosted by Peter Lalor (grandson of the leader of the Eureka Rebellion). Still afloat on the residue of the previous evening's intake, Bell asked Clark and Dymphna to join him for the weekend at his country house in the Cotswolds. When Dymphna pleaded that they were too hung over, he bellowed in reply 'Oh, I love an alcoholic woman.' Within minutes, they were on their way to Bell's estate, where the Balliol flag flew over the pigs, poultry and eight-children household, like the ensign of some eccentric medieval baron. When the Luftwaffe's bombs rained down on England in 1940, Bell ran a rest centre in south-east London; and after the war ended in 1945, he took up his new life as the parson in a small village near Coventry, where he remained until his death in 1953. For Dymphna, it was his 'quixotic' side that led him to look after Clark, but she also recognised that Clark and Bell had something in common. 'I think Manning thought there was a certain element of the mountebank in Kenneth Bell. Well, there was a certain element of the mountebank in Manning too.'[16]

For Clark, Bell's influence extended well beyond social lubrication. In its thematic presentation, his volume of documents, *British Colonial Policy from 1830 to 1860*, edited together with WP Morrell and published in 1925, served as a model for Clark's first major publications, the two-volume *Select Documents in Australian History*. Bell had also edited an anthology of British history, collecting the writings of the 'great historians', and, as his former student Anthony Powell remembered, he was a teacher who was always anxious to show that history was not a tidy cluster of political and economic theories but very much about 'human beings'.

In the months after his marriage, Clark's earlier indecisiveness concerning his course of study was replaced by a newfound sense of direction. Marriage had the desired effect. He felt anchored and secure, tethered to the world through his wife, at least for the time being. He quickly found tutoring work at Balliol, which eased the financial pressure on Dymphna, and by April had made the decision to work towards his Masters degree by writing a thesis.

If there was one person instrumental in guiding him to this point, it was his tutor, Humphrey Sumner, a man whom Clark felt drawn to as much by his 'beautiful face'—to Dymphna it was a 'monastic' beauty—as by the quality of his intellect and teaching. It was to Sumner, alone in the privacy of his rooms, that Clark read his essays aloud, his head bowed over his words in delicate apprehension, and it was to Sumner that he confided his anxieties and from whom he sought advice. Dymphna remembered Sumner, a World War I veteran, as a 'neurasthenic, eccentric bachelor' who revolutionised Clark's method of note-taking, making his reading far more productive. Clark's response to Sumner's lectures on late nineteenth-century Europe was underwhelming. He remarked on his 'patient' and 'cautious' approach and his desire for 'scholarly accuracy', which he thought might obscure Sumner's 'grasp of the main currents' in history. He was much more impressed by RW Seton-Watson's 'depth of culture' and AJP Taylor's 'more emotional' performances, which had the knack of heightening the 'dramatic moments' in the past.

While Clark in his later years derided Taylor as 'a show-off', as a young man he watched Taylor closely, enthralled by his panache, wit and command of historical knowledge. In 1939, Taylor was using his Oxford lectures on the Austro–Hungarian empire of the nineteenth century as a testing ground for his next publication, *The Hapsburg Monarchy 1848–1914*. Clark took issue with his interpretations, but he never left the lecture theatre anything less than impressed with Taylor's capacity to make history entertaining. To Taylor's example Clark owed more than he ever acknowledged. Few other historians in the late 1930s possessed his flair for teaching, prolific publication and unabashed self-promotion. Like the historians GM Trevelyan and Arnold Toynbee, Taylor, in his work and public commentary, reached far beyond the academy. When war broke out, his work was deemed to be of such national importance that he was declared exempt from service.[17]

Clark could not have wished for a richer and more intellectually stimulating environment than the one he encountered in Oxford. The prospect of war gave the study of history an even greater prescience, with every lecture—like the frequent public debates concerning the British government's response to Nazi aggression—riding close in relevance to the irregular pulse of day-to-day politics. Throughout 1939, his reading gradually forced him to reassess his position on Germany. Two works in particular—Hermann Rauschning's *Germany's Revolution of Destruction* and Guido de Ruggiero's *History of European Liberalism*—helped him to see the necessity of opposing Hitler with force. De Ruggiero's work reaffirmed the importance of liberal values in the face of Nazi totalitarianism, while Rauschning's polemic, widely read in England, argued strongly against appeasement and condemned Nazism as a 'transient disfigurement' of the true Germany, a betrayal of all the 'spiritual standards' of Western civilisation. In its abrogation of the rule of law, its denial of individual liberty and suppression of all dissent, Rauschning (himself a former party member) argued that Hitler's national socialism was little more than a dictatorship maintained by 'brute force'. Both writers paid a price for their views. Rauschning was forced to flee Germany, living in exile in Switzerland and England, while de Ruggiero was imprisoned by the fascist regime in Italy. Clark later claimed that few books had influenced him as much as Rauschning's courageous stand against Nazi tyranny.

By March 1939, the Wehrmacht's tanks were rolling across the Charles Bridge in Prague, making a mockery of Hitler's promises at Munich only six months earlier. Rauschning forced Clark to ask himself a fundamental question: what response should liberalism offer in the face of Nazi expansionism—and what would be the fate of liberal democracies if Germany emerged victorious? The march of fascism threw the history of liberalism into sharp relief. As he read more and more widely on nineteenth-century Europe, Clark saw how many of that century's political, social and economic struggles remained unresolved—the struggle between autocracy and democracy, between the propertied classes and the proletariat; the problem of national self-determination; and the increasing demand for social equality against the need to preserve the standards and traditions of high culture. Overlying these larger themes, he confronted a question faced by every historian in pre-war Europe: was the history of revolution and political change in Europe best understood by applying Marx's framework? (At each stage a new class replaces the old order: bourgeois revolutions wipe out feudalism and usher in capitalism, which is then overthrown by the communist nirvana—the dictatorship of the proletariat.) Or was Marx's schema merely another way of seeing the past as a prefigurement of the present? Next door to Humphrey Sumner's room at Balliol was the room of another of Clark's contemporaries and later his occasional correspondent, Christopher Hill. Hill, who was barely three years older than Clark, was then working on his first book, *The English Revolution*, in which he produced a powerful example of Marxist history, arguing that the English Revolution of 1640–60 was Marx's quintessential 'bourgeois revolution'. Clark, however, showed little sign of being persuaded by Marxism or by the willingness of communists to take up arms in their struggle. When the young Australian political scientist Fin Crisp came for afternoon tea to Clark's rooms in January 1939 and told him that socialists, if necessary, must use violence to achieve their ends, he recoiled, unable to share 'his faith'. For Clark, 'the human tie' was too strong—he could not condone the killing of others, regardless of the political imperative.[18]

As Clark began to focus his reading and to write essays for Sumner, he also faced the key questions of the day concerning historical method, so many of which remain just as pressing today—how should the historian weigh narrative against analysis, and are these two obligations mutually exclusive or complementary? Was history first and foremost a science, as the German historian Leopold von Ranke had stipulated; or was it rather, as Trevelyan insisted, a branch of national literature, the very building block of a nation's culture? Clark's natural inclination was to side with Trevelyan, but in 1939 he was far from being certain of his stance. Hovering constantly in the back of his mind was the question of his future work on Australia. At times he sounded like a bush bard, declaring his allegiance to Australia at the same time as he proclaimed his determination to produce a major work on Australian history. But equally, there were times when he merely echoed the same English prejudices that had so offended him. In February 1939, he complained that the scarcity of sources on nineteenth-century Europe in Australian libraries meant that he would have to be 'content' with Australian history. He felt repulsed by Australia's 'littleness' and 'mediocrity', and daunted by its 'vastness' and 'lack of order'. Yet he also believed that the big questions in Australia had still to be answered. His reading on the rise of nationalism in Europe made him ask whether Australia had produced 'a new race of men', just as his reading of Imperial history pushed him to understand the place of Australia in what he called the 'Europeanization of the world'. In Oxford, his perspective on Australia was both national and international. His work on Europe would serve as his intellectual grounding, and by early 1939 it was clear that his thesis would grapple in some way with the competing forces of autocracy and liberalism; at first he was drawn to writing on the English government's *entente* with Tsarist Russia in 1907, but Sumner persuaded him to turn instead to the nineteenth-century French historian and politician Alexis de Tocqueville.

In Tocqueville, Clark gradually came to see a man who was torn over some of the same issues he was grappling with in his own mind. Born a child of the aristocracy in 1805, and a liberal and democrat by intellectual inclination, Tocqueville rejected France's ancient monarchical regime yet remained deeply suspicious of the revolution of 1789–99, which had resulted in the execution of Louis XVI in 1793. In his monumental work *Democracy in America* he articulated, more profoundly than any other intellectual of his generation, both the irresistible logic of democracy and the potentially detrimental consequences of 'the tyranny of the majority'. Clark was attracted to what he saw as the tension in Tocqueville's thought—was it possible to have social equality without infringing on individual liberty? And what would be the fate of Europe's 'highbrow culture' in 'the age of the masses'? Then there was Tocqueville as prophet: would the old European powers such as England and France be forced to give way to the United States? Many of these tensions would reverberate in Clark's scholarship throughout his life, particularly the 'potential antagonism between aristocratic values and democracy'—or, as Tocqueville characterised it, the inherent friction between nobility and freedom. There was another more personal reason for Clark choosing 'Toccers'—he identified with him, projecting his own personality onto Tocqueville. As Clark explained, it was Tocqueville's 'sadness' and 'brooding self-dissatisfaction, mixed with the awareness of his own ability' that appealed to him. He thought Tocqueville was like himself—reluctant to 'form conclusions', timid and eager 'not to offend'. 'I may understand him very well,' he reflected. Clark needed to be involved deeply. To write on Tocqueville, he needed to inhabit him—to see his own soul mirrored in his subject.[19]

Throughout 1939, Dymphna and Max Crawford were, in addition to Humphrey Sumner, Clark's crucial intellectual confidants. Dymphna knew that Clark was disappointed by her limited grasp of international affairs, and she was keen to engage with him. When he read Toynbee, Lawrence or Dostoyevsky, so did she; when he read Tocqueville, she helped not only with French translation and the reading of sources but also in fleshing out Tocqueville's understanding of democracy. She sat next to him in lectures, sought out books in libraries, and listened attentively to his first ideas for a thesis. In his correspondence to Crawford, Clark thought aloud—a tendency which probably caused him trouble because Crawford and Augustin shared the same workplace and were in contact with one another. From the moment he arrived in Oxford until the day he returned home, he led Crawford through the drama of his ever-changing plans. His frankness with Crawford was driven by two motives: his eagerness to secure a teaching job at Melbourne and his determination not to burn all his bridges with the teacher to whom he felt so indebted. In early 1939, when he first realised that Crawford had considerable reservations about his new plans, he wrote anxiously to Anna Lodewyckx, asking if Crawford was 'angry' or 'disgusted' with him, imploring her to find out for him. 'I don't want to antagonise either you or Professor Crawford,' he told her, 'because my debt to both of you is too great to be ignored.' In June, when Crawford finally advised him that there was no

An Eye for Eternity

immediate chance of a job in Melbourne, Clark replied, laying down the course of his life for what turned out to be the next five years—obtain a teaching job in England, return home to Australia and secure one there, publish articles relating to Australia, and continue to work on his MA thesis on Tocqueville. His ultimate aim: a lectureship at Melbourne University. For all his anguished vacillation, Clark set his sights on his goals like a bird of prey, rarely deviating from the course he had laid down.[20]

In the summer of 1939, together with Dymphna, Clark spent three weeks working on the Tocqueville archives at the family's former home in Normandy. Travelling via Paris and Belgium, where they visited Augustin's relatives, they arrived in the nearby town of Cosqueville in the first week of August. On the journey through Belgium, in Antwerp and Booischot, Augustin's hometown, Clark was overwhelmed by the poverty he saw on the streets and 'the mediocrity of the people, their poor physique, and their ugliness'. He looked at the closely worked landscape of Europe with the eyes of a young Australian unaccustomed to material hardship and dense populations. Set against the vast, untamed landscape of Australia, the European environment appeared to be under tight control. Here was a country where 'every piece of land [was] used, the crops coming right up to the back door—vegetable gardens in between the rows of wheat. Fruit trees, & cows together. People everywhere—rubbing against each other—struggling [for] economic security'. In Normandy, the poverty was still visible; Clark found the villages 'backward, almost primitive'. Catching the autorail that conveyed them each day from Cosqueville to the Tocqueville chateau, he saw the children running to fill their buckets at the village well, the women washing in the street, and the old men driving their rickety horse-drawn carts weighed down with bundles of wood. Nearly all of the people he encountered in the villages were oppressed by what he called a 'drab level of mediocrity in dress, speech & manners'. In the simplicity of the village peasant's life, Clark saw something terrifying, a life cut adrift from the pinnacle of European culture by class difference. Turning away from the people, he looked to the landscape to feed his romantic imagination. When he contemplated the countryside around him, he found the passion he was looking for: 'the sea, the heath, & the colouring from the wild flowers'. But he also saw the figure of Christ, etched deeply in the fabric of the built environment, not only in the many churches and cathedrals but in the starkness of the lonely hilltop crucifixes that stared silently out to the Atlantic Ocean. Writing in his diary, he reflected that, in Australia, there was simply 'the earth & man', whereas in Europe, there was 'the earth, Christ & man'. Twenty years later, these thoughts would come back to haunt him, when he began to see that neither the Catholic nor Protestant visions of humanity would ever gain the same foothold in the Australian environment as they had in Europe.[21]

From a research perspective, the weeks Clark spent in France in the summer of 1939 were disappointing. Save one conversation in Paris with Tocqueville's biographer, Antoine Redier, he gained little from his time at Cosqueville, which ended abruptly on 28 August, when posters plastered throughout the village announced the mobilisation of the French Army. World War II was less than a week away. On 1 September, Germany invaded Poland. As Dymphna recalled, the Tocqueville archives were suddenly closed. They were told to pack their bags and cross the channel from Cherbourg to London. This was the end of Clark's original research on Tocqueville. Leaving Cosqueville, he saw people huddled in conversation, the 'women washing at the lavoir with frightened looks', speaking anxiously to one another of 'les Allemands' and 'la Russie'. People told stories of women bursting into tears as they heard the news that their husbands and sons had been called up. The apprehension he saw in the villages of Normandy only nourished his own fear. He felt engulfed by a 'vague foreboding of the future', the threat to his personal safety now more real than ever before. On the *Queen Mary*, on his way back across the English Channel, he was no longer certain that his existential dilemma lay in the choice between 'life according to the Catholic Church' and 'life, here & now—for humanity'. The walls of European civilisation were about to fall around him, and the outbreak of war only seemed to mock both God and man. He longed to return to the silence of his study to try and make sense of what was happening. During the weeks he spent in France, his thoughts flew away in conversation with Dymphna, lost in their togetherness. His hunger to write was so strong that he found his lack of independence irritating. He wanted more time to himself. The only way he could track the development of his thoughts and work out his response to the rapidly unfolding events in Europe was to find the solitude necessary to write. On the train from Southampton, he argued with Dymphna, and for the first time since their wedding, he felt 'deeply worried' about their compatibility. He was beginning to see that there were some thoughts he could not share with her, that within marriage it was possible to feel a special kind of loneliness. In his diary, he wrote of his 'yearning' for deep male friendship, preferably of the Australian variety—hearty and robust—unlike the repressed emotions of English men.[22]

Back in Oxford, he discovered that 'the foreign students' he had taught at Balliol had evaporated, leaving him penniless. There was no alternative but to find a position teaching in a school, where vacancies were increasing with the departure of so many men for military service. Five days after the German invasion of Poland, Dymphna wrote to her parents of Hitler's speech to the Reichstag, which she likened to the 'inhuman bellowing of a wild beast'. Clark followed events closely; he bought the morning and evening editions of the major papers and listened constantly to both British and German radio, combing the reports for some clue to the likely course of events. In September and October, he filled page after page of his diary with his reflections on the future course of the war, testing future scenarios against his knowledge of European history—would the war be short? Would Nazism collapse within Germany if an early peace could be secured? Could England defend herself if Germany invaded? Would liberal Europe survive years of Nazi tyranny? It was impossible to tell. But Clark was beginning to feel the strain. Within a week of his return from France he was already in discussion with Humphrey Sumner about the possibility of a job at Blundell's School in Tiverton, Devon, with which Balliol had long established contacts. He was convinced that for his 'own health', he would be best to find a teaching position 'in the country'. As the pressure mounted, he began to fear not only for his own life but for any chance of a worthwhile future should he survive, believing that all hope of building a better society was now lost. He knew that he could never align himself with the communists because it would mean the sacrifice of his 'individualism', nor could he stand with England or 'under the banner of the Church'—he was convinced English society was in its 'last rhythm', soon to be consumed by the fire of war or the processes of natural decay. In the midst of frequent but not unexpected bouts of depression, he felt more and more isolated by the descending chaos, a man living in a time of war without the crutch of a national, political or religious faith to guide him. With nowhere else to turn, he began to call out like a sleepwalker, writing down the biblical phrases that had stayed with him from childhood—'Father forgive them for they know not what they do', 'will some one have mercy on the sons of men, & forgive them?'. Every encounter suddenly became a sign of the future; even in 'the anxious expression on a child's face', he saw testimony that Europe was on the brink of total destruction. Underlying all of these fears was yet another guilt—he knew he could not fight. At times, he castigated himself for not being able to contribute more than thoughts and words. Writing history, he thought, was possibly his 'means of escape'.[23]

DEVONSHIRE: SPRING 1940

On 25 September, Clark heard that he had been appointed Senior History Master at Blundell's. He was overjoyed, convinced that he could build a 'personal' relationship with the boys and make a success of the teaching. Four weeks later, he received a telegram from the school's headmaster, Neville Gorton, asking him to take up his position immediately. Dymphna had already decided that if Clark found work, she would stay with the Reverend Layng and his wife in Oxford, where the couple had resided since their return from France, until she gave birth some time in early December, before joining him in Tiverton shortly afterwards. With the birth less than six weeks away, Clark left for Tiverton in early November. In the weeks that followed, they wrote to one another frequently.

As Clark attempted to come to grips with teaching teenage boys, Dymphna busied herself preparing for domesticity, purchasing cutlery and linen, and sending survival parcels to her desperate husband who, within a week of his departure, wrote to say that he was suffering from stomach upset and 'nervous strain' in her absence. Once again, without her at his side, loneliness and melancholy enveloped him. When he was with her, he longed for more time alone, when he was separated from her, he longed to be with her. He wondered what he would do if she died in childbirth—'could I endure life without her?' Alone for the first time since their marriage, he was reminded of his vulnerability. Without Dymphna, he felt the threat of war more acutely. In her letters, she told him in detail of the German radio broadcasts she heard from Leipzig, in which Beethoven's piano sonatas were followed by the bleating, 'bitter invective' of Nazi propaganda. When he managed to keep his anxiety about the war at bay, he worried instead about the sex of the child.

Dymphna and Sebastian,
Devonshire, England, 1940

I don't know how things will work out if it is a girl. I find it hard to like girls, or to understand them. In the first place, they are physically repulsive to me, and I don't want to see them naked, or enjoy them aesthetically. But I like boys, find them attractive, and so can warm towards them in other ways.[24]

He had already decided on the name of the child should it be a boy—'Johann, Sebastian, Wolfgang Clark'—a reincarnation of Bach, Mozart and himself. The approach of fatherhood brought out the nature of his ego. In another letter, he advised Dymphna of her coming duty.

I hope this letter reaches you before you have to go to hospital ... but I hope you will not be fighting alone if you realise that I belong to you, and that you must rise again triumphant to carry on our life together ... you have not lived in vain, because you have established contact with me, and now you are responsible for our earthly immortality, because you can perpetuate us in a third person ... birth, mating and death [is part of the cycle of life that has been ordained for us]. The greatest hell is caused by attempts to avoid it. Now it is your duty to complete the function of mating … In vulgar language, I think you will pop it out in record time with the minimum of discomfort. I would be the very reverse. I would anticipate hell on earth.[25]

About to give birth in Oxford, Dymphna had much to contend with. When she found the time to reply, she never responded directly to his concerns. Perhaps she was unsure of how to interpret his fears. Clark had grown up in a cloistered male world—Melbourne Grammar, Trinity College and now Balliol—a culture which repressed sexuality and circumscribed sexual behaviour. Young men and women could easily reach adulthood without seeing the opposite sex unclothed. The first woman Clark ever saw naked was probably Dymphna. Did he find young girls 'physically repulsive' because he had only ever experienced the female body in a sexual way? Was his 'repulsion' a symptom of his anxiety as a young father-to-be about finding a way to be physically intimate with a girl? Did he fear experiencing an attraction to the body of his young daughter? Or did it go deeper, did he feel uncomfortable with the female body, and was he still uncertain of his understanding of female sexuality? Whatever the answers, the strength of the word 'repulsive' can only make one wonder how Clark felt when Katerina, his first and only daughter, was born two years later. In the same letter, he declared that 'a woman should not appear naked before a man (figuratively)' because he would 'hate her for breaking his illusion'. He complained that 'modern women' were 'great image breakers', which he admitted was a problem for someone like himself, who wanted both mystery & understanding from a woman. While he expected women to refrain from revealing their vulnerabilities before him, he did not apply the same test to himself. Instead, he expected Dymphna to accept his nakedness, to be capable of absorbing his every trembling and trepidation. She needed to be both his muse and his therapist. Clark acknowledged this implicitly when he told her that her letters from Oxford made him feel 'so vivid and refreshed … spurred on to activity for the day', whereas his outpourings to her probably had 'the opposite effect', leaving her 'morose'. On the morning of 4 December, Dymphna gave birth to 'Johann Sebastian Wolfgang Clark'. When Clark's parents heard the news they demanded he change the child's name. The telegram arrived almost immediately—'Congratulations: forget name beginning W'. The baby's parents took Charles and Catherine's advice, allusions to Mozart were dropped and although Bach was still omnipresent, their final choice, 'John Sebastian', was slightly more discreet. Due to his teaching commitments, Clark could not arrange to see his son until three days after the birth. After going to see Dymphna and Sebastian at the hospital—'the hopeless crying and the peacefulness of his sleeping'—he held a small celebration in the Balliol Buttery, together with Fin Crisp and AGL Shaw, who had visited Dymphna daily, and Kenneth Bell, always at the ready for revelry. In the next few days, Clark felt nothing but 'bliss'; he saw Sebastian's birth as 'a stabilizing influence' and a strong 'incentive to respectability'. He joked to Dymphna that her nipples were his 'inspiration'. 'Heaven knows what else!' she replied. In moments of ecstatic love, he regressed to the language of childhood, adopting an infantile diminutive for Sebastian—'childie'—which mirrored his pet names for Dymphna—'Kleinie' and 'Dillsie'. Returning to Tiverton, he wrote her immediately of his first feelings as a father.

> I have had to fight my way from a very poor beginning, and childie will have a good start. He will be a continuation of me—a greater achievement. He may not be that type. We will see, but I will work for him ... [with the two of us] there is always a struggle, but we cling on ... I have known real peace, and have been as loving as a child. Besides, we have made something together now—something final ... I like childie. So far he is very like you physically—but spiritually (take that!), he is like me.[26]

Sebastian was born with the burden of being a 'continuation' of his father. Long before Clark became an established public figure, his first-born son was asked to carry the weight of his father's expectations.

Reading Clark's letters in the Radcliffe Infirmary, her breasts sore from the first rounds of feeding, Dymphna felt lonely. 'The other women,' she wrote Clark, 'had their husbands whispering into their ears from 8 until 9.' She was also having to explain to the whole ward that AGL Shaw was neither her husband nor the father of her child. Reading page after page of Clark's literary dispatches—'full of nice things'—she saw a glaring contradiction.

I tell you all my nice things when we cuddle in bed at night & you laugh at me. You wait till we are separated & then write me the most loving letters. There's the difference! You can imagine how pleased I am that you find <u>one</u> intimacy so satisfying—it is exactly the same for me. It is also very strange that you should think that I have more hold on society than you. The most casual kind of social intercourse may perhaps come more easily to me, but how seldom do I ever get on intimate terms with anyone! And yet look at the number of firm and valuable friendships <u>you</u> have made for both of us since we were married in Oxford … lots of love from Moocow.[27]

Unlike in his letters to Dymphna from Oxford before their marriage, Clark did not rebuke her. Now that she was both wife and mother, his tone shifted; he replied only with affection and torrents of starry-eyed prose. While she needed physical intimacy to express her love for him, Clark's love unravelled voluptuously on the page, feeding on the pain of separation, until he transformed their union into a sublime metaphysical vision.

While she wrote to him of the day-to-day experience of motherhood, he pondered the consequences for his future, describing Sebastian's birth as a 'deep inspiration' to his imagination and his 'baptism into life'. At times she embraced his romanticism, at other times she found it irritating, just as Clark knew full well that he needed her pragmatism yet longed for her to be more passionate in her prose. These differences, already visible after less than a year of marriage, would remain, but for both of them much of the anguish of the previous year had dissolved; having made the decision to marry and have children, they were now bound by a common goal. Dymphna wasted little time in letting Clark know that she would take control of his salary, reminding him that 'economy' was of 'paramount importance'. For his part, Clark quickly realised that fatherhood had given him a new sense of purpose. After reading 'the latest work' on Tocqueville by JP Mayer, he pronounced that he could write a much 'better work'—but not without her help; 'I have found a lot more reading for you to do,' he told her, 'mostly in German. If I can't do my degree, I will publish a work on Tocqueville or bust. You must help me, Dillsie'. In the midst of a post-natal high, and in a markedly different tone to her earlier letter, she left him in no doubt as to her answer.

Your letters still thrill me. Your enthusiasm is infectious and I am so well that I feel energy oozing out of me. I feel that the discipline imposed by having a child will help me to get more instead of less into my life. I will read anything, learn anything, teach anything for you. I am sure you can write a better book on Tocqueville than Mayer![28]

Her ambition had become his. In the first year of their marriage, there was relatively little negotiation between them about the precise nature of their respective roles as husband and wife. Instead, they took up the positions that were assigned to them. As Clark told her: 'I suppose that the child is your sphere & my work mine; that is the normal division.' Although he claimed that he wanted a 'real fusion'—'we both rear the child, & we both work intellectually'—Dymphna would rear Sebastian, while for the moment her 'intellectual' work was essentially her contribution to Clark's thesis on Tocqueville. Now that motherhood had stolen even more time from her, her chances of returning to study were slim.

After Sebastian's birth, Augustin remained sceptical of Clark's career prospects, and even doubted that Dymphna had made the right choice. All of her parents' reservations she passed on to Clark, and he vented his anger frequently. She tried to soothe him, explaining that her mother was actually 'happy' they were married; it was only Augustin who disapproved, she said, and besides, he was an 'enigma' before whom her mother refused to speak her mind. She was not overly concerned about his attitude to their marriage, only that Clark might feel 'insulted'. 'Just ignore it,' she implored him, but in the years ahead Clark would do the opposite, filing every slight in his memory and magnifying it a thousand times over. In his later years, with mischievous and scathing irony, he would refer to the home of his parents-in-law as the 'house of the long knives'.[29]

Once she had left Radcliffe Infirmary and returned with Sebastian to stay with the Layngs at Museum Road, Oxford, Dymphna became impatient to be reunited with Clark. As she stood naked in front of her bedroom mirror for the first time after giving birth, she saw how her figure had changed, and wondered when it would return to 'normal'. But the real change she noticed was in her face. 'I was astonished,' she exclaimed to Clark, 'I look like a real mother.' Lying in her hospital bed after 'lights out', she had heard the other women in the ward talking of when 'they had last slept with a man'. Like them, she wanted to remain attractive to her husband, but she also knew that her new role as a mother would change her sex life.

Clark was still in Tiverton, searching for suitable accommodation for his family, not only feeling lonely and depressed by the war unfolding around him but also experiencing a sense of 'acute discomfort' and 'failure' in the classroom. Teaching, he complained, was 'all giving and no taking'. The longer he was separated from Dymphna, the more 'restless' he became. 'It is a long time since we have slept together,' he lamented, and 'a very long time since I have known the peace of fucking.' No matter how hard he tried, he could not quell his sexual longing. He worked harder, but that only ended in exhaustion. His choice of fiction probably didn't help. Reading *Lady Chatterley's Lover*, where he found Lawrence's memorable description of post-coital contentment, he was reminded of his 'inner-loneliness'. Without the warmth of a woman to 'draw' on, he seemed incapable of intellectual effort, distracted and fatigued by the persistent pulse of his own desire.[30]

Dymphna did all she could to settle him. When she read his letter, she felt 'a sudden rush of love'. She was looking forward to sleeping with him too, but she was 'very much afraid' that John Sebastian would 'have a word to say in the matter!' As for his other problems, she explained that she didn't have time to address all of them by post. It would have to wait until she came to Tiverton in January. Clark had also asked her if she kept his letters. He wanted to know if they mattered enough to her, did she re-read them? Perhaps he was perturbed by the thought of his words disappearing into the ether—to discard his letters would be to discard his love. 'Of course I keep all your letters,' Dymphna reassured him, 'that is why I am so glad you are coming back—my handbag is so distended.' She was discovering that it was easier to deal with Clark in the flesh than it was by correspondence. In late December 1939, when she finally arrived in Tiverton, together with Sebastian, Clark was immediately quietened. 'A lot of my bitterness against the world,' he sighed, 'has been assuaged by being with Kleinie.' In the months ahead, he rarely wrote in his diary, his time consumed by teaching, parenting and his life with Dymphna.[31]

An Eye for Eternity

The English winter of 1939–40 was bitterly cold. The Thames froze over, public transport frequently ground to a halt and many people struggled to cope. The first house they found available for rent, 'The Larches', on the outskirts of Tiverton, made life even more 'miserable' for a couple with a young baby. Dymphna described it as 'a decaying, pretentious, semi-detached, middle-class house' built for a staff of servants which no longer existed. 'The basement kitchen,' she remembered, 'was just a messy wilderness with nettles and pools of water', and to run the house effectively 'you needed an income of a thousand pounds a year'. In early April, their luck changed when they found a small bungalow at Halberton in the Devon countryside. Although the pipes in the house still froze—Dymphna recalled waiting for them to thaw each morning before she could make a cup of tea—the spring soon revealed a flowering garden which ran down to the Great Western Canal. There, in the first days of April, she and Clark skated on the last floes of ice. At Blundell's, the call-up to the armed forces had depleted staff at such a rapid rate that Dymphna was asked to teach French in early May, only four weeks after they arrived at Halberton. The editorial in the school magazine claimed that, ever since the beginning of the war, tradition had 'gone by the board' and 'into a strictly male society Mrs. Clark has stepped'. As well as teaching classroom French, Dymphna gave private lessons in Dutch and Italian, cycling the eight-mile return trip from Halberton to Blundell's twice a day in order to give Sebastian his 2 pm feed. Meanwhile, Clark took his History Sixth to Exeter each Wednesday to practise their research skills in the town archives, and on Saturdays he coached a victorious cricket XI. As the summer approached, Dymphna was offered more periods due to the greater need for graduates with language skills. Unlike Clark, who found the increasing conflict in Europe nerve-wracking, she enjoyed this aspect of her life in wartime England, as she recalled later:

One of the secrets that keeps the idea of war alive is that when there is a war all sorts of human resources are rallied, emotional and in every other way, and people can come alive during war in a way that's much harder to achieve during peace. A lot of people are happier ... because they can't think about themselves.[32]

Two years earlier, when they had sailed from Melbourne, Clark told Catherine that 'if the worst should occur', he would return to Australia 'immediately'. By the end of May 1940, he sensed that the time had come. At night, the skies above Tiverton droned with the sound of German bombers on their way to Bristol. Clark's History Sixth 'shrank as the older boys enlisted one by one'. In May, the dithering Chamberlain finally resigned as British prime minister and was replaced by Winston Churchill. By the end of the month, Hitler's armies had invaded France, and Belgium capitulated. On 14 June, the Nazis marched down the Champs Elysées and the swastika flew from the Eiffel Tower. Not far away from Clark, at Monk's House in East Sussex, Virginia Woolf was also keeping a diary. She could see no way out—'this morning we discussed suicide if Hitler lands'. The war was like the onset of some 'desperate illness'. Every night Woolf felt the dread of the 'bomb terror … all the searchlights in extreme antennal vibration'. Walking in late May, she saw the 'first hospital train—something grieving and tender and heavy laden and private—bringing our wounded back carefully through the green fields'. As the strain of waiting for the attack mounted, each sight and sound became a potential omen of death. In Tiverton, Clark was almost as pessimistic as Woolf: 'I fear deeply that the spaciousness & the liberalism of the 19th century are over … we shall all be absorbed into something else … we may have to change our whole lives—or drag on as misfits in the new world.' Sketching a short story—'Moods in Wartime'—he described how 'the drone of the approaching planes' made him feel 'powerless and naked'. After the fall of France, nearly everybody in England believed that the German attack on Britain would come in a matter of days. Now there was no escape. Clark and Dymphna had to either stay in England and contribute to the war effort or flee home.[33]

In mid-June, as he had done ever since his arrival in England, Clark sought advice from Humphrey Sumner in Oxford, who suggested they return to Australia immediately: 'sail as soon as you can [Manning] … the right thing is to take Sebastian away now … how about money for the passage? Let me know if you are in bad straits.' Clark always acted 'on advice', perhaps because he knew that he would have to justify whatever decision he made to Augustin and Anna. In late June, they left Blundell's for Oxford to say their farewells. Passing through London, they saw the last-minute prep-arations for the German air raids. In September, as the Luftwaffe's assault on London began in earnest, a 'mass exodus' from the city began as thousands tried to escape the Blitz, many of them travelling to Oxford. Not everyone Clark had known left the city. Fin Crisp stayed on at Balliol, though the college was taken over by the Foreign Office in late 1940, and finished his degree. AGL Shaw, who had spent several weekends with them in Tiverton and addressed Clark's History class, decided to leave for Melbourne in August. Despite the war, Dymphna would probably have stayed in England if Clark had felt differently. As she later explained: 'I could have done some quite exciting things once the war started … even going to Bermuda as a volunteer interpreter for aliens suspected of being spies.' But Clark's mind was made up. In the first week of July, they sailed from Southampton on the *Orcades*, bound for Melbourne via South Africa and Fremantle.[34]

When the ship disembarked a 'whole troop of British marines' in Gibraltar, they suddenly realised the *Orcades* was 'a perfectly legitimate military target'. To avoid raiders and minefields, the captain struck well to the south, towards the 'freezing forties'. Dymphna remembered how, at every alert on board the ship, 'and there were many', Clark first clutched Sebastian, then his old briefcase, which contained his work on Tocqueville and his diary. In their luggage was every letter they had written one another since their departure from Australia two years earlier—the record of their love Clark couldn't bear the thought of losing—and the first layers of what would later become the edifice of his papers. Reaching for his briefcase as the alarm sounded on the *Orcades*, Clark grasped for the thing most dear to him next to his family—his writing. Before leaving Southampton, he made the last entries in his diary, and he was merciless in his verdict. He claimed his work had been a total 'failure', his output 'nil', his 'agitation very high'. He saw his marriage to Dymphna and the birth of Sebastian as a 'loss of independence' and, for a moment, he even doubted the wisdom of returning to Melbourne. Here and there, amidst the hail of self-laceration, it was still possible to dis-cern the first stirrings of the direction his writing would ultimately take. He detested his essay writing at Oxford, which he described as 'bodyless, form-less' and 'purposeless'. In 1940, and for a long time afterwards, scholarship was a domain in which the 'body' and 'form' of the individual voice was supposed to be invisible. Clark was beginning to see that he had tried to write like a scholar because he was afraid of giving himself 'away'. As he put it, he had to write in a 'less specialised and less intellectualised way'.[35]

Towards the end of his life, Clark spoke of his last months in England as 'a little idyll'. In his autobiography and in many interviews, he recalled his short time at Blundell's glowingly. The school, he said, established in the seventeenth century, had a proud academic tradition, preparing senior boys for scholarships to Oxford and Cambridge. The maverick headmaster, Neville Gorton, a renaissance man like his new recruit, inspired him, and he was fortunate to have 'a marvellous class' of twelve to fifteen boys, all of whom easily reached the standard of a 'second or third year honours class in an Australian university'. His memories concurred with the evidence in the school archives. In the *Blundellian*, Gorton described Clark as 'a brilliant and inspiring speaker' whose influence on the boys was nothing short of 'magical'. His short time at Blundell's—from the autumn of 1939 to the summer of 1940—made an indelible impression on both students and staff.

In the pages of his diary, however, Clark complained of the 'deadening effect of life at Tiverton' and described his frustration with teaching students below 'university standard'. The contrast between his later recollections and his feelings at the time is stark. Why did the older Clark wax so lyrical about a time that the younger Clark found so lacking in stimulation? The difference was not merely public memory versus private confession, but success. The old man was free to indulge in selective nostalgia about the 'influences' that had supposedly led to his exalted position. The young man, ambitious and frustrated, weighed his experience against the absence of the literary and scholarly success he so urgently craved. As he wrote at the time, he had learnt to pass on to the boys what little he had acquired, but he had not yet gone further himself. Living in the glare of fame, the old man forgot the pain of his youthful self.[36]

Shortly after buying his diary that first day in Bonn, he had inscribed on its front page the words from Romans 12:19 'Vengeance is mine and I will repay'. In 1940, and for the rest of his life, Clark understood his existence through biblical language, a language of trial and examination, of stern love and harsh punishment, of unremitting labour, guilt and torment. He knew how to punish himself. On nearly every occasion when he opened the pages of his diary, he faced an unforgiving court of his own making. As the war raged around him, he was at war with himself. His diary was not the place where he recorded his experience so much as the place where he reached for his literary persona. In one sense, to write in his diary was to constantly remind himself of the great gap between his ambition and what he had managed to produce. Beyond the diary's walls was the unwritten Clark, a person of many subtle gradations, a person who was forever giving lie to the man on the page.

Writing on the *Orcades*, as the ship headed south across the Atlantic towards Cape Town, he described the flight from England as 'the most difficult decision' of his life. But the further the ship sailed, the more convinced he became that he had made the right decision. Having just turned twenty-five, and finally on his way back to Australia, Clark felt 'complete release from the tension of life in England', from all its 'suspense and the anxiety'. He had no misgivings.[37]

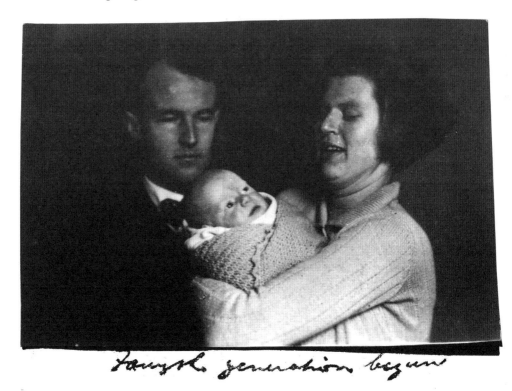

fourth generation begun

PART THREE

7: WHAT A LIFE: GEELONG GRAMMAR 1940–44

Experience of something different has made me critical … my embrace of Australia is not a lover's embrace.

—MANNING CLARK, AUGUST 1940[1]

Interviewed towards the end of his life, the American playwright Arthur Miller wondered what it would be like to live in a 'small country', a country unencumbered by the tag 'world superpower'. To be an 'American writer' was to write in the shadow of a culture preoccupied with the exercise of world power, a culture forever spinning the web of its own significance. Miller dreamt of freedom from America—he longed for a bit of insignificance. For most of the twentieth century, Australian writers, artists, and intellectuals longed for the reverse: well accustomed to insignificance, they longed to leave behind their life in a peripheral colonial society for the metropolitan heartland—London, Oxford, Cambridge—anywhere in England was preferable to living in a country thought to have so little history and culture of its own.[2]

Manning Clark struggled, during his last months in England, with 'the split in consciousness' he experienced living in Oxford. Australians had inherited English cultural and intellectual traditions, yet in every other way they were not English. He felt too uncultivated to be English and too cultivated to be completely Australian. Much as he resented the 'English assumption of superiority', he worried about returning home to a culture that was 'a bad imitation' of England … something half-formed, vague & incoherent'.

Having experienced life in England, he knew he would never see Australia in the same way again. In Melbourne, it was impossible to experience the depth of culture offered in Europe. In any case, to compare the old world and the new, he thought, would be like pitting 'Beethoven against mud pies ... the gulf could never be bridged.'[3]

On his way back to Australia, Clark toyed with the idea of making 'character sketches' of the English and Australians on board the *Orcades*. He observed the 'openness' of the Australians, men and women who endeared themselves to him with their naïve enthusiasm for life at the same time as they repelled him because their eternal cheerfulness seemed so superficial. When the ship docked in Fremantle on 5 August 1940, he looked on Australia for the first time in his life with the eyes of a foreigner. What he saw appeared both completely familiar and unusually strange; it was part of him, yet somehow alien, the newness of everything, the 'vulgar clothes' worn by people in the street, the glaring commercialism—such was the thin theatre of Australian culture—so much 'nothingness', so little depth. Like so many others who returned home after long periods in Europe, Clark was horrified by the shallowness and crude materialism of life in Australia. Dymphna was probably reminded of the last time she arrived in Fremantle, on the SS *Strathnaver*, in February 1934. Returning from Germany with Anna, when, after the usual 'farcical medical inspection', and five hours off the boat 'drinking in the smell of the Australian bush', she arrived back on board to find 'a very big crowd of Australians of the most obnoxious type' setting off on a cruise to Noumea. She found them 'impossibly dull', but was forced to 'grin and bear' them until Melbourne. 'Just imagine,' she wrote in her journal, 'there will be 1100 on board after Sydney for the cruise. What a life!'[4]

Arriving at Port Melbourne on 10 August 1940, Dymphna and Clark were shocked by the insularity of public debate on the war. Having lived with the threat of annihilation and experienced Nazi terror first-hand, they discovered that Australians were preoccupied with the government's plans to introduce petrol rationing. After the sights in Bonn, it all seemed so petty and self-centred. They were beginning to share an outsider's perspective on Australia. What Dymphna had already learnt from Anna and Augustin—to measure life in Australia against the high culture of a

European homeland—Clark learnt in England. Two years there had heightened his sensitivity to Australia's 'vulgarity' and 'littleness' at the same time as it gave him first-hand experience of English condescension. At Blundell's, he had been so offended by the other masters at the school, finding them boorish, overly 'refined' and painfully intellectual, that he longed to break free: 'I want to be really crude & vulgar for a night [and] sing dirty songs,' he confided to Dymphna. He knew that the coarseness and vulgarity of Australians that repelled him was inside him too. After two years in England, so much of his writing was increasingly propelled by the personal and intellectual tensions he experienced while he was away; everything kept coming back to the push and pull between Australia and England, to the dilemma of living in a society so far removed from the site of the history and culture that had given it birth. Even before he left England, he thought of writing an article on Anglo–Australian relations or 'the reflections of an Australian in exile'.[5]

When Clark looked at popular understandings of English history, he found that many English were deluded about their own past, clinging to the soothing fables 'spouted' by the likes of the British Foreign Secretary, Lord Halifax, who kept reassuring the English that they were a moral and respectable people. The English, Clark believed, had simply 'drunk in Macaulay & Trevelyan innocently' and seemed unwilling to look at their history critically. When he turned to Australia, he saw that the people had 'no historical sense' of their own. Aside from a 'diminishing shame' about the convict legacy, there was 'nothing else', save perhaps 'the tradition of Anzac'. If the English basked in self-congratulation, Australians lived in ignorance, as though they had no need of history. 'If I ever write Australian history,' he declared, 'I will tell them the truth and not tickle their vanity.' He wondered if the course of Australian history would prove Tocqueville correct. Would Australia, like America, become oppressed by the 'uniformity, mediocrity and indifference' that accompanied the 'tyranny of the majority'?[6]

Standing with Dymphna and Sebastian on the dock at Port Melbourne, his notes, diary and letters in hand, Clark saw the welcome-home streamers fly from the deck of the *Orcades* as he turned his eyes down the long timber jetty towards the shore. There to meet him was every member of his family: Catherine and Charles, Russell and Hope, together with Augustin, Anna, and Axel. Augustin immediately picked Sebastian up out of his basket and carried him in his arms as they walked along the jetty. Clark and Dymphna had both missed their parents. When they left for Europe they were still very much in their parents' shadow, a young, recently engaged couple heading abroad to further their studies. Now, they were adults eager to stake out their independence and their own family life. Although they were home, they had not left England behind. Just across the water was 'Princes Pier', named in honour of the Prince of Wales's visit to Melbourne in 1920. Together with Station Pier, where they came ashore, this was the most dramatic site of the colonial predicament—a life lived between adopted home and motherland, separated by more than a month's journey at sea.[7]

Clark was returning to an Australia that was about to be radically changed by the course of the war. In August 1941, the Menzies government fell, and two months later Labor's John Curtin took office. In February 1942, the fall of Singapore saw the British retreat from South-East Asia. For the remainder of the war, Curtin presided over a profound realignment of Australia's relations with Britain, until his early death in 1945 saw him replaced by Ben Chifley. Even before the war ended, the groundswell of interest in building a uniquely 'Australian culture' was undeniable. The impetus for the new national mood was not only social and political but economic. In late 1942, Curtin announced the establishment of the Department of Postwar Reconstruction, appointing 'Nugget' Coombs as director in January 1943. When Curtin ordered that 'Advance Australia Fair' be played alongside 'God Save the Queen' at the Australian War Memorial on Armistice Day 1941, he made a deep impression on Clark. Curtin's patriotism gave added impetus to the tension that was already driving Clark's first uncertain steps in researching and writing Australian history. For all its lack of refinement, he was about to discover that Australia was at least free from the burden of centuries-old traditions. Once the country began to loosen itself from the moorings of the British Empire, there would be an opportunity to create a distinctive culture, to forge new literary, artistic and intellectual traditions, and to rewrite Australian history for a postwar generation.

Manning and Dymphna with Sebastian and Katerina, Corio, Geelong, 1941

In August 1940, Clark was neither Anglophile nor Australian nationalist; he enjoyed playing both sides of the divide. In the pages of his diary—or
corresponding with someone he knew was bound to feel the same way—he
stepped into the shoes of the supercilious Englishman forced to suffer the
crass behaviour of colonials. In 1943, after the death of Beatrice Webb, he
wrote a letter of condolence to Sidney Webb (Lord Passfield), playing the
tune Webb wanted to hear. In his reply to Clark, Webb was in full agreement: 'I very much concur with your feeling that the Australian Colonies are
so backward,' he purred. At other times, especially in the company of his
male friends, Clark sided with Australians, mocking English pomposity. A
few years after he walked down the gangplank at Port Melbourne, aghast at

Australia's vulgarity, he returned to the same wharf to welcome home friends returning from a P&O cruise to the South Pacific. Hearing the prim English voices of the ship's staff as they stepped ashore, he tilted his head back slightly as if he were about to address the entire crowd, and shouted at the top of his voice—in a perfect mock-Oxford accent: 'Isn't it wonderful to hear those beautiful voices again!'[8]

GEELONG GRAMMAR

On Sunday 10 August 1980, the fortieth anniversary of his return to Australia with Dymphna and Sebastian, Clark remembered the occasion as one of high drama, calling it 'the day the Lodewyckxs snatched my child and my wife, and I saw my mother's tormented, broken face'. His recollection, injected with the accrual of four decades of spite towards Dymphna's parents and his eternal grieving for his mother's death, was less a memory of how he felt in 1940 than a reflection of how he felt in 1980 as he replayed the scene in his mind. Dragging the past with him as he aged, the old writer facing the blank page saw his life suspended as if in a timeless space. In 1940, however, things were not as clear-cut as they were to appear four decades later.[9]

As he travelled from Port Melbourne to Mont Albert, together with Sebastian and Dymphna, he was apprehensive at the thought of living with Augustin and Anna. He was convinced they had not approved of the couple's decision to marry in England, just as he was adept at turning criticism of any kind into personal rebuke. Still, they welcomed him warmly. Within days of unpacking his bags at Mont Albert, determined not to be dependent on his parents-in-law, he was already looking to leave. He asked Crawford about the possibilities of a position at Melbourne University but was told there was still little possibility for several years to come, yet another response which Clark took as a personal slight. On his first morning at Mont Albert, he wrote to the headmaster of Geelong Grammar, James Darling: 'I am anxious to obtain a [teaching] position in an Australian school ... I should point out that I have been certified as unfit for military service.' Darling, who had already had one enquiry from Clark in England, replied quickly, writing to him the following day that there was every chance of a vacancy coming up soon. Within four days of Clark's return, Darling had received Max Crawford's reference. Crawford was brutally honest. He told Darling of Clark's 'brilliance', recommending he give Clark 'a trial'—'he might, indeed, prove to be well worth permanent employment'. But Crawford's admission of those aspects he did 'not like' in Clark's record proved revealing.

It appeared to me in September 1938 that both he and his parents were expecting me to take a decision which was properly theirs, whether he should return to Australia or not. Moreover, the coincidence of his major move-ments with the tide of events is not altogether pleasing. There is, however, this to be said. It would be hard for any young man whose family admired him so much and made so much of a slight nervous disability (which takes the form of a very occasional faltering in step) to escape unscathed, and I believe that his intellectual brilliance might, under guidance, prove to be accompanied by intellectual courage. Strangely enough, I also believe that he is capable of taking the initiative, despite this wretched belief that he has to consult his superiors about every move. As a matter of fact, his various decisions have been his own, though accompanied by much consultation. His wife (she is Professor Lodewyckx's daughter) is a sensible intelligent person who may well prove to be his salvation.

Crawford knew Clark better than Clark knew himself. There were few more penetrating assessments of Clark's character. Despite his reservations, Crawford's letter clinched the job. Darling immediately invited Clark to make the 75-kilometre journey from Mont Albert to the shores of Corio Bay. Five minutes after Clark walked out of the interview, Darling offered him employment at 250 pounds per annum, together with free accommodation. There was every chance, he told him, that the position would be 'either for the duration of the war or permanent'. Judging from Darling's comments when he advised Clark of his timetable, preparation for classes would not be too onerous. 'I have been taking [History Lower VIth] myself and talking to

Geelong Grammar School, 1938

them about anything which came into my head … I suggest you give them a series of lectures on anything you particularly like … possibly the nineteenth century would be best.' In the third week of September 1940, the family moved from Mont Albert to Biddlecombe Avenue, on the school grounds, and Clark took over as Acting Senior History Master. In the space of two months, he had exchanged one High Anglican school environment for another. Instead of England, he now found himself in 'little England', and despite all his prior unhappiness at Tiverton, he knew he had little choice but to take Darling's offer; if he did not want to rely on others then 'Mr Clark' it would have to be. So much of his life to this point had been spent within the walls of grammar schools, tightly stitched worlds of god-fearing men, unforgiving military discipline and highly regulated behaviour.[10]

Geelong Grammar was founded in 1855 on the model of an English public school, to educate both local boys and the 'sons of pioneer pastoralists', and to become 'the Eton of Australia'. Unlike Melbourne Grammar, the school's semi-rural setting reflected its intention to be an entirely self-contained village community. When Clark took up his appointment the

An Eye for Eternity

school had its own railway station, fire brigade, sanatorium and resident doctor. In the years immediately following World War I, the sons of Melbourne's elite and urban middle-class began to board in greater numbers as road and rail links to the city improved. Clark's time at Balliol and Blundell's made him the ideal recruit for a school keen to establish its English credentials. The mock Englishness he scorned was his passport to financial independence. Darling, who had already been principal for a decade when Clark arrived, had come to Geelong from England in 1930, a servant of God and Empire, and he was devoted to bringing education and culture to the antipodes. Throughout the 1930s, he attempted to broaden the school's recruitment base and encouraged boys to think of careers beyond farming, particularly in the Commonwealth Public Service. As a member of the Labor government's wartime Universities Commission, Darling was a widely respected figure. In 1944, after fourteen years as principal, he remained fearful of the Australia that lay beyond the reach of his civilising mission, as he explained in the school magazine, *The Corian.*

> The Australian, when disciplined either by good government or even by circumstances, is as fine a man as any in the world, possibly better, for he seems to preserve a certain independence of judgment and freedom in initiative, even while submitting, but Australians and Australia without discipline, without the habit of obedience and thoroughness ... may become a self-seeking, contumacious and jealous rabble.[11]

Before he retired as principal in 1961, Darling established Timbertop, the bush outpost where boys honed their fitness and survival skills. It was there that the school's most famous student, Prince Charles, claimed he had the 'pommie bits bashed out' of him. Darling saw his mission as inculcating the principles of active citizenship, service and duty. A former member of the British Labour Party and a World War I serviceman, he exhibited a fervent imperialism accompanied by a healthy dose of noblesse oblige, together with a tolerance of free and open political debate, rare for a man in his position during a time of war. Historian Russel Ward, who taught at Geelong Grammar in the late 1930s, saw him as charismatic, 'the most humane, liberal and best employer I ever had'. Many former students agreed. Political scientist Jamie Mackie, who as a school prefect lunched with Darling once a week, remembered him as a man driven by a sense of duty to the great unwashed. In a manner reminiscent of the Toynbee Hall socialist schemes in London, Darling instructed Grammar boys to reach out to the local poor and unemployed, admonishing the 'children of the rich' during morning chapel, who, he claimed, had no right to be at the school unless they thought of those less well off than themselves. Another student, academic, editor and author Stephen Murray-Smith, felt indebted to Darling for his 'spiritual leadership'. Other students saw different qualities in him. Bruce Anderson remembers his unforgiving standards. 'When one boy, the son of a Western District squatter, was admonished by Darling for his poor academic record, he replied that it didn't matter because his father would "put me on the land". "What as?" asked Darling, "Manure?"' Anderson depicted Darling with a mixture of affection and awe.

> He had a sombre presence. Tall, stooped, London tailored—in three piece pin or chalk striped dark worsteds with large double breasted style lapels— and Oxford spoken, he walked with measured grace ... In his black academic gown and mortar board he looked like a somewhat arthritic crow ... When he folded his arm over your shoulder and told you that Bertrand Russell was a dangerous man or that Robert Bridges was the only poet of consequence in the twentieth century you were not disposed to argue. You were petrified.[12]

For Clark, teaching at Geelong Grammar quickly brought the memories of Melbourne Grammar flooding back. In early 1943, attending chapel, he suddenly recalled one Sunday night in 1929, when the house master came into his dorm in a rage, demanding to know why the boys didn't have their prayer books at Evensong. Twelve years later, he could still see 'his terrifying look' and the 'anger in his face', which left him 'cowed and trembling'. If he closed his eyes, it might well have been 1929; the tolling of the tower bell, the still mass of the school assembled in the Drill Hall, 7.30 am roll call at house assembly: 'Baker', 'Sir!' 'Dunstan', 'Sir!' 'Mackie', 'Sir!'— followed by porridge at 7.45, then to class. And overlaying it all, the solace of the chapel's sombre rituals, wherein Darling, like a frustrated actor, revelled in the theatre of reading the morning lesson and the chaplain held out the promise of eternal life to all who believed. At Melbourne Grammar, Clark was the receiver. Now, eleven years later, he was on the other side, and he was determined to buck the system. His pupils found him quirky and refreshingly non-conformist, unlike some staff members and parents, who were deeply suspicious of his unconventional views and doubted his loyalty in a time of war.[13]

When Clark walked into the classroom, he exuded a sense of theatre, a young man who was already 'conscious of leaving an impression', sometimes 'reserved and lacking in self-confidence', sometimes outlandish and uproariously funny, but always drawing others in, cultivating intrigue like an exotic foreigner. Wherever he was, Clark had the knack of appearing to be from out of town. In the classroom, he was 'passionately agnostic, with a quizzical look, a throaty warble to his voice and his pyjamas often showing underneath his clothes'. The first time he entered Bruce Anderson's class, he appeared hesitant but memorably attired, wearing a 'ginger, hand-woven tweed suit with four buttons down to a square return, over a white flannel shirt with homespun, electric green tie, plus black boots and white socks'. When one student enquired about the provenance of his tie, Clark explained that it was an offcut from 'one of the Führer's skirts'. 'What!' the student exclaimed, 'the Führer wears skirts?' 'Only in the evening,' Clark replied. After the more familiar train of reserved masters in their dowdy attire, Clark, at only twenty-six, less than a decade older than many of the boys he was teaching, appeared enticingly bohemian, a splash of youthful eccentricity in a school where most of the younger staff had been hollowed out by the war. Journalist and former student Keith Dunstan was struck by his 'wild sense of humour'. 'One time I arrived ten minutes late for his class. "Where have you been?" he asked. "In chapel," I replied. "The Jesus racket, [Dunstan?]" "We were praying, Sir." "[Ah], the Jesus racket. I suppose it doesn't do you any harm, all that standing up, all that getting down on your knees, very good exercise for young boys."' On another occasion he told Dunstan how much he loved Rimsky-Korsakov's *Scheherazade*. 'Very sexual music,' Clark intoned.

'I play it when making love to my wife … the only trouble is, I have to get out of bed to turn over the records.' Sensing Dunstan's liking for bawdiness, Clark played the rake; when he encountered students with different sensibilities, he donned the garb of the sensitive aesthete. Walking down Corio Avenue with his student Geoffrey Fairbairn, he declared in mellifluous tone: 'Come and meet my beautiful Nordic bride'; then, in Clark's recollection, like wistful figures trapped in the canvas of a landscape painting, they walked down the hill to his house on the school grounds, and so began a lifelong friendship. Bringing a drunken James McAuley home to Corio after meeting him at an AFL game one weekend in 1941, Clark flicked the switch to vaudeville, singing along while the poet 'played the pianoforte like a mollhouse piano'—Noël Coward, honky tonk, blues, gospel, Baroque … their repertoire seemed endless.

It was the same in Clark's classes. Students were often baffled. He seemed to have no fixed position—socialist parson one minute, bon vivant the next. Mackie, who, like other students such as Fairbairn, Anderson, Don Baker and Frank Kellaway, maintained a close friendship with Clark, recalled how he 'had the sons of the western district pastoralists eating out of his hand'. He was a tease: 'he was the only master in the school who would use the word *fuck* in public,' said Mackie, 'but he used it carefully.' Coaching cricket, he would stand on the sideline, point at the Bentleys and Jaguars parked around the ground and ask out loud: 'I wonder what the total value of these cars might be?' Former students such as Stephen Murray-Smith, philosopher David Armstrong, historian Don Baker, filmmaker Tim Burstall and journalist David Chipp remember Clark as without doubt one of the best teachers they ever encountered. He 'forced' them to think, 'encouraged' them to read, and introduced them to 'the glories of English scholarship and historical writing'. He was often 'perverse', but he accepted and encouraged argument. Rather than arrive at a definitive political stance, Clark relished the theatre of disputation. Jamie Mackie found his approach delightfully unorthodox.

There were only four of us doing Ancient History and Manning was a revelation. He simply decided to devote one class every week to discussion of public affairs. He seemed to us at the time to be taking the communist approach. I always thought he hovered on the doorstep of the Catholic Church and the membership of the Communist Party.[14]

In later years, Clark maintained that few people in Melbourne in the early 1940s were interested in his experience in Europe. Some of the Germans he had met in Bonn and Munich two years earlier had been killed on the French and Russian fronts, and in their grizzly fate he saw the 'tragic side of German history'. While he understood the German reaction to the Treaty of Versailles, and knew first-hand that the Nazis were not only wicked but also extremely clever, Australians appeared blissfully trapped in the thrall of British propaganda, unable to see Germans as anything other than stupid warmongers. Moreover, when Australians did engage in political debate, he found they usually played the man rather than the issue, allowing their arguments to descend into slander or crude moral attacks. Clark's impressions never wavered, but he probably overstated the ignorance of his countrymen.

While teaching at Geelong he was invited on many occasions, both within and outside the school's walls, to address 'the European situation', frequently impressing his audiences with his 'novel thinking'. He offered an international perspective, describing the 'atmosphere' of tension in Europe and exploring the 'psychology' of war, although he was apparently thin on 'actual facts'. He spoke many times to the Public Affairs Society, which had been set up by Darling to stimulate political debate within the school, and even started a discussion group himself—The Philosophical and Historical Society. To these discussion groups, usually held on Sunday mornings after chapel, Clark invited his university friends to speak. AGL Shaw spoke on Marx, philosophers George Paul and AC Jackson, acolytes of Wittgenstein, debated the left-wing historian Brian Fitzpatrick. At another meeting, Clark organised a Catholic priest to speak on behalf of 'the light of Rome', while he stepped up to play 'the voice from Moscow'. Most Sunday mornings, the students sat in a circle on his living-room floor, the room 'smelling of boys' feet' for days afterwards'. Unable to teach at University level, Clark attempted to recreate the atmosphere of undergraduate learning at Geelong Grammar.

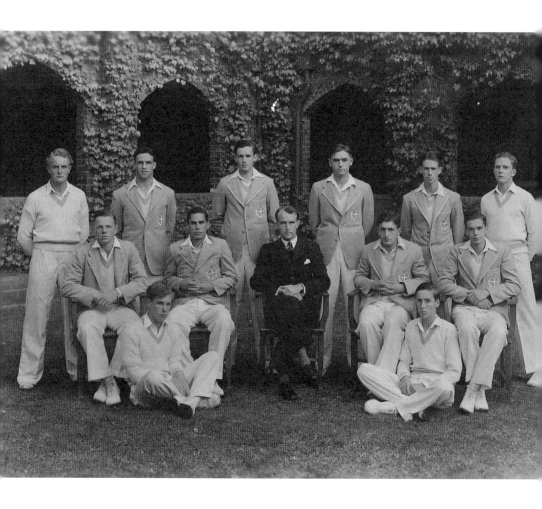

Manning Clark and the Geelong Grammar First XI, 1944

Every forum—whether it was the classroom, the discussion group or the sporting field—was an opportunity for political debate and philosophical reflection. Richard Woolcott never forgot Clark's insistence on discussing 'different forms of societies, different forms of civilizations, and different types of government'. Clark's sympathy for the German people and his appreciation of central European culture was often misread as disloyalty, just as his criticisms of the British, and his mocking of the 'Jesus racket', resulted in accusations from old boys and parents that he was a dangerous radical bent on revolution. His one and only editorial in *The Corian* castigated the 'Public School system' for its outrageous fees ('they are simply much too expensive'), wasteful indulgence ('we are waited on hand and foot') and

An Eye for Eternity

warped values ('the competition complex must be drastically reduced'), resulting in howls of protest. Darling claimed that he never received any formal complaints and, to his credit, he defended Clark on more than one occasion. Only six months after he appointed Clark, in his regular principal's report in *The Corian*, Darling produced some provocative political commentary of his own, reminding the school community that the war demanded a profound restructuring of society.

> We are not fighting this great war to preserve with all its injustices and false standards the world which we have known and—let us be honest—enjoyed for the last twenty years. We hope that there is an awakening in the community ... a clear realization of the weaknesses and injustices of the structure—some of Dr. Goebbels' criticisms find their mark, if we are at all honest ... we must try to build a society based on justice and equity, and we must develop a respect for duty at least equal to our respect for rights.[15]

This was a bold statement at a time when pacifists, socialists, and critics of capitalism were seen as the likely pawns of communist agents, and it says much for Darling's ability to foster an atmosphere of liberal tolerance at Geelong Grammar, when it might so easily have descended into jingoism. In the early 1940s, the climate was increasingly hostile to dissent. Every issue of *The Corian* listed the names of old boys and members of staff who were engaged in active service, including those who had lost their lives. Editorials quoted Kipling's rallying cry from World War I—'The Hun is at the gate'—warning readers that Australians had 'no excuse for idleness or complacency'. In this environment, even Clark's habit of listening to his shortwave radio—'he was the only person for twenty miles who could listen to Berlin, Moscow and the BBC'—aroused considerable suspicion. His youth also raised questions. Dymphna claimed that he was deeply uneasy about his failure to volunteer for military service. 'He was quite incapable of having a military career,' she said, 'he felt he would physically crumble under the strain—psychological and physical—he didn't talk much about it and he felt terrible guilt.' At the end of his life, Clark spoke compassionately of John Barber, his former colleague at Grammar, who was unable to serve on medical grounds but who was nonetheless possessed by the belief that people were persecuting him for not having enlisted. Barber's paranoia only increased as the war continued. Convinced that people were eyeing the lapel of his jacket to check if he was wearing an AIF badge, he wore a badge that could easily be mistaken for one. Clark's empathy with Barber was born of a shared sense of shame and guilt, and it remained one of the few abiding emotions he hid from public view. Even in the pages of his diary and notebooks, he chose not to confront his feelings, although on so many other fronts he was pouring out his frustration, anxious to realise his ambition to become a writer.[16]

'LIKE WATER WITH THE LIGHT SHINING ON IT'

In the three-and-a-half years during which Clark taught at Grammar, he not only kept his diary but began to keep a separate series of notebooks, into which he placed his thoughts on his reading, and sketches for articles, essays, novels and plays, usually on Australian themes. His first notebook contained a declaration of intent: 'I intend to write notebooks of fifty sheets per volume, and to write down all that passes through my mind. I hope this will provide the material for the articles, novels, plays, and books of the future.' Unlike the diary, his notebooks appear to be written more feverishly, and occasionally (particularly in 1943) they spill over into diary-like entries—immediate, intense, and piercing in their honesty. He certainly lived up to his declaration to write down all that passed through his mind. In between class, before and after class, or whenever he had a moment alone, he turned to the notebooks like a man opening a prison window, dreaming of life outside.

In the staff room, coaching cricket teams, or when teaching European and Ancient History, he was lively and witty, but when he came to write he measured himself against the ideal of the writer he aspired to be—the tortured, romantic artist—a man born with an irrepressible need to write but burdened by the pain and drama of the creative process. He believed that his 'anxiety' could be 'purged by creative work', that the very act of writing was a way to release his pent-up emotions and frustrations, a way of easing his pain, a balm for his anguished soul. In order to create, it was necessary to suffer. And suffer he did. He tried to welcome feelings of loneliness because he thought they would be good for his work. He dwelt on his feelings of guilt in the hope that the words he put on the page might wash them away. When he sketched his ideas, he was an historian one day and a novelist the next. 'I love fantasy,' he exclaimed. The only common theme of his 'roving mind' was 'the unutterable, unanswerable sadness ... the hopelessness, and the purposelessness' that he saw in 'most people's lives'. Looking out on the world, he cloaked all he saw in the darkness that enveloped his own soul.[17]

So much of Clark's writing became a litany of disappointment and self-disgust. Read together with the diary, his private writings between 1940 and early 1944 assume the thoughts of a man trapped in a kind of hell. He applied for university positions in Melbourne, Sydney and Perth, even the Australian mission to Moscow, but each application was unsuccessful. He visited Max Crawford regularly in an effort to press his claims for a position and to discuss his thesis on Tocqueville, but, as years went by and no position materialised, he began to feel caged. Every route out of Geelong seemed blocked. Repeatedly, he expressed his hatred of the school ('I must abandon this vile life'), he scolded himself for his failure to write, and he complained of the lack of intellectual stimulation in the 'sterile isolation' of Geelong ('Here, one has the worst of things—no experiences, just routine and dull people'). Now and then, he was cheered by the thought that, although his output was poor, at least he had the ideas—and 'that is a lot', he consoled himself. Yet for all his torment, he persisted with his goal—'I am more determined than ever to be a writer ... my forte will be with the pen'. Reading Freud's *Civilization and its Discontents*, he drew on its ideas and tried playing analyst to himself, observing how he 'transferred' his guilt to others, and seeing his intellectual work as the most effective 'sublimation' of his sexual energy. Even his compulsion to write, which he saw partly as a means of releasing 'the guilt that [he] always felt' but could never express, echoed Freud's conclusion: a 'sense of guilt' was the 'most important problem' in the development of civilisation; the price human beings paid for progress was the repression of their drives and a 'loss of happiness'. He also started to see religion in the same way as Freud—as a 'mass delusion', yet another escape from the reality man found too hard to bear, much like his frequent bouts of drinking. The role of the Church, he joked, was to ensure that no one was ever happy, that no one ever enjoyed 'a good fuck'. Thinking of his monogamous relationship with Dymphna, he began to doubt the virtues of fidelity. Freud stated bluntly that 'only the weaklings' clung to monogamy, 'stronger spirits' rebelled. 'Virtue is dull, duty is dull,' Clark exclaimed in furious agreement. He had a choice: either he spent his life 'too afraid to succumb to temptation' or he acted on his desires. Which was the more honest and truthful course—to hang his head in quiet desperation, living 'in agony of temptation', or to live freely?[18]

In *The Quest for Grace*, Clark rightly claimed that, while he was at Geelong, *Civilization and its Discontents* was as important to him as Dostoyevsky. As the pages of his diary and notebooks filled with all his emotional heaving and intellectual searching, Freud's critique of western civilisation as an agent of repression and control hit home. When he looked at what was happening around him—the brutality of much of the school's discipline, the refusal to accept adolescent sexuality, and the high-minded talk about Christian love—he saw nothing but cant and hypocrisy. Bruce Anderson, who remained close to Clark for most of his life, was one student at Grammar who felt the hands of 'civilisation'. Not long before he died, he expressed the thoughts on the school that he had felt unable to publish while he was alive. One thrashing from Darling stayed with him for life:

> He whipped me six times on two occasions. I was called to his study one evening. He told me to lower my trousers and bend over a chair. He selected a cane from what looked like an umbrella stand and struck me with all his strength. The cane whipped around my buttocks and thighs. When I awoke next morning I was stuck to the sheets, and under blanket of my bed, by dried blood.[19]

Anderson had boarded at Grammar from the age of ten to seventeen and, like many other boys, had lain awake in his dormitory bed at night, wondering if he would be chosen by one of the masters as the boy who would be fondled that evening. On the other hand, in the late 1930s, as master of one of the dorms, Russel Ward was instructed to patrol the dorm to ensure the boys were not ruined by the 'crippling effects' of 'self-abuse'; the masters either played God's policeman or clandestine sexual predator. 'Thus,' as Anderson explained, 'while everything was known, even to the boys who seemed to know, it was not supposed to be known. The basis of this so-called Christian education and character building was hypocrisy and humbug.' In July 1943, when he was caught fondling another boy, Anderson was severely reprimanded by Darling, his mother called in, and the usual corporal punishment meted out. Anderson confided in Clark, one of the few teachers he felt he could trust; Clark was appalled by Darling's 'methods in dealing with sexual conduct'. 'Can I stay at a school,' he wrote, 'where such methods are used to deal with sexual conduct ... Is the pistol pointed at me as well as Anderson?' For a moment, he contemplated resigning, disgusted with himself because he knew that he did not have the courage to stand up to the school authorities. Clark identified with Anderson's plight, not only because he was affronted by the school's double standards on sexuality but also because he had felt physically attracted to adolescent boys himself.[20]

Only three months before Anderson was shamed, Clark was trying to come to terms with his own feelings for 17-year-old John Ramsay, a tall blond-haired boy in his History class, who was also one of the school's best athletes. Drawn to gossip and intrigue, he became more curious about Ramsay when he discovered that he had written a 'love letter' to another student, PJ Hall. In his notebook, he tried to make sense of his feelings. 'Queer—my fascination for these affairs—half envy, half timidity of committing myself, & so deriving pleasure from knowledge of other affairs. I am attracted to Ramsay—note the type, sensitive, aloof, lonely—the desire to commune with the odd spirits. I suspect this is part of [my] search for a soul mate, for the perfect relationship.' A few weeks later, walking down the aisle of the classroom, he stood at Ramsay's desk and observed him more closely.

> Am interested in J.W. Ramsay. The curious thing is that I tolerate in him appearances, mannerisms and behaviour, which I would strongly condemn in others. Even the filthy fingernails were pleasing to me, and I lingered over

them fondly, indulgently. The scrawny, dirty hands and the careful ruling of each page—an action that normally amuses or infuriates me—I tolerated them all … perhaps this is just evidence for the proposition: love is blind. On the contrary lovers are extremely observant. Love and hatred affect our judgment, not our senses.[21]

Clark's attraction to adolescent boys—emotionally for their openness and impressionability, as well as physically—was something he did not seem to fully understand himself. Plagued by guilt, he felt he should control his inclinations: 'I must fight against the temptation to be attracted by adolescents.' One month earlier, he wrote down his feelings on same-sex attraction; he knew he could be 'sexually attracted or repelled by men', but he preferred to enjoy 'the contentment of contemplation' without 'the urgent desires of lust': 'one can enjoy the stimulus without the anxiety of the advance or the sordid elements in the physical embrace'. His attraction to Ramsay was both platonic and physical, but always from a distance, a desire to experience what he called 'the serenity of affection'.

Until this point in his life, he had longed for the company of men more than women. With the right man he could show his vulnerability, unlock his intellect and find spiritual communion through the consumption of copious amounts of alcohol. With his close male friends, he could reveal a side of himself he could not show to Dymphna. The language of men was not the language of husband and wife, and like so many men in the 1940s, Clark saw the coming together of select men as akin to the gathering of a superior caste. Only weeks before his notebook entry on Ramsay, after spending time with unnamed men on the previous weekend, he admitted that he felt less 'strain' and 'guilt' in their company; with women, he found it more difficult to disagree, he always felt as if, after speaking his mind, he had made an 'irrevocable mistake' and any chance of reconciliation was impossible. 'Perhaps men are more forgiving,' he thought, 'or more fond of harmony—women enjoy hatred—therefore reconciliation will be as extreme as the estrangement, will be closer to love than to friendship.' Clark had only ever known two kinds of love with women—sexual love and unwavering motherly adoration. Apart from Dymphna, he had no close women friends.[22]

An Eye for Eternity

The culture in which his sexuality emerged—the grammar schools of the 1930s and early 1940s—was one in which sexual contact between boys, and occasionally between boys and masters, was not uncommon. At Geelong Grammar, for example, in the decades before Clark was appointed, sexual acts sometimes formed part of initiation rituals in the dorms. More often than not, they involved coercion, manipulation, or abuse of power, both within and outside the dormitory environment, while 'homosexuality' was 'feared' but not 'talked about'. There are traces of the same fear in Clark's notebook and diary entries in 1943. While his attraction to Ramsay had homoerotic overtones, it was also an expression of his hunger for companionship and love. Aware of his desires, he tried to repress them, dreaming of escape: 'either I change my way of life or I leave this school'. 'Two things I fear very much', he confessed in his notebook: 'annihilation and being discovered'. He was not only afraid that his feelings for Ramsay and other boys might be discovered, he feared that his secrets might be laid bare—his 'self-disgust', his contempt for the values of Geelong Grammar, and the vast sea of loneliness that welled inside him. When he looked at the faces of certain boys, he saw himself at the same age at Melbourne Grammar; even his attraction to Ramsay was a bittersweet communion with his earlier self. The pain of his former loneliness rushed over him in waves; standing back, he saw that he extracted 'a curious pleasure' from recalling his own unhappiness. Feeling 'nostalgia' for his 'own tragic days at school', he was drawn back to the very past that another side of him wanted to leave behind, a young melancholic bathing in the exquisite joys of his own sorrow.

So many entries in Clark's notebook and diary possess an almost brutal determination to confront such feelings in himself. In these pages, his first audience was himself; yet even in 1943 there was no purely private realm in Clark's writing. He was a writer hunting for an audience. Whatever he wrote, the promise of an audience always beckoned because, at any time, ideas, phrases and whole paragraphs might be developed or recycled for future publications. Even as he wrote of his attraction for Ramsay, he couldn't resist the literary flourish at the end—'love blinds our judgment, not our senses'. His feelings for Ramsay, as with everyone he encountered, were potential vehicles for literary discovery. Writing was becoming his way of making sense of his existence. Experience—given shape and form through language—stopped the truth from running away. Life was his material—as much as, if not more than, the books and documents that lay piled on his desk. While there is no evidence that he acted on his desires for Ramsay or any other boy, the feelings of attraction he felt were powerful, and they caused him considerable distress, largely because he did not know how to deal with them. His attraction to Ramsay, and Darling's treatment of Anderson, only made his own feelings of hypocrisy and falseness as a 'Master' more acute. The 'gulf' between his 'values' and those of Darling was too wide. The only way out, he believed, was to leave Geelong Grammar, hopefully for Melbourne University.[23]

In early 1941, Clark told Crawford that he would find the means to complete his work on Tocqueville or 'bust in the endeavour'. Although Darling believed Clark was 'more suited to university work than school work', he, like Crawford, thought Clark's chances of immediate employment at Melbourne were little short of a 'mirage'. Meanwhile, Darling tried to stall the Victorian Education Department, which had continued to insist that Clark complete the mandatory teacher-training course if he were to continue teaching at Geelong. Clark did all he could to avoid the course, bringing GS Browne, the Registrar of Public Education, to the point of total frustration. Browne explained his position to Darling in November 1941:

> We have had plenty of good scholars & overseas men in the course—better ones than Manning Clark ... In Clark's case we feel that he regards the course as a nuisance & resents the fact that anyone of his high mental capacity should be asked to do it. The character of such work as he has done & some of his letters shows this ... we cannot give him the qualification just because he is a prodigy.

Shortly afterwards, following a series of haughty but pleading letters from Clark, Browne told Darling that he had never received such correspondence before—'from any students, anywhere in Australia'. Clark argued that, if he was forced to do the course, his 'nervous condition' might be placed under too much strain, accusing Browne of pursuing a personal vendetta

An Eye for Eternity

against him. Exasperated, Browne's tone became more agitated. 'There is no need for any undue strain on his nervous system,' he wrote to Darling, 'we have never had a student like this ... the idea that I have any sort of personal animosity towards him is absurd; but he is so apt to blame us for omissions and negligence which are due to him.' In April 1942, Browne lost his patience entirely, withdrawing Clark's permission to teach in Victorian schools. Only then did Clark enrol in the course. With no guarantee of a university position and his job at Geelong Grammar still temporary, he had little choice, limping through with a 'Teacher's Primary Training Certificate', which he was finally granted in November 1943. Forced to endure evening classes in Geelong, he had even less time to devote to his own writing. As he sat through those two-hour-long sessions, he had plenty of time to dwell on his future. For the first time, he faced the very real possibility that the life of a schoolteacher might well be his lot in life after all. He wondered if his aspiration to be an historian was nothing more than a foolish dream.[24]

In the winter of 1942, after learning that his application for a Commonwealth Literary Fund grant had failed, he went immediately to see Crawford and enrolled as an MA candidate to complete his thesis on Tocqueville. Over the next few months, and well into 1943, he struggled to rekindle his enthusiasm. He complained that he was no longer 'excited by the subject'; Tocqueville was now 'stale' and 'boring'. Yet, despite all his frustration with his lack of progress, and having to undergo a difficult appendix operation in February, he still managed to put pen to paper, completing his second draft as early as June 1943. By December he had finished the final draft, and in early 1944 the thesis was finally submitted. The writing had not been easy: in Clark's melodramatic description 'every word was agony'. Throughout 1943, as he pushed himself to finish Tocqueville, he read history greedily; especially the great New England historians of the mid-nineteenth century—George Bancroft's eight-volume history of the United States, William Prescott's *Conquest of Mexico*, Francis Parkman's comparative history of the English and French in seventeenth-century North America, John Motley's *Rise of the Dutch Republic*—and, of course, the English historians—Thomas Carlyle's three-volume *History of the French Revolution*, Thomas Babington Macaulay's five-volume *History of England*;

and finally, Edward Gibbon's *Decline and Fall of the Roman Empire*. All of these histories—grand, romantic, epic, character-driven literary narratives—were bestsellers in their day. Clark later claimed that they taught him one lesson above all else: to write history, he would have to tell a story, and to do this he would need to have 'an easily intelligible style'. In time, his multivolume *A History of Australia* would betray their influence in many other ways as well. But in 1943, he remained uncertain as to whether history was the best medium to tell the story he wanted to tell.

In one of his first articles, published in 1941, among a collection of essays for senior school students, he reflected that history was 'a dispiriting business' because it failed to satisfy the deeper needs of the human intellect. Impartiality in the writing of history was impossible, he argued—whatever the historian wrote would only be overturned by those who came after him. What was the point in writing history when the historian's ultimate fate was to be little more than a minor footnote in the dung heap of scholarly literature? In the few moments he had alone, in between teaching, family life and writing his thesis, he threw down his thoughts on historical writing in his notebooks. Prefaced by the now-familiar flagellations—'I very rarely convey on paper what is in my mind and am disgusted by what I write'—he cut to the core of his difficulty in thinking of himself as an historian.

> I think all historians are intellectually lazy. They have a predisposition to receiving ideas instead of creating ideas. In the republic of letters the historian performs a similar function to the translator in the study of literature. He is a re-creator … In a difficulty one can always fall back upon another man's opinion, use a quotation, paraphrase a passage. I believe that a historian's so-called creative work is one long quotation; that style for the historian, is the cloak with which he conceals his plagiarisms. A historian is incapable of distinguishing between borrowed ideas and his own embellishments to those ideas.[25]

Clark wanted to be much more than the chronicler, a historian who simply observed 'the succession of events'. He wanted to produce history that was prized for its originality and creativity. When he examined his intellectual predilections, he saw that his mind did not work systematically. He tried to see, but was unable to find, any logical relationship between cause and effect in history, and when he probed for scientific laws that could be applied to the study of the past, he came up empty-handed. The path to historical insight was to look inside himself: 'my ideas on the causes of historical events are beliefs or opinions to which I give my assent by an act of faith. My ideas on history will be determined by my beliefs.' He had no intention of writing history to 'influence the world for good'. Instead, he had a more selfish motive: personal glory. 'The confession must be made,' he admitted: 'my motive is to impress, vulgarly, to play to the gallery. It will satisfy my ego to produce a work which will bring publicity to me.' If he could achieve little more than being 'the low comedian in the republic of letters', this was infinitely preferable to being invisible; the latter was the fate of the detached scholar, and he wanted much more—notoriety, public acknowledgement, and sales.

In his notebook, he kept reminding himself to come back to the idea of the historian as an entertainer. The honesty of these entries shows Clark striving for something that, up to this point in his life, had eluded him: self-knowledge. As he kept his promise to himself to write down every thought that passed through his mind, his writing became a cathartic quest for artistic expression. Rather than being driven to explain historical or intellectual problems, he was motivated by the need to be the heroic artist whose work would be popularly acclaimed. Like the American historian William Prescott, who described history as being 'borne onward on a tide of destiny, like that which broods over the fiction of the Grecian poets', Clark saw himself as an instrument of the muses. When ideas came to him, 'the words raced through [his] mind, like water with the light shining on it'. Images rose before his eyes and fell away, as if his creative imagination was in touch with some power beyond himself. He felt his 'inspiration' received; creative ideas came in sudden blinding flashes, like religious epiphanies, and he had no choice but to follow them. To write as the artist–historian, to bring the past alive, and to create a truly redemptive tale, he would have to choose a subject that was 'close to [his] heart', even though the thought of exposing his emotions filled him with dread. Afraid of the 'choleric' men and women in academia—'the wolves' who would tear his work 'to pieces'—he wondered if he had the strength to withstand criticism, let alone the 'impersonal', 'lifeless' and 'pretentious' environment of a university history department.

When he submitted his MA thesis on Tocqueville in 1944, he put many of his thoughts on historical writing into practice.[26] The thesis opened with a bold declaration: 'historians and dramatists have always had one thing in common. Both have sought to entertain and instruct.' Throughout, the voice is distinctive: omnipotent, often portentous, a writer in search of majesty through grand, sweeping generalisations, an historian with a penchant for summing up human behaviour in aphoristic language reminiscent of the psalms. More often than not, Clark's searching for philosophical grandeur appeared strained, merely stating the obvious—'the opinions of a writer with prestige', he trumpeted, were 'persuasive only to those who are disposed to be persuaded'. Beginning with a discussion of Tocqueville's 'mind and heart', he explored the internal conflicts of his subject: a man of aristocratic birth who became intellectually drawn to liberty and democracy. Rather than be content with outlining Tocqueville's ideas, he took issue with them. Concentrating on Tocqueville's 'ideal', Clark rejected his proposition that religious belief was a positive and necessary restraint on liberty in a democracy, arguing that 'religious idealists' were often the most 'bitter opponents' of those who sought equality and a 'better society for all'. He was also impatient with Tocqueville's insistence that liberty in democratic societies be achieved 'without compulsion', putting forward his own strategies for converting the un-persuaded.

> What of the minority who refuse to conform or who use their liberties to destroy the good society? Let us be brutally frank: they must be compelled to conform … they must be prevented from influencing other members of society. This may mean imprisonment or exile, or, at least, a prohibition on their right to express their opinions in public, either in speech or in writing … [Only then will] the fatal helplessness of the liberal ideal … be avoided … This then is the task of the men who retain their faith in the future of mankind: to convert others to this ideal, and to devise humane methods to suppress the opposition.[27]

Clark's conclusion had little to do with Tocqueville. Instead, it showed the influence of Lenin as he wrestled with his own position on communism. When Clark walked the shores of Corio Bay with James McAuley, he listened as McAuley explained the position of his teacher at Sydney, the philosopher John Anderson: that the only answer to society's ills was to give up the need for political creeds altogether. If Clark had thought much about McAuley's warnings concerning human evil, he showed little sign of it when writing his thesis. He could not countenance violence to achieve 'the good society', yet he willingly embraced Soviet-style compulsion as a necessary strategy, seemingly oblivious to the fact that by sanctioning 'imprisonment' of his political enemies, whoever they might be, and condoning 'suppression' of the opposition, whatever that might mean, he was opening the door to the very violence and savage intimidation from which he recoiled. In the coming years, he would contradict his position many times, softening his stance to the point of doubting if any political ideology could safely deliver 'the good society'. Nor is there any evidence that he aired his views on compulsion in his public speeches in Geelong. Perhaps he was playing to his audience—thinking that his examiners might be sympathetic to such a strident view. Regardless, Crawford thought so highly of his work that he recommended it for publication. But Clark was more interested in publishing on 'exciting' subjects.

Throughout 'the four long years' of struggle needed to complete the thesis, Dymphna had made every step of the journey at Clark's side. She was there when the research began in Cosqueville; she accompanied Clark to libraries in Europe and Australia, researching, translating and copying; and at Corio, when 'there was not much time for the higher pleasures', with 'three not very obedient children under four and few conveniences', she typed the thesis on an old, secondhand typewriter, producing a top copy and three carbon copies. She also found the time to do occasional translation work for the government censor. 'Corio,' she said many years later, 'wasn't too bad, but I didn't fit in— even less than Manning I think.' In Biddlecombe Avenue, it was the home of the Classics Master Kay Chauncey Masterman and his wife Margaret that proved to be her 'oasis', a 'beautiful, tasteful, infinitely generous and hospitable' couple, who threw 'wonderful dinner parties with great food, music and invigorating conversation', placing on the table the wine that they were unable to afford themselves. Manning, said Dymphna, 'had his own cronies' at Geelong, but Margaret Masterman, together with the French teacher, Dorothy Wilson, who also lived nearby, her husband a prisoner of war in Malaya, offered much-needed companionship for Dymphna. For both of them, Geelong was isolated from Melbourne, almost 80 kilometres away. To reach their parents' homes, they travelled two hours or more by train, a journey Dymphna often made with the children. Catherine Clark, having suffered a series of strokes, was ill for most of the years they lived at Corio, and Clark felt the distance keenly, just when they both would have liked the children to spend more time with their grandparents.

In the pages of his diary and notebook, when Clark referred to Dymphna, he recorded his dissatisfaction—'too irritated by my wife's presence to write ... she is severe, ruthless, unconscionable'—no doubt dejected because she stood up to him. They argued over Sebastian's education, over money, over future plans, and over those seemingly 'little things' that can so easily become impassable mountains between lovers. Clark knew his temper was more 'volcanic' when he'd been drinking, continually berating himself in his diary. One morning in 1942, at Corio, they argued intensely, Clark 'railing' at her until she 'collapsed on the laundry floor' from nervous exhaustion. He found the experience 'painful' but 'necessary' and 'beneficial'. It had brought out into the open so many of the emotions they often repressed. With three young children, their sex life had been altered dramatically. Clark found the lack of sexual intimacy difficult to cope with, becoming 'angry' when Dymphna refused to make love ('the fury with the woman'). She no doubt found it difficult as well but she was fearful of another pregnancy and when the risk was too great she simply said no. These were not the only sources of tension between them. Augustin had not given up on his daughter. He could see that motherhood was depriving her of any chance of a career. She resented his interventions, while Clark, as he had done in Europe, encouraged her to assert her independence from her father. Ever since they had met at Melbourne University, Clark had struggled to free her from her father's influence. By the time they had settled at Geelong, he was convinced that Augustin held him in contempt. Until he could bring Dymphna completely into his orbit, he feared her love for him was always capable of being undermined. As he told her in 1943, '[I] suggest a firm line with your father. Why not answer him? Bullies are quickly thrown off their guard.' Most of the documentary evidence from the Geelong years features the couple's disagreements, leaving voiceless what must have been scores of hours and days that passed happily between them. Only rarely, in the most unexpected of places, does some light and joy shine through.

Finishing the draft of his first publication, 'Letter to Tom Collins' for the new literary journal *Meanjin*, Clark left a note at the top of the first page: 'Kleinie—please polish the rough edges, but do not destroy the fire'. At the end of the document, he dashed off another note to Dymphna: 'clothing situation is desperate … Kleinie this is the letter for *Meanjin Papers*. Would you type it out—two copies—also an envelope … send them to me, and I will send the article to [*Meanjin*] with a personal note. Miss you very much tonight. Hope you applaud my industry … I bleed for you.' Already his muse, lover and wife, Dymphna was also his intellectual sounding board, his laundry woman, his editor and his typist. Without her in his life, he went 'to pieces' and became like 'a little child'. The lines of the partnership that would ultimately give him the security he needed to write *A History of Australia* were already formed by 1943. He wanted from Dymphna the same love his mother had given him—devoted worship—but he received a clear-eyed love, grounded in genuine friendship, humour and shared interests. When adoration came, it came with a healthy dose of irony. Crawford couldn't have been more accurate. In every way, Dymphna was his salvation.[28]

TURNING TO AUSTRALIA

Even as he finished the last draft of Tocqueville in the second half of 1943, Clark's mind was already turning towards Australia as his subject. Completing a thesis had given him much more than first-class honours and a Master of Arts; it gave him the confidence to keep writing and to experiment with his ideas. In 1985, at the age of seventy, Clark picked up his 1943 notebooks and read them for the first time in many years. He was surprised by what he saw.

The genesis of *A History of Australia* was 'all there'; almost twenty years before the publication of volume one, in a few roughly hewn passages of a young schoolmaster's prose, he had mapped out some of his fundamental ideas. Speaking to historian and friend Don Baker in 1985, he sounded astonished—there was a clear path to his life after all. But in 1943 the path was not visible. He knew only that he wanted to write, and he frequently doubted what his subject would be.

Much as he wanted to escape Geelong Grammar, he wondered if he would ever succeed. From his first months teaching, he wrote opinion pieces on the politics of Australia's war engagement, then mailed them, unsolicited, to the editors of the *Age* and the *Argus*, and watched as they were returned with rejection slips. Not to be deterred, he wrote letters to the editor, which also went unpublished, like the one he wrote from Corio in 1942, warning that 'to make Hitler the personal agent of the devil absolves individuals from responsibility for their actions'. In 1941, he succeeded in publishing in the *Australian Quarterly* a small article on France and Germany in which he expressed a hope that, out of the 'common catastrophe' of war, Europe would somehow find cause 'for unity'. Wherever there was an opportunity, Clark sought to push himself forward. In January 1943, he sent a summary CV to Clem Christesen, the editor of *Meanjin*: 'Manning Clark: At present a school teacher at Geelong Grammar School, contributor to the *Australian Quarterly* and *Historical Studies*'. His was a voice that would out; even from his mid-twenties, he was a relentless self-promoter, a writer possessed of an inner conviction to succeed and an overwhelming hunger to be heard. He also had his ear firmly to the ground, sensing that Australia's cultural and political alignments were undergoing their most significant shift since Federation. Sketching his first ideas on Australian history in his notebooks in 1942–43, he struggled to give voice to what he saw as the inarticulate spirit of Australian independence. He was also feeding off the intellectual environment in Melbourne; swirling around him was a growing public discussion on the rise of a new national consciousness. [29]

The Melbourne to which Clark returned home in 1940 was vastly different from the city he had known when he was an undergraduate. Four years and the onset of war had changed much. Across the political spectrum, there was a renewed interest in promoting a uniquely Australian culture that had not been seen since the 1890s; even before war broke out in 1939, the end of the Depression saw a raft of government initiatives, all of which helped to create a professional class with an interest in promoting Australian identity. Universities would soon begin to expand, training a large number of public servants who would ultimately reside in Canberra, the new national capital, founded in 1927. Funding of the Australian Broadcasting Company (founded in 1929 and becoming a state-owned commission in 1932) was boosted significantly, allowing it to extend its reach, while the scope of the Commonwealth Literary Fund (1908) was broadened to provide funding for Australian writers. In 1938, in Melbourne, the Contemporary Art Society (CAS) was founded, among its more radical members, artist Albert Tucker and the solicitor and art patron John Reed. Less than a decade later, CAS and the Reed country retreat, Heide, on the outskirts of Melbourne, were at the forefront of a new wave of Australian modernist painting. From the late 1930s, a number of literary magazines 'swept onto the market'. These included, in 1937, *Venture*, the home of the 'Jindyworobaks', a literary movement led by Adelaide poet and critic Rex Ingamells, which drew on a new aesthetic of land and Aboriginal culture in order to cultivate a uniquely Australian literature that rejected 'foreign influences'; and, in 1940, *Meanjin*, founded in Brisbane by the poet–writer Clem Christesen, and *Angry Penguins*, founded in Adelaide by Max Harris. (The latter two would soon move to Melbourne.) Meanwhile, both the Left and the Right sought to speak to the upsurge in cultural nationalism. The success of PR Stephensen's polemic *Foundations of Australian Culture* (1936) led to the publication of *The Publicist* in the same year and, in October 1941, to the Australia First Movement. Stephensen's aggressive brand of anti-British nationalism quickly became tainted by fascism, anti-semitism and a rabid anti-communism, but not before his writings had encouraged a generation of intellectuals to think differently about the creation of a distinctively Australian culture. 'Here we are,' Stephensen trumpeted, 'on the threshold of self-consciousness.' On the left, Clark's friend, the historian Brian Fitzpatrick, published his groundbreaking study on the British Empire in Australia in two volumes, in 1939 and 1941. For Fitzpatrick, and for many fellow travellers, the underlying theme of

Australian history was class conflict—'the struggle between the organized rich and the organized poor'—which, as historian Stuart Macintyre explained, took the form of a battle between 'the radical nationalist ethos and the conservative British tradition'.[30]

In the late 1930s and early 1940s, across the political divide of this 'cultural watershed', two issues stood out above all others: the struggle to assert a more open and international Australian culture over an insular and backward-looking chauvinism; and, on the communist Left, the delicate act of appearing to be the vanguard of a cultural nationalism predicated on uniqueness at the same time as being beholden to the dictates of the international communist revolution led by Moscow. On the first, Clark was in no doubt: Australia needed to assert its own culture and independence in a way that did not shun the outside world. There could be no return to White Australia, as the flood of immigrants from southern Europe would soon demonstrate. On the second, he was undecided. Despite the widely publicised show trials of the Stalinist regime in the late 1930s, he remained romantically attached to the Soviet Union, because of both the promise he saw for 'humanity' in the 1917 revolution and his obsessive love for Russia's nineteenth-century literary culture. He refused to align himself exclusively with one political party or faction. Teaching at Geelong, he read Stephensen's *The Publicist*, read and wrote for *Meanjin*, and regularly cycled the 12 kilometres of open field that separated Corio from Geelong, to ensure that he had his copy of the *Worker's Weekly*. In July 1941, he made a point of keeping his copy of *The Publicist*, which carried Stephensen's 'Alphabet of Australian Nationalism'. Under the entry, 'history, Australian', Stephensen had written: 'extraordinarily ignorant of the details of Australian history, the overwhelming majority of Australians believe either that Australia has no history or such history as Australia has is not interesting'. Echoing Henry Lawson in the late 1880s, Stephensen condemned the preponderance of 'imported teachers' in Australia's education system, complaining that 'almost all Australian history has been written by non-Australians'. 'A nation without pride in its own traditions,' he argued, 'cannot endure'. Clark filed Stephensen's words in his papers and kept them for the rest of his life. In late 1940, at Grammar, when he opened the first issue of *Meanjin*, he read Christesen's call to arms:

An Eye for Eternity

A complete reorientation of national thought and consciousness is necessary before Australia thinks and acts as a united nation ... it is not only a matter of politics and economics ... it is also a matter of the spirit ... Australians have never loved Australia as a country should be loved by a strong and virile and devoted people. [31]

In 1942, Christesen devoted an entire issue of *Meanjin* to the question of founding a truly unique Australian culture. This, he argued, must 'grow out of the Australian situation'. It was precisely this sentiment that was beginning to drive Clark's work. The zeitgeist was now even more receptive to the mission he had first spelt out to Dymphna from Oxford in late 1938. Australian history was 'virgin soil' and he would do something about it. In a few short months, between late 1941 and early 1942, the intensity of the debate over Australian independence quickened dramatically. In December the Japanese bombed Pearl Harbor. In February 1942, Singapore fell to the Japanese Imperial forces and the British retreated to Europe. Weeks later, the Japanese Air Force bombed Darwin. In late May and early June, Japanese midget submarines bombarded Sydney Harbour, killing twenty-one sailors. Fear of a Japanese invasion soon spread throughout the country. At Geelong Grammar, in the pages of *The Corian*, principal Darling discussed evacuation procedures. By September, as the situation in New Guinea became more serious, Clark confessed that he was 'afraid' of the Japanese ending his way of life. In Melbourne, the philosopher Gwen Taylor, a friend of Clark's, who lived in a small flat on Exhibition Street, drew her curtains one morning in early 1942 to find Royal Park covered in rows of American army tents—'little wigwams'. As she gazed out at the streets below, she saw the roads 'bumper to bumper with Uncle Sam's jeeps'. She was relieved. John Curtin's appeal to the United States on 27 December 1941 had been answered. 'We really thought the Japanese were coming,' said Taylor. As panic spread, she remembered how Clark and Fitzpatrick scoured local government offices at Box Hill, Camberwell, Hawthorn and elsewhere throughout the city in a last-ditch attempt to save historical records before the councils, under instructions to destroy any documents that might be helpful to the Japanese, carried out the deed. When the realisation dawned on Australians that they could no longer rely on the British for help, a younger generation of intellectuals turned their minds to the task of finding an 'Australian answer' to the nation's predicament. Historian Geoffrey Serle explained the mood perceptively:

> I had my twentieth birthday in the month Australia's very existence was threatened as never before. Some of my contemporaries felt themselves to be a new generation of independent Australians, were fed up with the cringe to Empire, were inspired by idealism for postwar reconstruction (having grown up in the depression), and saw themselves as contributing to the description and definition of Australian society. [32]

Australia's sudden exposure to the threat of invasion also gave the Communist Party of Australia added impetus. After Hitler made the inexplicable decision to invade Russia in the second half of 1941, the Soviet Union, together with Britain, led the allied fight against fascism. Between 1940 and 1942 party numbers in Australia trebled. The British withdrawal from Singapore only heightened the radical Left's newfound appeal. It was in this environment, some time in late 1942—when he had begun to read WK Hancock's *Australia* (a paean to Australia as a British society, which betrayed Hancock's 'love–hate relationship' with the land), as well as Lawson's stories and poetry and Joseph Furphy's *Such is Life*—that Clark drafted a letter to the editor of the *New Statesman* in his notebook. Drawing on the upsurge of national feeling, he let his fury fly:

> Did you not notice the type who attacked [Curtin]? The conservatives, the tweed [jackets] who have always exploited the loyalty theme, [those who] ape the English way of life, the bishops and headmasters from England, the second-raters [with their] … contempt for the indigenous Australian? … The queer thing was that we were threatened with annihilation and our response—an appeal for help to the most likely source—provoked the English to accuse us of squealing … Perhaps if you recall what you felt after Dunkirk, you may almost understand how we felt after the Fall of Singapore and Java. I say almost because English comment seemed to

ignore the central fact that Australia may have been the first 'European' country to be occupied by the Japanese … our fevered minds recalled the pictures of Nanking, Shanghai & Chang-Sha, no wonder we felt afraid … we were defenceless, yes defenceless! … We believed that … the English would save us … generations of Australians have grown up with a blind faith in the English fleet … I think that many Australians were shocked by their personal reactions to the Singapore campaign. We were told we ought to feel anxiety for ourselves and sympathy for the British. Some may have felt anxiety for a time but I don't think anyone felt sympathy for the British (there was much pretended sympathy). On the contrary I think many were pleased. This may appear to be very shocking even to you. Do you remember Nehru's comment that he always experienced a thrill when the Asiatics defeated a European power? I think we experience a similar thrill when the English are receiving punishment.[33]

The letter was never published. In its visceral anti-Englishness, Clark's broadside certainly betrayed the influence of Stephensen, Furphy and Lawson. It demonstrated Curtin's stirring of Australian sentiment little more than a year after he became prime minister in October 1941. But it also revealed how Clark's experience at Geelong Grammar reinforced the negative impressions of the English he had gained while at Oxford. The school did its best to imitate English traditions and cultivate an English way of life. When Clark discussed the class system with Darling on one occasion, he was incensed when Darling used the analogy of breeding horses to justify the existence of a privileged class. 'Some are well bred, others not,' Darling told Clark dismissively. Recording the comment in his notebook he could barely contain himself. 'Do I object? Yes! This is a disgraceful argument—one ought to be ashamed to use it!' Darling's comment reminded Clark of everything he hated in the English and all those bourgeois Australians who did their best to ape the mores of the English aristocracy. Why are we enraged by the English?' he asked. 'I have it. They do not believe in Australia: they sneer at us, hold us in contempt, make us writhe—why? They make us aware of our swinishness—make us feel that servility is the only possible position for us.'

In the wake of Singapore's fall and the Japanese advance in the South Pacific, Clark's contempt for English arrogance, already seething when he arrived home eighteen months earlier, was given added intensity. Writing 'A Letter to Tom Collins' for *Meanjin* in 1943 (the centenary of Joseph Furphy's birth), he again drew attention to the 'sneer' of the 'upper one thousand at the vulgarity of things Australian'. While he rejected the cringe to Britain, he also distanced himself from the radical nationalism of Lawson and Furphy. Australia should not be a second-rate England—that much was clear—but there had to be a more sophisticated alternative than the sweaty, alcohol-drenched 'mateyness' of the working man. If Australia was to develop a new sense of identity there must be 'something more'; the 'myth' of 'mateship', he argued, was not enough. As if to write his own job description, he then asked his readers: 'Do we need a new prophet to preach a new myth?'[34]

In 1943, Clark had little idea of what ideas might serve as a substitute for the British myth. But, like the artist Sidney Nolan, he sensed the historical shift that was underway. Writing at the same time, Nolan also saw a move towards a more Australian-centred culture: 'If the Aussies stick close to what is before their nose,' he told artist Joy Hester, 'we might get somewhere after all.' Trying to make his own contribution to a genuinely new literature, Clark was still finding his way. When he searched for myths that might sustain Australia in the future, he looked to the mystery of Australians' relationship with the land—or, as he put it, the 'queer relationship between man and earth … how we treated her as a harlot, frenziedly raped her for her wealth', erected vulgar architecture, and created an 'artificial' civilisation which seemed to behave as if it were 'concealing some crime'. He wrote of his struggle for 'artistic' insight into the human condition in Australia, her people 'huddling on the brink of the ocean', 'insecure' and fearful of the heart of the continent. Inspired by Eleanor Dark's historical novel *The Timeless Land* (1941), in which she painted the land as 'gaunt' with magic and burdened by 'the secrets of its incredible antiquity', Clark confronted all the customary descriptors of the Australian environment—that it was hostile, harsh, empty, dry, drab and dreary—and tried instead to find the traces of Dark's magic. However, he was less preoccupied than Dark by the historical experience of Aboriginal people in the wake of colonisation. Dark depicted

Aborigines naïvely and romantically, yet she still recognised the violence done to them. The opening pages of *The Timeless Land* were nothing less than an attempt to see the arrival of the First Fleet in 1788 from the perspective of Sydney's Aboriginal people, the Eora. She also sensed a connection between the Aboriginal relationship to country and the possibility of a new environmental aesthetic in Australian literature. While Clark was enthralled by her writing on place, he looked, in his quest for new myths, not to indigenous people but to European literature. He knew that the English had committed a crime against the Aborigines—'these strange members of human society'—and he sensed the nation's repressed guilt that accompanied that crime, but he was too much a prisoner of 'European civilization' to embrace the history or culture of indigenous Australia.[35]

In early 1944, Clark's much longed-for escape from Geelong Grammar became a reality when he applied for a lectureship in Political Science at Melbourne University. His referees provided glowing recommendations. Macmahon Ball, remembering him as an undergraduate, claimed 'he possessed one of the most acute, sensitive and profound minds' that he had encountered 'during seventeen years as a University lecturer'. Darling added some reassuring words: 'he has a first class brain'. Ever since his undergraduate days, Clark had attracted impressive endorsements from his peers and superiors. Ian Milner, the New Zealand-born, Oxford-educated poet and communist who, in 1944, was acting head of the department during Macmahon Ball's absence, wrote to the vice-chancellor recommending Clark's immediate appointment without advertising the position. Between 1943 and 1944, enrolments had nearly doubled. The department needed another lecturer urgently and there was no better candidate. Clark urged himself on: 'Must win the Melbourne job.' At the same time, he applied for a position as chair of History at the University of Witwatersrand, in Johannesburg, and was so confident that he would win one of the two jobs that he offered Darling his resignation.

This is not an easy letter to write. Those who are striving for harmony on earth ought to stand together. And I believe that despite the obvious differences in personal beliefs, and the frictions caused by them, there is sufficient communion of spirit between us to say that we are after the same thing. I say this even though I know you would find your justification in Christ's "In as much as ye did it unto the least of my children", while I would look elsewhere for support. But then there is the question of where this work is to be carried out ... [Since experiencing the profound exhilaration of university teaching] I have ... decided to abandon the profession of school mastering, and to make every effort to enter that profession in which personal taste and capacity are both satisfied ... I realise that these applications may greatly inconvenience you, and, if you wish it, I am prepared to send in a formal resignation so that you can make more stable arrangements for the second and third terms. This is not perhaps the moment to thank you for your inspiration and guidance. I hope and believe that I can make a contribution to the education of this generation, and I am sure that some of the seeds were sown in Corio. [36]

Darling accepted Clark's offer, despite the fact Clark did not know whether he would be successful in his applications. Darling was willing to let him go and be free of the uncertainty. Clark, no doubt wishing he had remained silent, obediently kept his word, writing his brief letter of resignation and asking Darling if he could be held in 'sympathetic consideration' for a position at Grammar should his university applications fail. He was more than disappointed when he read Darling's reply: 'As to the future, if you don't get the job,' Darling said bluntly, 'I can promise nothing, except to do what I can in accordance with how I am then situated.' Darling had cut him adrift. The Melbourne position did not start until May, yet six weeks beforehand, in mid-March, he had managed to lose his job at Geelong without knowing if he had secured future employment of any kind. Between March and late April 1944, he could do little else but wait with bated breath. Knowing Dymphna's likely response, he kept everything to himself, sweating on the outcome.

On 1 May 1944, he was granted the entry to university teaching that he had longed for since arriving back from Oxford nearly four years earlier. Like Clark, Dymphna was more than willing to leave Geelong. She was determined not to make the mistake of living and working 'on site' again.

Clark was elated and relieved. Now he could write Darling one final 'good-bye' letter. Unfortunately, the letter has been lost, but Darling's reply tells something of its contents. Darling thanked him for 'his various acts of gracefulness in his going', regretted his departure, and assured him he would follow the instructions Clark had given him: '[I] shall strive to live up to the role for which you have cast me,' wrote Darling.[37]

At Melbourne, required to prepare lectures from scratch, and quickly, Clark's diary entries all but ceased. But he continued to use his notebooks, now filled with quotations from Australian literature. Throughout 1944, reading Eleanor Dark, Joseph Furphy, Henry Handel Richardson and Miles Franklin, he made a point of writing out the particular paragraphs and phrases that he found most striking. Again and again, he returned to the theme of place, drawn instinctively to metaphors of harshness, emptiness and melancholy exile. He wrote out each quotation, underlining key words. There was Furphy's description of Australia as a 'recordless land … cursed by no memories of fanaticism and persecution', Kylie Tennant's exhortation to her countrymen to 'serve the land as well as exploit it', Brian Penton's bleak image of life in the bush, 'the savage deeds, the crude life, the hatred between men & men and men & country, the homesickness, the loneliness & despair of inescapable exile', and Richardson's plea to Australians to learn 'to do without the promiscuity, the worship of money, the general loudness and want of refinement'. One of the longest passages that attracted Clark's attention came from *The Timeless Land*, in which Dark, through the voice of Arthur Phillip, described Australia as a 'harsh country, which kept its inner tenderness concealed; a country reticent of its beauty, demanding a wakening of the heart & a new perception in the eyes of the beholder'. Like Clark, Dark had read Lawrence's *Kangaroo*, a novel that exerted a profound influence on the generation of Australian writers who came to prominence between the wars. Clark would re-read the novel throughout his life, and on each occasion he became more and more astonished at Lawrence's 'genius'. Here was a writer who managed to find out more about Australia in ten weeks than most Australians discovered in a lifetime. Lawrence's evocation of the land and its people mesmerised him—his descriptions of a 'weird' country, 'hoary and lost' in time, one that exuded a 'far-off indifference', its

Garry Shead, DH Lawrence, Thirroul, *1992*

vast 'vacant spaces' and 'deathly stillness' lacking any 'inner meaning', its people locked in silence, suspicious of talk, their civilisation 'sprinkled on the surface of a darkness into which it never penetrated'—an 'Englishness all crumbled into formlessness and chaos'. Lawrence saw the possibilities of this 'raw, loose world' as well, the sky so open and uplifting after the 'old closing in of Europe', the air 'un-breathed'—the whole country 'unwritten'. That word told above all others—unwritten; a word blind to the presence of Aboriginal story, a word that valued the narrative of the exiled colonial, searching, like Clark, for what Lawrence (in an essay published in 1923, in the same year as *Kangaroo*) extolled as a new 'spirit of place':

> Every continent has its own great spirit of place. Every people is polarized in some particular locality, which is home, the homeland. Different places

An Eye for Eternity

on the face of the earth have different vital effluence, different vibration, different chemical exhalation, different polarity with different stars: call it what you like. But the spirit of place is a great reality.[38]

Lawrence's mystical, sensual vision, which emerged from his experience travelling in Mexico, America and Australia in the early 1920s, struck a deep chord with Clark, who imbibed its sensibility and language eagerly, Lawrence's words tolling like clarion bells in his mind. At the end of the anti-British tirade he had sent to the *New Statesman* one year earlier, he echoed Lawrence when he attempted to articulate the dissonance between man and his environment in Australia.

I know of many who have come here, felt the indifference, the apathy, struggled against it, then given in, and become apathetic. There is a spirit in the place that makes one feel the insignificance of human life, and all buildings dedicated to the spirit of man are incongruous.[39]

This was Dark's intuition too; mirroring Lawrence's description of an Australian civilisation sprinkled over the surface, she saw the Australian people beset by a 'spiritual malaise'—plagued by 'a curious sense of impermanence, of illusion, of drifting, as though they were ghosts or clouds, or brown shreds of smoke between earth and sky'. Free at last from the suffocating conformity of Geelong Grammar, Clark would soon take up Lawrence's challenge to articulate Australia's spirit of place, asking a question few others had the courage to ask in the 1940s: 'Do we belong here?'

His time at Geelong Grammar had been pivotal. The isolation he experienced there only hardened his resolve to become a writer and an historian. Within months of arriving at Melbourne University, his confidence buoyed, he spoke of Australia as 'virgin soil' for artists and intellectuals; Australians, he proclaimed, needed an 'interpretation of the past and the present', they needed 'prophets, poets and historians to enrich their appreciation and awareness of their environment'. Clark was starting to understand that he could deliver to Australia all three—the poetic artist, the enigmatic prophet, and the mystic keeper of the national past.[40]

8: JOURNEY WITHOUT MAPS

Happy, people used to say,
is the nation which has no history.
Australia has no history: things
have merely happened to us.

THE AGE, *Editorial*, 27 MAY 1950

Melbourne University, 1947: looking down from the top, the lecture theatre in the Old Arts building was steeply raked. A sharp cliff of 'brown varnished benches' descended to the lectern below, like columns of seating in a bygone playhouse. The space seemed cavernous; when latecomers walked up the aisle to take their seat, their footsteps echoed, amplifying their embarrassment. Law students, 'who had a reputation for being anarchic', would often drop marbles from a great height in an effort to create as much of a racket as possible. 'The whole appearance of the place was rather shabby.' Granite-like seats and the glare of yellow-stained light from bare bulbs overhead, in winter, the space was uncomfortably cold. Somewhere on campus, there lived a man whose job it was to stoke the coal heating. If he was late, 'everyone froze'. Once the lecture had begun, those who dared to speak were quickly called to order. Smoking was not allowed inside; 'it was all fairly puritanical'. Usually, the students had all taken their seats by the time the lecturer arrived. Hugh Stretton recalled the atmosphere from the back row: 'we didn't look up at a *duce* on a balcony, we looked down at a virtuoso on the stage'.

In the late 1940s, there was a new virtuoso on the campus, and he strode into the theatre in dramatic fashion. Bruce Grant, who remained Clark's friend for life, described the feeling of anticipation as he waited for

Clark's lecture to begin: 'He brought with him into the room a sense of excitement, that here, in this room tonight, something was going to happen. You had a sense that what he talked about mattered.' Sometimes, without saying a word, he would walk in and 'closely observe a woman' who was sitting in the front row. To many present he seemed 'a bundle of nerves'. Perhaps that was because the content of his lectures on Australian history was composed 'a bare hour ahead of his students'. Former student Sid Ingham never forgot Clark's unorthodox style in the classroom:

> He had the irritating habit of turning 360 degrees while making an important point. At 180 degrees, he communed with the blackboard. There were times when he stood gazing out the window, fiddling with the adjacent window-cord. Students, mesmerised, would follow the winding and unwinding of the cord around his right index finger.

In the lecture theatre his voice was 'hesitant', barely audible. There was also a 'slight impediment' to his speech, which only seemed to add to his appeal, transforming what might have been something 'dull and factual' into 'something spiritual'; each sign of nerves an invitation for his audience to come closer. He wanted his students 'to feel the issue'. For Clark, then just thirty, lecturing was no less of an art than writing—every hour on stage was an opportunity to make a lasting impression. His ability to create a favourable impression as a teacher was often hard to define. Historian John Legge remembered Clark's former student and historian Geoff Serle 'raving about him as a teacher' at Melbourne. 'Tremendous stuff,' he'd say. Yet whenever Legge pressed Serle to explain precisely why Clark was so good, he was stumped. 'Oh he's just tremendous,' Serle insisted. If Clark inspired his students, it rested less on the content of his lectures and more on his unconventional teaching style. He appeared to reveal himself, yet he managed to leave the impression that he was withholding something significant; what remained unsaid lured the students as much as his hour-long performances on the podium. He had the gift of making them feel differently about themselves, that they too could produce work of great importance. As Bruce Grant explained, 'he treated me as an individual with a mind of my own.

I felt as if emotionally we were travelling the same path and we communicated intellectually too.' Compared with other lecturers, such as Max Crawford or Kathleen Fitzpatrick, he was certainly more 'easy-going' and he could be tremendously funny, entertainingly funny; in fact, he was 'quite barmy in a way'. Outside the confines of the university, he could become even more unpredictable, especially when drinking.

A sip of sherry or cheap claret was enough to send him off. The first rush of alcohol liberated him, but each successive drink only made him appear more childish and often inconsolably maudlin. Don Baker, who drank with Clark at various watering holes in Melbourne in the 1940s, remembered him as 'subversive when drinking'. He was a binge drinker, said Baker, but 'when he was half drunk he was magnificent'. Peter Ryan, honours student and later Clark's publisher, gleefully recalled him, after having 'had a few', walking with him one evening on the way to the tram stop, when, coming in the opposite direction, they encountered 'a rather stuffy mathematician, who was all stitched up'. As he walked by, Clark went up to the unsuspecting professor and almost yelled in his ear: 'Goodnight Ned! Great fucking!' Clark's greatness when drinking was surely in the eyes of the beholder. In Exhibition Street on Friday and Saturday nights, Gwen Taylor would turn off the lights in her flat in order to fool him. Late in the evening, he would look up from street level in the hope of finding an all-night drinking partner. 'I'd pretend not to be at home,' Taylor would say, laughing. 'Once he got in, you could never get him out.' When he did get in, however, he could charm her. 'I suppose one always looks for a bit of light-heartedness in the grind,' she said, 'and in Manning there was always plenty of it available'.

Clark's more outlandish drunken behaviour soon earned him a reputation in the corridors of the department. At end-of-year parties, when the drink had run out, he could be found raiding Crawford's office in search of more grog, even breaking Crawford's desk drawer in the process. On one occasion, the office party continued at the home of his student Bid Williams' parents. 'Manning,' said Bid, 'was so drunk that my mother and I, together with one other woman, took turns to sit on the arm of a big armchair in which he was sitting in the kitchen so as to pin him down, so that he could not go into the other room and embarrass himself further; we simply put up with his drunken sexual advances.' In his last years at Melbourne he was viewed with wariness by both Crawford and Fitzpatrick. Fitzpatrick knew the damage alcohol could inflict all too well, having lived with a compulsive drinker—her former husband, historian Brian Fitzpatrick. Kathleen Fitzpatrick's slightly distant, 'dignified' composure irritated Clark as much as his childish antics riled her; Clark could often be heard 'railing against Kathleen', before the inevitable rapprochement was achieved. At another end-of-year students' party held at Bid Williams' family home, Crawford gave a short speech, eloquent as always. Manning then decided he would speak. He allotted each member of staff a character in a then well-known radio play, amusing the audience by profiling the personality of each one. To Kathleen Fitzpatrick he gave the character 'Aunt Kate', and while the whole thing started off quite hilariously, the atmosphere soon turned icy as Clark's comments became more and more cutting, eventually culminating in embarrassed silence. Clark couldn't bear the 'Matins and Evensong' atmosphere of the department, cultivated largely by Crawford and Fitzpatrick. Fired with alcohol, he found the freedom to send them up—the smashed court jester ad-libbing on a stage of his own making.

Several of Clark's former students remembered him occasionally being 'under the influence' in tutorials and a stream of anecdotes has survived testifying to the outlandishness of his alcohol-fuelled performances. Taxis were one of his favourite props. Creighton Burns met him in Martin Place in 1948 on a research trip to the Mitchell Library in Sydney. They jumped in a cab, with lecturer Clark in the front seat, giving directions: 'Driver,' he said, 'this man has made an indecent approach, please take us at once to the police station.' On the way, he changed his mind, instructing the driver to stop outside St Mary's Cathedral. Said Burns: 'Manning went inside for more than five minutes while I waited in the cab, wondering what was going on. Finally, he rushed out, jumped in and shouted: 'Ah, that's better!' The following day, unable to remember what happened, Clark asked Burns: 'Do I need to apologise?'

Of course, there were those for whom Clark's charm did not work. What some saw as enchanting theatricality others saw as fake, a person who was so much of an 'egoist' that he would pull any stunt to get the attention of others. Bid Williams saw him as 'a poseur'. For her, the impromptu taxi trips were not entertaining—they were simply irritating. A student in his Australian history tutorial in 1947, Bid remembered one class vividly: 'He arrived late, and instructed all the students to pile into two cars, one of which was driven by June Philipp. "I'm going to take you somewhere interesting," he announced. We simply drove around for an hour, without stopping. Manning seemed too drunk to know what he was doing.' In moments of reflection in his diary, recovering from the effects of alcohol abuse, Clark felt ashamed of his behaviour.

Interviewing many of his former friends and students from the 1940s, I was struck by the way they sought to capture the essence of Clark's personality through one or two anecdotes, as if one detail or observation—a way of speaking, a mannerism, or a memorable performance—might prove more revelatory than all that had been said or written about him in public. They believed, much like Clark himself, in the truth-telling potential of even the most fleeting variations of character. But there was something else. For some, the telling of their chosen anecdote tended to bring out the ·aspect of their own personality that had most gelled with Clark. Even for those who later became disenchanted, such as Peter Ryan, he managed to slip under the wall of resistance to become the lusty paragon of Ryan's ribald sense of humour. For others, such as Creighton Burns, who mimicked Clark's manner of speaking perfectly, even clearing his throat before speaking just as Clark did, it was Clark's delivery of wry, understated comic lines that endeared him. For Gwen Taylor, it was the forlorn figure of the midnight hours wandering the streets of Melbourne, looking for a comrade with a well-stocked bar. For John Legge, who drank with Clark in 1944–45 at Naughtons Hotel in Royal Parade, opposite the university, Clark was the larrikin and stirrer, a man for whom 'intellectual seriousness was simply not part of the equation'. For Sid Ingham, a Catholic, it was Clark the bishop, who assailed him with his musings on the 'true faith' and who left him with the impression of a 'rather deep person, his eye ever on eternity'. This was Clark's mercurial talent for etching himself into the memory of others; it was if he weighed up each person he encountered at close quarters, saw at once what they were like, and swiftly pulled out the appropriate character with which to charm them, usually a more extroverted version of themselves.

After his death, almost all the students who recalled Clark as a lecturer at Melbourne University in the 1940s did so, four decades later, with full knowledge of his later success. Remembering him from this vantage point, it was impossible to stop the older man's fame and notoriety from colouring their memories of the younger man. Having known Clark for nearly fifty years, their memories of him merged; in conversation, their 'Manning' became spirit-like, thirty-two years old one minute, seventy-two the next. And yet this is what the death of someone close to us demands; we comb the past for anecdotes that capture a true likeness, playing them over and over in our minds, as if somehow these allegories of spirit, ageless and prayer-like in their repetition, might embody the departed person in their telling. Interviewing Clark's former students, I saw a similar process at work. As with all oral history, the present continually infects the past; memories of the person are nipped and tucked in the telling with the sweet symmetry and heightened drama of narrative—and from the mouths of writers and scholars, they arrive gift-wrapped, almost ready made for biography. The lurking danger is that Clark's later fame appears pre-destined, when in 1946 he might easily have disappeared into academic life, leaving little trace of his existence. Yet for all these risks, there remains an underlying truth in the memories of Clark's former students.

For the generation who recorded their experience of his teaching at Melbourne University in the late 1940s, he was 'unforgettable'. The verdict was almost unanimous; in the words of one student, Gordon Fisher, being taught by Clark was 'one of the truly memorable experiences' of his life. Here was a university teacher 'with whom a boy could talk', someone whose theatricality and unconventional manner attracted attention and defied easy categorisation. Clark wanted to stand out, and he stood out. As Sid Ingham remarked, 'Manning would have liked a God very much modelled on himself.' Even in his thirties, long before he had written a word of Australian history, Clark was busy chiselling away at his own memorial.[1]

In 1945, as the war ended, and the number of students on campus surged, he found himself with a platform of authority, and the opportunity to give voice to a mood for national renewal that was rising steadily around him.

An Eye for Eternity

In 1944, in the last stages of the Pacific War, John Curtin's Labor govern-ment launched a renewed offensive against the Japanese. US General Douglas MacArthur had relegated the Australian Army to a largely subsid-iary role, which created mounting criticism. In Australia's cities and towns, American military and naval personnel were an all too evident reminder of the nation's vulnerability and dependence on outside help. With the Soviet Union's leading role in the defeat of Nazi Germany, many Australian ex-servicemen returned home sympathetic to communism.[2]

For Clark, there could be no more important time to be lecturing in politics and Australian history. Six years of world war and a total death toll of well over 50 million demanded a fundamental re-evaluation of the social order. The dropping of the atomic bomb on Hiroshima and Nagasaki in August 1945 filled Clark with dread, as it did many others. If a third world war followed, as World War II had followed the Great War, human societies faced annihilation on a scale previously unimaginable. Political reform was not optional; it was a necessity. Under Crawford, the discipline of History had come to occupy a central position within the Arts Faculty at Melbourne University. Like many new students, Clark believed that the study of history and politics would only help shine a light on the best course of action for the future. One year before he gave his first lecture in Political Science at Melbourne University, in May 1944, Clark professed his core political belief in his notebook: 'I believe socialism is the best organization of society ... I do not like the consequences of our [present social] organization—war, poverty, waste ... the bourgeoisie [are not humane], they have no want for the men and women who are distressed.' As the war drew to an end, like so many others filled with hope for a more equitable and just society, Clark was broadly sympathetic to the Left. Yet, unlike members of the Communist Party and the more radical activists within the broader labour movement, he failed to map out the precise lines of his future socialist state. His socialism was grounded as much in Christian compassion for the poor as it was in political theory. As he told his students in July 1948, there was 'a real affinity between the teaching of Christ and the aspirations of the left'. Remember, he said: 'I am come that ye may have life and have it more abundantly.' Only under socialism, he argued, would the most 'powerful causes of violence and cruelty disappear'.[3]

Lecturing in Politics, Clark found himself having 'to mug up to something' he 'knew very little about', working 'like a slave' to find out what he could say 'at five past twelve when the clock struck twelve'. Bob Phillips, who sat in Clark's lectures in 1945, quickly saw his political inclinations but remained impressed by his determination to provide a 'fair balance' between competing political ideologies. It was not the content of the lectures that stayed with him but Clark's personality:

> He was a very astute observer of the human heart and one of the few intellectuals who could mix it with the inner city working class boys with whom I grew up in the twenties and thirties, and with the boys from the bush with whom I served in the army, and mixed with in the post-war years.

When Clark arrived in Politics, Ian Milner was acting head of department. From 1944, until Max Crawford created a full-time position for him teaching Australian History in 1946, Clark taught British and Australian Politics—first under Milner, then under Macmahon Ball, who returned briefly in 1945 when Milner left to take up a senior appointment in External Affairs; and finally, as Acting Head, for a brief time in 1946, after Ball left to sit on the Allied Control Commission in Tokyo. In later life, Clark claimed he had never wanted to be in a political science department, yet in October 1946 he applied unsuccessfully to head the department following Ball's departure. The economic historian Herbert Burton, who sat on the selection committee, told Macmahon Ball that Clark had no reason to be disappointed; he was now 'held in very high regard in the University' and his future academic career was 'pretty well assured'.[4]

In his first year in Politics, Clark got on well with Milner, whom he described as 'a straight down the line Stalinist'; gradually, he was drawn into 'closer association with the Left'. He spoke for the Yes case in the failed 1944 'Fourteen powers referendum', arguing that the Commonwealth government

An Eye for Eternity

should have the power to legislate on issues such as the regulation of monopolies and corporations, national health, family allowances, and 'the people of the Aboriginal race'; he volunteered to work for the Brotherhood of St Laurence, and he spoke on public platforms both within and outside the university campus on any number of issues. Most days in 1945 he lunched with Jim Cairns, who was then teaching Economic History, and who would later become treasurer in the Whitlam Labor government, while Cairns's predecessor in that ministry, Frank Crean, took notes in Clark's politics lectures. In 1974, Cairns wrote in gratitude to Clark for the friendship they had shared while at Melbourne: 'I have often recalled our talks while walking around the University grounds between 1946 and 49, and I think our talks contributed considerably to my development.'[5]

Beginning his career as an academic, Clark planned to 'write a text book on Australian democracy'. Before his first year of lecturing had come to an end, he had changed his mind. Many years later, Milner recalled Clark entering his room shortly before he departed for External Affairs in late 1944 and, 'with an 'eagle flash of intellectual fervour in his eyes', confessing to Milner his 'real ambition'—'to write one day the history of Australia'. By 1946, when he was finally given the chance to flesh out the ideas that had been brewing since his time at Oxford, he used the lecture theatre and the tutorial room as a testing ground for his future publications, asking students to collect documents and proof-read transcriptions. From the outset, teaching fed his writing and writing fed his teaching; the two were inseparable.[6]

In March 1946, as he gave his first lectures on Australian history, the campus swelled with large numbers of ex-servicemen and -women. The federal government's support for returned servicemen and -women resulted in an influx of large numbers of students from working- and lower-middle-class backgrounds, many of whom would later find work as teachers and public servants. The atmosphere was one of barely managed chaos, temporary accommodation, classes full to the brim, and the ongoing rationing of essentials such as petrol and butter. Those who had served were already in their mid-twenties and, having been scarred by war, were eager not to waste time. Keen to learn, and keen to recapture the youth they feared they had lost, they were a generation that carried memories of the Depression and their parents' involvement in World War I. Many were sexually inexperienced, and for those who had gone from single-sex schools and colleges almost immediately into the defence forces, they had barely known the company of the opposite sex, let alone the pleasures of an intimate relationship. Some men addressed one another using their surnames, a common practice but one that was also seen by some students as a grammar-school affectation—the taut, hierarchical language of the parade ground. For those on the outside looking in, such as Hugh Anderson, it was a signal to students from different backgrounds to keep their distance. As for the ex-servicemen, in the words of Stephen Murray-Smith, they came back from war 'a mixture of naivety, ebullience, uncertainty, diffidence and arrogance'. Clark, himself launching forth as a university lecturer and, barely five years older than many of his students, felt the same mixture of apprehension and exhilaration. He had never taught women until he started lecturing in 1944, nor had he come into contact with such a broad variety of students. Clark was finally in touch with the Australia he had pined for—postwar Melbourne University was a world away from Balliol and Geelong.[7]

After the strict government control of information during wartime, there was also a sudden unleashing of political debate. The polarisation of international politics outside the campus walls was provoking a culture of activism within the university. By 1947, with the Cold War already under way, student politics was dominated by the Left. The Labor Club boasted 450 paid-up members, and left-wing representatives dominated the Student Council. The club's secretary, Peter Ryan, was selected as an independent candidate for Toorak in the Victorian state election. The Liberal Club, various Catholic associations and, for a while, an ex-servicemen's club vied with Labor to attract members on campus. In parliaments around the country, fear of communism fuelled a culture of paranoia as conservatives and right-wing Catholics mobilised to fight 'the red menace' and politicians branded academics who spoke in defence of civil liberties as communist revolutionaries. While the majority of students, as Murray-Smith admitted, probably belonged to the 'nothing party', public lectures and political meetings on campus sometimes attracted crowds of well over a thousand. Whether or not students were members of political associations, the culture was increasingly one of political engagement.

Political sparring spilled over into nearby Carlton pubs, with communists Ian Turner and Murray-Smith 'holding up one end of the bar' while non-believers like Bob Phillips occupied the other. It was a relatively small intellectual environment, but still 'invigorating'. 'After two world wars,' Sid Ingham recalled, 'everyone felt that a better world order was needed and possible.' While the onset of the cold war would soon temper that optimism, students on the Left maintained a 'great belief in a new order'. There were decisions to be made. How was wealth to be distributed, was Europe to be reconstructed under what some, including Clark, saw as a new form of American imperialism, or did communism represent the way ahead? Intellectuals believed it was their responsibility to be the vanguard of a progressive movement in postwar reconstruction; as Clark wrote to Eleanor Dark in September 1946, 'if one is to do anything worthwhile about Australasia we must work very hard'. The election of the Attlee Labour government in Britain in 1945, together with Ben Chifley's victory the following year, only nourished their optimism and verve.[8]

THE LONE EXPLORER

In 1946, Clark 'arrived at the lecture-theatre rostrum virtually breathless,' as one of his students would later put it, 'quoting from his latest documentary discovery made that day in the Melbourne Public Library'. He gave the impression he was sailing in uncharted waters, as if Australian history had never been attempted before. His message to students—that they were studying a largely unknown past—dovetailed perfectly with the postwar mood. Individually and collectively, they were a generation who felt they were forging a genuinely new path. With every gesture to the *terra incognita* of Australian history, Clark demonstrated his solidarity with them. 'Hatless and beardless', effortlessly spinning Dostoyevsky-like asides, he left them, as Jamie Mackie felt, with 'a sense that a new, less derivative civilisation might be emerging' in Australia. Clark and his students were on the same journey. In later life, he was fond of giving the impression that he had single-handedly discovered Australian history. 'In the late forties and early 50s,' he reminisced, 'the historical map of Australia was almost a blank: I had to set out on a journey without maps'. While it was true that no scholar would imagine a historical canvas as vast as the one Clark would soon bring to Australian history, in 1946 historians such as Ernest Scott, Keith Hancock, Brian Fitzpatrick, Stephen Roberts and Eris O'Brien had certainly done some mapping of their own.[9]

In the decade since Clark completed his undergraduate degree at Melbourne, Max Crawford had already encouraged a more Australian-centred approach in the department. Gone were the days of the mid to late 1930s, when it was common to hear academics such as the economic historian Gerry Portus confidently proclaim that Australian history was not deserving of being a university subject. Crawford, who in the mid-1940s had plans of his own to write a substantial history of Australia, had begun teaching the subject himself. In 1941, he edited *Ourselves and the Pacific*, a book that was widely used in Australian schools and influenced a generation of scholars and teachers. In 1940, he helped found *Historical Studies*, a scholarly journal devoted to 'Australasian history' as well as the work of Australian historians on 'non-Australasian subjects'. At Sydney University, from the time of Gordon Wood's forays in the 1920s through to Stephen Roberts' in the 1930s, there was already a strong tradition of research and publishing in Australian history. From Wood, Crawford brought with him the idea that sparked Clark's imagination in the late 1930s—that to write history was not to write a clinical report but to write literature. Preparing his lectures, Clark was heavily influenced by Brian Fitzpatrick's anti-imperialism and the Catholic Bishop Eris O'Brien's history of first settlement, *The Foundation of Australia* (1937). He drank regularly with Fitzpatrick and saw him as both friend and rival. One evening in 1946, lounging in front of his fireplace over a drink, Fitzpatrick asked Clark, 'So what do you want to do with your life, Manning?' 'To be as good a historian as you, Brian,' Clark replied. Eris O'Brien was another matter. A man whose status in the Catholic church intrigued Clark as much as his work, O'Brien was already lecturing part-time in Australian history in Sydney, and Clark admired him so much that he invited 'the Bishop' to give guest lectures. Clark was far from being alone in his interest in Australian history; he simply chose to dismiss most of what had gone before him. He knew that the drama in his lectures would come from his own research and his own discoveries; this was infinitely more exciting than the prospect of summarising the work of 'imperialists' like Scott or any number of dryasdusts who preceded him. That way lay torpor, somnolence and death.[10]

Thanks to Crawford, in 1946 Clark became the first historian to teach a full-length course in Australian history, and he was conscious of the new ground he was breaking. His feverish enthusiasm, maverick humour, unpredictable insight and ungainly manner brought the subject alive in a way no one had done before. This was where his originality resided. In his three years' teaching at Melbourne, he would do more than any other academic to shift the perception that Australian history was dry, peripheral and second-rate—not even worthy of bright young minds. By 1949, Crawford was complaining of the increasing numbers of students wanting to take Australian history. Decades later, Geoffrey Serle, one of Australia's most outstanding historians of the postwar era, recalled that the late 1940s and early 1950s 'were the greatest years of the Crawford school'. 'History,' he said, 'attracted a remarkably high proportion of the best minds of my generation.' Together with Serle, so many fine historians of Australia emerged from under Clark's wing—Geoffrey Blainey, Ken Inglis, Ian Turner, Jamie Mackie, Weston Bate, Michael Roe, Noel McLachlan, Don Baker, John Mulvaney, Miriam Dixson and— the list could go on. Most if not all of these students experienced Clark in the more intimate environment of tutorials, where they found him an even more effective teacher. The lifelong debt they felt they owed him began here.[11]

Teaching classes in groups as small as eight or ten allowed Clark to get closer to his students. When he questioned them, he not only wanted answers to historical problems; he wanted to know what made them tick. For their part, they saw his vulnerabilities all too easily. He was 'shy, highly-strung and insecure', a 'timid, passionate man' who, in the company of so many ex-servicemen, appeared embarrassed by his failure to enlist. Drink covered up his insecurities, and by the end of the day he'd leave a nearby pub to take his last tutorial, arriving 'relaxed and informal'. There was always tension in the air. You had to do your work, and when he asked you a question 'he'd make you jump'. 'And what would you say to that?' he'd ask, eyeballing the student intensely. He pitted students against one another: 'Ingham, you survey Australian history from the Roman Catholic viewpoint. Turner, you do the same from the communist viewpoint—and please! No jargon.' The dramatic intensity of the discussion mattered as much as the content. You had to be more than interested: 'You had to be "moved".' If students were too deferential, Clark would wipe his arms down, as if to dust off sycophantic praise. Master of the enigmatic phrase, he would sometimes disarm a student with an unexpected remark—'Today, I won't ask you to give a paper, but I'd like you to tell me about the wattle instead.' Many female students found him attractive, 'a popular subject of intrigue and gossip'. Ann Moyal remembered meeting Clark in 1947, in the cloistered silence of the Mitchell Library reading room in Sydney, and being swept away by his 'quiet voice and pensive face, his sudden gay gusts of laughter and his mocking objection to pomp'.[12]

He often accompanied his students to the State Library of Victoria, searching for documents neither he nor they had set eyes on before. Ken Inglis never forgot the excitement of that journey, walking up the library steps with his lecturer, peering into the past together. Clark's enthusiasm was infectious. Occasionally, he invited writers from outside the university, such as Eleanor Dark and Leonard Mann, the author of anti-war novels, to talk to his Honours students. His sense of the past was so much broader than that of his peers, constantly reaching beyond the walls of the university and Australia's shores. Like other members of staff, such as Kathleen Fitzpatrick, Clark addressed his colleagues on 'teaching history by the tutorial method'. His instructions bore overtones of an evangelical crusade: 'communicate your enthusiasm to students,' he told them, 'inspire them to do history themselves, let them see you at work, prepare thoroughly, be sure to have clear themes, test the evidence before drawing conclusions, practise the art of putting questions (study The Dialogues of Plato!)', in discussion 'bring in the least of the children'. And remember, 'don't talk too much yourself, don't read long extracts, use humour', and 'treat them all as of equal significance'.

An Eye for Eternity

He finished by reminding his colleagues that they needed to do more than impart information—they had taken on a moral and creative responsibility: 'Teaching a lesson is a work of art,' he asserted. 'Both you and the class should feel as one does after an act of creation.' In 1946, after Stephen Murray-Smith gave a paper in one tutorial, Clark wrote him a personal letter of thanks. 'It was very good of you to lead the discussion on communism for the … tutorial. It was apparently a great success. You should make an excellent teacher—with the skill in presentation and having something to say. Many thanks, yours ever Manning Clark.'[13]

Clark knew the impact personal communication from a lecturer could have on students. It alerted them to their own potential at the same time as it imprinted his memory on their hearts and minds for the rest of their lives. He aspired to be their teacher as well as their spiritual guide. Clark's influence in this respect was profound, not only in turning the minds of his students to Australian history but in reinforcing the concept of history that ran right through Crawford's school. Above all, this translated into an acute moral sensitivity—a conviction that history held the answers to 'the deeper problems of human existence'. As Crawford saw it, the historian's task was to 'teach students to see beyond the surface of things, to be honest with themselves and their evidence, and at least to understand ideals beyond the gratification of private self-interest'. To study history was akin to studying the Bible and the past was a bottomless well of parable; with enough persistence and patience, and a close reading of the sources, students might even learn how to live. John Mulvaney remembered that Melbourne was then one of the few history departments in Australia where it was possible to study the Theory and Method of History. And 'no matter what subject you were doing', said Mulvaney—'Rome in the time of Augustus, Athens in the fifth century BC, or the French Revolution—the bourgeoisie always seemed to be rising'. It was also at this time that a fourth year of study was added for honours. Crawford wanted his staff and students to be self-reflective and to put their knowledge to some higher purpose. So much of Clark's approach was explained by the progressive, devotional and almost 'religious' intellectual culture. Yet few lecturers were capable of breathing quite the same magic and life into their subject as he managed to do. Sketching his first plans for

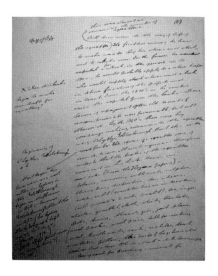

a course on Australian history, he immediately saw how to make the subject attractive. 'What to do?' he wondered. His answer: 'Make the events romantic.'[14]

Clark's handwritten lecture notes from the late 1940s survive today, the script so small it's a wonder he could read the words out; the paper yellowing slightly as it decays, giving off a dry, earthy smell, a visceral reminder of how different this time was for teachers; no visuals and no props, save chalk, the blackboard, the odd map and the drama of the teacher's soliloquy. Every word was painstakingly written out, even down to introductory remarks ('Today I want to'), tiny asides ('So you see'), self-assessment ('this is badly presented, make the point more clearly') and jokes ('Today I will indulge in broad and billowing generalisations'). Occasionally, the older Clark intrudes, writing his epistles to the biographer—'This was written in 1949—before the disastrous decision to move to Canberra.' At other times, he made corrections, clearly planning to recycle the lectures or to use them as the basis for future publications. The notes were clearly structured, each lecture falling naturally into paragraphs and concluding with a tidy summary of the questions asked at the outset. What is most striking about Clark's lectures today is just how conventional they appear. He offered a standard chronological overview of nineteenth-century Australia—'the British background' convicts, transportation, squatters, working conditions and immigration, the labour movement, responsible government and federation—all peppered with frequent statistical breakdowns, the same statistics he would later mock as the narrow domain of 'the measurers'. Covering the squatters, he relied heavily on Brian Fitzpatrick's analysis of colonial society, portraying them as an elite class bent on exploiting the lower orders. Dealing with the convicts, he attacked the 'birth stain myth'. When he discussed the Aborigines, he depicted them as one of the 'challenges' facing the squatters. This was Australian history from the settlers' perspective. The whites' actions had provoked the blacks to violence, but aside from a brief coverage of the Myall Creek massacre, there was little mention of white violence or the impact on Aboriginal people of the white man's land use practices. Ken Inglis saw Clark's approach as sympathetic to Marxism but certainly not Marxist. At the time, 'the Marxist interpretation was … the default position', he said:

> it's what you used unless you opted out of it, and it was perhaps a bit easier to be a Marxist than not: if you didn't use the Marxist dialectic, the onus was on you to show why not. This had to do with the spirit of the age, though it also might have had more to do with Melbourne University than some other [universities]. For Manning … Marx was always the moralist and [the] politician rather than the theoretician of society.[15]

John Mulvaney, who credited Clark with 'winning him over' to Australian history, kept his lecture notes for over sixty years. Mulvaney was struck by Clark's mention of the Aborigines; however cursory, it sparked an interest that would eventually guide much of his life's work. He graduated with the belief that he too could be a 'pioneer in Australian history'. 'This was the sense that Manning gave us,' he recalled, 'and for that I owe him a great deal.' He spoke fondly of Clark's amusing depictions of the squatters' leisure activities ('more fertile than their rams'), and how his obvious passion for Australian literature (Mulvaney remembers him praising Eleanor Dark's *A Timeless Land*) made cultural history significant in a way he had never encountered before. The study of history was no longer headed 'Britain and …' but 'Australia and …' The starting point was right in front of them—every aspect of their society—its politics, environment and literature, its art, music and humour. Suddenly, the past that had previously seemed so dull had come alive. It was also politically relevant. Clark's final lecture for the year began with the question 'Was Australia a true democracy?' 'Imagine this,' beamed Mulvaney, 'it seemed so daring at the time.' Many of the lectures in Australian history that have survived in Clark's papers were first delivered in 1948, no doubt revisions of those given in the previous two years, which by that time were slowly beginning to resemble the structure and interpretations in the first volume of *Select Documents*, published in 1950.[16]

Manning Clark, Collins Street, Melbourne, 1947

In August 1948, Clark gave a lecture on 'Periods and Themes' in Australian history. Using the lecture as a rehearsal for an essay he hoped to publish, and a seminar he would later give to his peers, his notes were quite detailed—so detailed, in fact, that it's possible to imagine what it might have been like to sit on the rock-like seats in the Old Arts' lecture theatre in the spring of 1948 and hear Clark deliver the words from the lectern below.

Every generation creates its own picture of the world ... historians search the past to explain the present, and, perhaps, predict the future ... the creators grope for the pattern which will evoke that recognition from their contemporaries. They will say, when they read or look at their works: this is us—this is our world ... To know so much, and to appreciate so little: that is the curious paradox of the white man in Australia ... For the serious minded, the 'classics' of English literature, the events of European history, still provide the content of cultivated conversation. Australian scholars, with an insensitive indifference to their own past, vie with their European colleagues to add a mite to the colossal stores of knowledge on European civilisation. The student who 'finds' Australian history is puzzled by this indifference, sometimes even hurt by the condescending inquiries made by those who find their comforters 'overseas'. The odd thing is that those who seek refuge from the Australian scene in the culture of Europe are themselves fossils from the Australian past, fossils from the time when there was no indigenous culture, and the only contribution possible for Australians was to European culture ... the indigenous culture has not enjoyed the prestige of the imported ... The past, too, was no guide. For this was a new country, a country on which the books were silent, a country whose original inhabitants kept no historical records ... For the first century ... Australians developed a way of life that was not conducive to intellectual inquiry ... They were indifferent to their past ...

There is however one task which the professional historian has always so far neglected. He has not sketched the main periods and themes in Australian history ... There are four distinct periods in Australian history: 1788–1815, the time of the penal colony, a period rich in human drama; 1820–1856, the period of the squatters' power and pastoral civilization; 1856–1890, the period which saw the decline of the squatters and the rise of the bushman's creed—mateship[—and] the first signs of Australian national sentiment were appearing in print; and finally, 1890 to the present day, the period when Australia became an imperial power, [and began to see itself] as an outpost of white civilisation in the Pacific.

The [recent] economic changes in Asia, the conversion of primitive rural communities into modern industrial powers, the hardening of Asiatic sentiment against the white man, and the corresponding growth of national sentiment have raised the whole question of white civilization in Australia … Australia faces the future with a community divided on the question of social organization, and uncertain in its relations with its northern neighbours … will Australia remain a capitalist society? Will Australia remain almost entirely a white society? … Merely posing these questions implies that Australia might be on the verge of a new period, that a fifth is [today] taking shape … Perhaps if Australian history and society had been studied more intensively we would see the outlines, or at least perceive what was likely to occur, and not exhaust our energies in the repair of all that time has eroded.[17]

Clark sensed that Australia was on the cusp of a new, uncertain era. Rapid industrialisation, de-colonisation and war had washed away the old verities—white Australia, the British myth and the natural supremacy of capitalism. Postwar Australians had been pushed back on their own reserves. Would they have the courage, intelligence and imagination to organise society in a more equitable fashion and to forge a more independent national culture? Australia's move away from Britain in the twentieth century would prove to be so piecemeal and tentative that in different guises Clark continued to ask similar questions until his death in 1991. He finished his lecture by quoting from the last line of Federation poet Bernard O'Dowd's 'Australia', which again pondered Australia's future:

A new demesne for Mammon to infest?
Or lurks millennial Eden 'neath your face?

Four decades later, in the 1980s, he recommended that O'Dowd's words grace the Federation Pavilion in Sydney's Centennial Park, where they stand today, inscribed on the sandstone frieze of the pavilion just below the dome. Asked why he chose the words, Clark explained that O'Dowd's poem reflected the principal obsession of the intellectual community at the time—will Australia become a country of corrupt, 'ill-gotten' wealth or will we create a paradise that will last for a thousand years? He asked the same question in 1948 and his students remembered its impact. He forced them to confront in a new way not only their nation's past but the role each of them would seek to play in securing O'Dowd's 'millennial Eden'. When he finished writing up his ideas on 30 August 1948, he was dissatisfied, wondering if he had become 'stale'. 'Make the essay livelier,' he scolded himself. If he was to avoid his work disappearing into obscurity, he had to be 'in step with the sympathies and intuitions of the people'. Only when he wrote in the language of the ordinary Australian could he begin to find the popular audience he craved. That audience, however, could not be found through writing alone—he knew that he had to reach out to the public in other ways—through radio broadcasts, public lectures and speaking on political platforms. Committed as he was to the restructuring of society along social- ist lines, his views quickly attracted opposition. As the postwar climate of McCarthyism intensified in the late 1940s, politically engaged academics sympathetic to the Left soon found themselves under surveillance.[18]

In early 1944, virtually from the moment he took up his appointment at Melbourne, Clark provided political commentary for the ABC on the last throes of the war. Late the following year, he took part in a series of evening radio discussions—'International Co-operation or Conflict? 1920–1945'—organised by Macmahon Ball. These appearances were unex- ceptional; they were simply part of the wider public role any lecturer in Politics and History might play. Gradually, however, the tenor of Clark's commentary changed. As he gained in confidence, he provided more stri- dent, idiosyncratic critiques of Australian politics and culture. Whatever the theme, he emphasised the importance of restructuring society on a more equitable basis, both within Australia and internationally. When he spoke on anti-Semitism, he argued that the only way to put a stop to racial hatred was to ensure that economic conditions were improved. Only then would marginal groups not be made the scapegoats for unemployment and social inequality. When he dealt with the economic future of postwar Europe, he depicted the Marshall Plan as just another form of imperial domination. If it were introduced, he told a radio audience in February 1948, it could well 'split the world into two camps, the capitalist and the communist'. In yet another radio discussion, he addressed the question of Australian security in the South Pacific, supporting de-colonisation in the South Pacific and insisting that the only way to make Australia safe from attack was to assist Asian nations to free themselves from the yoke of 'western imperialism'. There was no point in 'rigid exclusion of Asians from Australia', he declared. It would only antagonise them further; far better to engage with Asian countries. 'We have a great deal to offer one another,' he enthused. 'Here we are, nurtured in European culture, and influenced by the wonderful sky and the bush of Australia. Maybe something even stranger will happen in this environment—the meeting of East and West on a footing of equality and fellowship. I wonder whether we will be capable of this great achievement.' In 1946, few nationalists saw Australia as a potential site for marrying eastern cultural traditions with those of the West. Unlike Lawson and Stephensen, Clark's nationalism was open and inclusive. But he had not deserted his stalwarts entirely. Much as he recoiled from the crudity, racism and anti-intellectualism of the radical nationalist tradition, he envied Lawson's passion and larrikin gumption. The 'period piece' nationalism of HV ('Doc') Evatt, for example—who in the late 1940s argued that there was no incompatibility between Australian independence and the continuation of the British connection—irritated Clark because he found it too tame, dry and legalistic. This was the tension in Clark's first nationalist urgings. Yearning for a more independent Australia, he stood between the old radical Labor nationalists and those such as Chifley and Evatt, an intellectual searching for a new language in which to make an old argument. Yet another tension was emerging in his politics, one that would remain unresolved for years to come.[19]

An Eye for Eternity

Like many on the Left, Clark placed his faith in an intellectual vanguard, a political class that would benignly engineer a better future for humanity. He believed that the path to social justice, equity and a more active, responsible citizenry was through government intervention, regulation and control. He also rejected the liberal faith in 'enlightened capitalism', guided by the United States, which was fast-driving the postwar reconstruction of Europe. Acutely aware that the fundamental division between Left and Right 'on how society should be organised' threatened to plunge the world into yet another war, he pleaded that 'the decision between the two should be reached by a counting, and not by a breaking, of heads'. 'All men,' he argued, should be encouraged to 'settle their disputes by discussion'. Clark wanted a bloodless revolution. Superficially, he appeared to support many of the aims of the Communist Party while still clinging to the principles of liberal democracy that had formed the bedrock of his education. As more and more news of Stalinist brutality in the Soviet Union filtered through to the outside world, he came under increasing pressure to forsake his faith in the Left. One source of pressure came from his most frequent correspondent in the late 1940s, Geoffrey Fairbairn, his former student at Geelong Grammar, who, in 1946, was studying in Cambridge after serving in the Royal Australian Navy.

Fairbairn's first letter to Clark, in May 1945, spoke of his horror at the killing and violence of war. There were probably two responses to witnessing death in wartime: returning home determined to fight for political reform so that war might never happen again; or turning away from politics altogether, sceptical of all human endeavour to secure peace and harmony on earth. Fairbairn took the former course. His early letters to Clark, written from Europe in the late 1940s, show the enormous hope so many returned men and women had for a better world. As Fairbairn told Clark in 1945, 'The left must avoid bloodshed but act quickly, determinedly, concertedly … the formation of a spiritual popular front with the progressive section of the bourgeoisie will be a great asset in peaceful transformation of society.' Alone in Cambridge, he found in Clark's letters 'the breath of a kindred spirit', and he produced a torrent of letters in reply, many of them extremely passionate, searching and open, driven by an obsessive questioning of the future form society would take. Few of Clark's correspondents pushed him to question his political beliefs as Fairbairn did. Hearing the news of violence and intimidation from Russia, Fairbairn's anti-communism became more and more virulent. 'Surely you agree,' he wrote Clark in 1948, 'that servility must be the result of communist methods?' Referring to Stalin's purges, he couldn't have been more direct: 'It is the police state that is coming in, [Manning]. Don't let's kid ourselves it's a better world that is being ushered in. It is barbarism.' Unfortunately, Clark's replies to Fairbairn are lost, but from the comments Fairbairn quoted back to him, it is clear that Clark stood his ground, believing that the Left, if not Stalinist communism, offered the only way ahead. To let go of his faith in socialism, and his romantic ideas of Russia, Clark had to forsake an ideal, to live without the dream of a future utopia. For the romantic that he was, to relinquish the ideal was unthinkable, even in the face of Fairbairn's cross-examination. Despite their differences, Fairbairn was resolute: 'whatever happens Manning, our friendship must never break. It is the best thing in life I know of. It must be honest. It must face the personal divisions.' He could also deflate Clark's earnestness with humour: 'how is your temperance campaign progressing? Well, I'll write again soon. I hope by your next letter you will have found a rough Aussie who admires Picasso and Virginia Woolf.'[20]

As Clark received letter after letter from Fairbairn, grilling him over his political views, he found himself the subject of political controversy. Although the war was over, the culture of surveillance that accompanied it carried over into the postwar environment. During the war, German or Japanese infiltration was the major source of paranoia. In 1943–44, Dymphna's family had been subjected to security checks by ASIO's precursor, the Commonwealth Investigation Branch. Anna's endorsement of Hitler in the early 1930s, Augustin's links with the German community, and his role as a translator for the government censor were more than enough to arouse the suspicion of the authorities. Reading the Lodewyckx security reports—which describe Augustin as 'a general nuisance'; his son, Axel, then serving in the RAF, as a 'definite security risk'; and Dymphna as 'harmless' but as someone who could 'find other employment' if the Censor could possibly do without her—one wonders if the government knew who its real enemies were. In the postwar climate, the fear of internal subversion continued under a new guise. Now, for very different reasons, it was Clark's turn to be the object of suspicion.[21]

In 1946–47, riding on a rising wave of anti-communist hysteria in Truman's USA, Australian conservatives turned their sights on home-grown dissidents—vocal academics, members of the Communist Party of Australia, and all those on the Left who displayed the slightest sympathy for communist principles. In Melbourne, Frederick Edmunds, the Liberal member for Hawthorn and a shrill wowser, led the charge against the Left. A former (and not very successful) student of Ernest Scott's in the 1920s, Edmunds had managed to convince himself that the Melbourne University History Department was a seething cauldron of communist dissent. In November 1946, together with former Victorian Premier Albert Dunstan, he named Max Crawford as one of several 'pink professors' in the university. Even before the war, Crawford had long been 'one of the most vocal academics on campus', denouncing government infringements of civil liberties and championing progressive causes. In his role as president of Australia–Soviet House, the Melbourne branch of the Australia–Soviet Fellowship of Writers, Crawford was considered suspect. Moreover, he had a professional interest in the cultural history of the Soviet Union and at Evatt's instigation had accompanied the first Australian diplomatic mission to Russia in 1943. Academics at Melbourne, Ernest Scott included, had always been involved in political debate, but the lines of ideological division had sharpened considerably since the Spanish Civil War debate in 1937 and they left politically engaged scholars such as Crawford and Clark increasingly vulnerable to allegations of bias and political subversion. Anyone in a position of authority who dared to question or criticise the status quo ran the risk of being tarred with the communist brush.[22]

In May 1947, Clark 'debated' Edmunds on ABC Radio, the topic: 'Is communism white-anting our education system?'—a clear invitation for violent disagreement. Clark 'introduced himself by way of a disclaimer: He was 'a lecturer … not a communist'. In fact, he had never been a communist, and he had 'no intention of becoming one'. The students, he asserted, were capable of deciding for themselves if lecturers were not presenting information impartially. Edmunds delivered the predictable retort—History and

Politics lecturers at Melbourne were peddling communist propaganda under the cloak of tertiary education. If a generation was to be saved from communist propaganda, there was an urgent need to 'weed out' the reds. Within weeks of the debate, Clark was the subject of a security report. He won the radio debate easily, an outcome Edmunds obviously did not forget, describing Clark shortly afterwards on the floor of the Victorian Parliament as either 'a highly overpaid ignoramus or an evilly disposed wrong-headed person'. Edmunds alleged Clark was 'a paid agent of the Communist Party', a dangerous intellectual bent on exporting the Marxist revolution to the world. Overlord of this conspiracy was apparently none other than the Renaissance man Max Crawford. To Edmunds, Clark was just another academic in the line of fire. In 1947–48, as hundreds of students rallied to defend their lecturers from accusations of political bias, it was clear that Edmunds' attack was aimed at the independence of the university itself. It was nothing less than a volley of abuse intended to silence political dissent. The tactic was transparent: all those on the Left—Labor, communist, or the politically non-aligned—were impugned with the charge of disloyalty. Once seen as disloyal, their political credibility was undermined. Remarkably, this was where Clark's secret life as 'a communist spy' would begin. Fifty years later, when the Brisbane *Courier-Mail* accused Clark of being a Soviet spy, it opened its case against Clark with Edmunds' smears and innuendo. All this when Clark, in the 1940s, could be accused of nothing more than defending 'academic freedom' and 'promoting the study and criticism of the existing order'. However, much larger than individual reputations, the basic right of academics to design their courses free of political interference was at stake here, as was their freedom to go beyond the role of academic expert and engage critically in political debate, either as commentators or as political actors. Clark was one of many academics who, in 1948, signed an open letter drafted by Brian Fitzpatrick and the Council of Civil Liberties calling on the Australian Government to recognise a 'Jewish state in Palestine, together with a neighbouring, independent Arab state'. As academics spoke out on any number of issues, the press gave their views more attention, and this fuelled the interest of crusading politicians such as Edmunds. Extremely concerned, the university administration insisted that the vice-chancellor,

An Eye for Eternity

John Medley, be consulted before any public communication by staff was made, particularly those of a political nature. Medley defended both Crawford and Clark, but warned all staff to be 'extremely careful' in their public appearances. If Clark escaped unscathed, Crawford did not.[23]

As head of department, Crawford was surprised and wounded by the vehemence of Edmunds' denunciations of his professional integrity. The liberal principles that had guided so much of his professional and public life since his appointment in 1936 were steadily being eroded by the ferocity of the Cold War. In 1947, Crawford resigned from Australia–Soviet House, worried that Edmunds would 'raise the political reputation of the department in the Legislative Assembly'. This was the beginning of his retreat from championing the causes of the progressive Left. Over more than a decade, from the mid-1930s until the late 1940s, he had helped to define the intellectual culture within which Clark's understanding of the historian's professional and public roles was formed. As Crawford withdrew, Clark would step forward. Ever since he had come to Melbourne as a student in the 1930s, Clark had looked up to Crawford. It was Crawford's lectures that had first sparked his imagination, it was to Crawford that he looked for advice while he was in Oxford, and it was Crawford who had finally secured him a university position. By 1949, after four years of lecturing, Clark was no longer under Crawford's wing—he had established himself as an outstanding teacher and a scholar of exceptional promise. Approaching thirty-five, he was ready to strike out on his own.[24]

ANOTHER LIFE

While Clark was immersed in the university career he had long hungered for in Melbourne, Dymphna's life was somewhat different. In 1944, when the family moved from Geelong, she was barely twenty-seven and already mother to three children under the age of five: Sebastian, Katerina and Axel. As they waited ten long months for their new home to be built at Croydon, some 30 kilometres east of Melbourne, she lived between Mont Albert and

The Clarks' house, Croydon, 1946

Mentone. 'We were the travelling Clarks,' she recalled, more with irony than resignation—'yo-yoing from one set of in-laws to the next'—unable to afford wartime rents, forced to move on whenever the children ('who were no angels') became too unruly or simply wore the patience of one grandparent too thin. To pay just over 1400 pounds for the house and land at Croydon, they'd been forced to borrow money from Augustin and Anna, and from Charles Clark. Living in between their parents' homes, Dymphna sometimes felt dependent. Since marrying Clark in 1939, she had moved incessantly, each move burdened with greater responsibilities as her family expanded. In April 1945, when they finally moved into Carroll Avenue in Croydon, it was the first opportunity she had had to make a home of her own.

'The A frame timber house faced east down a broad hillside, looking across the Lilydale valley and up to the Dandenongs in the near distance', 'it was semi-rural and idyllic', 'a real hill-billy life'. The Clarks had no car, no phone, no refrigeration and no washing machine. All the roads were dirt and

An Eye for Eternity

the house was surrounded by scrub and a climbing sea of grey-green bush beyond. The small suburb of Croydon boasted one teahouse and one pub—social life was 'thin on the ground'. But at least there was space, and 'plenty of room for the children to build cricket pitches and to get into trouble firing detonators on the railway line'.

While Clark was in Melbourne, Dymphna's 'only link' with the world beyond was the Melbourne *Age*, which was delivered along with the milk every morning. Melbourne was one hour away by train. Fortunately, she was still close to her parents' home at Mont Albert, just several stops away on the same line. Without a car until 1949, she walked everywhere. It was 2.4 kilometres to the station and at least 800 metres to the nearest bus.

In later life, Dymphna didn't mind revelling in the heroics of her younger self. In 1999, long before I floated the idea of writing Clark's biography, I walked over to see her at Tasmania Circle in Canberra, late one Sunday afternoon. She was in the front garden, digging up gum seedlings that had sprouted in the lawn, potting them up ready to pass them on to friends and neighbours. As I walked down the steep drive holding my four-year-old's hand, with my two-year-old on my shoulders, she looked up and shouted: 'That's not as impressive as my efforts at Croydon!' She told me of her regular trips to and from the shops, walking along the railway tracks with Axel on her shoulders, one or two shopping bags dragging on her arms, and Sebastian and Katerina trailing behind—'how much further Mum?'—a return journey of at least 4 kilometres. These were the days when she needed to go without to stretch the weekly grocery order, when she'd rather walk than wait for the bus. Wartime austerity measures were still in place. Meat: 1.84 pounds (835 grams) per person per week, butter: 6 ounces (170 grams) per person, sugar and petrol were rationed as well, and clothing was only available by coupon, so expensive that worn family clothes had constantly to be patched and rejuvenated. What had to be done was done. Painting bedrooms, stocking the kitchen, finding furniture, sewing the children's clothes, cooking, cleaning and entertaining—the life of the tireless, effervescent, bountiful young mother. Outside, Dymphna set about creating a vegetable patch and flower garden 'from nothing'. Rather than re-create the oak forests of Europe, as her father had done at Mont Albert, she planted Australian natives from seedlings cultivated by friends and neighbours. At Croydon, as Clark's mind turned on all things Australian, she discovered a love of the Australian bush.

Russell and Eirene Clark lived close by. Russell had applied for the chaplaincy at Geelong Grammar, but Darling, having already had the pleasure of one Clark, was in no mood for another. In 1946, Russell took up the appointment as vicar at Croydon instead. 'We didn't see Manning and Dymphna at church much,' Eirene would later recall with a smile, 'but we did see one another fairly often. Dymphna was always pushing prams, and she'd walk everywhere, struggling along.' With only a lecturer's income, loan repayments and increasing expenses, her budget was tight. Picturing Clark with the family, Eirene described him as an 'involved father'—cricket impresario, rabbit trapper, a fine hand with the scythe, a sharp eye with a shotgun (he had several black snakes to his credit) and always attentive to his children's needs—but he was a weekend father. Most of the time, Dymphna was at home alone with the children. Clark often arrived home late at night, sometimes due to late classes and sometimes after drinking sessions with the classicist John O'Brien, who, after leaving his wife, was holed up in Trinity College and eager for company. Clark's eagle eye for the Irish Catholic 'communion rail' frequently lured him away from Carroll Avenue to the pub. In Melbourne, there was the Mitre Tavern, where in 1943, Arthur Boyd had first opened his eyes to Vermeer; and the Swanston Family Hotel, a popular haunt of Brian Fitzpatrick; or, just a few hundred metres from the university, in Lygon Street, Jimmy Watson's Wine Bar— one of the few public houses in Melbourne where women could feel comfortable drinking with men. On weekends, Clark could occasionally be found at the Croydon Hotel with another O'Brien, his neighbour Denis, an Irish-Australian veteran of World War II. Today, O'Brien's name stands on the war memorial at the top of Croydon's main street; he was killed in action in Korea. Clark always remembered his naïve enthusiasm as he left to fight in the Korean War. 'I'm going off to get the commies,' O'Brien had announced, beaming.

For all Clark's alehouse wandering, he brought home more of his social life than he kept to himself. Much to the horror of some of Clark's other friends, Denis O'Brien's drunken renditions of 'Hail Queen of Heaven' were often performed in the living room at Croydon. Compared with that of most families nearby, the Clarks' life was positively bohemian. Flagons of cheap wine and meals that appeared like manna from heaven kept a constant stream of visitors afloat. The novelist Martin Boyd, returning from Europe in 1948, came to sit at Clark's table, telling him that he should try to do for Australian history what Boyd had already done in fiction: place 'European values in an Australian setting'. Ex-students from Geelong Grammar came too, as well as university colleagues and the usual trail of family friends. It was just as exciting a time for Dymphna as it was for Clark. Their lives were opening out, independent of their parents, and they were making their first connections with what was then the tiny world of Australian artists, intellectuals and writers in Melbourne. On the weekends, Clark often invited students home to help 'work the farm'—fencing, clearing and digging drains on the one-and-a-half-acre property, with the promise of a game of cricket and a meal when the work was done. Sid Ingham was always struck by the way he simply 'expected her to provide'. Dymphna never disappointed, somehow capable of feeding a tribe of students and her own children at the same table, her hospitality completely 'unconditional'. From her mother, she had learnt frugality, and hospitality cost 'practically nothing'. Throughout her adult life, she could always hear Anna's voice: 'You won't find nightingales' tongues on my table.' As a young girl, she had watched as Anna retrieved from the garden a thrush, a bird with a song-like call and curious nature her mother loved more than any other. Taking the dead thrush into the kitchen, she plucked, cooked and ate it immediately. When Dymphna asked why, Anna replied: 'So that it might not have lived in vain.'

If Dymphna's childhood had been dominated by periods of loneliness and occasional boredom, her own children would later tell of a more chaotic, exuberant existence. Sebastian remembered how loudly the noise echoed throughout the house at Croydon. Together with Katerina and Axel, he played 'the dolls' game', standing at the top of the stairs, throwing the dolls down to his sister and brother below; interchange every 60 seconds, the sound of their running feet on the timber floor like an express train. 'Stop the noise!' Dymphna would shout, trying to make herself heard. Amid the

Manning and Dymphna, with Sebastian (centre), Katerina and Axel, Croydon, 1946

chaos, Clark sometimes tried to work upstairs, his study the last room on the eastern side of the house, almost twice the size of the couple's bedroom, his desk positioned under a large window facing the morning sunrise over the Dandenongs.

As neighbours moved in around them, the family's isolation was slowly whittled away. Before long, to the north, returned serviceman 'Brigadier' Williams saw Clark take his naked walk each morning from the outside bathroom: 'Put some clothes on you swine!' he would holler. To the east, Clark had a clear view from his study window of the home of Charlie Cone, a heavy drinker and the owner of a much-coveted Wolseley. Early one morning he saw Cone stumble out the front door of his house, his wife's shouts of 'get out' trailing behind him. Cone opened the boot of his Wolseley, jumped in with his beloved whisky bottle and pulled the lid down.

These are typical of the stories that have survived from the years at Croydon, the 'remember when' stories, the 'you should have seen' stories, the stories of a more rustic and uncomplicated life, all the finer details of life reduced to one or two abiding impressions. Buried beneath the stories of Dymphna's indomitable spirit and Clark's backyard antics lies the largely unreachable story of their first years with young children. There is no wad of correspondence, for they were nearly always together; there are no notebooks, and no diary entries, save a few stray remarks from Clark. If there was time for reflection, there was little or no time to write it down. All we have is anecdote and the late-life recollections of Dymphna and Clark, so often tinged with world-weary emotions grafted on to another, earlier life, when they were in their early thirties—ambitious, hungry to make a contribution to their country and still deeply in love. In these years, they took their summer holidays at Phillip Island, often scaling the windswept slopes of pigface together, carrying their buckets full of snapper and whiting as they looked down on the black rocks below, the children running along behind them. Looking at family photos from these years at Croydon, it's possible to feel something of the sense of promise in their relationship and to see hints of a marriage that was in some ways a genuine partnership.

At times, Dymphna surely felt lonely on those many long days at home, looking after three young children, her intellectual stimulation gained largely through Clark's work and whatever he brought home—ideas, half-finished articles, colleagues and students. There was not much time for anything else. Yet somehow she made time, just as she had done at Corio, breast-feeding Axel as she read *The Fortunes of Richard Mahony* aloud, unable to know that he would one day become Henry Handel Richardson's biographer.

Whenever Dymphna accompanied Clark to the university for social gatherings, she felt out of place: 'there was always an intimidating hush in the History tea room at Melbourne University,' she said, 'where cultured, if not holy, quiet was breathed.' She found many academics distant and self-important, obsessed with their tiny empires of arcane scholarship. There were exceptions: the philosophers Alan ('Camo') Jackson and George Paul, a Scot, who amused her with his take-off of Wittgenstein's mannerisms when arguing, and Paul's wife Margaret, an economist who ran the communist bookshop in Camberwell and who quickly became a close friend. But the 'hush' of academic life she remembered as a child, exemplified in her father's stern silence, was a way of life she had no desire to return to. Dymphna's university was off campus, in the noise of the conversations rising around her family table, and the countless impromptu dinner parties she and Clark held at Croydon, where ideas flew free from the rigid constraints of academic etiquette.

Throughout 1948, Clark worked tirelessly on the first volume of *Select Documents*, making countless 'checking' trips to the State Library. To expedite the process, he persuaded some of his students to perform the tedious task of proofreading. In August 1948, when he heard from Colin Roderick that Angus & Robertson would publish both volumes, he was ecstatic. Immediately, he imagined the book standing on the shelf, and he wrote excitedly to Roderick, explaining his vision for the cover.

> Would it be possible for the book to be bound in the same way as your firm bound 'National Buildings in Australia'? I suggest the title on the cover should be: Australian History, Select Documents, Clark, Star—the star would indicate that it was Vol.1—I am working on Vol.2—a colossal task!

Clark was busy building his first monument. When Roderick received the first draft, the number of errors staggered him. Clark thanked him profusely for his 'spot checking', which he admitted had probably saved him from a 'damaging and crushing review'. The errors, said Clark, were the fault of his typist. Next time, he would check the manuscript himself.

Later that year, seeing that the chances for promotion at Melbourne were slim, Clark started to look further afield. He applied unsuccessfully for a chair in History at the University of Adelaide. While teaching at Geelong Grammar, he had applied for university positions interstate and overseas. Now, eager to leave Melbourne, he was equally uncertain as to his destination. He might easily have found himself in South Australia, Sydney or Perth, but in early 1949 he happened to read an advertisement for a Chair of History at Canberra University College and applied immediately. Although Crawford and many others spoke highly of his teaching at Melbourne, he had no doctorate, unlike a growing number of younger academics, and only a few, relatively minor publications. Beyond all this, there was an even bigger question hanging over Clark's future in 1949. For all his ambition, would he ever be capable of demonstrating the self-restraint necessary to achieve his goal of writing a history of Australia?[25]

Early one evening in May, one of the neighbours in Carroll Avenue came over to say that Herbert Burton, since 1948 the inaugural principal of Canberra University College, was on the phone. Clark had been appointed Chair of History. It was startling news. There was no need for discussion. With a Canberra professorship, his salary would double. Clark would accept the appointment and Dymphna would follow with the children as soon as accommodation could be arranged in Canberra. Within weeks of Clark's appointment, the Victorian Government announced the Royal Commission on Communism, with Melbourne University one of its prime targets. Many of Clark's former colleagues, friends and students, such as Brian Fitzpatrick and Ian Turner, would be hauled before the commission. The intense climate of suspicion engendered by the Cold War was beginning to fasten its grip. In October, fears of Australia being surrounded by communist nations to its north were heightened when Mao Tse-tung led the communists to power in China. Before appointing Clark at Canberra, Thomas Owen, the University Registrar, asked the Commonwealth Investigation Service for a security report. An informant was quickly found: a staff member at Melbourne

University, a person who claimed to know Clark 'intimately'. Judging from his handwritten report, he knew him very well indeed.

> Clark is essentially a Socialist and may have thoughts in common with Communists, but this would be academic only ... as a lecturer in history ... he would be above reproach insofar as he would not use his appointment as a means for propagating his views, whatever they might be ... His sentiments ... are motivated by a feeling for the 'underdog' ... [and he] is not a person who would submit himself to the dictates of others, whether they be Party or otherwise, and his loyalty to his country is beyond question.

The report appeared so benign that the Director of the Commonwealth Investigation Service suggested it be treated 'with considerable reserve'—'it appears a partisan rather than a judicious opinion,' he concluded. Years later, Clark joked that the intelligence operative understood his beliefs better than he did himself. He would be appointed Chair of History at Canberra, but he would remain under surveillance.

When Geoffrey Fairbairn heard the news of Clark's move, he was despondent. Clark had tried to convince him to leave England and join him in Canberra, and despite Fairbairn's attempts to persuade him otherwise, he remained sympathetic to the Left. When he read Fairbairn's reply, he was disappointed. Fairbairn saw Clark's refusal to condemn communism as the beginning of a parting of ways and beliefs: 'My life will irrevocably be devoted to opposing all you stand for,' he declared to Clark. 'You will be part of a movement trying to destroy ... the vision of life that has come to be mine.' The looming ideological war was inescapably personal, and it would cut deep, dividing friendships, families and marriages. To be non-committal was cowardly. The stakes were too high. Clark may not have been a communist, but in Fairbairn's eyes his refusal to distance himself from Soviet totalitarianism made him just as guilty.[26]

On 1 October 1949, Clark arrived in Canberra, relieved to be free from 'the large classes in Melbourne, the steady stream of student enquiries, and the difficult people'. Initially, he had no more than a dozen diplomatic cadets to look after. After Melbourne, there was a sense of freedom. He had time to think, time to write, and time to plan his future. To Crawford, he wrote frequently of his indebtedness, fully aware that he needed to keep the channels of communication open if he was to have any chance of returning to Melbourne in the future. Crawford regretted his departure—by the late 1940s there were more than thirty students enrolled in Masters or doctorates on Australian topics—yet equally, he was looking forward to taking over the reins in Australian History. For the moment, Clark tried to come to terms with his new position and the strangeness of his new environment. Living in the Kurrajong Hotel, close to Parliament House, he was horrified by the 'inner emptiness' of the 'hostel' life of so many of Canberra's academics and public servants, many of them in a similar predicament to himself, either waiting to find accommodation at a time of severe shortage or scanning bush paddocks for a building site to establish a new home. Like other 'bachelors' in town, he could 'float through the weekend on parties', but that was only short-term amusement, like his all-night drinking sessions at the Museum Tavern in Civic with Don Baker, who arrived from Melbourne shortly before him. The first thing that struck Clark about Canberra was its 'provincial savagery'. Meeting teaching staff from a local high school, he was unimpressed: they were 'rather low middle class, heavily blinkered types', he thought, 'without any of the graces or the refinements of life'. Still the Melbourne Grammar boy at heart, he told Dymphna that this was a mark he did not want to see 'imprinted' on his 'children'.

It was more than a decade since Clark had been apart from Dymphna for any length of time. Immediately, he cast his mind back to the day when they separated in Sweden, in the autumn of 1938. Seeing her depart for Germany, he went 'to pieces'. Now, happily married with a promising academic career, he felt 'more contented and less anxious'. Compared to the outpourings of angst and grief that flowed from his pen ten years earlier, his letters to Dymphna from Canberra in 1949 appear, at first glance, to be almost banal. Hopeless with the washing machine, he put his new 'purple underpants' next to his 'old white shirt', with the inevitable result. He wrote to her of his treks to and from the washing line (it's best to get them off the line 'before tea') and his understandable frustration with petrol rationing, worried that he would be unable to obtain sufficient petrol tickets to return to Melbourne, let alone enough for weekend drives outside Canberra. The last months of 1949 would be among the few times in his life when his correspondence to Dymphna was free of discontent and unfulfilled longing. She was there whenever he needed her. She checked the proofs of *Select Documents* and mailed them back to him; she sent him parcels of food and clothing, as if he were a soldier on the front line; and, in between tending the children and looking after the house, she found time to write to him. 'Hugs-rolls-wrestles-everything,' he replied, 'I hope Andrew is walking by now.' Beneath the surface, however, it wasn't hard to see that Clark could bear her absence for a brief while only. He wrote to her daily, and he looked for her letters every afternoon, always disappointed when his mailbox was empty. Troubled by insomnia, he took sleeping pills to get through the night. He needed her with him, he told her, to 'cushion' him from the 'shocks' of life. In order to write, he had to be alone, but he could not live alone. The knowledge of her love freed him to work. It was both the foundation from which to launch his ambition and the refuge of comfort if he fell behind. By December, he would be back in Melbourne and they would leave Croydon, together with the children, making the 800-kilometre journey to Canberra.[27]

Dymphna was not keen to leave Croydon. She had only just begun to establish the house and garden; Sebastian, Katerina and Axel were already at school. 'Relieved' to have a miscarriage in 1947, she had found herself pregnant shortly afterwards with Andrew. In 1949, with four children, and after four years of toil to build up her first home, she did not want to be uprooted again. Many years later, she told Sebastian of her reluctance to leave Melbourne. 'I created Croydon with my own hands,' she reminded him.

In 2007, Sebastian and I visited the Clarks' former house in Carroll Avenue. The house itself had changed little. Inside, the old kitchen was stripped bare, ready for renovation. We walked upstairs to Clark's study, the view east to the Dandenongs now shrouded behind tall gums. Outside, what once was a stretch of bush paddocks was now suburbia. Sebastian pointed out the patch where Dymphna had started her vegetable garden sixty years earlier. With every step his recollections came back; each door in the house opening a long-locked door in his mind. The house had only recently been sold. The new owners, a builder, his wife and their young family, were only

The Clarks, Croydon, 1949

vaguely aware of their home's first occupants. 'The agent told us he was famous,' they said, 'but what did he do?'

In the 1950s and 1960s, on return trips to Melbourne, Clark and Dymphna often took the children back to Croydon, driving down Carroll Avenue, parking opposite the old family home at the bottom of the hill. If the occupant was agreeable, Clark took the children inside, keen to revive old memories. Sometimes, they would stay for more than an hour, the children playing in the backyard while Clark reminisced. On every occasion, and there were several, Dymphna remained in the car, refusing to go inside. Sebastian remembered her silence, and how, as they tumbled out of the car, she would turn away, as if even to set eyes on the house brought her too much pain.[28]

9: THE CROSSING

8 September 1969

'Hoping for better things...'

Long after Catherine Clark's death in March 1943, Manning Clark was 'haunted' by the 'odour' of death as her body lay in the family home at Mentone. The mere thought of those days of 'agony' made him nauseated. In the months that followed, he struggled to understand. 'Here is a curious thing,' he wrote, as if startled by the strangeness of his own thoughts, 'I have always believed that I will never die.'

The loss of his mother shook him more than his father's death, not only because the death of her adoring love revealed the certainty of his own death but because he was so much closer to her than to his father. In Canberra, in the years ahead, the memory of the smell of death, which rose involuntarily, like a terrifying dream, served as a constant stimulant, awakening Clark from the comfortable sleep of an ordinary life and pushing him to be extraordinary. Success as a writer would bring some kind of compensation for his inevitable extinction. Like the words of Thomas Carlyle, which Clark saw etched into the sandstone walls of the foyer in the Mitchell Library in Sydney ('In books lies the soul of the whole past time, the articulate audible voice of the past, when the body and material substance of it has altogether vanished like a dream'), writing, and a library tomb, promised him immortality of a kind. Only through writing could his voice be heard beyond death.

Not to achieve literary success would, as he told himself, leave exposed his 'rotten, slimy self ... something bare for the sun, the wind and the rain to hasten into putrefaction'.[1]

The day after Charles Clark's death in January 1951, Clark drove to the Lodewyckx family home at Mont Albert, where Dymphna and the children were staying. He walked inside, gathered the children together and asked them to follow him outside. They walked down the front-yard path, through the gate, and stood silently in front of the house. What he had to tell them, he could not tell them in *that* house. 'Your grandpa died last night,' he said. Katerina burst into tears. Clark continued, 'I walked alone on the beach at Mentone. I went down to the sea to see the sunset. Your grandfather loved the sea.' The funeral took place a few days later, 'a gloomy and dreadfully serious affair', attended mostly by 'men in black'. There were no anecdotes about Charles Clark's fun-loving nature, no uplifting stories from his family life. In death, the Church of England claimed the Reverend Charles Clark completely.[2]

Years later, talking about Charles while promoting his autobiography, Clark explained that he never knew his father as he knew his mother. What he did know, however, was that Charles was a Labor voter. Unlike Catherine, who had always voted for the conservatives, his father's solidarity with ordinary people led him to vote for the 'enlargers of life'. The story fitted comfortably with Clark's tale of his divided inheritance—the class-conscious world of his mother's family set against the earthy working-class nature of his father. Yet Sebastian Clark recalled being in a car with Charles shortly after the federal election in December 1949, when Robert Menzies led the Liberal Party to power. 'Charles and another fellow were talking about the election which had just taken place,' Sebastian remembered. 'My grandfather said that he had voted for Menzies. I never told my father. He would have been too upset—it's not good to have your illusions taken away.'[3]

Charles died only twelve months after Clark arrived in Canberra. Clark was now setting out in a new life in every possible way. At only thirty-five, he had lost both his parents. His sudden geographical isolation represented much more than severance from his former life at Melbourne University; he was leaving behind the first part of his life, the life of childhood and adolescence, the life of the promising, brilliant young man. His family connection with Melbourne was now limited to his siblings, Hope and Russell, and Dymphna's parents, the pair he cursed every time he hit his finger when chopping wood in the backyard at Croydon: 'Lodewyckx swine!' With him to Canberra came the memory of his parents' unstinting devotion and the most abiding constants of his life to that point: the literature of Fyodor Dostoyevsky and DH Lawrence, and that great 'confused novel', the King James Bible. Together, this cultural inheritance constituted Clark's eyes onto the world. Through literature he sought solace from death, he found the principles that would guide him in love, in religious belief and as an historian.[4]

Dostoyevsky suffered from epilepsy after his experience in a Siberian labour camp. Clark, similarly afflicted in his youth, found this similarity a 'source of strength and comfort'. In reading Dostoyevsky, especially *The Brothers Karamazov*, he also admitted he was 'trying to sort out his religious beliefs'. From the first moment he read the novel in 1934, and in every re-reading thereafter, particular paragraphs and phrases resonated deeply, as did certain passages from Ecclesiastes—'all is vanity', 'there is nothing new under the sun'—seeping into his everyday experience and becoming voices that lived inside of him, ever-present in the 'prayer-like communion' of his writing, their meaning changing as he aged, like a mirror giving different reflections of the same person over time.[5]

In 1941, his daughter Katerina was named after Dostoyevsky's mother. It was only because of objections from Katerina, having been teased at school because she 'had a foreign name', that her brother Andrew was saved from being named Dimitri Alyosha, after two of the Brothers Karamazov—the believer and the Dionysian, but not the atheist. As Katerina remarked in 2007, 'In giving his children names from Dostoyevsky he was less naming us than himself.' At Geelong Grammar, he persuaded students such as Bruce Anderson to spend their holidays reading Dostoyevsky in the Melbourne Public Library. In Canberra, Clark would tell his students and tutors that reading Dostoyevsky was more important than reading any work of history. Shortly after his arrival, journalist, Tom Fitzgerald dubbed him 'The Dostoyevskian from Canberra', a scholar who perceived an 'abnormal sense of the desolation of things in Western society'.[6]

From 1938 until he arrived in Canberra in 1949, Clark measured himself in his notebooks and diaries against fictional characters. 'Like Father Sergius [a Tolstoy short story], I strive for approval, esteem—not betterment of mankind.' Not long after he settled in Canberra, usually after a specific incident had upset him, he would pace up and down the hallway of his home, 'ranting and raving' like an actor delivering a soliloquy on stage, shouting out random words and phrases—'what torment!' 'I'm a swine!'—cursing the Lodewyckx family, until the words became unintelligible, merging into one raging torrent of abuse. Benedict, his youngest son, saw much later how many of Clark's outbursts that had so scared him as a child resembled those of the self-pitying Marmeladov, the failed public servant in Dostoyevsky's *Crime and Punishment*. 'My father,' said Benedict, 'wasn't totally connected to the world.'[7]

In DH Lawrence's short essay 'Why the Novel Matters', which Clark read while he was in Oxford, Lawrence observed that 'books are not life'. 'They are only tremulations on the ether. But the novel as a tremulation can make the whole man alive tremble.' As David Malouf found, Clark was 'always presenting' in his everyday life. Living through the heightened, fabulous 'tremulations' of fiction, he sought to make the same life-changing impact on others that the characters of Dostoyevsky had made on him. By 1949, his sense of himself as a writer was taking shape; to be taken seriously, he not only had to write well, he had to learn how to 'fashion his life on literary models'—in other words, not only to read and write literature but to live it. In 1950, on a return trip to Melbourne, repelled by the 'the great oblivious poseurs of the Melbourne History School', he wrote to Dymphna: 'I felt yesterday that I should shout out in anger against them, drive them out of their temple of learning with a whip.' In so many of his letters, up until 1950 by far his greatest literary output, he spoke through biblical parables. While he no longer believed in the Church's teachings on eternal life and an interventionist God, he continued to speak through the moral and allegorical language of the Old and New Testaments. That Dostoyevsky was the novelist who came to mean so much to him was hardly surprising.[8]

In Dostoyevsky's final novel, *The Brothers Karamazov*, his narrative at one celebrated point played into the story of the gospels through the parable of

An Eye for Eternity

the Grand Inquisitor. Told by Ivan, an atheist, to his brother, Alyosha, a novice monk, Dostoyevsky's fable sees Christ return to earth at the time of the Spanish Inquisition. He performs miracles and thousands follow him, recognising him as the Son of God, until he is imprisoned and sentenced to death. The Grand Inquisitor, denouncing Christ as a prophet who condemned humanity to a life of suffering and torment, visits him in his cell the night before he is to be burnt at the stake. The Inquisitor tells Christ that human beings are not equipped to cope with the freedom of choice he has given them—that they prefer to be bound by miracle, mystery and authority—to have someone to 'bow down' to. Throughout the Grand Inquisitor's prosecution, Christ remains silent. When the Inquisitor is finished, he waits for Christ to reply. Christ approaches him quietly, and kisses him 'on his bloodless aged lips'. Shaken, the Inquisitor sets Christ free 'into the dark alleys' of Seville. Dostoyevsky never answered the Grand Inquisitor's case against Christ, except to follow the chapter with the life story and teachings of the monk, Father Zossima, before continuing his themes of philosophical and religious ambiguity through the story of the three brothers.

Writing the novel in St Petersburg in the 1870s, Dostoyevsky asked similar questions in his correspondence to those he asked in the novel: 'Why should I live righteously and do good deeds if I am to die entirely on earth? ... After all, I shall die, everyone else will die, and nothing will be left.' Drawn back continually to the parable of Christ's forty days and nights in the desert, he imagined Satan taunting the 'omnipotent' Son of God: 'You see these stones, they are legion. You have only to will it and the stones will be turned into loaves of bread.' Christ answered that man 'did not live by bread alone'. For Dostoyevsky, Christ's reply gave expression to a fundamental truth— man was 'spiritual in origin'. The great flaw in socialism, he thought, was that socialists in both Europe and Russia denied these spiritual origins. They had set out to 'eliminate Christ from everything', as if man's problems were due solely to his 'corrupting environment' and material conditions, as if bread alone could satisfy him. All of man's strivings for 'universal' happiness on earth were doomed to failure if he refused to acknowledge his spiritual nature and the 'immortality' of his soul. A Godless existence was untenable. Human beings, endowed with consciousness and reason, existed 'above and outside everything on earth'. Therefore, they 'must be of a higher order'. The meaning of life, however, was hidden from us. It would always remain a mystery. In the words of Father Zossima:

> Many things on earth are hidden from us, but in return for that we have been given a mysterious, inward sense of our living bond with the other world, with the higher, heavenly world, and the roots of our thoughts and feelings are not here but in other worlds. That is why philosophers say it is impossible to comprehend the essential nature of things on earth ... if that feeling [of contact with other mysterious worlds] grows weak or is destroyed in you, then what has grown up in you will also die. Then you will become indifferent to life and even grow to hate it. That is what I think.[9]

When Dymphna was having difficulties in Bonn, Clark suggested she read the words of Father Zossima as consolation. In *The Brothers Karamazov*, Dostoyevsky achieved something remarkable: he created a language of faith that embraced doubt and ambiguity. His mysticism, his pessimism concerning political theory, echoing the fatalism found in the scriptures, wherein human beings were created as 'fallen', and his depiction of characters instinctively driven to 'touch other worlds', fell on Clark like a benediction. Walking along the shoreline of Corio Bay with James McAuley in 1943, listening to McAuley hold forth on Eastern religions in the same breath as he explained his Catholicism, Clark was intrigued and bewildered by his willingness to 'stand on entrenched ground'. When he moved to Canberra as the Cold War escalated in 1949, his sympathy with the broad ideals of the Left existed side by side with the more mystical view of human nature espoused by Dostoyevsky—the belief in 'the fundamental mystery of man'. Clark lived out these contradictions: revolutionary one moment—calling on opponents of the Left to be silenced—Russian holy man the next. 'Men are as they are,' he declared in 1943, 'they will never tolerate harmony, the contentment of a Utopia—they will smash it up.' The influence of Dostoyevsky on his thinking went far beyond his struggle to work out his political and religious beliefs.[10]

In 1943, searching for a structure to explore his interest in Australian history, Clark drew on Dostoyevsky's schema in *The Brothers Karamazov* as his model—revealing philosophical differences through opposing characters. He set out to speak through two characters—'the enthusiast for change, the optimist with the vision of the future—and the aloof, mystic—the pessimist'. Historical parallels emerged too: both Russia and Australia suffered from 'a raging inferiority complex' as against Western Europe. As Clark put it, they were 'isolated from the main centres of culture, London, Paris and Berlin'. And like the United States, 'they used a slave labour force to create wealth'. Dostoyevsky believed that Russia had to protect its innocence from European decadence and corruption. Clark, in the 1940s, looked out from his distant outpost in Australia, and saw Europe with the same eyes. Europe was 'a fantasy', the home of class prejudice and old-world traditions, which were fundamentally foreign to Australian conditions. Reading Freud's essay on Dostoyevsky and parricide, he became even more convinced that the mission of the creative artist was the only path worth pursuing. Unlike the 'corpse-like' academics, men and women who had 'no contact with life in the raw, no horrors, no glows, no guilt and no remorse', and who 'had their brief season and then are heard no more', he would produce work that would last. All of these ideas were firmly embedded in Clark's mind when he arrived in Canberra in 1949—Dostoyevsky in one pocket, Lawrence in the other.[11]

When Clark left for England in 1938, Tampion Daglish, a friend from Trinity College, gave him a copy of *Phoenix: the posthumous papers of D.H. Lawrence*, published only two years earlier. It was in this collection that Clark first read Lawrence's essays on Dostoyevsky, art, and the novel, while in Aldous Huxley's edited collection of Lawrence's correspondence, published in 1932, he discovered three letters written from Thirroul, the small coastal town on the south coast of New South Wales, where Lawrence and his wife Frieda lived between May and July 1922. In a handful of correspondence, Lawrence offered a condensed version of his impressions, which would later appear in *Kangaroo*. Writing to author and friend Catherine Carswell, he described Australia as an 'untouched' land—'strange', 'empty and unready'— 'older' and more 'nerve worn' than the mother country. In awe of the country's antiquity, he felt like 'the errant dead or the as-yet unborn'. The land was 'too far back'. He sensed an overwhelming indifference to the 'soul or spirit'—everything was 'so convenient', yet there seemed to be no 'inside life

of any sort'. Alone in Canberra, in the spring of 1949, Clark was 'both fasci-
nated and appalled' by the life he found there. 'All one's material needs were
catered for,' he wrote to Dymphna: if it was cold, there was central heating;
if it was warm, there was the electric fan. Food, drink and sport—'all were
there in abundance'. Yet, much like Lawrence, Clark found that there was
something lacking. He couldn't explain it—this 'mystery' of the land's 'hollow
shell'. Still, he could appreciate its beauty, its liberating 'sense of space'.
Unlike the mountains around Healesville, near Melbourne, the bush surrounding Canberra revealed almost 'no undergrowth, no vines climbing up
the trees, and no darkness'. Instead, there was 'dry soil, stones', 'a great variety of wild-flowers' and 'marvellous bird life'.[12]

As Clark moved to Canberra with dreams of writing the spirit of place
into his history of Australia, Patrick White, preparing to write *Voss*, was
reading the journals of the explorer Ludwig Leichhardt. In 1949, Sidney
Nolan was flying over central Australia, working on a series of paintings of
the MacDonnell Ranges, Ayers Rock, and 'unnamed' ridges, sandhills and
plains, flooded in what he called 'a transparent floating light'. Nolan was also
reading the diaries of Burke and Wills in preparation for the first of a stunning sequence of paintings based on their ill-fated attempt to cross the continent from south to north in 1860–61. At Melbourne University, in 1946,
Clark saw an exhibition of Australian 'contemporary art' which featured
Nolan's early Ned Kelly paintings, Albert Tucker's 'Images of Modern Evil'
and two of Arthur Boyd's most important works from the 1940s, *The Mockers*
and *The Mourners*, paintings which echoed Bruegel and Bosch in their use
of biblical narratives and their hellish visions of humanity, except that Boyd's
work was set against the background of the Holocaust and Hiroshima, and
placed in an Australian landscape. Sitting with Clark in Melbourne's Mitre
Tavern, Boyd had talked of the continent's 'fragile beauty'. Shortly afterwards, like Nolan before him, he too set off into the bush, travelling through
the Wimmera district of Victoria to paint its dry, desolate plains. Boyd and
Clark shared the sudden sense that the work of Australian artists and writers
mattered in a way it had never done before. 'It was a core of something',
said Boyd, 'of which you thought there was nothing else like it, either in
Australia or elsewhere'.[13]

In Sydney, in early 1949 and in 1950, unknown to one another, Patrick White and Clark both saw Nolan's paintings that had resulted from his journey to Central Australia, with their aerial views of an empty, rust-red landscape. Remembering their impact, White would later ask Nolan to provide an illustration for the jacket of *Voss*. In his notebooks, Nolan claimed that he had painted mountains of bare rock as Australia's 'cathedrals', dwarfing the trees and shrubs below them, which appeared as little more than a 'dotted veil above the landscape'. From Cairns, in 1947, Nolan told John Reed of his difficulty in 'understanding the country' he encountered. It seemed impossible, he said, to 'be articulate about it from our own particular level and tradition … we have only experienced the fringe of what we know to be indigenous'. Reed had already seen Nolan's first Ned Kelly paintings that year and was thrilled by his 'inspired realisation of the Australian bush'. Nolan, Reed argued, had penetrated beneath the harshness of the landscape that had so alienated Europeans in Australia and 'revealed the deep soft beauty of the bush', 'with all its subtleties'. In fact, he had glimpsed something of an 'authentic national vision'. Here was the expression of everything that cultural nationalists such as Vance Palmer, 'Inky' Stephensen, Clem Christesen and Max Harris, albeit from extremely different standpoints, had pined for—the creation of a national mythology.[14]

Reading Clark's memoirs it is easy to get the impression that he was the only person in Australia in the 1930s and 1940s reading Lawrence and Dostoyevsky. In 1940, indebted to the inspiration he received from his writings, Nolan painted Lawrence's portrait, a daubed, almost primeval vision of the author who had opened his eyes to the mystery of the Australian landscape. The Kelly paintings that Clark saw at Melbourne University in 1946 were not only about Kelly but about Nolan's 'psychological situation'. 'I was a loner' too, said Nolan. 'It was this sense that everybody, without exception, was against you. Dostoyevsky went through it too.' Nolan, a writer and poet who had contributed frequently to *Angry Penguins*, spent almost as much time as Clark in the public libraries of Sydney, Melbourne and Brisbane, in search of 'indigenous' historical narratives to feed his painting. Dostoyevsky, Lawrence and Rimbaud were the writers who contributed most to his early landscapes and history painting.

At Open Country, the Boyds' family home, in Murrumbeena, Victoria, the young Arthur Boyd heard the Melbourne literary graduate Max Nicholson read the work of Dostoyevsky aloud. His father Merric was an epileptic, and Boyd was particularly struck by Dostoyevsky's description, in *The Idiot*, of the silent screams and uncontrollable spasms of an epileptic seizure. Listening to Nicholson read from *The Brothers Karamazov*, Boyd was captivated by the Russian's ability to depict the private lives of his characters so vividly. From the moment he met Clark in Melbourne in the early 1940s, a shared love of Dostoyevsky was one of the bonds that kept their friendship alive. Like Nolan's Kelly paintings, with their unforgettable evocation of the lone individual in the Australian bush, Boyd's religious allegories of the 1940s attempted to portray the psychological state of Europeans in the Australian environment—not only the strange beauty of the land but the inner loneliness, the isolation and the silence that the bush seemed to impose on all those who inhabited it. In doing so, they drew on European traditions and Australian history to create a genuinely new mythology. In 1950, Nolan, Boyd, White and Clark were all beginning a journey into the Australian spirit of place that would unfold steadily over the next three decades. With these singular artists, Clark had more in common than he did with any historian in the corridors of Melbourne or Canberra universities.[15]

A few weeks before leaving Melbourne with his family in January 1950, Clark stood on the verandah of Dymphna's family home at Mont Albert together with her father. Conversation between them was, as always, laboured. 'What will you be working on in Canberra?' asked Augustin. 'I want to write a history of Australia,' Clark replied. 'What history has Australia got?' Augustin answered dismissively. Clark paused: 'I will prove it to you.' To realise his ambition, he could not have chosen a better site than the new national capital.[16]

On 6 October 1949, Clark shared a picnic lunch with friends at Mount Franklin, in the hills outside Canberra, inside of him, the ghosts of Dostoyevsky, Lawrence and the countless hours of his father's sermons and his mother's pious injunctions, of Sunday school lessons and chapel hymns, with their earnest, sombre cries to God above. He was as much shaman as intellectual, his inspiration rising from blinding artistic impulses. So much

Dymphna and family farewelling Anna, Mont Albert, January 1950

of his writing to that point was a response to his personal suffering. The vast space that surrounded him that spring day was a metaphor for all that remained to be done. It was 'one of those really halcyon days, not a cloud in the sky', and he was in awe of the country around him—the 'transparent air, the deep blues in the sky', the whole 'world stretching out' before him. DH Lawrence's 'unwritten land' would soon be written a million words over.[17]

Today I fear ... been drafted. Hoping ... and am very unhappy about it. I ... to be leading a more disciplined ... an unhappier life so to ... work well ... for myself ... anxious ... and know ... such by my wife ... over ... taken over me.

"Be

hes

, an

inter ...

dicalest ms

al 7 themes

PART FOUR

10: CANBERRA

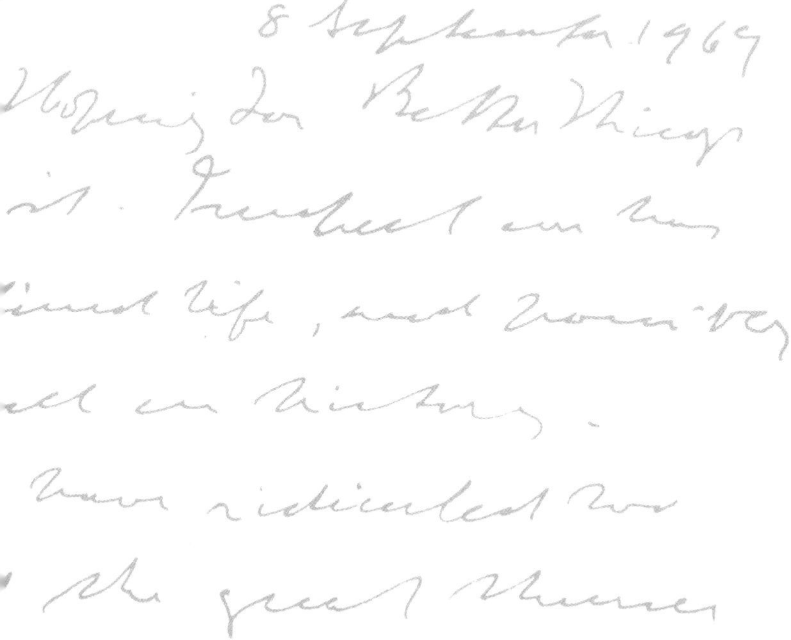

8 September 1969

[handwritten text, largely illegible]

Hoping for Better things

... life, and ...

... history.

... ridiculed ...

... the great ...

With its black leather seats and wide running boards, the Clarks' first family car was a gangster's dream: MK 869—the sleek, blue-black 1948 Austin 16. Even while the car was moving you could steady yourself on the boards, take aim and fire. In the winter and spring of 1949, on weekend afternoons, Clark would drive his new acquisition out to Steel's Creek, near Yarra Glen, passing Dame Nellie Melba's house at Coldstream on the way, nine-year-old Sebastian surfing the boards beside him, shotgun at the ready. There was no better car for shooting rabbits.

When Clark returned from Canberra that summer, he helped Dymphna pack the boot of the Austin, ready for their departure from Croydon. Uncertain as to how long they would stay in Canberra, they decided to lease out the house rather than sell. They had invested too much of themselves to cut their ties so quickly. While removalists transported their belongings to Canberra, the family travelled in the Austin. Clark drove all the way. Dymphna sat in the front passenger seat and in the back were Sebastian, nine; Katerina, eight; Axel, six; and Andrew, nearly two. Until then, they had driven no further than from Melbourne to Phillip Island. Most couples driving 800 kilometres with four young children would have taken the Hume Highway; it was by far the easiest route. But Clark made the decision to

The Clarks' Austin 16

travel east, then north along the coast before turning inland for Canberra. He had never seen the far south coast of New South Wales before. He was keen to explore the country and its history, particularly Boydtown, south of Eden, the site of the failed pastoral empire of the Scottish entrepreneur Ben Boyd, whose arrival in Australia in 1842 was greeted with the fanfare usually reserved for royalty. Setting off in the Austin, suitcases stacked a metre high on the roof, Clark told his family the story of Boydtown, how Boyd had dreamt of building a village on the sea, a replica of what might be found in his native Scotland, only to flee when his funds dried up, leaving a church without pews, a lighthouse unlit, an inn deserted. Only when Clark saw the lie of the land could he begin to understand its past. The decision to travel via Boydtown illustrated one aspect of his character. From here on, Clark's journey was the family's journey too: one way or another, they would all be implicated. His passion for history would never be his private possession; it would be something he shared with them. Ultimately, it would come to define them as a family.

An Eye for Eternity

The journey was 'a real saga'—three days in all, much of it along a goat track illustriously named the Princes Highway. To Orbost, in north-east Gippsland, with its 'rushing river', where they spent their first overnight stop, the highway was sealed, but from there on the road was little better than a narrow, potholed dirt trail. From Orbost to Eden, across the New South Wales/Victorian border, a distance of nearly 200 kilometres, there was little human habitation. The forest enveloped them in darkness, the gums so tall and impenetrable that sunlight rarely struck the surface of the road. The few towns along the way seemed to have a tenuous existence, little more than small frontier settlements in the wilderness. At Cann River, smoke from the local sawmill filled the sky, the ash falling on the road like black confetti. Reaching Eden, in southern New South Wales, Clark saw the Australian coastline that James Cook had first encountered in April 1770, when, sailing in the *Endeavour* from New Zealand, he reached the east coast at Point Hicks and continued north to Botany Bay, naming mountains, bays and rivers on behalf of King George III along the way, the smoke from the distant camp fires of the Aborigines trailing in the salt air behind him.

On the second day, they reached Bega, only 30 kilometres south of Wapengo, where, eighteen years later, they would purchase 400 acres of prime coastal land. The smell of cow manure was a constant companion, the herds on the highway causing them to stop frequently. Creeks and rivers, clogged with soil and sand, the vegetation cleared right down to their banks, wound their way through the green pastures of the Bega Valley. The names of the small towns around them—Pambula, Merimbula, Wolumla—were testament to the Aboriginal history Clark had yet to contemplate. As they turned off the Princes Highway and headed up Brown Mountain to the Monaro, he talked with Dymphna about his plans for writing a history of Australia while the children squabbled in the back seat. What kind of a life could they build there? Were they leaving civilisation behind them? The climb up the mountain was steep: 10 kilometres of winding, slippery, dirt road lined with tall tree ferns and majestic mountain grey gums, some soaring up to thirty metres high. Occasionally, the road detoured around giant gums, their trunks immovable, like the pillars of a stone temple. Frequently shrouded in mist, the route could be dangerous even in the height of summer.

There was little margin for error. The Austin, forced to stop several times due to overheating, struggled to the top.

Up on the Monaro, between Nimmitabel (with its mock-Tudor pub) and Cooma, little more than 30 kilometres away, the land suddenly stretched out into dry grassy plains, which ran all the way to the foot of the Snowy Mountains on the western horizon. To the east, in the distance, they could see the peaks of the Great Dividing Range. After the intensity of the mountain forests, the light seemed harsh. Out on the plain, a train cut its way across the lunar landscape. As the Clarks drove on, lines of roughly hewn telegraph poles followed the course of the road, dwarfing the few white-sallee gums that stood bent and twisted by the wind. In the late afternoon light, the whole scene exuded a stark, alluring loneliness. To the west, the grasslands were relieved only by small mesa-like obtrusions jutting gently above the plains, having long ago inspired the local Aboriginal people, the Ngarigo, to name their country Monaro—'like a woman's breast'.

Leaving Cooma the next morning, and driving the last 100 kilometres of the Snowy Mountains Highway to Canberra, they finally returned to a sealed surface. In the towns along the way, small wooden churches and old colonial pubs skirted the road, and behind them fields of straw-coloured grass ran down to railway sidings and tiny clusters of bleached weatherboards, peeling in the sun; beyond, dirt driveways lined with pine trees climbed to bare hill-tops where homesteads once stood. Every structure the early settlers built on the Monaro appeared transient, every building ancient and worn, much like the land itself. On the approach to Canberra in the mid-afternoon, waves of heat shimmered above the tar. Here and there, patches of the road were burnished blood-red, the crushed, carrion-picked carcasses of kangaroos strewn along the roadside.[1]

As Clark began the descent into Canberra with his family, the sense of starting life over again overwhelmed him. Dymphna felt a mixture of excitement and apprehension. Like the thousands of newly planted deciduous trees, everything they saw around them was in a state of formation. After Melbourne, nothing seemed settled; there was only this vast open plain. The so-called 'national capital', ringed by an 'amphitheatre of hills' covered in scribbly gum and stringybark, was a city in waiting; a parliament house here, a war memorial there, and across the wooden bridge that straddled the Molonglo River a series of white colonnaded buildings that went by the anodyne name of 'Civic'. Sheep kept the grass low. The sky above was an eternal cobalt blue, the light bright and harsh, the space allotted to the future city cavernous. The sound of the birdlife, not always song-like, was louder than the din of human traffic. There were more streetlights than houses. Residents joked that at night Canberra was 'the best illuminated paddock in the world'.

After a protracted debate, the federal government had finally decided on Canberra as the nation's capital in 1908. Sydney and Melbourne were both determined to oppose the choice of a coastal site, largely to avoid the development of a rival port city, while the mantra of 'developing the inland' worked in Canberra's favour. Forty years later, the city's population was just over 19,000. Viewed from the air in 1949, it was little more than two hubs of fledgling settlement: on the north side, Civic and the recently built suburb of Reid, the Canberra University College, and the 'sheds' and 'cottages' on the Australian National University site at Acton; and on the south side, Parliament House and Manuka. Elsewhere, dirt roads crisscrossed the land-scape, the first signs of the development to come. With the war, construction had almost come to a halt, with funds, labour, materials and housing in short supply. Depression and war had postponed the transfer of federal government departments from Melbourne and slowed the development of the city. When the war ended, the population grew quickly. In 1950, more than two thousand families waited for housing. In the meantime, hastily erected temporary accommodation filled the gap. In the circumstances, Clark was lucky to find a house not far from the university, at 41 Froggatt Street, Turner, the house of Jim Hill, a friend who worked in External Affairs and had just been posted to London. As the Austin 16 parked in the drive, there was no curious cast of neighbours there to greet them. At first sight, they had arrived in a place much like the one they had left behind: a house on a bush block surrounded by 'vacant land'. Froggatt Street lay just before the pine-break. Beyond the pines and Macarthur Avenue, there was 'nothing'; barely a few hundred metres from their front door, Canberra came to an end.

The Clarks, Todd Street, O'Connor, 1950

Nine months later, Hill was recalled by External Affairs and the Clarks were forced to move out. Luckily, they found a house nearby, at 4 Todd Street, O'Connor. To cope with the housing shortage, the authorities moved more than 200 houses from the Tocumwal air-force base in New South Wales to Canberra. These simple, three-bedroom timber houses arrived en masse, creating instant neighbourhoods overnight. Near the Clarks lived the King family, with their eleven children. Sebastian and Katerina remembered their years at Todd Street fondly; with the King children they organised 'The Todd Street Olympics'. They were also allowed to roam: 'we used to wander all over Black Mountain, Mount Ainslie and so on, by ourselves,' Katerina recalled. 'We had a lot of freedom.' Like Clark's years at Phillip Island in the 1920s, theirs was a bush childhood. While Clark cycled the 2 kilometres to university most mornings, Dymphna tried to come to terms with her new environment. 'Shopping was extremely primitive'—tired with making do, many people drove the 80 kilometres to Goulburn for their supplies. Fruit and vegetables were of 'poor quality' and clothes were 'few and far between'. She washed the family's laundry in a copper and trough and relied on an old Bega wood stove for cooking. Years later, her memory of Todd Street was still vivid.

An Eye for Eternity

There were no drives. There were no paths. [When it rained] it was very often just a sea of mud, but by degrees the government put in two strips of concrete along the drive and a couple of garden paths near the back door and to the front porch. And every time they put in an improvement like that they added sixpence or so to the rent, so the rent rose by degrees over the three years we were there, from, I think 37/6 a week to in all two guineas a week but for that we got an electric stove, to supplement the old Bega fuel stove we had in the kitchen, and an electric bath heater and these concrete strips ... the legend was, before we ever came to Canberra, that in Canberra you were put into a house in a street and everybody in that street had the same salary... Well, Todd Street certainly gave you the lie to that—absolutely. It was a really good mix.[2]

In 1996, Dymphna insisted that she had not found Canberra 'desolate' in the early 1950s, yet both Axel and Katerina thought their parents felt 'the emptiness' of Canberra keenly. For most who came from Melbourne, Sydney, or Europe after the war, Canberra was a bewildering place. Immediately after the war, Clark's friend Gwen Taylor left her flat in Exhibition Street, Melbourne, to work in Nugget Coombs's Department of Postwar Reconstruction in Canberra. She encountered a tiny outpost run as the private fiefdom of the city administrator, who also decided the bus timetable. At first, she recoiled in horror: 'there was not one restaurant in Canberra, and only one fruit shop where you could get bacon and eggs at 6 pm. Everyone ate at home.' Since 1929, few shops had been built in the city. Five hotels serviced the entire population. Publicans struggled to cope with the six o'clock swill. Women were banned from drinking in public bars, which in the late afternoons were packed with a rising sea of sloshed, carousing men. In the *Canberra Times*, drinking conditions were described as 'deplorable'; barmen regularly complained of physical 'harassment' when they refused men drinks at 6 pm closing.

Anne Gollan, who arrived in Canberra 1951, felt 'suffocated' by the city's smallness ('every one knew everybody else'), and stifled by a public service culture in which women were treated as second-class citizens, forced to resign if they fell pregnant. She also detected a sense of insecurity permeating the entire social fabric: 'I was struck by the fact that Canberrans would always ask me what I *thought* of Canberra?' The itinerant population resembled a shipload of colonists that had suddenly disembarked to begin the task of settlement anew. Everyone was from somewhere else, either telling one another the story of their arrival or dreaming of their imminent departure. Adelaide-born Walter Crocker, foundation professor of International Relations at the ANU, who spent much of his early career in the British Colonial Service, initially declared Canberra 'better than the South of France', 'better than Arizona' and 'better than Morocco'. Within three years, Crocker had flown his nirvana, contemptuous of what he described as 'the cult of excessive social security, of bets & beer and all that'.

Bob Hawke, who arrived in 1956 to complete an MA at the ANU before taking up a position with the ACTU in 1958, shared a flat close by with his wife Hazel. In the adjoining unit were Peter and Verna Coleman. Hawke found Canberra 'incestuous but exciting', whiling away his spare time in the public gallery at Parliament House, watching Menzies and Evatt trade blows over the Suez Crisis. Verna Coleman found the city formal: 'if you weren't in the diplomatic cadets you didn't matter', she said. Reactions to the city varied enormously. Some found the concentration of professionals, politicians and scholars 'exhilarating', and for all those who were terrified by the city's open spaces, there were just as many who felt liberated by the proximity of the bush. But one thing seemed undeniable: there was an inescapable sense of being 'isolated from the world beyond', of living on the thin line of an imported, frontier civilisation, surrounded by the indifference of nature.

Poet Bob Brissenden, a colleague of Clark's at Canberra University College in the 1950s, saw the comic side of Canberra, a seat of federal government that demanded the performance of starched academic, military and political protocols in the middle of the bush: 'within this sparsely settled and desolate territory,' he wrote, 'strange tribal rituals were carried out with grave punctilio and an obsessive concern for the formalities of dress and precedence … diplomats and bemused local residents lurched from one dreary cocktail party to the next.' In the midst of the oppressive, baking, dry heat of Canberra summers, every blowfly buzzing in the ear of polite society seemed to ask the question: who in their right mind would build a national capital in the middle of a sheep paddock? Even today, the collision of bush and society can still appear incongruous. Driving into Canberra from the south, along Mugga Way, visitors pass from barren scrubland to the manicured lawns and smooth pavements of Red Hill in less than a few hundred metres. Half-starved kangaroos one minute, Manuka matrons the next. There is no time to adjust the eye; no hiding the fact that you are living in an invented city, a model capital, rather than an organic capital.[3]

Manning Clark would spend the next forty years in Canberra. Towards the end of his life, he learnt to forget his earlier misgivings—the city's lack of 'refinement', the shallowness of its spiritual life, and the burgeoning 'rash' of suburbia. He spoke only of the city's 'beautiful natural setting' and its nearby hills and rivers, places like the Cotter Dam and the banks of the Murrumbidgee, to which he would escape, like 'a pilgrim to the holy waters', and be 'washed clean'. Contrasting Canberra's natural beauty with the 'corruption', 'greed' and 'smugness' of Melbourne, he dismissed all criticisms of Canberra as a reflection of the critics' lack of sensitivity and imagination. It was not Canberra that was dull but its detractors. As early as the 1950s, he claimed that 'Canberra was more intellectually interesting than Melbourne'. This was the memory of an elderly man who knew he would never again live in a different city, praising his place of residence as an Arcadia. But the younger man held no such illusions. As soon as he arrived in Canberra in early 1950, he plotted to return to Melbourne.[4]

Teaching a handful of diplomatic cadets in the college's makeshift rooms in West Row, Civic, he struggled to find the same satisfaction he had gained from teaching Australian History at Melbourne. He found the students smug and distant, interested more in their future career paths than in history for its own sake. From the first class he took, he was convinced they were contemptuous of their work. In 1952, when the College moved to the 'more spacious' rooms of an old builders' hostel in Childers Street, Clark revelled in the Common Room discussions he shared with other foundation professors such as AD Hope, Fin Crisp and Heinz Arndt, and the impromptu parties that flowed constantly from one academic's house or makeshift embassy to the next. Together with Dymphna, he threw himself into

Canberra's nascent dramatic arts scene, writing reviews of Canberra Repertory productions for the *Bulletin* in exchange for free tickets to the next production. When he needed more earthy entertainment, he drank at the Civic Hotel, only a short walk away. There, one evening, he was rescued from a drunken stupor by Bob Hawke, a 'good Samaritan' who picked Clark up out of the gutter and drove him home, only to 'cop an earful' from Dymphna for leading him astray. In Hawke's eyes, when Clark was on a binge, 'there was something pathetic about him'.

For all Clark's frantic social activity, he remained shocked by Canberra's 'microscopic scale'. As the plans for the national research university emerged, he became increasingly concerned about the institution's 'elitist' direction, worried that he would soon be surrounded not by cultivated men with a broad education but by men 'who spent their time teasing formulas and arid generalisations out of the figures produced by the Commonwealth Bureau of Statistics'. When he wrote to Max Crawford, he sounded like a long-lost son, cajoling him, 'desperately anxious' and 'so vitally interested' to know when he could secure his return to Melbourne and continue his 'teaching of Australian history'.[5]

In 1951, a few days before Christmas, Clark was in Canberra Hospital, seriously ill with rheumatic fever. He suffered weeks of high fever, severe pain and stiffening joints before a fortnight of cortisone injections restored his health. After his Melbourne GP, Clive Fitts, read him 'the riot act', he threw away his pipe and tins of Benson and Hedges 50s, vowed to give up drinking and retreated for a month's convalescence to Broadleaf Park, Tumbarumba, the property of an old school friend, David Rayburn Brown, in the foothills of the Snowy Mountains. He drove all the way, stopping off to buy a packet of Minties at Gundagai and picking up four young hitchhikers at Batlow, before arriving to begin four weeks of hot baths, 'sleep-ins' and 'long breakfasts'.

Forced to rest, he saw the path he had to take, telling Dymphna in March 1952 that he would 'finish' teaching the diplomatic cadets at the end of the year and return immediately to Melbourne as a senior lecturer, even if it meant a drop in salary. He would have a builder extend their house at Croydon and would look forward to years of 'working' with her 'on Australiana'. He had heard from Crawford of a possible vacancy, and with good sales and glowing reviews for the first volume of his *Select Documents*, published in 1950, he felt he would walk into his former position, even boasting to Dymphna that the only obstacle he needed to overcome was Crawford's and Kathleen Fitzpatrick's fear of having him 'in a subordinate capacity'. In the wake of his illness, his letters home lurched from over-confident declarations of his own superiority to bitter denunciations of Melbourne intellectuals— 'those hard cruel people'. One moment he was complaining to Crawford of Canberra's provincialism, almost begging to return; the next minute, writing to his family, he portrayed the Melbourne History Department as a nest of vipers unworthy of his prodigious talents. Although the vacancy Crawford mentioned never materialised, Clark remained convulsed by his love–hate attitude to the university that had given him succour.[6]

In February 1953, after winning a scholarship, Sebastian started secondary school as a boarder at Melbourne Grammar, sent by the man who later told his sons how much he had 'hated' the school. Clark argued with Dymphna over the decision. There were 'perfectly good schools in Canberra', she said, and having just moved from Melbourne, she was reluctant to see her eldest son leave home at only thirteen years of age. What's more, she doubted they could afford the financial outlay. As it was, they struggled to make ends meet on Clark's income, despite the royalties that had come their way from the sale of 1000 copies of *Select Documents*. For Sebastian, the decision had 'unfortunate consequences' ('in retrospect I don't think it was a good thing ... but I was very happy to go'). The disagreement over his schooling affected not only his parents' relationship but also his relationship with his mother.

> One of the simple reasons that it wasn't good was because I can remember my mother saying ... that because of having been to boarding school she felt that she lost us ... she definitely said that to me ... it had taken away something in the relationship between her and me and I'm sure she would say the same about my brothers.[7]

Clark wanted Sebastian at Melbourne Grammar regardless of where the family lived. His eldest son would walk in his footsteps, be shaped by the same forces and carry the same imprint on his soul. This would be his first step in fulfilling his father's expectations and creating a family tradition.

In the early 1950s, as Sebastian began his first years as a boarder, Clark travelled to Melbourne frequently. Canberra University College was still administered by Melbourne University. Clark made the journey to finalise student results and course outlines and to continue his research at Melbourne Public Library. Despite all his reservations about the city, it was still his spiritual home. Melbourne and Phillip Island held the key to his childhood, which he was now beginning to relive in his mind. He thought of buying a block of land on the island. 'I feel I belong there,' he told Dymphna. Since arriving in Canberra, he had enjoyed his short forays into the Brindabellas and his fishing trips to the Murrumbidgee, just as he took pleasure from his excursions in the country around Tumbarumba, lying 'in front of a camp fire for hours in the eerie mountain ash country', yarning 'while the moon rose like a silver ball over the dark outlines of the hills'. But his sense of belonging to Canberra would take decades to evolve.

Although he could not see it at the time, his arrival there dovetailed perfectly with his own ambitions. The city was an experiment in creating a national culture, and Clark was about to embark on a parallel journey: to write the nation's history, each mammoth volume another pillar in the edifice of Australian identity. Living in Canberra would give him proximity to the seat of commonwealth power, the press gallery and national institutions. Some thought that by leaving Melbourne, Clark had left 'the centre of things'; but Canberra, being such a small national capital, meant that when writers and intellectuals visited from overseas, as Bertrand Russell did in 1950, he was more likely to meet them. Unlike Melbourne, Canberra was a city in which Clark had the space and freedom not only to write but to build his own empire. There was no one 'lording' it over him. The city's provincialism was his point of opportunity.[8]

Entering his forties, Clark belonged to neither Melbourne nor Canberra. Wherever he was, he longed for somewhere else. After recovering from rheumatic fever, he joked that he wanted to 'resume' his 'role as M. Clark', and Melbourne was the stage where 'M. Clark' had performed most regularly, usually to wild applause. Visiting Melbourne in the early 1950s, he was

Clark about to board his daily transport to the ANU, Canberra, 1950

unhappy; returning to Canberra, he dreamt of a return to Melbourne. He preferred exile to belonging. And for the writer he yearned to be, exile was a far more productive state of mind. Alone, riding the ferry across Sydney Harbour on a humid, overcast spring day in 1953, he looked out across the 'leaden' water and thought of Kenneth Slessor's 'Five Bells', reciting the last lines of the poem over and over in his mind:

> [I] tried to hear your voice, but all I heard
> Was a boat's whistle, and the scraping squeal
> Of seabirds' voices far away, and bells,
> Five bells. Five bells coldly ringing out.
> Five bells.

11: TASMANIA CIRCLE, FORREST

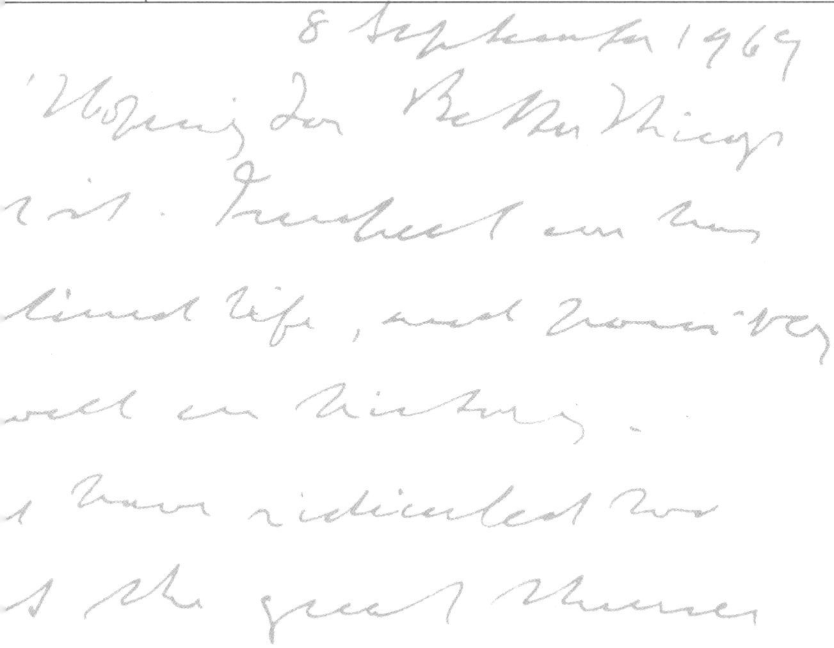
8 September 1969

From the southern end of the street, the road climbs gently. Looking east, glimpses of inner Canberra, stretched out on the plain below, appear through stands of birch and oak. The houses are stately, their gardens and the nearby parkland spacious. On the northern side of the hill, as the road starts its downward slope, the driveway to Manning Clark House begins its steep descent under the blue-grey leaves of a magnificent Argyle apple.

Walking down the drive, the house seems refreshingly unpretentious compared with the cold façades of the modern concrete-and-glass temples nearby. Situated on two-thirds of an acre, it nestles into the southern end of the block and looks out on an extensive garden that falls away gradually to the north. At the bottom of the drive, underneath a timber pergola covered in the fan-like leaves of an ornamental grape vine, the glass-framed corridor that divides the house is the first thing to catch your eye. Even before you set foot inside, you see through into the living room on the eastern side of the house and through the glass door, to the north-facing sitting area outside. There were few places for the Clarks to hide.

Inside, light floods the foyer, intensifying the rich reds of the Persian rugs on the pine floorboards. The leaves of a Japanese maple in the garden outside brush up against a wall-sized glass window in the living room.

307

(top) Front entrance, Tasmania Circle, Canberra
(bottom) Living room, Tasmania Circle, Canberra

There, in the corner, the piano Clark learnt to play in his fifties, a gift from Dymphna's Swedish grandmother, stands next to the antique Flemish furniture inherited from Anna and Augustin. The overwhelming impression is one of earthy simplicity. In the dining room, a long trestle table with bench seating sits in front of shelves of classical vinyl records that Clark loved to play at ear-splitting volume. On the kitchen wall, his old fishing hat; on the bookshelves nearby, his books and publications concerning his life and work. If there is something unsettling, it is the same quality that can be found in many homes of cultural figures that have been preserved as monuments to their memory. Time stands still. Everything is as it was. The paintings hung on the wall, the photographs of the children on the sideboard, the cutlery and crockery in the kitchen; everything remains the property of the past.

In 1953, the Clarks' choice of Tasmania Circle as the site of their future home was entirely accidental. At first, Clark wanted to build a house 'facing the blue hills behind Canberra'. He bought a three-acre block of land at the foot of Red Hill but immediately worried that it was completely 'naked', marooned 'on the outskirts' of the city, near an 'ugly rash of suburbia'. The idea of building was attractive because it offered him the opportunity to defy 'the all pervading uniformity' he saw around him. When Sir John Eccles arrived in Canberra in 1952 to head the new John Curtin School of Medical Science at the Australian National University, he insisted that the Department of the Interior find him a block of land commensurate with his standing. For his nine children, Eccles needed room for 'a square dance lawn, a swimming pool and a tennis court'. A department official asked Clark and Dymphna if they would exchange their three-acre block at Red Hill for the much smaller one close by. They took one look at Tasmania Circle and agreed. In early 1952, to cheer Clark up after his rheumatic fever, Dymphna suggested they engage Robin Boyd to design a house for the new site. She had long admired the simplicity of Boyd's modernist buildings, which featured regularly in the *Age* when they lived at Croydon. Through Brian Fitzpatrick, Clark had known Boyd as the brother of artist Arthur and novelist Martin, a 'fastidious, thin-lipped' man who despised beer drinking, mateship and the crudity of so much that passed for culture in Australia.[1]

Canberra in the 1950s was a *tabula rasa* for architects keen to experiment. In April 1952, Boyd responded enthusiastically to the opportunity to design his first house in the city. The Bauhaus school of the 1920s and the 'binuclear house' designed in the 1940s by Hungarian born architect Marcel Breuer had heavily influenced him. The core idea of Boyd's plan for Tasmania Circle—living and sleeping wings separated by an entrance hall—drew on Breuer's concept of divided 'cells'. As he finalised the design, Boyd consulted Dymphna on the finer details of interior design. He wanted 'dark soft red' for the living room ceiling; she settled for 'galah pink'. He wanted as much light as possible; she worried about the 10-square-metre glass window in the living room, the bagged walls and the outside brick walls which she thought would need to be painted often. Boyd reassured her: 'bricks look good when the paint is peeling off'. His dealings with Clark were more cavalier. Rushing to catch a plane back to Melbourne, Clark called out to him as he walked onto the tarmac at Canberra airport. 'Is the house going to be single storey with my study in the basement?' After a moment's thought, Boyd shouted back: 'Single storey with the study upstairs.'[2]

In February 1953, Clark and Dymphna had word that their house in Croydon had sold for 4500 pounds. They made it clear to Boyd that they could only afford the 'cheapest house possible'. The total cost of building was 7300 pounds. The budget was tight—so tight that, as construction began, Clark was hunting around for more cash. When he heard unexpectedly that some of his father's shares had been sold, he wrote to his brother Russell, executor of Charles's estate, demanding to be paid a percentage of his portion immediately. Russell had just led a memorial service at Mentone on the second anniversary of Charles's death.

Dear Russell

It was very good of you to send me so promptly a description of the service at Mentone. I was really very upset at not being there … I can well understand your exhaustion at the end of the service. I am sure, however, that you would be deeply satisfied that you had done it for Dad.

Now for some sordid business. I want you to pay 15 pounds immediately from Dad's estate into <u>my</u> account at the University branch of the National

Bank. I will tell you why when I see you. Do not panic. You do not have to go to university to do so. Just post it to the manager, National Bank, University of Melbourne. Deduct this from my amount [of the shares]. Please do it immediately. I need the [money] to bridge the gap for the new house, I need it <u>immediately</u> … the sale of [the shares] is a great godsend to me. I am in no hurry for the rest. <u>Do not</u> refer to this in correspondence to me. Do it now. Do it now.[3]

If anyone was panicking, it was not Russell. He did as he was told, and paid the money into Clark's account. With extra income from Dymphna, who taught English part time to recently arrived migrants, Clark's royalties from Angus & Robertson and a substantial bank loan, the couple managed to scrape together the 7000 pounds. Boyd agreed to take on the job in April 1953 and by the end of the month construction was underway. Like Boyd, Jack Dorman, the Italian footballer Clark employed to build the house, was trying out a few ideas, never having built a house before. But his rates were competitive. During construction, he fought frequently with Boyd, who came up from Melbourne on at least three occasions. When Boyd was back in Melbourne, the builder clashed with the Canberra-based architect whom Boyd had appointed as supervisor. The only person he managed to get on with was Dymphna, who relied on her Italian to talk through any difficulties. During the six months between commencement and completion, they developed a strong friendship, and she remained in touch with him for the rest of her life. Almost fifty years later, he arrived on her doorstep like the prodigal *pater familias*, bearing flagons of wine from his family's vineyard near Shepparton.

Sebastian was already at Melbourne Grammar in October 1953 when the Clarks moved in to Tasmania Circle. Fortunately, over the course of their family life, there were few periods when all six children lived at home. The four-bedroom home was barely big enough for four children. It was also the second time in seven years that they had moved into a newly built house. They were starting over yet again, and so much of their first years in Forrest reminded them of their time at Croydon: the bush setting, the gravel road, bread delivered by horse and cart, the manure collected for fertiliser, working weekends in the garden, cutting the lawn with a push mower, establishing a vegetable patch, building a chook shed (Clark's architectural offering) and ensuring that the children had a cricket pitch and room enough for badminton and tennis. Rene McGuire, a Tory 'homemaker' who lived with her civil engineer husband, Reg, in the mock-Tudor mansion next door, struggled to match her neighbours' backyard peasant farm with Clark's professorial standing. Canberra's inner suburbs, built largely by a migrant force in the 1950s and 1960s, were more stratified than most cities. While there were exceptions, the size and position of 'a man's house' depended on his position in government, academic life or the public service. In Canberra, it was impossible to escape being themed: wooden cottages for the artisans, modest brick houses for middle-income earners, and architect-designed houses and large estates for the elite. Clark had claimed a place on the upper rung of the ladder, his simple, 'grey painted white-trimmed house' set in a suburb inhabited by judges, academics, politicians, journalists, foreign diplomats and top-ranking public servants, the streets nearby named after many of the explorers he would soon write about—Flinders, Dampier, La Perouse and Cook.[4]

Clark and Dymphna were to live out their lives together at Tasmania Circle, Dymphna mostly in the kitchen or garden, Clark upstairs in the study, writing *A History of Australia*. It was here that they were to create a milieu of their own—'the Clarks'—a family renowned for its hospitality, quality of conversation and irrepressible *joie de vivre*. And it was here that they would lay down the small rituals of their daily lives, Clark writing in the mornings and teaching in the afternoons, Dymphna bringing him tea mid-morning and doing whatever was necessary to hold everything else together. The most important things that they achieved, both as individuals and as a couple, were achieved within the walls of Robin Boyd's light-filled house. It became their one true home.

Eighteen months after they moved in, the *Sydney Morning Herald* despatched a journalist to write a feature article on the house for its lifestyle section. The result was a full-page spread replete with crowning clichés— 'An ivory tower for a Professor (absent-minded or not), a home for a family'—and detailed descriptions of design features, colour schemes and the layout of every room, especially the living area, which was described as ideal

Surrounded by his family

for 'the entertaining that members of the Faculty are frequently called upon to do'. The house was photographed from the north, its simplicity and modesty accentuated by the starkness of its surroundings, Clark's study soaring above it all like a solitary watchtower. Before he left, the journalist asked for a photograph of the whole family in the study. The result—'Professor Manning Clark receives his family'—was an image of rare clarity. Dymphna, in her late thirties, reclines on the back of Clark's desk, her arm around thirteen-year-old Katerina, while Sebastian, fifteen, stands to her right behind Andrew, six; and Axel, eleven, closest to his father.[5]

Clark looks settled, his books in the shelves behind him, copies of the first volume of *Select Documents* on his desk, his children at his side. Yet, over the next two years, he would come close to giving it all away. He would try hard to secure a Chair in History at Melbourne University and be prepared to leave his new Canberra home. He would almost lose Dymphna and his family. At times, he doubted if he would ever be capable of writing a major work. Approaching forty, his love for Dymphna and his determination to write Australia's history were about to be tested.

12: FIVE BELLS

Manning and Dymphna,
Canberra, early 1950s

Before the National Library opened in Canberra in 1968, part of the collection was located in the basement of Parliament House. While this was vastly superior to the corrugated iron huts that housed the National Archives down on the shores of Lake Burley Griffin, it was rudimentary compared with the grand old libraries of Melbourne and Sydney. Space was limited, and there were few creature comforts, not even a cafeteria. There was also an endearing informality about the whole building: politicians came downstairs to the reading rooms in need of respite from the debates in the House, readers casually strolled upstairs in need of stimulating theatre. There was no security. Dymphna and Clark wandered in and out of the visitors' gallery at will, recalling the 'tiny and malicious' Billy Hughes; the 'dignified' speaker, Archie Cameron; and the 'lumbering' Menzies, who 'looked down on everything he surveyed'. They had been regular visitors since the late 1940s, when Clark began to collect material for his first volume of documents.

Until he arrived in Canberra, Clark's only research assistant was Dymphna. Even after his professorial position provided him with a succession of research assistants, usually attractive young women, she was his most important collaborator in every stage of production—research, writing, editing, proofreading and rapturous reception of the finished product. She was the only one who could be honest with him: 'this is too scattered', this 'a bit wooden', this 'not so good'. Travelling up from Melbourne, she had always felt guilty when she left the children with her parents at Mont Albert. In Canberra, working in the library with Clark, she sometimes felt shunned. 'Occasionally Manning would be invited by a member to lunch but not I, and of course there was not so much as a crust of bread available, there was no cafeteria for miles, sometimes I had no lunch.' Wives were not fit for certain company. This was her recollection after Clark had died. In her old age, she often seemed eager to cast herself in the role of the long-suffering wife. But her pleas were also understandable. She wanted others to know what it was like to play the supporting role to the 'great man'.

Dymphna would later describe a vivid image of one particular day spent with Clark in the National Library. Working on original documents, her table was separated from his desk by a glass door. 'If I found something interesting,' she said, 'I'd knock on the glass, hold it up, and if it interested him I would have to transcribe it. That was before the days of photocopiers, and I would transcribe it [there and then] by hand.' She felt they were like Pyramus and Thisbe, the two lovers in Ovid's *Metamorphoses*, whose parents refused them permission to marry and who received each other's messages through the chink in the wall that separated their houses. For much of her married life in the mid-1950s, Dymphna felt herself like Thisbe, struggling to break down the wall that separated her from the man she loved.[1]

In early 1954, shortly after moving in to Tasmania Circle, Dymphna fell ill with rheumatic fever, the condition that had afflicted Clark just over two years before. She thought she had managed to escape the illness, but a number of factors had combined to run her down. In February, she played 'hostess' to a house full of scholars from interstate who had come to Canberra for a conference, which Clark had helped to organise. The city was also in a state of heightened readiness for the visit of the young Queen Elizabeth II. Public buildings had been subjected to aerial bombardment with DDT to ensure that not one fly or mosquito marked Her Majesty's milk-white skin. The children wanted 'to see the Queen'. If Dymphna wasn't entertaining the children, she was entertaining her guests; then there was the added responsibility of moving into a new house. Sebastian was also deeply unhappy at Melbourne Grammar. Late in her life, Dymphna gave a detailed account of her responsibilities during the conference.

After breakfast they would all disappear and I had no car because the car had taken them all over to the conference so I had to clean up the whole place in the heat of course; clean up the breakfast, and then set out on a bicycle with a rucksack to go and buy food for them for the rest of the day, bring it all home on my bike, tidy up, get the lunch ready, and in the afternoon once again they'd all clear out and I'd have to do it all over again and they'd all come back for dinner. Anyway, I was feeling pretty weary and there was a knock on the door about half past three on a very hot afternoon and I went to the door and there was this most extraordinary figure. She was the daughter of Dr. Fritz Loewe, a refugee from the Nazis whom our family had known very well. She was about 18, just started at university and chasing some philosopher I think, but she had hitchhiked from Melbourne to come to this conference. She was wearing boots, huge boots, she had a waist of about 18 inches with a great white belt pulled round her and red hair. She was quite a spectacular sight ... I don't think she had walked very far in those boots, she was spectacular enough to get lifts all the way. Before long, Manning came back in the car and I could see him stagger up from the garage, back bowed, and he came in and said: 'I'm absolutely done.' 'Well,' I said, 'that's too bad but I guarantee you in 20 minutes you won't be done.' 'What do you mean?' [he asked.] 'Well you just wait,' I said. 'I'll make tea and in 20 minutes you'll be feeling fine.' And of course, before 20 minutes were out Ruth Loewe had appeared from her shower, resplendent in clean clothes ... and Manning was sparking on all 16 cylinders during the afternoon tea.

Both Katerina and Axel spoke later of the 'terrible drudgery' of Dymphna's life during these years. Before the inheritance from her parents made life easier in the 1960s, she did virtually everything by herself. Isolated from her family, and living in a 'senior kind of suburb' like Forrest, where 'there was absolutely no exchange over the back fence', she had no 'support system'. In

1952, when Clark was hospitalised, and with no one to mind the children, she was sometimes forced to leave them at home, cycling to the hospital and back as quickly as she could. When Clark was ill, she got by, but when the tables were turned Clark was unable to cope alone.[2]

Once the fever hit, Dymphna was bedridden. By early March 1954 she was in hospital. For seven weeks, Clark hired domestic help—an ebullient woman from Kiev who came for four hours each weekday afternoon and continued to help out occasionally after Dymphna returned home. In April, when she finally recovered, there was no possibility of convalescing at the rural retreat Clark had enjoyed two years earlier. He was already writing to Max Crawford that he desperately needed the second volume of his *Select Documents* to come out 'to help pay for the catastrophic costs of Dymphna's illness'. She came home immediately to Clark and the children, and what she later described as her 'occupational therapy'—the proofreading of Clark's manuscript. During her absence, Clark had been consumed with his own troubles. He complained of having 'no sap' in his system: '[I] am not in love—with the plan [for my writing], with a person, or with my job, so [I] am bored—which is curable—but [I] am also lonely—and not taken up with any of the deeper subjects or issues.' Without the feeling of being in love, he found writing difficult. He was also increasingly seeing marriage as an instrument of oppression.[3]

Reviewing two books on marriage for the *Age* in May 1954, he appeared to be speaking for himself in his opening paragraph. 'Human beings seem to enjoy torturing one another. One of the ways of doing this is by creating an ideal standard which only very few can achieve, and then punishing each other for not attaining the ideal. One simple example of such an ideal is monogamous and indissoluble marriage.' On campus, he encountered ideas of free love and 'uninhibited sexual behaviour'. Many of his closest friends and colleagues, such as Don Baker and Russel Ward, were openly having sex outside marriage. Even chance encounters brought up the subject. Driving from Canberra to Wollongong along the narrow, winding, Macquarie Pass with the rain 'pelting down', he picked up a hitchhiker, 'an old-age pensioner puffing and wheezing on his pipe'. When the subject turned to sex and religion, the old man asked Clark whether he remembered the scene between

Christ and the woman at the well, then exclaimed wryly: 'they shagged too, then—didn't they!'[4]

In Clark's early twenties, during the first years of his courtship with Dymphna in Germany, he tried to possess her, terrified by the thought that she might go out with another man or make love with someone else. Now, after fifteen years of marriage and with four children, he felt restricted. There was never enough sex; that much he had discovered long ago. But it was more than that. In exchange for security, social respectability and the pleasures of family life, did he have to give up the possibility of ever knowing the pleasure of loving another woman? Did he now have to say to himself that he belonged totally to Dymphna, that he would never again experience the rush of Eros that came with the first moments of a new love? He longed for a sexual relationship that was untainted by the politics of domesticity. Writing in his diary, he observed with brutal honesty his own marriage as well as the failed marriages of his friends. His observations were potential material for short stories. Soon, they would become a means of fleshing out historical characters. For the moment, he seemed incapable of controlling his fury with Dymphna.

In marriage there are some conversations with one's wife which make one furious—angry—the anger which can only be appeased by tearing some-thing—or shouting—or throwing something against the wall. [As]Axel [Dymphna's brother] once said: 'It makes you feel as though you want to tear them in pieces.'

e.g. He: 'I am going to collect the wood to-morrow.'

She: 'Oh don't bother. I've arranged for a carrier to bring it.'

He: 'What did you do that for?'

She: 'Oh you're always so busy—and haven't got time for the simple things.'

Now, one reason why we feel maddened by it is because we have not got an easy mind on the point. They put their knife into the sorest part of the wound. But, what is worse. This provokes men to anger—Lose their temper—say unkind, cruel things—then have to make amends—promise to get the wood to-morrow—and so twice lose their self-respect.[5]

The constant point-scoring within his marriage, which saw him feel guilty for enjoying 'trivial pleasures' such as 'going to a football game … reading the paper, or having a sleep after the mid-day meal on Sunday', made him feel 'hunted'. At these times, he turned with even more abandonment towards alcohol for relief. When Dymphna called him 'Daddy' and 'bubbled over with happiness', his mind 'blackened over' and he wanted 'to hurt her'. He didn't want her to call him 'Dad'; he wanted her to see him as her lover. He was also plagued by thoughts of his own sinfulness and 'wickedness'. One night in November 1954, he dreamt he 'came across a naked woman':

I asked her why she was crying [and] she said it was because she was expecting a child. I then asked her whether she prayed. She said she did. Then I asked her whether she prayed not to have the child. Again she said she did. So I said: I used to be spiritually sick like you. You should rather rejoice & thank God for the child. Next morning I thought—Well! Well! Sir Harcourt Reilly [a character in TS Eliot's *The Cocktail Party*] has free drinks while he is discussing the spiritual health of his patients. At least in my dreams I go one better, and see them in the nude! I also put my arms around them![6]

Clark's extramarital sexual longings were locked in the chains of the religious dogma he imbibed as a child and which would cause him much pain and anguish throughout his life. The desires of the flesh were evil. They were an example of mankind's baseness. Unless they were kept under control by God's holy sacrament of marriage, men and women risked losing their souls. No amount of reading about the need for sexual liberation could wash these tormenting thoughts from his being.

One of the few things that gave him guilt-free pleasure was seeing his own work in print. In December 1954, he was so keen to hold the second volume of *Select Documents* in his hands that, on the day of its arrival from the printer to Angus & Robertson, he piled the family into the car and dashed to Sydney to take official delivery. When his six complimentary copies arrived in the mail in February 1955, he was ecstatic. 'We are delighted

An Eye for Eternity

with it,' he wrote to George Ferguson, 'and I must thank Angus & Robertson for clothing my imperfect work so attractively. We are all very proud of it.' Dymphna, who had worked so hard collecting, transcribing and editing the book, shared his excitement, writing to friends immediately with the news. Clark asked Ferguson for another six free copies ('the longer you stay in the academic world, the wider become your obligations!'), and sent him a complete list of newspapers, magazines and academic journals in Britain, America and Australia to which Angus & Robertson should send review copies. Later, unwilling to trust Ferguson alone, he wrote personally to the literary editors of major broadsheets in an effort to ensure that the book received the attention he thought it deserved. When Ferguson telegrammed him on 17 February to let him know that the book would be in Melbourne bookshops by the second week of March, he immediately planned a trip to Melbourne. Once there, he rushed headlong into an affair, which was to have serious implications for both the future of his marriage and his career.[7]

One weekend in the winter of 1947, alone with Sebastian and Katerina at Croydon and without a car, Clark asked Pat Gray, who was then lecturing in British history, to drive out from Melbourne to see him. There was a large covering of snow on Mount Donna Buang that he wanted the children to see. He had also had a crush on Gray since VJ Day 1945, when they stood in the quadrangle near the Law building, picking flowers from the camellia trees. Gray drove her Morris Minor out to Croydon and picked up Clark and the children, then drove them out to Mount Donna Buang, where she stood with Clark as Sebastian and Katerina played in the snow. One year later, he said goodbye to her on the steps of the Melbourne Public Library before she left Melbourne to read sociology at Columbia University. To that point they had been friends, although seven years later, he wrote that he first 'fell in love' with Gray that day she walked away in 1948. He would not see or hear from her again until she returned to Melbourne on sabbatical, in the summer of 1955. Then in her early thirties, Gray was highly regarded at Melbourne. Crawford, who knew how gifted she was, had hoped to bring her back from America with the offer of a lectureship but the position eventually went to Clark's old friend at Oxford, AGL Shaw. Gray, who had since moved to London, was strikingly beautiful, a woman who had had several

Pat Gray, circa 1955

affairs with married men before she returned to Melbourne in 1955 and who had already established a relationship with the man she eventually married, the German-born sculptor and printmaker, Erwin Fabian (she would later change her name to Ailsa Fabian).

Gray arrived in Melbourne on holiday, keen to see her family and old friends. Clark arrived in late February, awash with pride on the publication of *Select Documents* and plagued by doubts about his marriage to Dymphna. Within days of seeing Gray, he had fallen for her completely. On 25 February, after drinking at the Curtin Hotel, they walked through the grounds of the Melbourne Cemetery where Clark 'fell in love with her again'. The following morning, they met again, Clark measuring the hours in his diary ('I saw her on Friday from 10 am to 2.15'). On the Saturday he telegrammed. He needed to see her immediately. He could think about nothing else. This was 'the spell' that Clark had longed for. The following weekend, late on the Friday afternoon, one day after his fortieth birthday, he was sitting in the passenger seat next to Gray as she drove out of Melbourne. Gray, who subsequently moved to London, later recalled what happened next.

> I remember setting off with Manning in my mother's Daimler on a Friday afternoon, for our house at Portsea, which was empty, where we spent the weekend. Or rather, didn't quite, because Manning prevailed on me to drive on Saturday all the way from Portsea to Geelong Grammar and then back to Portsea, while I idled in the countryside somewhere near. It seems to me now a severe imposition and also a more gruelling drive than I would willingly undertake, though I don't remember much inner protest at the time. Another anti-romantic feature of the weekend was that Manning made it somewhat public by insisting on visiting his friend John O'Brien with me

An Eye for Eternity

before we set out, and then meeting Creighton Burns [another of his colleagues at Melbourne] when we returned. With Creighton in particular there was the sense of forming an intimate little group bound by an emotional intensity of loyalty, affection and secrecy. I accepted all of this because of Manning's powerful dominating charisma though (I think now) I was old enough to know better.

Clark was keen to let his friends know that he was having an affair. As he boasted to friends in Melbourne afterwards, 'I'm in love with Pat Gray!' Back in Canberra, unaware of the affair, Dymphna sent Clark's research assistant, Ailsa Zainuddin, a copy of *Select Documents*, signing off flippantly: 'Manning celebrated his fortieth birthday with black crepe and wailing last week.' Although Clark talked little to Gray about his marriage, she sensed his loneliness. 'He was quite an intuitive person, an egoist, and he had a great urge to talk about everything, he wanted the truth to come out,' she reflected, but 'of course, if the truth is out things can be made worse'.

When Clark returned to Canberra he immediately told Dymphna of the affair. She was overcome with a mixture of rage and despair; convinced that he 'loathed' her, she threatened to commit suicide. Day and night, she argued with him over the same things that they had argued about beforehand, his drinking and his constant 'baiting' of her in public. She could not bring herself to ask him about the details of the affair and Clark, in any case, was fearful of telling her lest she tried to 'kill herself'. He felt his affection for her 'draining away'. In his first days back home, he did not feel 'sorry or penitent'. Instead, he wondered whether he and Gray would 'suffer' for the 'stolen pleasures'. In his diary, he documented Dymphna's response—she was cold towards him and collapsed into tears—as well as his own reaction—he hated his wife more because she was 'keeping him away from his pleasures'. The mere sight of her stirred his 'guilt' and 'anger', but not his shame.

Even as his marriage threatened to collapse, his writer's eye scoured the emotional fallout, hunting for material that might be useful for the short stories he planned to write. Clark was incapable of living completely within his experience. He was either playing to his audience or sitting in the stalls, watching himself from above, his self-consciousness at once his greatest gift and his greatest affliction.

Some time in the next few days, Dymphna sent the children to stay with friends and left for Sydney, taking a room at the YWCA in Liverpool Street. Before she left the house, she gave Clark an ultimatum. Either he finished the affair with Gray or their marriage was over. As soon as Dymphna was gone, Clark telegrammed Gray, who recalled that Clark asked her to stay with him:

> Dymphna must have heard about the weekend, because the next thing I knew was that she had left Manning and gone to Sydney, and I was summoned by Manning to Canberra, and went. I spent a night in their house (no children there) and a second night at Russel Ward's—a damage limitation exercise of Manning's. Technically speaking, we didn't make love in the house. No doubt Manning was preserving some sense of loyalty to Dymphna. He also made the visit public with the opposite motive to the one he had in Melbourne—taking me to lunch at the University, with the idea that we were bound to be seen together, and that if he didn't make a secret of it the implication would be that it was innocent. I never had any thought of causing a permanent split between Manning and Dymphna, and I returned to Melbourne knowing that sexually at least, it was over.

From this point, Clark directed both Dymphna and Gray to secure the outcome he desired. When he asked Gray to come to Canberra, he was intent on continuing the affair. But in the space of a few days reality soon set in. When she departed for Melbourne, he returned to an empty house. For the first time he faced the real possibility of losing Dymphna, his children and everything that they had built together. Ever since he had fallen in love with her, nearly twenty years earlier, he had been incapable of living without her. As Gray recalled, 'he was appalled at the prospect of her leaving him'. Two weeks of 'stolen pleasure' was beginning to give way to waves of guilt. With the affair with Gray all but over and Dymphna exiled in Sydney, it did not take Clark long to come to a decision. He had to persuade her to return home. He decided that the best way was for Gray and Dymphna to meet.

Over the next few days, Clark was a frequent visitor at Manuka Post Office, where, in a flurry, he sent telegrams to both women. When he telegrammed Dymphna, it was in German or French, occasionally under a Dostoyevsky alias—'Forgive me, I need you … Remember the first line of High Noon ['I do'] and come back to me—Marmeladov'. Meanwhile, he sent another telegram to Gray and asked her to write to Dymphna. Only days earlier he had written to her with 'declarations of eternal love'. Now he wanted Gray to ask Dymphna for forgiveness on his behalf. She demurred.

Two days later, he telegrammed her again with the same request. She had planned to write to Dymphna in her own time, when she was 'calmer' (they had known one another briefly, at Melbourne University). But Clark wanted Gray to write immediately. 'With misgivings,' she did as he asked her to do, explaining to Dymphna that she had never wanted to hurt her or the children. She was honest. She could 'not resist' the affair with Clark, but she was all too aware of the pain that it had caused. She asked Dymphna 'to forgive and accept Manning'. This was the 'only way', she argued, that they could all avoid being 'engulfed in a real tragedy'. Clark had what he wanted. Dymphna was now confronted with both her husband and his lover pleading for her forgiveness. Replying to Gray, Dymphna was philosophical. The seeds of the affair, she said, were written in all three of their personalities long before they met. Over the next two weeks, the triangular correspondence continued in an effort to arrange the meeting between Dymphna and Gray that Clark had first insisted on. In late March, Dymphna finally went to Melbourne. Gray remembered little of the meeting except for her appearance. She was 'run down' and had 'let herself go'. Well before Gray left for London on 19 April, Dymphna and the children had returned to Tasmania Circle. She was pregnant with their fifth child.[8]

For the remainder of the year, Clark could not bring himself to write directly about the fallout. Instead, he turned his eye on the marriages of his colleagues at the ANU, filling his diary with pages of observations on his friends' failing relationships. Coming close on the heels of his marital crisis, many of the entries offer pessimistic generalisations concerning the difficulty of relations between men and women—'the really big thing about … my generation is our confidence that we have solved the problem about human relations—no more war—no more sense of sin—no sense of guilt, psychologists would fix that up, yet we are probably far more miserable than any other generation—especially in our married lives—torturing and tormenting each other.' They also reveal how troubled his feelings were towards women in general. Writing about the wife of one colleague who he believed taunted her husband unnecessarily, he was consumed by rage.

> What is it in her which makes one want to destroy her?—to shout at her— Why does she make one feel murderous—& then, of course, ashamed of feeling like that? Why does she make men feel they want at the same time to murder her, and to fuck the arse off her—and, yes, realise that even after they had done that she would still look at them in the same way—that look which stirred up such terrible thoughts in their minds … I felt maddened by her—just as all men are maddened by women who always wound their husbands—a curious sensation, murderous, as though you wanted to strike her, to shout, to give vent to the most tremendous anger—But … after anger he must ask to be forgiven, and that makes him hate her more.[9]

The same anger Clark felt towards Dymphna was more vehemently expressed when he directed his attention to other women in his diaries. The entries are disturbing because of their barely contained violence, the urge to hurt, silence and conquer women, the image of sex as a means of asserting male dominance, and what appears superficially to be little more than thinly veiled misogyny. Many of the diary entries that follow in the wake of his affair with Pat Gray show him enraged by women who played God's police, curtailed men's freedom or refused to forget men's past transgressions. At the same time he was tormented by his desire for women, which he knew he could not satisfy without giving way to a flood of self-laceration. His rage was an expression of his own frustration and feelings of inadequacy, just as his boasting about the affair reflected his inability to come to terms with his own sexuality. In the short time she shared with him, Pat Gray sensed his discomfort.

> Manning was not at ease with his own sexuality. There was a big gap between moments of passion and how he felt and talked at other times. His

An Eye for Eternity

dominant memory of his sexual encounters, at least extra-marital, seemed to be not of mutual pleasure and shared emotion, but alternated between guilt and triumphant conquest—that drunken boasting. Macho!

Gray looked back on her relationship with Clark from a distance of more than fifty years. The man she remembered was filtered through her subsequent life experience. What the older woman condemned as 'alienating behaviour', the younger woman, seduced by Clark's 'powerful dominating charisma', either did not see or tolerated. In 1955, Gray told Dymphna that her exile from Australia would not be 'voluntary'. Later, she was astonished at what she had written fifty years earlier. 'The suggestion that when I left Australia again in 1955 I was going into involuntary exile is nonsense, although I appear to have written it.' Her visit to Australia, she explained, was never intended to be anything but that—a short stay to see her family. To remember her affair with Clark was to confront aspects of her past self, which she sometimes found difficult to share. ('To talk about Manning is to tell you more sometimes about myself than him'.) She remained in contact with Clark intermittently over the years, both in London when he visited, and in Melbourne, when she lived there with Erwin Fabian and her children from 1962 to 1966.

When Dymphna was with Clark in London, Manning and Gray did not meet, although he continued to make 'surreptitious phone calls'. 'In general', they met as 'affectionate friends with a past of greater closeness', as she later explained. But Gray was let down 'in a painful and unexpected way' after the death of her daughter, Sarah, when Clark refused to 'hear anything' of her loss or 'say anything' in sympathy or understanding. Clark's silence exposed other grievances. She decided to write and tell him of her disappointment 'with his boasting all over Canberra about having had me'. She thought that perhaps, by mentioning it, she might help to 'dissolve the barrier' between them. But he ignored her, replying that he was sorry if she 'still felt bitter'. Yet it was Clark, not Gray, who harboured bitterness. She later discovered what he had said about her marriage: 'I will never recognize Pat Gray's marriage to Erwin Fabian.' Nor, presumably, would he under any circumstances recognise the children from their marriage. Gray could not have known, but Clark's behaviour towards her was similar to the possessiveness he had displayed previously towards Dymphna. If he was not the sole object of affection, he responded petulantly. Despite Clark's pettiness, and her 'mixed feelings' about their brief relationship, Gray had no regrets.

> There was behaviour towards me that I condemn and that was alienating, and scenes that I accept with a sort of astonished awe; a mixture of betrayal and loyalty; but I also feel that it was a privilege and a gift of fortune to have known someone with his enormous range of knowledge, understanding and appreciation of literature, music, people and life, and his gift for (at least temporary) intimacy ... It is somehow pleasant to remember from this all-too-sober distance, that I once enjoyed [this] exhilaration.

Gray never forgot Clark's brilliance and charisma, but she also realised that she would be better off without him. She saw the brief affair with Clark as 'a turning point' in her life. He was the last of 'several dominating high-powered men' who had their own 'flattering but flimsily based notions' about her. 'Intoxicating' as they were, she saw that they were 'no basis for making a life'. She decided to return to London and stay with Erwin Fabian, to have children and consequentially to marry. In her late eighties, she confronted the irony that a few weeks of her life in 1955 were being publicly remembered. Dredged up from 'another country', it seemed both 'distant' and 'shocking'. The story of her affair with Clark allowed her to see what she could never have seen at the time: 'the context of Manning's fury and unhappiness about marriage and his longing for new loves'.[10]

For Dymphna, if she did speak of how Clark's affair had affected her, she did so privately. Her humiliation was public, as many of her friends knew about the affair. When it ended, she was in the early months of pregnancy and she returned to Tasmania Circle uncertain about the future of her marriage. At times, when her domestic burden seemed too much to bear, the memory of the affair rankled. But she was not one to nurture grudges or to brood excessively. And she returned to Clark because she chose to do so, because her life with him was much more than domestic drudgery: it was rewarding and stimulating. The common past they shared, and the family they had created together, mattered too much to her. Traces of her lasting disappointment, however, survived in the stray notes Clark kept in his study. Clark not only recorded his own response to the affair, he occasionally recorded her most cutting remarks, as if compiling the case for his own prosecution. In 1956, he dated a remark from Dymphna, which he later filed in a special folder marked 'letters from my darling Dymphna': 'What hurt most of all: You are able to say with complete conviction what you obviously don't mean—16 May 1956'.

Clark begged her 'not to look back in anger'. This, he said, 'was the story of our marriage'. Yet he was no different. If Dymphna looked back in anger he looked back like the Pharisee in the gospels, pacing the village square eternally pleading for forgiveness. He was incapable of leaving the past behind him. On a different piece of paper, filed in the same folder, he left another message to the future: 'Jeremiah: God to the people of Israel after their religious infidelities such as the worship of idols. And thou with many lovers have been unfaithful; come back to me, and thou shall find a welcome.'[11]

For Clark, the affair with Pat Gray would have unfolding consequences in the three most crucial aspects of his life: his search for faith and redemption, his resolve to write the history of Australia, and his relationship with Dymphna. The intensity of his emotional life in the autumn of 1955 laid his vulnerabilities bare. He vented his anger, frustration and hatred, he felt himself 'in love', and for the first time in his life he seriously contemplated the end of his marriage. His moral life was held in the most fragile tension.

As a 'memento' of their 'closeness', Pat Gray kept the book that Clark accidentally left behind at her parents' cottage at Portsea in March 1955: Kenneth Slessor's *One Hundred Poems*, the same copy that Clark carried with him in Sydney when he rode the harbour ferry in the spring of 1953, chanting the last lines of 'Five Bells'; 'the boat's whistle', the 'scraping squeal of seabirds' voices far away' and 'five bells coldly ringing out'. As a 'voluntary gesture', she sent him a tiny edition of Schubert's *Goethe Lieder*. Some years later, Clark mailed it back 'without comment', which to Gray seemed an 'unnecessary act of rejection'.[12]

13: AN UNCHARTED SEA: REWRITING AUSTRALIAN HISTORY, 1954–55

Shortly before Christmas 1954, only three months before his affair with Pat Gray, Clark was convinced that his former colleagues in Melbourne thought him 'madder than ever' because of his flamboyant behaviour. Wounded, he saw the effect criticism had on him—'it leaves me like a whale with a harpoon in its back or like a puppy which goes into a corner to whimper, while he licks his sores'. Unable to control his drinking, he confronted the real possibility of failure. To edit a book of documents was one thing; to write a history of Australia would require discipline, restraint and self-denial. In his darkest moments, swaying from self-knowledge to self-pity in his diary, he feared that even if he succeeded in 'mastering' himself, the time required for writing might well take from him the 'one thing [he had] in the world': the love of his children. Only prayer, he said, gave him the strength and conviction to control his self-doubt. In the autumn and winter of 1955, in the aftermath of his relationship with Gray, there were few signs that he was any closer to achieving the self-discipline he desired. Neither he nor Dymphna had found a way to put the affair behind them. In the weeks that followed her return home from Sydney, he applied for the newly created Ernest Scott Chair in History at Melbourne University, despite his certainty that he was the victim of a malicious campaign designed to scuttle his chances. Reading

Manning Clark delivering a public lecture at the ANU, early 1950s

reviews of *Select Documents*, he attacked anyone who dared to criticise his work. If the world was not at his feet, the wolves were at his door. He could find no equanimity.[1]

While Clark's private writing overflowed with self-criticism, his public writing bristled with confidence. Reviewing books for the *Age*—European, Asian and American history, sport, travel, fiction, papal biographies, almost any publication for 'the serious-minded'—he put himself forward as one of Australia's most formidable public intellectuals, the arbiter not only of local culture but of international literature. As he sifted through historical

An Eye for Eternity

documents, reviewing allowed him the freedom to hone his style and find his voice as a writer. The tone was lofty, ironical and quizzical; invariably, there always seemed to be as much room for Clark's views as for those of the author whose book he was reviewing. His by-line was 'Professor of History at the Australian National University', yet he wrote like a journalist, observing academia with bemused indifference. Eminent historians were ticked off for not 'having a view of the world' and lending an all too 'attentive ear to the Oxford dons'. AJP Taylor, for example, was chastised for strutting like a peacock in his biography of Bismarck, busily scoring 'off his colleagues in the common room'. The bane of good writing was 'a mountain of scholarship', which obscured the author's 'love of his subject'. 'Academic people', Clark protested, were responsible for 'soul deadening' and 'soul destroying' prose. Given the opportunity to review Gordon Greenwood's multi-authored collection—*Australia: a Social and Political History*—a book that would sit with Clark's *Select Documents* as a standard text for matriculation and university students for the next two decades, and to which Clark was invited to contribute but declined—he was far from generous. 'What do these six university men make of our past?' he asked dismissively, before concluding: 'it is not clear what new ideas they propose … one wonders what it is all about.' Clark criticised Greenwood for failing to look to Australia's creative people, to her poets, writers and artists. The implication was clear. Academic historians had made a 'negligible' contribution to Australian history. Only Clark, it seemed, was capable of writing literary history for a popular readership.[2]

When he delivered his inaugural professorial lecture in Canberra on 23 June 1954, Clark set out to be controversial. The *Canberra Times* reported the lecture the following day under the headline 'Need for a New Approach to Australian History'. Decades later, it would be seen as Clark's manifesto, the moment when he laid down his plans to rewrite Australia's past single-handedly. Even from his opening sentence it was clear that a powerful and original voice had emerged. His audacity was astonishing. With the other foundation professors sitting in the audience—the poet AD Hope, the economist Heinz Arndt and the political scientist Fin Crisp—Clark began by quoting from the first book of Samuel—'David took a harp, and played with his hand; so Saul was refreshed, and was well, and the evil spirit departed from him'—followed by the Dostoyevsky quote that had already become the touch-stone of his historical writing. To write history, he suggested, was one way to 'understand what it had all been for'. Was Clark a prophet or a scholar? All his literary heroes were wheeled out, some for inspiration, some for denuncia-tion. DH Lawrence's fear that there could be no 'inner life' in a country like Australia was groundless, he said. Australians needed to reject the idea that they were little more than 'second-rate' Europeans, condemned to live in a 'cultural desert'. Their history was not dull and lifeless; on the contrary, it was the site of drama and deep divisions, especially the sectarian divide between Catholicism and Protestantism. Clark rejected the comforting notion that the convicts were saintly innocents forced into crime. They belonged, he argued, to a 'professional criminal class'. The radical tradition of historical scholarship, which found the progressive ideals of equality and democracy in the Eureka rebellion and mateship, was deeply flawed. It completely ignored the racism of the *Bulletin* and the Labor nationalists, and it bowdlerised the history of the squatters and all the pillars of bourgeois civilisation in Australia—'the cathe-drals, town halls, universities, schools and banks'. But who would write the new history that Australia so badly needed? It would not come from the universi-ties, those 'bankrupt defenders of the liberal ideal'. Nor would it come from the 'radicals' or the 'measurers'; they were tethered to 'a rigid creed' and refused to acknowledge the mysteries of human existence. It had to be written by some-one with 'something to say about human nature', someone who had pondered deeply over the problems of life and death'. Leading by example, Clark quoted Kenneth Slessor as his lodestar, drawing on the poet's image of the souls of the dead calling out to the living in 'Five Bells', the past beating on the door of the present, desperate 'to make its fury heard'. The historian's task was to hear the voices of the dead, bring them into dialogue with the present and 'put forward new ideas for [his] generation'. Like the music of David's harp, history was a source of spiritual solace for the living. By the time he had finished cutting a swathe through the nascent historical profession, demolishing the con-servative apologists for the British Empire, condemning the Left for its romantic view of labour history and its reluctance to embrace 'the mystery at the heart of things', there was only one man left standing: the artist–historian Manning Clark.[3]

In the autumn of 1955, when Clark's peers read his introduction to the second volume of his *Select Documents*, they confronted a maverick voice, which swung from biblical solemnity to wry humour in the space of a few lines. While Clark's chapter headings—economic history, social history and political history—were little more than pedestrian, his treatment of them was highly unconventional. St Paul was conscripted to begin the introduction, Goethe to introduce the goldfields, while Dostoyevsky was given free rein, cited in the book's epigraph but echoed throughout in much of Clark's provocative and often purple prose. Along the way, Clark took a swipe at what he called the 'synthetic ... vitamin pill' culture of his day, and mocked historians whose reverence for manuscript material was excessive, as if such material held 'the keys to the great truths'. No historian in Australia had written like this before. By producing the first substantial collections of historical documents, Clark had not only helped lay the groundwork for establishing the study of Australian history in its own right, he had also made the case for a return to the grand literary history of the late-nineteenth century, a history intent on bringing out 'personalities, narrative and drama'. The past had to come alive. If Henry Parkes's handshake was 'as cold as that of the proverbial fish', and it was, then this fact needed to be included when the historian dealt with him. If the fact was omitted, Parkes became little more than 'a name'.

Part of Clark's originality lay in his perspective on Australian history; he stood outside the British inheritance, and he was captive to no school of historical thought save one—that of CMH Clark. Yet this was precisely the quality that so often irked his colleagues—his breathtaking arrogance. As early as 1949, Kathleen Fitzpatrick remarked on Clark's 'lordly manner'. Asked to write references for others, he was the master of damning with faint praise. Three years before the 1958 publication of Russel Ward's *Australian Legend*, a book that found a uniquely Australian ethos in the egalitarian ideals of the bush worker and would prove to be one of the most significant works of Australian history in the postwar era, Clark, who disagreed with Ward's argument, offered this appraisal of his talent.

Ward is not an original thinker, and he would not start a new theory of history, or put forward a major interpretation of any period or episode in history. He has, however, the ability to keep in touch with what creative people are doing, and to pass on their ideas to students.[4]

It was not difficult to guess who the first of the creative people might be. Some reviewers of *Select Documents* noted the 'Olympian attitude' of Clark's introduction, which showed 'no scholarly humility'. Humility, at least when it came to competing with his academic colleagues, was not Clark's forte. His bravado clashed with the unwritten code of academic behaviour—not to self-aggrandise—just as his willingness to expose his inner feelings embarrassed others in an academic culture that prized a man's ability to repress emotion. In their correspondence, Crawford, Fitzpatrick and other staff members frequently joked about Clark's florid and melodramatic style of writing. (He had once written 'I look forward to seeing you possibly in May, when the autumn has softened some of the harshness out of the sky'.) When he wrote to Clark, Crawford always reassured him that he was highly thought of in Melbourne, which was certainly true so far as Clark's scholarship and teaching were concerned. However, Clark's personal qualities were another matter. Early in March 1955, Clark explained to Crawford that he resented his teaching and examining of students in Canberra being judged by others in Melbourne. Consequently, he had decided to pass the teaching of Australian History to Don Baker, who was more in agreement with 'what goes on in Melbourne'. Clark had long been riled by his loss of independence since he came to Canberra, being forced to secure Melbourne's approval for his courses and grades. The tone of his letter was typical of his response when he felt aggrieved. He was the sensitive creator, misunderstood and piqued ('I have been a failure in Canberra'), but still reluctant to hurt Crawford ('my feelings for you remain as warm as ever'). Crawford was amused by Clark's tender plea for his affection, telling his colleague Margaret Kiddle soon afterwards:

I've had two letters in two days from Manning—'not to be shown to anyone'. Should my male colleagues in other universities write to me in the tone of a distracted lover seeking to repair or avert a non-existent quarrel? But you will know all! I think there is a lot to be said for plain blokes who have never

An Eye for Eternity

read a word of Dostoyevsky. I shall not quote because you would laugh &
then you would be forced to 'bellow' (your own word, my dear, with pain).[5]

If the memory of Clark's antics at staff gatherings in the late 1940s was
not enough to damage his chances of returning to the History Department
in Melbourne, his affair with Pat Gray, which quickly became common
knowledge in the corridors, provided further evidence of his erratic behaviour. After hearing Clark deliver a version of his 'Re-writing Australian
History' lecture in Melbourne, and reading his introduction to *Select
Documents*, some of his former colleagues believed he had 'gone religious'.
June Philipp, a colleague and friend, whom Clark had supported when she
was hauled before the Royal Commission on Espionage in 1954, tried to be
honest with Clark. A close friend of Pat Gray's, she wrote to him shortly
after the affair to tell him gently what others had been saying much more
maliciously. She thought he had changed since he left Melbourne. She wondered whether he had developed 'an obsession with death' and 'embraced the
Christian faith'. She was also concerned by his behaviour when he visited
Melbourne; many of her colleagues saw him as 'eccentric' and 'irresponsi-
ble … making deliberately shocking or outrageous general statements and
taking cracks at people'. 'Making a fool of himself', she told him, only dam-
aged his academic credibility. Then there was the more serious matter of his
recent lectures and publications.

> It seems to me that of late years, when you have written or spoken (publicly
> I mean privately doesn't count in all this) about History you have really
> been only partly concerned with history—you've also been concerned to say
> things which had, often, nothing much to do with history. At some times
> you have been concerned to shout the name of the Lord from the hilltops,
> you have been making a confession of religious faith, you have been con-
> cerned to make prophet like remarks & sometimes, I think you have been
> laying bare the 'soul' or personal problems of Manning Clark … I do think
> it 'queer' in the sense of inappropriate, & in a way almost obsessive, that at
> almost every opportunity you should feel the need to bare your soul publicly,
> to all & sundry, friends & foes alike—especially in the guise of history …

the same sort of thing, I thought, (& was not alone in thinking it) ran through the talk you gave here last year. One example that has stuck firmly in my memory runs something like this—'there is only one or two alternatives in this day & age—the way set out in the Communist Manifesto or the way set out in the Apostles Creed' … Please remember that I write at least with a very warm friendliness & esteem for you.[6]

Interviewing Philipp in 2007, I asked her if she remembered writing this letter. 'No,' she replied, 'but I agree with every word of it.' Her frankness only fuelled Clark's paranoia. As Pat Gray left to return to England, and with his marriage still to be healed, he heard that the Ernest Scott Chair in History would soon be advertised. The university was expanding and Australian history was proving extremely popular with both undergraduates and postgraduates. In part, the creation of the Chair was a direct result of Clark's success during the late 1940s. In Canberra, he had 'ideas but no opportunities'. Only by returning to Melbourne could he rekindle the intellectual stimulation he experienced teaching Australian history in Melbourne six years earlier. Dymphna understood his reasons for wanting to apply, but after having worked so hard to establish their home at Tasmania Circle, she was in no mood to uproot the family for the second time in five years, and the dramatic circumstances of her homecoming in early 1955 only made her more reluctant.

The combination of the affair, the publication of *Select Documents* and the newly created Chair in Melbourne, all in the space of a few weeks, exacerbated Clark's fraught emotional state. In March and April 1955, he sent a barrage of correspondence to Crawford and his former colleagues, seeking endorsement for his application. He came across as anxious, hurt and distressed, eventually managing to convince himself that Crawford did not want him to apply. Crawford, who was recovering from a severe bout of hepatitis, was placed under great pressure. Clark continued to ask him for his unqualified support, constantly fretting that he was unwanted in Melbourne. Hearing that Kathleen Fitzpatrick, one of Crawford's two preferred candidates, had dropped out of the race, he went so far as to remind Crawford that in 1952, when he was eager to return to his old position, he had been told by

An Eye for Eternity

John La Nauze (right) and 'Nugget' Coombs, Oxford, early 1930s

Crawford to wait until 'new chairs were created in Melbourne'. Now the Chair had been created, and Clark wanted his due. Crawford was annoyed, drafting a letter that accused Clark of being unfair. 'Your letter does rather place on me the responsibility for your not returning here earlier to your old position, that is hardly fair; for I kept things fluid, with great difficulty, for a long time to enable you to return here if you decided to do so.' He encouraged Clark to apply for the Chair, but of course he could not guarantee the outcome. Time and time again, he assured Clark that there was no hostility towards him in Melbourne and that his application would be welcome. The new Chair was also not exclusively in Australian history. If it were, Clark would have been Crawford's first choice. That the Chair was in general history, rather than Australian history, was a pointer to the real truth. Crawford was happy for Clark to apply, but he did not want to see him appointed.[7]

Throughout April and May, despite the fact that he knew John La Nauze was the 'hot candidate' and could virtually 'have the job for the asking', Clark chose to confide in him. La Nauze, known more accurately as 'Jack the Knife', was an outstanding scholar and historian and in many ways Clark's opposite. Shrewd and aloof, he possessed a fierce intellect, encyclopaedic knowledge, an austere manner and an acerbic tongue. While Clark danced across the stage parading his feelings in public, La Nauze was secretive. In late March, La Nauze travelled from Melbourne to Canberra, where he spent a night at Tasmania Circle talking with Clark about the Chair and his coming review of *Select Documents*, a publication he once referred to as a 'book of snippets'. Clark laid bare his frustration and anxieties concerning the Chair while La Nauze listened attentively, giving away none of his inside knowledge. He was on the selection committee. As La Nauze returned to Melbourne the following morning, Clark was already writing to him, confiding that he felt 'hurt, humiliated and angry' because his application would be 'unwelcome'. Crawford, he declared, had a 'moral obligation' to explain to him his reasons for not wanting him to apply.

The few hours La Nauze spent with Clark had exhausted his patience. When he arrived in Melbourne and read Clark's letter, he was exasperated. Clark continued to off-load his 'inmost feelings' to him, not to mention his criticisms of his colleagues in Melbourne. La Nauze felt compromised. He was tired of being the sounding board for Clark's angst. 'I left [Canberra] with my tranquillity shattered & facing my ever-present horror of sleeplessness. I don't suppose you could possibly have known that I was in a state where I could hardly bear additional burdens; but I wonder whether it ever occurs to you that other people <u>can</u> be in such a state.' In the same letter, he sent Clark a copy of the selection criteria for the Chair. Clark, stung by La Nauze's criticisms, replied instantly:

> I cannot thank you for the material on the Chair in Melbourne—which I am returning to you with this letter ... I realise now it was a great mistake to write to you. The heart, I believe, is a lonely hunter, and, in the past, I have always chosen to hunt alone. That will again be my policy. Certainly I shall never hunt in Melbourne ... I deeply regret writing to you ... I don't give a damn when the review of Select Documents appears. It seems an utter mockery for people in Melbourne to go on yattering away about the 'quality' of my work when everyone knows quite well that I could not even become a tutor there ... I am disgusted by the whole academic game at the moment & my own sordid role in it. So say what you like about the book. It was produced in faith, and fundamentally, that's all that matters.[8]

Two weeks later La Nauze apologised and praised *Select Documents*. Clark forgave him. 'Write to me about history or literature or cricket or life and death,' he suggested. But Clark could not let go. 'The shock' of his rejection in Melbourne, he divulged to La Nauze, made him 'sit up in bed in the small hours of the morning'. Still, he reflected, 'everyone has their wounds, and only mongrels lick them in public and whine about them'. As the deadline for applications approached, Clark decided to apply. On 2 May, the Melbourne Registrar received his application for the Chair. Two weeks later, John La Nauze withdrew from the selection committee and was appointed to the Ernest Scott Chair. Clark was devastated and embarrassed. He told several people that he had decided to withdraw his application at the last minute, possibly after he heard that La Nauze had been successful. But Clark's letter of withdrawal was never written. He spread the rumour to give the impression he had not been passed over. When the selection committee sat for its final meeting on 24 May, he was one of the four shortlisted candidates. Unbeknown to Clark, Herbert Burton, his superior at Canberra University College, had not helped his chances, describing him in his reference as 'touchy' and 'argumentative'. Crawford thought Clark's claim of withdrawal 'a joke'—'if Manning can get some face-saving satisfaction out of supposing the result might have been otherwise, let him do so'. The saga had ended as it began. What Clark saw as betrayal and victimisation others saw as yet another example of his childishness and vanity.[9]

Throughout the crisis surrounding the chair, Clark's dealings with literary editors revealed just how easily he could be unsettled. When a mildly critical review of *Select Documents* appeared in the *Age* the weekend after his affair began with Pat Gray, he telegrammed the reviewer: 'astounded and shocked by your review believe it a gross misrepresentation'. Clark complained that the review had made him feel 'miserable', which elicited a sympathetic reply from the penitent reviewer, Ian Mair, who pleaded that the editor had 'mangled' his words. A few weeks later, when the *Age* failed to publish one of his reviews immediately, Clark asked if the literary editor was unhappy with the quality of his work. 'There is absolutely nothing wrong whatsoever with your reviews,' Mair replied, 'I sincerely hope this note soothes your troubled heart.' At the same time, Clark was beating on the door of John Douglas Pringle, literary editor of the *Sydney Morning Herald*, demanding to know why he had not yet reviewed *Select Documents*. Again, in his dealings with Clem Christesen, editor of *Meanjin*, Clark's testiness was on display. Pressed for time, he often rushed his contributions, telling Christesen to 'throw them in the rubbish bin' if he thought them not up to standard. But when Christesen did criticise his work, or refused to publish his contributions, Clark threatened to withdraw his subscription to *Meanjin*. Behind the brilliance of Clark's intellect and the self-assertiveness of his prose lay a deeply ingrained, profoundly troubling insecurity.[10]

In December 1955, six months after John La Nauze's appointment to the Scott Chair, when his admiring review of *Select Documents* finally appeared, he recognised Clark's potential to 'write a general history of Australia which, combining scholarship, understanding and vision, will make us see what, if anything, our history means.' Clark quickly forgot his earlier resentment and telegrammed La Nauze immediately: 'Overwhelmed and deeply pleased by review, feel am unworthy, agree with criticism the overflow of a passionate heart, ready big work thanks Manning'. The criticism to which Clark referred was La Nauze's dislike of his 'tendency to express repugnance, even to acknowledge nausea, at the thought of various types of Australian historical work'. Clark enjoyed dishing out criticism of others but he found criticism of his own work and character intolerable. While many of his colleagues were probably guilty of the same double standard, they were more skilled at disguising their hypocrisy. Clark was the man with the transparent soul, the effete historian with an emotional fragility, which proved embarrassing for many of his colleagues in the starched confines of the academy. As Crawford remarked two months before the Chair was advertised, Clark's 'imagination and personality' were 'not fully in control'. Although he had 'the imagination to write a great book', he could easily 'irritate and even alienate'. Crawford, who drove La Nauze to work every day and considered him his best friend, was relieved when Clark was not appointed. He knew instinctively that La Nauze would pose no threat to him, that he would be a far better administrator and much easier to manage. Since discussions surrounding the Chair began in 1954, both men had worked to ensure that the selection criteria would conspire to deny Clark the Chair. When La Nauze was finally appointed, Crawford told Clark that there was nothing but goodwill towards him in Melbourne, which was far from the truth.

Clark may have exaggerated the hostility towards him but he did not imagine it. He was seen as capricious, unstable and risky, a man who fell prey to unfortunate 'eccentricities of mind'. Neither Crawford, Fitzpatrick nor La Nauze wanted him as their colleague. His company was tolerated with 'amusement' or 'sustained' through gritted teeth, his talent best kept in Canberra. For Crawford, La Nauze was the path of least resistance, an appropriately sober and 'mellow' man who would also share his administrative load. Sobriety was not one of Clark's ideals. For him, the civilised behaviour in the Melbourne History Department was prim and suffocating. And for every rebuke he received, he had an even more outlandish response. Early in 1958, when his dream of returning to Melbourne had long faded from view, he visited the department to attend the funeral of his former colleague and friend Margaret Kiddle. The day was cold and wet. With cars in short supply, staff members stood huddled in small groups in the tearoom, discussing who would drive to the church, when the door opened suddenly. Everyone in the room looked across to see Clark, dripping wet, wearing a huge oilskin coat and a broad-brimmed bushman's hat. Just off a plane from Canberra, he looked like the vagrant drover blown in from the bush. The room fell silent. Clark stretched out his arms, the water dripping off his coat onto the floor. 'I am distraught, like Hamlet I am forsaken,' he exclaimed.[11]

Several months later, when Clark heard that his application for an 800-pound grant from the Rockefeller Foundation had been successful, his disappointment at being rejected in Melbourne subsided momentarily. At least he would have time to devote to writing. The funding would allow him to travel through South-East Asia to collect material for 'a two volume history of Australia' and to develop his main theme: 'that the history of Australia [was] part of the history of the Europeanisation of Asia'. Combined with the study leave granted by Canberra University College for all of 1956, he was now free to visit England to work in the Public Record Office and begin writing the history at Balliol College, Oxford, where he had arranged accommodation and an office. He thanked Crawford for his 'generous testimonial', convinced that his work remained the object of scorn: 'To my surprise (in Melbourne I imagine this would be astonishment) they told me last week they had decided to make me a grant'. Crawford's reference had described

Clark as 'the outstanding authority on Australian history … a man of ideas and imagination'. Clark, however, preferred to think of himself as an outcast. Believing that his peers held him in contempt incited his ambition. He would show the doubters what he was capable of. His bitterness over the disdain he felt from historians in Melbourne would fester inside him for the rest of his life. He did not forget.[12]

Although relieved of the problem of moving to Melbourne, Clark and Dymphna were now faced with the dilemma of what to do with the children during their time away. After the emotional trauma of Clark's affair, they believed they needed to travel alone, both to save their marriage and because Clark needed Dymphna's skills as a translator in the libraries of South-East Asia. Reluctantly, they decided they would leave the children behind in Melbourne and travel in December. Rowland, born in October, would be placed in a Melbourne hospital for children, while Sebastian would remain at Melbourne Grammar. Katerina, Axel and Andrew would stay with relatives and join them three months later in Bombay, before they all set out for England. As the time for departure grew near, the reality of leaving behind a six-week-old baby proved extremely distressing for Dymphna. The separation from all the children was painful, especially from Rowland. She was forced to wean him quickly. Until she was finally reunited with him in India, in March 1956, every sight of a mother breast-feeding her newborn child tore away the thin layer of resolve she had managed to sustain in order to live without him.

Before Clark and Dymphna left Melbourne for Singapore, they visited Dymphna's parents at Mont Albert. So many of Clark's strongest memories of coming home after living overseas, or of leaving Australia to live in Europe for extended periods, were associated with the old colonial house at Mont Albert. Now, with both his parents dead, he felt himself even more isolated in the company of the Lodewyckx family. He knew that they did not think highly of him; on that score, nothing had changed. As usual, nothing was said. Everyone acted his or her role as required. The relationship between Clark and Augustin remained tense. Dymphna had not told her parents of the crisis in her marriage. When she left Tasmania Circle, she chose to go to Sydney partly because she did not want her family to know. Her privacy was

Manning and Dymphna and their children (left to right: Axel, Andrew, Sebastian and Katerina), early 1950s

sacrosanct. While Dymphna imprisoned her feelings, Clark's emotions streamed onto the pages of his diary and correspondence. As they entered their sixteenth year of marriage, setting out for Asia and Europe, alone together for the first time since 1940, this remained the biggest gulf between them: Clark, gushing, vulnerable, ever needy; Dymphna, self-contained, independent, steadfast.[13]

PART FIVE

14: TO SOUTH-EAST ASIA, 1955–56

On Tuesday 6 December 1955, Manning and Dymphna Clark left Melbourne for Singapore and Jakarta via Sydney and Brisbane. Just over a week later, at Thursday Island, they left Australian territory behind. When their pilot boat pulled away from the shore, Clark wondered what they would find in Asia. Looking out on the waters of the Torres Strait, intimations of mortality rose inside him, as if, in the emptiness of the sea, he saw the reflection of death itself. As Dymphna stood next to him, she was fighting her instinct to remain at home with her children. By the time the *Sydney* was cutting its way through the Pacific Ocean, they both knew they were returning to the sensory environment of their first journey abroad in 1939: the bracing air on deck, the ship's rise and fall and the land slowly receding, until, finally, they were alone with the sea.

The three-month journey would take them to Jakarta, Malacca, Rangoon, and Delhi, then by train across India, through Agra, Varanasi, Calcutta, Madras and Bombay. Along the way, they would work together in the Singapore University Library, the Djakarta Museum Library and the National Archives in Delhi and would meet with professional historians, novelists, priests, librarians and journalists. It was the first of Clark's journeys of historical discovery and there was much hinging on the months ahead.

He left Melbourne knowing that his work had made a significant impact on his country. Oxford University Press had already contracted him to produce a one-volume collection of documents for the international market. The *Argus* described him as the historian who 'deflated Australia's legends'. The *Age* noted his departure and promised the readers of its literary pages that he would be back. Enthused by the publication of *Select Documents*, the *Sydney Morning Herald* devoted an editorial to his work, demanding that a Chair in Australian History be established at Sydney University. His work had sparked the interest of the postwar generation in Australian history. In 1955, Australia was establishing stronger relations with a score of countries outside its traditional British association and, as the *Herald* recognised, its proximity to Asia called for some revision of the country's historical perspective. Clark's grant from the Rockefeller Foundation rode on the back of an increased Australian and American interest in Asia, especially among Left intellectuals.[1]

Heading for Singapore, Clark was fully aware of the historical circumstances that were shaping the postwar world around him. The end of the war had left a new geopolitical environment in its wake. Press reports covered the rise of independence movements across Asia, while academic interest in 'Asian Studies' grew quickly, as did the numbers of Asian students enrolling in Australian universities. By the middle of the decade, to claim that Australia was 'part of Asia' was already a well-worn cliché. Clark saw quite early that Australia's future was tied inextricably to Asia. In 1954, writing an opinion piece for the *Argus*, he could not have been clearer: The 'superiority of the white man', he argued, was still something many Australians took as given. But the European domination of Asia was over. 'With India and China holding the balance of power in the world, it was surely just common sense not to insult them.' There were also 'moral reasons' for racial equality. Put simply, he insisted, White Australia was a phase in Australia's history that had to end lest the country find itself isolated in its own region.[2]

Within a decade after the war's end, the dominance of the old imperial powers—Britain, France and Holland—had given way to a succession of autonomous republics. Indonesia declared its independence in 1949, two years after India and the same year as the communist takeover in China. In

An Eye for Eternity

1954, the French withdrew from Indo-China after a major military defeat, and by 1955 Vietnam had already split into the Viet Minh–controlled north and the anti-communist south. Burma gained its independence in 1948, and Laos and Cambodia in 1954, while Australian soldiers battled communist insurgents in Malaya in the early 1950s and fought in the Korean War until the armistice was signed in 1953, remaining there as part of a United Nations force until 1957.

As Clark headed for Singapore, back in Australia, Menzies was doing his best to exploit the population's general fear of communism. After promising to reveal details of Soviet espionage in Australia, the Russian diplomat Vladimir Petrov defected, while his wife, Evdokia, whom Petrov had not included in his plans, was forced onto a plane at Sydney airport by KGB agents, bound for Moscow. When her plane landed in Darwin to refuel, Evdokia was granted political asylum on Menzies' instructions. Soon afterwards, Menzies announced a Royal Commission into the affair and won his second election in two years. Labor, led by 'Doc' Evatt, alleged that Menzies had prior knowledge of Petrov's intentions and had merely timed the release of the scandal to coincide with the election. A few months later, Labor's conservative Catholic Right, led by BA Santamaria, split from the Party and formed the Democratic Labor Party (DLP) in order to take a more vigorous anti-communist stance. Fear of communism was also driving much of Menzies' foreign policy. The signing of the Australian, New Zealand, United States (ANZUS) Security Treaty in 1951 and the South-East Asian Treaty Organisation (SEATO) Alliance in 1954 attempted to bolster Australia's security in the face of communist expansion. Clark suspected that India and Indonesia might well choose socialism and, along with many other Australians, he believed that the world was drifting towards yet another war. At the same time, he longed for a more substantial debate on Australian independence; but with Australia's ties to Britain given their most mawkish expression during the 1954 Royal Tour, there was little debate on Australian independence to be found. Like AD Hope's poem 'Australia', published in 1955 in the collection *Wandering Islands*, which Clark read before he left Port Melbourne, he wondered if Australians would ever aspire to being more than 'second-hand Europeans' who clung timidly 'on the edge of alien shores'.[3]

On Wednesday 21 December, Clark and Dymphna arrived in Singapore, its harbour dotted with small islands covered in palms—'a dull green and a ripple of light on the water'—the gardens of stone houses on the water's edge resplendent with flowering trees and shrubs. Ashore, three porters in white trousers, straw hats and bare feet carried Clark's bags to a Morris Minor taxi and they were driven to their accommodation overlooking Keppel Harbour. Clark was impressed with the city: 'I suspect the British have helped to keep it clean,' he wrote. However, within two days, in Jakarta, his first thoughts would turn to his own safety. After living the last six years in suburban Canberra, he was shocked by what he saw. The poverty and squalor, the oppressive heat, the frightening noise of the traffic, the dirty, fly-infested *kampong*s, the over-crowding; at times, he flinched in horror at the 'filth' he encountered on the streets, the smell of mud, food cooking, human sweat, open sewers, the stench from the ponies, the steam rising off the bitumen road, the men in shorts, tattered shirts and hats, bare-footed women in sarongs, 98 per cent humidity and rain teeming down constantly. Everyone was on the move and the politicians were talking of West Irian and planning a mass anti-imperialist meeting. Now that colonial rule was at an end, Clark feared for Indonesia's future. He wondered if extremists would take power. Perhaps the 'Moslem fanatics', or the communists or even the nationalists would make a 'scapegoat' of the Dutch, or of foreign capital, or of colonialism, spark the 'lumpen proletariat' and bring on civil war. The situation, he thought, was explosive. For the first time in his life he was suffering from culture shock. Now he truly knew what it was like to be an outsider. Much as he wanted to gain a broader perspective on Australia's historical relationship with Asia, his perceptions were still grounded in a European sensibility. He felt isolated and unwanted and he yearned for European food, conversation, tea, music and books—anything that would make him feel at home. Only reading DH Lawrence's poems made him 'come alive', their language and imagery from a familiar world, unlike the strangeness of his surroundings. Incensed by the hypocrisy of some of the Europeans he met, he grew weary of the role of the observer:

We don't belong here—[we] are alien … we are always doing the anthropo-logical approach … [Australians] are the great thick skins in the East. We have the colossal cheek to talk about social consequences of miscegenation to a people which has lived for a thousand years in appalling material hardship without losing its dignity.[4]

Clark also encountered Europeans and Australians who were doing their best to foster good relations with Indonesia. In Jakarta, during the first two weeks of January 1956, he visited contacts from Australia: his research assistant and former student from Melbourne, Ailsa Thomson, and her Indonesian husband, Din Zainuddin; and Herbert Feith, the Viennese-born scholar of Indonesia, who had come to Australia as a refugee in 1939 and who, like Clark, had studied under Macmahon Ball in Melbourne before initiating the Volunteer Graduate Scheme, which encouraged Australian graduates to work inside the Indonesian Public Service on Indonesian salaries. Ailsa would later remember Clark and Dymphna's visit fondly, particularly a Christmas party at Feith's home, where they had enthusiastically joined in the singing of carols. Forty years on, reading Clark's diary, Ailsa was surprised to find that Clark was 'embarrassed' by the 'crude' Christmas decorations and appalled by Herbert Feith's lacklustre performance on the violin, not to mention the quality of the singing, which Clark thought 'out of tune'. She was unable to reconcile the vivacious person she remembered in Jakarta with the 'profoundly depressed' person she found entombed in the diary, the person who wrote only days after seeing her that he was a poor father, his work was a 'failure', and his writing was 'hopeless'.[5]

Back in Singapore by mid-January—'the sky melting, mysterious, impenetrable—very far off', he felt safe after the 'anarchy' of Indonesia. The British, he thought, had 'immunised the place'. Everything seemed more ordered and controlled. He soon realised that this impression was superficial. At Singapore University, the students he addressed were critical of Australian policy on west New Guinea as well as its role as a colonial power in Papua New Guinea. Speaking to the University's Socialist Club, he told his audience that 'the colonial English were resented and even hated in Australia—though not by all people'. He noted how this 'appealed to them'—though he suspected their bitterness and loathing 'cut much deeper'. He was embarrassed when asked to explain Australia's foreign policy: 'how foolish Australia looks in Asia having to explain at diplomatic and official gatherings: "You know, we don't recognise China—and we have no diplomatic relations with Russia." The Asians and other Europeans rightly think Australia too small a beer… for not taking a stand on their own.' Talking to students in Delhi a few weeks later, he was again reproached about Australia's treatment of the Aborigines, its policy in New Guinea, ('was it to prepare the natives for independence or for annexation by Australia?'), Australia's support of the Dutch in west New Guinea, and, of course, SEATO—'the subject' that, as Clark noted, 'every Asian interested in politics trots out sooner or later'.

> [I] felt embarrassed by this persistent questioning, and the attempt to make me responsible for the policy of the Menzies Government. Later, in a calmer moment, [I] saw all four, Aborigines, Papuans, Dutch New Guinea, S.E.A.T.O. & White Australia as the residue of colonialism—a residue which must be removed as soon as possible if we are to win the confidence of Indonesians, Malayans, and Indians and Chinese (let alone the Russians.) Before 1941 we could blame it all, except White Australia, on to the British & pose as the friends of all opponents of imperialism. We were the innocents, or even minor victims of imperialism. Now we are tainted—and the taint comes in the main from an attempt to preserve a standard of living, to exclude others from our creature comforts etc. & in part the price of American assistance and in part the price for joining in the crusade against communism.[6]

Even before Clark arrived in India, his experiences in Jakarta, Singapore, Malacca and Rangoon had convinced him that White Australia was the main barrier to Australia's relations with the new nations of Asia. Until Australia's immigration policy treated all people equally, the country would look 'ridiculous and contemptible' in the eyes of its neighbours. In India, he was asked repeatedly to explain Australia's insistence on clinging to ideas of racial superiority. His embarrassment was fuelled by a sense of indignation. Seeing first-hand how many Asian intellectuals had fought to shake off the yoke of colonialism and were still fighting to express their country's independence, he was ashamed that Australia appeared to have no comparable movement. Instead, Australians preferred to play the role of Little Britain in the South Seas. Less than a decade after the declaration of Indian independence, the Indians he met tended to know only one of two things about Australia: that it was racist and that it was good at cricket. Clark was doubly ashamed that Australia was not known 'for her ideas, or her literature'.

The English historians whom he met in Singapore and Jakarta, such as Cyril Parkinson, Clark saw as 'pretentious mediocrities', academics whose work on Asia would be pushed aside when Asian peoples wrote their own history. What the new historians would do in Asia, Clark imagined himself doing in Australia: writing history from a post-colonial perspective. In some ways, he was beginning to see Asia as a role model. In the 1950s, when South-East Asia surfaced in Australian political debate, it usually appeared as a threat, a spectre or a warning, either as descending yellow hordes, a lurking economic powerhouse, or the site of burgeoning communist expansion. Clark saw a different story; the response of South-East Asian nations to the waning of imperial power after World War II also held out a positive example. It highlighted the need for a more independent Australia. In Singapore, on Australia Day 1956, attending dinner at the home of Australian diplomat Sir Alan Watt, he drank the toast of Australia, raising his glass to Queen Elizabeth II and noting later, 'Remember the toast of Australia—the first time I have ever drunk it. Put this with point about Australian independence'.[7]

After facing so many questions from Asian students about the White Australia policy, he saw Australia's history in a much more critical light. Reflecting on the 1901 *Immigration Restriction Act*, he could barely contain his rancour:

> What impertinence, brashness and confidence and ignorance to speak in this way of people who … created the Hindu and Buddhist civilizations … the back bench men were ignorant and could not know what they were doing, but what of men like Deakin, Reid, Barton and Hughes, who had the chance to know, but who remained silent or did not bother to find out? All this from a people with a spurious boast about themselves as pioneers of democracy, and apostles of mateship.

Manning and Dymphna, India, early 1956

As for the racial equality clause at Versailles: 'Australians thought Hughes was doing a great thing—fighting courageously for our salvation—but he was fighting to perpetuate an injustice—fighting for a lie.'

Clark arrived in India in February 1956. More than any other country he visited, India demonstrated to him the virtues of independence from Britain. On the train from Madras to Bombay, the train shaking violently, he managed to steady his hand to write graffiti-like across the page of his diary: 'Imperialism: Evil; one group assumes [it can] decide what is good for another.' In January 1950, dissatisfied with the status of dominion after independence, India had become the first republic in the Commonwealth. By 1956, Jawaharlal Nehru, who had become prime minister on independence in 1947, was pursuing a policy of non-alignment, attempting to maintain good relations with both the United States and Soviet Russia. Clark was impressed by Nehru's attempt to forge an independent foreign policy during the Cold War despite the simmering conflict with Pakistan and the ongoing struggle with Lisbon over the Portuguese colony of Goa. For India, the benefits of independence transcended the political sphere. Clark noticed the cultural revival that followed the Indian nationalist revolution. Thinking of Australia's future, he wondered if India's experience after independence was proof that nationalist movements were more stimulating to artists and writers than class movements.[8]

India also forced Clark to confront his privileged position. Each day when he stepped out onto the streets from the flat where they were staying near Delhi University, he was overwhelmed by the poverty. Late in the evening, the images of squalor and destitution replayed over and over in his mind like a nightmarish film trailer: small boys in rags carrying babies; the maimed and deformed, crawling, hobbling, or kneeling with their hands outstretched; blind beggars; one-legged beggars; toothless women touching their lips in mute appeal; men in rags rushing up to trains and buses, banging on the windows, the unforgettable sound of their razor-voiced cries; flies crawling over food and in the eyes of children; people defecating on the street; children with running sores over their faces begging for food or money—this was life sustained at a level that Clark could not begin to grasp. In Madras, when Dymphna refused to give money to one young woman, the beggar shouted after her. When she refused to pay a second time, the beggar began hitting Dymphna on the back. In Calcutta, another woman came out of the shadows with a child suspended over her left arm, emaciated by undernourishment. Clark gave her half a rupee and fled. Later, two women waited for him outside a bookshop. As he left, he gave one of them a small coin, but they followed him, whining in a low moan 'Sahib'. Panicking, he ran to get away from them. What a sight, he thought later, 'The Sahib fleeing from the great inequality between East & West'. He lay awake at night, haunted by the beggars, still hearing their desperate, frantic voices rising like a wave to engulf him—'This way Sahib. Yes, Sahib, Sahib! Sahib!'

The extreme hardship Clark confronted made him question his presence—'every enjoyment here must be a sin until the poverty goes'. Like Dymphna, he was repelled by the sight of the American tourists, haggling over the price of saris, waddling through the hotel foyer with their bottles of Vichy water, shouting to the waiter: 'Bring me a jug of hot water, and that <u>can</u> of Nescafé, I'm goin' to mix myself a decent cup of <u>corfee.</u>' Soon, Clark thought, they would travel with their own kitchens, and the whole of India would be made aseptic for them. The tourists' only aim in India seemed to be to 'have fun'. It staggered him to see their wealth displayed in this 'oasis of luxury', with India's poverty kept at bay only by the high walls of the hotel. Dymphna never forgot looking out from her boat on the Ganges in Varanasi and seeing a houseboat 'festooned with flowers', full of 'happy and cheerful' Americans. She could hear Indian music playing, the American women wearing saris, their men in pantaloons, as the smell of incense drifted across the water. Sitting in the corner of the boat was a young Indian boy about fourteen, dressed in jeans, chewing gum and reading from an 'American cartoon book'. He was the only Indian on the boat.[9]

In Agra, the sight of the Taj Mahal brought tears to Clark's eyes, but his appreciation was held back by what he saw on the streets nearby, the overcrowded homes and workshops of the tailors and hawkers plying their wares, families asleep on makeshift beds on the roadside, miraculously untrampled by the passing parade of buffalo-drawn carts, mangy cows with their dry udders and bells clanging, pedestrians shouting and cyclists blasting their horns. Overhead, between the tops of the buildings on either side of the street, 'as though through a slit', Clark saw the sky, the intense blue 'powdered by the dust' that rose up into the air from the streets below. Again, he was overwhelmed by the seeming hopelessness of the task in India: 'how tempting it must be to give up', he thought. What saved him from giving in to despair was the same thing that had saved him during his few days in Burma, 'the great well of mystery' that pervaded everything in the East—'movement, speech, houses, decorations, dress, the grace of the dancers'; even the nights seemed mysterious, the air steamy and thick, laden with humidity.[10]

At Varanasi, on the morning of Friday 2 March, Manning and Dymphna stood on the stone-rimmed banks of the Ganges. What they saw there that morning—as they watched the Hindus perform their religious rites—stayed with them till the end of their lives. Walking down the steps to the river, they passed the *sadhus* (holy men), with their beads and long, black, grey-flecked beards, holding their staffs and begging bowls. Dymphna thought them so 'weird' that she could not bring herself to look at them. Clark, ever fearful of playing the anthropologist, felt 'obscene', as if he were intruding. As they walked on, they passed the beggars, cripples and old women, their backs bent, their breasts 'long and dry', their bodies 'shrivelled up'. The sound of flutes, brass and drums from a nearby wedding procession filled the air. At the edge of the bathing ghats, below the 'flaking' line of temples, palaces and shrines that straddled the river, people washed, prayed or swam beneath the rising sun. Across the water, in the far distance, funeral pyres were burning on bamboo rafts. The draped bodies were dipped slowly into the water before the fires were lit and the ashes scattered in the Ganges. In these rituals of spiritual cleansing, death and salvation, Clark again saw his own mortality writ large. All this 'superstition' and ceremony for 'Paradise', he reflected, so the faithful might be delivered to a place without heat, dust, mud, thirst or hunger, a place free of suffering and death.[11]

Part of the reason for Clark's coming to Asia had always been to make a comparative study of religions. He wanted to understand the role of the Christian, Buddhist, Hindu, and Moslem faiths in the successive waves of colonisation in Asia. Only then could he understand the coming of

Catholicism and Protestantism to Australia. Weighing against one another the faiths he encountered, he observed their doctrines and rituals through his own yearning for spirituality, faith and eternal life. Whenever he could, he attended Church services, scouring the congregation and service for signs of Christ's love and compassion, which he believed to be the source of the true Church. In Indonesia, he found Protestant Christianity 'dead'—'a miming show where the players have lost the meaning'. Islam was the binding force, the 'national cement' that Indonesians had lived by during 'the long night of the Dutch occupation'. In Delhi, at dusk, as a 'dust haze' settled on the city, he attended Evensong at St James Church in Kashmiri Gate. Looking around him, he saw how the Protestant religion in post-colonial India attracted a middle-class minority solid in the truth of its convictions. In Rangoon, in early February, thinking about Buddhism, he realised that it clashed with Christianity and one of his most powerful wishes, the survival of his own soul. Buddhism aimed to stop the craving for eternal life, which 'Catholic Christendom' purported to answer. It was also unsatisfactory on the problem of human evil—too detached, not sufficiently concerned with others, and perilously close, he sensed, to turning its back on society completely. He felt much the same in Madras, when he finished reading Gandhi's autobiography, finding Gandhi's 'quest for salvation' selfish, a running away. Why, he asked, should Gandhi want to be released from the cycle of birth and death? Why strive not to be born again? Buddhism remained a mystery to him, like the Indian music he heard in Rangoon, music of heat, of 'life at breaking point', seemingly 'on the verge of hysteria'. Listening to the interplay between sitar and tabla, he imagined himself walking along a narrow ledge, his body at an angle, the wind pushing him towards the precipice. What he heard was totally unfamiliar to his western ears, a music that was not personal or individual in creation but one in which individuality dissolved, as if to prepare the listener for 'transition into another state of being', 'illuminating life and making it bearable'.[12]

In Madras, he talked with an historian who told him of the Tamil legends in lands to the south and east of India. At once, he wrote, he 'began to see the world through the eyes of a Tamil—for here Hinduism was created which colonised south-east Asia—the religion, the drama, music,

An Eye for Eternity

sculpture. This was its cradle.' Although he was repelled by the commercialisation of Hindu temples, he appreciated the sophistication of Hindu culture (the mother of the religions, the arts, the skills which spread all over South-East Asia) and the 'purifying influence of its religion, music and dance' in the midst of India's grinding poverty. One faith, however, spoke to him more than any other—Catholicism. In Singapore, Jakarta, Rangoon and throughout India, Clark attended the Catholic Mass whenever he could. He went to ask forgiveness for his sins against Dymphna and to drink in the ceremony and ritual—the singing of the credo, the raising of the host as the bells rang, the chanting of the Lord's Prayer ('Lord Have mercy on us'), the white trails of incense rising above the altar—and the solemn theatre of the communion procession, in which the faithful waited patiently, their hands clasped and heads bowed like innocent children. The sight of the poor in the congregation could move him to tears. In Rangoon, he watched as an old Indian man moved his lips in adoration at the elevation and consecration of the host. He marvelled at the way local cultures cast Catholicism in their own image. In a tiny wooden church outside Malacca, in a village inhabited mostly by poor Eurasians, one matriarchal figure sat in a special pew, 'crowned by a long black lace mantilla, which was carried behind her by two tiny serving girls'. Just to be close to the faithful was sustenance enough, to see men and women with the unquestioning thirst to believe that his own intellectual pride would never admit him to hold. The Catholic Church claimed to be the true church, the one and only faith that led to eternal life with God; but, after seeing the religions of South-East Asia, Clark knew this to be false. Faith and life everlasting were not the exclusive property of Rome. In Calcutta, he was shocked to hear the priest stressing the importance of Catholic doctrine 'in a country where charity and love of God [were] desperately needed'. In Malacca, after hearing a sermon that painted hell-like visions of the Second Coming, he wondered how a faith with such beautiful music could revel in such 'terror, and deception'. In Rangoon, when he encountered the parishioners genuflecting before the Cardinal and kissing his ring, he saw that the priests had turned themselves into kings, distorting everything Christ had stood for. In the midst of all his musings on faith and religion, he grappled with the question of how to begin his history of Australia.[13]

While he was noting his general impressions in his diary, he also kept a separate notebook in which he jotted down ideas on history. In these pages, he tried to come to terms with the early histories of conflict in South-East Asia and the coming of 'the Hindu, Chinese and Mohammedans'. To write about the past, Clark needed to feel its material legacy. History was a sensory experience before it was an intellectual one. Visiting Malacca, wandering the streets and talking with the descendants of the Portuguese, he began 'to understand the Portuguese in South East Asia'. As the general shape of volume one of his history of Australia formed in his mind, he asked himself a series of questions: 'The three invasions of Australia—Aborigines Europeans and Asians? (this leads me) into a discussion of Indian, Javanese, Malay, Chinese & possibly Japanese interest—then the explanation of why Asian interest waned', 'did the Asians know about Australia before the Europeans (before Wilhelm Jansz discovered it in 1607)?' 'Why then did the English take interest in second half of eighteenth century? I need to examine the Dutch records thoroughly to understand their attitude to the South Land.'

Clark's gaze was panning as widely as any historian of his generation. This was the mark of his originality. His decision to travel in Asia had broadened his perspective far beyond Australia's relationship with Britain. He wanted to understand Australia's history in its broadest possible context. Until he understood the history of European imperialism in Asia, and the result of European interaction with the great civilisations of Asia, particularly the collision of Catholic and Protestant Christianity with the Hindu, Buddhist and Moslem faiths, he could not begin to write about the British experience in Australia. In the Djakarta Museum Library, he read of the Hindu fables about the land to the south of Java and the Chinese stories of the 'kingdom of women' south of Timor. In Malacca, it is possible to see how his personal experience ignited his historical imagination. At Malacca Museum, he bought two portraits—of Magellan and of Francis Xavier—both of which he later pinned on the walls of his study in Canberra. With Dymphna, he visited the Dutch-built Stadthuys before climbing the hill to

St Peter's Church, where the statue of Francis Xavier stood overlooking the harbour. In the ruins of the church, he saw the tombstones for the Dutch who died in Malacca in the seventeenth and eighteenth centuries—men and women 'who died there while the civil war raged in England and the 30 years War in Europe, and the Dutch were exploring the west coast of Australia'.

One of the most striking features of Clark's history notebooks is the occasional appearance of Dymphna's handwriting, which takes the form of translations of archival sources and memorial tablets found in churches and cemeteries. Without her skills as a linguist, much of the primary source material in the Asian libraries was lost to Clark. She was the first to read and understand the Dutch and Portuguese sources, and initially she decided what was important. In Jakarta, she discovered that the Bugis maritime traders of Macassar had their own name for the north coast of Australia— Marege. Ever since Clark began collecting primary material for *Select Documents*, in the late 1940s, she had sourced, read, sorted, transcribed, translated and collated—and, most importantly, talked with him about—the material they discovered. Implicitly, Clark acknowledged her assistance in the second volume of *Select Documents* when he used the first person plural throughout his introduction ('we decided'). She was his eye onto the past. But she was also his collaborator, his de facto colleague, and his first admirer and critic.

In late March 1956, Manning and Dymphna were finally reunited with Katerina, Axel, Andrew and Rowland in Bombay. For the children, the three-week journey by sea had been trying. Rowland was now four months old, his face unrecognisable from the baby Dymphna had left behind in Melbourne. All the children seemed noticeably older, especially Katerina, who was now fourteen. Dymphna held Rowland in her arms, leaning him against her shoulder, her hands wrapped tightly around his back. On her left hand, she wore the sapphire ring Clark had given her in Singapore to mark their seventeenth wedding anniversary on 31 January. At that moment, as the children milled around her, Clark knew their fates were tied once again. In a few weeks, Dymphna would be pregnant with their sixth child.

15: TO ENGLAND AND IRELAND, 1956

The Clark family,
Bonn, 2 September 1956

In 1938, on arrival in Europe in his early twenties, Manning Clark had filled page after page of his diary with political analysis. As war approached, the young historian recorded his thoughts on every major political development, distilling the outside world onto the page. Like almost everyone else in England, his private affairs were shaped by public events. It was impossible to live free from Hitler's threat to the continent. Returning to Europe on 27 March 1956, shortly after his forty-first birthday, the political context he confronted could not have been more different. In England, the postwar hopes of Labour had long since dimmed. Although the country had recovered from war—there was now almost full employment—it remained uncertain of its international role as its imperial power waned. There was also the prospect of yet another conflict with the Soviet Union. When Clark stepped ashore with Dymphna and the children at Tilbury Docks, Conservative Prime Minister Anthony Eden, who took office after Churchill's retirement, had recently been returned with an increased majority. In October, determined to stop Egypt from nationalising the Suez Canal, Eden decided to join France and Israel in the invasion of Egypt, only to be forced to make a humiliating withdrawal after Eisenhower refused to support the invasion and the United Nations intervened. The political environment may have been less threatening to Clark's personal safety than it was two decades earlier, but it was potentially no less absorbing for an historian who wanted to address contemporary political problems, especially decolonisation. For many observers at the time, the Suez debacle was seen as the death throes of British colonial power. Yet throughout all of Clark's notebooks and diaries in 1956–57, he made no mention of Suez, nor did he offer any reflections on British or Irish politics.

During his stay in England, Clark became close to the journalist and diplomat Bruce Grant, one of his former students from Melbourne University. After the war, Grant worked in Fleet Street and for a time was a foreign correspondent for the *Sydney Morning Herald* and the *Age*. With Grant, Clark talked about the things he no longer wrote about in his diary—the Suez Crisis, Russian aggression in Eastern Europe, the arms race and the Cold War. As Grant remembered, 'Europe in '56 was boiling in many ways. I think Manning needed help. He would ring me at any hour just to talk. I think he thought I might have understood something about secular humanism. I always felt as if he wanted me to throw some kind of light on it … I was more in touch with the world at that time than Manning.' As if to make Grant's point, one day Clark rang Grant in his Fleet Street office from the British Museum. 'Can you come quickly? Can you come now? I will be standing on the steps of the British Museum,' said Clark. Reluctantly, Grant agreed. He walked out into the London rain, hailed a cab and made his way to the museum. Fifteen minutes later, as he climbed out of the taxi in Great Russell Street, he looked across the road to the front steps of the Museum and saw Clark standing on the steps in the rain. He was wearing his large hat (an essential component of his attire since his departure for India), a long overcoat and ankle-high boots. Grant ran up the steps to greet him. 'Well, did you count them?' asked Clark. 'Count what?' Grant replied, bemused. 'Count the steps,' said Clark. Grant went back and walked up the steps again. 'Eleven, Manning; there are eleven steps.' 'Yes,' Clark intoned, 'you are standing on the eleventh step and it was on the eleventh step of the sacred staircase that Luther had his doubts.'[1]

Reading Clark's diaries after his death, Dymphna was struck by the difference between his first diaries and those of his middle age. She saw how political analysis, which had dominated his earlier entries, gradually gave way to more idiosyncratic, literary observations. It was not that Clark lost interest in politics but that his way of understanding the world had changed. He had started to see the limitations of liberalism and socialism. As a young man, he tried to work out his position—where did he stand on Chamberlain's policy of appeasement? What historical circumstances had given rise to National Socialism in Germany? To find the answers he tested and weighed the evidence before arriving at his conclusion. Returning to Europe in 1956, he had completely abandoned any pretence to academic objectivity. Rather than *determine* the truth, he wanted to *divine* the truth. By the time he arrived in England, his diary was not so much a record of his daily life as a portrait of his creative imagination. It read like a series of visions; the journal of a solitary pilgrim who travelled in search of the past, faith, and the lives of his literary heroes. Only many years later, when Dymphna stood photocopying his diaries in the National Library, did she understand the extent to which Clark had 'confronted Catholicism' in 1956. She was astonished not only by what was missing from the pages—so much of what she remembered from their time in England and Ireland—but also what was there. Here were the voices of Manning Clark she had heard either faintly or not at all.[2]

Clark had come to Europe to work in the Bodleian Library and the British Museum on the discovery and foundation of Australia, to visit Dublin and Cork to research the early history of Irish transportation to Australia, to finish editing his next collection of historical documents for Oxford University Press and to begin writing his history of Australia. As if this were not enough, he would also spend time teaching at Balliol College, and he would also research the history of Dutch exploration in the southern oceans at the Royal Library in The Hague. All of this he would achieve. And he would also retrace the steps of his younger self, searching out the places that once signalled a way of life far deeper than anything he had known before. Renting a small, two-bedroom house at 13 Raleigh Park Road, Botley, a dreary suburb on the western side of the railway line in Oxford, he set about planning his first pilgrimage, to Eastwood, Nottinghamshire—the birthplace of DH Lawrence.[3]

As he drove through Leicester and Nottingham in the cold mist of an early April morning, he saw the coalmines through the car window: the huge heaps of slag piled high, the black-stained grass at the pithead, and the great dark wheels against the skyline. Here was the coal town that had nurtured the writer who had taught him almost as much as Dostoyevsky. On arrival in Eastwood, he went straight to 8A Victoria Street, the house where Lawrence was born, visited his first school and entered the Congregational Chapel where his family had worshipped. He even managed to speak to a woman who had known Lawrence as a boy. In the faces of the people on the street he saw a 'different race of men from the genteel born in the south'. The pages of his copies of *Sons and Lovers* and *The Rainbow* were almost in tatters from use. Looking at the landscape around him, he was staggered at what Lawrence had achieved. 'How did he do it?' he wondered. 'A prophet of industrial civilisation rising out of the slag heaps, the coal dust, [and] the ugly houses to damn them all.' Walking in Lawrence's footsteps, Clark was searching not only for Lawrence but also for some spark of inspiration that might endow him with greater insight as a writer.

As he set out to write the first words of his history of Australia, he scanned the past in the same way as he read Lawrence and Dostoyevsky, searching for moments of revelation. He knew instinctively that his history would take the form of a 'well constructed play'. In his hands, the past would behave itself. Events would unfold before the reader like actors moving on and off stage; the future would appear as natural, almost inevitable. He travelled through England and Ireland, visiting libraries for material and walking the streets for inspiration. In the notebooks he kept along the way, which contain some of his first sketches and ideas for *A History of Australia*, the sensuality of his historical imagination shines through.[4]

Spring in Oxford was the beginning. 'May in England,' he thought, 'the First Fleet sailed in May … the flowering time? the buttercups, the hawthorns (were they out?) [I must] compare [this] with what they would see at Botany Bay.' Driving across the moors in Yorkshire, before he descended to the coast at Whitby, the workplace of James Cook, he encountered three 'big things'—the ruins of the Abbey on the headland, the poverty of the area, and the call of the gulls that circled above the coastal villages, which nestled into the rocky headlands facing the North Sea. These were the sights and sounds of Cook's childhood. It was the same wherever he travelled. Like a film director in search of atmosphere, Clark drank in the sense of place, hoping to colour his history with the same moods and feelings. In a whirlwind tour of Edinburgh, he wondered if the soot-blackened walls of the city's buildings mirrored what Calvinism had done to her people. Here, the cold hurt. The wind pinched his face. He saw the streets and churches cluttered with war memorials that 'shouted' about the Scots' military prowess, then he walked through the slum areas, shocked by the distorted, hideous faces of the men and women, swollen and stained by drink. Attending a Welsh Congregational service in Clifton, he saw how the harshness of the Old Testament stories had permeated the entire culture, producing a people who denounced the evils of drink, equated sex with sin, and feared their bodily desires. At Cork, he tried to imagine the world the Irish convicts left behind as they sailed for Australia. Standing with Axel, he looked out on the mouth of the Lee River and pictured the convict ships moving out to sea, bound for the distant shores of Sydney Cove. He could see the scene unfolding before his eyes, the Irish prisoners under the command of English officials, the shoreline littered with refuse and reeking of fish, the fierce, desperate faces of the Irish men and women on board, a people who lived close to religion, with crucifixes and statues in their homes and the sign of the church on their door, their priests hovering all the while with stories of damnation and salvation. What did they feel as they left their homeland behind? In the Cork of 1956, Clark found a people drained by the past and the church, their flesh cold and damp, the bones on their fingers hard as they shook his hand, a city waiting for the resurrection of the dead, gloating over the wounds of its ancestors, its ballads soaked in Guinness, which, as everyone told him, tasted as soft as cream. These were the images that moved through Clark's mind as he sat down to write, a montage of the visions that had 'entered and taken possession' of him, as if delivered miraculously by some power beyond himself. Sensing that he had finally found a way to begin, he was determined to write history in a way that no Australian historian had dared write before him.

Delicacy of feeling, grace of bearing, shades of emotion and sentiment. All these have been dulled for a long time, dragged into quiescence, generally suppressed, or ignored as too painful, or starved for lack of food and warmth of other human encouragement. But also, the task is clear, the loneliness accepted, or endured as a necessary condition of fulfilling the task. Can I retain the vision … [and] the faith in the days in which the punishment will be visited on me for past squandering of talents, past cruelties, past bullyings, past tormentings? Can I live without mockery and destruction? Can I create anything?[5]

Clark was striving for a history that was fully alive to the sensuality of existence and human emotion, something that might come close to what Sidney Nolan described in 1956 as a 'sacramental feeling', a history that captured 'the magic' of the continent that had so frightened DH Lawrence. He was attempting to do for Australian history what Nolan was doing for Australian painting and Patrick White was doing for the Australian novel. In 1958, after the publication of *The Tree of Man* (1956) and *Voss* (1957), White explained that, in writing *Voss*, he had wanted to give the book 'the textures of music [and] the sensuousness of paint, to convey through the theme and characters of Voss what Delacroix and Blake might have seen, what Mahler and Liszt might have heard'. Beginning his history, Clark thought of Beethoven and Mozart, who met in Vienna for the first and last time in the very month in which the First Fleet sailed for Australia. As Clark railed against the lifeless prose of his academic colleagues, White attacked Australian novels that resembled 'the dreary, dun-coloured off-spring of journalistic realism'. All three men were convinced of the superiority of their vision in a country blind to the originality and power of their art. While Clark steeled himself against the 'jeerers, mockers and sneerers', White condemned the dingoes that howled unmercifully at his door. Nolan, meanwhile, spoke of Australia as a 'ghost civilisation' based on a 'kind of cannibalism—eat the land. Eat the trees. Eat the artists'.[6]

For Dymphna, Clark's determination to follow his creative instinct wherever it might take him meant that she shouldered an even larger share of the parental burden than usual. Since they were reunited with the children in

Bombay, Clark had fought with Katerina, now aged fourteen. He was convinced that she wanted to punish him for his 'cruelty' to her when Dymphna was in hospital, when he had insisted that she take on more of the domestic labour in Dymphna's absence. One episode in particular riled Clark. Leaving Bombay, he had paused at the Customs shed door before he boarded the *Arcadia*. He wanted to 'say goodbye to India'. Overwhelmed by a feeling of calm and possessed by 'a mystical vision', a 'great flow of tenderness' and gentleness for everyone passed through him. He wanted to say 'thank you to India'. Seeing him standing alone, away with his thoughts, Katerina shouted at him: 'Why do you want to make a fool of us by stopping here?' When Clark explained that he merely wanted to say goodbye she 'snorted with disgust'. At least this was Clark's reading of his daughter's reaction. Complaining in his diary, he transformed his troubles with Katerina into yet another example of his failed relations with women.

With Katerina one lives with a permanent void in the heart—and where love, affection, trust, compassion, joy should be there is irritation, anger, and no faith. Like the Lodewyckxes, my relations with her have drifted to a point where there can be no peace, only turmoil—and when she uses my past, that part of the past of which I am ashamed to haunt me, to torture me, to tantalise me till breaking point occurs, and I turn on her in blind rage—which, of course ... increases my guilt. All my relations with women tend to lapse into that pattern which makes me so sad, sometimes so bitter that I feel like crying out in anguish 'For God's sake, stop tormenting me—I can't stand it.' ... I find it terribly hard to live with a person who treats me in that way. How can one enjoy even a cup of tea, or a swim, or a game of ping-pong if one is haunted, tortured, punished by the past? Have I been a fool to bring her with us? How dare she cast such a shadow over my one year of recuperation after all the lonely struggle of the past? Why should one's daughter be added to the legion of women who start by being friendly, and end as tormentors? Where is the refuge? Perhaps there is none ... God, what an unhappy family we can sometimes be, and what insecurity we have plunged the children into. People who torment each other create an atmosphere of suspense, of tautness. I am too miserable to write more—too distressed by what has happened—To the world I must appear a bad tempered swine—and yet [I] am not convinced the sins deserve such cruel, relentless, never ending punishment. Is there anywhere someone who can lighten the load, lift some of the burden off the heart?[7]

In moments like these, Clark sounded more like a child than a father. Sometimes he felt Dymphna was siding with Katerina, which only entrenched his besieged mentality. When Dymphna wanted to hurt him, she knew his most vulnerable point, sarcastically telling him that she 'couldn't keep up with his finer feelings'. Clark retreated, convinced that she viewed his artistic sensibility with nothing but scorn. Depressed, he saw all tension with Dymphna or Katerina through the prism of his own guilt, as if his wife and daughter had condemned him to plead eternally for their forgiveness. His only relief was a 'volcanic' eruption of anger that released what he felt to be his 'bile and wretchedness'. In June, watching John Osborne's *Look Back in Anger* at the Royal Court Theatre in London's Sloane Square, he felt as if he were reliving the story of the early days of his marriage. At a performance of *The Seagull* at the Saville, he saw his own 'guilt sodden, petty, unhappy self' before the work of a giant like Chekhov, a writer who had the courage to see the world 'without illusions, prejudices, pettiness, spite, malice and self-pity'. Driving with the children through Europe in August and September, he continued to feel constrained by the family. He complained frequently of the boys' bickering and Katerina's rebellious nature. Even carrying Rowland around wearied him.

In early September 1956, Clark and Dymphna returned to the site of their courtship—Dietzstrasse 4 in Bonn—the home of Frau Unger, Dymphna's landlady in 1938. Crossing the channel from England to Holland, where Clark worked in the National Library in The Hague, they were forced to wait for a week while their Austin sedan was repaired. The huge expense—more than 50 pounds—put added strain on an already tight budget. Clark 'felt angered' by their bad financial position. 'Why have we not enough money to buy a meal? Why must the spending of every penny be explained, defended, justified—until the nerves are frayed, & all privacy destroyed? Even the children have a voice, and complain if I have a pot of tea. Who said we had a large income?' Writing in his diary, Clark could turn the slightest display of prickliness on the part of a shopkeeper into the symptom of a national pathology. The parsimonious habits of the Dutch irritated him—'Holland is the only place where I have had to pay to urinate'—as did their zeal to protect property—'Calvinism makes for hard people.' Once the car was repaired, he wasted little time in leaving: he picked up the car from the mechanic at 9 pm in The Hague and was driving the family to Germany one hour later. In the early hours of the morning, with the children asleep in the back seat, Clark parked the car outside Frau Unger's house in Bonn. They slept in the car until 6.30 am, when Clark was woken by Herr Unger's tapping on the car window—'Herr Professor!' As they walked inside, Frau Unger ran down the stairs in her dressing gown and threw her arms around Dymphna—'Frau Clark! Frau Clark!' For both Clark and Dymphna, this was a homecoming. Seventeen years after they sat at the Ungers' table talking of Hitler, England and Australia, they now listened to them talk of the Americans and the 'shallowness of their civilisation'. The Ungers, Clark believed, had no 'anger about the war, no remorse, only a reminder: "you don't know how much we suffered and how much it meant to hear from the outside world that we were not forgotten"'.[8]

Staying at the Ungers with four children for more than a few nights was impossible. After three days they were on their way to Basel to visit a friend of Dymphna's from her student days in Bonn, Hans Ehrenzeller. As they drove through the south of rural Germany, past the 'gaudy, painted statues of the crucified Christ', the family was bickering all the way. Clark insisted that they stop in Baden Baden to visit the Casino where Dostoyevsky had gambled away his last rouble in 1871. There, as Clark knew, Dostoyevsky had written to his wife, Anya, whose possessions he had pawned, pleading her forgiveness—'Anya, I prostrate myself before you and kiss your feet … this was the *very* last time … now I will put my mind to worthwhile things.' In Dostoyevsky's struggle with gambling, and his remorseful flight to priests for absolution, Clark saw his own battle with alcohol and infidelity.

Late in the evening on 4 September, they finally arrived in Basel where they slept on Ehrenzeller's living-room floor. The host gave them a warm welcome, but he quickly became annoyed by the intrusion of six people into his tightly ordered domestic space, just as Clark became irritated by his 'unc-tuous, two-faced behaviour'. The next morning, Clark suddenly announced to Dymphna that he was leaving the family in Basel and would travel alone to Italy. As Dymphna recalled after his death, Clark was by that time 'thor-oughly sick of travelling with the family'.

> [Manning] went to Rome ... He decided that he had never been to Italy, that it was part of his education, and should be repaired, so he just suddenly announced to me—'I'm going to Italy'. [He planned] to rejoin us in Basel and we'd drive back home to Oxford ... [But] he got desperately sick in Rome [with gingivitis] and we had our bookings on the ferry because we had to be back in Oxford so that the children could go back to school ... With Gingivitis—you have this terrible inflammation of all the gums. Manning just rang up [from Rome] and said he couldn't come back to Basel. He would come, he said, when the doctor allowed him, he would come back to Oxford by train. [He told me] that I was to proceed ... and so I just had to do it.[9]

While Clark recuperated in Rome, staying with the Australian immigra-tion doctor Alec Reith, Dymphna, who was then five months pregnant, set off in the prewar Austin, chugging along at 35 miles an hour. She was alone with the four children, including Rowland, who was not yet one, as she drove through Germany to Holland, then on to Oostende, across the Channel, north to London, and finally to Oxford.

About his reasons for leaving them in Basel, Clark remained silent. In his last autobiographical work, *A Historian's Apprenticeship*, he described his visions in the Uffizi Gallery in Florence and St Peter's in Rome, but little else. In the pages of his diary he was in Basel with his family one moment and in Rome alone the next. The closer he moved to becoming the writer he always wanted to be, the more his daily life escaped the pages of his diary. In Rome, running a fever, with his mouth full of ulcers and downing a cocktail of aspros, sulphur and penicillin, Clark wrote Dymphna longing letters, des-perate for the same loving care that had brought him back to life in 1952 when he was stricken with rheumatic fever—'In this sort of ordeal I miss you terribly'. The same family he had flown from in frustration less than a week earlier now appeared before him in the early hours of the morning as a series of apparitions, the sight of their faces 'cheering' him on through 'some dreadful, dark, low moments' when the disease seemed to make his whole world shrink to one room. Dymphna replied from Antwerp, where she had been staying with relatives on her way back to Oxford.

I could write [so much] about all that I felt when I at last got your card and letter yesterday & about what happened since we last saw you—but I only have till the others come home from a shopping trip & the letter will be truncated. I often felt desolate and alone. I had not heard from you. When the boys fought & Rowland screamed and Katerina would not take him on her lap because she had a good skirt on, I cried quietly sometimes and wished all sorts of things were different. But I gave them a good trip I think … There were some low moments on the trip too—a disgusting night in a little hotel near Metz, where everything really stank—waitresses who scowled at Rowland—fights between the boys—the children's greed for souvenirs … every now & then Axel's face would light up & he would say 'I bet Dad's all over Italy by now!' … The children are alive, receptive, absorbent … I hope this reaches you on Monday, Darling.[10]

As a young man in Germany, wanting ever-more romantic declarations of love, Clark had read so many of Dymphna's letters in disappointment. When he read her letter from Antwerp to Italy in 1956, he knew that he could ask for nothing more. How much more could she give him than this? Telling the story of Clark's trip to Rome years later, Dymphna emphasised her shock:

I was a bit shaken at the thought that from then on I was on my own until he came back and that he didn't want to stay with us [in Basel] but well, what could I do? He wanted to do it, and so he had to do it … and I didn't raise any objections, it was just the way the cookie crumbled.

She was also determined not to lose him. Her need of him—much less demonstrative than his need of her—was lived out through her unstinting devotion. The brief moment of separation in the autumn of 1956, their first since she had left him eighteen months earlier, had actually brought them closer together. To be apart in Europe took them back to the last months of 1938 before they were married. They had come so far together since then. Working in the British Museum, only a few days after his return to England in early October, Clark sent Dymphna a postcard: 'the big thing about this trip to England is that it has brought me back to you'. Nevertheless, close as he was to her, he kept his inner longing for faith to himself. His short visit to Ireland in June, like his trip to Rome, was made without her.[11]

In May, at Balliol, Clark asked the Roman Catholic Church for a series of leaflets on the Catholic faith to be sent to him by mail. Ever since his affair with Pat Gray, he had toyed with the idea of becoming a Catholic. His trips to Ireland and Italy were as much about his own spiritual searching as they were about history; the two quests were inseparable. Torn between his image of Christ—compassionate, independent and anti-establishment— and his disdain for Church authority, he was unable to commit himself. If anything, his pilgrimages to Ireland and Italy only deepened his scepticism. In Rome, he was disgusted. At St Peter's, the Church encouraged the worship of statues and relics, the faithful queuing to view the embalmed body of Pius XI like the Russians in Moscow, who stood in the freezing cold to view Lenin's body in Red Square. Everywhere he turned, he saw the Church busy securing its power, degrading Christ's work to the level of 'mystery mongering, magic spells and charms'. Clericalism in Italy only retarded the country's intellectual life. Meddling in the private lives of their flock, the priests dared to tell people how to conduct their sex lives. Clark claimed that the Church, in its 'savagery against fucking', was simply trying to deny others the pleasures it had denied its clergy; and this from people who allegedly had no experience of sex. The religion he saw propagated by the Catholic Church was little more than 'mumbo jumbo'. Where was the other side of the faith, he wondered; the side that had inspired the Masses, the paintings and statuary? Great music and poetry might allow him to believe in his 'secret longing and hope', but not Rome.[12]

In Ireland, three months earlier, Clark had the impression that the Church was choking the country. On the streets of Dublin, he saw the clergy dominating life, stalls selling religious literature, plenary indulgences for sale, 'Fatima Cafes', vast numbers of priests and nuns on the street, the city's life-blood 'dried up', as if the sexuality of its people had been killed by fear and 'drowned in stout', the whole city preoccupied with death, the eyes of its people 'fixed on eternity'. He wondered what became of those who could not accept the authority of the Church, the ones who hated saying 'Yes father, no Father, certainly Father' and wanted to yell out 'Take your lily white hands off me!' In the ubiquitous statues of Christ, he saw the faces of the Irish youth; the only thing missing was 'a cloth cap and a cigarette dangling from Christ's mouth'. 'Talk about God making man in his own image,' he joked. 'Here is man returning the compliment.' As with the churches he visited in South-East Asia, the one thing that redeemed the Catholic Church was its embrace of the poor and downtrodden—'persons of all classes and all colours of skin'. The mere sight of the poor could wash away all his contempt for the Church hierarchy. At the end of his life, he grew fond of telling the story of how he had watched an unshaven man in Cork—his skin blotchy, his suit brown and dirty, his shoes without laces, his body stinking of whisky—as he walked by the church crossing himself reverently. In these images of the faithful poor, Clark found his vision of Christ, a vision which mirrored Christ's teachings in the gospel: 'I tell you solemnly, in so far as you did this to one of the least of these brothers of mine, you did it to me.' Standing with the poor in the Catholic Mass, watching them kneel in whispering prayer as the music and poetry of the credo soared in the nave of the cathedral, Clark composed his personal God, a God of the Muses, a God of the little man. About this he uttered not a word to Dymphna. 'We didn't talk about it,' she admitted.[13]

By the time he returned to Oxford from Italy, Clark was ready to begin writing. On 1 October, in the upstairs bedroom of a rented terrace in Botley, looking out across an autumnal Raleigh Park to Tom Tower and the spires of Oxford in the distance, Clark pushed the boat out on his tormented sea. Describing Governor Arthur Phillip at Sydney Cove taking possession of the continent in the name of the Crown, he began with echoes of Genesis: 'It was all there in the beginning, that seventh day of February 1788 ... It was all there—the European past, the seeds from

Raleigh Park, Oxford

which it all developed—the protestant view of the world, the catholic view, the enlightenment, and that other one—man and his environment ... European man under the gum tree, not the oak.' Thirty years later, with the publication of volume six, the gum tree and the oak would become 'the old dead tree and the young tree green'. Oxford, the site of his perceived rejection at the hands of the English at Balliol in 1938, was also the place where his history began. His first drafts were written in his customary scrawl. Remarkably, there were few crossings-out. Reading the drafts today, one has the feeling that the words flow effortlessly from his pen.

In the margins, Dymphna's editorial comments can be read more clearly than Clark's text: 'This is not another book of documents! ... What about Bennelong? ... Amend first sentence ... A curious way of expressing yourself ... can't you stand the word discipline?' She also wrote out the transcripts of longer documents, which Clark then inserted into his draft—not only the Dutch and French translations, but the statements of Banks, Phillip and other English officials as well. She corrected factual inaccuracies, she drew his attention to inconsistencies of argument, and she told him bluntly

An Eye for Eternity

what she thought. Given the ant trail that passed for Clark's handwriting, his notes squeezed in at the bottom of each page in even smaller script, his corrections written over the top like graffiti, the potential for error was enormous. The first pages were a struggle. He had no idea of the period he would cover and he was still six years out from publication. But he had begun. Having secured his marriage and re-committed himself to Dymphna, he had finally found the will and the sheer bloody-minded persistence to write.[14]

Manning Clark began his history in the shadow of Patrick White's *The Tree of Man*. In White's character Stan Parker, the small farmer whose life is consumed by the desire to understand the mystery of God, Clark saw much of his own spiritual searching. White's themes resonated with the themes Clark was struggling to articulate in Australia's past. Parker sensed the divine in the Australian landscape, a moment of revelation for Clark, as he prepared to explain the fate of Catholicism, Protestantism and the Enlightenment in the unforgiving environment of Australia. Reading *The Tree of Man* inspired him to deal with the universal themes of human existence and to write history as art. If a novelist could do it, Clark thought, then he wanted to show that an historian could do it. He had to find a way to show the unspoken and undocumented lives of his characters and imagine his way into their hearts and minds. The figures of the past would move in his hands like characters in a novel or film, their actions lit intensely for brief moments, coming and going on the page as people moved in and out of his own life.[15]

Virginia Woolf, grappling with the task of writing her autobiography, reflected that her life was made up mostly of 'moments of non-being', moments forgotten. She could only recall 'moments of being', those moments of intense experience, which resulted in the transcendence of the everyday, which had cut through the habitual experience of her life and allowed her to see life anew. As he prepared to leave Europe for Australia in December 1956, clutching the beginnings of his life's major work, Clark lived and wrote for moments of being. From now on, his life would be the quest for the transformative moment, the moment when the veil, for a brief moment, is pulled back and life is seen for what it is.[16]

16: TO RUSSIA, 1958

On Tuesday 11 December 1956, Manning, Dymphna and the children boarded the Shaw Savill liner *Southern Cross* at Southampton, bound for Australia via the Panama Canal. Before he boarded the ship, Clark broke down at the thought of leaving England. Departing Oxford early that morning, he walked in Raleigh Park for the final time, collecting the last of the autumn leaves. Standing on the deck of the *Southern Cross* three hours later, he threw the leaves onto the Southampton docks like a man scattering the ashes of a friend. As they spiralled downwards, Clark looked back wistfully on his time in England. In the background, through the drizzle and the morning's dim winter light, he could see the factories and houses in the distance, their wet bricks gleaming under the white glare of the port's streetlights. Wherever he travelled, Clark found leaving difficult. Every departure was a death of a kind, as if he were being asked to leave part of himself behind.

Walking inside the ship, his nostalgia quickly turned to anger. Shaw Savill's idea of 'the south' reminded him how difficult it was for Australians to escape the colonial straitjacket. In the dining room, reliefs on the wall showed Australians, New Zealanders and South Africans as cricketers, surfers, soldiers and mountaineers. As ever, Clark complained, 'we are seen as simple men of action, men of physical courage, not men who dream dreams, and have visions'. The experience only made him more determined to cling to his own visions. On the voyage home, he continued to work on his short stories and the first chapter of *A History of Australia*.[1]

The family had secured a six-berth cabin below the waterline for the five-week passage that would take them to Trinidad, Panama City, Curacao, Balboa, Fiji and Tahiti, where Clark saw the bay from which Cook observed the Transit of Venus in 1769. In Dunedin, at a conference held on 17 January 1957, he delivered a paper on the discovery of Australia. Four days later, the *Southern Cross* finally arrived in Sydney. The journey represented Clark's temporary farewell not only to England but also to the countries of Asia and the Pacific, 'those non-Australian societies' that had shown him just how insular Australian society was. As in 1940, when he left England to return to Melbourne, he had 'very mixed feelings' about coming home. After Oxford and the stimulation of Europe, he was fearful of returning to a country 'without illusions', a country where people lived in 'the raw', unprotected by 'buildings and manners'. Australians were a people who seemed content to live without 'magic and mystery'. In Europe, Clark felt 'clothed' by history and the 'sad note' of church bells, buildings and trees, as if the continent's cities and towns sounded a melancholy tone that was inaudible in Australia.[2]

Meeting Australian officials and diplomats overseas had also made Clark more critical of his countrymen's tendency to ape the British and Americans. In Europe, as in Asia, he found that Australians did not get to know the locals. They failed to speak their languages, read their journals or listen to their leaders of public opinion. Australians, Clark believed, were not makers, but followers, of policy. It was not that he was anti-British. In Ireland, he was critical of the republicans who hugged their hatred of the English like a 'sore leg', blaming the English for everything. Hatred and contempt were just as debilitating as fawning allegiance. Clark wanted Australians to develop a more positive, 'distinctive' culture, an Australian 'atmosphere' that could be recognised as easily as French, British or American culture. Returning to Canberra in 1957, he felt himself an outsider, unable to align himself with the 'vulgar, rough-mannered, insensitive planners and improvers encouraged by Doc Evatt', or 'the sycophants and career men of the Menzies circus'.[3]

Although his travels and research made news in Canberra, Clark had no shattering findings to report. He told journalists that he was the first historian to express interest in the history of Asia's contact with Australia, but he also had to admit that Asian explorers had not proceeded far beyond Indonesia before the arrival of the Dutch, French and British expeditions. If there was a breakthrough it was in Clark's attitude to Asia. He returned even more convinced that White Australia was doomed, supporting an increase in Asian immigration and dreaming that Australia would one day become a 'synthesis of east and west', a place where 'eastern transcendentalism' would be married with 'western science'. Delivering a public lecture in Canberra in May 1957, he warned of the effects on Asia of rapid industrialisation, fearing it would continue until 'the anthropologists had made their last tape-recording of Asian music and the whole of Asia looked like Ashfield, Braddon and Turner'. On his way home through the South Pacific, he saw societies in the 'twilight' of colonialism, where racism continued to pervade the European mentality. The language of Shaw Savill's travel brochure on Tahiti was one example—'when pure, this is one of the finest and most handsome races in the world'. Clark wrote immediately on his return to the company's management: '[your statement] suggests, or, rather, implies, that the people of mixed race are not so fine. The tone too, is patronising and liable to offend Polynesian and Asian ... May I suggest you leave this sentence out?'[4]

The richness and sheer vitality of the cultures in Asia and the Pacific had woken Clark's senses. For all the deleterious effects of empire, and the relative poverty of countries like India and Indonesia, he came to see their societies as far more authentic and vibrant than countries like Australia. Compared with the racially mixed societies of Asia, the largely homogenous and derivative culture of Australia appeared mediocre and dull. During his short stay in New Zealand, he was irritated by the boasting of local officials, who kept telling him that New Zealand had the biggest library 'south of the line', 'the purest democracy in the world' and the 'best apricot country in the world'. In the 'drab, grey streets of Dunedin', he saw a 'prim' people who busied themselves 'aping Scotland'. He wanted 'to scream', to wake them up from their 'welfare coma and complacency'. Was being 'second-hand' Britons all that Australians and New Zealanders could aspire to, he wondered. Back in Canberra in late January 1957, like many artists and intellectuals who returned home after long stints in Europe, Clark complained of the spiritual aridity of life in Australia. Writing to him from Ireland, the poet Vincent Buckley offered Clark some sage advice. 'The aridities', he said, were 'as much possibilities as obstacles.'[5]

On 31 January 1957, Clark and Dymphna's eighteenth wedding anniversary, Dymphna gave birth in Canberra to Benedict, 'the child of recommitment'. On the *Southern Cross*, she was so heavily pregnant that the crew had run a book on whether she would give birth on board. As with the birth of Katerina, Andrew and Rowland, Clark made no mention of Benedict's birth in his diary. Only Sebastian, his first-born, provoked him to write at length, while Axel's birth, which occurred in the shadow of his mother's death, was recorded without comment.

Dymphna remembered their homecoming as difficult. The tenants had left without paying their rent, taking many of the household appliances with them. For the next eighteen months, paying back debts, making the necessary purchases, they struggled to get by on Clark's university salary. If not for the royalty cheques from the sale of both volumes of *Select Documents* (more than 200 pounds per annum in 1956–57), they could never have afforded to travel in Europe without borrowing money. Back home and unable to afford a car, Dymphna was forced to do everything by bike, including the shopping. With Rowland still in a pram, and Benedict only weeks old, she made her way to the Manuka Baby Health Centre pushing two prams, 'one in each hand'. Shortly after Benedict's birth, she decided to take part in a scheme initiated by Lady Bailey, the wife of the Commonwealth solicitor-general, Kenneth Bailey, designed to induct migrant women into the 'Australian style of housewifery'. Dymphna received 'Mrs Pidder', a Polish woman with a razor-like wit, who had once worked for a German-speaking doctor in Warsaw. She always remembered her arrival at 8 am each day. 'I was getting the kids ready for school and everything was flying about in total chaos and she'd walk in the door and exclaim—'Was für ein Theater!' (What chaos!)

Clark in his study shortly after returning from Asia and Europe, 1956

Then, glancing up to the relative quiet of Clark's study, where Clark would sometimes be working, she'd raise her eyebrows and shout: 'Das Herren Kabinett!' (The men's chamber!) Dymphna and Pidder remained friends for life.[6]

During their first years in Canberra, Clark's correspondence with Dymphna and the family during his trips away in 1957 and 1958 revealed his impish sense of humour. Writing to the family as 'Manning & Dad' from Queenstown in Tasmania, he played the clown in his opening line: 'This will be the last letter of this trip. I have eaten so much roast mutton that it would be easier to baa than compose.' Again from Hobart: 'At last I have found a country with the best sheep, the best cattle, the best railways … and the best harbour in the world. Please warn New Zealand about its rival—or rather, in this respect its twin'. To Axel, then fifteen, and about to play cricket for Melbourne Grammar: 'when not facing the bowling try to soothe yourself with a tune from Bach'. In another letter to Axel, who shared his father's roguish humour, Clark described Sebastian's driving: 'Like a man possessed with a devil … with a curl of the lip [and] a baring of the teeth, he pressed harder on the accelerator … and we plunged, careered madly into the night.' For a man who spent so much of his time apart from his family—teaching, socialising, travelling or entombed in his study—Clark could break down weeks of distance between them with a flourish of his pen. Within the pages of his correspondence he worked a kind of magic, creating a reality that dissolved all others, washing away any hint of bitterness and doubt until it appeared that he held only unadulterated love in his heart. To Dymphna, he wrote from Hobart on 19 May 1958: 'Everyone here asks after you—I think too they see what I feel, how much I miss you but, more important, that I, without you, [am] incomplete—and without the children too.'[7]

When Clark returned to Canberra in late December 1956, he had already completed the first chapter of *A History of Australia*, although he was far from happy with the result. In the six years between the writing of his first sentence in Oxford in 1956 and the publication of volume I, in 1962, he would rework the opening chapter several times. The writing was slow. He was always uncertain of its quality—'finished a second version of Chapter one. It does not satisfy me at all. Damn it!' Before 1957, he had not written an article or essay longer than a few thousand words and the scale of the work was proving daunting. At first he thought he would write a two-volume textbook of Australian history, covering the period from 1788 until the fall of the Chifley government in 1949. But the more he wrote, the more he found himself immersed in the story of the first years of settlement. The long gestation of the *History* was also explained by the fact that he was often preoccupied with other writing—theatre and book reviews for the *Bulletin* and the *Age* (on average, at least one per fortnight), correspondence, diary keeping, lecture writing and, most importantly, his short stories. When his first short story was published in the *Bulletin* in 1957, he was ecstatic. 'On Monday 18 March [I] received £13:13:0. from The Bulletin for A Democrat on the Ganges. This is the first work of this kind by me ever to be published.' Clark's story was an ironic take on the cultural prejudices of Australians in post-colonial India, brief and inconsequential. But its publication spurred him on. In the late 1950s, he devoted more and more time to writing up the autobiographical sketches that would be published as short stories in the 1960s. His themes were universal: childhood, family, love, marriage, faith and death. Thinking of himself as a writer of fiction set him free. In the academy, he felt insulted and humiliated by criticism, backbiting and gossip. As a creative writer he could fly above it all, or so he thought.[8]

In October 1957, when he received his first copy of *Sources of Australian History* from Oxford University Press, he confronted the strangeness of his own creation. Reading his introduction to the collection of historical documents—from the Dutch explorations of the seventeenth century to the end of World War I—he discovered an 'incomplete person'. He tried to convince himself that *Sources* represented everything he 'thought about life and death between 1955 and 1956', but he knew that the book only hinted at his emotional life. 'I am in the book,' he thought, 'but only in jumps and starts.' He could hardly have expected more. In style and tone his introduction to the documents was everything Oxford University Press would have expected of conventional academic scholarship. Throughout 1957, as he continued to write the *History*, he searched for a way to reveal himself in his work—not directly but implicitly, through the words of others. In this respect, his historical writing was no different from his fiction. It had to be animated by the drama of his inner life: his voice, his narrative, his arrangement of the past, every aspect of his work had to be true to 'the man within'.[9]

In the late 1950s, fresh from his spiritual quest in Asia, Ireland and Italy, Clark rekindled his friendship with the poet James McAuley. Whenever he visited Sydney, Clark sought him out. With McAuley, he could talk freely of all that he had felt as he attended Mass in the Catholic churches of Asia and Europe. Attracted by McAuley's Catholicism and his knowledge of eastern religions, Clark saw him as a kindred spirit, someone with whom he could discuss his struggle to write Australia's history. In December 1955, McAuley persuaded Clark to join the editorial advisory board of *Quadrant*, the new journal of politics and culture founded by the Congress of Cultural Freedom specifically to counter the 'leftism' of journals such as *Meanjin*. As *Quadrant*'s editor, McAuley was keen to bring Clark into the fold of intellectuals who opposed communism and who held a less parochial view of Australian literature. Sensitive to Clark's mysticism, he also thought he would make an ideal recruit for the Catholic Church. There was one more bond between them: a love of alcohol. In Sydney they often drank together, Clark, eager for an opportunity to talk about his search for faith over the communion rail of a Sydney bar, McAuley, with his roguish, leprechaun face and uncompromising intellect, always willing to take Clark on. The friendship blossomed at a critical time for both men.

Clark had begun to see the importance of the Portuguese navigator, Pedro Fernandez de Quiros (1563–1615) to his vision for writing *A History of Australia*. In December 1605, Quiros set out to find the fabled *Terra Australis* on behalf of the Spanish King, Philip III, and the Catholic Church. Mistaken, he attempted to found his New Jerusalem in present-day Vanuatu, which he named 'La Austrialia del Espiritu Santo' (Australia of the Holy Spirit). Rejected by the island's indigenous inhabitants, he was forced to flee, although until his death in 1615 he never gave up his dream of founding a new Catholic kingdom in the Great South Land. In the failed journey of a romantic idealist and religious zealot such as Quiros, Clark saw the origins of the story he wanted to tell, 'how three quite different visions of god and man—Catholic Christendom, Protestant Christianity and the Enlightenment—confronted each other in Australia'. Like many Catholics who knew the story of Quiros, he also recognised the dream of an alternative history—Australia settled by Catholic Spain rather than Protestant England. Writing at the time of the Cold War and in the wake of the Labor Party split in 1955, a time when sectarianism still bitterly divided many Australians, Clark conceived Australian history as a clash of ideologies, one that mirrored the climate of ideological and religious conflict in which he lived. In 1958, he published a short essay—'Quiros'—in which he argued that Quiros's vision of Catholic Australia, like the dream of Magellan, had survived nonetheless, 'sustained, nursed and kept alive' until it eventually rose 'triumphant out of the ashes'. Clark was beginning to see the past through the prism of his personal life, his historical writing and his quest for faith becoming one and the same journey. Even before he read Clark's article, McAuley was inspired by Clark's ideas on Quiros and his tripartite vision of Australian history. In 1959, McAuley began work on his epic poem, *Captain Quiros*, which many regard as the summation of his life's work, both as a writer and as a Catholic. As Clark imagined Quiros's vision surviving through the ideas of the English convert Cardinal John Henry Newman (1801–93) and his Catholic followers in Australia, McAuley imagined the ships of Quiros riding 'in upon the present from the past', inspiring a vision of faith that would transform Australian society in the future. Clark's epic history and McAuley's epic poem both owed much to their conversations in the late 1950s.[10]

James McAuley, circa 1960

After seeing McAuley in October 1957, Clark felt his faith in Australia restored. Feeding on the poet's conviction, he attended High Mass at St Mary's Cathedral, carried away as the slowly ascending scales of the Kyrie Eleison quelled the doubt within him. Back in Canberra, he continued with the writing of history, occasionally receiving supportive letters from McAuley—'how goes the intellectual turmoil?' Through McAuley, Clark had also met some of the key figures in the Church hierarchy, men such as James Murtagh—priest, journalist and historian of the Catholic Church in Australia. Murtagh, 'a slick salesman of grace and salvation' (as Clark described him), was also a confidant of Archbishop Daniel Mannix and Clark quickly persuaded him to arrange an appointment. On Wednesday 27 February 1957, Murtagh obliged, driving Clark from Melbourne down to Sorrento to see Mannix. In the car, Clark thought of the last time he had driven along the same stretch of road, in March 1955. Then he sat next to his lover. Now he sat next to a priest. Thinking of his weekend with Gray, with the befrocked Murtagh beside him at the wheel, his affair seemed 'foul'. As they approached Sorrento, he was 'riddled with un-cleanliness' and increasingly anxious about what he would say to 'the great man'. Writing about the meeting later that afternoon, Clark's talent for character description was on full display. His portrait of the 93-year-old Mannix was unforgettable.

We arrived at Sorrento at 2.30pm. Dr. Mannix walked on to the verandah, wearing a beautiful light purple beretta, a cape edged with red, a cassock with flannel underwear visible [underneath], black stockings and slippers with golden buckles. His face was heavily lined, [his] cheeks sagging, though not flabby, the eyes moist, tinged with a faded yellow, a thin line of red along the edge of both eye-lids. The general effect, in repose, was impressive—solemn dignity which often collapsed into an impish twinkle, or chuckle. He coughed a lot. His voice still bears an Irish accent though not often—pitch, generally a mumble at a low pitch. We talked at first about Cork, and I muffed my first compliment. Later, much later, when with more confidence I told him the people of Cork looked on him as one of their proudest sons, he said scornfully, though with that impish twinkle, 'They must be short of people to admire' ... When we left Murtagh genuflected, & kissed the ring of the Archbishop. I shook him by the hand—At the door of the car I turned & it looked as though he was blessing me, & I was doubly moved. Also, he looked like a man for whom it all happened years ago, and like a man who had been stunned, knocked down by a great force, but had the courage, the faith, to stand up to his oppressor, & not to whine in the gutter—supine—and a sadness deep down because...he could not explain why it happened to him & Ireland. [Mannix was] too lovable to make people afraid or angry ... These men, these Catholic Bishops are spiritual men.[11]

For all his love of Catholic ritual and spirituality, Clark was still unable to join the Church. Despite his affection and respect for them, not McAuley, not Murtagh, not even Mannix, could bring him to take the final step. Preparing to visit the Soviet Union in late 1958, he continued to be preoccupied with questions of mortality and religious belief. So much of his writing from these years reads like the words of a man unwilling to accept the certainty of his own death, a man who stands paralysed between doubt and faith, unable to give himself over to institutionalised religion. Yet Clark was convinced that the Catholic Church had managed to preserve a vision of faith closer to Christ's gospel than any other Christian denomination. In his study, he kept the leaflets on Catholic instruction he had received in England, singling out one Catechism question in particular for special consideration.

An Eye for Eternity

Q. After your night prayers what should you do?

A. After my night prayers I should observe due modesty in going to bed; occupy myself with the thoughts of death; and endeavour to compose myself to rest at the foot of the Cross, and give my last thoughts to my crucified saviour.[12]

In moments of despair at his own sinfulness, Clark turned to Catholicism for support. He could not manage to get through life without accepting the existence of something beyond himself. He felt trapped by his own failings—binge drinking, the affair with Pat Gray, his bragging about sexual conquest and his hurtful comments to others, many of whom he counted among his friends—a litany of wrongdoings that made him feel 'unworthy of belonging to other people'. His reading of the Catechism and the Bible, his visits to the church to pray before the statue of the Virgin Mary, and his conversations with Catholics who believed in God as he could not—completely and wholeheartedly—were all cries for help. Reading Christ's teachings, he felt humbled. We were all like 'the lame, the halt and the blind' in St John's gospel. Before God, we were all 'impotent'. In April 1958, he read 'The Double', Dostoyevsky's story of the clerk, Golyadkin, a man who believed his evil actions were performed by his alter ego, Golyadkin junior, who could possess his soul at any moment. Captivated by Dostoyevsky's image of a man undermined by a fraud self, Clark marked the following passage: 'suddenly, in a matter of seconds, a person notorious for his evil intentions and brutish impulses in the shape of Golyadkin junior appeared, and by so doing demolished at one fell swoop all the glory and triumph of Golyadkin senior'.[13]

In Dostoyevsky's Golyadkin, Clark saw something of his own struggle, a man who wanted to be virtuous and loving but who suddenly found himself 'eclipsed' by forces beyond his control, forces that 'dragged him into the mire'. Clark feared his other self, the 'IT' that 'possessed' him, the person whose actions made him feel that his transgressions could 'never be atoned for or forgiven, either by God or man'. 'That is the meaning of sin,' he told himself, 'and of self-destruction.' Wanting to believe, and not being able to, was the greatest 'anguish' imaginable. For Clark, 'unbelief was unbearable'. Without faith of some kind, all 'the mystery' and 'wonder' in life would be drained away. After he tried to talk to others about these things, he was 'terribly hurt' when they shunned him as if he were 'mentally maimed'.[14]

As Clark prepared to embark on his next trip, to the Soviet Union, his beliefs and preoccupations could not have been further removed from the communist view of the world. Day and night, he reflected on the words of the 39th Psalm:

> Lord, let me know my end,
> and what is the measure of my days;
> let me know how fleeting my life is.
> You have made my days a few handbreadths,
> And my lifetime is nothing in your sight.
> Surely everyone stands as a mere breath.
> Surely everyone goes about like a shadow
> Surely for nothing they are in turmoil;
> They heap up, and do not know who will gather

KHRUSHCHEV'S RUSSIA

When Josef Stalin died in March 1953, two and a half million people were imprisoned in the Soviet Gulag. During his three decades in power—in purges and political repression, forced collectivisation and famine, deportations to the Gulag and random shootings and executions—well over fifteen million people lost their lives. The duration and scale of Stalin's terror exceeded the Holocaust and rivalled Russia's enormous losses in World War II. In February 1956, in a 'secret session' at the Communist Party's XXth Congress, Stalin's successor, Nikita Khrushchev, delivered a four-hour-long speech in which he denounced Stalin's crimes. The Soviet delegates were dumbfounded; Khrushchev had publicly admitted Stalin's regime of torture and murder. It did not take long for the news to reach the outside world. Historian Eric Hobsbawm, a leading member of the British Communist Party, recalled the shock felt by many in the West at 'the sheer extent, hitherto not fully realised, of Stalin's mass murders of communists'. After Khrushchev's speech, 'no thinking communist', Hobsbawm admitted, 'could escape asking himself or herself some serious questions'.

Khrushchev's outburst might have appeared surprisingly frank, but it was also a shrewd exercise in political survival. Stalin was saddled with sole responsibility for the crimes committed in the Party's name. As Khrushchev reassured his comrades, 'we all worked with Stalin but that does not implicate us'. His litany of crimes was extremely selective. While he admitted that communists had been persecuted, he said nothing of the millions of non-communists who had died. In the months after his speech, he watched nervously as the ripple effects destabilised the Soviet bloc in Eastern Europe. In East Germany, the already large numbers fleeing across the open border in Berlin soon became a flood. In Hungary, student protests sparked a revolution against the country's Stalinist regime, eventually leading to the installation, under Imre Nagy, of a new socialist government that proposed free elections and termination of Hungary's membership of the Warsaw Pact. At first Khrushchev hesitated, but he soon saw that Hungary was demanding nothing less than complete independence from Russia. Fearful of the effect on other Soviet satellites in Eastern Europe, he decided to intervene.[15]

On the morning of 4 November 1956, Soviet tanks entered Budapest. Within two weeks, Hungary's short-lived revolution was brutally crushed. In the process, 2700 Hungarians were killed, 13 000 arrested and imprisoned and 350 executed (most of them young workers), while more than 200 000 escaped to the West. Imre Nagy was arrested, languishing in prison until 1958 when he was executed—yet another 'enemy of the people' despatched to an early grave. When Clark, listening to the BBC, heard the reports of the Russian invasion, together with the stories of public hangings on the streets of Budapest, he felt 'sick'. The thought of the violence made him 'faint—as in a swoon'. Khrushchev had set the example he intended, but it was now clear to the outside world that the communism practised by Soviet Russia and her satellites was simply another form of tyranny. Despite the post-Stalinist 'thaw', Khrushchev's Russia appeared no more defensible than Stalin's dictatorship.

After 1956, no one could plead ignorance of the Soviet Union's brutality or its ham-fisted imperialism. In Western Europe and in Australia, Communist Party membership declined. Clark might have felt sickened by the violence in Hungary, but his position on communism remained just as ambivalent as his attitude towards the Catholic Church. On the one hand, he doubted 'whether any people accepting Marx and opposing religion [could] understand the human heart' and he deplored the savagery employed by the Communist Party in the Soviet Union. On the other hand, he opposed all those who wished to persecute communists for their beliefs as much as he despised those within the ALP who wanted to crush anti-communists like BA Santamaria. When his Melbourne friend June Philipp appeared before the Royal Commission on Espionage in 1954, he wrote immediately in support:

> Don't let your tormentors make you feel guilty or ashamed. We all know you joined the Communist Party for noble and high-minded reasons … it may be, of course, that the Communist Party is wrong in its methods—terribly wrong—as I believe it is. But I know that you were in it for what it wanted to achieve and not for the methods it used … listen to the choral movement of the 9th symphony—and if you are a believer (as I am) you will find strength to stand up to your oppressors.[16]

Too independent to align himself with one political party or position, and too romantic to forsake the dream of equality and brotherhood that he saw in communist philosophy, Clark left behind trails leading in different directions. Sometimes, even his closest friends weren't sure where he stood on communism. Before he visited the Soviet Union in 1958, he lived through a decade of anti-communist hysteria: the 1949 Victorian Royal Commission into Communism, the Petrov affair and the 1954 Royal Commission on Espionage, the Labor Party split in 1955 and Menzies' failed attempt to ban the Communist Party in 1951—a political climate of intimidation and fear, fuelled by the Cold War, a nuclear arms race and regional instability and stoked by the covert activities of ASIO, which kept Clark (and anyone else who dared to be critical of Australian government policy) under constant surveillance. To dissent was to be accused of being communist. To be communist was akin to supping with the devil. In the wake of Vladimir Petrov's defection from the Soviet embassy, Menzies severed diplomatic relations with Soviet Russia for five years.

Clark saw what was coming: 'I believe the Petrov episode ... will be the beginning of a movement for revenge on the intellectuals of the Left. The bohemians, the drinkers, the free lovers, the emotionally unstable will be persecuted, and made to suffer.' Attending the Royal Commission hearings in Canberra, he noticed how the trial-like atmosphere created barriers between people, making them 'suspicious' of one another. Meeting Labor Leader Doc Evatt in October 1955—a 'powerful personality' who 'sucked ideas and life from others'—Clark saw that Evatt too had fallen victim to the atmosphere of mistrust, seeing blackmail and conspiracy in every new development. No section of Australian society was left untouched by the witch-hunt orchestrated by the Menzies government. One way or another, everyone was expected to declare their allegiance. The Catholic clergy instructed the faithful that a vote for the communists was a vote against the official doctrine of the Church. Government appointments were screened by ASIO, as were Commonwealth Literary Fund grants and university appointments. When he was nominated as president of the Convention on Peace and War Committee for Canberra, External Affairs asked for 'urgent consideration' of Clark's position teaching the diplomatic cadets at Canberra University College. Early the following year, he was 'relieved' of his position, despite the fact that he had decided not to chair the committee. Clark was deemed by ASIO to be 'someone to be watched', a possible 'secret party member'. It was not long before some on the conservative side of politics believed they had proof.[17]

In early 1954, as the French Government continued to fight Ho Chi Minh's Viet Minh forces in Indochina, the American Secretary of State, John Foster Dulles, proposed that the ANZUS signatories (Australia, New Zealand and the United States of America) join forces with France and Britain and intervene. Richard Casey, Australia's Minister for External Affairs, told federal parliament that if Indochina fell to the communists there was little doubt that 'the whole of South East Asia would be threatened'. Clark was one of four 'concerned' Canberra citizens (including the

Anglican Bishop of Goulburn, Ernest Burgmann) who signed a letter published in the *Canberra Times* warning Australia not to support the 'firebrand developments in American policy towards Asia'. Australia, they insisted, should consult with other Commonwealth countries first. They also pointed out that the 'Viet Minh movement' had emerged in Indochina as a legitimate nationalist movement to end French colonial rule.

In parliament, Casey's colleague William Wentworth accused all four signatories of 'following the Soviet line', arguing that the Vietminh were communists and needed to be opposed at all costs. Labor MPs accused Wentworth of McCarthyism—whipping up hatred against intellectuals who questioned government policy. Gough Whitlam mocked Wentworth's 'midget pomposity'. Meanwhile, ASIO noted Clark's views and continued to keep him under surveillance, tapping his home phone and screening his application for the Rockefeller Grant in 1955. Clark's public stand also provoked a rift with his friend and former student, Geoffrey Fairbairn, now even more fervently anti-communist. Throughout 1954 and 1955, Fairbairn pushed Clark to declare his hand, just as he had done in the late 1940s:

> It was you who taught me a long time ago that political cruelty was indefensible and monstrous. It was you who taught me what totalitarianism was … let me make my position clear: I am fighting and shall continue to fight the Communist movement. I was not suggesting that you would approve of political murder; what I was suggesting, nay demanding, and what I do demand of my friends is that they bear witness against these things … I repeat: I am fighting communism. Are you for or against it? I don't know.[18]

Pushed up against a wall and asked for a clear statement of his beliefs, Clark instinctively demurred. He refused to answer Fairbairn's question directly, accusing him of 'snapping at the heels' of Dr John Burton, the former Secretary of the Department of External Affairs, who had condemned the show trial atmosphere of the Royal Commission into Espionage and who Fairbairn had inferred was a 'communist apologist'. Clark's confrontation with Fairbairn was just one example of how the ideological and political contest of the Cold War pitted colleague against colleague and friend against friend.

In such an intense and volatile political climate, intellectuals and writers were divided about the role they should play. Some believed that writers had a responsibility to speak to the issues of the time and that they should defend the principles of academic freedom and freedom of speech. Others believed that writers, especially those outside the academy, should remain above politics. This was almost impossible at this time. Politics infiltrated every aspect of the nation's culture. Overlaying these matters were differences concerning the general direction of Australian culture—should it be focused exclusively on the creation of a national literary culture, or should it be more international in its outlook? In the mid-1950s, small independent literary journals such as *Overland* (founded in 1954), *Quadrant* (1956) and *Meanjin* (1940) fought for their fair share of Commonwealth funding as they staked out different positions across this political divide. *Overland*, bearing on its masthead the words of Joseph Furphy—'temper democratic bias Australian'—was aligned with the Communist Party; *Quadrant*, funded through the Congress of Cultural Freedom by the CIA, was trenchantly anti-communist; and Clem Christesen's *Meanjin* was determined to advance a cosmopolitan and uniquely Australian literary culture. Clark agreed to sit on McAuley's editorial board at *Quadrant*, where he was publishing his short stories, and he defended McAuley against attacks of *Overland*. As a contributor to *Meanjin* he was appalled when Clem Christesen was brought before Menzies' Royal Commission in 1954. While others stood clearly in one camp or the other, Clark stood above the fray. As he told John La Nauze in 1957, he was depressed by the 'overbearing intellectual conformism in Australia', which assumed that there was 'only one correct view of the world' and remained ignorant of all others. Clark was describing both the Left and the Right, the people he believed were 'steeped in liberalism, socialism [and] rationalism, but nothing else'. He wanted a less doctrinaire approach. Rather than trying to find 'homo Australicus', a nationalist project that was in any case doomed to fail, Clark believed Australian intellectuals needed to follow Tocqueville's example. They had to show 'the field of the possible' and point the way to a more visionary, pluralist and outward-looking Australia.[19]

In July 1957, Clark's reputation for standing apart was rewarded when he was elected president of the ACT branch of the Fellowship of Australian

Writers, a federal body founded in 1928, which had tried to remain above the politics of the Cold War but which, like so many cultural organisations, frequently found itself accused of being a communist front. After the relaxation of visa restrictions and contact with the West under Khrushchev, cultural and professional organisations in many countries sent to the Soviet Union delegations comprising architects, town planners, lawyers, health workers, writers and artists—all eager to see what life was like behind the 'Iron Curtain'. Such was the spirit of Arthur Phillips' letter of instruction to Clark as well as to communist writer Judah Waten and the Catholic poet Jim Devaney when the three men were selected to visit the Soviet Union as representatives of the Fellowship of Australian Writers.

> Professor Manning Clark should act as spokesman for the delegation. [The main task is to seek answers to the following questions:] How do writers get their start in Russia? How long is government support given? What restrictions are placed on the choice of subject matter and approach? What is the attitude to the paying of royalties on Australian work published in the USSR? … hoping you will puncture a large cultural hole in the curtain.[20]

Clark was elated. He started learning Russian and even introduced Russian 'conversation' into evening meals at home. For all his reservations about communist methods and Khrushchev's invasion of Hungary, he could not pass up the opportunity to visit Russia, the land of some of his most cherished authors. Like a latter-day Tocqueville, he would make the journey to a foreign country and report back on his findings. Only months before Phillips' letter, the Soviets launched the first satellite into space—*Sputnik*. Shortly afterwards, they sent up another, this time with a dog called 'Laika' on board. The Soviet propaganda machine wasted little time in boasting that these flights were symbols of Russia's modernisation and emerging technological superiority. Clark, lying in a hospital bed in Canberra recovering from a ruptured hernia and still half-delirious from the after-effects of the anaesthetic, heard the news of Laika's voyage into space and wrote to his friend Bruce Grant, imagining packs of dogs sniffing, scratching and hunting their way through the universe until the entire cosmos was charted as

An Eye for Eternity

Flinders had once charted Australia. He fantasised about the dogs spreading suburbia to the edges of the universe, destroying all mystery and hope not only for people on Earth but for all those who lived on planets millions of light years away. Khrushchev's Soviet Man—technocratic, godless and entirely disconnected from Russia's pre-revolutionary past—had as much chance of converting Clark to communism as Laika had of returning to the streets of Moscow. Yet there were things that Clark should have acknowledged about the Soviet Union before he boarded, on 30 October 1958, the Air India flight that took him to Moscow, things that he decided to either dismiss or ignore.[21]

Hungary alone would have provided sufficient grounds for many writers to decline the invitation to visit Russia. The historian Ian Turner, a former student and friend of Clark's, was expelled from the Communist Party over his stance on Hungary. Despite Khrushchev's freeing of political prisoners and his acknowledgement of Stalin's crimes, the 'thaw' was not what it seemed. The historian Orlando Figes has maintained that while the Soviet intelligentsia spoke more openly about the terror, 'ordinary people were still too cowed and frightened by the memory of the Stalinist regime to speak openly or critically'. For ordinary Russians, 'stoicism and silence' were far more common reactions. Russia was a country that had known little else but authoritarian rule for centuries. Under Khrushchev, the Soviet State was still bent on manufacturing social and cultural reality. Communist ideology was all consuming. There was no possibility of deviating from the Party line; all dissent was ruthlessly crushed. Underwriting Soviet propaganda and the slavish mentality of Communist Party apparatchiks was an intellectual crudity of frightening proportions. Khrushchev soon demonstrated his own iron-fisted approach to Russian culture, closing down churches and forcing university students to study 'scientific atheism'. Only a matter of days before Clark left Australia, news broke that the writer Boris Pasternak had been expelled from the board of the Soviet Writers' Union for refusing to attend a meeting in which the renowned poet Anna Akhmatova, a friend of his, was to be denounced. Soon afterwards, Pasternak was attacked in *Pravda*, the official organ of the Communist Party, as being 'alien' and 'remote from Soviet reality'. Depressed by the return of Stalinist intimidation, he withdrew from public life to finish his greatest novel, *Dr Zhivago*, a plea for the retention of the values of Russia's old intelligentsia set at the time of the 1917 revolution. Published in the West, the novel's success saw Pasternak awarded the Nobel Prize for Literature in 1958. For this achievement, he was reviled in the Soviet press and forced to decline his Nobel Prize. As historian Humphrey McQueen would later acknowledge in his book *Suspect History*, Clark, the historian and devotee of Russian literature, chose to continue with his visit to the Soviet Union despite the Soviet government's treatment of Pasternak; however, Clark 'the citizen should have stood down'.[22]

Soon after leaving Australia, Clark discovered the depth of indignation that Pasternak's victimisation had aroused overseas. At a press conference in Delhi, en route to Moscow, the Australian delegation faced 'angry' questions from Indian journalists about Pasternak. One asked why Soviet politicians should 'pass judgement' on literature. Wasn't this yet another example of the Soviet government's intimidation of writers and artists? As spokesperson, Clark fielded the question and hesitated, telling the journalists that, as Australians, the delegation had no 'moral authority' to condemn the Soviet response to Pasternak. He knew instantly that he had failed, admitting afterwards that he 'spoke badly' and paid the price for being 'non-committal'. When Clark, Waten and Devaney finally arrived in Moscow in early November, they found that the British embassy, which 'normally showed hospitality to distinguished visiting Australians', declined to entertain them. The British did not want to risk being seen as tacitly endorsing the Soviets' bullying of Pasternak. At heart, Clark found Pasternak's treatment abhorrent, but like many unsettling aspects of Soviet Russia that he encountered during his brief, three-week visit, he could not bring himself to state his beliefs without equivocation. In each of Clark's literary responses to his experience in the Soviet Union—his diary, his letters home, his letters to the press, and *Meeting Soviet Man*—his impressions of Soviet Russia oscillated wildly between naïve enthusiasm and outright rejection. He did not travel as a political analyst, journalist or even as an historian. Instead, he flew to Moscow like a child journeying to the land of his darkest dreaming, the land of Dostoyevsky and Holy Russia.[23]

SOVIET MAN

When the Air India jet took off from Delhi at 7.10 am on Wednesday 5 November 1958, Clark's stomach remained on the tarmac. Within minutes the plane had shot up to 35 000 feet, cruising at 520 miles per hour. After an hour he was flying over the Himalayas. 'Have you said your prayers, Sputnik III?' the *Age* literary editor asked Clark before he left Canberra. At cruising altitude, Judah Waten looked across at Clark and saw a nervous man downing pills to control his anxiety, 'the most frightened man I've ever looked at'. His performance in Delhi had convinced Waten that Clark was a 'fence-sitter', a 'tongue-tied' dreamer who took refuge in Dostoyevsky every time he was called upon to make a decision. At first Clark thought Waten 'loveable'; but, as the trip progressed, his impressions of Waten became less sanguine. Waten's unblinking support for the Soviets troubled Clark—'he attributes the basest motives to imperialists, Americans and Australian liberals … [and he seems willing] to trample on everything that impedes the great march forward'. Pasternak, Waten told Clark, was 'a man who had allowed his ideas to be used as ammunition in the Cold War', while Khrushchev had 'nipped' the problem of Hungary 'in the bud'. As for the Catholic Devaney—an aged, tall, thin and completely 'imperturbable' man—Clark knew that he would not give himself over to Waten's faith in communism. In Moscow, the three men stayed on the seventeenth floor of the Hotel Ukraine, Clark's room looking out across the city's expanding fields of apartment blocks, a sea of concrete towers and construction sites washed in Russia's grey winter light. Muscovites had a nickname for the new flats— 'Khrushoby'—'merging Khrushchev with the word truschoby ('slums')'.[24]

In his first letters home to Dymphna, Clark could barely contain his excitement: 'I love every minute of it: the people are so tremendously alive & proud of what they have done, and confident … the whole thing is fabulous, I still think I'm at the films.' The lack of 'social pretension' on the streets and the desire for equality impressed him. Compared with the entries he was making in his diary at the same time, Clark's letters sometimes read as if they were written by a different person; the prose is far more animated and

Judah Waten, Manning Clark and Jim Devaney, Moscow, 1958

enthusiastic, the person within their pages more rounded and more recognisable. In a reference to the family's washing machine, he wrote: 'I have just put on the clothes washed by M.C. They have not that snowy whiteness which the Thor creates.' While he made it abundantly clear to Dymphna that he detested the compulsion inherent in Soviet communism—'here they are trying to persuade, cajole, bully everyone to like art, culture etc; I do not like the way they press people to behave, to be cultured etc …God help those who just can't agree'—Clark, for once, saved his lightness for her. She replied with the details of the 'minutiae' of her daily life: 'as all the big questions remain unanswered, this is no occasion for comment, and I can only continue with the catalogue of small and smaller events. Rowland has been quite sick with tonsillitis … you are gone but not forgotten.'

More than anyone else, Dymphna understood the depth of Clark's attachment to Dostoyevsky. Now, finally, he was in Russia, and he had to let her feel his elation. He hinted of his deeper doubts, telling her of his fear that the communists had 'snuffed out the inner life' of man and impoverished the people's 'spiritual life', but his overall reaction was one of infectious enthusiasm. Driven around Moscow and Leningrad by his hosts from the Soviet Writers' Union, visiting museums, universities and libraries, enduring earnest talks at collective farms on the quantity of milk produced and the number of potatoes harvested per hectare, and knowing full well what had happened under Stalin, Clark wrote to Dymphna that Russia had entered 'the great moment in its history'. 'It may be', he told her, that 'the creative burst' was over, that the communists would now bring to everyone 'the fruits of that colossal bursting forth'; such was their belief in 'enlightenment and progress' and their 'high seriousness, enriched by gaiety and tenderness'. To witness this historical moment, which Clark believed began in the 1860s with the emancipation of the serfs, was 'one of the greatest experiences' of his life. But to describe what happened in Russia between the 1860s and the Khrushchev era as a 'creative burst' borders on farce. The Russia held in Clark's heart, chiselled from the pages of Dostoyevsky, combined with his attraction for the utopian vision of Lenin, blinded him to historical and political realities.[25]

Sitting in his hotel room each evening, after writing at least a thousand words to his family, Clark put his correspondence to one side of his desk and picked up his diary. He then summoned the energy to write for himself. As in England two years earlier, his diary writing became increasingly epigrammatic. Words and phrases stood alone, as if asked to carry more weight, as if waiting to be 'written up'. They also recorded the one aspect of Clark's inner life that he continued to hide from Dymphna: his yearning for eternal life. While he was exhilarated about Russia when he wrote to her, in the diary he complained of feeling bored, tired and listless: 'I am not alive, my sensibilities atrophy in this sort of society.' At times, he sounded like a priest in exile, depressed at the sight of the churches 'toppling down', sceptical that members of an atheist society could show compassion to one another, and convinced that Soviet Man held little sympathy with his beloved 39th Psalm. 'Sometimes I yearn for a society influenced by Rome,' he pined. 'This is Byzantine—continental—There is something indefinable, yet alien here.' Clark's torrid quest for the certainty and consolation of religious faith was slowly changing his diary writing. Line by line, his language was becoming more confessional and prayer-like. On the page, his spiritual searching appeared fervent, yet away from his desk it could easily appear comic.[26]

On 8 November, in Moscow, Clark met Harry Rigby, an Australian Sovietologist then working in the British Embassy. As he was unable to see Clark on the embassy grounds due to the British Government's stance on Pasternak, the pair met at a Moscow restaurant, the Armenian. Rigby remembered the evening as 'rather Kafkaesque—and very long'. After queuing for ages to get in, they entered a 'surreal' dining room. Tables were piled high with dishes and cutlery, while 'cooks' moved customers from one table to another as if to discourage them from ordering. Finally, they found a table and refused to move. Two Stasi officers who had travelled from Berlin for a 'police conference' soon joined them, communicating through Clark's rough German and the clinking of vodka glasses. By the time they had finished their meal it was midnight. Out on the street, Clark and Rigby were unable to get a taxi, so they set off along the embankment of the Moscow River in the direction of Hotel Ukraine. 'Miraculously', after at least half an hour's walk in the freezing night air, Rigby managed to flag a taxi down. As he opened the cab door, Clark, who already had a track record of outlandish performances in taxis, suddenly changed the conversation: 'Harry, I've been meaning to ask you,' he said: 'What is your view of the apostolic succession?' Rigby was stumped. About such matters, he had to confess that he had 'no position'. 'It's very important,' Clark insisted, 'I'll show you the key to it when we get to the hotel.' When they finally arrived back at the Hotel Ukraine, Clark went straight to his Bible, searching for the passage that 'would clinch it'. Rigby waited with bated breath. Clark turned the pages furiously until he finally made his announcement: 'I can't find it!' he exclaimed. The page had been torn out. Forced 'to forego (sic) clarification of the apostolic succession', Rigby bid Clark farewell, rushing home to prepare for his departure back to Melbourne. One night with Clark in Moscow, never to be forgotten. Four decades later, Rigby still enjoyed telling the story, relishing the opportunity to relive Clark's vodka-fuelled zeal to find just one biblical passage. Well aware of his friend's talent for acting, he nonetheless saw something 'deadly serious' in Clark's intent.

> Manning regarded our particular variant of Western society as fatally faulted, but he could not make up his mind about the remedy: was it to be found in Rome or in Moscow? He was inclined to accept the claims of Lenin's Bolsheviks to be their true heirs, via the French Revolution, of the Enlightenment. But what if it was precisely the Enlightenment where it all went wrong? Should we ever have rejected the authority of the See of Peter, the rock on which Christ built his Church?[27]

In the few hours he spent with Clark, Rigby saw a man who confronted the ideological choices facing the postwar world from an extremely unorthodox perspective. Rather than relying on political or social analysis, Clark employed his knowledge of European history and Christianity to intuit metaphysical truths—an Australian mystic wandering the streets of Moscow in search of his elusive *éternel*. Like every other conflict in his life to that point, Clark sought the truth through Russian writers—in this case, the fate of Tolstoy, Dostoyevsky and Chekhov in Soviet Russia. Driving to Yasnaya Polyana, the home of Leo and Sophia Tolstoy, in the 'sapless month of November', the frost 'lying thick on the ground', the landscape 'vast and brooding', the sky clear and blue above him, Clark looked out on the villages he passed along the way and saw 'the guts of the old poverty, vermin, filthridden Russia being ripped out and replaced by bricks, concrete and chromium'. The new architecture was utilitarian but 'uninspired'. At Tolstoy's estate, he walked through the house, down to the author's grave, set 'deep in a birch forest of unbelievable beauty' where he pocketed a stone as a memento. What angered him was the way the communist authorities emphasised Lenin's view of Tolstoy, expecting visitors to believe that Tolstoy's flight from home days before he died represented his rejection of the nobility. Class, it seemed, could explain everything in Tolstoy's life.

A few days later, in Leningrad, while visiting the house in which Dostoyevsky had died in 1881, Clark realised that much of the author's legacy had been suppressed. The Soviets might have been proud of Dostoyevsky but they were not confident enough to publish *The Devils*. As with Tolstoy, Clark found the doctoring of Dostoyevsky's past 'patronising and arrogant'. It permitted only 'one vision of the world', as though the Tsars, the Church and the aristocracy had never existed, as though 'the faith by which men had lived for thousands of years, their hopes, their aspirations, fears, dreams, visions had never been, or what had been was worthless before the coming of Soviet man'. The 'tragic grandeur' of Russia that Dostoyevsky and Tolstoy had revealed to Clark twenty years earlier was precisely the vision denied by the communists. The Soviets wanted to 'prune away all the inwardness and sobbing souls and stress hope and strength'. Clark thought of all this 'with sadness'.

By the time he finished writing up his Soviet diary some weeks later in Paris, he had made up his mind about communist Russia—not by examining the policies of Stalin and Khrushchev but by reading St Augustine's *Confessions*. In a literary epiphany that echoed Dostoyevsky, he remembered attending High Mass in the Brompton Oratory in Chelsea only days earlier, writing of how his body shook during the Kyrie of Byrd's *Mass for Three Voices*. As he gazed at a woman whose face seemed lit by piety, charity and the most beautiful resignation, he saw why he could never accept the view of humanity put forward by Soviet Russia. The scene was contrived. But Clark was also being truthful. 'I cannot abandon the hope [of immortality] … the brotherhood of communism is not enough. Who gave them the right to decide for others?' Racked by a 'profound sense of incompleteness', he finished the diary with the words of St Augustine:

Thou hast made us for
Thyself and our souls will not
Rest till they find
Repose in Thee
Now for Home[28]

When Clark arrived home in mid-December 1958, the picture he presented of the Soviet Union was radically different. The articles he had promised to the *Age* before he left Australia appeared in January 1959, and they provoked a lively debate. Clark suggested that the Russian people were as free as they wanted to be, insisting that over 90 per cent of Soviet citizens 'agreed with the policy of the party'. This was precisely the impression that his minders from the Soviet Writers' Union wanted to impart. Remarkably, Clark appeared to accept their propaganda uncritically. The Soviets, Clark proclaimed, had 'begun the greatest revolution in human history'. The events of 1917 were the people's 'great inspiration'. They had provided Soviet culture with its 'creative drive'. More articles appeared in the current affairs magazine *Nation* in February and March, some containing prose of which *Pravda* would have been proud. Arguing the Communist Party line, Clark insisted that restricting certain freedoms was a temporary measure necessary until such time as the revolution was completed. Khrushchev, he implied, had little choice but to invade Hungary because the communists' hold on power was so tenuous. He praised the Soviet Government for extending culture to the masses, raising the standard of living and 'spreading enlightenment'. The prose was reminiscent of the letter of thanks to the Soviet authorities signed by Clark, Waten and Devaney and published in the *Moscow News* on 20 December 1958, with its gushing description of communist Russia's 'cultural flowering'.

At times, in his articles for the *Age* and *Nation*, Clark seemed oblivious to the suffering of Stalin's victims. It was possible to read his reflections on Russia and conclude that he was willing to justify the deaths of millions for what he saw as a worthy and noble cause. '[When the serious-minded Russian] sits back now … after war, revolution, civil war, industrialisation, collectivisation, treason trials and the great liberation after Stalin died, and all the achievements in science, sport and culture—it would be very odd indeed to be a doubting Thomas.'[29]

In April, the letters he had written to Dymphna from Russia were typed by his research assistant, then edited lightly and published in the *Bulletin*. By now, little that Clark wrote was exclusively for a private audience. Photographs showed him sporting his new Lenin-like goatee beard; and, in the *Bulletin*, his chorus of praise for the Soviet Union continued. 'Forget all about the miserables in the Soviet Embassy in Canberra,' he enthused. 'I don't know where they found them, nor how they persuaded them to behave like that, [but] before you die, you must see a Chekhov play, a Tchaikovsky opera, you must see the people.' He referred to his meeting with Alexsei Surkov, Secretary of the Soviet Writers' Union, the man who had led the denunciation of Pasternak, and described him as a 'very great man'. Reservations, however, did begin to surface. Clark expressed his concern about Soviet Russia's break with religion, its lack of charity to those who failed to toe the party line, and the shallowness of 'social realism'. Yet the impression left by his journalistic reports from behind the Iron Curtain was overwhelmingly positive. Clark was proud of his efforts too—cutting, dating and filing every article that appeared in the press, sending copies to his old friend Ian Milner, with whom he had spent a few days in Prague on his way home, and to Helena Romanova, his friend from the Soviet Writers' Union. These letters offer some insight into why Clark's initial public statements on Russia were so enthusiastic; on a personal level, he was keen to repay the hospitality of his hosts. As he told Romanova, she would see from the articles 'just how much we came to admire what you have achieved in the cultural field, and, above all, that continuation of high seriousness and gaiety, that capacity both to weep and to laugh from the heart'. He was also determined to provoke public debate. Clark boasted to Milner that 'the articles in the Age stirred up a good controversy'. It was 'tremendously important', Clark told him, to get Australians to see that Soviet Russia had 'a noble dream', even if it had been imperfectly carried out, just as it was important to get Russians to see that 'people may want something more than what they are offering'.

Clark took it upon himself to decide what the Australian people needed to know. And he knew full well that praising Soviet Russia in Menzies' Australia would ignite controversy. On the Left, many (such as Ian Turner) saw his articles as outspoken and courageous, while on the Right the response was one of dismay. The most eloquent expression of disappointment came in the form of private correspondence. The poet Vincent Buckley, now back in Australia and one of the leading Catholic intellectuals at Melbourne University, wrote personally to Clark and offered him a frank assessment of his articles in the *Age*.

> You will probably be as distressed to receive this as I am to write it. But I have thought hard, and decided that silence would be an implicit acquiescence in what you are doing … In 1959 naiveté is a crime, and self-deception is a betrayal of other people as well as of oneself … Your articles in The Age are not merely a most trivial, naïve, second hand and question begging hand-ing-on … of the Soviet cultural line, but are also disturbingly unhistorical. In your first article, you carefully refrain from making the two points that you made to me in private conversation: that the present activity in Russia is part of a post-Stalin thaw, and that you are still irrevocably opposed to communism both as an ideology and as an international conspiracy. Instead, you present yourself to your readers as the utterly captivated man, gratefully sucking the fresh air of the expansive State into tired lungs, and conscious of no wrong behind the grandiose gestures of murderous Caesar … I didn't

think the day would come when I would feel obliged to attack you for doing a job which even Judah Waten would baulk at doing. No Australian writer will believe your account, though many with devious motives will pretend to … I write to you not only from personal friendship, but because I think that, of all people, a distinguished, original, and vital historian should refrain most scrupulously from the stupidest and most harmful fairy-story of the century. Believe me, your articles can achieve nothing but harm.[30]

Coming as it did from someone Clark respected, Buckley's criticism unsettled him. He knew that Buckley spoke at least one truth: Clark played to his audience, saying one thing in private and another in public. Just as he told Buckley that he was opposed to communism, privately Clark told Waten that, although he found Russians to be 'loveable people', he 'did not share their Marxist philosophy'. He was never so blunt in print. Buckley demanded that Clark be more consistent, but consistency was not something to which Clark aspired. In June, he heard that Angus & Robertson had agreed to publish a 'small edition' of *Meeting Soviet Man*. As he prepared the manuscript, he started to rethink the enthusiastic endorsement of the Soviet Union he had offered in his articles. By the time he sent a draft of the manuscript to Waten in July, he found reason to vent the deeper doubts he had expressed earlier in his diary. Waten was shocked. The positive tone of Clark's articles in the *Age* had been replaced by 'anti-communism'; Clark had gone from one extreme to the other. When Waten reviewed the book on its publication in early 1960, he condemned it as a 'great disappointment', accusing Clark of being swayed by his critics and retreating to an 'each-way method' of analysis. Privately, he told Clark that he had done nothing more than add 'to the vast assemblage of anti-Soviet and anti-communist books continually pouring off the presses of the capitalist world'. Dymphna's telegram to Clark on the day the book was launched could not have been more ominous: 'today you cast the pebble tomorrow comes the ripple'.

Clark knew from the moment he completed the book that, for different reasons, Waten, McAuley and Buckley 'would not like it'. Reading the reviews, he suddenly discovered what it was like to face a barrage of criticism. McAuley sent him his 'critical' review before it was published in *Quadrant*, telling him that most of the book was little more than 'a guided tourist production, mid fifties style'. Douglas Stewart called it 'extremely muddled'. Donald Horne labelled it 'a flop', astonished at its provincialism, 'its look-at-me-mum quality'—there was 'not one new fact in the book', said Horne. In Moscow, when Oksana Krugerskaya from the Soviet Writers' Union finished reading the copy that Clark mailed her, she was extremely disappointed. In his reply, Clark attempted to explain his thinking: 'it was not my intention to say anything uncharitable about the people we met,' he told her, 'but that does not mean … that I share their view of the world'. Clark had achieved what he would manage on many occasions in the years to come—to antagonise both Left and Right. Tom Fitzgerald, the editor of *Nation*, probably put it best of all: Clark was 'a sensitive, religious, Canberra radical', who had an 'abnormal sense of the desolation of things in Western society'. It was also true that much of the criticism of Clark's first major essay in print was accurate.[31]

Meeting Soviet Man read like the work of a writer still undecided about the philosophical and political principles that underpinned his worldview, a writer who approached the Soviet Union as 'a boy from the bush'—naïve and misty-eyed—his eyes fixed on a romantic ideal. It was also the work of a man who had never personally experienced violence or intimidation. When he referred to the millions who died under Stalin, Clark weighed 'the cost of human lives' and suffering against 'the price of defending the revolution'. 'Is it worth it?' he asked. Never once did he quote the numbers killed, or detail the methods of persecution. These horrors had merely 'muddied the waters' of his precious Revolution. Nor did he devote even one chapter to the Soviet State. At the beginning of the book he argued that, by 1958, few in Australia were taking Soviet Russia seriously, but, after three weeks there, he was convinced that it was time to do so. This was the naïvety of the book's premise: that three weeks in Moscow and Leningrad might explain the future course of a lumbering, totalitarian state that was slowly emerging from the barbarity of the Stalin era. As an outsider, Clark could do no more than look at the people on Moscow's Red Square and proclaim blithely that they 'seemed to believe in getting there'.

The other problem was style. Clark's opinions were often shrouded behind the scenes and actors he was describing, particularly when it came to his view of Lenin. On the surface, he appeared to think to himself that Lenin was 'Christ-like', but he was referring to the Soviet portrayal of Lenin in memorials and museums. In fact, Clark revered Lenin as one of 'the great teachers of mankind'. Again, he seemed to overlook the fact that Lenin was more than willing to employ violence ruthlessly, particularly through the operations of the Cheka—the Bolshevik secret police. He seemed unable to appreciate that Marx, who was much more a scholar 'in the stream of the enlightenment' than Lenin, was far more deserving of his praise. In Tiflis, when Clark looked at Lenin's portrait on the wall of a railway station waiting room, he joked that he had the appearance of a man who 'had just tapped impatiently those notes on the drum at the beginning of Beethoven's violin concerto'. Even though Clark was trying to reveal the absurdity of communist propaganda, his allusion to Beethoven jarred because it seemed to trivialise the seriousness of what he was attempting to understand. For the anticommunists like McAuley and Buckley, Clark provided more than enough inflammatory material. For communists like Waten, Clark performed the same service. Waten accused him of 'giving pleasure to Cardinal Gilroy, the Right Hon. R. G. Menzies and James McAuley and Co … the reactionary establishment of this country'.

Indeed, there were times when Clark let his revulsion at Soviet intimidation show, especially in his chapter on Pasternak, where, after reading the letter written to Pasternak by the editorial board of the literary magazine *Novy Mir*, he saw that it 'stank to high heaven of spiritual popery'. All the criticisms of Soviet Russia that he had voiced in his diary were also written up and given more force. Waten no doubt squirmed when he read Clark's pessimistic conclusion. Soviet man, Clark decided, would never produce great music or great literature because he refused to accept the great mystery of the struggle between good and evil; the communists denied the possibility of a religious view of the world.[32]

Before he left for Russia, Clark sent McAuley 'Monologue of a Man in Black', his short story exploring the anti-communist hysteria in Canberra in the 1950s, which McAuley eventually published in *Quadrant* in the autumn of 1959. But, after reading Clark's articles on the Soviet Union in the *Age*, he became increasingly 'worried' about Clark. In his short story, McAuley thought Clark had 'left himself in the rather fashionable position of deploring both the Communists and the anti-Communists as equally horrible', while in his pieces for the *Age* he appeared to have reverted 'to a fellow-travelling position'. Buckley had given McAuley his explanation—Clark was 'fighting against the strong pull towards Catholicism which he has felt over recent years'—but McAuley remained undecided and wrote to their mutual friend Eris O'Brien, now Catholic Archbishop of Canberra, hoping that O'Brien might talk to Clark: 'I don't know what the explanation is,' he said, 'but [Manning] seems to me to be in a very desperate and ambiguous condition.' McAuley thought Clark so fragile he decided not to give him his opinion about the articles in the *Age*, lest Clark react as he expected—hurt and angry—which would have left him with little choice but to remove him from *Quadrant*'s editorial board. 'And I don't want that,' he admitted to O'Brien. Both men hoped that Clark would soon join the Catholic Church. Eight months later, in January 1960, Clark picked up his first copies of *Meeting Soviet Man* from the offices of Angus & Robertson in Sydney and then met McAuley in Crows Nest, on the city's north shore, to give him one. Settled in a bar, they talked about Rome and Kyrie Eleison, about McAuley's capacity for faith and Clark's longing for the same. McAuley told Clark that, in all the religions of the world, there was only one true revelation. Clark replied that Rome and the Eastern churches were the only ones to 'preserve the image of Christ'. As always, after talking to McAuley, Clark felt 'deeply happy and secure'; even being close to the faithful buoyed his soul. When McAuley got home and began to read *Meeting Soviet Man*, he was perplexed. What did Clark truly believe?[33]

Early in 2007, I found a first edition of *Soviet Man* on the shelf of Clark's study in Canberra. At first, I noticed only faint markings on the text. Some weeks later, when I removed the dust jacket, I saw that Clark had written in pencil on the inside of the back cover. The handwriting was not that of the older Clark; the script flowed too freely. The note was written some time after the publication of *Meeting Soviet Man*, probably in the mid-1960s, although it is impossible to be certain. It was another of Clark's notes to the future, in which the truth arrived as an afterthought. 'The truth with the boy from the bush is that he [relies] upon beliefs deeply shared emotionally by

Meeting Soviet Man, *first edition, 1960*

Lenin and Dostoyevsky, and approaches Soviet Man with too much reverence and too much awe. Because it contains the element of fear [the book] tends to inhibit the discovery of truth.'[34]

Clark knew that *Meeting Soviet Man* was deeply flawed. His yearning for a utopia led him to say many things about communist Russia that he later regretted. But, unlike his friend James McAuley, he could not stand on one side of the divide, knowing who his enemies were, giving himself completely to one ideology or to one faith. To those around him, Clark often appeared non-committal and confused, a man crippled by his own indecisiveness. But, as he often said years later, he was never a joiner; he looked on life as a stranger. The darkness that plagued him, the fear of his own annihilation, was also the fear that would drive him to write *A History of Australia* in the years ahead.

ANNA KARÉNINA

A NOVEL BY
LEO TOLSTÓY

Translated by
LOUISE *and* AYLMER MAUDE

With an Introduction and Notes by
AYLMER MAUDE

LONDON
OXFORD UNIVERSITY PRESS
NEW YORK   TORONTO

Oxford University Press, Ely House, London W. 1

GLASGOW NEW YORK TORONTO MELBOURNE WELLINGTON
CAPE TOWN SALISBURY IBADAN NAIROBI LUSAKA ADDIS ABABA
BOMBAY CALCUTTA MADRAS KARACHI LAHORE DACCA
KUALA LUMPUR HONG KONG TOKYO

PART SIX

17: A VIEW FROM THE STUDY

The view from
Clark's study, 2010

The steps of the ladder are designed to discourage 'frivolous visitors'—only ten steps at an angle of seventy degrees, so steep it's a wonder Clark didn't die falling down them. Halfway up, bookshelves already line the walls, Lawson and Jung less than an arm's length away. At the top of the stairs, the eye is drawn immediately to the room's one source of light—a large north-facing window—before which sits Clark's wooden desk. The view is expansive. Looking out across the garden below, shrouded behind a rising sea of eucalypt and oak, the flagpole of Parliament House on Capital Hill pushes above the skyline. From here, anything seems possible.

The study is barely twelve square metres, an isolated tower where Clark spent so many hours in the last three decades of his life. In the 1970s and 1980s, when journalists came to interview Clark at home, they almost always ascended the steps to the study, like scribes entering Valhalla. For his children and many of his admirers, it remains a special place, so closely identified with Clark that it has become a shrine of remembrance. Despite the fact that Robin Boyd added additional sun screening, the room is a furnace in summer. Clark usually dressed in trousers and long-sleeved shirt regardless of the temperature. His routine rarely varied. He took his first cup of tea upstairs in the study at 7 am as family life stirred below him—the background music to his prose. At 10 am he descended the ladder, a book tucked under his arm, walked out the front door and round the back of the kitchen to 'Clarkie's corner'. There, he stood near the chook shed, his feet just touching the lawn as he peed. 'Bloody embarrassing', he'd say if anyone walked by. Then another cup of tea and back up to the study until lunch, all service dutifully provided by Dymphna. Each climb up the ladder was a reminder of the struggle that lay ahead.

By the early 1960s, Clark's life had become one with his writing. Every day was marked by familiar rhythms, thousands of mornings that began in exactly the same way—the pen, 'the blank page', the view to the north. When Clark first looked out his study window in 1953, save the spire of St Andrew's church to the north-east, he saw only cleared paddocks and bushland. In the 1960s and 1970s, the paddocks became the tree-lined streets of Canberra's inner south. By the 1980s, he could see Australia's new Parliament House. In his last years, the trees gradually obscured his view, as if slowly closing his world down.[1]

To walk into Clark's study today is to enter something like a crypt. He had entombed there everything that was precious to him. His ink bottle and nib pens in the desk drawer, his correspondence from Dymphna, the letters from his children, old family photographs, memorabilia and awards, and the most precious items of all—his books ... the things he placed between himself and the world because he could not face reality. At first sight, the study has the appearance of an unexceptional museum exhibit—the writer's study circa 1980. But, on closer inspection, Clark's personal touch soon emerges from the shadows. Pinned on the back of the study door are the works of art and figures from whom he drew his inspiration—John Curtin, James Cook, Ferdinand Magellan, Fyodor Dostoyevsky, Robert O'Hara Burke, Edward Munch's *Scream*, Rembrandt's *Prodigal Son*, Arthur Boyd's *The Mourners*, Stefan Lochner's *Madonna*, and Jesus Christ—the colour draining from their faces as the ink and paper slowly disintegrate. On top of the filing cabinets are the photographs Clark held dear: the beatific Catherine Clark, a dapper Henry Lawson and different versions of himself—the historian at his desk, the historian as Aussie Rules star, the historian as family man. Around the room, on the bookshelves squeezed into every available bit of

wall space, are Clark's 'abandoned loves', the books that represent different stages of his life. Shortly before he died, Clark imagined his books calling out to him: 'Why did you forsake me?'[2]

One of the most extraordinary aspects of Clark's study is that he conceived it as a future reading room for biographers. In the last few years of his life, he checked that each book was named and dated, sometimes placing a question mark ('Canberra, 1973?') if he was uncertain, or adding a comment in brackets ('Dante's *Divine Comedy* bought in Oxford in 1939 in Italian'). Standing in front of his bookshelves, he wrote down his directions to his future chronicler, inserting comments in the preliminary pages of his books. While similar to the ones scattered throughout his papers, they never fail to surprise. It's as if Clark imagined the biographer opening his books and requiring assistance. Hence, he left comments such as these: 'bought in Melbourne, 1936—not my underlinings! 'Re-read 1973 and March–April 1979 for volume four, see passage on railways'. From the comments he entered in the various editions of his histories, it is possible to appreciate the extent to which he foresaw his work as an historical artefact. In the copies of his early publications, such as *Select Documents*, he simply entered 'Manning Clark, Canberra'. With the publication of *A History of Australia*, his inscriptions changed, reflecting his increasing hope to be remembered by posterity. Inside the hardback of Volume III: 'seen first at Middletown, Connecticut, 27 November 1973'; inside the hardback cloth of Volume V: 'Manning Clark, Canberra (Bound by 15 September, seen on Friday 18 September 1981)'. Even the first sighting of his work was for him a momentous historical event. Clark imagined his future biography reading something like this: 'Manning Clark first set eyes on Volume Five of *A History of Australia* on Friday, 18 September 1981.'[3]

Every period of Clark's life is represented in the books in his study. Books from his father's library at Mentone, one or two of his mother's school textbooks, the books he read in his teens, his first copies of Lawrence and Dostoyevsky, the volumes of Carlyle he bought at a secondhand bookshop in the 1930s, shelves of Australian history and multiple copies of his own works, including the editions translated into Japanese, Italian and many other languages. Inscriptions in books Clark and Dymphna gave one another record their moments of separation ('For the Russian journey October 1958') and bittersweet reunion ('for the one who provided the bridges to cross those oceans. From the one who was sometimes mad enough not to use those bridges, Manning, Anniversary Day, 31 January 1978'). Others remain ambiguous. In a copy of Joyce Cary's novel *The Captive and the Free*, which Dymphna gave to Clark, she left the following inscription: 'For Manning. From one captive to another. September 1959'.[4]

Clark devoted a whole section of his study exclusively to the giants of Russian literature, with Ibsen the lone intruder. Sitting above the volumes of Dostoyevsky, Chekhov and Tolstoy are a pair of Clark's old walking boots and a bugle. As Clark put it, every book 'mapped the country he had travelled'. Acquiring books also helped him to belong in Canberra. With every extra volume he purchased, his attachment to Tasmania Circle and his study grew. Sebastian never forgot the day in 1950, when, as a young boy, he saw his father's books arrive in huge tea chests from Melbourne. As Clark opened each chest, carefully pulling the books out one by one, he became more and more excited—as though, with his books stacked around him, his own arrival in Canberra was now complete. Unlike many academics, Clark kept the majority of his books at home. His university office was for teaching, not writing. If he wanted a book, he stopped at nothing to obtain it, even writing to secondhand bookshops in London to order the books he could not find in Australia. Axel remembered accompanying his father to bookshops in Canberra, where Clark, piles of books already under his arms, would beg Axel to 'get him out of the shop' before he bought any more. Benedict recalled Dymphna's reaction to each new purchase in the 1960s, when the family's finances were still tight. 'Dad was always buying books … Mum would see a pile of books come through the door and she'd sort of faint, then go around and show him the place on the bookshelf where he already had them all.' As Clark's hunger for books increased, new bookshelves had to be added down-stairs, his collection, finally totalling 10 000 volumes, eventually overtaking the children's bedrooms, a creeping Leviathan halted only by his death.[5]

Every writer's study is the relic of a lifelong conversation with literature, a midden of intellectual influences, discarded ideas and creative inspiration. Clark's study was no different, but he used books in a way that few others do. His life is written in the pages of the literature he treasured. He treated his books like correspondence, as if each novel was addressed to him personally. And he responded immediately. Over time, his replies merged with the orig-inal text, until each novel in his collection read like a dialogue between Clark and its author. He recorded the place and date of the book's purchase, as well as each subsequent reading. He marked resonant phrases and passages, wrote comments in margins, and scribbled pages of notes on jacket covers with every reading. Re-reading his favourite novels, he saw his original markings and recognised his younger self. Each new reading brought a new perspec-tive, tracking changes in his intellectual trajectory, even marking milestones in his life. If he knew that a major event was about to occur—publication of the next volume of *A History of Australia*, a book launch or perhaps the announcement of a literary prize—he re-read a favourite novel (usually Dostoyevsky) to mark the occasion, then noted the event on the inside cover of the book ('re-read for launching of volume five, 8 October 1981'). In this

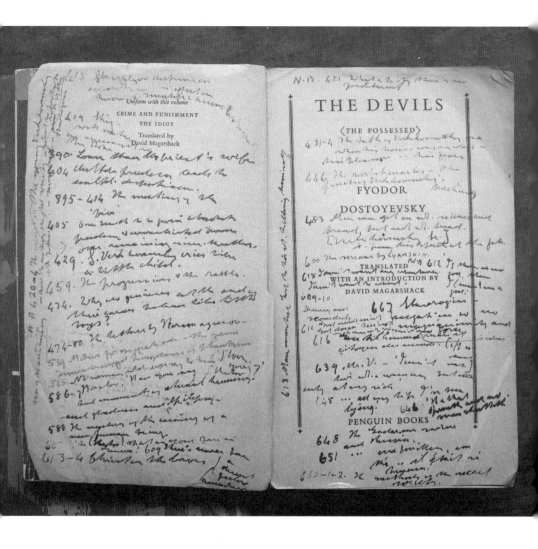

way, he turned his library into yet another diary, layering the text with his own thoughts and feelings, over and over, until they became a tableau of his most intense lived experience, his interaction with literature.[6]

Occasionally, Clark cut out paragraphs from articles in the press or requested that his research assistant type particular passages from novels or biographies. He then left them in his papers, as if leaving clues to his state of mind. On one piece of paper, Clark noted Tennessee Williams' reply to a journalist's question in 1962. 'Interviewer: What is it actually that you despair

An Eye for Eternity

of?' Williams: I despair sometimes of love being lasting, and of people getting along together as nations and as individuals.' Elsewhere, he recorded a
passage from Albert Schweitzer's biography of Bach: 'When asked how he
had managed to bring his art to such perfection, Bach usually answered: "I
have had to work hard; anyone who will work equally hard will be able to do
as much."' In the pages of his most cherished works, it's possible to see him
using literature as an instruction manual on how to live. In Townsville, in
1973, he marked a passage from Ibsen's *Wild Duck*: 'There are people in this
world who dive to the bottom the moment they're winged, and never come
up again.' In Sydney, after seeing John Bell play Uncle Vanya in *The Seagull*,
he raced back to find his copy of Chekhov's work, making special note of one
comment made by 'Nina' towards the end of the play: 'What really matters
is not fame, or glamour, not the things I used to dream about—but knowing
how to endure things. How to bear one's cross and have faith. I have faith
now and I'm not suffering quite so much, and when I think of my vocation
I'm not afraid of life.' Year after year, Clark re-read the passages that had
struck a chord with him, until the words fell naturally and became his own.
As he returned to the Bible for sustenance, so he returned to literature, reading novels, biography and plays for guidance and wisdom, like a creative
preacher returning to the gospels, spinning new allegories from each reading. From the insights he gleaned, he created his own Book of Life.[7]

More than any other books in Clark's possession, his copies of Dostoyevsky
appear the most worn. Often, his annotations are written in different ink,
each variation in colour signalling new discoveries at different points in time;
the young Clark marks one passage, the older Clark marks another, but the
one constant in his life is this same well of creative inspiration and spiritual
nourishment. Clark reserved his readings of Dostoyevsky's novels for
moments of exultation, despair and self-transformation. In 1981, he turned
again to *Crime and Punishment* after his 'resurrection to a new life'. Typically
cryptic, many of Clark's later annotations upon re-reading Dostoyevsky
mimic the author's mysticism. Conscious of the moments in his life that he
associated with reading particular novels, Clark saved his re-readings for
those times that reflected his spirits at the time of first reading, pulling novels
from the shelf as emblems of his mood and state of mind. His copy of *The*

Idiot, which he bought in 1938 in Stockholm as he set off for Oxford, when his life's work was still ahead of him, he chose to re-read fifty years later at the point of its completion. 'Re-read early September 1987 after David Malouf launched vol. 6 and after seeing Wagner's Lohengrin at Sydney Opera House.'[8]

Reading Dostoyevsky's personal correspondence, Clark looked for the patterns of his own life mirrored in the life of his literary hero. As Dostoyevsky pleaded with his wife Anna to forgive him for his gambling, so Clark pleaded with Dymphna for forgiveness of his adultery. As Dostoyevsky acknowledged that Anna did everything for him to enable his writing ('you not only run the whole house and take care of all my business affairs, but you also manage your fussy and troublesome family'), Clark knew the same was true of Dymphna. But he also saw the differences, enviously making a note of Anna's reply to Dostoyevsky: 'I find myself loved by the most magnanimous, noble, pure, honourable, and saintly of men! ... you are on top of the mountain while I lie at the foot of it ... I do not just love and respect you, I actually adore and worship you.' And what of faith? Dostoyevsky saw the most pressing question in the problem of faith to be 'whether a man, as a civilised being, as a European, could believe in the divinity of the Son of God, Jesus Christ'. Clark saw the central question of faith as 'the Godhead of Christ', and whether a man of his generation could 'venture such a belief'. Like Dostoyevsky, Clark's 'image of Christ' was not that of the Church but one drawn from his own reading of the gospels. All of these affinities would inform the writing of Clark's *History* in the years ahead. But Dostoyevsky's influence on Clark's historical writing went far beyond his philosophy of religious belief and love; it extended to the very concept of the *History* itself. In 1869, Dostoyevsky conceived the idea of writing a series of 'epic legends' for Russian school students. He wanted to show 'the whole of Russian history from a Russian perspective'.

> [The legends would distinguish those places], those moments and points at which Russia ... seems to have focused and expressed herself at once in her entirety. In the thousand years of the country's history, there are as many as ten, or possibly even more, such all-expressive moments. And it is these

Clark at his study desk, 1984

moments that must be seized and related in the epic, to be conveyed to one and all, not, however, as an ordinary chronicle, no, but rather as a stirring poem which, even without strict adherence to the facts …will lay hold of the main point and convey it in a way that shows the idea from which it emerged as well as the love and the suffering that brought forth that idea. But there must be no egoism in it, no personal note, it must be ingenuous, as ingenuous as possible, with just the love of Russia gushing from it like a hot spring—and nothing else.[9]

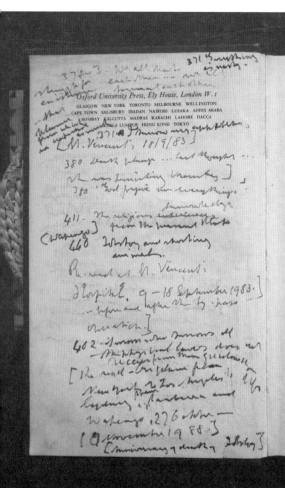

ANNA KARÉNINA

A NOVEL BY
LEO TOLSTÓY

Translated by
LOUISE *and* AYLMER MAUDE

With an Introduction and Notes by
AYLMER MAUDE

LONDON
OXFORD UNIVERSITY PRESS
NEW YORK   TORONTO

When Clark read Dostoyevsky's letter he recognised something of his own ambition. Dostoyevsky's romantic nationalism was akin to Clark's aspiration: to reveal the character of the Australian people by writing their history. The parallels were striking. Clark noted Dostoyevsky's elucidation of his own work: to explore Russian character, 'straight from the heart', to devote himself entirely to Russia, both to the distinctiveness of her people and to her 'national roots'. Dostoyevsky hoped that his ballads and epic legends might become 'a national book', contributing to a resurgence of 'self-awareness in the Russian man'. Between 1958 and 1991, as Clark sat in his study writing *A History of Australia*, short stories, autobiographies and

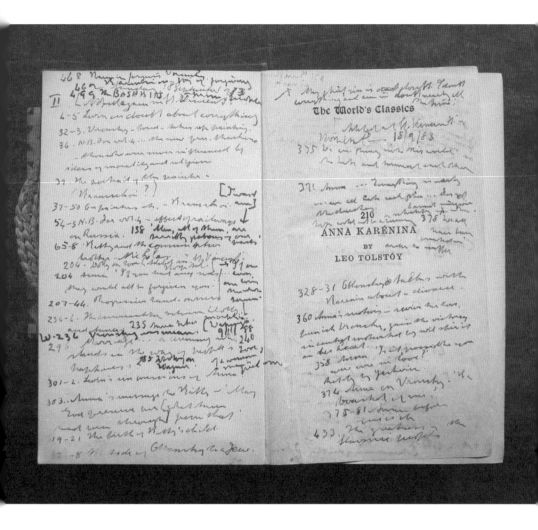

countless articles and letters, he wrote every word with Dostoyevsky as his constant companion.[10]

Photographs of Clark in his study show a man almost submerged by reams of paper, photocopies and transcripts of historical sources piled high on his desk, colonial office despatches, newspaper reports and the journals of English officials and settlers, a writer looking earnestly down at the desk or out through the study window to the bush beyond. His notes and historical documents were his raw materials, but behind him lay the bank of European literature that he had already read several times over when he finally set out to write his country's history.[11]

18: THE HISTORIAN

It is hard to hear a new voice, as hard as it is to listen to an unknown language. We just don't listen.[1]

DH LAWRENCE, 'Spirit of Place', 1923

Sidney Nolan, Central Australia, *1950*

Australia: a country in which the songs and gods of the old world do not seem to fit. The dryness of the earth pierces the soul: a young country with a vast, waterless heart, more ancient than Babylon or Constantinople.

On a night during Ramadan in 1890, French novelist Pierre Loti stood on the Galata Bridge in Istanbul and looked across to the European side of the city.

> An arm of the sea stretches out its calm, empty space between the deafening neighbourhoods I have just crossed and another great, fantastic looking city that appears beyond it—a black outline jagged with minarets and domes against the starry backdrop of the night…I can't wait to be over there; an attraction, the indescribable emotion of memory makes me quicken my pace in the darkness of this endless bridge that leads across the sound, to that terribly black city.

Later that day, visiting the Topkapi Palace, built on 'the extreme tip of eastern Europe', Loti was spellbound as the citadel gates of the Sultan's residence opened before him. He felt himself being 'gathered in' by the 'dead past' and 'the delightful melancholy of inner things'. Loti's romantic evocation of Istanbul's melancholy could easily have applied to many ancient cities in Europe, Asia, Africa and the Middle East, cities like Istanbul, Jerusalem and Venice, where the remains of past civilisations can still be seen and felt, where it is impossible to escape the feeling that you are walking in the footsteps of others, and that, for good or ill, you are the inheritor of things past. The feeling of melancholy these cities evoke comes both from the survival of the past and from the visibility of its decay, a decomposition of such grace and beauty that it seems to invite death itself. For Europeans who settled in Australia, their experience could not have been more different.[2]

From the moment the British arrived in the late eighteenth century, Australia was seen as a land without history. Although the settlers walked on earth imprinted with the stories of thousands of human generations, they saw themselves standing at the beginning of history. Behind them, 'all was waste and barbarous'. Like DH Lawrence, they believed they would need to 'people' the land 'with ghosts and catastrophes and water it with blood', before they could possess a history that was truly their own. In time, history would happen.[3]

At first, the newcomers had no eyes for the country around them. They shaped the land in the image of their ancestral memory, dreaming of verdant hills and inland seas. Disconnected as they were from Australia's Aboriginal past, their feeling for history was fixed firmly on their distant homelands. Now surrounded by so much newness, they found their colonial culture to be brittle and thin against the cavernous space of the land around them. They were not only exiled from their loved ones; they were exiled from their past— free and prosperous, but rootless nonetheless. One of the things that made life bearable was the consoling thought that they were connected to Europe's deep past—'the history of times immemorial'. Their British heritage was the only antidote to the shallowness of everything they saw around them. If European societies could not escape history, colonial societies craved history. So many of the dilemmas they confronted in living in a country 'without history' have remained part of the Australian experience.

The mystical connection that Europeans felt with ages past had always been dependent on the architectural scaffolding of their history: on the

An Eye for Eternity

churches, public buildings, cottages and roads of their villages, towns and cities. The Australian environment could not be understood the same way. If historical melancholy could be felt in Australia, it could not be found in the built environment; it could only be found in the land itself. This was the realisation that dawned slowly. In Australia, the land and Aboriginal cultures that had existed for millennia were the true source of connection with 'time immemorial'. But how to gain access to a culture and history that stepped so lightly on the landscape and seemed inseparable from the earth itself?

Unlike Europe, where the land was under the control of human hands and every patch of earth was managed, mastered and accounted for, in Australia the land seemed to mock all human endeavour. It could not be tamed. The melancholy felt in Australia came from the awareness that victory over the land could never be had. In the coastal cities, when the hot northerly winds arrived in summer, the sky filled with dust, carpeting city pavements in the red sands of the interior. When bushfires raged, ash fell like rain on the streets of Melbourne and Sydney. The harshness of the climate kept tearing at the walls of civilisation. Settler society appeared vulnerable and ephemeral against the 'howling wilderness' of the bush, an emptiness that seemed to add an extra terror to death.[4]

Until the first volume of Manning Clark's *A History of Australia* was published in 1962, no historian had dared contemplate the existential dimensions of life in Australia. What impact did the Australian environment have on the inner lives of those who settled here? What did it mean to live in exile, to feel one's soul cut adrift from every structure and life force that had previously given it meaning? To live in a country in which the external world did not align with one's internal world, where the land and its rhythms cried out in a frightening, alien tongue? The same questions were being posed in the late 1950s by writers such as Patrick White, Judith Wright and AD Hope: were we strangers? What were we doing here? Where did 'the mystery and the poetry' lie that might make life bearable in Australia? Or, as Clark himself asked, 'What [was it] like to be a human being in this harsh, weird and beautiful land of Australia', and how had the environment shaped the character of her people?[5]

In the 1960s, these were not questions academic historians were supposed to ask. The historian's task was to investigate the documentary evidence, to remain detached and objective, much like a laboratory technician, to record the events of the external world, and to leave the emotions of human beings to the creative artists. But Clark was determined to explore the inner lives of his characters, to see inside their souls and to hear their voices. He understood the poetics of the land and confronted its strange, ancient pulse, one he thought 'cursed by some malevolent being'. As Thomas Keneally saw when he first read *A History of Australia*, Clark was obsessed with the solitary human figure in the Australian landscape, the figure that was also Orpheus descended into a nether-world, a European Hades, the one man who struggled to understand, like Patrick White's Voss or Sidney Nolan's Ned Kelly. While other historians busied themselves with questions of class analysis or argued over issues of historical interpretation, Clark set out to write history as myth; not myth as the opposite of truth but myth as a story that was universal and instantly recognisable, at once ancient and modern. 'We in Australia have no history,' he declared in 1961, 'no tradition, no legends, stories [or] heroes, nothing between us and the sky, nothing between us and the present to cushion the squalor, the misery, the ugliness, and the emptiness.' Clark tried to fill the vacuum by modelling his work on the vision of one of his own heroes, Thomas Carlyle, writing narrative history that was 'a true epic poem of mankind'. He sensed that the country without history was heavy with story. Beneath the surface of everyday life, beneath the materialism and ugliness of so much of the built environment, beneath the matter-of-fact conversations and a culture that pretended life in Australia could never be tragic, Clark found pathos, an epic confrontation between the belief systems of European societies and a continent that seemed to exist outside of time and history, a country indifferent to the ways of the old world. His was a vision suffused with melancholy, the melancholy that he saw in the land and that he carried within himself. His struggle to tell Australia's story was born not only of his love of the country but also of his repulsion and horror. At times, he expressed exhilaration at his progress, but each return to the blank page brought a phase of melancholy even deeper than the last. The possibility of rescue lay in completing a project that might be too big to ever be completed.[6]

A MOMENTOUS EVENT

The 1960s were the most productive decade in Clark's life. Between 1960 and 1971, he published *Meeting Soviet Man* (1960), *A Short History of Australia* (1963), one volume of short stories (1969) and the first three volumes of *A History of Australia*. He was already forty-one when he began to write the *History* and his best work would be written in his fifties. He was a late starter. But by any measure the scale of this achievement was remarkable. As the vastness of the project unfolded, Clark lived every day with the thought of writing the next volume in the back of his mind. Getting out of bed each morning, he heard a voice calling to him: 'Clark, I'm still here, get upstairs and start again.' The history became 'a monster' that consumed not only his life but much of his family as well. For Dymphna and the children, the arrival of each successive volume marked the passage of time—'it was around the time of Volume III'—as though Clark's work stepped out the progress of their lives, a monster carried not by one man but by his entire family.[7]

Flyer for Volume I

Shortly before he turned fifty in 1965, Clark claimed that he had stopped drinking. The victory was never complete; there would always be breakouts. But compared with his binges while teaching at Melbourne University in the 1940s and his fondness for the communion rail of Hotel Civic during his first decade in Canberra, the 1960s were a relatively sober period. As each year passed without drinking, Clark marked the anniversary in his diary and knelt in prayer in St Christopher's Cathedral at Manuka. It was not union with God that he sought, but solace in Christ—the only one, he imagined, who could understand him and forgive him everything. Now in middle-age, he was already suffering ill health—problems with his gums, permanent deafness in his left ear and a ruptured hernia. Giving up alcohol may have steeled him to write but it did little to alleviate his anxiety or hypochondria. Throughout the writing of every volume, he appeared to exist in a constant state of nervous tension, playing out the drama of his creative life in his diaries like an actor delivering a nightly monologue: 'my confidence is destroyed. I doubt my powers. My wife hates my work. Am terribly depressed. I am close to a breakdown.' When his work was praised, he 'wept tears of joy', taking care to document the most glowing endorsements he received:

> on Tuesday night at the Publishers' dinner at the Hotel Canberra, John Pringle, in his speech in reply to the toast to Australian literature, said he was proud to live in the same town as Alec Hope and Manning Clark—who had written a great book on Australia, and, in his opinion was a very fine writer. I was deeply moved at the time—and went home and played part of a Bach Partita and part of Vaughan Williams' The Lark Ascending—and hoped the gods would make one worthy of such esteem.

When criticised, Clark doubted he could go on: 'I despair of ever communicating anything to anyone, and even doubt or wonder whether I have anything to say.' If his diary were to be taken as the only gauge of his life, he would have lived in one of only two states—either high on accolades or wilting before criticism.[8]

Sitting at his desk in his study, Clark read over his previous diary entries before he poured out his anguish or joy onto the page. With the pen in his hand, the external world blacked out. Everything else dissolved before the silent space of his writing. Each entry was a release, a melodramatic high-wire performance, but it was also a way of working up the dramatic tension that he needed in order to write *A History of Australia*. Despair and suffering were part of Clark's creative drive. Historians, he believed, 'should wear vine leaves in their hair, and have blood and not ink in their veins'. Clark wanted to be seen as a mixture of Apollo and Dionysus, the passionate seeker of truth whose stories would comfort and heal all. But his magnum opus was not simply the product of a tortured soul. It was also the product of an iron-willed discipline, a calculated and opportunistic determination to push his name and work before the public, and the supportive domestic environment provided by Dymphna. While Clark sat in his loft study writing *A History of Australia*, Dymphna held everything else together below—Hestia to Clark's Apollo.[9]

Equally important was the historical context in which Clark's work was written. Australia's intellectual and literary circles in the 1960s were incestuous. The most common way of talking about the country was through the metaphor of maturation—Australia was described either as pubescent or as forever 'coming of age'. To visitors from Europe or the United States, it was all rather amusing. As the US academic Norman Mackenzie remarked in 1964,

> it is an open question whether Australia has a distinctive culture: the debate on this question is a favourite parlour game among Australian intellectuals and those who visit them. The society is relatively new; its origins and development comparatively simple and documented; its small scale enough for writers, artists, and academics not merely to know what their contemporaries are doing but to know many of them personally.

In one year, he met virtually all the major players, Clark included.[10]

The idea that Australian society was an inferior offshoot of another world, significant only because of its connection to Britain, was pervasive. In 1950, the Melbourne literary critic AA Phillips dubbed this pervasive sense of inferiority 'the cultural cringe'. Yet by the early 1960s, Australian intellectuals were giving voice to a more assertive national mood. Writing *The Lucky Country* in 1964, Donald Horne stirred the possum at every available opportunity. Australia, he said, did not 'have a mind'. Intellectual life existed, but it was still 'fugitive, emergent and uncomfortable'. Compared with other liberal democracies, Australia seemed to be in the grip of some kind of torpor. Serious discussion appeared to be almost non-existent. Spurred on by what he described as the 'collapse of European colonial empires, the strength of communism in South East Asia, and the emergence of anti-colonialism and anti-racialism', Horne called for public intellectuals who could 're-visualise images of the nation'. Over the next three decades, his wish was granted. With the expansion of universities and the Commonwealth bureaucracy came the rise of an educated middle-class and a marked increase in media outlets; knowledge, expertise and opinion increasingly became valuable commodities. A public intellectual class began to emerge.

As the Australian economy boomed in the 1950s and 1960s, the country's traditional ties with Britain—in trade, defence, foreign policy and culture—were fraying rapidly. This was the nationalist turn in mid-twentieth century Australia, the moment when questions of Australian identity and national consciousness dominated in a way that had not been seen since the late nineteenth century. The new national mood was epitomised by the publication in 1964 of Australia's first national daily newspaper, Rupert Murdoch's *The Australian*. The publishing of Australian literature rose sharply, assisted by increased government subsidies. In 1962, when Penguin began to publish in Australia as a separate entity, Australians were already spending more on books per capita than any other English-speaking country. New literary journals appeared—*Australian Literary Studies*, *Art Australia* and *Australian Book Review*. Inside the universities, courses in Australian history, literature and politics were flourishing. The number of historians and postgraduates researching and writing on Australian topics increased significantly in the 1960s as the historical profession expanded.

In Canberra, Clark's work was at the forefront of this national awakening and, like Donald Horne and Geoffrey Dutton, he saw himself as part of an intellectual vanguard whose members believed it was their duty to articulate a new direction for the country. In 1961, together with the anthropologist Bill Stanner, Clark arranged and introduced ten programs for ABC TV. Entitled 'Australia's Story: the Beginnings', it was one of the first documentary series on Australian history made for Australian television. Shortly after the publication of Clark's *History of Australia Volume I*, John Douglas Pringle asked him to write a 1200-word article for *The Observer* on the future of Australia and New Zealand, to be published at the time of Queen Elizabeth's visit in February 1963. Pringle's letter of request to Clark said much about the new environment in which Clark's work was now being received.

> We are not really interested in the Queen's visit though you might care to mention it. What I think we would like to know is how Australians and New Zealanders are reacting to the great events of the last two or three years, e.g. Britain's attempts to enter [the European Economic Community], the nuclear stalemate, President Kennedy's policies, the rise of China, and the emergence of Indonesia as a possible threat, though personally I think Australians are inclined to exaggerate this … Presumably, too, Menzies is nearing the end of his career and Australian politics should begin to move again. Is a new Australia emerging, politically as well as culturally and socially? Is immigration beginning to have a marked influence?[11]

If Pringle had hoped for a straight answer from Clark he was surely disappointed. In his article, Clark bemoaned the rising tide of consumerism and doubted the moral fibre of a society that no longer 'produced bread by the sweat of its brow'. Australia's people, he said, were still unaware of their past and culture. And until they gained that awareness, the vision of a genuinely new and independent Australia could never be realised. The implication was clear. Clark's work would help to prepare the ground for a new vision of the nation to emerge. As *A History of Australia* gathered momentum throughout the 1960s, the story of Clark's writing of the history became an ongoing public drama. No other historian or writer was seen explaining his work in the context of the new national consciousness as frequently as Manning Clark. As he filed each successive instalment, the media trailed every stroke of his pen. Despite the fact that Clark's *History* was written in an archaic, angelic tongue, his struggle to write the six volumes captured the attention of the Australian public, as if the nation waited eagerly for the next chapter in the story of its own creation. By the end of the decade, the historian and the nation were seen to be on one and the same quest.[12]

When Clark's first volume appeared in September 1962—'From the Earliest Times to the Age of Macquarie'—its impact on Australia's burgeoning intellectual culture was profound, in part because Clark attempted to see Australia as whole, of itself and without apology—a unique site for the transplanting of European civilisation. So great were the themes, so grand was the vision, so vast the imaginative landscape and so deeply personal the prose, that its very scale seemed to dwarf anything that had gone before it. Clark had, almost single-handedly, given Australian history its human drama and depth of feeling. Gone was the 'positivistic spirit' and 'objective reality' that characterised scholarly history. Here was an historian who claimed to be concerned with 'beauty, symbolism, subjective meaning' and artistic truth, a historian who had not one territory but many. To add to the sense of occasion, Volume I was one of the first 'event' publications in the history of Australian literature. Reflecting what was fast becoming 'the fashion for new books', it was launched in Melbourne with great fanfare by Clark's former teacher and mentor, Max Crawford. Clark spent hours choosing the guest list, writing several letters to Peter Ryan (who was now head of MUP) in the weeks beforehand, planning his 'party' with great care, like a director choreographing his opening night. For Dymphna and Clark, the launch of the book was the culmination of so many hours spent together in libraries in Australia and abroad. Finally, there was a book to show for their efforts. The morning after the launch, Dymphna pressed the carnation flower she had worn the previous evening and placed it inside a sealed envelope, which she kept for the rest of her life. On the front of the envelope, she wrote the words: 'A History of Australia, Cathedral Hotel Melbourne 7-9-62'.[13]

Barely two months later, the first print run of 2500 copies had sold out. Ryan, already hungry for more, ordered a reprint and confirmed that MUP would publish an overseas edition. Clark's *History* awoke Australian publishers to the market potential of Australian history written in a lively and accessible style. Before 1962, single-authored volumes on Australian history

A MENTOR BOOK

MT522
75c

An account of the continent's development—from
its first scattered settlements of aborigines to its
emergence as a prosperous and dynamic power

Manning Clark

A SHORT HISTORY OF
AUSTRALIA

First paperback edition of A Short History of Australia, *New American Library,*
September 1963

tended to be small narrative histories written very much from the vantage point of Australia's place in the British Empire—Ernest Scott's *A Short History of Australia* (1916), which had been a standard text for four decades, being the prime example. Bestselling works such as WK Hancock's *Australia* (1930), Max Crawford's *Australia* (1952), AGL Shaw's *The Story of Australia* (1955) and Russel Ward's *Australian Legend* (1958) resembled extended interpretative essays rather than substantial histories. Clark's was the first multi-volume history of Australia since GW Rusden's in 1883 and its scope was far in excess of that adopted by anyone who preceded him.

His research in South-East Asia and Europe in 1955–56 had proved crucial. By placing the British settlement of Australia in what *The Economist* called the context of 'the broader cosmic process', and beginning with the history of Asian contact with Australia rather than Cook's 'discovery' of the continent, Clark offered a view of Australia's past that was written from *outside* the British orbit rather than from within. Australia, for so long on the periphery of world history, was now at its centre—Clark's perspective was genuinely post-colonial. And 'for the first time', as Keith Hancock told Clark, Australian history had 'become part of man's spiritual pilgrimage'. Peter Coleman, associate editor of the *Bulletin* in 1962 and a former leader of the Liberal Party in New South Wales, recalled the sense of excitement felt by many writers in the country at the time. 'You have to remember,' he insisted, 'Australia hadn't seen anything like this before; the range and depth of Clark's interpretation [were] revolutionary at the time.'[14]

In a seminal collection of essays, *Australian Civilization,* published in the same year, Coleman championed Clark as the most important Australian historian of the postwar period, the man who would lead 'the counter-revolution in Australian historiography' against the 'standard radical–leftist interpretation' of the past. Clark's essay 'Faith', in which he argued that Australia's future lay either with the men of 1917 or with Christ, Coleman thought highly original. Years later, he changed his mind, believing that he had been 'conned by Clark's style'.[15]

In the early 1960s, Clark was the great shining hope of conservative intellectuals, the man who would show that Australian history was a much richer tale than mateship, the workingman's paradise and the march towards

Labor's light on the hill. In 1965, Robert Menzies told the American Ambassador: 'we have an eminent historian in Australia—Manning Clark … and I advise you to read his work'. Across all sides of the political and cultural divide, Volume I would generate enormous interest, both in Australia and overseas, but nothing could have prepared Clark for the intensity of criticism and controversy the book would provoke. When he wrote his first words in Oxford in 1956, he dreamt of writing history that betrayed 'delicacy of feeling, grace of bearing, and shades of emotion and sentiment'. He was about to discover that a history so intense in emotion could also incite an equally negative response.[16]

In the weeks before the launch, brooding on the fate of the book, Clark took the trip he would make on so many occasions in the years to come as he searched for inspiration, riding the ferry across Sydney Harbour to Manly. From there, he walked through the rain to North Head, thinking of all the people he had written about in Volume I. After Max Crawford described the work as a masterpiece at the launch, Clark was ecstatic. But his more lasting feeling was one of fear. Until he held the book in his hands, he worried about the quality of certain chapters, yet even when he had the opportunity to make changes he admitted that he was 'incapable of doing anything other than to amend a sentence here and there'. The more he read the manuscript, the more it seemed to resist alteration. Long before one review had been published, he was 'terrified of the assassins'. Somewhere inside him, the fear of failure lingered, as if he knew there would be errors of fact that would leave him open to attack. To steel himself he could always replay the words of encouragement from his friends. Bruce Grant, who had read the manuscript before publication, told him that his first three chapters 'offered a fantastic repositioning of Australia'. James McAuley encouraged him, telling him that he had given 'colour and resonance to that deathly-grey stuff they thrust down my gagging throat at school as Australian History'. From his first glance at the manuscript, Gwyn James, who preceded Peter Ryan as director at MUP and had commissioned Volume I, knew that it would be a long time before anyone attempted to tackle Australian history on such a scale again. As a historian himself, James recognised the work's originality. Before he was replaced by Peter Ryan in June 1962, he wrote to Clark, 'hurt beyond words' that he would not be there to oversee the launch of the book he had nurtured, yet equally determined to tell Clark what he believed he had achieved. 'This is a landmark in Australian history writing. No one else is even trying to write for the community as well as fellow scholars. No one can or will do a full-length history again for decades.'[17]

By writing of Australia in geological time, and telling the story of the first waves of indigenous migration to Australia, together with the Greek, Roman, Chinese Hindu and Moslem fables of an unknown land in the southern oceans, Clark had opened up the sense of what Australian history could be. John Manning Ward, Professor of History at Sydney University, probably explained this aspect of Clark's work best of all: 'Everyone who writes on Australian history after him,' he said, 'will have to come to grips with what he has written, not because it compels assent, but because it indicates so powerfully that earlier viewpoints were too narrow.' Clark had devoted nearly four hundred pages to the first three decades of settlement, which was a period that other historians glossed over in a chapter or less. James realised the uniqueness of Clark's treatment as early as 1961, telling him excitedly: 'as the instalments arrived I could hardly keep pace with you … it seems that the whole work could take four or five volumes, with publication spread over the 1960s.' As Volume I progressed, Clark wrote of the heroes of exploration who had captured his imagination in South-East Asia, of Quiros, Magellan and the spirit of Catholic idealism. Then he turned to the first European contacts with Australia, the Dutch Protestants such as Tasman and Hartog, men who were unmoved by the land they saw, believing that there was nothing good to be done in this wasteland of sand and flies. It was all written in a startling voice that Australians had not heard before—sonorous and majestic, biblical and outlandishly grave—a voice that seemed to elevate Australia through style and tone alone.

Reviewers were quick to point out that there was considerable overlap between Clark's grand themes. Men of both Catholic and Protestant traditions were also men of the Enlightenment. In his eagerness to make his themes work, Clark failed to acknowledge that the intellectual and spiritual heritage of so many officers of the First Fleet was a dual one. Yet, as Max Crawford admitted, nothing could undermine his achievement. Clark had managed to produce 'one of the most exciting works to appear in Australian historical writing'. There was no hint of the materialist, progressive history that characterised so much Australian history. Clark had accomplished what Alan McBriar, one of his old drinking partners and colleagues from Melbourne University, had instructed him to do years earlier: 'to prophesy again in a great work before many people'. Brilliant as his opening chapters were, he had not entirely deserted the scholarly tone of his two volumes of documents. With hindsight, Volume I would prove, in method and style, to be the closest of the volumes to academic history, but it was still not close enough for most of Clark's peers. Enrolled in a third-year Australian history course at Sydney University in 1963, Lyndall Ryan watched as her lecturer, Duncan MacCallum, walked in to the seminar room, held up Volume I and declared to the students: 'No one is to read this. It is disgraceful.'

In Volume I, Clark drew on many of the documents he had already published. He told the story of James Cook ('the son of the Enlightenment'), and the British government's choice of Botany Bay to found a penal colony, before moving through his cast of characters, chiefly colonial governors, finishing with four chapters on the 1810–21 governorship of Lachlan Macquarie, the visionary builder of Sydney brought down by vanity. Along the way, Clark nodded slightly to 'social history', by devoting a chapter to the society of New South Wales in 1810. His chronological structure was the standard approach of historical writing at the time. What was unusual, and would irritate so many of his critics, was Clark's determination to speculate on what could not be known from documentary sources and his audacity in thinking that he could get inside his characters' minds. Clark also broke an unwritten rule of academic culture in the 1960s: men did not air their emotions in their work, nor did they show their hurt when their work was criticised. Historians lived with the pretence that their scholarship could be criticised without any loss to their self-esteem. Clark saw no difference between his own flesh and blood and the words he inscribed on the page—'they are me'. While his colleagues talked of a spirit of academic debate and inquiry in which scholarship was continually reappraised, Clark, having invested so much feeling in his work, felt that he had laid himself open, and he trembled like a child in search of approval at the thought of his creation being subjected to censure or derision. 'Whoso attacks my [work],' he maintained, 'is undermining my deepest self.'[18]

To ensure that Volume I was widely reviewed, Clark wrote to literary editors personally. He left nothing to chance. The morning after the book launch in Melbourne, over a hotel breakfast with Dymphna, he read the first review, a glowing endorsement by Stuart Sayers in the *Age*, who described the book as 'a major work, not only of scholarship, but of Australian literature'. Two weeks later, when the critical reviews came in, Clark doubted if he would ever bother to write another work of history. 'I wonder if it would be better to publish things posthumously.' On 22 September, the *Bulletin* published a review by Malcolm Ellis under the headline 'History Without Facts'. Clark was devastated. Ellis, the Sydney journalist, biographer and historian with whom Clark had been on largely friendly terms since the early 1950s and whose work he had encouraged at every opportunity, had betrayed him. Since 1959, Ellis, who was then in his early sixties, had been a regular visitor to Canberra, brought there through his contact with Professor Keith Hancock, eminent Australian historian and Fellow of All Souls, Oxford, who was then guiding the establishment of the *Australian Dictionary of Biography* (*ADB*) at the Australian National University. Historian Ann Moyal, who was closely involved with the project, remembered how Ellis revelled in the Oxbridge rituals at University House. Sitting at High Table, his 'currant bun face glowed' with delight. A fettler's son, Ellis was entirely self-taught, and for someone who was in close contact with academics, his lack of university qualifications was a constant source of insecurity. As Moyal recalled, 'he carried a very conspicuous chip on his shoulder and was watchful of honour'. Ellis, president of the Australian Pioneers Club and a suspected ASIO informant, was also a deeply conservative man who saw Clark as a 'crypto communist', especially after the publication of *Meeting Soviet Man*.[19]

In October 1959, Ellis and Clark were appointed as co-editors of the first volume of the *ADB*. It was a short-lived working relationship. Clark found Ellis officious, controlling and vain. Ellis was infuriated by Clark and Hancock's reluctance to let him have his way with the *Dictionary*. As the conflict intensified, Ellis and Clark could not bear to be in the same room together. Ann Moyal recalled Clark dropping by her office with a 'consoling posy of flowers', pondering on what he called 'the bizarre and humiliating contradictions in the lives of all of us'. By February 1962, Ellis had resigned as co-editor, telling Hancock that he could not work with Clark, a man who had 'publicly sneered on more than one occasion at the spiritual values of western civilisation'. Only weeks later, Clark resigned, telling Hancock that he had decided to devote his time to writing the *History*. By the time Ellis came to review Clark's *History* six months later, he had accumulated more than enough bitterness to write a damning critique. Rather than write a review, he produced a litany of Clark's omissions and factual errors, questioning his use of sources and interpretations. He accused Clark of impugning the honour of John Macarthur, Lachlan Macquarie and the whole Protestant inheritance in Australia. The tone was carping, eviscerating and malicious, enough to send anyone into fits of despair. Ellis could find nothing redeeming about Clark's work. Clark was concerned not with the facts of history, said Ellis, nor with what men did, but only with the 'little things of the mind and spirit', a comment that revealed more about Ellis than it did about Clark.

The day Clark read the review followed close on the heels of a major altercation with Dymphna. As was often the case after they had argued, she was not speaking to him. But this time she wilted quickly, realising that Clark was distraught. On reading the manuscript before publication she had expected criticism, but she was surprised by Ellis's savagery. In the days that followed, 'the effect on family life was negative', Clark was wounded and she tried to lift his spirits. He wrote to friends of his hurt and loss of confidence, receiving many consoling and supportive letters in reply. Don't worry about Ellis, Crawford told him, 'you see your path and must pursue it'. But Clark was floundering. And before another review had appeared, he received two letters that further shook his confidence.[20]

Clark's former student, Geoff Serle, now a leading Australian historian, wrote from Melbourne to tell him privately of his thoughts after reading Volume I. He reassured him: the book was a 'distinguished achievement'. But Serle was also honest: Clark had overlooked too much—trade between Australia and Britain, for example—and he was guilty of almost 'total neglect' of women such as Elizabeth Macarthur and Elizabeth Macquarie. His chapter on William Bligh was 'flat'. His way of introducing characters—'x was born in'—was 'wearisome'. All too often he allowed his 'personal distaste' of his characters to intrude. Serle, who knew Clark's sensitivity well, wondered if he should mail the letter, but sent it in the hope that Clark's future writing would benefit from his criticisms.[21]

A few days later, Clark opened a letter from his friend John McManners, the English historian and clergyman who was then lecturing at Sydney University. McManners had reviewed Volume I for *Nation*, and the piece would be published within three weeks. As an act of collegiality, he sent Clark the review beforehand, a common practice in the academy, one which many journalists would have found unethical. McManners had accepted the invitation to review the book from *Nation*'s editor, Tom Fitzgerald, who was Clark's friend, 'not knowing he would disagree with it so violently'. He couldn't pretend that he was 'anything other than exasperated' by Clark's treatment of European history and intellectual movements. What angered McManners in particular was Clark's contemptuous reading of the Protestant tradition, in which he cast Protestants as morally upright, bourgeois and self-serving, as opposed to Irish Catholics, whom he saw as compassionate people who had managed to keep 'the image of Christ alive'. There was no other way of putting it. Clark's view of life was jaundiced and 'peculiar'.

Within minutes of reading the review Clark dashed off a reply. He considered his friendship with McManners finished. McManners had 'excited passions' in him which 'disgraced' their relationship. Clark did what he would do whenever someone he considered to be an ally let him down: he pretended they did not exist. McManners replied immediately. He was 'deeply unhappy' with Clark's response, telling him that he was prepared to suffer the 'personal loss' in order to stand up for 'justice to the past'. Clark would not rest. Still shaken by the Ellis attack, he set out to control the response to his work. He decided to ring Fitzgerald and ask him not to publish the review. Fitzgerald refused. Clark decided that he would 'keep out of McManners' way' in the future. And he wanted the right of reply. He was extremely hurt by the 'malice and spite' in the review. Would Fitzgerald publish his response? Fitzgerald was reluctant to agree: *Nation* did not normally publish authors' replies to reviews. In the next few days, Clark wrote again to McManners, harping on the unfairness of his review. Determined to stop its publication, he became increasingly desperate. He decided to send the review to the two most powerful figures in the historical profession—Keith Hancock and Max Crawford—and asked them both to lean on Fitzgerald to pull the review. The result was a messy compromise.[22]

When Fitzgerald phoned McManners and told him that Clark had sought to enlist Crawford and Hancock to his cause, McManners began to have second thoughts. Some time over the course of the next week, in discussion with Fitzgerald, he made an extraordinary decision. He would publish an addendum to his review. In effect, he would apologise. In the same issue in which his critical review was published, on 20 October 1962, McManners' retreat appeared on the letters page. In his 'anxiety to defend Protestantism against Professor Manning Clark', McManners claimed that he had treated Clark unjustly. 'This is simply the impact of the book on me,' he confessed, 'the result of my harsh, personal selection from so many riches and insights.' Nor had he recognised that 'the personal idiosyncrasy of an historian is often the very groundwork of his insight and originality'. He had failed to pay 'tribute' to Clark's vision. While he admonished himself in public, his correspondence to Clark was quite different. He apologised, but he also stood by his argument. It was Clark's depiction of Protestantism that was unfair.

> You must understand ... however hurt you feel, you too had struck a blow, and I believe, an unjust blow, at things I respect and love, even though I do not adhere to them intellectually. I cannot accept that religion of any kind has reinforced the base materialistic greed [in Australian society] ... I have given a great deal of thought to the other points you make but I honestly cannot follow them or see that I was wrong. I will not write more. I am doing now what you do, writing from the heart & this has its dangers.[23]

This was surely one of the least edifying episodes in Clark's career. Because his work was the subject of criticism from a friend, he threatened to withdraw his friendship, which clearly upset McManners more than it did him. He had also placed Crawford and Hancock in an extremely difficult position. By sending them the review before publication and asking them to intervene on his behalf, he had tested his friendship with both men and brought his professional integrity into question. He wailed about unfair treatment until he extracted a public apology from McManners and forced Fitzgerald to compromise. He was true to his word: whoever condemned his work condemned his deepest self. And he would stop at nothing to protect himself from attack. In the last months of 1962, his spirits were buoyed briefly by a run of laudatory reviews in the press—'the greatest work on Australian history so far published', 'compassionate, ironic, lucid, it is history of a unique order'. James McAuley stood by him, refusing to join the Ellis attack, commissioning a sympathetic review from Clark's former student, Michael Roe, for *Quadrant*. At MUP, however, Ryan was worried by the errors that Ellis had highlighted in Clark's work and he was concerned about the 'over lavish praise' of Clark's defenders. He wanted Part One to be recast before a new edition was published: 'too many of the factual details need to be corrected', he told Clark. It was the beginning of Ryan's doubts about the quality of Clark's work. At the same time, Ryan saw the market potential in an historian whose writing could arouse such passionate reactions.[24]

The Ellis review provoked enormous controversy in Australia's literary circles, both for the vehemence of its criticism and its exposure of Clark's errors. Ellis's final paragraph was an open invitation to Clark to defend Volume I before his critics. In August 1963, journalist Peter Coleman decided he would invite Clark to respond at a special seminar convened by the Australian Congress for Cultural Freedom, the conservative, CIA-funded think tank behind *Quadrant*. 'There was a question I wanted to answer,' Coleman explained later: 'who was right—Manning or Malcolm Ellis?' There were those who thought Clark's vision transcended the factual errors while others thought that he had so many facts wrong—who cares about the vision? For Coleman, and all the historians who attended the seminar in the ballroom of the Belvedere Hotel in Sydney, the occasion was unforgettable. There was Ellis, 'one of the last pre-academic historians', whom Coleman remembered as 'a man of great passions, sustained by an inner rage', a 'natural scholar who lived for history'. And there was Clark, who accepted the invitation knowing he would be criticised—not only by Ellis and his old friend AGL Shaw, whose critical review had by now appeared in *Meanjin*, but also by John Forsyth, a Sydney solicitor and historian of European exploration in the Pacific, who had written to the *Bulletin* complaining of Clark's many 'misconceptions and mistakes'.

When Clark arrived at the Belvedere Hotel on the morning of 25 August he was in high spirits. Bursting into Coleman's office, he was already fired up. Coleman never forgot Clark's dramatic entrance: 'He came through the door waving his hands, exclaiming "If they are going to challenge me about the length of Henry Parkes' prick, then I've got the evidence."' As they walked together to the seminar, Clark walked so fast that Coleman had to skip to keep up with him. Inside, Clark's critics awaited him. Clark spoke first. He said nothing of the criticisms of Ellis or Forsyth, nothing of factual errors or differences in interpretation. Instead, he delivered a defence of his personal view of history, beginning with a story from a dinner party he had attended in Melbourne a few years earlier. Around the table, a group of academics were in heated discussion; 'What you say is not clear! Is that a verifiable proposition?' Bored, Clark's eyes were drawn to an Arthur Boyd painting on the wall behind them. Boyd's canvas depicted David playing the harp to Saul, refreshing his spirits until the evil spirit departed from him. Clark saw his own reflection. He would play David's harp. Like Boyd, he was a 'representative of one of the muses'. At this point Ellis was beginning to grow impatient. How was it possible to argue with a historian who saw himself as an artist? Clark claimed he wanted to understand 'the conflict between good and evil'. He spoke of moral conflict, the fundamental mystery of life and man's tragic flaws. Ellis wanted to speak about the building blocks of history, about facts and interpretation. Responding, he recited Clark's errors in exhaustive detail. Historian Archbishop Eris O'Brien, Clark's friend since his days at Melbourne, stood to defend him. By discussing the foundation of Australia in the context of moral and religious principles, O'Brien argued, Clark's work was groundbreaking. By the time Forsyth came to speak, the mood of the audience had shifted.

Armed with a mass of paper documenting Clark's mistakes, as if he were a prosecuting attorney, Forsyth warned the audience that he 'might go on for some time'. At one point, when he queried one of Clark's translations from the Dutch, Clark accused him of insulting his wife, who had translated the passage. 'I did not know that you were married,' pleaded Forsyth, 'I did not know she did the translation.' Clark would not let up. He found it 'offensive', Dymphna's 'honour was at stake'. As Dymphna watched in silence, Forsyth, ever the gentleman, apologised profusely. It was the high point of drama in the seminar. Later, many of those present felt that Clark had manipulated the situation. Rather than reply to legitimate criticism, he had sought to humiliate Forsyth by accusing him of disparaging his wife. In Coleman's eyes, it was 'a dirty trick'. Shaw thought much the same. Although he was impressed with Clark's defence of his work, he was appalled by Clark's treatment of Ellis and Forsyth. '[Manning] lost his head in the discussion and was extremely rude to Ellis and Forsyth of whom neither on this occasion said anything but the politest of legitimate criticism. I don't think he came well out of it, and I cannot feel that his book really does him credit as a historian.'[25]

Hurt by Shaw's criticism of his work, Clark refused to speak to him. Shaw, who had stayed with Clark several times in the 1950s during his visits to Canberra, often playing golf with Clark, never visited Tasmania Circle again. Later that evening, a few hours after the seminar closed, Clark and Dymphna flew out of Melbourne for San Francisco. Clark had decided to take up the invitation to be a guest professor at Duke University in Durham, North Carolina, during the fall term of 1963–64. The day after they arrived, Clark bought an old Rambler station wagon for 600 dollars and set off with Dymphna and their two youngest children, Rowland and Benedict, to drive across America, reading the novels of William Faulkner along the way. Faulkner was Clark's preparation for the South, a novelist whom Clark thought one of the greatest in the English world, and who had died little more than a year earlier, shortly after he arrived in Virginia from Oxford, driving his red Rambler. Clark had chosen not only Faulkner's novels but his car as well. As he drove east from California to North Carolina, through New Mexico, Kansas, Missouri, Illinois, Indiana and Virginia, Clark's deep sense of grievance over the criticism of his work did not leave him. The majority of reviews, both in academic journals and the press, had been extremely positive, many gushing in their praise, and the book had received wide coverage overseas, particularly in England. No other Australian historian had made such a significant impact. But Clark could not let the handful of criticisms go. He seemed incapable of leaving his anger behind him. In his heart, the months ahead in the USA and Europe would feel much like the months he experienced in Australia before his departure. He wrote to Axel, now aged twenty, complaining that the memory of the attacks had 'wrecked' his time overseas. Researching Volume II, he often felt paralysed, a victim of the 'savageries' meted out by the 'whipping boys' such as Ellis and Shaw. For encouragement, he read the letters of Thomas Mann, trying to see himself, like Mann, 'as someone ... who had reached across and beyond the wild conflicts of his time', and produced a work of lasting significance.[26]

To ease his pain, he created caricatures of his critics. While he was the man of boundless vision, they were spiritual bullies with 'hearts of stone', soulless men who waded in the sewers of 'historical enterprises limited', obsessed with the little things of life—petty facts and arcane detail. He was selective too, in showing his hurt, playing for sympathy or admiration, depending on his audience. While he told Dymphna and the children that he was thinking of giving everything up—'my temperament will not stand much more'—he told Crawford that the Ellis attacks had 'not touched him deeply'. Although he insisted that he took no notice of academic reviews, and that the only response to criticism was to 'produce another great work', he would go on complaining about critical reviews for the remainder of his life, letting nearly all his friends and colleagues know how sensitive he was, as if to foreclose future criticism. 'Don't worry about what other historians say,' he declared. Yet it was the praise of his peers for which he hankered most of all—'recognition by a peer is the deepest pleasure a writer can know', he admitted. And he took their advice, noting the factual errors listed by Ellis, Forsyth and others, instructing Peter Ryan to make the necessary changes in later editions; albeit with an important qualification. He insisted that Ryan signal changes under the heading 'alterations'. 'I think it better than the word corrections.'[27]

Looking down on Clark's life through the forensic eye of biography, with all his contradictions laid out on the table, it is all too easy to pass judgement. The voice caged in the documents is so often earnest and self-serving.

Reading his correspondence and diaries, many of his former friends were later shocked to find how crippled he was by criticism. Bob Reece remembered how Clark would often joke about the Ellis review, pretending to stagger about his office from a sudden stab wound in the back. John Legge recalled him laughing off bad reviews, referring to Ellis sardonically as 'the great biographer of Lachlan Macquarie'. In his dealings with his close friends, Clark sent up the grave character he left behind on the page for posterity. Hurt as he was by criticism, he found relief in levity and self-irony. He also felt compelled to minister to his enemies. In 1969, when Malcolm Ellis was dying in hospital in Sydney, Clark travelled from Canberra to make his peace with him before he died.[28]

THE CREATOR

Among the portraits and photographs that hang in the living room of Clark's former home in Tasmania Circle, Canberra, there is a pencil sketch, *Drifting*, by Charles Blackman. Out on the water, two men sit in a boat with no land in sight. Another figure, completely white, stands just behind the bow: an apparition defying the current. In 1965, Clark saw himself much like the ghostly figure in Blackman's sketch. His was a singular vision—emotive and mischievous, tortured and divine—like that of no other Australian historian or writer of his generation.

Clark spoke often of his connection with ordinary people: his audience was not the academy. And publishers would bid avidly for the work of a historian who saw himself as akin to 'an actor on a revolving stage'. Historians, said Clark, 'should be judged by their success in increasing wisdom and understanding and their capacity to entertain'; writing history was like dancing, composing music, or painting. It was enough to make his colleagues shake their heads in dismay. They did not see themselves as artists or entertainers. As Clark pushed ahead with the second and third volumes of *A History of Australia*, his philosophy of history began to emerge in both his historical writing and his public reflections on his work. Today, the six

Clark in his living room, above him,
Charles Blackman, Drifting, *1966*

volumes appear to have a natural coherence and purpose, as if Clark knew that he would finish his story early in the twentieth century. At the time of writing, however, the direction and end point of the project were in a constant state of flux. Clark was always uncertain of when he would finish, always doubtful of the work's integrity, always in need of reassurance from his publisher, and always in need of more time to travel in Australia and overseas to find the inspiration for the next volume.[29]

After Volume II, published in 1968, each volume was potentially the last. Sometimes Clark thought he would bring the story down to the gold rushes of the 1850s and end the *History* there. But the direction of the work was shaped partly by the responses of other historians. He had to keep going to prove them wrong. 'I want the third volume to reassure those who are still worried by my carelessness. I also want it to reassure those who think all the old material of the historians (land, squatters, immigration etc.) has been dropped'. Peter Ryan also played a role in directing the course of the *History*. On several occasions, he lost his temper with Clark because he seemed so undecided about the work's future. 'I can't see the staying power to carry it through & he's getting older and older. One always suspects, of course, that he'll then switch instantly to (say) Cassells for an advance of $10,000. Do we care?' MUP's files are full of letters from bookshops and the reading public craving the release of the next volume of Clark's history. As Clark attracted more and more readers, Ryan helped to persuade him to keep writing.

> Don't underestimate the importance of the work, nor the impact it has made upon historians and plain readers alike ...When our sales representatives call upon bookshops or meet history teachers, the question they are most likely to be asked is: 'When will there be another volume by Manning Clark?' It continues to sell steadily. Not one day passes without orders ... We regard the history as one of the most important works ever entrusted to MUP... Whatever form you wish to give the History will be acceptable to us, but if it is possible to persuade you to carry it on to more or less modern times, upon a grand scale, then that is what we would prefer ... There is no historian writing in this country whose work arouses anything like the interest yours does, or has half the influence. Short, middling and long histories of Australia appear almost annually in hard covers or paperback; they are reviewed, read, and very nearly forgotten before the year is out. But your work is not forgotten, either by those who agree with you or by those who don't.[30]

Ryan knew he had 'a tidy little earner' for the publishing house. And his judgement was astute. Clark's work would not be forgotten, although most historians who have written about Clark's place in Australian historiography seem happy to leave him hovering in a no-man's land, somewhere between nineteenth-century literature and an antiquated form of epic history. There is a broad consensus that Clark simply does not fit into the schema of Australian historiography. Few historians have sought to engage with his work, save for one or two embarrassing attempts to imitate him. For Clark, the feeling was mutual. Although he read the work of his peers, he rarely referred to the work of another historian in his text—he preferred to plough his 'lonely furrow'. He was also out of step with the intellectual fashions and preoccupations of his colleagues—the great generalist in a time of increasing specialisation. The revisionist history of the 1960s and 1970s had little impact on his work. Throughout the six volumes, Aboriginal people appeared not as individuals but as a group that shadowed the advance of white civilisation. Clark was compassionate towards them, but he also felt estranged from them. Unlike his portraits of individual colonists,

Peter Ryan, circa 1962

Aborigines were portrayed simply—either as victims or aggressors—a fact Russel Ward noted as early as 1962: 'we are shown the aborigine through European eyes'. Then there was the question of style. Clark's dogged pursuit of a prose style recalling Macaulay or Carlyle was already passé by 1962, when volume I of *A History of Australia* was published. As he joked at the end of his life, 'there's always a terrible danger that if you're new you might just be trendy, and trendies don't really last for long'. Because Clark's work was so far removed from nearly everything written by his peers, it came as little surprise that so many members of the historical profession were critical of his *History*.[31]

In 2005, I interviewed the historian AGL Shaw, a former friend of Clark's. Shaw had known Clark nearly all his life, from Melbourne Grammar and Balliol in the 1920s and 1930s, eventually suffering Clark's opprobrium when he criticised his work in the 1960s. Shaw is one of Australia's finest historians—a humane, gentle man with a deep commitment to the traditional values of scholarship. In his nineties, he continued to give lectures gratis to the University of the Third Age. Sitting in his study overlooking Melbourne's Botanic Gardens, I asked him whether Clark's *History* would endure. There was a long moment of silence, his face limpid. Finally, he shook his head and uttered emphatically—'No.' Clark's work was too personal, he said, too focused on individuals at the expense of economic, political and constitutional history. Shaw's view mirrored the views of several of Clark's former colleagues who took the trouble to write long letters explaining their views of Clark's work. Robin (Bob) Gollan, Clark's former colleague at the ANU, who succeeded him as professor of Australian History in 1975, considered Clark's work was 'not real historical writing'. 'His method was that of a novelist,' said Gollan, 'and I find him impossible to read.' Frank Crowley, who had been so impressed by Clark's volumes of documents that he was inspired to publish his own documentary history of Australia, wrote to explain how disappointed he was by the six volumes. 'I was appalled. Archival fidelity, my inheritance from the Melbourne History Department, had been slaughtered. Clark's many solecisms crystallise the flaw in his histories; the tendency to move into historical fiction, to alter facts to suit explanations, to be imaginative in order to bolster an over-riding generalisation.' Clark's daughter, Katerina, a historian of Soviet Russia, admitted that she had never read her father's work in its entirety. It was simply not 'her type of history'. John La Nauze refused to read Clark's work because, he said, he didn't 'read fiction'.

Historians who looked for depth of historical context rather than vivid character portraits and wanted (at least in a general history) a more systematic account of Australia's political, economic, social and cultural history found Clark extremely difficult to read. In their own work, they sought to create distance between themselves and the past, while Clark, like a historical novelist, sought to break that distance down. They also wanted less of Manning Clark and more of the past, as well as a more nuanced reading of the primary sources. While this was the response of many of Clark's peers, the reaction of his readers was quite the reverse. He had achieved something that few of his colleagues could manage: a large popular readership. Long after the writings of most of his contemporaries had been consigned to library shelves and secondhand bookshops, Clark's *History* still graced the shelves of major bookshops. What was it, then, that made his work so memorable, and how are we to understand its value?[32]

On the publication of Volume I of *A History of Australia*, Max Crawford noted 'the very distinctive personal vision' that Clark brought to his subject.

As each subsequent volume appeared, Crawford's remarks were replayed. Reviewers described Volume II as 'personal and burning, and fascinatingly readable', 'highly personal', 'idiosyncratic' and 'highly original', but few sought to explain exactly how his voice made itself felt. Clark's personal voice was grounded not in political statements or in any prefiguring of postmodern scholarship but rather in a profound religiosity, and it is this highly individual understanding of the religious—ecumenical and spiritual, in the broadest sense—that gives Clark's work its depth of feeling and its distinctive, redeeming personal quality. 'What is deep inside you,' Clark said in 1969, 'will come out, and it must come out and you must let it come out.' Some of his readers thought they could hear his voice when they read his prose. Helen Garner felt she could hear him speaking like 'an ordinary human being, full of sad and humble questions'. His nephew, Philip Ingamells, heard his voice so clearly that he found it difficult to read his work, so powerfully did it sound his presence.[33]

Clark did much more than let his personal voice come out. The very structure of the first four volumes—the struggle between Catholicism, Protestantism and the Enlightenment—was Clark's personal struggle writ large. Clark wrote Australia's history through the prism of his personal experience. And he wanted it no other way. In 1976, he acknowledged that many of the central conflicts in his history—especially that of the English inheritance versus the native born—were, as he put it, 'in my veins'. All of the lead characters in Clark's *History* carried his personal conflicts within them. In 1965, writing the chapter on Governor George Arthur for Volume II, Clark described his feelings as he tried to portray Arthur's character: 'Am big with Arthur child, but [I] fear that after delivery the child will not have any of the beauty or grandeur or wit or interest I want to give him.' The birth analogy was apt: Clark felt his characters part of himself. His description of Arthur betrayed his own feelings of passion and guilt:

He wore black clothes. He walked with a stoop, as though his shoulders were weighed down with the burden of human depravity. The pallor of the cheeks, and the tight-lipped mouth, which rarely broke into a smile, seemed a fit instrument for those passionless petitions he sent up daily to his God.

Only the huge lack-lustre eyes betrayed at times those moments of hysteria, those days when the gusts of passion swept over him, leaving that huge deposit of guilt, which had been washed away by God's saving grace.[34]

It was fanciful but brilliant. Character description was one of his greatest talents as a writer. In the late 1960s, gazing at a portrait of the New South Wales Colonial Secretary Edward Deas Thomson in the Dixson Galleries in Sydney, he divined that Thomson was a good family man and loved his wife. Sometimes, it was hard to know where Clark's personality ended and his character's personality began. In Volume III, William Charles Wentworth often seemed to behave like Clark, the lover of bawdy jokes, a person at ease with the native-born Australian, and a man who lived with a dark secret in his heart. But while historians rightly accused Clark of inserting into his characters personal qualities and thoughts for which he had no evidence, readers were enthralled. They saw Clark's characters as if they were standing before them, like the gold digger Edward Hargraves, 'a mountain of flesh, the quintessence of the vulgarity, brashness and coarseness of the men of the New World'. They saw the colour of the characters' hair, eyes and skin, even the scar on William Bligh's cheek. And they heard the sound of their voices— the songs and ballads of bush workers, the revelry and drunkenness in the streets of gold rush Melbourne in the 1850s, and through the windows of the ballroom of Government House in Hobart in 1828, the 'lap, lap of the waters of the Derwent'.[35]

Clark's audience was pulled along by the emotional drama as much as his love of bacchanalia. Some historians, however, winced at the purple prose ('early one golden Sunday morning'), the clichés ('all creatures great and small'), the Punch and Judy language ('the heart dampeners' and 'whip wielders'), the shameless borrowing ('tiger tiger burning bright'), the wild excess ('with the madness of that bitch goddess of success stirring in his blood'), the unrelenting fatalism (Macquarie: 'the tragedy of a man whose very creation swept him aside'), the enthusiastic repetitions (in one paragraph, Parkes loses the 'kingdom of heaven', then tries desperately to put 'the kingdom of greatness' between himself and the 'kingdom of nothingness', only to find that the 'tragic grandeur' of his life foreshadows the 'coming age of ruins'), and the Messiah-like conclusions. ('For just as the history of a man turns some to a tragic vision of life, the history of men's dreams prompts others to work for the day when that wealth of love which used to be lavished on Him is turned upon the whole of nature, on the world, on men, and on every blade of grass.') As one reviewer remarked, Clark piled words on top of one another 'like icing on a wedding cake'. Every character seemed to exist in a permanent state of moral hypertension. It was quite a heady brew, yet Clark's work somehow rose above the melange of banality and hyperbole. For all its faults, his history was animate. Suddenly, readers of history were privy to individual passions. Clark lived up to his promise: he made the dead live. In 1968, he advised Ryan to advertise Volume II with the following slogan: 'For four hundred passion packed pages buy Clark; only two pennies per passion packed page.'[36]

Battling to abridge Clark's six volumes down to one in the early 1990s, historian and broadcaster Michael Cathcart struggled to understand Clark's approach to history until he finally saw its personal dimensions. 'Once I realised it was about him I had it. All those indirect narrators were just Manning in fancy dress,' said Cathcart. 'And why did Manning hate Deakin so much? Because Deakin reminded him of that side of himself he hated so much, the playing to Yarraside.' Clark took his father's advice: 'You mark my words, boy. It's what happens to individuals which is the stuff of history.' The books' individuals carried the drama of *A History of Australia*. Clark's succession of flawed, tormented males—such as William Wentworth, Henry Lawson and John Curtin—were divided personalities brought down by their 'fatal flaws'—self-righteousness, pride, lust, ambition, vanity and avarice. Like Clark, they were burdened by the 'private hell in the heart' and drawn to confess their sins to the reader. In Clark's hands, their lives lurched from the inspired to the droll, with tragedy, pathos and existential crisis lurking on every stump and street corner. Women appeared in the lives of Clark's male characters much as they did in Clark's diaries—as figures of mystery, whose beauty and sexual power threatened to belittle men and expose their weaknesses. Nor were they capable of the same spiritual sensitivity as men. Take, for example, Clark's description of Wentworth's wife, Sarah Cox: 'It was not given to her to know the Dionysian frenzy of the heart which drove her husband on to glory, and damnation'. In Volume IV, describing morally upright women who lived in the bush in the late nineteenth century, Clark wrote his negative feelings about his marriage to Dymphna straight into the heart of the bushman of the 1860s. 'Being good … was precisely what a man could not endure … [it] brought out the devil in him. The man, tormented by guilt at what had come up from inside him, asked the woman to forgive him and then hated her all the more as the one who knew what he was like.' Solipsism was Clark's trademark. Yet for all his self-centredness, there was also something translucent about his character portraits. As EM Forster wrote of Dostoyevsky's characters, they always 'stand for more than themselves; infinity attends them, though they remain individuals they expand to embrace it and summon it to embrace them'.[37]

In Volume II, Clark chose characters to represent different dramatic elements of his narrative. Richard Johnson played the role of the Greek chorus, entering the narrative to make 'gloomy remarks about the human situation'. Then, in the language of Shakespeare, he selected characters to play 'mighty opposites': the Reverend Samuel Marsden, Lieutenant-Governor Arthur and John Macarthur stood for 'darkness', while William Wentworth, Governor Richard Bourke and Chief Justice Forbes were examples of men who were 'moving towards the light'. At the very end of Volume I, he told the story of a man in Tasmania printing an edition of Charles Dickens' *Pickwick Papers* because he wanted to introduce Dickens as a symbol of hope. Clark's characters operated as both historical figures and emblems of classical dramatic art. Driven from elsewhere by some unknown force, they struggle to attain a moral sensibility and control over their own destiny. They fight to assert their own conscience, naïvely cling to the dream of human perfectibility, doubt the existence of God and strain to find purpose and meaning in life. Like Clark, they suffer because of their knowledge of human beings' capacity for evil—a capacity that they know is also inside them—and they are confronted with the conflict between the desires of the flesh and the needs of the spirit. And, now and then, like the explorer Robert Burke and Clark himself, they are brought down by a 'fit of the sillies'. Although Clark claimed to be the type of writer who did not intrude into his narrative, the truth was that he intruded nearly all the time. Clark's characters and scenes became unwitting carriers of his own ghosts, psychological infirmities and obsessions. His tracks were emblazoned across every paragraph, not only because he lived in his characters but also because of the way he used primary sources.[38]

During the writing of this biography, historians and students would occasionally alert me to examples of Clark's 'plagiarism'. They almost always involved cases where Clark had quoted from primary sources without acknowledgement. Years earlier, as a postgraduate student, I had been guilty of much the same excitement, thinking I had caught Clark out, but I discovered that chasing the trail of his footnotes was a fruitless task. Like many before me, I could not crack Clark's code. Passages frequently appeared in his work that seemed to bear no relation to the sources in the notes—or, as was more often the case, they blended so seamlessly with his own prose that it was impossible to tell who was speaking. Scribbling notes for Clark's obituary in 1991, Ken Inglis offered this staccato-like description of Clark's historical writing: 'Prose glowing, incantatory, allusive, evocative, archaic, banal, repetitive, threadbare. Mixed with prose of subjects in a baffling compound.' No one has put it better. If the academic definition of plagiarism were applied to Clark's work, he would stand guilty of plagiarism on every page, not because he stole the ideas of others but because he often failed to acknowledge his sources. Quotation marks are not always used when they should be. Written in the present tense, his own words mix with those of his characters, creating the illusion that the reader is present in the past, as though they were eavesdropping on conversations, or actually witnessing events, like cinema audiences watching a documentary. After Keith Hancock read Volume III he told Clark that he had come 'as close as any historian can come to "re-enactment"—not of the "total past", which is a mirage, but of the past which lives again when mind meets mind: when Clark meets Wentworth, Marsden, Scott, Darling—and Betsy Bandicoot'. For many readers, the effect was electrifying. Clark's technique immersed the reader in the language and spirit of the time, transporting them back to the streets of colonial Sydney or Hobart. Clark wrote in period dress—'My Lord Bathurst'—he was the lyrebird of Australian history.[39]

Sitting in his study, with photocopies of his primary sources laid out on the desk in front of him—newspaper articles, colonial despatches, letters and diaries—Clark transcribed passages straight into his narrative. He used historical sources in the same way as a musician uses a musical score. The original documents were a form of notation upon which he would improvise, providing a magnificent libretto. Like a Handel oratorio, voices rose up to take their designated role in the score, given an added touch of Clarkian drama here, an extra bit of Clarkian pathos there. His work was polyvocal; it teemed with voices, and the voices within Clark's text mirrored those within his mind: he often referred to himself as a polyphon, a man of many voices. He claimed to hear the future-of-humanity voice, the sceptical voice, the eye of pity, the voice of doubt about everything, the voice of 'Mr Passion' and countless other nondescript voices within 'Mr Passion'. In Clark's mind, these played constantly, usually in unresolved tension, conveying 'an eternal restlessness and discontent'.[40]

Captivating as this method of writing history was for so many of Clark's readers, it brought him nothing but trouble from his editors and reviewers. Shaw, for example, was irritated by the way Clark's polyvocal technique appeared to turn his characters into historical authorities; they were both actors and commentators, argued Shaw, and the result was confusing. Editing Clark's manuscript of Volume IV for MUP, Carol Bram chastised Clark for the way he lumped all his footnotes together, making it 'virtually impossible to tell which note belonged to which statement'. This was precisely what other historians wanted to know. Clark, she said, required 'gentle disciplining'. He needed to 'be more aware of the distinction between the persona Manning and other persons'. Clark's illegible handwriting only increased the likelihood of factual errors, as did his massive output—over 1000 words per day. Yet he did care about factual accuracy. In fact, his inability to stop making mistakes caused him great anguish.[41]

In late 1963, three weeks after Clark arrived in San Francisco, as he was settling in to his office at Duke University he collected the mail that was waiting for him. When he opened one of the largest envelopes, his first copy of *A Short History of Australia* fell onto the floor. He had written the book in the space of nine weeks in 1962, eager to collect the 900-pound advance from the New American Library so that he could buy his family a new car. Picking the book up off the floor, he plucked up the courage to check the details of Wentworth's birth, which he feared were incorrect. 'They were.' He rang the publishers in New York to see what could be done. They would insert an erratum slip. His confidence shattered, he waited for the 'jeers and sneers of the Australian mockers' to crucify him. Overcome by fear, he turned to his diary. 'My words seem to incite people … to hatred and derision.' For the next few days 'death seemed the only escape' as the thought of suicide crossed his mind. He prayed for the strength not to run away, to face up to his tormentors and put down on paper all that was in his heart, 'that little candle of light in the heart of an immense darkness'.[42]

The avalanche of criticism that Clark feared never eventuated. When the reviews appeared the book was praised as 'a personal triumph'. Predictably, Ellis took him to task again for factual errors and his trenchant criticism of postwar anti-communists ('I had to check that the author's name was Clark and not Marx'). Unlike Volume I, Clark's narrative in the *Short History* rushed along. The story was one of moral decay, in which the fledgling nation was left prey to the materialism and greed of the bourgeoisie, a nation 'stripped bare of all faith … left comfortless on Bondi Beach'. It was a bleak view. By 1988, the *Short History*, having found its way onto school reading lists, had sold well over 250 000 copies. The style was racy, even journalistic, the tone lighter, the perspective closer to traditional Left, class-based analysis, the content largely free of Clark's God-like intrusions. It was by far the most successful popular history of Australia in the postwar period, being serialised in tabloid magazines like *Pix*, where Clark's book was promoted on the front page, flanked by bikini-clad models and man-eating crocodiles.[43]

The issue of factual accuracy, however, continued to plague Clark's multivolume *History*. In 1963, as he left the *Short History* behind and started work on volumes II and III, he spent much of his time in a constant battle with MUP over the quality of his manuscripts. Peter Ryan, on receiving the manuscript of Volume II in 1967, was furious. It was 'full of mistakes, overflowing with errors of fact and severe blemishes of spelling and syntax'. In a fit of rage, he rang Dymphna, shouting a 'stream of vituperation' so loudly that she was forced to hold the phone away from her ear. Dymphna knew the manuscript was 'awful' but she 'never dared' tell Clark about Ryan's call. Ryan decided to send his tenacious copy editor, Barbara Ramsden, to Canberra to 'sort out the text'. When Clark discovered that Ramsden was on her way to Canberra he responded in predictable fashion, declaring his 'incompetence': 'It was my mistake ever to begin the work.' In his Melbourne office, Ryan could 'set his watch' by Clark's calls at 9.30 each morning. He did what had to be done, humouring and flattering Clark until his anxiety abated. As the manuscript was edited, Dymphna recalled Ramsden climbing the ladder to Clark's study each morning. She handed Clark a list of his mistakes and stock phrases—'the men in black', 'the fatal flaw', 'tragic grandeur'. Insulted, Clark was 'speechless with rage': '[I am] still depressed and shaken about the manuscript … Why can I never transcribe a sentence accurately?' Eventually, he saw his good fortune. Ryan and Ramsden had saved him from another caning from critics such as Ellis, just as Carol Bram, Ramsden's replacement, would later save him in preparing the manuscript of Volume III. The pattern continued with successive volumes, Clark spotting mistakes at each stage of production, right down to the galley proofs, exasperating Ryan and his editors.[44]

Dymphna had long been Clark's most valuable critic and was always the first person to read his manuscripts. Because she saw them in their original state, she played a crucial role in improving Clark's prose, breaking up his 'inordinately long sentences', correcting errors of syntax and grammar, questioning the accuracy of details and the validity of his interpretations, and 'suggesting adaptations to make his work more accessible to an ordinary reader'. As she acknowledged after Clark died, they were 'a team', two 'very different people' whose talents were complementary. She did not have his 'compulsive interest in the deeper questions of life'. And besides, she was 'far too busy changing nappies, cooking dinners and cleaning up mess to think too deeply about those things'. By bringing 'her critical faculties' to Clark's work, she was forced to tackle the worst excesses of his romantic temperament; essentially, to stop him from 'letting his imagination run away with him'. She paid a price for her honesty. Clark responded to her criticisms petulantly, lamenting that he was saddled with a wife who 'savaged' his work and wanted only to hurt and punish him. 'Is my wife right? Is my second volume self-conscious and diffuse? She is neither malign nor benign—just a vast, painful indifference and contempt for me in my strivings.' How much of this Clark told Dymphna is difficult to tell, but his hurt certainly surfaced at times of heated argument, judging from his diary entries. The differences in their intellectual dispositions added yet another layer of tension to their marriage. While Clark longed for a woman who would swoon for him each evening with flirtatious adoration, he also knew that he needed Dymphna's pragmatism to temper his worst excesses as a writer. Her unyielding, clear-eyed assessments of his work were indispensable to his success. As the volumes progressed and Clark's writing became more dramatic and apocalyptic, he sensed that her criticisms and reservations as an editor went far deeper than she let on, that she actually found his work self-indulgent. It was this suspicion, and his need for intimate, deferential praise, that would spark his attraction to other women in the years ahead.[45]

Dymphna's understanding of history was radically different from Clark's. She valued traditional scholarly principles—fidelity to documentary evidence, factual accuracy and the necessary limitations of historical truth—above and beyond artistic expression. She did not seek emotional involvement with her material. While Clark believed that there wasn't 'very much difference between fiction and writing history', at least not his type of history, Dymphna saw fiction and history as different branches of literature. She read nearly all the reviews of Clark's work and knew that some of the reviewers who criticised Clark's unreliability on matters of historical detail actually had a point.

In 1967, Clark claimed that the only difference between his form of history and fiction was that, as an historian, he could not 'invent facts'. While he never invented facts, his factual errors undermined his work because they occurred too frequently. For historians who read Clark's work closely, troubling questions arose. A factual error in itself was trifling, but when Clark based his interpretations on facts that were incorrect, where did this leave the validity of his interpretations? In Volume II, for example, Clark has Samuel Marsden preaching a sermon at a service he did not attend and also gets the details of the service wrong. Yet he invests Marsden's sermon with great significance. On his first reading of Volume I, Shaw counted 'thirty-four mistakes without checking'. Some were trivial while others were consequential. In Volume VI, Phar Lap won the Melbourne Cup twice. In Darwin, there was hanging of Aborigines who in fact had their sentences commuted. In Volume V, Sir John Forrest gave speeches he never made ... and so the list goes on. If every footnote were checked in Clark's six volumes—a task that no one would want to take on—many mistakes would be found. While every work of history contains mistakes, Clark's mistakes have long been a bone of contention for historians, especially because of his public profile. He frequently received letters from colleagues and members of the public listing his many errors. Even those historians who reviewed his work favourably acknowledged his mistakes, arguing that Clark's 'novelist's insight' and 'sheer story-telling' ability outweighed them. Yet underlying the criticisms of Clark's factual accuracy was one fundamental question. Do Clark's evocative portraits enhance our understanding of Australian history? Or, as John Manning Ward asked, if his vision had so little to do with what happened, what was to be said in its favour, save that it was fascinating? Had Clark written history or had he, in fact, written 'something else'?[46]

THE TRAVELLING HISTORIAN

Flying over the Western Australian coast just before dawn on 23 December 1975—'the silver beam of a full moon over the water'—Clark saw the desolate coastline first sighted by Dirk Hartog in 1616. To understand what Hartog had seen and felt, he knew he had to return. In April 1976, he flew to Perth to meet Suzanne Welborn, a former student and friend who had promised to help him get there. Clark waited in the foyer of the Parmelia Hotel, wearing his old boots, khaki shirt, battered Akubra and torn, baggy trousers. In the plush surroundings of the hotel lobby he looked out of place. Welborn saw the incongruity as Clark intended her to. A lean, erudite man who looked like a dishevelled fisherman blown in from the east greeted her. That day, they set off together to drive the 800-kilometre journey north to Shark Bay, the most westerly point of Australia.

Clark was determined to reach Dirk Hartog Island, where the Dutch explorer had come ashore 350 years earlier. When they finally arrived, the island station manager drove them the last 100 kilometres to the northern tip of the island where Hartog, in October 1616, had nailed a plaque to a wooden post on the cliff's edge. Hartog's plaque was long gone, having returned to Amsterdam with another Dutch sea captain, Willem de Vlamingh, who landed on the island in 1697, and had the presence of mind to leave a replacement behind. Welborn watched as Clark stood on the spot where the first known landing by a European on Australian soil had taken place. The sea was calm. Unexpectedly, Clark faced the waters of the Indian Ocean 'and in a deep baritone, sang the Dutch National Anthem'. He was singing as much for Welborn as he was for Hartog. When he first saw Shark Island from the air eight months earlier, he was already infatuated with Welborn—'I returned with the person I had thought much about on that moonlit night on 23 December 75.'[47]

Clark's performance at Shark Island was just one of hundreds of journeys he made in his lifetime in search of historical atmosphere. His papers in Canberra contain many folders of maps, postcards and brochures relating to his travels, all grouped under the simple title 'Journeys'. Ever since he stood among the British tombstones at Fort George in Madras, in 1956, he knew that he could only write history as art by trusting his senses. Standing among the gravestones, he voiced the inscriptions as he wrote them into his notebook, like a priest reciting the psalms. He saw the ideals of the British colonists crystallised in their epitaphs, their work for religion, their service to the East India Company and the Crown, and their sense of themselves as the new Romans, bringing the rule of law, roads, bridges, education and a common language to the world—'the Pax Britannica'. In the thirty years that elapsed between his journey through South-East Asia in the mid-1950s and his completion of *A History of Australia* in 1986, Clark travelled incessantly—in Europe, in America and throughout Australia and New Zealand. Even before the age of mass air travel began in earnest in the late 1960s, when he travelled with Dymphna he would leave the younger children at home in the care of friends, relatives or their older siblings, having written ahead to historical societies and libraries asking to be shown the sites. For

Australian historians in the 1960s and 1970s, Clark's restless journeying was highly unusual. He was Australia's first travelling historian. For more than three decades, he walked almost every line of *A History of Australia*.[48]

As the youngest child, Benedict often accompanied Clark on 'spontaneous drives into the country' in the 1970s. 'I remember in my teens driving to historical sites with Dad. We'd drive for hours sometimes and he'd get out of the car, scribble a few words in his notebook, these tiny squiggles that nobody else could read, and after five minutes he'd get back in the car, look at me and say, "I think I've seen enough now."' In 1985, Benedict, aged twenty-eight, accompanied Clark on a whirlwind tour of Gallipoli and the battlefields of Europe. 'I thought it would be impossible on our schedule to see the French battlefields but he drove himself to do it. And we saw Proust's hometown too. After he returned from travelling he was almost always exhausted. But this didn't stop him. He didn't know what he would say until he'd been to a place; once there, he would feel something or work something out.' The historian Bill Gammage, Clark's former student, travelled with him on several occasions. 'You could almost see him stripping away time and imagining what it felt like for the people who were there … and when you read him you can see that experience of country infuses what he says about it.' In Clark's letters home, he referred to his travels as 'sniffing around for atmosphere'. He was either in libraries or in cemeteries, lingering in the homes of former literary greats, sniffing for Ibsen in Bergen, hunting down Dostoyevsky in St Petersburg, or simply enjoying the scenery. In May 1964, he wrote to Andrew and Axel from the British Museum of his trip to Ireland. 'We drove around the island, sniffed the cream, the cow shit, heard the human jungle in the lanes, and the rosary beads in the churches.' Clark lived every day with the ghosts of the past singing in his mind. As he walked along Sydney's Macquarie Street to the Mitchell Library, he would halt suddenly and exclaim: 'This is the spot where James Macarthur stopped his carriage and invited William Charles Wentworth to step inside and have a conversation.' Historian Lyndall Ryan, Clark's research assistant in the early 1970s, was with him often in Sydney. 'We'd walk along Macquarie St, past all the landmarks, Parliament House, Sydney Hospital, the Mint, The Hyde Park Barracks, and Manning would have a story for every 10 metres.' Every statue told a story—Henry Lawson, James Cook, Governor Richard Bourke and Robert Burns—Clark conversed with them all as if they were still alive.[49]

He travelled to London in 1964, searching for the atmosphere that would infuse the opening pages of Volume II. As he stood in front of Adelphi House, where a public meeting had been held in 1833 to discuss the founding of the new colony of South Australia, he looked across the waters of the Thames, 'that river of beauty and horror', to the place where the prison hulks were moored, and saw at once how the sight of those ships would have further entrenched the view that South Australia should remain free of convicts. On the night of Monday 12 May, 'incurably romantic as ever', he went by train to Portsmouth, to be there for the 177th anniversary of the sailing of the First Fleet, taking a ferry ride round 'those sacred waters'. Alone, out on the waters of Portsmouth Harbour, Clark imagined the fleet sailing for Australia, Arthur Phillip at the helm of the *Sirius*, the convicts chained in filth in the holds below him, the mist rising off the water, the ship's bow slicing through the waves, the cacophony of English voices on deck, and in the eyes of every man and woman aboard the shared sense of leaving their homeland behind, perhaps forever. Back in London, he walked to the Old Bailey where Newgate Prison had stood until 1904. He read the newspaper reports of Newgate's brutality, but he had to walk the streets and sit in the public gallery of the Old Bailey to imagine the scene he wanted to paint in the opening pages of Volume II.

> From the East End of the great city of London, right to the outskirts of Westminster, unwashed, unshaven, squalid and dirty men constantly raced to and fro ankle deep in the filth and mire. In that mass of dirt, gloom and misery drunken tramps jostled with the rich and the titled. Men and women craving for booty, their bellies filled with beer and gin, committed crimes for which they were hanged by the neck until they were dead after which their bodies were cut down and given to their friends.[50]

Painting this Bruegel-like canvas, Clark provided what he called the 'backdrop' to his story, a theatrical term that betrayed his true purpose. Unlike other historians, he did not talk of context or consider circumstances.

Instead, he fed his instinctive readings of historical places straight into his work. Inscriptions on the walls of churches Clark visited were scribbled into his notebook and found their way into his history. He searched too for William Wentworth, visiting Elm Court, where Wentworth had lived in the early 1820s, and the Temple Church of St Mary, where Clark saw the Ten Commandments carved in gold above the altar and imagined Wentworth 'pondering their meaning'. In Volume II, he placed Wentworth in the church, mixing fact and invention in the way a novelist uses his personal experience:

> There [Wentworth would] go each Sunday against his will to that church in the Middle Temple where, through the dreary, if edifying, prayers and sermons, he could read cut in gold letters those words on the tablet behind the Lord's table, that law of God, the violation of which had cheated his father of his place in society—'Thou shalt not commit adultery.'

Clark had no evidence that Wentworth had actually thought these things, but for the type of history he was writing he needed physical evidence only as a launching pad for his imagination. With each volume of *A History of Australia*, the gap between the factual foundations of Clark's work and his interpretations became wider. Joseph Conrad, describing his own use of personal experience in *Heart of Darkness*, explained how he had 'pushed' it 'beyond the actual facts' in order to bring his story home to the reader. Conrad wanted to give his story a 'tonality of its own', a 'sinister resonance' that 'would hang in the air and dwell on the ear after the last note had been struck'. And so it was that Clark's method embodied that of a novelist: he pushed beyond the particulars in order to write history that revealed universal truth—not historical fiction, but fictional history.[51]

The research method of the travelling historian was intuitive. Clark wanted 'to feel his way into the two great experiences of William Wentworth's life: the life of the son of a convict woman, about which he was silent for the rest of his life and went to great lengths to conceal; and the life of a man tenuously connected with the ruling families in England and Ireland. So he sought out Wentworth's aristocratic heritage in England and Ireland, 'noting the irony of Wentworth's father coming from the same town in Ireland as Ned Kelly's mother, Ellen Quinn'. In 1964, he journeyed to Peterhouse in Cambridge, the college where Wentworth was enrolled as a student at the time when he submitted his poem *Australasia* for the Chancellor's prize. In the chapel, Clark noted 'the sombre wooden pews—the diamond-shaped black and white stone floor—the painted ceiling—the simple altarpiece bedecked with a woven cloth— the candles on the pews—dark … austere— man and his God'—to whom, as far as he could see, Wentworth made no response. In order to know Wentworth, Clark tracked down every detail of his life that he could possibly find. He gave himself completely to the task— physically and mentally. Where Wentworth had stood he would stand too. Inevitably, when he came to write up his experience as history, the result was a mixture of Wentworth and Clark. Thus, when Clark describes Wentworth's marriage in Sydney in 1829, it seems that Clark himself is marrying Sarah Cox. 'Wentworth went down on his knees at the fatal rails in St Philip's Church, and swore before Almighty God that he, 'the Don Giovanni of Botany Bay', would now forsake all others, and love, honour and cherish Sarah Cox until death did them part.' Wentworth, like Clark, is a haunted man, a man threatened with exposure—rushing on towards his goal but casting his eye back over his shoulder lest anyone he knew was looking. At Vaucluse House, the Wentworth family home on the southern shores of Sydney Harbour, Clark was mesmerised by the painting of Mary Magdalene ('La Maddalena')—'a sorrowing woman, her breasts bare, the fingers of her right hand touching the crown of thorns and the linen of the one without sin'. In her plaintive face he saw the repentant sinner seeking forgiveness and his own guilt revealed, later writing up Wentworth in Volume III as his alter ego, the man who collected paintings of Mary Magdalene 'not so much in the hope that those who had loved much would one day be forgiven, but rather that they would be understood'. Clark's bleeding heart lingered in Wentworth as it did in every one of his fallen heroes.[52]

It was in the USA and Europe in the 1960s that Clark found his inspiration for his next three volumes. Driving across the southern states of America in 1963, abused by white drivers for picking up 'negro hitchhikers', he saw something of his own purpose in William Faulkner, 'the historian of the

South's glory and doom'. Standing in Mark Twain's house in Hannibal, on the Mississippi, or in the garden of Abraham Lincoln's home in Springfield, Illinois, he 'groped for' their America, the one submerged beneath the highways and 'the Coca-cola motel America'. Whether it was Faulkner's home and grave at Rowan Oak in Oxford, Mississippi, Dickens' haunts near Marshalsea Road, in south London, Thomas Hardy's grave at Westminster Abbey or the home of Thomas Carlyle at 24 Cheyne Row, Chelsea, Clark stalked the scene, rummaging around, surveying the site, winding back the years in the hope of finding some eternal truth.[53]

At musical concerts in London, Clark saw his path as a writer more clearly. In 1964, at the Royal Albert Hall, listening to Alfredo Campoli play Brahms's third violin sonata, he felt Brahms trying to tell him that the strong could learn to endure, 'without flinching'. Hearing Handel's *Messiah*, he perceived majesty, harmony and the sweetness of melody, but not darkness or terror. Mozart's *Don Giovanni* reminded him that 'only an artist's vision of life', either in sound, words or paint on canvas, could purge his mind of its pettiness and illnesses and lift him 'up to things eternal'. More than any other composer, it was Bach who strengthened Clark's artistic resolve. From the days of his father's services in Belgrave and Mentone, and morning chapel at Melbourne Grammar, Bach's cantatas, masses, and music for keyboard had been at the centre of his spiritual life. As recorded classical music became more accessible, Clark wrote from Canberra to London in 1960, enquiring about recordings of the *Well-Tempered Klavier*, before deciding to buy Rosalyn Tureck's landmark 1954 recording with Deutsche Grammophon. In 1964, he heard Tureck play Bach in London and was stunned by the capacity of Bach's music, after more than two centuries, to still the London audience and soothe the anxiety within him. Later, attending a performance of the *B Minor Mass*, he felt 'hushed awe ... the burden of the mystery ... and decided never to touch again petty things in literature'. Bach taught Clark to maintain his vision, to write history as a 'hymn of praise', just as the architecture of Venice revealed to him 'that something else, beyond what we can see, touch, smell and hear'. Although Clark had no faith or belief in God, he knew, rationally, as he walked the streets of London and the alleyways of Venice in 1964, that 'we are alone'. Yet coexist-

An Eye for Eternity

ing with this rational belief was a sense within him of something that transcended the everyday, a sense of infinity that he glimpsed, as if from a distance, like the sound of music heard from far away—faint, alluring, otherworldly and undefined.[54]

So much of his time away from Australia was devoted to music and art. While he visited the British Museum Library for material, he spent many days searching for inspiration in London's galleries. He took extensive notes on his response to particular paintings, even making special trips to Madrid's Museo del Prado, in 1964 and 1968, to view the work of Francisco de Goya. Early in 1964, he attended a Goya exhibition at the Royal Academy of Arts. It was the beginning of a lifelong fascination with the 'contrast between darkness and light' in Goya's work. So many of Goya's subjects, Clark remarked, were consumed by 'a frenzy of [violence], guilt and passion'. Clark was drawn to Goya's hellish depictions of humanity as much as he was by the questions of faith he saw posed in many of his paintings and drawings. Giving a lecture at the Institute of Commonwealth Studies in London, in March 1964, he referred to the Royal Academy exhibition to illustrate his artistic vision for writing *A History of Australia*. Goya's art, he told his audience, offered moments of illumination, confronting both human stupidity and horror, as well as holding out sympathy and pity for all of us. Clark saw this as akin to his own task. In writing history, he had to offer his readers more than the past. He would give them his 'tragic vision of life'. His characters would have 'moments of awareness', despite the fact that 'they very rarely' experienced such moments. Like a novelist, he would decide their fate according to their role in the story. As Goya manipulated external reality in order to reveal greater truths, he would 'impose a pattern of achievement, pride and retribution' on the past, even when the facts pointed only to chaos. This was the art in Clark's history—the ability to recreate the past both as history and allegory. After attending the Goya exhibition at the Royal Academy, he saw immediately how he should open Volume II. Goya's portrayal of barbarism alerted him to a passage in John Henry Newman's *Apologia*, which he first read as an undergraduate in the late 1930s. His copy still back in Australia, Clark found another in a secondhand bookshop on Charing Cross Road, and marked up the passage:

And so I argue about the world:—*if* there be a God, *since* there is a God, the human race is implicated in some terrible aboriginal calamity. It is out of joint with the purposes of its Creator. This is a fact, a fact as true as the fact of its existence; and this the doctrine of what is theologically called original sin becomes to me almost as certain as that the world exists, and as the existence of God.[55]

Acknowledging his debt to Newman, Clark began Volume II by combining Newman's image of humanity as fallen with his Goya-like depiction of depravity on the streets of London in the 1820s. He entitled the chapter 'Darkness'.

> Some who came to man's estate in the cities and country districts of the British Isles in the decade between 1820 and 1830 who knew the defeat of good, the success of evil, the physical pain and the mental anguish considered the human race was out of joint with the purpose of its creator ... In Vauxhall Gardens, orgies of lust and drunkenness prevented the industrious in the neighbourhood from sleeping, and the dying from departing in peace. In the streets, ragged and half-starved Flemish boys importuned females, and thrust forth from under their coats disgusting monkeys, to terrify the women ... Women gave birth to children in public places, because of their extreme misery and degradation ... Bishops [and] priests [explained that] ... as punishment for that offence in the Garden of Eden all creatures great and small were condemned to live in a vale of tears for the term of their natural lives.[56]

Clark would soon lift his convicts out of one hell and place them in another—the Australian colonies. Goya had helped him to cast *A History of Australia* in mythical language. This was the other dimension to Clark's history. Volume by volume, he dragged Australians into a Dante-like inferno, setting hell against heaven, drought against flood, and darkness against light. His fidelity was not to the past—quite the opposite. His intention was actually to make the past obey the dictates of his tragic vision and to shape and mould Australian history into a story that transcended history and became timeless; a story of flawed heroes who were elevated to the realm of the

Gods. Clark, however, had not come to Goya, or the idea of writing history as myth, alone.

In London, in the spring of 1964, he and Dymphna were in close contact with Arthur Boyd, Sidney Nolan and Barry Humphries. Humphries had been living and performing in the city since 1959, later describing London in the early 1960s as a Mecca for Antipodean painters. Boyd had set up a studio in Highgate. In summer, Sidney Nolan's Kelly and Gallipoli paintings were exhibited in Piccadilly. Clark attended both exhibitions. At first mystified as to exactly what Nolan was trying to say, over the next five years he gradually became more and more inspired by his work.[57]

When they arrived in London in January 1964, Clark and Dymphna found an old gamekeeper's cottage at Twickenham, on a narrow lane that ran down to a pub on the river, with nothing but a small copse between them and the water. Around the cottage, Dymphna remembered an acre of garden and, 'in the days when Manning was still quite social', long dinner parties with the Boyds, Nolan and Humphries that ran well into the dawn. While Clark had known Boyd for nearly fifteen years, he got to know both Humphries and Nolan more intimately in London and, through them, was drawn into closer contact with Patrick White. Meeting Humphries for the first time, on Charing Cross Road in March 1964, he immediately felt a 'deep bond with him'. In Humphries—his black hair swept long on one side of his face, his voice darting in and out of character—Clark saw someone like himself—'damned, doomed, vulnerable and anxious to uncover themselves—another Don Juan in hell', an artist who had been 'savaged by the reviewers' and his fellow Australians. Eager to let Humphries know of his feelings, he wrote to him in London to tell him that his stage performances had managed to lift Australian suburbia 'into an epiphany of the human situation'. 'So, go on,' he told Humphries, 'give us more of those moments of illumination, we desperately need them.' So well did he get on with Humphries that Clark felt Dymphna was 'wildly jealous' of their 'intimacy'. No doubt she also resented Clark's 'childish excitement' when he came into contact with 'great spirits' in whom he saw his own reflection, an excitement from which she immediately felt herself excluded, or beside which she was cast suddenly into an accessory role.[58]

In August, when Clark met up with Sidney Nolan at the exhibition of his Ned Kelly paintings in the Qantas building in Piccadilly, he pursued the same theme that had drawn him to Humphries. They talked of 'the mockers' in Australia who failed to understand their work, unlike the critics in London. Patrick White, they agreed, was in much the same position. Over coffee, Clark told Nolan about the particular moment in which they found themselves. This was Australia's chance to 'discover' itself. For Nolan, it was also a moment of opportunity. He saw that Australian artists had 'something to paint or to write about, which [hadn't] been worked over … hadn't had odes written to it'. As they parted, Clark felt at peace. He was in the company of a kindred spirit. Since 1961, he had filed every press clipping on White and Nolan, and would continue to do so until his death. He craved their acceptance and friendship as an implicit recognition of his own artistic endeavour, none more so than from Patrick White, with whom he 'fell in love' at first sight.[59]

When Clark wrote to White in 1961, after reading *Riders in the Chariot*, he drafted his letter three times, so anxious was he to impress. *Voss* and *Tree of Man* had already made an enormous impact on him. Now White's story, set in the 1950s in the fictional Australian suburb of Sarsaparilla, had overwhelmed him too. To show his excitement and 'tremendous gratitude', he sent White records as gifts—his favourite recordings of Bach and Beethoven, including Wilhelm Kempf's recording of Beethoven's late piano sonata (opus 111). Clark explained that in the slow movement, Beethoven, like White, had communicated the vision of a man who had 'climbed a mountaintop'. The image was reminiscent of the Caspar David Friedrich paintings that so often graced the covers of recordings of Beethoven and Schubert for Deutsche Grammophon, that of the artist–hero who stands alone on the cliff and gazes out to sea, seeking sublime inspiration. Clark told White that he had given Australia a novel that reminded him of the story of Christ visiting the house of Simon the leper, and the work of Dostoyevsky. His letter was fawning and romantic but sincere nonetheless. White responded warmly, inviting Clark to dinner. Shortly after his conversation with Nolan in London, Clark received White's response to Volume I. It was a 'truly wonderful and live work', said White; he felt 'humbled'. A few months later came Nolan's response to

Clark's 'gift'. He was 'thrilled': 'I feel so much in sympathy with what you have discovered.' Reading Clark, Nolan 'felt that tingling of recognition and sense of exact place and time similar to the effect of the wind on the emotions'. Two years later, after going to dinner at White's house in Martin Road, Centennial Park, the poet David Campbell, one of Clark's closest friends, told him how warmly White had spoken of his work, describing him as 'one of the few writers of understanding and imagination' in Australia. Even before Volume II was published in 1968, Clark had entered the court to which he had always sought entrance, the court of the artists—and in 1960s Australia there was no higher court than that of Patrick White, the only writer who had achieved significant international recognition.[60]

As Clark settled down to write volumes III and IV in the late 1960s and early 1970s, Nolan and White's influence on his work deepened. Writing the history of the spread of settlement and the great journeys of exploration, his travelling increased. As often as possible, he set out like Voss, to cross the continent from one end to another. His plan was to finish Volume III with the story of his 'beloved Burke and Wills'. As it turned out, his work on Burke and Wills would not appear until Volume IV was published in 1978, but in the interim he made two journeys into the heart of the continent in search of the two explorers. Nolan's Kelly paintings had already shown him how the bush 'alienated' many Europeans, reducing them to 'unfeeling, unaware' people, preoccupied with the question of their own survival. In 1966, when Clark saw Nolan's *Riverbend*, he realised something far more profound. Before he left Canberra in August 1967 for Menindee on the Darling, reading the fiction of André Gide as he searched for Burke and Wills, he wrote to Nolan to tell him how moved he had been by his 'Bend in the River paintings'. In September, as Nolan prepared for a major retrospective of his work at the Art Gallery of New South Wales, Clark wrote again, reminding him that, together with the poetry of AD Hope and White's novels since *Voss*, *Riverbend* was one of the few works of Australian art with a vision to match 'the one of those who first dreamt of planting civilization in the South Seas'. Two weeks later, in Melbourne, addressing the Victorian Historical Society, Clark told his audience that Australians were living in 'a most exciting moment in the history of the arts'. Nolan, White, Hope,

Dobell and McAuley had produced groundbreaking works of art, argued Clark, 'not through insular nationalism, but by painting and writing about the universal problems of mankind'.[61]

In Sydney, on 12 October, Clark saw the Nolan retrospective featuring the Kelly and Gallipoli paintings he had seen in London three years earlier, as well as Nolan's luminous paintings of Burke and Wills at the Gulf. Immediately, he felt 'uplifted', overcome by a feeling of 'serenity and joy'. Then came the moment of realisation. Nolan's mythical figures were also Clark's figures. Pulling out his notebook, he scribbled down his response as he walked through the gallery: 'Myth—my myth too, of Kelly, Burke, Leda, Frazer, Eureka, Gallipoli'. Nolan had helped Clark to see what he was trying to achieve in writing *A History of Australia*. Five days later, he wrote to Nolan in London: 'I cannot find the words to do justice to what you have seen. For me it was like listening to one of the preludes of Bach.' Even before the publication of Volume II, Clark saw the tragic vision he wanted to convey in Nolan's haunting images of Kelly and Burke and Wills, stories of failure set in a 'primeval landscape that stretched on forever'. In Nolan's Gallipoli paintings, Clark felt the Anzacs were 'flesh and spirit fused into one unity with Olympian gods and ancient heroes'. Now he had to do the same for his characters, especially Burke and Wills. For Nolan, meanwhile, reading Clark's work helped him to understand how so much of Australia's history was the story of settlers penetrating the country and 'not finding the garden, or the great river, or the place where you can grow crops and raise cattle'. By capturing both the delusions and disillusionment of his heroes, Nolan told Clark that he had put 'a snake in Australia's paradise'.[62]

In the story of Burke and Wills, Clark came to see the embodiment of everything he had tried to convey in writing Australian history. It had all the necessary ingredients—grand visions, majestic ambition and fatal mistakes—European explorers who were lured by fame into the heart of the continent and slowly undone. All that he wanted to say about man and his environment in Australia could be said in the telling of their tragic story. As he wrote volumes III and IV, the two explorers became more and more beloved in his imagination. In 1973, he visited Burke's birthplace in Ireland, slightly east of 'the gaunt beauty' of the Connemara's bare hills, and discovered for

Sidney Nolan, Riverbend [panel 3], *1964–65*

the second time the stables, the gardens and Burke's grey-faced sandstone
house, not far from where the swans sported, like the wild swans of Coole in
the poems by WB Yeats, whose summer house was close by. Shortly before
he left to follow in Burke and Wills's footsteps in May 1975, he saw Nolan's
Burke and Wills series in Melbourne: 'Burke on the camel, Wills on Billy,

Arthur Boyd, Portrait of Manning Clark, *circa 1972*

the grey charger, luminescent water, Burke on hump of camel, the monarch of all he surveyed, larger than life, the three [scorched] trees in rear, foreshadowing the disaster, surrounded by water'. Nolan depicted Burke and Wills naked; their bodies yielding completely to the land around them, their flesh seeping into the earth and sky. Perched on his camel, Burke looked like a strange, dazed intruder. When Nolan flew over Australia for the first time in the late 1940s, he realised the debt Australia's poets and painters owed to the explorers, 'with their frail bodies and superb willpower'. He thought of Burke and Wills as his 'predecessors', describing his paintings as an attempt to portray 'the actuality of the landscape' they encountered, 'intensified to the point of a dream'. As Clark left Canberra for the inland, Nolan's images of Burke and Wills shone in his imagination, informing his own impressions of the land he encountered.[63]

Travelling to Menindee in the far west of New South Wales, Clark followed Burke and Wills's tracks to Coopers Creek in the top north-eastern corner of South Australia, then headed north to Birdsville, where Nolan had been more than twenty years before him. From there, he turned back, retracing his steps to Coopers Creek, before making brief visits to Mildura and Melbourne and embarking on the second leg of his journey, driving north through Victoria, New South Wales and Western Queensland all the way to the Gulf Country. In total, Clark drove well over 10 000 kilometres, through some of the most sparsely settled and desolate parts of the country, and he took great pleasure in recording in his notebook the distances between each town, as if with each kilometre travelled he was another step closer to knowing Australia. He also calculated his budget, albeit in one sentence: 'stay in pubs or motels: accommodation 1000 so take 2000 dollars'. The small blue-covered notebooks in which he wrote down his immediate impressions later became one of his most important sources. Unlike the content of virtually all his other diaries, Clark's *plein-air* entries were immediate and intuitive responses to his surroundings. There was no time for lengthy reflection or self-analysis; he simply stood at the site, notebook and pen in hand, scanning the horizon.[64]

Menindee 12 May 75
Site of Burke's camp, dawn on the Darling … first light [on the] … surface of the river, the flock of crows, the seagulls. This is the place from which Burke wrote the letter about success & failure.

Mootwingee: Seen as the place of desolation by the man who knew the grasses of Galway

Giles Rock, Mootwingee 13 May 75
What did he say about the Aborigines? Did he have any ideas on them as a people who could teach the white man anything?

Sidney Nolan, Robert O'Hara Burke, *16 May 1950*

Milparinka 14 May 75
Where Sturt stayed, called it 'the dreary country', the site of his despair, the heat, the death of Burke. Is it only a hard country for those who want to change it? To make it bear fruit?'

Innamincka 17 May 75

They were not lost, they were abandoned, not by God, he was not there ... so [how could they be helped] but by men?

Coopers Creek Innamincka 17 May 75

But why, in this place where life abounds and thrives ... should they die in despair? ... Burke's grave, one hundred yards from the Cooper, the waters of life, [he] died under the tree of life, staggering over the sand, in that time of year when the tiny blue-bells were in flower ... why did Burke abandon Wills? ... [they] died wresting the heart from the continent, the silence that was before sound'.

Leaving Innamincka for Birdsville 18 May 75

[Departing Cooper's Creek camp at 7.30 am], the light—pelicans, brush swallows, corellas ... Stony plains ... which have only known the silence or the calls of the birds, red sand ridges covered with spinifex, stunted trees, dead wood standing, limitless horizon, indifferent ... the country where the creeks run dry.

Birdsville 19 May 75

Sun on the horizon, the drunken school teacher, the aboriginal children ... 'Mummy, there is nothing wrong with being white is there?' ... hearing Verdi at dusk.

Back at Cooper's Creek 20 May 75

Sturt: 'I hope never to see such a country again'

Mildura 24 May 75

The cold at Barra, the gales of wind, the clouds skidding across the sky, the sleety rain, but still the dust dominates.

Normanton 21 July 75

If only Burke had come in the dry time of the year, all would have been well ... he would have seen the blue waters of the Gulf

Arrived here at 2.30 pm on mouth of Norman River, saw the sea at the point, the slime and slippery mud on the rocks at low tide, treacherous place. Across the mouth of the river can see the mangrove swamps in which Burke and Wills floundered and sank at the end of the journey and Burke wrote the words about not seeing the sea … the scene of Burke and Wills floundering in the mud, the horse bogged, the just desert for the madness in Burke's heart.

22 July 75
Why didn't he make a boat, and row to the Gulf? the scene of the Aborigine looking at Burke and Wills.

Weipa 26 July 75
The spirit of the place, a place which belongs to those who do not crack up.[65]

It was the kind of notebook that few historians keep, a record of personal experience and sensory impressions. As a landscape painter took his brushes, paints and canvas out into nature, Clark took his notebook to historical sites. His method was that of a painter. He painted scenes and sketched the country around him. His keenest memory was visual and auditory, a memory wired not for dates but for atmosphere, colour, sound, movement, feeling and human emotion. His notebooks give the impression that he was trying to haul the past back in front of him, as though he stood in the desert and called out 'action!'—then watched as his characters began to move before his eyes. When Clark finally came to write the story of Burke and Wills in Volume IV, he produced one of his most evocative set pieces. He began by setting the scene.

Melbourne: August 1860, the Victorian Exploration Committee selected Robert O'Hara Burke to lead the expedition to cross the continent from south to north. The race was on to beat the South Australians. 'Chance or the gods had planted in Burke an insatiable hunger for glory and public acclaim but had mocked him by also planting in his clay forces which always cheated him of what he coveted.' The die was cast. Burke's 'mighty spirit' would not tolerate the questioning of his decisions. He 'danced divinely' but he had a tendency to 'lapse into savage rages', typical of 'the hasty impulses of the Irish'. William Wills, who had just turned twenty-six, was an English surveyor and astronomer. 'The gale of life blew high through Mr. Burke' but not through Wills. He was a scientist—a 'methodical and meticulous' man, 'not given to rash, impulsive decisions'. On 20 August, as Burke and Wills and their party left Melbourne, 'everyone who was anyone was there to wish them god speed. Mr. Burke, wearing the tall hat of a gentleman rather than the wide-awake of a man about to move into the outback, his eye single, and his whole body full of light, looked quite transfigured on his grey charger Billy'. As the party camped at Essendon for their first night, Burke galloped back to Melbourne 'for a last look at the woman who was all in all to him, entertaining some mad hope that on this great day she would give him that other glory a man could receive from a woman. She gave him no such sign.' How Clark knew such things, he did not say. Two weeks later, 'as the huge cavalcade rolled over the bridge at Swan Hill and made for Menindee on the Darling River, they moved away from civilisation into the great silence'. The image was reminiscent of White's character Voss, who journeyed into the interior of the continent awed by 'the volcanic silence of solitary travel through infinity'.[66]

As he wrote the melancholy tale of the Burke and Wills journey, Clark relied on his notebook entries, sourcing whole paragraphs to footnotes headed 'Personal visit to site'. He described the scene at Mootwingee, 100 kilometres north of Menindee, 'the gaunt gidgee trees, the wattles which emitted an unbearable stink before rain, the fragile, sombre mulga, the tussocks of grass, the rock pools, the flat, uninviting bare earth, and the apostle birds'. Instead of looking at the rock carvings of the Aborigines, Clark claimed that Burke's party 'shuddered and went on their way to the Cooper'. More than likely, the shudder ran through Clark, not Burke, but his evocation of the environment was the most powerful yet for an Australian historian. As Peter Ryan enthused when he read the manuscript, it was 'vintage Clark'. Clark captured Burke's ignorance and his fear of Aboriginal culture, as well as the more subtle details of the Aborigines' knowledge of the bush, how they learnt to find the fish in mud holes of Coopers Creek and dried pelican flesh for tucker in the years when the waterholes evaporated. Burke was convinced that the Aborigines were opponents of all he had come to achieve. His eyes were on the prize; he could not understand 'the fragile beauty beneath the barbaric exterior of the country'.[67]

Clark painted Burke as Nolan's portrait had painted him. He gave Burke 'huge eyes', the eyes of a desperate man, 'a man possessed by some demon or torment he either would not or could not control'. He turned Burke into a figure of classical mythology, a man who could be 'swayed by some malevolent spirit like the Greek goddess Ate who prompted men to acts of aberration and folly'. 'For a brief season' Clark imagined Burke as 'God-like'. Then he brought him down. After Burke's fatal decision to proceed to the Gulf as the wet season set in, the party became bogged in a sea of mud. Forced to leave their camels behind, Burke and Wills proceeded alone to the Gulf, 'floundering knee deep in water', only to be compelled by torrential rain and boggy ground to turn back to Coopers Creek without setting their eyes on the open ocean, despite coming within a few kilometres of their goal. As they started to make the long walk back to Coopers Creek, Clark, like the lord of creation, ordered the birds and beasts to mock Burke's foolishness: 'wild geese, plover and pelicans, all living creatures cackled and cried and grunted while they floundered around in the mud'. Then, with Burke and Wills struggling back to Coopers Creek at the rate of four miles a day, so 'done up that they could scarcely crawl over the desert', he conjured an image of broken, desperate men punished by an environment they did not comprehend; dogged by persistent rain, suffocated by humidity, their rations depleted, they stumbled into the heart of the continent, disorientated and bewildered, completely blind to its beauty. Approaching Coopers Creek, Clark instructed the wind to draw 'weird shapes out of the shadows cast by the moonlight'. Burke 'coo-eed into the night air but no human sound broke the eerie silence of the Australian bush, except the echo of his own voice'. The country was taunting him. Devastated by the departure of the base party from the campsite, the crazed Burke made a series of blunders that finally brought the two explorers to their deaths. Clark turned the fearless death of the atheist Wills into a triumph: 'he faced the silence with a nobility which transfigured the sandy waste in which he lay into a mausoleum fit

Sidney Nolan, Burke and Wills at the Gulf, *1961*

for a hero'. His description of Burke's death allowed his readers to see Burke as if he had died in front of their eyes—'clothed still in a manner befitting a gentleman, the pistol in his hand being the sole reminder of his one-time frantic quest for military glory, he died, his huge eyes still staring at the sandy wastes, and his back facing the bidi, or great source of life in Cooper's Creek'.[68]

In Robert Burke's epic journey and tragic death, Clark created a synthesis of all that he had learned about the Australian bush since he read DH

Lawrence and Eleanor Dark in his late teens and early twenties. Clark's Burke was Nolan's Burke and White's Voss, a man driven to penetrate a country in which 'men's souls were more woundable than flesh', where Europeans stumbled in the dark, lost and exhausted, while Aboriginal people moved with grace and confidence through the very same country that the explorers encountered as a kind of hell, a land beyond time and history, a land outside of God's creation, possessed of an infinity all of its own. Slowly, they were brutalised by the environment, brought to their knees by starvation and thirst. Even the face of their treasured Christ was reduced to a mirage shimmering on the edge of the horizon. All the trappings of their cultural superiority were rendered ineffectual until, like Voss, they could 'advance no farther' and waited to die in what White called a country of 'rock and scrub, of winds curled invisibly in wombs of air; of thin rivers struggling towards seas of eternity'.[69]

Clark's description of Burke's death scene was also painterly. The image carried the interpretation. Clark offered his readers no analysis—he simply described what he saw in his imagination. He placed his characters in the landscape like figures in a landscape painting or dramatis personae from a classic Greek tragedy. Reading *A History of Australia* is like moving through the rooms of a gallery. Scenes are rendered, captured, stilled, evoked and framed in succession, as if they were hanging side by side on a wall. When Michael Cathcart abridged the six volumes down to one, he compared the task to 'hanging a painter's best works'. Clark illustrated moments in past time, stringing them together in a dramatic, film-like narrative, shifting his point of view from one part of Australia to another as a camera shifts its gaze from one scene to the next. The result is a series of panoramic tableaux, a series of historical impressions, shot through with all the hallmarks of Clark's style—repetition, exaggeration, cliché and patches of intensely purple prose. It was all part of Clark's glorious fresco. Instead of condemning Clark's work for what it is not—scholarly history—it makes far more sense to celebrate it for what it is—a flawed attempt to write history as a revelation of the human condition.[70]

19: THE TEACHER

Clark at his office desk,
ANU, mid-1960s

Canberra: 1983. A group of twelve students sit in a tutorial room listening to a paper on the convict period. The student giving the paper is nervous. Clark is taking the class as a guest tutor, a man who knows more about the convicts than anyone else on the campus. Wrapped in his anxiety, the paper-giver talks faster. His hands tremble as he turns the pages of his notes. Eager to reach the finish line, he remains fastened to the lifeline of his text, never once looking up at the other students in the room. They grow impatient; what was to be a fifteen-minute paper goes on and on. The wait seems interminable. Clark remains unruffled. He appears to be paying attention. Finally, after more than half an hour, when the monologue comes to an end, no one seems any the wiser about the convict system and no one asks a question. There is a long, drawn-out pause. Clark clears his throat and looks across at the student who now sits frozen with apprehension. 'Remember,' he intones gravely, 'in life, always hold something back.'[1]

Next to writing *A History of Australia*, teaching was Clark's greatest passion. From his first full-time teaching position in 1940, at Blundell's School in Devon, Clark understood the performative aspect of his profession:

one has to show them that you are cunning and can see right through them. Then one must remain a mystery to them, because they will always believe in you so long as there remains a part of you which they can't unravel. There I have an advantage which I hope never to fritter away.

He never did. For Clark, teaching was 'an act of creation'. 'I thought of every class rather like a piece of music, which would have a definite form, it would have the statement of a theme, the development of a theme, and the reca-pitulation.' In the twenty-five years Clark spent teaching Australian history in Canberra from 1950 to 1974, he cultivated an academic environment that valued teaching above publication. At Clark's instigation, teaching was a frequent focus of staff discussion—how to become a better lecturer or tutor—and his message to staff never wavered: 'the reason you are here is first to teach and then to research'. To be an intellectual in Clark's History Department was to read widely, to inspire students and to sparkle in erudite conversation. To be a good teacher was to be 'a good human being'. It was a 'noble calling'. Teachers of Australian history had to be 'in love' with their subject and willing to use it to 'move the minds of the students to ask funda-mental questions of life'—questions on religion, politics, art, literature and love. A university was more a spirit of enquiry than an institution. 'You don't have to have a building to have a university,' Clark reflected. 'You can have a log of wood and sit on it; if somebody's got something to say, then you're deep into a dialogue.'[2]

In tutorials, Clark's conversation 'didn't flow'. He dropped pearls of enig-matic wisdom and waited for the students to respond. When questions were asked, they tended to be open-ended, usually delivered with delicate flip-pancy: 'Can you lend some light to our darkness Miss Mesurier?' Ken Inglis, a former student from Clark's days in Melbourne and later his friend and colleague at the ANU, recalled his style in tutorials, seminars and meetings: 'It was not really to discuss; but rather to converse and to declare—his mind was not really analytic.' Some former students, like Bob Reece, felt overawed by Clark's high expectations of them, as if every remark they made had to be 'earth shatteringly brilliant'. 'Since that was rarely possible,' said Reece, 'we were left feeling inadequate and crushed.' While the smarter students quickly saw through Clark's performances, his combination of levity and seriousness baffled others. Better with the brighter students, who also saw through his performances more quickly, Clark's combination of levity and heaviness required more translation for others.[3]

In lectures, usually given in the afternoons before honours classes, Clark had 'a reputation for being well-prepared'. While the content was almost always drawn directly from the particular volume of the *History* he was working on at the time, diversions were to be expected. A lecture on Governor Gipps and the squatters could easily end with reflections on Stendhal or Dostoyevsky. Shock was a common tactic. Humphrey McQueen, appointed by Clark as a senior tutor in 1970, remembered Clark entering the lecture theatre, locking the door behind him and proceeding to sing the popular songs of the nineteenth century. If he wanted to stir the students up, he would quickly drop his voice and pronounce tentatively: 'I hope you don't misunderstand what I am going to say', then proceed to talk of the explorer Ludwig Leichhardt 'taking another man in a manly embrace'. After 1962, as he began to concentrate more on the writing of *A History of Australia*, Clark's lecturing style gradually became more predictable. He tended to read more, and by the end of the decade some students found his lectures dull, although he was 'generally forgiven on the grounds that he was occupied with higher matters'.[4]

His best teaching in Canberra was done in the 1950s and early 1960s. For students who arrived on campus with only 'the dreary desert of Australian history' that they had endured at school, Clark's lectures placed Australia on a stage of high drama. Jill Ker Conway, coming to the ANU in 1956, was first taught Australian history badly—'nothing but a sequential roll out of colonial despatches'. Then she was lucky enough to have Clark. 'It was Manning's sensitivity to place that opened my eyes. I was writing a thesis on the history of the wool industry in Australia, and wanted to understand how the farmers had related to the land. Manning helped me to do this.' Rather than train imitators, Clark saw it as his responsibility to encourage his students to find their own subjects of interest and trust their own voice. His ability to make Australian history come alive resulted in many developing a lifelong interest in the subject. Hooked on history, they never forgot the debt they owed him. Yet Clark's theatrical style resonated with some students more than others.[5]

Historian Iain McCalman, a member of Clark's honours class in the late 1960s, was one student who saw through Clark's performances. Like his fellow student, friend and historian Ian Britain, he saw the subversive side of Clark. 'Manning's seduction of each of us,' observed McCalman, 'was that he was able to make us believe that we had possession of the real Manning Clark. Everybody wanted to own him, he was like Bloom, an everyman—there was always this incredible lightness about him.' In the same honours class was McCalman's friend, Steve Christiansen, son of the Marxist and Communist Party member Ted Hill. In April 1970, the bicentenary of James Cook's first sighting of the east coast of Australia, Clark decided that he and Dymphna would take a party of students and academics on a tour of the far south coast of New South Wales—among them, McCalman, Christiansen, postgraduate student John Thompson and Bruce Hodgins, a Canadian professor visiting the ANU. The aim was to reach Cape Everard, close to the border of New South Wales and Victoria, the headland that Cook had sighted from the deck of the *Endeavour* in 1770. Thompson would recall the group's departure from Tasmania Circle in the early afternoon:

> Dymphna, who welcomed us warmly, had done all of the work to get the party provisioned and packed and ready to leave. Manning appeared at the last minute impatient to leave and dressed rather oddly with his street clothes over a pair of pyjamas. Perhaps this was his way of dealing with the early onset of the Monaro winter. But my lasting impression of that journey was the contrasting personas of Manning—on the one hand seeming venerable and aged, hesitant, tentative, emotional—and on the other, highly driven and with an amazing (aggressive) force behind the wheel of his car.

On arrival at Cape Everard, Clark conducted the students along the bush track that wound its way from the car park; with every metre, his pace quickened with excitement. After a long and difficult walk, the group emerged onto a shoreline of massive, smooth boulders. Again, Clark led the way, skipping from rock to rock like a man half his age: the mere thought of looking out on the Pacific Ocean and imagining the *Endeavour* sailing north along the coast had given him a newfound agility. Standing on the rocky headland, with the party gathered around him, Clark read from Cook's journals, his voice rising above the crash of the waves below them. At one point, he stopped, turned to Christiansen and asked him directly: 'Do you or do you not think there are moments of greatness in James Cook?' 'I wouldn't have a clue mate,' Christiansen replied. 'At this point,' remembered McCalman, 'I knew Steve was destined for second-class honours—he wouldn't play Manning's game, he was unavailable for seduction.' For Thompson, the experience was different. The magnificence of the site and Clark's own excitement had provided 'a powerful stimulus' to his historical imagination. He felt privileged to be part of the excursion: 'there was something mysterious and wonderful looking out at that amazing large empty sea and at the vast sky above us and actually being called on to imagine that tiny ship approaching the enormity of the place we call Australia.' Together with the rest of the party, including Dymphna, Thompson signed his name in Clark's diary as requested, as if recording his presence in an explorer's journal. For those open to seduction, Clark's performances were inspiring. He conjured the illusion that the moments of existence he shared with them were transcendent, that somehow, they all shared a 'unique closeness to him'.[6]

At the ANU in the 1960s, the top students completed undergraduate honours, in which they undertook additional studies from their first year, culminating in a special fourth year. 'Brutally competitive', the honours program was also characterised by a 'strong sense of community' in which students and staff socialised together, on and off campus. Academic life in Canberra was about 'rapping'—in pubs, at parties and wherever the wine flowed—often to the point of 'social claustrophobia'. Honours students were Clark's chosen ones, the students for whom he had the highest hopes and on whom he placed the greatest expectations. They were also the ones who witnessed the exercise of his power at close quarters. Until the Faculty of Arts finally put a stop to the practice, Clark held private sherry parties for his honours class, usually in the late afternoon the day before their final results were due. Handing out glasses of sherry as he walked around the room, Clark whispered the students' results in their ears: 'by the way you got a very good 2A'. For every student, it was a nerve-racking experience and a reminder of Clark's God-like status. Ian Britain thought Clark took an almost sadistic pleasure in watching students quiver in apprehension as they waited to hear their results. Before the first-class honours were announced, Clark occasionally made a personal visit to the student's home to bestow the news. Nearly every year, he asked Dymphna to weave a crown of laurels from the bay tree in the garden. Then, in front of the class, he crowned the student to whom he had awarded a first. Not content with the university's recognition of academic excellence, Clark invented his own honours system, a blend of Ancient Greece (where the laurel wreath was bestowed as a symbol of victory), universities in Europe and America (where the laurel was sometimes awarded to postgraduates), and Tasmania Circle, Canberra, where the Clarks created a court with its own rituals and symbols. Thompson saw Clark's laurel crowning as an example of his elitism—an attempt to 'out-Melbourne Melbourne'. His 'blessing of the gifted ones', 'like a benediction or laying on of hands', Thompson read as building on the culture of Crawford's department in Melbourne, where it was 'the first-class minds that really mattered'. Clark, as the historian Margaret Steven remembered him at the ANU, 'smelt of Melbourne'. In Clark's imagination, his top students were all set apart through their contact with him. His imprint would stay with them for life.[7]

Jill Waterhouse, an honours student of Clark's in the early 1960s who later became a close friend of the Clark family, was charmed by Clark's playfulness when she first encountered him at the ANU. Once he gained her confidence, Clark quickly dissolved the hierarchical barrier between teacher and student: 'he enjoyed dramatizing situations of affection,' said Waterhouse. 'Crawling towards you on hands and knees was a familiar and amusing, if initially alarming, gesture.' Playing the affectionate puppy was a role Clark did not perform for male students or colleagues. But Waterhouse was not put off. She accepted Clark's eccentricities and found a loyal, generous man who enlarged her experience of life. In 1972, when the women's liberation movement was active within Clark's department, one honours student, Moira Scollay, decided to represent the concerns of other female students and ask Clark why Waterhouse had been the only woman to achieve first-class honours in recent years, going to his office to confront him. Clark walked around his desk, pinched her on the bum and said: 'You've got a spunky arse, your face isn't too bad, you're going to get married, and you don't need first-class honours.' Scollay stormed out of the office, slamming the door so hard that its frosted glass inset shattered behind her. The anecdote, told years later in Canberra before a large audience gathered for the memorial service for Scollay's friend and colleague Bob Gollan, revealed one truth about Clark but left out another. Conscious that he was being accused, and unaccustomed to being challenged in such a provocative fashion by a female student, Clark played the sexist pig, knowing full well that it was precisely this reaction that would incense Scollay most of all. As for the women's movement on campus, his record was mixed. While he was suspicious of birth control—'I don't know which is worse—aborting the foetus or stopping the sperm from reaching its goal'—and sceptical of the aims of women's liberation—'I didn't know they were so unhappy'—he also supported the establishment of Women's Studies in the History Department, although not out of political solidarity—'I wish there would have been courses like this in my day, then I would have understood what goes on in the heart of a woman.' To the same end, Clark played the slightly barmy romantic to select female students and staff.[8]

Joan Lemaire, a night student at Canberra University College in 1950, Clark's first year of teaching in the city, remembered him driving her home after dinner one night. 'We drove up the top of Red Hill to look at the stars, and though he was driving, he really was looking at the stars. He did leave an impression on me—he had a nose for people's private lives.' When Clark found out Joan had just become engaged to his former student at Trinity College in Melbourne, Jim Lemaire, he stopped the evening lecture midflight to hand out glasses of Spanish sherry to the eight students in the class. 'We were all bewildered. He waited until everybody had the sherry in their glasses before he announced the toast.' It was in the early 1950s too, when librarian Verna Coleman watched Clark walk between the rows of books in the college library as he hummed *The Rock of God* for her to hear. His unconventionality lightened the strangeness of Canberra. For Verna, 'the sun was always shining, the weather was brilliant and the world seemed a wonderful place with this beautiful, tall, bearded man about the campus.'

Clark's sexism—a label that only gained currency after the movement for women's liberation emerged in the late 1960s—is more visible in retrospect than it was for most of his twenty-five years at the ANU. As Anne Gollan remarked, 'Yes, Manning was sexist, but they all were in those days.' In 1964, women comprised less than 10 per cent of the 337 staff at the ANU. Equal opportunity for women would not arrive until the 1980s. Women were often written off as serious scholars; marriage and secretarial duties were considered the best they could do. When they did study at university, they were rarely expected to proceed past a first degree. Patronage and encouragement were reserved for men. For the few women who did infiltrate the male-dominated world of the academy they encountered men who did their best to marginalise women and 'devalue their work'. Ann Moyal, assistant editor of the *Australian Dictionary of Biography* from 1958 to 1962, claimed that exceptions were rare. Moyal admitted that many women seemed eager 'to take on the task of satellites around a distinguished male'. She also recalled the strangeness of the sexual politics of the postwar years: 'When I arrived in Canberra I was astonished how many men invited me out to dinner. They simply pressed my hand. They were strange days.' In the early 1960s, when Clark kissed Moyal in a lift in the old Anthony Hordern's building in Sydney, he was doing what he did with many women who attracted him—'he tried it on'. Moyal had no romantic interest in Clark but, like Jill Waterhouse and so many other women, including staff and students who joined the liberation movement in the 1960s, she felt that Clark had a 'deep understanding' of women.[9]

Clark's gift for communicating with students in a way that few academics could manage ensured that he was a figure of intrigue on campus. His talent for set piece performance made him stand out. It was also another way of setting himself apart from his peers. He did not want to be seen as an academic. From his first years at the ANU he was often uncomfortable in seminars and meetings. Troubled by the self-importance of many of his peers and the conventions of scholarly discussion, he had an acute eye for academic pomposity and vindictiveness.

The ANU professors always arrive late at seminars—enter with a mumbled apology—as though what they had been doing was very important. Some of them then fall promptly to sleep. Later in the discussion they laugh at each other's feeble jokes—turn on anyone who is a visitor when they speak, and tear them to pieces. As soon as the visitor opens his mouth, a sea of hostile eyes swims in front of him—and tongues dart like snakes to a dog—that curious solidarity of a group intuiting that it may be under fire ... hence the flow of display conversation after each paper—and the tendency to raise remote or trivial issues.[10]

Clark could not find a way to deal with the rituals of academic criticism. To criticise the work of another was like 'taking the flesh off the bone'. Long after seminars were over, he could still hear 'the horrifying cynical laughter' of his colleagues. Overcome by feelings of revulsion or inadequacy, he dumped them straight onto the pages of his diary, which he carried with him at all times. His discomfort was explained not only by his disdain for academic backbiting but also by his own hypocrisy. There were many times when he joined in the chorus of denunciation or filled his diary with spiteful criticism of colleagues and friends. The customary round of seminars and conferences in academic life were not Clark's natural habitat. He did not seek kudos or self-worth from asking the most penetrating question after a paper. Nor did he preen himself with lengthy displays of erudition in front of his colleagues, partly because he felt easily threatened by rivals or anyone who appeared hostile to his ideas. In seminars, his face appeared 'carved in stone, and he would often leave before the end, after total silence or one gnomic observation', especially if his friends were being attacked. For more than two decades, Clark's professional life was characterised by a nagging contradiction. In public, he traded on the authority of his professorial position at the same time as he distanced himself from academic life. He regularly mocked the 'divinity of Australian professors' and the dry empiricism of academic historians. Yet he craved academic status and recognition. As a teacher, a historian and a public intellectual, Clark owed much of his success to his academic standing. His career paralleled the postwar expansion of universities and the belief that increased access to tertiary education was a core component of Australia's civic society.[11]

When Clark arrived in Canberra as foundation professor in 1949, the new University College had barely a dozen staff and relatively few students.

Even in the 1950s, student and staff numbers remained small, while postgraduate theses were so rare that on the few occasions when they were awarded their recipients made national news in the *Canberra Times*. It was 'a university stranded in a sheep paddock', where internationally reputable scholars like Sir Mark Oliphant, foundation Professor of Physics, led their respective fields. Stranded around them, engaged in this unique social and intellectual experiment, were the other foundation professors like Clark, Professor of English AD Hope, and Professor of Economics Heinz Arndt. While Canberra University College remained under the control of the University of Melbourne until late 1960, development of the ANU continued apace. Set up with the backing of Ben Chifley's Labor cabinet and Nugget Coombs's Department of Postwar Reconstruction in 1946, the ANU was slated to become one of the world's leading research universities, similar to Princeton or All Souls. The university's charter spelt out its mission to foster the study of national institutions, history and culture. Doc Evatt, in particular, was keen on the ANU becoming 'a research factory on Australia and the Pacific'. Scholars were expected to play an advisory role to government, as Washington consulted academics from Yale and Harvard. Throughout the 1950s, Clark remained concerned that a research university 'ran the risk of seeming to be elitist in a country where the ethos was firmly against elitism'. 'The Oxbridge model', epitomised in the concept and design of the ANU's University House which had been built in 1954 as a place of research rarely visited by undergraduates and where no formal teaching occurred, suggested Clark's fears were well founded.[12]

To divorce teaching from research went against all of Clark's instincts. When Keith Hancock, who had been closely involved in the initial stages of recruiting a professorship for the fledgling institution, returned to the ANU from Oxford in 1957 to take up the Chair of History and directorship of the Research School of Social Sciences, Clark, 'naturally allergic to rivals', was 'cool towards him'. However, as he got to know Hancock, his initial frostiness subsided—they shared a bond. Ex-Balliol men, they were both sons of clergymen, and their fathers had known one another well in Melbourne. Talk of amalgamating the University College, where teaching did take place, with the ANU, where research scholars resided, had been floated since

Clark at home, circa, *1980*

Clark's arrival in 1949. Like Clark, Hancock was a great supporter of the idea. He also introduced joint seminars, shared supervision of postgraduate students between college and ANU historians, and worked closely with Clark to lay the foundations of the *ADB*. Clark was relieved. Under Hancock, who pursued 'excellence without pretension', he felt they were 'all historians together'. In 1960, when amalgamation finally arrived, Clark became head of History in the School of General Studies in the ANU's Faculty of Arts. Yet the old divisions remained. The research arm of the university—the Institute of Advanced Studies—remained separate from the teaching departments in the faculties. The distance between Clark and his counterpart in the institute, John La Nauze, who arrived in 1965, exemplified the disunion. La Nauze was scathing about Clark's posturing and thought little of his *History*, joking that 'there was a man on campus who thought all history was tragedy', while Clark, who had not forgotten that it was he who had stopped Clark from claiming the Ernest Scott Chair in 1955, saw La Nauze as emotionally repressed, aloof and too convinced of his own superiority.[13]

After Hancock's retirement in 1965, Clark's animosity towards the research historians deepened. One of those historians, Robin Gollan, who eventually took over Clark's Chair of Australian History in 1975, explained that 'the bad blood' that existed between the institute and the faculties at the ANU carried over from the period before amalgamation. 'There was a feeling on the part of some Institute people that they were superior to the college types and a feeling on the part of many of the College people that they were better than many of the institute people, who led a very privileged life.' 'And remember,' said Gollan, 'Clark, Hope and Arndt were at the top of their professions.' Clark explained the same divide more graphically. In the late 1960s, when Peter Ryan asked him during a visit to Canberra why he had so little time for historians in the institute, he took Ryan by the arm and said, 'Look, how would you feel if I told you I was working in that building with the advanced fuckers, and you had to stay here with the ordinary fuckers?' During the fourteen years that expired between amalgamation in 1960 and Clark's retirement in 1975, his disdain for the concept of non-teaching academics never diminished. While teaching, he managed to produce three volumes of *A History of Australia*, a rate of productivity that easily exceeded many of those who lived in 'the mansion on the hill'. As staff and student numbers rose dramatically in the 1960s, the increased activity in Clark's department contrasted more dramatically with the tranquil gentility of the institute, where scholars ambled out from their research hives to be greeted by tea ladies who served morning and afternoon tea with Arnott's biscuits.[14]

Clark's tenure as head of the history department in the Faculties coincided with the rapid growth of Australia's university sector. In the late 1950s, the Menzies government substantially increased funding to Australian universities and Menzies took a personal interest in the development of the ANU, approving construction projects and even holding his daughter's wedding reception at University House. Outside the campus, the face of present-day Canberra began to take shape. Lake Burley Griffin was filled in 1964, while Menzies opened the neo-classical National Library in 1968, the first of the imposing buildings along the southern lakefront to be completed. The High Court and the National Gallery would not follow until the 1980s. Planned satellite centres emerged around the city and by 1968 the population of Canberra exceeded 100 000. Streets of new houses in treeless suburbs marched out into the bush, where they stood, like hastily erected military encampments, marooned under a blazing sun. Although the inner suburbs slowly began to lose their frontier feel, some who arrived from Sydney or Melbourne found living in Canberra unbearable—alcoholic stupor or Friday-night escape to Sydney being the most popular coping mechanisms.[15]

After his retirement, Clark claimed he never foresaw that the city's sudden rush of growth would be accompanied by an increase in student numbers. Enrolment numbers at the ANU, about a thousand in 1961, had swelled to nearly 5000 by the early 1970s. By then Clark's permanent staff in History numbered well over twenty, while student enrolments approached a thousand. It was a far cry from the handful of students Clark had taught in the early 1950s. Although History continued to offer a broad range of courses—everything from the history of Christianity to ancient, medieval and British history—after 1965, the department increased its offerings in Australian history, reflecting the shifting research interests of both staff and students. The rising awareness outside the campus of a more Australia-centred outlook in foreign affairs, politics, culture and the arts was mirrored in the sudden interest in Australian history in Canberra, where the sons and daughters of Commonwealth public servants and politicians flocked to university. Throughout the 1960s, Commonwealth and state government scholarships assisted almost one in two of the student population. In Canberra, the city where the architectural scaffolding of the new nation would be built, Clark, with his long-standing passion for Australian history, was ideally placed to lead the surge of interest, both on campus and beyond. As head of department, he managed to build what was unquestionably one of the most outstanding departments in the country for the study of Australian history. In his last few years at the ANU, he worked tirelessly to establish the major in Australian History. It was an impressive legacy to bequeath his successors. As always, Clark's methods were unorthodox, but his achievement was no less remarkable for that.[16]

Like other 'god professors', Clark had the right to control the department budget (which funded his personal research assistants) and appoint his own staff. He exercised his prerogative to the full—it was 'Manning's department'. On the rare occasions when he did make it in to work early, he made a point of sitting at the head of the table at department morning teas, a religiously observed ritual that was nearly always performed collectively. Because the rate of expansion in the 1960s was so fast, lecturers and tutors often had to be found immediately and Clark soon gained a reputation for spontaneous appointments. In choosing his staff—both men and women—the last thing he looked for was 'specialist scholarly knowledge'. The spirit of his formative years as a lecturer in Max Crawford's generalist department in Melbourne was carried through to Canberra. Clark's criteria for selecting staff reflected his own interests: Is he a Catholic? Is he a communist, or even better, is he both? Has he taught fourth-form boys? Did he control them? Does she care about 'the things that matter'? Does she have a vision of life? Does she possess the qualities that will make her a good teacher? Clark was not interested in appointing disciples or establishing the Manning Clark School of Australian History. Instead, he gradually created a department that was akin to an ideological map of the twentieth century—employing Protestants, Marxists, Catholics, Socialists, agnostics, atheists, 'religious

An Eye for Eternity

fanatics' and the undecided. He wanted to expose his students and staff to different belief systems and different approaches to the study of history.[17]

Positions were rarely advertised. Clark heard of 'good people' through his network of contacts and met them for lunch, usually leading the candidate in a meandering conversation that had little to do with the job on offer. Occasionally, after meeting someone whom he sensed would make a good teacher, Clark offered the person a tutorship on the spot, much to their astonishment. Whether his tutors-elect knew anything of Australian history mattered 'not a jot'. He seemed to have an uncanny eye for recruiting able teachers. Humphrey McQueen, whom Clark appointed in 1970 as a senior tutor, thought Clark made appointments according to 'the lame dog principle—you took in lame dogs, drunks and Catholics'. Clark loved nothing more than to 'rescue' talented people. In 1962, after his former Melbourne student Ken Inglis lost his first wife in a car accident, Clark travelled to Sydney to console him and talk about his future. He then asked Hancock to secure a position for Inglis at the ANU: 'I am very anxious indeed for Inglis to be a member of this university. I believe he is one of the few people in Australia who has something to say about the shape and direction of our society. [We should] get him now … and tide him over this difficult period.' In 1964, John Molony, who, like Inglis, later became one of Australia's foremost historians, was working in the Heinz Tomato factory at Dandenong when he was recruited to translate medieval Latin in history in the Research School of Social Sciences at the ANU. A former priest, Molony had no qualifications in History. In 1965, he stood in Robin Gollan's office, discussing the possibility of further employment. Gollan looked out his window and saw Clark strolling across the lawn. 'There goes Manning,' exclaimed Gollan, 'he might have something for you.' Within days, Clark, who was intrigued by Molony's earlier life as a priest, offered him a tutorship in British History. Like so many of Clark's appointments, Molony learnt on the job, discovering his subject at the same time as his students. As well as more astute appointments such as McQueen, Inglis and Molony, Clark also found employment for people who would probably never have managed to secure a position in Sydney or Melbourne. Bill Mandle, whom Iain McCalman remembered as 'a raving right-winger', was persona non grata in the academy but an outstanding teacher, as McCalman discovered when he took Mandle's Renaissance and Reformation course. Clark's eye for the ability of fellow mavericks to communicate with students was part of his department's success.[18]

Administration, however, was another matter. As his department grew, Clark's lack of interest in staffing formulas, school budgets and the more mundane matters of daily administration was compensated for by the extra work of his secretarial staff. Aware that Clark often failed to read official mail, they arranged to have the correspondence mailed to them as well, then informed him of his obligations in person and took control of his appointment diary. In 1968, Clark interviewed Shirley Bradley for the position of secretary of the History Department. Bradley, a vivacious North Londoner who arrived in Canberra in 1956, was unprepared for Clark's opening question: '"You won't try to organise me, will you?" Of course, when he gave me the job, that's exactly what I did,' Bradley would later say with a smile; 'in a discreet way—he needed it.' She quickly learnt to cover for Clark's lack of administrative acumen. 'He hated brown envelopes. He'd throw them straight into the garbage bin. After he left the office at the end of the day I'd rummage through his waste paper basket. Sometimes I would find cheques, which I'd leave on his desk for him to collect the next morning. He really needed nursing.' Bradley spent much of her time excusing Clark for making double appointments and trying to learn the foreign script that passed for his handwriting. Occasionally, she sat up till midnight typing up his hastily written notes on administrative matters. Indebted to all women who performed the thankless task of decoding his scrawl, Clark relied on the charmer's traditional cache of gifts—chocolate, flowers and perfume. In 1973, he gave Bradley a bottle of perfume: 'You don't need to be made any nicer than you are, but here is a bottle of fluid which some need.' Long after she left the ANU, Bradley kept Clark's letters. Her abiding feeling remained one of deep affection for him. 'I suppose I played a mother role,' she would say. 'I always felt like he needed a good scrub—Dymphna dressed him in these old suits she bought from the Salvos at Fyshwick.'[19]

Bradley saved Clark from administrative embarrassment, but she could not save him from the criticisms of his colleagues. Some members of staff resented Clark's absence in the mornings, arguing that, while he sat in his study writing, more of the administrative load was foisted onto them. When Clark was preoccupied with his latest manuscript, Don Baker, his closest ally, would cover his administrative responsibilities. Without Baker's loyalty, Clark would have been far more exposed to criticism. For his part, Clark felt that too many of his colleagues revelled in the petty theatre of department and faculty meetings, extracting their sense of professional standing from committee power plays rather than their ability to publish major work. In department seminars, Clark was hardly the paragon of traditional scholarly standards. Reading Dostoyevsky, he told his staff, was more important than reading the next article from the house of Historical Enterprise Pty Ltd. Ian Hancock, who joined Clark's department in 1970, found that Clark's skill as an administrator was to encourage his staff in their teaching and writing without interfering in their affairs. To avoid administrative tasks swamping his writing time, Clark quickly learnt to spread the load—delegation was part of his survival strategy.[20]

Marking students' essays, he rarely offered more than cryptic one-line comments, gazing out the window in lofty silence as he handed out the essays in class. 'On such occasions, the eyes of the student and teacher should never meet,' he would say. At the same time, he was lax with closing dates for essays—'as long as they come in before the exam results are due'—and he was always willing to invent rules to allow students to pursue certain courses of study—'I seem to remember that when I came from Melbourne, there was a rule.' In his official dealings with postgraduate students and staff, Clark could often disappoint. Supervising, marking, writing references, attending meetings and forming committees—the academic's daily stock-in-trade— were not Clark's forte. Nor was he very interested in the majority of post-graduate thesis topics—they sought to explore historical problems rather than sing a hymn of praise to life. He saw his role as inspiring and empower-ing others. The rest was up to them. In his final years of teaching, there were some historians who believed that an academic reference from Clark 'wasn't worth the paper it was written on'. He was notorious for his lordly one-line references: 'He cares about the things that matter.' 'He has a big heart.' Ken Inglis found his references illegible and not very helpful, reflecting Clark's 'esteem for the candidate but not the grounds for it'. It was a similar story with postgraduate supervision and the examination of doctoral theses. Heads of department in other universities, like Frank Crowley at the University of Western Australia, stopped sending Clark doctoral theses because he failed to give candidates adequate reports. David Carment, who enrolled in early 1972 as a doctoral student under Clark's supervision, learned much from the breadth of his knowledge but soon realised that Clark was 'not particularly interested' in his thesis when he returned drafts quickly, with 'very few comments'. Clark was too preoccupied with his own writing to devote hours to reading the work of his students.[21]

His understanding of teaching was not based on principles of pedagogy, institutional models or even classroom-based learning—his course was life—and he taught every day, wherever he was and with whomever he shared his company. Clark's most profound impact on students and friends was not the knowledge he imparted but the doors he opened. He had the rare ability to give others the sense that life was richer than they had imagined. Tasmania Circle was his true house of learning, the place where he would bring his honours and postgraduate students for dinner and where Dymphna, performing miracles of hospitality at short notice, would feed all who dropped by—students, colleagues, visiting academics, writers, artists, journalists and politicians. When the numbers grew too large, the ping-pong table would be dragged into the living room and draped in a table-cloth, and the guests would sit wherever they could find room. The atmosphere was convivial, bohemian and, for young Australians in the 1960s, exotically European. In a relatively small kitchen, Dymphna served food cooked on a wood stove while Clark sat at the head of the table like paterfamilias in an open-house dacha, Bach's *Mass in B Minor* belting out from the speakers behind him.[22]

As a student at Melbourne University in the 1960s, Helen Garner, née Ford, knew both Sebastian and Axel Clark and she visited Tasmania Circle several times, catching the train to Canberra from Melbourne. For a young woman from working-class Geelong, entering the Clark household was like passing into another world. 'When I first saw them they looked weird to me, they were unusual people and terribly impressive; they didn't have the

An Eye for Eternity

same aspirations as other middle-class people at that time, they were just different'. Garner and fellow writer Drusilla Modjeska, who was then a student at the ANU, invented the term 'Clarkery' to capture the unique milieu at Tasmania Circle. 'They were like robber barons', recalled Garner, 'big sociable story-telling drinkers and they were all fiercely loyal to one another'. In Garner, Clark saw a person who was open to his brand of education. He gave her the Henry James short story 'Madame de Mauves' to read—the story of a man caught in a web of uncertainty as to whether he should commit adultery. It was a typical Clark test. Garner, all too aware of the enormity of the task, nervously offered Clark her 'modern' interpretation—'I don't know why they didn't just go ahead and have an affair,' she told him. Clark gave a 'wry smile and turned away'. She felt he was 'disappointed' in her. Years later, Garner 'blushed with embarrassment at the thought of how shallow and unsophisticated' her response had been. She had other things to thank him for as well. Clark had opened her eyes not only to James but to music.

> Often after breakfast Manning would be in the kitchen, standing near the record player, and he'd say to me (dropping his voice) Listen to this Miss Ford. And he'd put on Bach's Partitas, or a Sibelius Symphony. He lent me the Mozart Piano Concertos when I was at Janet Clarke Hall and for someone like myself who grew up in a house without an intellectual life, this music was a revelation—I think it is through music in particular that I can feel Manning's influence. It was heartening to see a man in his 40s learning to play the piano. I can still see him sitting at the piano, his feet crossed under the bench, picking away at Bach's Preludes.

Looking back from the vantage point of her later success, Garner saw how both Clark and Dymphna noticed and cultivated 'whatever hint of talent' people around them showed. When she gave her first reading, from *Monkey Grip*, in the tent at Adelaide Writers' Festival in 1978, they were there. When she gave readings in Canberra in the 1980s, they came too, Dymphna on one occasion bringing a bright-red geranium from her garden and pinning it on Garner's jacket. 'They understood what it was to be someone who wanted to write,' Garner reflected. Yet it was this and more. It was a way of living in the world, condensed now in Garner's memory of Clark's lyrical tuition, Axel's 'roaring laughter and huge gestures', and the packed lunches that Dymphna gave her for the train journey back to Melbourne from Yass Junction, thick sandwiches with 'cucumber cut in chunks' that told her she was 'cared for'.

Helen Garner's story is reflected in the experience of other writers who visited Tasmania Circle, such as Tom Keneally, who first met Clark and Dymphna in 1967. 'Manning encouraged me to take up the career of writing,' says Keneally. One of his strongest memories is of standing in the garden discussing Australian history with Clark. As Keneally read Clark's work— 'the Augustan style', the characters 'weighed down by original sin', Australians 'subject to the same pressures as Ulysses'—and returned whenever he could to see Clark at Tasmania Circle, his mind turned towards writing Australian history. Clark had brought the subject alive for him. Alex Miller, bored in the Canberra public service in the 1960s, went to see Clark in his ANU office to ask if he could enrol in a postgraduate degree in History. They talked for an hour or more, Miller telling Clark of his ambitions to be a writer. At the end of the conversation, Clark offered Miller some unexpected advice: 'You are very welcome to join us here, Alex, but you've just made it very clear to me that your first love in life is to be a novelist. If you do your masters you'll finish up in the academy and you'll never write your novels.' Clark confessed to Miller that his first love was fiction, but that he was committed to writing *A History of Australia* and would put off his plans to be a novelist until the next life. Miller left Clark's office feeling buoyed and grateful to him, not only because he encouraged him to follow his 'true path', but, as he explained, 'for believing that I had the capacity to do it. His evident belief in me was what impressed me and sustained me later when I doubted myself.'[23]

Clark's greatest gift as a teacher was to see in young men and women what they could only half-glimpse themselves, to impart conviction, aspiration and self-belief. If he had left no other legacy to his country, this alone would be significant. He understood the potential of personal words of encouragement from on high. As he told young scholars like Susan Magarey and Jill Roe, 'we need to open a woman's window on our men of iron'. He also knew how to use telegrams for dramatic effect. Iain McCalman was not particularly close to Clark as a student. On his first day as a tutor at Macquarie University in 1972, he received a telegram from him: 'Never mind the harpoon throwers, get on with your own work.' 'Imagine the effect that had on me,' said McCalman. 'Manning took the time and made the effort. He simply knew how I would be feeling, it shows such an acute sensitivity.' In November 1952, Clark mailed a good luck note to George Virtue, a Bachelor of Commerce student who worked in the Treasury, before he sat his exam in Australian History. 'Dear Mr. Virtue, This is to wish you the best of luck on Friday. You have read widely, and have a lively interest in the subject. So you have every reason to be confident.' Nearly forty years later, Virtue sent a copy of the note back to Clark with a covering letter.

> The letter is one to which I attach great value. I have preserved it, with its original envelope, inside Volume I of your six volume opus; all volumes take pride of place in my big bookcase ... open to all to see ... Except for you, none of my lecturers or professors sent me a message of support and encouragement before end-of-year examinations, or gave me the slightest amount of hope. They were hard times for me and for most of my fellow students, generally ex-servicemen like myself. We were trying to re-establish ourselves after six virtually lost years, trying to make our way in the world and at the same time trying to get a home together, attend to children and maintain marriages. Some failed, I am sorry to say. Perhaps you sensed the problems, the desperate inner-feelings, the lack of confidence, the seemingly overwhelming weight upon your students.

Clark's sensitivity to his students' emotional life resonated and left a lasting impression. As a teacher, he shared their curiosity about life. The child within him was always visible. Outside the lecture theatres and seminar rooms, he matched his students' youthful exuberance with a certain wildness, like the Clark whom Bob Reece remembered driving past St Christopher's Cathedral at Manuka in the 1960s—like Flash Jack from Gundagai—pointing out the car window at the cathedral and exclaiming to Reece: God is in there, you know, Reece.'[24]

20: THE MUSES

Lyndall Ryan, 1978

In the European summer of 1964, six months after their twenty-fifth wedding anniversary, Clark and Dymphna left their cottage at Twickenham in London's south-west and departed England for the continent. The youngest children, Rowland and Benedict, had returned to Australia to be cared for by Katerina, who was then in her early twenties. For the first time since their marriage in 1939, they were alone again in Europe, free to pursue their individual interests. While Dymphna travelled to Rothenburg to take up a German-language course at the Goethe Institute, Clark, riding on the royalties from Volume I and *A Short History of Australia*, journeyed alone through Norway, Sweden, Poland, East Germany, northern Italy and Austria, searching for Ibsen, Bach, Mozart and the 'music of the spheres'. The six-week period of separation brought them back to the days of their courtship—Dymphna studying in Germany, Clark lonely and longing for her return, now wondering if he could uncover his former self—'the man of 1938'.[1]

Solitude, the necessary condition of Clark's occupation, was something he always found impossible to bear. During his Odyssey around Europe, he shielded himself from the loneliness that gnawed at his soul by writing letter after letter. In July 1964, he wrote to Dymphna daily, hoping that his avalanche of letters and cards would bring her closer to him. The slow dance of correspondence between them—writing, mailing, waiting for and reading one another's replies—had long been the means through which they expressed and understood their love for one another. The mere sight of Dymphna's handwriting on the face of an envelope was enough to send Clark into a lather of child-like excitement. Each word from his distant beloved had the potential to keep him afloat for the rest of the day. With her at his side, he knew he could endure the attacks of the 'whipping boys' in Australia. If his diary was the keeping place of his discontent with Dymphna, his correspondence was the place where he wove 'the spell' that kept their marriage alive. As they parted in London, Dymphna suspected that she would soon find herself inundated with mail, but she had no way of knowing just how intense Clark's letters would be. In 1938–39, his passionate out-pourings had brought her to Oxford and an early wedding. Now Clark would try to erase the doubts and bitterness that had plagued them since his affair with Pat Gray in 1955.[2]

As he travelled through Norway in the second week of July, awed by 'the elemental mountains' that towered over the valleys, the wildflowers in the meadows and the stands of birches set on the edge of fir forests, their white bark 'gleaming against the sombre background', Clark's imagination soared. Immersed in one of the most romantic landscapes in Europe, the homeland of Ibsen, Munch and Dymphna's grandfather, he set out to remake his love for Dymphna. Alone on trains and ferries, he had time to think. He saw how his infidelity had failed her and the children. He knew he had to 'repair the outrages' he had committed against them. From now on, he told her, there would be no more 'sad sack face' or 'tragic impotence'. In Dymphna's absence, Clark saw what he was never capable of seeing in her presence. The act of writing to her made everything clear in his mind. Even if there was no 'life hereafter'—'no God and no justice', he knew now that it was only through her that he could find 'meaning purpose and joy'. There was no need for other women in his life; she was his one and only.[3]

As he moved through Norway, Clark's daily schedule was structured around his compulsive need to write to Dymphna. On the morning of 8 July he caught the early train to Oslo, having implored her in a letter sent the night before to write to him at Stockholm, where he would arrive two days later. There was still no letter from her. A whole week had passed. He wrote again: 'For God's sake,' he shouted in Christ-like admonishment, 'write something and write it quickly because the whole of my being needs you. Don't give me a stone when I offer bread, or when I ask for fish give me serpents.' From Oslo, Clark took the train that 'wound its way along the edge of lakes and fjords on the way to Skien'. There, the lonely pilgrim took a taxi to Ibsen's childhood home. After walking four miles to the church where the playwright was confirmed, and a further two miles to the Ibsen statue, he rushed back to the train station to return to his hotel in Oslo, eager to share what he had seen with Dymphna. If Clark failed to give his experience shape and form through prose, his day had not been lived.

After writing and posting another letter to Dymphna that evening, he lay in bed, unable to sleep, until his next move was 'borne in to' him. The following morning, before leaving for Stockholm, he attended Mass at St Olaf's Church. Before the statue of the Virgin, flanked by 'nuns with beautiful faces', he lit a candle and prayed that his love for Dymphna would not founder because of his 'pride, waywardness, vanity and deceit'. Standing with his head bowed in prayer, Clark beatified her, imagining Dymphna not as his judge, tormentor, or thwarter—the images with which he filled his diary—but as someone who 'appeared' before him as his 'beloved', a 'vision of life and eternity'. All of this he wrote to her after returning from Mass in a frenzy of passion, only to find that in her two letters that arrived that morning she seemed relieved to be apart from him. Clark found her letters too matter-of-fact, but it was an old complaint. He wanted her to show more passion, to be a female version of himself. She again told him she could never possibly fulfil his romantic visions. She didn't like him 'being off in that way'. But Clark was writing for himself as much as for Dymphna, wrestling with his demons and trying to convince himself of his love for her. Deaf to her pleas for a more grounded approach to their marriage, he pressed on regardless. He wanted to recapture his youth: the 'old Mariner and mystic Manning'. The epiphanies piled up one after the other, as if Clark imagined their love undergoing a transfiguration. On 12 July, having lain awake until 3 am in a Warsaw hotel, he got out of bed to write to her. It was the only way to deal with 'the cruel agony' of their separation. In a few days they would meet in Rothenburg but first, she had to know what he was now about to tell her. For a long time, he had resisted her, thinking that she was not really the one who could fulfil him completely. Still trying to make sense of his affair with Pat Gray a decade earlier, he saw how she had 'suffered from that savagery'.

> Now I see face to face, and know that you are that one I want, that you are not the hunter but the one I have been hunting … [I should have seen it years ago when I was chasing after false gods] … One of those gods is your body: another is your soul: my third god will be when we bring those two bodies and those two souls together into that oneness. Then, I take it, we shall understand that great mystery of the three in the one … our kingdom.[4]

It was not only the savagery of Clark's affairs that Dymphna had to contend with; for a woman who was not prone to religious epiphanies, it was also the savage intensity of his love. Although she could barely recognise herself in some of Clark's reveries, she was swept away by his romantic readiness. The letters she received appeared to be written by a man who was permanently giddy with love, his need for intimacy always snapping at her heels, overpowering in its melodramatic expression and never subsiding as the years passed. How many women married for twenty-five years received such letters of love and affection from their husbands? In one way, she was extremely fortunate. As she told him twelve months later, she kept the flood of letters she received from him in the summer of 1964 with 'poignant gratitude'. His need for her was humbling. Even if she could never rise to his exalted heights in her replies, his letters brought her back to him, just as they had done in 1939. When they met for a few days in Rothenburg, Clark's missiles of tortured affection ceased for three days. The meeting he had dreamt of so feverishly for the past three weeks had finally come to pass. Less than a few hours after they parted on 21 July, he wrote to her from Munich Post Office on his way to Venice, 'hot, tired and shaken', uncertain of his demeanour over the previous three days. Seeing her was not how he had imagined it would be.

I was so shy, possibly even remote, because after my outpourings on paper, which will go on for a while yet, being with you seemed not so much surreal, or a strain, but a joy which was beginning in passion, restrained though that way, and leading up to all those things which have become the guiding lights for me on this storm-tossed sea of life. Today is a blank ... I who have known all the beauty and the wonder of your body also know that without tenderness and pity between men they face each other in eternal isolation.[5]

Unable to match the passionate intensity he created in his letters with the more elusive reality of loving Dymphna in person, Clark had brought himself to the point of nervous exhaustion. Compared to the heights his emotions scaled on the page, everyday communication with her seemed prosaic. He struggled to marry the woman who stood before him with his rapturous visions. To calm himself and replenish his romantic imagination, he re-read *The Brothers Karamazov*. Within days, he had rekindled the fire of his earlier letters, writing to her from Vienna, uplifted by the sight of the Danube and the city's musical riches, the choral performances in St Stephen's Cathedral, his visits to Beethoven House, Mozart's grave and the musical performances he attended in the city's concert halls. The cultural riches of Vienna gave Clark 'a sense of oneness in the numen'. He wrote to Dymphna that she deserved 'a Mozart vision of life', insisting that only he could provide that rare sense of ecstasy and fulfilment.[6]

In the three weeks before they returned to Australia in late August 1964, Clark returned to England while Dymphna completed her course in Rothenburg. The deluge of letters continued. At his favourite haunt in London, the Brompton Oratory, Clark heard the choir perform a Palestrina Mass. The slowly ascending scales of the Renaissance music cleansed him of all feelings of 'rancour' and 'revenge'. He wanted Dymphna to have the same experience, to feel the same sense of spiritual euphoria that he felt in the presence of religious music. If she did have the same response when she returned to London from Germany, he asked her, would she then accompany him to the Oratory, tell the priest what had happened and ask him what they should do? Unable to wait for her answer, he decided to telephone her from London. Returning to his hotel room, he wrote to her immediately, leaving a space at the bottom of the page for his post-conversation comments. On the phone, they argued. Clark was unhappy with the general mistrust he sensed in her letters. She had already told him that, while she was willing to accept his overtures of unconditional love, her mind still had difficulty assenting to 'what her heart affirmed'. Hundreds of passionate letters could not erase her experience. She still doubted Clark's capacity to live up to his ideals and promises. Clark was furious. Putting down the phone he turned to write the final words of his letter: 'I hoped [the call] would be a note of joy. You crushed that. I do not take back or withdraw anything I have written to you over these last four or five weeks. You, I take it, have rejected it. The rest is silence.' Despite Clark's petulant reaction, Dymphna's reply was warm. But it also showed how far removed she was from Clark's sensibility.

On Tuesday night you were a little tactless, and I responded with envy, jealousy, malice and pride... I am sorry. We are both unworthy, and immature. What an example for our children! Please forgive me. Please be happy till my return. Let us both do what we can to rise above our imperfections. Though it may not be very much! If you ever want to go to the priest I will go with you if you want me to. But we had better not wait till I have a mystic experience too, because, in view of my coarser clay, I may be some time.[7]

Clark returned to Australia alone, via Madrid and Rome, while Dymphna completed the last days of her course in Rothenburg. A few days after reading Dymphna's letter, Clark replied while flying from Calcutta to Singapore. Reading Hardy's *Tess* ('I have never been so moved by prose in years'), he had already climbed his way back to heaven, suggesting that she lacked courage: 'I have that other life which you do not want to enter, for fear of what you might see. But all I have said stands. Build on that, and we can come into our kingdom. And for God's sake, have faith ... you see, I am swept back to you even if your lack of faith shook me to the foundations.' Clark was unwilling to accept Dymphna's 'coarser clay'. Like a deluded evangelist, he asked her to forsake her doubts and follow him to the paradise garden.[8]

The gap between the ardent fancies of Clark's correspondence during his periods of separation from Dymphna and the everyday experience of their

An Eye for Eternity

marriage, largely lost to the written record, sounds a warning. The letters capture Clark's struggle to compose an image of Dymphna, to define the chemistry of their love, to make their relationship behave according to his romantic fantasies, and to dictate how things would be between them. Like all his writing, they reveal his emotional neediness, his melancholy and his hunger to transcend his own death through art, but they say little about the way he and Dymphna interacted on a daily basis. This was more often embedded in Dymphna's letters, as were many of the more practical needs Clark had for her while he was away, as in her letter of September 1965.

> Of the allotted tasks I have performed: 1. Typing title page of vol.2 … 2. Delivery of same to Keith Hancock. 3. Taken car to garage, where they fiddled with the carburettor, greatly improving performance. Today they are jacking it up to attend to noise in back wheels, by now very ominous. 4. Read manuscript. Will type same soon. We give what we have. 5. Given your farewell messages to Mrs. Bateman for Joe B.[9]

When Clark was the one left at home while Dymphna was away, his amorous letters relied more on humour ('I miss my headmistress very much'). He joked about his domestic helplessness ('the Falstaff of the chromium plated suburbs' who scrambled to deal with an overflowing washing machine 'because you, my dearest one, forgot to take the plug out of the sink'), the poor quality of food in her absence ('last night we survived on eggs, we all badly need one of your meals') while also relying on schoolboy titillation ('with my love and hugs and many naughty thoughts about my secret places—and bays—and openings'). Helen Garner remembers one evening in particular when she was a visitor at Tasmania Circle in the early 1960s. Clark wanted Dymphna to go with him to a party but she was cross with him for some reason. 'Dymphna,' said Garner, 'jacked up when they were supposed to be going out together.'

> But Clark flirted with her and teased her until she gave in: 'Oh Dymphy darling—please come. Dymphy, won't you come with me? Oh do come!' I watched this out of the corner of my eye in amazement—I had never seen a husband and wife being flirtatious with each other. It was thrilling.

Wooed by Clark's advances, Dymphna changed her mind and went to the party.

Alone on his cultural pilgrimages through Europe, America or Australia, Clark relied on other means of seduction.[10] In one of his first letters to Dymphna from Norway, Clark referred to the '*Sehnsucht*'—a longing or yearning—that stirred in him. Clark's letters to his 'distant beloved' show him longing for 'an ideal state of being'—the infinite—a longing which he knew he could never really satisfy, but which he was also unable to live without. 'In love with the idea of being in love', Clark appears to have existed in a permanent state of *Sehnsucht*, without which he was unable to write, teach and love. He was always feeling 'incomplete', restlessly drafting a better world beyond the present. And yet it was this very sense of incompleteness that he sought to remedy through his writing. His letters to Dymphna in 1964 also contain the psychological seeds of much of their future conflict. Clark not only idealised Dymphna, he idealised himself, dissociating himself from his past behaviour. He told Dymphna that the actions which had caused her so much pain were only his 'surface behaviour', the 'perverse me'. Behind this Manning, he insisted, lived another one, the man who reached out for her. In effect, Clark created a double—the pure, all-loving Manning who wanted nothing more than union with his beloved—and the deviant Manning, 'the madman' upon whom he heaped all of the actions for which he felt embarrassed, ashamed or guilty. Bifurcating his idea of self, Clark avoided taking responsibility for his behaviour. Any unpalatable action could immediately be shafted onto his alter ego. It was self-deception of an ingenious kind, but as time passed experience taught Dymphna to be wary of the spell cast by his letters. She was not the only woman to whom Clark wrote his passionate epistles.[11]

Throughout the 1960s and early 1970s at the ANU, Clark worked and socialised in a liberal academic environment. His last fifteen years on campus coincided with the years of sexual revolution, women's liberation and radical student politics. In 1960, when the pill became readily available, the fears of generations of women—unwanted pregnancy, forced marriage or social banishment—subsided. Many women, some of whom had married young in the 1950s and later enrolled in tertiary institutions, suddenly found themselves in a radically different world. Canberra's 'hothouse atmosphere', in which an unusually high proportion of academics, public servants, diplomats, politicians and 'fly-by-nights' partied vigorously on Friday and Saturday nights, provided the perfect environment for sexual experimentation. Susan Magarey (then Eade), Clark's research assistant in the early 1970s, was one of those young married women. She arrived in Canberra from Adelaide in 1967, aged twenty-four, and together with her husband lived in a small flat provided by the ANU, huddled in front of a three-bar radiator in winter, watching *The Two Ronnies* on a rented TV. Because of the pill, women no longer needed to 'be careful', while men, more than aware of the new opportunities, 'expected women to come across'. The pretence of a monogamous culture was shattered. Attending student parties in Canberra in the early 1960s, novelist Roger McDonald had his eyes opened. 'Girls boasted about their abortions' and used four-letter words loudly. Their boyfriends sang bush songs and drank red wine. There was universal admiration of Manning Clark (down to affectations of clothing) and pride in the cheekiness of AD Hope, who led the 'Acton Poets', a group devoted to bawdy verse and bacchanalian festivities. Others described the atmosphere in Canberra in the 1960s as 'mad'. On campus, student–staff relations were common, as were affairs between members of staff. As Anne Gollan put it, 'the intellectuals were always changing beds'. Jill Waterhouse claimed that she didn't know many academics in the 1960s who weren't 'off with someone else', usually the wives or husbands of their colleagues. The climate of sexual liberation coexisted with a culture of heavy drinking in which some men, usually drunk, 'thought nothing of coming up to you at a party and unzipping the back of your dress', said Waterhouse. 'But that was read differently then.' Inspired by the debauchery, Bob Brissenden turned to comic verse to capture the spirit of the time:

> Got no little girlie to cheer up my life—
> If I ever get any loving, it's with somebody else's wife.
> I've got those bad Canberra blues...
> those governmental, bureaucratic, university, academic, matrimonial, very adulterous, always alcoholic blues.[12]

It was a far cry from the starched academic formality that Clark had rebelled against in Melbourne in the 1940s. Two of his closest friends—historian Don Baker and the poet David Campbell, a former boxer, rugby player and war veteran and a man with a bricky's face and the pen of an angel—played the Canberra blues at every opportunity. In Campbell especially, Clark saw the man he wished he could be: the rugged, handsome, devil-may-care Dionysus. Although he saw advantages in the relaxation of sexual mores, Clark's sexuality was held fast in the chains of his early twentieth-century Protestant upbringing—sex was naughty, an act of procreation ordained by God. He was also suspicious of the new roles being sought by women. When Lyndall Ryan, his research assistant between 1966 and 1968, showed Clark the front cover of the women's liberation magazine *Refractory Girl*, edited by Anne Summers, Ann Curthoys and herself, Clark was appalled. The photograph was a microscopic image of swimming sperm. Before the next issue had appeared, said Ryan, Clark had cancelled his subscription. 'It was too much for him—he had a very frail sense of masculinity—I always remember him telling me that he didn't believe in contraception. Poor Dymphna.' Clark was also fond of joking about his sexual advances, occasionally revealing that much of his extramarital sexual encounters were either imagined or frustrated in their consummation. Anne Gollan recalled one of Clark's favourite after-dinner brags: 'Manning would often tell me that he was fond of putting his hand up women's dresses and encountering their suspender belts long after they'd stopped wearing them.' Attempting to describe Clark's sexuality, his friend Ann Moyal made a distinction: 'Manning was a sensitive man—he was not a sensual man.'[13]

On campus, Clark's intimate contact with women came through his association with students and staff, and particularly his research assistants—a string of young, attractive women in their twenties who worked with him at close quarters: Barbara Penny, Deirdre Morris, Lyndall Ryan, Susan Magarey and Beverley Hooper. Every woman whom Clark knew intimately had to be seduced—if not physically, then spiritually. Thirty years older than most of Clark's assistants and burdened with domestic responsibilities, Dymphna felt both protective towards them and threatened. She was well aware of Clark's propensity to be flattered by bright young women and equally conscious of their vulnerability before the aura of the great historian. At university parties she often felt uncomfortable, wanting to leave early or arguing with Clark afterwards about his behaviour. She was not one for sexual liberation. The libertarian values of the academics were anathema to everything she had lived as a married woman. And besides, by the time the pill arrived she had six children and was approaching menopause, while Clark was entering the peak of his career and fame, surrounded by young women who were in awe of him. Nor was she the kind of woman who played by the rules of more polite Canberra society. As Jill Waterhouse explained: 'She'd think nothing of taking a pair of socks that needed darning to a dinner party.'[14]

While Clark wrote letter after letter pleading with Dymphna to forget his past infidelity, she knew that the milieu in which they moved was likely to see him do the same again. She never disguised her lack of trust and Clark harped endlessly in his letters and diary that she lacked faith in him. In moments of self-pity, he continued to complain that she hated his work, his view of the world, his conversation and appearance, and his behaviour—'Which part of me does she like?' he moaned. After the death of Augustin and Anna in the 1960s, whenever Clark fought with Dymphna he projected much of his disdain for her parents onto her: 'She must despise and hate me as deeply as her parents despised me.' Approaching the end of the third decade of their marriage, the couple appeared to be heading for another crisis—she, suspicious of his pledges of loyalty and reluctant to live in a marriage sabotaged by his indiscretions; he, helpless before his need for constant injections of affection, flattery and clandestine intimacy with other women. In the late 1960s and early 1970s, Clark's close friendship with three women—Daphne Gollan, a colleague in the History Department whom he had appointed as a tutor in Russian History in 1963: Lyndall Ryan, who began work as his research assistant in January 1966; and Susan Magarey, who started in the same position in late 1971—allowed him to reveal different sides of himself, which he could not reveal to Dymphna without being reprimanded or spurned.[15]

Daphne Gollan, a member of the Communist Party until the 1970s, separated from her husband Bob in the 1960s. Only three years younger than Clark, she was an outstanding teacher and a committed feminist. At

Susan Magarey, 1979 and Daphne Gollan, 1971

first, Clark's contact with Gollan was mostly as a mentor as she began her teaching career at the ANU, but by 1967 it had grown to an 'affair of the heart', Clark's euphemism for his extramarital relations. Lyndall Ryan understood Gollan's attraction for Clark. 'Manning saw Daphne as a woman of the world,' says Ryan. 'She was worldly, and he thought he could go to the pits with her ... she was not afraid to speak her mind with him ... I think he always felt that there was a madness within him that had to be contained.' With Gollan, Clark could express his sexuality without fear of rebuke, writing to her from London in 1969, in a thinly veiled case of projection: 'Needing you in this huge dirty whore of a city, which I love to distraction', or telling Gollan of sitting next to Dymphna in Washington twelve months earlier, listening to a reading of *Ulysses* and 'hearing Mollie Bloom say that what she liked most of all was to suck a man's cock'. With Gollan, Clark could say the things Dymphna would never have tolerated. He could also ask her to do what Dymphna would never have done for him—crawl on the floor on all fours as a demonstration of her affection for him—a request with which Gollan later regretted com-plying, because it suggested Clark had little respect for her. On campus, Clark loved nothing more than to leave flirtatious notes in Gollan's pigeon-hole: 'Daphne, come to my room as soon as possible'; 'My dearest Daphne, I must see you this afternoon. Would 2pm be possible? I'm in despair. Your mate (always deep down) Manning.' In his letters to Gollan, only rarely did Clark describe their physical embraces—'those mouvements agités in the car'—and even then his language suggested a sexual passion that was thwarted, a bodily experience that was an all-too-inferior expression of the florid cartwheels of his prose. Between 1967 and 1969, as Clark wrote some of his most passionate letters to Gollan, he continued to write to Dymphna in the same vein as he had done in 1964.[16]

Travelling in Europe in 1969, fleeing Australia in the wake of the publi-cation of Volume II, Clark wrote Dymphna another box of lovesick correspondence. She was, he said, his 'earth queen', his *allgemeine*, his 'queen of blue bell forests and seas that fret in coves', his 'great receiver & giver back of all that makes one feel glad to be alive'. Thinking of her, he was overcome by that 'oceanic yearning for another creation', the 'ache' which 'only great art' or her presence could soothe. 'Love me and make me me again' he implored. Next to her, as Lawrence wrote in *The Rainbow*, 'all other women were shadows'. 'Have you thought of the meaning of trinity,' he asked her: 'man, woman earth, you, me earth'. By now, perhaps because she suspected the affair, Dymphna was telling Clark that his romantic outpourings were little more than 'rhetoric'. Her instinct was canny. To Daphne Gollan, sometimes within days of writing to Dymphna, Clark described his feeling of an 'eternal bond' with her. He wanted to take her up into 'the highest mountains', from where she could see 'the kingdoms of the world', in all their 'horror and beauty'. In London he felt 'an oceanic sense' of her everywhere he went. Through Gollan, he was put in touch with 'the wonder and the mystery' of life. 'Your bush fire of a man trembles for you and always will,' he told her.[17]

Set side by side, Clark's correspondence to both Dymphna and Gollan appears more contrived, its intensity of feeling feigned simply by virtue of its duplication. But Clark's duplicity lay less in his choice of language than it did in his pretence that each woman was the only one to whom he could confess his innermost feelings. As Lyndall Ryan would realise years later, 'Manning was fond of telling me you're one of a very small number of people I can talk to … It was a lie of course but I was too young to see it at the time.' Clark may have been fond of syndicating his favourite phrases of affection, but he was not faking the emotions that writing letters allowed him to tap. As he told Gollan, he needed someone to whom he could 'pour out everything', with whom he could 'be emptied and then be refilled'. He lived with an irrepressible need to know his beloveds and to be known, the drama of the courtships keeping his emotional life strung at fever pitch, without which he easily lapsed into depression, unable to work to his satisfaction. Nor did Clark see his affection for Gollan in opposition to his love for Dymphna. Writing to Gollan from London in May 1969, in the same breath as he confided the depth of his longing for her, he told her that his feelings for Dymphna had 'deepened too'. With a muse to sing to, Clark was momentarily free. His darkest fears and dreams were expelled onto the page, the place where his only chance of perfection in life resided.[18]

In January 1966, when Ryan became Clark's research assistant, she was twenty-three. He was fifty. Her father had died when she was fourteen, and at first she saw Clark as a substitute. 'I felt as if our relationship was one of father–daughter, I was flattered I suppose. He was very interested in my work on Tasmanian Aborigines.' Clark told Ryan that he had chosen her because she liked Erik Satie's wistful pieces for the piano (the *Gymnopédies*), barracked for Carlton and read Balzac. 'A little innocent', Ryan was charmed by Clark's 'solicitous' manner. She could also feel his intensity. He was 'a nervy type', unusually prone to emotional or physical sickness. 'I remember him often talking about the way artists or writers had to retire to bed sick. He enjoyed cultivating illness. It was his artist's cross, a fever which when cleared, brought him inspiration and insight.' Or so he claimed. Because of Ryan's youth, Don Baker took it upon himself to look after her. 'Don was Manning's ears and he knew I was the youngest research assistant to that point. He effectively managed my relationship with Manning, and I was grateful for that because especially in that first year I was very unaware.' Mindful of Clark's liking for young women, Baker warned Ryan 'not to go to Tasmania Circle alone'. She took his advice. 'You avoided Manning when Dymphna was away.' In the three years Ryan spent as Clark's research assistant, Clark grew increasingly fond of her. But when Ryan moved to Sydney in 1969 to begin her postgraduate degree, he was forced to find a replacement. Infatuated with Daphne Gollan throughout 1968 and 1969, his attention was diverted by Susan Magarey's arrival at the ANU. As soon as Magarey began working as Clark's research assistant in 1971, she found notes in her pigeon hole similar to those Clark had sent to Gollan; 'Susan, the Kind, See the undersigned. Manning the Solitary. As soon as you come in.' As one passion subsided in Clark's mind, another rose instantly to take its place. Without the rush that he experienced from becoming intimate with another person for the first time, and without the challenge of etching his presence forever onto their soul, Clark was condemned to a life in which he would never again know the feeling of falling in love—that sense of abandonment, discovery and excitement that pushed him beyond the humdrum of everyday existence and put him in touch with his creative instincts. Even his letters to Dymphna could be read as a decades-long attempt to sustain a permanent state of infatuation, while his relationships with his children reflected similar tendencies— 'Katerina: am in love with her again', 'Benedict: my new great love'.[19]

Although Susan Magarey would never become the muse that Daphne Gollan had been to him or Lyndall Ryan would soon become, in 1971 Clark quickly developed a deep affection for her. Shortly before Magarey left Clark in early 1972 to take up a doctoral scholarship in the Research School at the ANU— 'a double betrayal, I had gone to the enemy and left him before Volume Three was finished'— Clark flirted openly with her in front of Dymphna during a party at Tasmania Circle. It was not the first time that Dymphna had found herself relegated to the role of caterer. Incensed, she packed her bags and left a note on Clark's bedroom pillow. He woke the next morning to find that she had left him. Immediately, he resorted to pen and paper, writing to her that his 'erratic' behaviour was merely 'a surface bubble' of his present problems—drinking breakouts, his 'deep loss of faith' in the *History*, his dwindling prestige with students and colleagues and his 'general carrying on'. Lying in bed, 'drenched in moonlight', he saw again the error of his ways. He had committed no 'physical infidelities' as he had done in 1955. His sin, he told her, was a succession of 'spiritual treacheries' in which he had confided in others instead of her, his 'eternal mate'. Of all his friends— David Campbell, Don Baker, Lyndall Ryan, Daphne Gollan and Geoffrey Fairbairn—no one understood him like she did. Alone at home with fourteen-year-old Benedict, Clark shamelessly milked Dymphna's love for her son in order to persuade her to come back. 'Once, I noticed tears in Benedict's eyes. We sat together for a while in front of the kitchen fire reading our several books—both of us aware of the absence of a mighty spirit, both of us feeling that wound of the deprived.' Pleading for forgiveness, he promised her that he would search the world over to find his 'pearl' and bring her back home. A little over a week later, Dymphna returned to Tasmania Circle. Clark's letters, with their gilded promises of 'autumn days of love and splendour' had helped to soften her resistance.[20]

Within weeks of Dymphna's return, Clark, now briefly estranged from Daphne Gollan, turned to Lyndall Ryan for solace. In November 1971, entering the last stages of writing Volume III, he needed much more than his 'eternal mate'. He needed his fix of female sympathy and admiration. Now living in Sydney, Ryan had other men in her life, 'much younger than Manning', but she had never received letters like those that flooded her mailbox in the first months of 1972. Clark rang her at 9 o'clock many mornings, suffering from writer's block. 'I would pick up the phone and there was that voice at the other end of the line—as if coming from beyond the grave. "I can't find the muse, she's not there today." He needed to talk. After 10 minutes, he would be buoyed enough to continue writing.' In April that year, Clark wrote a piece for the press on the importance of women in his life. He mailed a photocopy to Magarey: 'here is another good laugh'. He sent another to Ryan. 'Talking with a woman with whom he had a great bond,' said Clark, 'was like listening to a great work of music or looking for a long time at a great painting ... a woman can give me that moment of heightened awareness ... despite death's untimely presence ... in our secular era men [who are artists] turn to women for their muse'. Dymphna read the article as well, one of the few women to appreciate just how difficult it was to play the lofty role Clark had assigned for her. Clark wrote of women as if they were merely the means to his own artistic fulfilment. In the same month in which his article appeared, Clark's letters to Ryan increased dramatically. He rang to tell her that he was coming to Sydney 'just to see her'. He asked her if he could 'unbutton' his soul, if he could risk 'showing the view'. He felt 'lifted up' after talking to her. She was his 'pyscho-delic girl', his butterfly, the one woman who expanded his 'whole psyche', the one whose face reminded him of one of those women in Renoir, with their unbridled gaiety and 'the hint of being acquainted with grief'. In the space of a few months, Clark's missives built to a wild crescendo. Layering his prose with quotes from Shakespeare, Blake and Dante, and delirious with love, 'the great enemy of doubt', he told Ryan that through her he could see all the poetry, music and painting in the world 'as if for the first time'. After every meeting in Sydney, he left feeling high on the 'after-glow', a trance-like state that allowed him to push on with his final draft of Volume III.[21]

The love letters Ryan received were from the country's most renowned historian. As Gough Whitlam prepared to lead the Labor Party to government for the first time in twenty-three years, Clark appeared in the press regularly—advocating a vote for Labor and musing on the country's future direction. The pressure that was slowly building in his private life seemed to mirror the increasing commotion of his public life. Ryan read Clark's opinion pieces and heard his public pronouncements at the same time as she received letter after letter from him professing his love for her. She was flattered by Clark's overtures of affection but she was not fooled. His letters bore little resemblance to her experience of their friendship. Reflecting on Clark's correspondence years later, Ryan explained that 'Manning saw more in the relationship than there was.' She denied any suggestion that she had an affair with Clark. Once, on a night ferry to Cremorne, when Clark tried to kiss her, she pushed him away. She had no interest in him as a lover. But she was willing to provide him with emotional support. 'I was the muse for volume three.'

Clark's relationship with his close friends followed similar patterns. Judy Campbell, wife of David Campbell, thought Clark imagined a deeper bond with her husband than actually existed.

> I always had the sense that the friendship between Manning and David mattered more for Manning than it did for David. David was more the dominant one. I can recall David saying that he felt he 'ought' to go and see Manning. David was certainly drawn to Manning's knowledge of Australia, and Manning could talk about anything and that suited David. But Manning needed David and sometimes I thought he leant on David.

Campbell also lived as Clark could no longer live. Some time in the 1970s, Clark told Dymphna: 'Last night David Campbell came by at 6 pm, but by 9pm after half of the white flagon and one third of the Fuji, he was like a Renaissance prince. My love for him deepened last night.' Only with his other 'great friend', Don Baker, on whom he had relied so many times at the ANU, did Clark find 'a shared sense of love'.

Throughout 1972, Clark's battery of words to Ryan climbed to the heights that he had reached in 1964 when writing simultaneously to Dymphna, and again in 1968–69, writing to Daphne Gollan. If the three women could have come together and laid out Clark's correspondence on a table in front of them, they could have picked up any letter and seen something of what they thought was their own private possession: the needy declarations, the secretive confessions that no one else could share such a deep level of intimacy with the bushfire Dionysus, and the same soaring phrases swept along by Clark's splicing of phrases from the literary canon, words of devotion that floated so high above them they were unable to recognise the scenes Clark described.[22]

In the first weeks of December 1972, only days after Gough Whitlam's victory in the federal election on 2 December, Ryan decided to tell Clark to back off. She could not reciprocate on the level on which he seemed to want her to respond. She told him that he was asking too much of her, that she needed more space. It was impossible to focus on her thesis with Clark constantly beating at her door. Predictably, Clark was hurt. He told Ryan to burn every letter he had written to her and to cut his name out of the books that he had given her. On Thursday 14 December, Ryan lost her patience. She rang Clark and told him that she never wanted to speak to him again. Then, while he was at work, she rang Dymphna and talked to her about her difficulty in persuading Clark to desist. Clark was about to lose not only Ryan but Dymphna as well. The morning after Ryan's phone call, Dymphna left Tasmania Circle, telling Clark that she would never return. This time, she fled not to Sydney but to Brisbane, where, with the help of friends, she secured a job as a nurse's aid in the Infectious Diseases Ward of the Women's Hospital—scrubbing floors, changing sheets, washing clothes—the same labour she had performed for years at home. Clark was left alone with Benedict. Initially, Dymphna decided that she would write only to Benedict. But when Clark found one of her letters to Benedict in the mailbox, he opened it and found her address. Before he had a chance to write his first plea for her return, Dymphna tried to ward him off. She knew he would dislike her bitterness, forget everything she said and 'plunge into another eloquent sea of rhetoric hoping by this means to bring [her] round'. But she decided to write in any case. Her letter was searing in its honesty.

This time no amount of eloquence will bring me home. And perhaps this is a good thing…when I was 37, and pregnant, I first left home and struggled to start a new life. You brought me home by your wonderful letters—can you remember to what? And how many times has that pattern been repeated since then? For what? But not again. It may be that you are a deeply divided person, with a 'double standard'. I look forward to your account of its origins with mixed feelings. Are you going right back to before the Swedish girls of Cosqueville? It will be a long account ... wanting to change ... and writing wonderful letters will not change things one iota.

... I left home with feelings of great guilt, and fear of failure. But there are already signs that I could make some kind of a life for myself—nothing that would impress you, but a life. My guilt was at abandoning you at a time of crisis, but what could I do for you? What was in my power I have done, to no avail, a thousand times. But I felt great guilt towards Rowland and Benedict, to whom I should be available at least until they leave school, however unwelcome and unpalatable our presence may be ... [but] how can I live with them as long as the nightmare cycle of my life with you continues? And how could you be expected to leave your books, your study, your music, your piano?

Let us accept the fact that we two have become allergic to each other: that you feel you cannot live completely with me, that I feel there is no spontaneity in a relationship where most things are clouded by memories, or weariness, or strain. Let us cut the cackle: Not one of the children really believes in marriage or 'morality'. They will not mind anything you do. I am too naïve to live among intellectuals and artists. Their values hurt me, they laugh at mine. The golden autumn of your life will be spent not with me but among great names and young grass. This is what you have talked and dreamt about for years. You will thank me for making it possible without your having to wail for the death of your wife.

Remember to cancel the bank's order paying part of your salary into my account. You will need to pay the bills.[23]

The children—especially Katerina, Axel and Benedict—quickly became embroiled in the impasse. Clark read Dymphna's letters aloud to Benedict, who was fifteen. Then he asked Katerina, who was thirty-one, to write her mother a Christmas card and plead for her return. She obliged but then wrote another letter to Dymphna in a tone that was much more critical of Clark. 'Which is the true tone?' Dymphna asked him. By now Clark was firing from every cache of his literary arsenal—telegrams, letters and cards arrived in Brisbane daily. Dymphna thanked him for the 'anguish' he put into his letters, his 'generous cheques' and implored him not to read her letters to Benedict. 'The thought that you might share my letter prevents me ... from writing with any frankness.' Nor did she want Clark to read his letters to her to Benedict. Did he have to make their every private pain public? 'Do not show this to [Benedict] or I cannot write again.' Benedict later recalled his parents' distress. 'Manning,' he said, 'was handwringing, forlorn, self-critical and desperate to find a way to get her back. Reading her letters to me was one way of achieving that.' Benedict helped Clark with the housework and tried to keep him calm, the adolescent son ministering to his father. At the Women's Hospital in Brisbane, Clark's letters kept arriving, begging for Dymphna's forgiveness and beseeching her to come home. After finishing her shift in the wards, she re-read them time and time again. Still, she held out.

> I have just re-read the letters I had from you yesterday ... [I] feel the tug very strongly. But although I want to resist all temptation to bitterness, I cannot say yes to your pleas ... This time I must not give way in the face of your rhetoric, must not throw away all I am starting to build up here, to fall back into desolation. Canberra is desolation to me—emotionally and socially. At the moment I don't particularly ever want to see it again. It is an infinite relief to be away from those cruel and unhappy intellectuals, from their pretensions, and from everlasting strain. Here I have nothing except a menial job and a hot mean little room ... but here is peace and absence of tension, and a chance of a better job and a profession—at my age! ... by next year I could probably offer Ned a pleasant home here, if he wanted it. None of this is what I have spent my life looking for, but it is infinitely better than what I have achieved hitherto. Why should I go back to a place where all our sordid intimate affairs are now an open book not only to all our children, but to the whole academic community? Where I am dung on the employment market and a domestic slave? ... If you have always adored me so madly, <u>why</u> Lyndall, at 55+?

I fear it is mainly my absence that makes you want me as ever. On my return you would be weary and oppressed as ever. I cannot bear the prospect, much as I would love to live the life you picture so glowingly in your letters. I am very glad to hear about your confident ending to the 3rd draft, and the themes you hope to express—but where will you find the strength for a fourth draft? For this reason alone I must urge you again to have a major talk to a doctor—someone who really studies the whole man ... And I think Father [John] Molony would be a wonderful confessor ... But please oh please take time and rest to restore yourself—for the sake of the fourth draft and of your loyal Ned.

... Goodbye, be of good cheer, as you say, life is immense ... Love to Ned Love D.[24]

Clark was so distraught that he could not bring himself to write in his diary. Confronted with the possibility of living without Dymphna, he conscripted others to his cause, visiting Tony Proust, a Canberra physician, and talking with his colleague John Molony. 'Manning,' Molony recalled, 'was asking Dymphna to separate his womanising from their relationship. He also knew that Dymphna respected me, and my wife, Denise. He rang me tearfully and asked me to give her a call. In the weeks before Christmas 1972, I rang Dymphna several times.' Molony may have left the priesthood years earlier, but for the Clarks he was still 'Father Molony', confessor, mediator and possible saviour. At the same time as he asked Proust to ring Dymphna and vouch for his potential to reform his ways, he persuaded Molony to write to Dymphna, setting out the conditions of her return. Molony obliged.

I have had a long talk with Manning regarding the problem. I am personally convinced that you have the solution this time. To reinforce the conviction you have agreed to seek medical advice—or sooner if required. I am willing to play a supervisory or advisory role. Manning asks me to ask you to come home ... he is so repentant that if necessary he will come to Brisbane.

Molony was convinced that this was the guarantee that persuaded Dymphna to return. On Christmas Eve, she finally wilted, telegramming

Clark with some of his own medicine, quoting Barkis, the wagon driver in Dickens' *David Copperfield*, who courted his servant lover by repeating the phrase 'Barkis is willin''.

Dear Manning,
This is a strange Christmas Eve for all of us, let's hope all the succeeding ones will be better.

Thankyou for your telegram. I am endlessly grateful to Tony Proust, and to John Molony—I don't think I said so on the phone to either of them … I have just sent you a telegram about my return—Flight 425 TAA, arriving Canberra at 5.10 pm Wednesday 27th—in case telegram goes astray.

You win—or do I? Who cares? Least said soonest mended
Barkis is willin'—but only a 'uman bein'.
Love to Ned
Your Dymphna[25]

Benedict remembered Dymphna's homecoming: 'She just seemed to slip back in. She was a very undramatic person.' Her resistance had dissolved for the second time in twelve months. Beyond the anguish of her correspondence lay the allure of Clark's moody, seductive charm and her playful response, caught momentarily in that one phrase—'Barkis is willin''. For all his duplicity and unreliability, Clark made her feel loved. As always, her need of him was less visible than his need of her, but no less great. After her return, he filed the letters she had written him from Brisbane in his study, describing them as 'documents on what I hope will be my last quarrel with my darling Dymphna'. Among them was the note she had left on his pillow the morning of her departure: 'Over the past couple of days you have made it pretty clear that Canberra is not my rightful place. I am removing myself. Please look after Benedict.' Clark added a note in brackets, attentive to archival accuracy: '(15 December 1972—Dymphna returned on 28 December 1972)'. He hid the folder of letters in the bottom drawer of his filing cabinet, and requested that they be destroyed on his death. In effect, he left the decision to her. Combing through Clark's papers twenty years later, Dymphna decided to leave her letters in the papers that remained at Manning Clark House. Unlike

Manning and Dymphna,
Cape Everard, 1970

so much of the material stored in Clark's study, these few pages from Brisbane in 1972 told her story of the crises in her marriage. But unlike Ryan, Gollan and Magarey, all of whom kept Clark's extraordinary outpourings, she destroyed the letters Clark wrote to her while she was in Brisbane. These she did not keep in poignant gratitude, as she had done in 1964.

Of all Clark's correspondents, Dymphna saw the shallowness of words left unsupported by actions—the sheer lightness of his weighty prose. Perhaps she also destroyed his letters because she could not bear to be reminded that, even in 1972, they had still managed to break her resolve, bringing her home for the third time in sixteen years. Although she came back to Clark in 27 December 1972, Dymphna's view of her marriage had shifted unalterably. Her trust in Clark had been shaken too many times. For the rest of her married life, she kept in her wardrobe a bag packed with clothes, ever ready for a quick departure.[26]

PART SEVEN

21: WAPENGO

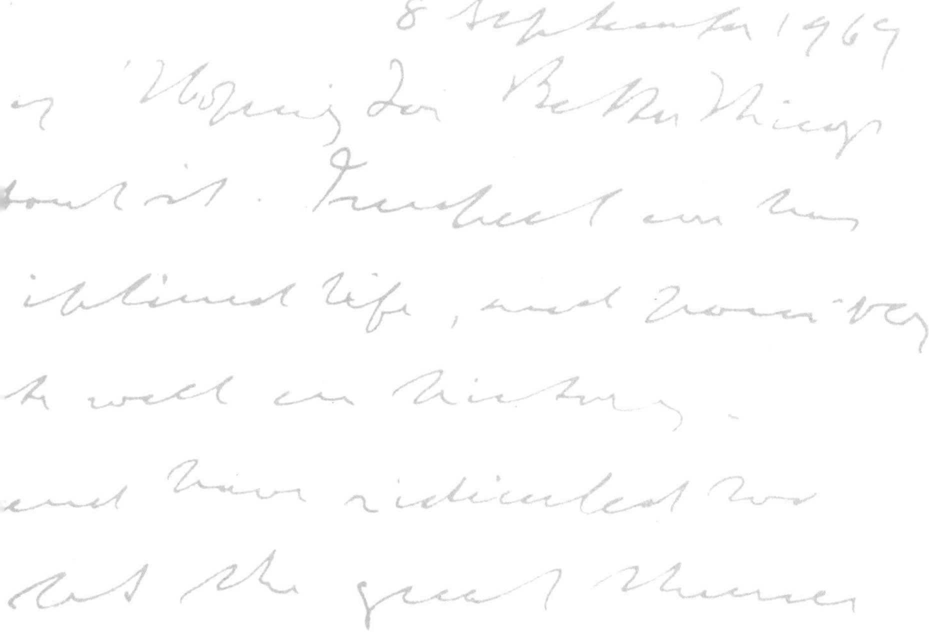

8 September 1969

The simplicity is disarming; a low-lying timber house fronted by a bush pole verandah, which stands discretely on the northern headland of the estuary. Nearby, a narrow track leads through knotted stands of banksia and ti-tree down to the sea. On the beach, looking south across the waters of the tidal inlet to the coast beyond, a landscape unfolds that has changed little in the past five thousand years, since the sea levels rose during the last ice age.

In November 1968, using the inheritance from her mother's will, Dymphna purchased 400 acres of coastal land barely twenty kilometres north of Bega, on the far south coast of New South Wales. Dymphna and Clark called the place 'Ness', a playful reference to nearby Lake Wapengo and the nose-like prominence of the headland that formed the property's eastern boundary. Later on, they erected a sign beside the driveway adorned with a picture of the Loch Ness Monster. Dymphna, who had long wanted a property with ocean frontage, drove the three-hour trip from Canberra to take first sight of the place. At Wapengo, she found a large tract of land bordered by a mile of estuary shoreline and the Pacific Ocean. The rough dirt road that led to the headland skirted the northern edge of Wapengo Lagoon, passing oyster farms and paddocks cleared by the dairy farmers who

The Clarks' house at Wapengo, 2008

were now desperate to get out. It was country in the middle of a long drought. The small subsistence dairy farms that had survived the Great Depression were no longer viable; the more the native forests were cleared, the faster the topsoils washed away.[1]

When Clark camped for the first time at Wapengo, he became aware of the Aboriginal campsites and ceremonial grounds that had once ringed the lake's shoreline. Removed from 'civilisation' in Canberra, surrounded by the bush and the sea, he saw how the white man had 'ignored' what the Aborigines had done to the land. When he visited the Aboriginal settlement at Wallaga Lake, thirty kilometres to the north, he sensed how the Europeans in Australia could eventually be dispossessed in the same way as the Aborigines. The ancient continent would outlive all its invaders. Standing on the beach at Wapengo, he imagined James Cook, in April 1770, sailing north along the

An Eye for Eternity

east coast. To think that he now owned land close to where Cook had first glimpsed the smoke from Aboriginal campfires gave him great pleasure. Years later, in front of journalists and television cameras, he strode the beach reciting lines from Cook's journal, pointing out to the sea as if the *Endeavour* were still sailing off shore. At Wapengo, he found a way to align his personal sense of place with the first moment of British settlement. Within months of Dymphna buying the property he was already attached to 'its broad acres ... its sights and sounds—especially the silhouettes of the she-oaks against the night sky, and the thud of the surf on the sand'.[2]

In 1970, barely more than a hundred years since the first wave of free selectors had taken up land on the south coast, Clark and Dymphna erected the first building to stand on the northern headland at Wapengo. Wanting a retreat rather than a grand statement of their presence, they asked Clark's nephew, Philip Ingamells, then a student architect at Melbourne University, to design the house. Ingamells fondly recalled how Clark would arrive on the site to deliver urgent pronouncements: 'We need electricity, I need civili-sation.' But it was Dymphna, he said, who was the main source of ideas regarding the design of the house. Inspired by reading the British economist EF Schumacher's *Small is Beautiful* (1968), a cult classic which rejected unbridled capitalist growth and consumerism in favour of a simpler environ-mental aesthetic, she set out to make Wapengo the epitome of the values she had carried with her since childhood. The house would not dominate the surrounding environment; it would merge with it. Over a period of more than thirty years, she planted hundreds of native trees along the lake fore-shore, shaping a vista that was akin to one of her first memories, when her child's eyes gazed upwards to the branches of giant fig trees as her parents pushed her pram through the tree-lined avenues of Melbourne's Fawkner Park in 1918.

To help with the work on the property Clark invited students down from Canberra for weekends, joking that if they worked four hours a day they could have a pass degree, if they worked six hours a day they'd get a Masters and if they worked eight hours a day they'd get a PhD. When Ingamells lived for a time at Wapengo in the mid-1970s, and Clark was often brooding over the fate of his work, he would confide in him.

One time while I was there I remember Manning came to me quite troubled. He wanted to re-write the first volume to revisit the Aboriginal question, over which he had profound regrets. Ryan told him not to do it, to leave it as it was. Manning seemed very worried that he'd accepted Ryan's advice. My impression was that he wanted to rewrite, and I regret not advising him to do so.

In all of Ingamells' contact with Clark at Wapengo, it was Clark's wit that left the most lasting impression. 'One day, I was mopping the back verandah and Manning arrived back after his daily walk. When he saw me he said: "Blessed are the moppers for they shall be mopped."'[3]

When the house was finished, Dymphna filled the living room with the antique furniture she had inherited from Augustin and Anna, its sombre European tones darkening the interior, a foil for the bright Australian sun. As more and more weekend visits were made, the house filled with Clark's books and music. The minimalist aesthetic reflected Dymphna's disdain for ostentatious display. The house was merely a vehicle for connecting with the environment, while the emphasis at the Clarks' table was on conversation that moved easily from politics and art to literature, sport, history and culture. For some outsiders, like Suzanne Foulkes, who lived nearby, the dinner-table jokes could seem slightly esoteric. 'Once the conversation stooped to the name of Dostoyevsky's dog I switched off.'[4]

The Clarks' arrival at Wapengo was part of a wave of city dwellers seeking seaside properties. In the space of twenty years, from the early 1960s through the 1970s, artists, writers, academics and architects bought up large tracts of the south coast. Land was available cheaply after subdivision of the old dairy farms. It was a moment that would never come again. By the early 1980s, the New South Wales Labor government had assigned most of the remaining coastal land to form Mimosa Rocks National Park. Across the water from the Clarks, barely 300 metres away, was the property of Roy Grounds, the Melbourne architect whose prominent geometric dome construction, inspired by the design philosophy of American architect Buckminster Fuller, failed to impress Clark and Dymphna. Ken Myer, the Melbourne philanthropist and businessman, shared the property with

An Eye for Eternity

Wapengo Lake, 2008

Grounds. David Yencken, head of the Australian Heritage Commission, owned land along the same stretch of coast. So too did novelist Rodney Hall, Sydney architect Phillip Cox, the photographer of Aboriginal sites and country, Wes Stacey, and historian Bob Gollan, Clark's colleague at the ANU and former husband of Daphne. Sprinkled up and down the coast were alternative lifestyle communities, many of their members eventually finding their way to Wapengo, where they would work, party and camp out for long periods of time. Some, like John and Mary Anderson, friends of the Clarks' third son, Andrew, would later found a community 200 kilometres south-west at Pericoe, not far from the Victorian border. The Andersons became the Clarks' caretakers in the early 1970s, building a cabin that they called 'The Clearing', a small cement, stone and timber hut nestled in an open patch of ground only fifty metres from the sea, which soon became a favourite spot for many of the Clark children.[5]

Although Clark and Dymphna were generous towards, and supportive of, the younger men and women who sought to break away from conventional ways of living, they were always suspicious of anyone who appeared to be 'wasting their talents', or who merely 'lounged about' on unemployment benefits. At the same time they excluded no one, picking up hitchhikers on their way from Canberra, sometimes allowing them to stay for a few days. As Bob Gollan explained, 'in those years people often set up semi-permanent camps along the coast and marijuana was usually growing along the creek banks. Long-standing locals built their own houses, some were on the dole and spent their days fishing, but they all turned out for the Clark cricket matches at Wapengo.' One of those cricketers was John Blay, the writer who founded a community at Umbi Gumbi, just south of Bermagui, and who first visited Clark at Wapengo in 1972, shortly after Blay finished the script for a radio play based on the Battle of Vinegar Hill, funded by a Commonwealth Literary Fellowship. 'I had gone to Manning's *History* only to discover that the dates and names for the battle were wrong. So I went to Wapengo to tell him. He wrapped his arm around me and said "My Dear Boy—does that matter? What's important is to have something to say."' Clark was more interested in giving Blay the sense that his writing was worthwhile, and he encouraged him as he set out to write his first book at Bermagui—*Part of the Scenery*—a blend of nature writing and personal memoir of which Australia had then seen few examples.[6]

At Wapengo, the tiny community soon realised whom they had in their midst and Clark and Dymphna did all they could to make their presence known. They adopted the same open house approach as they did in Tasmania Circle, bringing friends and extended family from Canberra and Sydney, and inviting virtually everyone they met on the coast to join them for lunch. One frequent guest was Phyllis Hunter, the local postmistress, who knew everything that went on in Wapengo, especially because, in the days when telephone exchanges were still manual—right up until 1974 when underground cables were finally laid—she listened in on everyone's calls, including the Clarks'. Her son, the moody oyster farmer Denis Hunter, whom Clark respected for his knowledge of the surrounding country, was dubbed 'the Patrick White of Wapengo'. Together with Mick Otton, who managed a local cattle and horse business nearby, the Hunters looked after the Clarks' property when they returned to Canberra.[7]

The house at Wapengo was built six years before Clark's retirement from teaching at the ANU. As his teaching commitments decreased, Clark came to Wapengo more often. Removed from the intensity of his working life in Canberra, he seemed bored if he stayed at Wapengo too long. The ideal remedy was fishing, a pursuit Rowland remembers sharing with his father. 'We used to go rock fishing. Point fishing was for salmon and tailor, and estuary fishing for bream, flathead, blackfish and whiting.' Fishing off the rocks at Wapengo became another of Clark's muses, a mark of his masculine communion with nature. As he told Peter Ryan in 1987, '[I] am off to Wapengo today in search still for the big fish. Fish are like women—When they are 'ON', it passeth all understanding!'[8]

Clark never wrote at Wapengo, except occasionally in his diary and to send postcards and letters. It remained a place of retreat and relaxation. There, he could more easily forget the pain that criticism brought him. He liked to think that coming to know Wapengo had rejuvenated his literary imagination, instilling in him even greater drive and energy as he pressed on with the *History*. For amusement, he placed Wapengo on a map of key places of settlement in early New South Wales, inserting it as an illustration in Volume III. He wrote fondly of the property to friends, exhorting them to come and stay. To make the point even more strongly he sometimes phoned them from Wapengo. In the early 1980s, the phone rang at AD Hope's house in Canberra while the poet Mark O'Connor was visiting. Hope took the call, which lasted only a few seconds. 'Who was that?' asked O'Connor. 'It was Manning,' said Hope. 'He just rang to let me know the ocean is making a very pleasing sound tonight.'[9]

Much as he loved Wapengo, Clark struggled to see the land and sea free from the biblical metaphors that had framed his life since childhood; for him, the sea represented the promise of spiritual 'healing'. Like the Hindu people he saw bathing in the Ganges in 1955, he imagined the waters of the Pacific washing his transgressions away. Living at Wapengo, Clark returned to his old themes. DH Lawrence at Thirroul became CMH Clark at Wapengo. In 1976, sitting at his bedroom desk, looking out the window to the ring of bush that sheltered the house from the fierce coastal winds, he felt frightened by 'the silence'. It was the same silence, he thought, that pervaded nearly all the Australian landscape, 'an intimation of emptiness'. In contrast to the English and Americans, he believed Australians had grafted an artificial life onto the land. Unlike the generation of writers that followed him, many of whom had already begun to find their sense of belonging by exploring Aboriginal understandings of Country, Clark remained a European in melancholy exile. Like a reincarnation of so many of the men he had written about—Burke, Leichhardt and Macquarie—he wondered whether he belonged in Australia. One of his most poignant expressions of his relationship with Wapengo came in an undated, unsent letter to Sebastian, probably written some time in the late 1970s.

A letter from the Zen Country

My Dearest Sebastian

I am writing to you from Wapengo. It is one of those exquisite days when the gulls look more white than usual. I can see them from my window as I sit writing to you, diving for fish, or those fragments of small fish the tailor leaves on the surface after they have taken what they want. And yet the curve of the dive is so beautiful, the day so balmy, that one is not tortured by what that entails. I mean the strong preying on the weak. Yes it is one of those days on the south coast when a man can accept everything. Yet so black is my mood that I do not feel a celebrant amidst all this beauty of sky and sea, that vast sea, heaving away, to the horizon, on the cliffs, gaunt, desolate with the ti tree and banksia, bent by the nor'easters into a straight line from shore to cliff top. No. I am so fearful for our future that not even the splendours of nature, the everlasting recurrence, can reassure me that all is well, or all will be well.[10]

Clark fishing on the rocks at Wapengo, late 1980s

The future for which Clark was so fearful was Australia's in the late 1970s. Dymphna had purchased Wapengo at the very moment when he was about to become a national celebrity. When the travelling and media appearances became too strenuous he retired to the silence of 'Ness', which held its own sense of foreboding. But even there, the media would find him, travelling to interview him in light aircraft and helicopters from Sydney and Melbourne to Wapengo, where they found a tousled, unshaven man holding a bucket of bait and a fishing rod, an old man of the sea.

22: THE PROPHET

Fame is like a river that beareth up
things light and swoln, and drowns
things weighty and solid.
FRANCIS BACON 1612[1]

'I feel like a person who is watching people on the other side of thick glass.' So wrote Manning Clark to David Campbell from Durham, North Carolina, in the American fall of 1963. As Clark entered his late fifties and early sixties, the image occurred repeatedly in his letters to friends and family. He imagined himself standing behind a thick pane of glass, like a prisoner condemned to life behind bars, separated from his fellow human beings.

All writers are observers, but Clark's feelings of separation went far beyond the necessary detachment required to write. As a child, he heard his father read from I Corinthians 13:12: 'For now we see through a glass darkly, but then face to face.' On earth, men and women had a restricted view of spiritual life. Only after death, he believed, could oneness with God be attained. Clark, the eternal doubter, carried the image with him throughout his life, nurturing and adapting it as a metaphor for his own sense of isolation.[2]

Clark's depressive episodes increased after the deaths of several of his close friends—David Campbell in 1979 and Geoffrey Fairbairn in 1980—with his second son, Axel, having been diagnosed with a brain tumour shortly after Clark's return from America in 1979. As Clark aged, he saw people disappear from his life like actors shuffling off stage. The experience was dream-like—a parade of brief encounters that dissolved into silence—all played out under an intense Shakespearian light. As his health began to deteriorate with age, he often wished he could go back to his fortieth year and start life over again. In the late 1970s he was afflicted with severe stomach pain. Despite tests, no serious cause could be found for his dyspepsia. Dymphna thought Clark's pain was 'largely psychosomatic'. By 1980 he suffered from hypertension. Blood pressure and heart problems surfaced. Taking medication now became part of his daily routine. He struggled to muster the strength to continue writing. In September 1983, he had coronary bypass surgery in St Vincent's Hospital in Sydney, an operation that convinced him he had little time left.[3]

In the last years of his life, the pages of Clark's diary became his wailing wall. Read continuously, the diaries are both tedious and moving. Clark's loneliness was expressed through a moribund litany of self-pity, in a chant-like prayer to a new-found 'God above'. Time and time again, he cursed his sins and prayed for forgiveness from 'someone who might forgive us all', as if asking his future readers to embrace him in sympathy, offering to his memory the love and absolution that had eluded him in life. He refused to let the past go, convinced that Dymphna would never allow him to atone for his infidelities, certain that she would never trust him again. In early 1973, only months after returning home, she made her feelings clear to him: 'Dear Manning, about acceptance, I think we ought to accept a future in which you live according to your instinctive principles and I react according to mine. Assurances, written or oral, are to be avoided. The ensuing disappointments are unhelpful.' In public, Clark referred to his blissful marriage. Writing for the *Australian Women's Weekly*, he wondered if younger Australians had experienced the same feelings of 'symphonic harmony' he had shared in his marriage with Dymphna. Four weeks later, he lamented in his diary that they seemed unable to say anything meaningful to one another. Each of the children had their own image of their parents' marriage. Benedict, during his late teens at Tasmania Circle, slept in a room next to his parents' bedroom. Lying in bed at night and in the early mornings, he often heard the sound of their laughter through the bedroom wall. When he left home in the late 1970s, Benedict carried the image of his parents' largely happy marriage away with him.

Throughout the 1970s, Clark was disgusted by his own drinking habits. Historian Ross Fitzgerald, whose work Clark encouraged at every turn, later recognised as a recovering alcoholic himself that much of Clark's demeanour resembled that of an alcoholic. He suffered episodes of amnesia after drinking binges, was embarrassed by his behaviour when drunk, and found himself incapable of giving up alcohol completely. Often, he felt himself directed by forces beyond his control, chastising himself for his 'never-ending identification with characters in novels'. 'This: I am Marmeladov etc, "who am I?" he cried.' Unlike his friends Fitzgerald and Barry Humphries, he never sought assistance from Alcoholics Anonymous and he never managed to completely shake his dependence on alcohol.

At every stage of life, Clark had found nourishment in teaching, especially the adulation he received from some of his favourite students. As he approached retirement, his best years of teaching were already behind him. With his 'old bag of tricks' starting to prove less effective with students, he began to fill the vacuum in his life by reaching out to a new audience beyond the academy's walls. And like so many other occasions in his life, he followed in Dostoyevsky's footsteps.[4]

Dostoyevsky, after reading his speech 'The Lovers' to a packed hall in Moscow in 1880, was overwhelmed by the rapturous response of the audience. He later spoke of 'the universal union of men' and the spiritual bonds of the Russian people. People 'wept and sobbed', rushing to the podium to embrace him. 'You are our saint, our prophet,' shouted the crowd. Writing to his wife, Anya, Dostoyevsky was in awe of his ability to arouse emotion in the audience who, for a brief moment, saw him as their Messiah. During the last decade of Dostoyevsky's life he became a cult figure throughout Russia. As his biographer Joseph Frank explained, 'it became customary during these years, even among people who disagreed violently with Dostoyevsky on social-political issues, to regard him with a certain reverence, and to feel [that] his words incarnated a prophetic vision illuminating Russia.' In the pages of the Dostoyevsky novels that Clark devoured at every stage of his life, prophecy—mystical, enigmatic and deeply religious in its expression— was a consistent tone of voice. In Dostoyevsky's prose, which had given him so much sustenance since adolescence, Clark recognised the moral dilemmas

and cadences of speech that he heard in his father's sermons as a child. He also found the model of the preacher in his literary heroes, such as Charles Dickens, whose storytelling ability as a public speaker kept his audiences spellbound. Then there was Yeobright from Thomas Hardy's novel *The Return of the Native*, the character who had 'meant so much' to Clark. He:

> found his vocation in the career of an itinerant open air preacher, speaking not only in simple language, but in a more cultivated strain elsewhere, from the steps and porticoes of town halls, from market crosses, from conduits, on esplanades and on wharves, from the parapets of bridges, in barns and out-houses and all such places in the neighbouring Wessex towns and villages.

Clark's last years were not dissimilar. After his retirement from teaching, he addressed Australia Day events and citizenship ceremonies; launched books; opened art exhibitions, fetes, music festivals, opera and theatre productions; endorsed rock bands; and spoke at school speech nights, ALP campaign rallies, anti-woodchip meetings and church services. As the electronic media expanded, Clark became one of the first Australian intellectuals to extend his reach beyond the press. He appeared on national radio, current affairs

An Eye for Eternity

and midday television and on house and garden programs, even managing a cameo acting role as the preacher in the 1985 film production of Peter Carey's novel *Bliss*.[5]

Unlike novelists, historians are rarely read beyond their deaths. History is continually rewritten in the image of the present. As an historian, Clark understood how to make history. In order to be remembered, it was necessary to do things that others would write about, rather than merely write about the things that others did. To witness the scale and magnitude of Clark's public life between 1972 and 1991 is to confront the capacity of his energy and determination. Against any measure, his output was staggering. Rather than becoming quieter with age, Clark's life became busier, his daily schedule more frenetic, his emotional life even more intensely felt. Despite his ailing health, he pushed himself to complete the last volumes of *A History of Australia*, which, together with his correspondence and diary entries, comprised a literary output of well over a thousand words per day. At the same time, his appointment diary became cluttered with commitments to address public forums, launches and political rallies. The mountain of documents that Clark left behind—speeches, interviews and opinion pieces—reflected his hope that biography might do for him what no one else could do: grant him another life.

'The bitch goddess of success', as he so often described it, lured him to the point of distraction and exhaustion. He seemed both unable and unwilling to decline requests for public appearances. Yet his craving for public adulation was not only due to vanity; at some deeper level he was driven by a genuine sense of missionary zeal. In the tradition of Thomas Carlyle's romantic hero—the writer who utters forth his 'inspired soul' to the soul of all and becomes 'the light of the world'—Clark attempted to minister to the nation as a kind of spiritual soothsayer, uttering gnomic words of guidance in the form of historical parables. Although he had precursors like Arnold Toynbee, the British historian whose earnest pronouncements on current affairs, historical, religious and metaphysical questions saw him become a national figure in postwar America, Clark's compulsive ministering set him apart from so many other historians who had played prominent roles in public life. He aspired to be much more than an historian who could make his history politically useful or dutifully advance the discipline's civic relevance; he aspired to be one of the gods. His personal life was little different. In his dealings with friends and family, Clark ministered to others constantly, drawn as he was to people experiencing moments of personal grief and those making life-changing decisions.[6]

Heather Rusden, who came to Canberra from Adelaide in 1971, met Clark through David Campbell, and they quickly developed a close friendship. When Clark agreed to give Heather away when she was married in 1981, she was unprepared for the preliminary activities he had in mind. On the day before her wedding, Clark told her: 'Today is not the day to be with your fiancé. If I am to give you away, then you must come and spend the day in our house, the women will prepare you in their way and I will prepare you in mine.' When Rusden arrived at Tasmania Circle, Clark played her his favourite arias from *The Marriage of Figaro* and *Don Giovanni* and read the verse of John Donne and Ben Jonson. In the 1980s, when Rusden suffered several bouts of cancer, he visited her frequently, sometimes daily. Telegrams arrived in Italian and Clark gave her a copy of *Anna Karenina*: 'You're going through a terrible time,' he told her, 'and you should read about another woman going through that and then we'll talk about it.' Giving literature to friends in moments of crisis was Clark's form of pastoral care. 'Manning was always concerned with people's suffering,' Rusden later remembered. 'He suggested praying to me. He wanted to explore how people live, how they approached life and how they coped with what life dealt them. He had this largesse. He was a true friend, I felt I could ask anything and when one did ask the world was offered.' Rusden kept the cards Clark sent her when she was ill: 'ask for strength and all will be well'; 'read the last paragraph of Anna Karenina and ask for strength. Keep your courage up'; 'music love and belief are the three great mysteries, love Manning'.[7]

Many of Clark's friends told similar stories. In October 1970, when the question of Humphrey McQueen's reappointment as a tutor at the ANU came up for consideration, Clark sat in on one of McQueen's tutorials. During the class the phone rang. McQueen answered only to be told that a friend in Queensland had committed suicide. He said he'd ring back and continued with the tutorial. Later that afternoon, McQueen ran into Clark in the corridor and explained the phone call. Clark was understanding. At that moment McQueen felt he knew that he would be reappointed. 'Manning saw my response to what had happened as an example of my closeness to the "great questions of life".' This was Clark's sixth sense: to recognise sensitivity and vulnerability in others. His talent for penning moving condolence letters revealed another side to his ministering. Death was an opportunity. In obituaries and notes of sympathy he could say something that memorialised both the deceased and himself. His letter to Barbara Todd, on the death of her husband Murray, an old friend of Clark's in Canberra, was typical:

> This will be an all too inadequate attempt to express sympathy to you … [Murray was] a passionate pilgrim for the meaning of life. I remember moments of great pleasure with him in pursuits as varied as the shooting of rabbits and the discovery of truth … I shall remember coming to Canberra partly because it meant meeting Murray … I would like to say something to comfort you. During the last visit to Hobart I sensed in both of you a spiritual strength which is not given to many human beings. That will sustain you during your terrible deprivation. I lit a candle for Murray in St. Christopher's on the day he was buried because he would like to be remembered there, and because one wanted to do something in tribute to what you both had achieved in our hearts. That candle was quickly consumed, but as I walked home one felt that people like Murray reminded me of what a tremendous thing a human being is, for even if he was cut down just when he was beginning to enjoy the prizes of his worldly endeavours, one could say: This was a man.
>
> In sympathy, yours ever, M. Clark[8]

The secular priest in Clark ministered to both friends and enemies. After Malcolm Ellis died in 1969, Clark wrote a moving letter to his widow, Gwen. He tended the sick and the dying whether they had been close to him or not. Bid Williams, whose husband Mick had been recruited by Clark to the History Department at the ANU in the late 1960s, found Clark's behaviour on the death of her husband and son upsetting.

Mick thought Manning was selfish, particularly because he was forced to shoulder much of the administrative load in the department. In 1987, as Mick lay dying in hospital, Clark suddenly became a regular visitor. I found this offensive. He gave me one set of the six volumes, inscribed of course, and then shortly afterwards, forgetting he had done so, he gave me another set. Mick was Manning's hostage to fortune. He wanted to make a sacrifice of Mick, an offering to the Gods in place of himself.

When Bid's son committed suicide shortly before Mick died, Clark attended the funeral, standing up at the wake to 'make a highly theatrical and flowery speech'. This was despite the fact that Clark had had little contact with her son for years. 'One had the impression,' said Bid, 'that he was granting us a favour.' Unlike Dymphna, whom she admired for her loyalty, hospitality and dignity, she found Clark's behaviour 'deeply hurtful'. 'Manning would refuse to acknowledge me, although I was a former student of his in Melbourne and I had been inside his own home. Whenever he passed me in the street, he would fix his eyes firmly in the middle distance and pretend I wasn't there.'[9]

Clark's hunger to minister was often more about his own needs than his concern for others. He thought of himself as a 'soul doctor', a counsellor who sought out those whose flaws and weaknesses were visible. Witnessing their distress was an opportunity for Clark to make what he called a 'creative response to suffering', pouring all that he had learnt from the vulnerability of others into his writing. It was also a chance to mimic Christ. His obituaries and letters of condolence raised the dead to eternal life—'the earth would never see their like again'. Poet and friend Douglas Stewart, who died in 1985, Clark praised as 'a man who will be read in centuries to come for his wisdom', his 'mighty spirit encased within his frail clay'. Adept at entombing the dead in his own mythology, his benedictions managed to move even those who were deeply suspicious of him, such as John La Nauze, who thanked him for his 'very moving' letters. Words were the currency of Clark's friendship and love. When the postmaster at Manuka spotted him approaching the counter, he immediately reached for his book of stamps. Clark's postcards, with their one-line messages—'trumpeter—what are you sounding now?'—were memorable for each recipient, despite the fact that he often repeated the same lines to different correspondents, just as he did when he inscribed his books to friends: 'in memory of so much'.[10]

As Clark's fame rose steadily in the 1970s and 1980s, he tended to the nation as if it were a friend in need. American historian Edmund Morgan, who formed a close friendship with both Clark and Dymphna during these years, was struck by his love for Australia. 'I think he felt a responsibility to speak out, for he became "Mr. Australia",' Morgan recalled. 'What many of his detractors could never really grasp was what a profoundly patriotic Australian he was.' Unlike Patrick White, who reflected the day after he won the Nobel Prize in 1973, 'I don't really feel Australian', Clark made a career out of feeling Australian. By the mid-1960s, the ideological cornerstones of the political and social environment in which his worldview was formed had started to crumble. The last decades of his life straddled Australia's involvement in the Vietnam War (1965–72), the groundswell of revisionist history, Aboriginal protest, women's liberation, Britain's entry into the European Economic Community in 1973, the election and dismissal of the Whitlam Labor government (1972–75), the Australian Bicentenary in 1988, and finally, with the fall of the Berlin Wall in 1989, the end of the Cold War. Throughout all this time, Clark played a central role in historical and political debates, cavorting on the national stage in his slightly tattered, black, three-piece suit, his watch chain dangling from his fob pocket, his long, thin legs anchored in paddock-bashing boots and, atop the lean, grave, goatee-bearded face of the old man, his signature—the crumpled weather-beaten hat.[11]

The story of Clark's public life lies at the heart of one of the great political and historical shifts in twentieth-century Australia. The decline of the idea of Australia as a fundamentally British nation combined with the surge in non-British immigration during the postwar period forced to the centre of public debate the question of Australian identity, both cultural and political. Australia, for so long deemed to be without history, suddenly needed to narrate its history in a way that it had never had to do before. So many of the tensions that had long informed Clark's intellectual life were now beginning to animate Australia's political and cultural life—the end of the White Australia policy, the relationship between Australia and Britain and the historical foundations of a new national identity. Clark not only observed these

Clark at Dunkeld, Victoria, 14 September 1980

changes; he inflamed them. And he found himself in an unusual position: as an historian on the national stage he attempted to step up and play the role created by the very same historical moment he observed. Like virtually every aspect of his life, his public roles were ambiguous; he espoused radical positions but he eschewed radical politics; he dressed like the rural parson but he embraced modish political causes. Throughout all of these stances, the one consistent and abiding theme of his life, both as historian and public intellectual, remained his passion for Australia. While so many other writers and intellectuals of his generation left for Europe or the United States, never to return, Clark didn't for a moment doubt that his creative path lay at home. As the person so often credited for arousing public interest in Australian history, the story of his final years is inextricably linked with Australia's struggle for political and cultural independence in the late twentieth century. Yet the story is not simply one of Clark's will alone. At the end of the twentieth century, the Australian people were looking for guidance. Manning Clark, the national sage, was Australia's creation as much as he was a product of his own self-invention.

THE PROPHET AND THE PRIME MINISTER

At 2 pm on a Sunday afternoon in October 1963, Clark accompanied two New Zealand graduate students, John Salmond and Michael Bassett, to a White Citizens council rally in Durham Stadium, North Carolina, where Alabama's newly elected Governor, George Wallace, was the featured speaker. The crowd was hyped up. Race relations in America's South were on a knife's edge. Only weeks earlier, four girls attending Sunday School in Birmingham, Alabama, had been killed when a bomb exploded in their Baptist Church, the place where many of the city's civil rights meetings had also been held. Six months earlier, police in Birmingham had turned fire hoses and attack dogs on black protesters. The situation was volatile. As Salmond walked into the stadium with Bassett and Clark, he was greeted by a sea of Ku Klux Klan, many in full regalia. 'Dressed in black, with his beard and bush hat', Clark, as Salmond recalled, 'cut a conspicuous figure'. Offended by the simmering undertones of violence towards black Americans, Clark suddenly began to shout out 'derogatory remarks' at the top of his voice, deriding the Klansmen as 'strutting galahs'. Salmond and Bassett, both of whom had lived in the South for some time, were alarmed. Clark seemed oblivious to 'the ugly mood of the crowd'. As Salmond remembered: 'We decided we needed to get him out of there without delay. I don't think Manning had any sense of the danger he was in. Certainly he did not want to leave and was somewhat reproachful of us for insisting that he do so.' Although the Klansmen were most likely unfamiliar with the galah, Clark's tone was 'contemptuous'. He did not lack courage in speaking out. Nor was he afraid to stand alone with his views.[12]

By 1964 Clark was already well known for his unorthodox public stances, both at home and in the United Kingdom, where *The Times* described him as one of Australia's 'prominent names abroad', impressed as much by his hat as by his ideas. A few weeks later, when Clark met the poet Philip Larkin in Hull, Larkin told him that, after reading the article in *The Times*, he had the impression that Clark was a wild man from the outback. Clark's theatricality was having the desired effect—his costume drama was attracting much attention. The publicity spurred him on. At home, newspaper editors asked him to write on everything from the erection of the Berlin Wall in 1961 to the historical context of Beethoven's fifth symphony, the meaning of Christmas, and man's landing on the moon in 1969. He rarely declined requests to write feature articles or opinion pieces. Given the chance to write for a public audience, he wrote effortlessly, the handwritten manuscripts in his papers revealing few corrections or amendments.[13]

One of the most striking features of Clark's archive of public writings is the moment when their volume rises sharply: between 1968 and 1972, the folders almost double in size. These were the years in which he began to receive more and more correspondence in response to his publications— hopeful authors sending poems, articles or whole manuscripts, artists and novelists writing out of admiration, his peers asking him to recommend books for publication, speaking invitations from every conceivable organisation, overseas enquiries and many referee requests. The demands on his time increased significantly. Before 1968, Clark wrote more book and theatre reviews than opinion pieces. In the late 1960s, he began to address the linked questions of Australia's national identity and the country's future. 'New nationalism', a term coined by Donald Horne in 1968, was beginning to drive much of the public discussion on Australia's position in a post-imperial world. Australian intellectuals and writers had been in search of a 'new national idea' since Clem Christesen founded *Meanjin* in 1940, but only in the 1960s, driven by Britain's retreat to Europe, did the idea gather any sense of urgency. The Liberal Prime Minister John Gorton, as soon as he succeeded Harold Holt as prime minister in 1968, lent his voice to the new national mood. With the bicentenary of James Cook's 'discovery' of the continent approaching, Clark was increasingly asked to explain the relevance of the nation's past to the Australian people. From the moment he stepped up to the pedestal, the question of Australia's independence from Britain began to infiltrate and guide the direction of *A History of Australia*, his public role gradually coming to define his historical writing. Yet long before Clark rose to the level of a national celebrity in the early 1970s, much of the ideological perspective that informed his view of Australia's future was firmly set in place.[14]

As early as 1960, with the Cold War at its height, he described Australia as a 'derived ... civilisation in decay', characterised by the 'dreariest hedonism'. The threat of a nuclear war between the United States and the Soviet Union fuelled his apocalyptic vision. Australia, he prophesied in 1962, would have to choose between 'dullness and destruction'. He warned of the 'holocausts to come' and wondered if Australian society would even survive in the near future. Had Australians woken too late, he wondered, to the fact that their society still championed racial inequality? Would they be punished? Clark's opposition to the Vietnam War—he insisted Australia support Vietnamese 'self determination'—and his call for an Australia fully independent from both Britain and the United States placed him at the forefront of progressive thinking. In other ways he was defiantly old-fashioned. Deeply suspicious of industrialisation, suburbia and new technology—the forces that shaped Australian society at the end of the twentieth century—Clark was at once forward looking and regressive in his public pronouncements. What marked him out from almost every comparable intellectual of his generation was the breadth of his historical gaze. He saw Australia's future not only in terms of its historical relationship with Britain but also against the history of the rise and fall of human civilisations—from Ancient Greece and Rome to the Portuguese, Spanish and Dutch empires—a background that made the settler grip on the ancient continent of Australia appear tenuous.[15]

In 1968, shortly after the British Government announced that it would withdraw its armed forces east of Suez, Clark wrote a long article for *The Times*, wondering whether the end of European domination in Asia might eventually mean 'the end of Europe in Australia'. If the country continued to side with the old imperial powers in Asia and the Pacific, those destined for the 'dustbin', he thought it might well be invaded or overrun by a more enlightened Asian power. Between 1968 and 1972, spurred on by the public interest in all things Australian and in the lead-up to Gough Whitlam's election as Prime Minister, Clark produced a stream of articles and speeches that laid the foundation for his ascending status in the years to come. It was the first burst of the intense public activity that would dictate nearly every day of his life from now on. Taken together, Clark's writings repositioned Australia at the end of the twentieth century. In July 1971, he was asked to speak on

ABC radio and address the question of Britain's entry into the Common Market. The result was a speech that crystallised nearly all his thinking over the previous decade on Australia's future.

All that a historian can do in our age of great confusion is either to preach a secular sermon, or to make a few prophecies. I am going to have a shot at prophecy. First I am going to prophesy that Britain's entry into the Common Market will hasten our becoming what Charles Darwin prophesied as long ago as 1838 we would become—namely, a commercial and manufacturing nation rather than a primary producing nation ... The question is: what is going to happen to us if and when we cease being British and become Australian? That takes me to my second prophecy: that we may soon suffer for having remained British for too long. That may seem like an extraordinary thing to say. So let me try to explain what I have in mind. Up to a point we are what we are in Australia—an outpost of British civilisation ... At the end of the eighteenth century the British transplanted their civilisation to various parts of the world—to North America, to South Africa, to India, to Malaya, to New Zealand and to Australia ... What we are living through [now] is the ebbing tide of British civilisation. That tide has gone out to sea in South Africa, India and Malaya. What is going to happen to us if the tide recedes from our shores? That will mean that for the first time in our history we will be in charge of our own destiny. That may prove too much for us. But if we cling to what remains of that tide are we not in danger of stepping out of the great river of life, and becoming like a billabong— stagnant, putrid and slimy ... My third prophecy—or forecast—is a much more hopeful one ... I suggest, or rather, prophesy, if that does not sound too pompous, that the entry of Britain into Europe strengthens the possibility of a third free force in the world.—This will give us an alternative to the greyness of Moscow and Peking and the over-ripe free enterprise society of America ... we have the chance to make our contribution to and comment on the human situation. We have a chance to tell people why things are as they are in Australia and about that complex fate of belonging spiritually to an older civilisation and yet being born in this weird, harsh, uncouth, but very beautiful country. We have a chance to grow up, and stop being

An Eye for Eternity

boastful about things Australian with a snarl on our lips for the rest of the world. We have a chance to become citizens of the world.[16]

Here was Clark's talent for speaking as the voice of his generation. He spoke as if he was conversing with his audience on the other side of the kitchen table. Rather than talk down to them, he asked their permission to speak—'let me try to explain'. Instead of preaching he sounded puzzled—'sometimes I wonder'. And although he was reading from a script, he appeared to be thinking things through as he spoke—'it looks as though'. Clark had the ability to place himself on the same level as those listening to him, articulating the same hesitancy, curiosity and half-glimpsed under-standings of the world shared by ordinary people. But behind his humble delivery lay a rare perceptiveness that set him apart from so many of his contemporaries. Well aware of 'the ebbing tide of British civilisation' and the parallel rise of the Asian powers, Clark dreamt of an Australian nation that would have the confidence to reject both the unfettered capitalism of the West and the oppression of the communist East. He diagnosed the transi-tional stage in which Australia found itself: a nation grappling with the problem of finding a new national mythology at a time when all the tradi-tional bases of nationalism—race, ethnicity and a common culture—had either been discredited or undermined. His answer was an Australia that dared to be a nation without nationalism, a nation that was post-racial, post-ideological and post-British, in which patriotism would not be insular or parochial but genuinely outward looking. In a world in which globalisation was 'whittling away differences between nations and peoples', it appeared to be the only sensible path. In many of his opinion pieces, Clark laced this progressive philosophy with an old-fashioned Protestant moralism, berating Australians for their materialism, of which Bondi Beach was his favourite symbol. He wrote about the importance not only of a new national identity but of the architecture and living conditions in Australia's cities, including 'the pollution and conservation problem', issues that he gathered under one banner: 'quality of life'. Occasionally, he gave voice to the view that was being heard from the emerging Aboriginal protest movement in the wake of the Cook bicentenary—'we are invaders too, we invaded this country in

1770 and became stewards for a great past'. What Australians seemed unable to accept, said Clark, was that there were 'two cultures' in the country—'one Aboriginal, occupying 99.5 per cent of human history on the continent, and the other mainly European'. By 1971, Clark had channelled all of these ideas into the mounting tide of expectations surrounding the election of Australia's first Labor government in twenty-three years.[17]

Whenever the mood took him, Clark wrote to Gough Whitlam just as he had written to former Labor leaders Doc Evatt and Arthur Calwell. But his relationship with Whitlam was different. Clark admired Whitlam more than any other Labor leader since John Curtin. After Whitlam became Leader of the Opposition in 1967, the two men gradually developed a friendship. When Clark donated money to ALP election campaigns, he always sent the cheque to Whitlam personally. For Whitlam, he preserved a mixture of flattery and hyperbole. Only months before his election in December 1972, Whitlam received a letter from Clark telling him that he would become prime minister on the anniversary of the Battle of Austerlitz (2 December 1805), when Napoleon routed the Russo–Hungarian coalition that threatened the French Empire. The comparison played to Whitlam's tendency to hubris and it formed part of a long correspondence of mutual admiration. Whitlam was Clark's Pericles and Caesar in one—the erudite, imperious visionary who would lead Australia to the 'great river of life'. Clark told Whitlam that he was the only man who could give Australians pride and confidence in their politicians and their country—not in a jingoistic or arrogant way, he suggested, but by building a vision of 'better things for mankind'.[18]

From the publication of Volume II in 1968, Clark made a point of sending Whitlam a signed copy of each volume of *A History of Australia*. Whitlam responded warmly: 'I can think of no book of which I would rather have two copies than Manning Clark's *History of Australia*. One will be at the Lodge; the other at Kirribilli. For all that, I have yet to read it, but will no doubt do so with the greatest pleasure. I have no doubt that it is in the highest tradition of scholarship we have come to expect from Australia's most distinguished historian.' Whitlam was well aware how valuable Clark and the new vanguard of pro-Labor intellectuals had become to securing the Party's success. On 23 November 1972, Clark, together with Patrick White, Judith

Wright, David Campbell, Kenneth Myer and Keith Hancock, was one of sixteen signatories to an unprecedented open letter, published in every national capital daily, which urged Australians to vote for a change of government. The letter was couched as a plea. After 23 years in opposition, 'the top 16' argued, if the people did not elect Labor, the Party was in danger of 'disintegrating as a force in Australia's political life'.[19]

In the weeks after Whitlam's election on 2 December, Clark's correspondence alternated between maudlin, pleading letters to Dymphna in Brisbane and euphoric letters to the new ministers in the incoming Labor government in Canberra. 'God be praised,' he exclaimed to his old friend Jim Cairns; 'it has happened at last. Now we can move forward into the light … you, my dear Jim, have fought a great fight. Now you will make history.' With Whitlam in power, Clark's adulatory letters reached new heights of aggrandizement. He told Whitlam that he had 'rescued Australia' from the colonial white man's club. On matters that touched the nation's 'honour and conscience', Whitlam, he said, led by example. He had removed the stigma attached to attitudes towards the Aborigines. Across Australia, he had converted 'despair and uncertainty' about the future of the country into 'hope and confidence'. The prophet had found his Messiah.[20]

Sitting at his desk in his study, Clark looked out towards Capitol Hill, Whitlam's office in Old Parliament House barely two kilometres away. The two men's correspondence captured something of the innocence of Australia in the early 1970s—Clark's hieroglyphic script no different from any other letter he wrote, Whitlam's handwritten letters dispatched on notepad-size A6 paper, with a tiny coat of arms and the words 'Prime Minister Canberra' at the top of the page. In retrospect, it all seems so endearingly unpretentious.

Within months of Whitlam's election, newspaper editors sensed the 'sudden change in the cultural climate'. Novelist Robert Drewe, then in his late twenties, was features editor at the *Australian*, where the paper's new editor-in-chief, the 'fervent nationalist' Owen Thompson, 'a conservative larrikin in the classic News Ltd. mould', agreed to Drewe's suggestion to run a series of articles on the new nationalism. With Thompson's support, Drewe joined cartoonist Bruce Petty, travelling around Australia trying 'to gauge the change in mood', soliciting articles in the meantime from intellectuals such as Clark and Donald Horne. As Drewe recalled, Clark responded to his requests with vigour.

> Clark didn't offer himself, or step forward, so much as respond to the invitations. He gave good copy. He replied quickly, politely and professionally, and his answers were direct and full of rich imagery, without (importantly) any academic waffle or hedging. He was a pro. It was like dealing with one of the better novelists or poets—which I had to do in my other job as literary editor. And, I must say, I liked the idea of having such a seminal figure on board. I respected him, and so did the paper, when faced with the copy I'd got from him. In contrast to The Australian's take on him a generation and a dozen editors later, I can't recall a single argument about him, or any of his expressed views.[21]

Clark's contribution to Drewe's series was an example of his ability to be the mouthpiece for virtually every new political cause. Australia's 'new nationalists', he proclaimed, had acquired 'a deeper hope and confidence than their nineteenth century counterparts'. The old xenophobia was dead. Australia's male-dominated society, in which women had no place 'except in the kitchen and the bed', was also doomed. He finished on a note of doubt. Australians wanted to shed 'the last vestiges of British colonialism' but they still did not seem to know the answer to one simple question: 'Where did they belong?' Clark's skill was to pick up the threads of ideas already circulating in the culture and hold up a mirror to his readers and listeners. This was the art of becoming a public intellectual; synthesising and explaining what people already knew rather than telling them what they did not know. For Clark, the timing could not have been more propitious. At the very moment when he was preparing to retire from his position at the ANU, Whitlam's election had carved out a new role for him. By 1973, he was responding to invitations not only from the media but from government as well.[22]

Herbert ('Nugget') Coombs had chaired the Australia Council for the Arts—the body he had persuaded Prime Minister Harold Holt to establish the previous year—since he had retired as governor of the Reserve Bank in

1968. Coombs wrote to Clark regularly, seeking his assistance. Asked by Coombs to prepare material for Liberal Prime Minister William McMahon on 'general Australian questions', especially for McMahon's overseas trips, Clark obliged, always careful not to 'provide material which could be used for political purposes'. When Coombs was appointed as Whitlam's personal 'consultant' in 1972, Clark's connection with the incoming government strengthened. Eager to cement the ties between the Labor government and the intelligentsia, Coombs sought Clark's advice on a wide range of issues, even asking him in September 1973 for an 'assessment of the government's performance' and 'aspects of policies to which you believe greater attention should or should not be given'. One of the keys to Whitlam's initial success was his government's embrace of intellectuals who were sympathetic to Labor's cause. As Clark believed in the potential of a Labor government to act as an agent of national renewal, Whitlam and Coombs believed in the potential of intellectuals and artists to boost popular enthusiasm for the government's program of reform. The relationship was symbiotic. Yet there was an even more significant and long-lasting connection being forged. Whitlam's rise to power coincided with a period in which interest in Australian history intensified. As Whitlam's Minister for Immigration, Al Grassby, explained in 1973: 'Australians are only now beginning to discover their history ... Australian history has never adequately been written. The saga of the Australian people remains to be told.' For Labor, Clark was the historian who was writing Australia's story. But in that endeavour, he was not alone. Geoffrey Blainey, his former student from Melbourne, had already made an impact with his groundbreaking work *The Tyranny of Distance*, published in 1966. But unlike Clark, Blainey's work was not explicitly devoted to discovering 'who Australians were'. Nor, in the wake of Whitlam's election, was he as visible in the public eye.[23]

With every article Clark published praising Whitlam, he aligned the Labor Party with the positive and progressive trends in Australian history. Thus Whitlam became the first Australian prime minister in the post-British era to successfully identify his party with a patriotic vision of Australia's past. In this unofficial department, after only twelve months in government, Clark was already Whitlam's most energetic scribe. He not only popularised

Australian history, he helped to establish the nexus that would become an increasingly common feature of Australia's political landscape at the end of the twentieth century—between historians, the writing of Australian history, and the nation-defining mission of federal government. In the politics of vision, this was the beginning of Labor's temporary superiority over its conservative opponents and the basis of many of the spiteful attacks on Clark in the years ahead. Whitlam, together with Clark—the country's first professor of Australian History—created the impression that the Labor Party was the bulwark of an Australian historical tradition, one on which the nation's new identity was steadily being built, whereas the conservatives were portrayed as backward-looking philistines, their beady, mist-laden eyes gazing ever in the direction of England.

When Whitlam called a double-dissolution election for May 1974, Labor did not wait to be endorsed by the intellectuals who had lent the Party their support two years earlier. In April, Whitlam instructed his press secretary, Evan Williams, to invite prominent Australians to sign an open letter calling for the government's re-election. An election rally was planned for the Sydney Opera House on 13 May, only five days before polling day. Invited to speak, Clark telegrammed Whitlam offering the Prime Minister his enthusiastic endorsement. Whitlam was overjoyed: 'I was heartened by your telegram. Together we will write a new chapter—perhaps a new volume—in the history of Australia.' This was the apogee of Whitlam's personal alliance with Clark. In the weeks before the election Clark surpassed Whitlam's expectations, writing several opinion pieces which declared that the election was one of the most 'decisive moments in the history of mankind'. He even penned a personal letter for the press: 'Why I will vote for a Labor government, by Manning Clark', an endorsement which contained all the hallmarks of Clark's political interventions—dollops of hyperbole, stark moral choices and dire warnings of the violent overthrow of the social order. A vote for Whitlam, proclaimed Clark, was a vote for a man who had 'dreamed a great dream', a man with charisma, the leader of a party who saw 'a way forward for humanity without the evils and suffering of a revolution'. A vote for Billy Snedden and the Liberals was a vote to defend 'an unjust and corrupt social order' in which there would be wealth for a minority, and the strong would oppress the weak. If elected, the liberals would 'put the clock back' and Australia would run the risk of being convulsed by revolution in the future.[24]

A few weeks earlier, Clark was awarded the *Age* Book of the Year prize for Volume III. Reports in the press described him as the man whose 'history books were well known to probably every Australian student, school and university, for at least the past twenty years'. Clark's public declarations of support for Carlton, the VFL/AFL football club of which he became a member in May 1972, helped to endear him to a wider audience. In interviews, Clark spoke of his love of Carlton as he pulled photos of Henry Lawson from his wallet and exclaimed 'I'm passionately fond of Australia.' The popularity of his history was feeding directly into his new role as Whitlam's court his-torian. Each spurred the other on. Already, Clark was showing signs of being willing to write on any topic, unable, for instance, to resist the temptation to hold forth on the Pope's Easter message in March 1974, reminding his readers that 'the representative of the Galilee fisherman' had turned the minds of Australians 'towards the things that matter'— mystery and reverence. When Clark arrived at the Sydney Opera House on 13 May, the scene he encountered revealed much about the forces that were helping to shape his emergence as one of the nation's leading public intellectuals.[25]

In the Concert Hall, twenty handpicked 'writers, painters, sportsmen, academics, and theatre people' declared for a Whitlam government before a 'wildly happy' crowd of more than 3000 people. It was a new style of political campaigning. Led by Patrick White, whose Nobel Prize for Literature in 1973 had energised the entire arts community, Labor's celebrities ascended the stage one by one to announce their support for Whitlam and denounce the conservatives. Among them were painter Lloyd Rees, actor and theatre director John Bell, writer Frank Moorhouse, and actor Kate Fitzpatrick. White amused the audience, claiming the Opposition parties were 'mentally constipated'. Playwright David Williamson warned that a Liberal government would see Australia become a 'whingeing, selfish, crying, sycophantic little infant'. For colourful overstatement, Clark topped them all, cautioning that the Liberals would construct 'one huge second-hand car yard between

Sydney and Alice Springs' as soon as they were voted into office. Outside, unable to gain entrance, thousands of people sat on the Opera House steps, applauding enthusiastically. Clark was inspired by the atmosphere—what 'a great day, he wrote in his diary, '[I felt] in touch with the people, like being at Carlton football ground'.[26]

Labor won the election in May 1974 with a slightly reduced majority, but it still lacked control of the Senate. Since coming to power, Whitlam had succeeded in branding Labor as the party of ideas and culture, the only political party that would cultivate and protect Australia's emerging sense of national independence. For the coterie of writers and artists gathered at the Sydney Opera House, there was also a palpable sense of release: Whitlam's election two years earlier had represented an all-too-belated expression of cultural awakening. Finally, it seemed that Australia had a government that recognised the importance of intellectuals and artists, a government that had the courage to break with Australia's colonial mentality and 'go it alone'. Whitlam's urbanity was also the antithesis of the more vulgar images of Australia that so offended Clark and White. Accepting his Australian of the Year award in January 1974, White praised the likes of Clark and Barry Humphries for their telling critiques of Australia. Clark, White suggested, had shown Australians that their essential characteristics were the same as their nineteenth-century forebears, 'the same politicians abusing one another in larrikin style, the same class-consciousness in a classless society— money consciousness might be nearer the mark—the same violence and drunkenness in the streets'. In private, White made the point more bluntly, telling Clark that his work had shown that Australians remained 'the same pack of snarling mongrel dogs'.[27]

In the early 1970s, White and Clark were in their honeymoon period, sharing dinner occasionally at White's home in Martin Road, overlooking Sydney's Centennial Park. As always, the gossip-hungry novelist with the scalpel-like eye was extremely perceptive on the foibles of those closest to him. Attending a production of *The Magic Flute* with the Clarks at Sydney Opera House in early 1974, White admitted that he found Dymphna 'difficult to come to terms with'. 'I'm told she only blossoms when he isn't there,' he wrote to Geoffrey Dutton. 'That must go for both of them.' The two men's correspondence continued to reveal their mutual admiration for one another's work. Clark confessed to White that he envied his 'power to evoke the frame of life' that surrounded everyone in Australia. Meanwhile, White read Volume II of Clark's *History* as he wrote *The Vivisector*, just as Clark had read *Riders in the Chariot* and *The Solid Mandala* during the writing of Volumes I and II. Sending Clark a copy of *The Eye of the Storm* in 1973, White flattered him after reading the beginning of Volume III: 'I see you have lost none of your power.' Eight months later, accepting his Australian of the Year award, White used the same volume as 'a pivot' to help him through the ordeal of public performance, chuffed that his speech, despite being delivered without his false teeth which broke up while he was eating an hors d'oeuvre, had given offence to the establishment.[28]

Although Clark's enthusiasm for White was more gushing, both men had the sense that they were ploughing parallel fields, following in the tracks of Australia's explorers and painters, writing over the country's silence. Since their first meeting in the 1950s, they shared a love–hate relationship with Australia. While they were both deeply devoted to understanding the country's environment and its effect on all who lived there, they recoiled from their fellow countrymen, described by Clark as sitting mindlessly 'with their two car families and their boat culture' and by Barry Humphries with 'their belly telly, their tinnies, their tubes, their snow bunnies and no complications'. This was White's 'great Australian emptiness' and Clark's 'greed and titillation culture'—suburban, materialist and anti-intellectual—everything the two writers despised. Their model was European high culture—Mozart, Bach, Rembrandt and Dostoyevsky—the cultural heartland with which they hoped their own work would one day help to connect their fellow Australians.

With a Labor government in power, Clark and White both felt a duty to assert a more sophisticated and cosmopolitan image of their country. Writing was not enough. 'Gough Whitlam and other politicians of like mind,' Clark insisted, 'badly need the help of the leaders of opinion ... to educate us all on what this is all about.' Whitlam's office felt the same way. Graham Freudenberg, Whitlam's speechwriter, wrote to Clark to convey his admiration: 'Your unique insights are needed, now as never before, to explain to us the grand themes of our history ... we need an understanding of the whole story. If you fail to find the meaning of that whole story, we shall all fail in the search for the true meaning of our existence in Australia.' Freudenberg saw that Clark's achievements went 'beyond scholarship'. Clark, he said, had the 'capacity to instil an understanding and inspire a kind of love, not only for the history, but for the historian himself.' Like Freudenberg, Whitlam and Clark believed that they were on the same mission. It was incumbent upon intellectuals and political leaders to provide the country with an ambitious, even epic, political vision. Power was a creative opportunity. During the twenty-three years of conservative government from 1949 to 1972, many intellectuals and artists felt unrecognised and undervalued in their own country. In April 1973, when Clem Christesen invited Clark to contribute an essay on the Menzies years for *Meanjin*, he managed to express the frustration that drove so many writers and artists to align themselves publicly with Whitlam.

Despite the teach-ins, the peace campaigns, the protest marches, the gaolings of war resisters, the political squabbles, the tensions generated did not provide high drama (in the sense of what happened in France during May 1968, or over many years in the USA, etc.) No imperative notes sounded above the general dullness and flatness, the suffocating blandness, the 'steak-fed vacuity' of Australian life. We all tended to march, or sleep-walk, under a 'dun-coloured banner'. A contributing factor was of course the long divorce between intellect and political power ... the mindless clichés of the Menzies government resulted in a sort of intellectual torpor. Can you recall a single utterance from a political leader during those long years which quickened our artists and intellectuals? There was absolutely nothing resembling that brief period when American intellectuals did quicken to the stimulus of the Kennedy era ... [but] I hope [this] will now happen during the Whitlam era. During the Long Wait, no wonder our writers failed to develop techniques, energies, moral and nervous recognitions similar to those evident in certain foreign literatures ... I think it is true to say that our political leadership has never made manifest a belief that it is through the various forms of art that the inherent tendencies of a society are made manifest, made visible and potent ... during the Big Drought lots of artists got well and truly clobbered; indeed lots of them finally fled the country.[29]

When Clark put his mind to writing his contribution for *Meanjin*, he fulfilled Christesen's brief, casting the Menzies era as 'the years of unleavened bread', an image that neatly captured Left stereotypes of the Menzies government for decades to come. But the euphoria that accompanied Whitlam's election blinded many writers to the political consequences of being seen as partisan warriors. Their relationship with Labor quickly became a cosy marriage. In the media and at formal ALP meetings, Clark continued to heap praise on Whitlam at every opportunity—'you are making us all proud again to be Australians'—often in such grandiloquent and fawning language that, well before Whitlam lost power in 1975, Clark was already a marked man in some conservative circles. At the ANU, many of his colleagues grew concerned about his public affiliation with the Labor Party, not to mention his sage-like demeanour.[30]

Within two years of Whitlam's election in 1972, Clark was appointed to the new Australian Literature Board and to the committee to judge a new national anthem. David Malouf, then in his late thirties, sat in on the first meetings of the Literature Board with Clark. Among others, he was joined by poets AD Hope and Elizabeth Riddell, Geoffrey Dutton, Judah Waten and, in the chair, Geoffrey Blainey. In his short eighteen-month stay on the board, Malouf was amazed at the behaviour of some of the older members of the board.

After lunches, when some would consume a considerable amount of wine, it was quite common for them to doze off in the meeting. Geoff would be in the chair and Manning, interrupting, would simply blurt out the first thing that came into his head, such as 'Geoff, have I ever told you I was at university with Ted Heath?' 'Go on, Manning,' Geoff would say.

As a member of the Literature Board, Clark did everything he could to assist and encourage Australian writers. This was the opportunity he believed Whitlam had given him—to foster the development of Australian culture.

And he took his responsibilities far beyond the boardroom, making a concerted effort to correspond with younger writers. By the mid-1970s, he had received letters of thanks from Murray Bail, Christopher Koch, Tom Keneally and many others. Later, he supported literary critic Peter Craven's efforts to secure funding for the literary journal *Scripsi*. Clark's work and his public statements inspired Craven, who saw that he had enlarged the possibility of what Australia could become. He had given so many writers a stronger belief in their own potential. For Robert Drewe, Clark's encouragement proved crucial in determining his future career.

> Manning was extremely encouraging to me as a young writer and I believe he was instrumental in my gaining a literary grant to complete my first book, *The Savage Crows,* which though a contemporary novel had an historical basis in the genocide of the Tasmanian Aborigines. I'd written half the book at the kitchen table at night, after work, but had no idea if I was on the right track, imaginatively and creatively. It wasn't much money: $9000, but the grant meant peer approval for my manuscript. In that sense Manning was responsible for changing the direction of my life, giving me the confidence to leave journalism and become a novelist at 28, and I've always been grateful to him for that.[31]

Australian writers and artists had never occupied the exalted position they found themselves accorded under Whitlam. Novelists, playwrights, painters, actors, dancers, musicians and historians were not only respected, they were seen as cultural engineers. In June 1975, when Whitlam announced the first recipients of the Companion of the Order of Australia under the new Australian honours system, Patrick White, Nugget Coombs, Dame Joan Sutherland and Clark were among them. When Clark received Whitlam's telegram telling him of his award he was elated: 'I little thought … that I would receive recognition from your "creative fire". But I think you know how pleased I am.' Taking the opportunity to remind Whitlam that Australia had the chance to 'show the world there was another possibility than the American answer or the Soviet answer to the problems of the world', Clark asked him to work with him to achieve the goal. 'The fruit, as you know,' he told

Whitlam, 'never falls far from the tree.' Throughout 1975, as Whitlam's government continued to lurch from one crisis to the next, their friendship deepened—Clark sending more donations and telegrams of support as he urged Whitlam to end mining on Fraser Island, and Whitlam, after a thousand days in power, even more appreciative of Clark's assistance: 'Dear Manning, Many thanks for your telegram. Your support will make the next thousand days much easier to bear, much richer in inspiration, and even more certain of completion.' Whitlam felt 'honoured' to speak on the same platform as Clark. No other intellectual had given him such unqualified public endorsement.[32]

During the tense weeks of October and early November, when the Liberal Opposition Leader Malcolm Fraser blocked the government's supply bills, Clark walked down to Old Parliament House several times to observe the train of events at close quarters. On one occasion, he met Drewe.

They were politically tense times and I was there to spend the day with Malcolm Fraser for a *Bulletin* cover story. I saw Manning on the Parliament House steps, we said hello, he inquired what I was there for, and I told him. He seemed very jolly for 10 a.m. in the morning. Then he said something that has stuck in my mind because of its risqué Aussie quirkiness. He said, 'Here's something to ask him: Malcolm, let's have a look at your cock.'

Clark's presence at Old Parliament House was one indication of his growing concern that Whitlam's days were numbered. As early as April 1975, he had feared Australia was about to pass through 'a terrible time', one that might involve widespread violence. Confronted with radical student politics in his last years at the ANU in the early 1970s—sit-ins, student protesters taking over the Chancellery and increasing disrespect for the authority of teachers and staff—Clark was disillusioned. As his colleague Ken Inglis has explained, 'the whole rhetoric of Maoism in those years made Manning feel that there was a kind of iconoclastic cultural revolution in the air which had no time, no place for people like him. The radical students, in their turn—or enough of them to distress him—heard in his lectures a vacuous, gentle (even worse, gentlemanly) liberalism'. Clark's sense of alienation from university life in Canberra was now complete. Unlike the Old Left, which had 'compassion and moral passion', Clark believed the New Left were bent on making life 'hideous'. He felt intimidated by 'revolutionary students who threatened to tear down everything that was worthwhile', fearing that, if Whitlam lost power, the radical movements might gain an even stronger foothold. The constitutional impasse—Fraser, in control of the Senate and blocking supply, and Whitlam, the recently re-elected Prime Minister refusing to call an election—continued into the first weeks of November.[33]

When the Governor-General, Sir John Kerr, resolved the crisis by dismissing the Whitlam government on 11 November 1975, and Fraser, as caretaker Prime Minister, called an election, Clark was in his office in the Chifley Library at the ANU. Contacted by the *Australian*, he blamed 'the petty bourgeois attitudes of the Australian people' and warned that, if a conservative government came to power, 'the next step forward for change would be much more likely to be violent'. Any temporary government of Fraser's, he argued, would not be allowed to govern. The unions, students and intellectuals would see to that. The issue was too serious, Clark said, for him to do 'a eunuch act of academic detachment'—he had to nail his colours to the mast. Six weeks later, when Whitlam's government was decimated at the election on 13 December, Clark had just arrived in England, on his way from the east coast of the United States, where he had been on another mission on behalf of Whitlam—establishing a Chair of Australian Studies at Harvard. It was one of the rare occasions in the 1970s when his diary recorded a political event: 'that fatal election result, avalanche against Labor, punishment for their weaknesses'. From Derby, he telegrammed Whitlam a message of sympathy. Then he wrote to Dymphna of his 'spiritual anguish' at the 'terrible punishment handed out to Gough Whitlam'. By the time he arrived back in Canberra two weeks later, there were two letters waiting for him from the former Prime Minister. In the first, written three days after his drubbing at the polls, Whitlam distanced himself from Clark's warnings of violence and revolution—'I know, from my personal association with you, that you are a man of the highest principles. I trust that democracy and justice will always prevail and that the parliamentary system will remain the sole tool of reform.' In the second, with more time to reflect on the result, Whitlam offered Clark a brutally frank assessment of his government's defeat.

An Eye for Eternity

Dear Manning

Your message of support was, as always, a comfort and an inspiration to me. Whatever the future may hold I shall value beyond words your continuing friendship and understanding. There are few people to whom one can express a candid view on recent events without seeming to be grumbling or looking for excuses. I suppose the simplest explanation of 13 December is that any government that presides over a recession and inflation—whatever the cause or whatever its response—is headed for electoral defeat. Perhaps we are too fond of believing that Australians would behave differently from any other people. Yet perhaps, had it not been for the constitutional issue and the emphasis we gave it, our defeat would have been greater. Do we thank Kerr for that?

Yours Ever, Gough.[34]

Whitlam had a far more realistic view of his government's failings than Clark. In the months after the 1977 election and well into the 1980s, Clark continued to cast Whitlam as a victim of forces beyond his control. In January 1976, he wrote for the *Australian* a feature article, 'History will be kinder to Labor than the People', which provoked a storm of controversy. Whitlam's years, said Clark, were the 'days of glory'. His government was like 'beautiful birds … trapped under the nets of the fowlers of this world … the men in black, those last-ditch defenders of a corrupt, decaying and obsolete society'. Australia had lost a prime minister who had believed in 'the cultivation of an Australian national sentiment', in contrast to the 'pro-British, archaic, anachronistic philistinism of their predecessors, men with the values, hearts and mental horizons of the bookkeepers, the accountants, the gravediggers of society'. It was Clark in full flight—thunderous polemic from the prophet who felt Australia had been cheated of its one chance of being led by a truly visionary leader. Although bitter, Patrick White told him that he was being too gloomy: 'Bad as things are, I can't feel quite as pessimistic as you.' But for Clark, Whitlam's dismissal, with its symbolic overtones of colonial dependence epitomised in the top hat and tails worn by Sir John Kerr, sharpened the old divisions in his thinking.[35]

After Whitlam's departure as prime minister, Clark began to cast Australia's quest for independence as an aspiration impeded by the British imperial legacy. The Dismissal, as it became known, coloured his view of Australia's past. The complex themes of his earlier volumes were reduced to one polarised struggle—the battle between Henry Lawson's 'old dead tree' and the 'young tree green'. Unlike in much of his earlier work, British characters became caricatures, as did conservative Australian politicians—a prime example being Clark's telling of the story of Australian federation in Volume V, in which 'the federation fathers' were condemned for tugging their forelocks to the British. Nor did he give up his apocalyptic pronouncements. He continued to warn of a violent revolution engulfing Australian society, most famously in 1978, in a speech delivered at a graduation ceremony at Wollongong University, where he spoke like the Old Testament God of Wrath, as if punishing the people for their sins.

> At the moment there is a lull: a great dullness so deep that no one can even fathom it has descended on us. But it looks as though this might be the calm before a great storm: a tempest or, to change the image, a cleansing fire, or a destructive fire may sweep over our ancient continent, stirring up the madness in men's and women's hearts—maybe a fratricidal war. We might all be tried in a fiery furnace ... the great question we have to face is whether we human beings will be able to rise out of the ashes after the fire has passed through ... [but] don't lose heart or faith, there is an eternal city and remember there are dogs outside the eternal city. Do not let them in ... Even after terrible things happen in our country—and I think they will—those who stand on entrenched ground will still hear the music of the spheres.[36]

At face value, the rhetoric appeared fanciful. Clark was not a supporter of revolution. Fond of prophesying violent conflict, he admitted to ABC TV's *Four Corners* in 1978 that he was not one to fight. Nor did he wish for a violent struggle to bring down the conservatives; 'that way madness lies'. Yet he seemed unable to appreciate that his comments could easily be read as condoning revolution, insisting he did not understand why he had been 'bombarded' by the media after the speech. When pressed, he explained his thinking. Perhaps the New Left would seize power in a revolution. How this might happen he did not say. Many intellectuals read the events of 11 November 1975 as treachery, blaming Malcolm Fraser, Sir John Kerr, and the Australian people for failing to return Whitlam to power in the election that followed. Writing to Geoffrey Dutton, Patrick White could barely contain his rage: 'this rotten hypocritical country really deserves a revolution'. Clark took the same sentiment one step further, delivering across the country lectures and speeches in which he appeared to relish the prospect of Australia being cast into an inferno. Ever fond of complaining about Australians' petit-bourgeois values, Clark knew that the chances of revolution in the 1970s were almost non-existent, just as they had been for nearly all of Australia's settler history. Why, then, did he persist with his prophecies of destruction for several years after Whitlam's dismissal? One of the passages Clark marked up in Dostoyevsky's letters offers part of the explanation.[37]

In 1871, Dostoyevsky was writing *The Devils* at the time of the Franco-Prussian War. In St Petersburg, the war had dried up credit and generally made life more difficult. But Dostoyevsky saw the war as a necessary corrective. 'Without war,' he stressed, 'man becomes sclerotic from living in comfort and wealth and completely loses his capacity for generous ideas and feelings, and imperceptibly becomes brutal and lapses into barbarism. I am speaking here of whole nations. Without suffering, happiness cannot be understood. The ideal passes through suffering like gold through fire. The heavenly kingdom is attained through effort.' Dostoyevsky's thinking, like Clark's, was deeply influenced by Christian notions of sin and salvation. War, famine, flood, fire and destruction were acts of heavenly speech, God's way of punishing the morally corrupt. Clark's call for a cleansing fire was a cry for spiritual redemption. His visions mimicked those of Dostoyevsky, who was fond of 'predicting the downfall of European civilisation'. As Clark told his former Melbourne colleague Kathleen Fitzpatrick in late 1976, 'our present society is sick … I believe there will be one or two hundred years of near anarchy in the world, during which monsters will appear as saviours … those monsters will be well dressed, and have good manners. Dostoyevsky saw the English country gentleman as a devil.'

In a more worrying fashion, Clark was starting to believe in his prophetic powers. 'I think there are people who have "seen" more than most people,' he reflected.

> Vision is 'to see', it comes from the Latin words 'to see'. There is also the Greek word 'psychedelic' which is used a lot at the moment, psychedelic drugs. Now, ethnologically, the word 'psychedelic' means to expand the mind, and I think a person who has seen a lot can help others to expand their minds, and to see more than they normally see.

By the end of the Whitlam era, Clark saw himself as one of the mind expanders, someone with profound insight into the human condition, a prophet who had a responsibility to lead his people. As he grew older, his appearance began to resemble his manner of speech: his bearded face gaunt, his expression grave, his clothes swimming on his angular frame like the robes of a holy man.[38]

In the years following the Dismissal, the intellectuals and artists who had forged an alliance with Whitlam remained loyal to him. After losing two elections, Whitlam resigned as leader of the Labor Party in December 1977. At a public testimonial given for him in Canberra's neo-Georgian Albert Hall the following January, the arts community chanted in unison: 'We want Gough'. Clark and White were there, believing like Judith Wright that 'Australia would never see another Gough Whitlam'. The atmosphere was not one of defeat but of a 'relaunched political crusade'. In April 1978, at yet another testimonial dinner in Canberra, Clark presented Whitlam with five books, three of them in classical Greek, including the works of Homer. One book—*The Hellenica*, by Xenophon of Athens—Clark selected for Whitlam because he believed the events it described (the battle between the oligarchs and the democrats) paralleled Australia's political turmoil in 1975. The Spartans, he claimed, with their belief in toughness and discipline, had values more like Fraser and the Liberal Party. Even after Whitlam's political defeat, Clark could only see his idealism, and he was reluctant to let the dream go. His association with Whitlam bolstered his confidence and ego. Praise from his hero was the highest praise of all—'Sydney 4 August 1981: Gough

Whitlam launched the illustrated edition of *A Short History of Australia* at Co-op Book Shop, Bay St Broadway. He praised my contribution to Australian History, spoke of me as a man who had changed the attitude of Australians to their country.' When Whitlam reviewed Volume Five later that year, he offered an interpretation of Clark's work that was unsurpassed for its glowing endorsement:

> Manning Clark is responsible above all others for the creation of popular interest in Australia's history. No one has done more to refute the myth that Australia has no history, the myth used for generations to keep Australian history out of our schools and even our universities, reinforcing the dominance of the imperial and provincial ethos in Australian life and character ... Clark belongs to that select band of historians who by writing history, change history ...That is the highest measure of all art, philosophy, literature and historiography ... [He] has changed the way we think about ourselves, and therefore, the way we act, the shape we try to give our nation, the contribution we believe we can make to civilisation ... In all Manning Clark's works, there is one central theme, one central question, the question 'Who are we?' ... Manning Clark's greatness is that he first, and for a long time alone, addressed himself to this supreme question. He has tried to give, to the people for and about whom he has written, the answer to that question with more success than any historian since Thucydides. He is not a vainglorious historian. Athens and Sparta were not superpowers, nor is Australia. Manning Clark not only asks the question, 'Who are we?', but is himself part of the answer. Whatever else we have done, Australia has produced Manning Clark. We claim him entirely for ourselves, though he does indeed belong to the ages. And a nation which produced a Manning Clark and a nation and a generation which can claim a Manning Clark as its representative, need not entirely fear the verdict of history.[39]

Whitlam's extravagant praise and shrewd judgement could not hide the fact that he said nothing about the quality of *A History of Australia*. He reviewed Clark's public life, not Volume V, and he kept his views on the quality of Clark's historical writing to himself. As Clark refused to

Gough Whitlam and Manning Clark at the launch of Volume V

acknowledge Whitlam's political flaws, Whitlam refused to engage in critical discussion of Clark as a historian. In public, both men preferred to cling to the myths they had helped create of one another—Clark busily spinning the rhetorical halo around Australia's saviour and Whitlam sculpting Clark in the image of Thucydides, the historian who gave life and meaning to the ideal of the nation for which Whitlam had fought and died a tragic political death. In the 1970s, so many Australian writers and artists were as one with them, hungry for the inspiration and idealism both men provided, long lamenting the loss of their 'beautiful birds trapped in the fowlers' net'.

THE COUNTERATTACK BEGINS

In May 1975, Clark asked himself a question he would go on asking for the next sixteen years: 'Can I live without an audience?' He saw public speaking as akin to 'partaking in or of a sacrament'. Hearing the waves of applause from the crowd, his self-doubt was washed away. In the three years since Whitlam's election in 1972 he had become a celebrity, Australia's first modern public intellectual. Letters poured in to Tasmania Circle. Could he help with a school student's history assignment? Would he contribute to a book of favourite recipes by 'well-known Australians'? Could he possibly write a foreword, launch a book, open an exhibition, endorse a political campaign or give a public lecture? Before speaking in public, he jotted down notes in his diary, pulling the small blue notebooks from his jacket pocket as he stepped up to the podium. Pressed for time, his letters became briefer, his complaints about the strain of public appearances more frequent, and time with Dymphna and his family more intermittent. Every month, his calendar was clogged with appointments. He began to wonder if he was being used. As his public profile grew, his private life shrank to the stolen moments in between performances. His children began to worry that he was pushing himself too hard. Katerina noticed that when he sat at the dinner table 'he wasn't really there'.[40]

Through Clark's ever-widening circle, Dymphna came into contact with the political and cultural elite. As a young woman, she had sensed that Clark was gifted but never once did she imagine that his prominence would be such that she would entertain prime ministers and Nobel laureates in her home. While she supported Clark's willingness to speak out 'on the great issues', she was not one to bask in the reflected glow of his success. At official functions, she was often left standing alone, as journalists, camera crews and groups of admirers flocked to surround him. 'It was Manning they wanted to see,' she acknowledged. 'I did feel that if people spoke to me at a function and asked, "What do you do?" And if I couldn't say I was a professor of something or other or that I was on the board of a Bank or something they would move on and talk to somebody else. I didn't let it upset me ... but I was conscious of it.' Late in her life, Dymphna offered a very different view of the Whitlam era. 'Unlike Manning, I was never drawn into the euphoria or the enthusiasm [surrounding Whitlam] because to me he was just another politician—imperfect—and surrounded by other imperfect politicians.' For Dymphna, Whitlam was 'no demigod' and, in sharp contrast to Clark, she felt little disappointment when he lost power.

Dymphna saw through her husband's public façade better than anyone, joking to him about the different characters he inhabited—M Clark historian, M Clark mystic and M Clark fisherman. Clark, meanwhile, taunted her for her refusal to succumb uncritically to his romantic overtures: 'I'm still in love with you, and, as you don't want me to say that, or talk about THAT, I will say no more today.' Dissatisfied and exhausted from travel and public speaking, he wrote to her from Perth in April 1976, eager to convince her that the time of their deepest love lay ahead of them.

> You deserved a better fate than to be mixed up with this fag of melancholy for so long. You are the greatest girl in Australia and I treasure you now more than you will ever know. Why can't we talk and enjoy the autumn of life! We are capable of great love—if only we would not be haunted by the past. Goodbye till tomorrow.
> Your wild, loving Manning.[41]

In the years following Whitlam's dismissal, with his public role attracting more controversy, Clark's need of Dymphna's support became even more pronounced; every attack on his work, his public statements and his credibility, only deepened his insecurity. What he could not see was that many of his comments appeared to invite criticism. On New Year's Eve, 1977, he sat at his desk in his study, clipping an article from the *Sydney Morning Herald*. 'Sayings of the Year' offered a selection of comments over the previous year from notable Australians. Clark's contribution was pithy and typically melodramatic: 'our civilisation is a graveyard'. Lifted out of its original context, the remark appeared ridiculous.

Well into the 1980s, Clark warned that capitalist, consumer society would soon collapse. 'Ballet,' however, 'would live on,' he argued, 'if only because its delights were eminently safe and harmless.' After the Iranian revolution in 1979, Clark predicted that Europe and America might be 'knocked sky high by an explosion in the Moslem world, an explosion of the have-nots lifted into fanaticism by talk of a Holy War against the diabolism of Western capitalist society.' The comments were typical of Clark's public statements after 1975—prescient one minute, bizarre and unfathomable the next. His dire predictions reflected the bitterness felt by many Australians after Whitlam's dismissal and the polarised political culture that Kerr's decision left in its wake. In this climate, Clark's enemies and supporters were no longer confined to the corridors of history departments but were now found across the full spectrum of Australian culture—from journalists and politicians to fellow writers and political ideologues.

Many commentators who had praised Clark's earlier volumes now turned against him. In 1968, Max Harris, leading columnist for the *Australian*, had described Volumes I and II as 'vast, original and great'. In 1977, in a mock trial of Clark's work in the same newspaper, he derided Clark's writing style as 'faintly comic'. 'The man writes ghastly prose,' blasted Harris, 'full of portentous abstractions.' By the late 1970s, as the excesses of the Whitlam years were frequently condemned in the media, especially in the Murdoch press (which had strongly supported Whitlam's election in 1972), Clark's work and public alliance with Labor became the subject of intense critical attention. For the new Liberal government and an increasingly vocal set of conservative commentators, it was one thing to have removed Whitlam from power, quite another to dethrone the cultural ascendancy of the intellectuals and artists who had given him succour. By now, Clark had emerged as one of the nation's most prominent activists. But again, he could not foresee the consequences of his political campaigning.[42]

In 1976, together with Donald Horne and Patrick White, Clark joined the new republican movement, Citizens for Democracy, addressing large crowds at Town Hall meetings in Sydney. Clark's vision of a republic—'a democratic, socialist Australia with a fundamental change in the ownership of wealth'—was founded on the demolition of 'the last vestiges of colonialism'. Popular sovereignty, he argued, must be explicitly vested in the people. Australia had to finish the job Whitlam had begun and slay 'the giant of British philistinism'. He called for a new national flag, a different national day and a new national anthem. 'Advance Australia Fair', the same anthem he had endorsed only a few years earlier, was now embarrassing. 'You could hardly call the Aborigines young and free, they've been here for 50,000 years.' In the same year, he published an article in *Meanjin*—'Are we a Nation of Bastards?'— in which he described the Coalition government as a party with the 'moral values of a troop of boy scouts'. By removing from power 'the man with the great dream', Australia, he claimed, had entered a 'time of shame'. When it was announced that Clark would give the ABC Boyer lectures in 1976, a furore erupted as the Liberal Party senators John Carrick and Peter Sim attacked him in federal parliament.[43]

In 1976, the Boyer Lectures occupied a privileged position in Australian culture. Broadcast nationally on ABC Radio, published soon afterwards and syndicated to the press as they were delivered, they were projected as the pinnacle of intellectual contribution to public debate at a time when the media environment was easily dominated. Clark had been chosen to give the lectures the day before Whitlam's dismissal. On 22 September, Carrick stood in the Senate and described Clark's views on Whitlam's removal as 'bigoted and fascist'. Still smarting from Clark's description of the Liberal Party in *Meanjin*, Carrick impugned his professional integrity, condemning him as 'a political partisan and apologist for the Labor Party'. Two days later, Keith Mackriell, assistant manager of the ABC, stung by Carrick's broadside and disturbed by ABC Radio *Lateline*'s decision to broadcast the Citizens for Democracy meeting at Sydney Town Hall, demanded that Alan Ashbolt, the head of ABC Radio, hand over a copy of Clark's lectures for his perusal. Mackriell alleged that Ashbolt, whom he knew to be a member of the ALP, had given too much airtime to the Town Hall meeting and failed to broadcast a 'balancing program'. Ashbolt was outraged, accusing Mackriell of wanting to censor Clark's lectures. He defended his decision to broadcast the Town Hall meeting, which he argued 'marked the beginning of a movement … towards republicanism'. If the ABC was expected to 'assess the suitability of material on whether or not it could be balanced', he said, it would end up 'rejecting large slabs of spoken word in every sphere of specialist programme activity'. Well over a hundred ABC employees signed a petition denouncing Mackriell's intervention. The story made national news, with Whitlam coming to Clark's defence. 'Australians ought to be able to hear the views of Australia's greatest historian,' he commanded; they should not give way to the 'petty McCarthy-ites'. The public stoush over Clark's lectures was one sign that the culture wars that would continue to plague Australia for the next three decades had their origins in the bitter divisions created by Whitlam's dismissal. Conservative allegations of ABC bias, the demand for 'balance', and the political sensitivity over the representation of Australian history, with which Clark was by now so powerfully identified, would all become a regular feature of Australia's political landscape.[44]

Interviewed in the ABC studios by the *Australian* only hours before his first lecture was recorded, Clark appeared depressed by the controversy. 'I'm much too emotionally vulnerable to be caught up willingly in [politics]. I am wounded too easily,' he lamented. By speaking at the Town Hall meeting, he pleaded, he was not trying to become a political figure. He merely wanted to draw attention to the major issues of the day. This was his duty as an historian. When the Boyer Lectures were over, he thought he would write a short article on the 'historic situation' and point out 'only the factual alternatives' that faced Australia. In the face of public criticism, Clark displayed his wounds and retreated behind the façade of the academic historian. He told the *Australian* that his opinions, including his conviction that a republic was nigh, were all based on 'historic facts'. Five days later, news broke that the ABC board had rebuked Mackriell's intervention and given its commitment that the lectures would be broadcast uncut. Clark was relieved but despondent. All 'the mudslinging' had been too much of a strain on him. The lectures, he told the Melbourne *Herald*, 'were not very good'. It was false modesty. The Boyer Lectures showed why Clark had found such a large public audience. Delivered in his trademark conversational tone—'you probably know already but let me try to tell you'—Clark conjured the illusion that Australia's history could only be truly understood through his personal testimony. First and foremost, the lectures were about him. They told the story of his journey of discovery in Australian history. On radio, the sound of Clark's soft, gravelly and slightly hesitant voice gave him an air of humility. He told his audience that he wanted to answer Hamlet's question 'What is a man?' All that he knew and had ever wanted to know about Australia's past had grown out of his personal experience. In the Boyers, he began to tell his life story to the nation, revealing his family background, relating his journeys to collect material, and conveying his epiphanies of mind and soul. As Whitlam had said, Clark himself had become part of the answer to Australia's quest for an independent identity. No other writer had managed to make his own life so pivotal to that endeavour. When Volume IV appeared in March 1978, with its title taken from the Book of Ecclesiastes—'The Earth Abideth Forever'—it was reviewed as the work of a 'prophet who was awakening Australians to the void in their national experience'.[45]

In the space of six weeks, Clark saw the publication of both Volume IV (which had taken him six years to write) and *In Search of Henry Lawson* (a short book of 60 000 words inspired by Clark's ten-year fascination with Lawson and published by Macmillan, written in just four weeks). Peter Ryan, who privately mocked Clark's growing sense of self-importance and unorthodox requests for advances ('Manning Clark wants to buy a new car. Guess who is supposed to finance it?'), was instrumental in steering Clark's work towards an even more popular audience as his fame spread. Ryan had already declined an offer from Macmillan to publish volumes I to IV in paperback, believing that Clark's prestige was worth too much to MUP. Instead, he arranged for MUP to publish the first four volumes in paperback. Promoting Clark, Ryan used the press skilfully. In the lead-up to the launch of Volume IV, he arranged for Stuart Sayers, literary editor at the *Age*, to 'scoop' his competitors by sending him the proofs. 'You must swear your reviewer to secrecy about this early start,' he told Sayers, 'and especially it must be kept secret from M.C. who will drive me demented with daily phone calls—"What do you suppose he will say etc. etc."' The two men, who both thought Clark's eccentricities amusing, were beginning to share some fun at his expense. For the moment, Clark's mind was concentrated on securing Patrick White to launch the book. After assuring White that he would not be forced to endure 'the agony' of AD Hope's attendance, Clark was elated when he agreed to launch it. This was White's first book launch. 'I've never launched a book in my life,' he wrote to Ryan. 'I'm more concerned with other people's landings ... [but] I accept to launch Manning's Fourth Volume because of my admiration & affection for him.' When the day came, White belied his novice status. With Whitlam, Clark, Xavier Herbert and Tom Keneally looking on, he described Australia as 'an increasingly abhorrent place for all men of good will'. 'I like to think that the evil forces, both formless and only too loathsomely palpable, will be routed by the flood of light [Clark] lets in'. But where White saw light, others saw darkness.[46]

Volume IV told the story of the goldfields and the emergence of national sentiment, with Henry Lawson (the Australian nationalist) and Henry Parkes (the Australian Briton) as Clark's indirect narrators. The juxtaposition mirrored the struggle he saw happening in front of his eyes, in a society 'still divided between the supporters of Australian nationalism and the Anglo-Saxons, one side wanting to retain the Union Jack and God Save the Queen, the other side fighting for the independence of Australia, republican political institutions, and the end of all formal legal ties with the United Kingdom'. There was little doubt as to which side Clark was barracking for. He played up the contrast by describing Lawson to the press as a man much like himself, a person who suffered more 'metaphysical anguish than most people, a mighty spirit who had terrible weaknesses', alcohol being the most glaring example. Twelve months earlier, in February 1977, the *National Times* asked 'experts' to nominate Australia's best history books. Clark nominated Geoffrey Blainey's *Tyranny of Distance* and Keith Hancock's *Australia*. 'I suppose I can't nominate my own books,' he laughed. Of the other historians consulted—Russel Ward, Ken Inglis, Geoffrey Blainey and Humphrey McQueen among them—not one nominated Clark's *A History of Australia*. Only his *Short History* was included. When the reviews came in for Volume IV, the distance between the enthusiasm of Clark's popular readership (his *History* was increasingly found on the 'Australiana' shelves in bookshops) and the cool response of his colleagues was glaring. As historian Beverley Kingston noted in her review for the *Weekend Australian*, thanks largely to the Boyer fiasco, his public defence of Whitlam and his republicanism, Clark's name was 'a household word'. But his notoriety, she argued, 'had little to do with his profession of history'.[47]

Criticism of Volume IV struck familiar chords. Clark had 'Banjo' Paterson sitting in a chapel at Sydney Grammar School before the chapel was built, while in the 1870s girls from Presbyterian Ladies College in Melbourne sang hymns that had not yet been written. He spent too much time on writers and artists such as Lawson and not enough on social, labour and economic history. He seemed more interested in writing 'psychological drama', the story of men's souls—a 'salvation history'. His style tended towards cliché and his short sketches of individuals tended towards caricature.

Kathleen Fitzpatrick devoured the book but she told Clark bluntly of its failings: 'in a way, the history of Australia makes me feel a homeless person—it has no place for women. I think more space is given in Volume IV to the tiny minority of Chinese than to the whole female population.' Others were more complimentary. Battling illness, writer Alan Marshall homed in on the sleight of hand in Clark's style: 'you sacrifice facts for truth … truth is slightly coloured with the character of the historian and thus becomes a living thing. This is how you write and I love it.' Journalists and writers were also willing to forgive Clark his sins, praising his narrative verve, despite the many repetitions. But there was also a new criticism: Clark's melancholy eye had become too pessimistic, even cynical. Surely Australian history was more positive than the story he portrayed. In a country in which the idea of the emerging nation was so closely tied to history, Clark's work appeared to leave no hope. As Bill Mandle, his former colleague at the ANU, suggested, Clark's 'Australian Gothic' failed to find 'a residue of optimism in the national story'. This shift, towards metaphors of light and darkness in critiques of *A History of Australia*, was the beginning of what Geoffrey Blainey, in 1993, would call Clark's 'black armband history'. In May 1978, with academic reviews of Volume IV yet to appear, concerns about Clark's bleak view of Australia's past were temporarily postponed by the drama that accompanied the publication of *In Search of Henry Lawson*, a book that showed all the signs of being hastily written.[48]

Clark's obsession with Lawson flowered after Whitlam's election in December 1972. Intrigued by the writer's Norwegian background, he even travelled to Norway in search of a possible connection between Lawson's grandfather Peder Larsen and the playwright Henrik Ibsen, who lived only thirty kilometres away. The only connection between them was in Clark's imagination. In Sydney, he became a frequent pilgrim to Lawson's grave at Waverley Cemetery, a place he loved as much for its dramatic setting—a wide hill of marble gravestones that rolled down to the sandstone cliffs facing the Pacific. There, often in the early morning, when the sea of white stone was drenched in the yellow light of the rising sun, he thought of Lawson—'those eyes, the one who had wisdom'. Standing in front of the grave, he filled pages of his diary with notes on his life. Lawson, he wrote, had 'bequeathed such a precious gift to us all'. In Henry Lawson the alcoholic, the thwarted, romantic nationalist, and the jaded seeker of 'some eternal harmony', Clark saw the mirror image of himself (again). The book that emerged from his obsession was nothing more than an extended love letter to Lawson. It was one of his most personal books and he poured his soul into his subject, something which reviewers were quick to point out. Two reviews in particular cut him to the core, managing to turn his slight book into a matter of national controversy.[49]

Colin Roderick, whose own biography of Lawson was so terrifyingly thorough as to be almost unreadable, described Clark's book as 'a tangled thicket of factual error, speculation and ideological interpretation'. The respected

Sidney Nolan's sketch
of Manning Clark

literary critic Dorothy Green, who knew Clark well, claimed that it was neither biography nor a history of the times. It was merely Clark's view of Lawson. The scholarship was 'scrappy', she argued, and Clark's prose, unlike Lawson's economy, understatement and lucidity, was clichéd, ponderous and predictable, little more than a poor pastiche of biblical allusions and other writers' work. From Roderick, whose doctoral thesis Clark had failed many years earlier, he might have expected as much. But Dorothy Green's criticisms hurt him badly because he thought so highly of her.[50]

Clark was mortified by the attacks. He rang Peter Ryan claiming that Roderick's criticisms were part of a plot by the conservative establishment to put him down. 'I think they've decided that it's time to get rid of me,' he told Ryan. Then he added: 'But you mustn't think I'm the victim of persecution mania.' Clark let family and friends know of his hurt. Even when he tried to use humour to dismiss the criticisms, he could not disguise his pain. Shortly after the appearance of the reviews by Roderick and Green, he sent David Campbell a postcard from Johannesburg. The front of the card showed a statue of Hercules, with a woman in a black dress using a hammer and chisel to dig away the fig leaf in front of his genitals. On the back, Clark wrote to Campbell: 'This can happen to you if you write a book on Lawson.' As Clark penned Robert Menzies' obituary in May 1978, the controversy over Lawson flooded the media. Patrick White, whose earlier novels had also been savaged by Roderick, came to Clark's defence, exchanging blows with Roderick in the letters page of the *Sydney Morning Herald*. Roderick charged that Clark's scholarship was so shoddy he should resign from the Australia Council. 'Roderick comes out of the affair looking like a very jealous man,' taunted White, 'perhaps because he's a dab hand at romance himself.' Sending a copy of his letter to Clark, White added a PS regarding his reading of Menzies' legacy: 'I felt you were kinder to Menzies than you might have been. Don't let them soften you up. Never was there so much Australian dry rot gathered together as at that funeral.' Meanwhile, Dorothy Green wrote to Clark several times complaining about his bad-mouthing of her name in academic circles. Her motives were 'scholarly not political', she said. She told him to grow up and get over it, reminding him that, although he did not respond to criticism of his work in public, he certainly did so privately. 'Repeat your accusations to my face,' Green exclaimed. Clark would not apologise, nor would he admit that he had impugned her honesty: 'Please do not write in the same vein again ... I hope you will consider this correspondence is now closed.' What Clark did not know was that Green had written to Senator John Carrick in 1976 to defend Clark against 'unfair' political attacks. The exchange of letters between them reflected poorly on Clark. It was certainly true that he had spoken ill of both Green and Roderick. From a scholarly perspective, Green's criticisms of *Henry Lawson* were valid, but Clark could not bring himself to accept that his work was flawed. Nor could he be content with the public acclaim for the book.[51]

In the first four months after publication, *Henry Lawson* sold over 10 000 copies. And this figure came on the back of aggregate sales of well over 40 000 for *A History of Australia* since 1962. Few of Clark's readers cared about the condemnation by academics. They were enthralled by Clark's style. Instead of writing about the historical Lawson, Clark wrote from inside the man ('Lawson was also finding there was a more gentle, more tender feeling inside him'). The majority of readers had no way of knowing that Clark's depiction of Lawson was a projection of his own character. Only scholars like Dorothy Green knew the facts of the matter. Others, such as Clem Christesen, wrote to Clark to pick over the facts of Lawson's death: 'you say that Henry was found dead in the backyard of the house in Abbotsford—lying there. In 1958 Vance Palmer told me in strict confidence that Henry was found propped up against the fence—and a blowfly flew from his mouth.'[52] What was unusual about the controversy over *Henry Lawson* was the way in which an essentially academic dispute went far beyond the walls of universities and broadsheet literary pages and became a matter of national importance. Entire newspaper editorials were devoted to the drama. The *Sydney Morning Herald* insisted that it was Clark's responsibility to reply to the criticisms of his work. Feature articles in the *Australian* led with headlines such as 'Manning Clark: for and against', and asked: 'Is this the beginning of the end for Manning Clark?' Cartoonists depicted Clark's supporters as disciples ('Hail Manning'), and his detractors as ideological zealots' ('Anti-Manning').

Clark's name had become a lightning rod for political and cultural division, so much so that he was relieved to leave Australia in July 1978 to take up the Chair of Australian Studies at Harvard University, a gift of the Australian government to mark the two-hundredth anniversary of Australian independence. The three months he spent at Harvard between September and December that year provided one of the most rewarding teaching experiences of his career. He gave two lectures per week, offering a survey course on Australian history drawn from *A History of Australia*, with the search for a national identity a constant theme. Students applauded after every lecture. Finishing his final lecture, he was given a standing ovation ('I have never taught so well'). In Harvard, Clark was incognito. Everything he said was heard for the first time. He could leave the controversies behind him and begin life again. Walking into the American Airlines office in Boston to buy his return ticket home, he broke down, telling the sales representative that he did not want to leave America. Back in Australia in early 1979 he learnt that Volume IV had won the 1978 FAW Barbara Ramsden Award for a book of quality writing in recognition of the contribution of both author and editor. Elated, Clark went straight to his record player to play Samuel Barber's *Adagio for Strings* as 'tears of joy' formed in the back of his eyes. It was a short-lived moment of euphoria. The bitter polemic surrounding his work and politics was about to reach an entirely new level.[53]

In January 1981 Clark was named Australian of the Year, proof that respect for his contribution was capable of transcending the virulent criticism of his work. As the *Bulletin* trumpeted, 'few leading figures are so unmistakably Australian in manner and accent: no one has done more to arouse Australians, through his teaching, his books, his prophecy and general intellectual head-thumping, to a clearer understanding of their own country'. Later that year, shortly before Volume V was released, Clark was waiting at Canberra airport. He had driven from Tasmania Circle to stand in the terminal and watch 'the plane arrive with vol. 5 in its cargo'. Then he returned home and waited. At Tasmania Circle later that afternoon, when Ward's Express handed him the parcel that contained the book, he was overcome with emotion: 'I took it to the lawn under the clothes line and cried.'[54]

Launched by Gough Whitlam, Volume V provoked a critical response more disparaging than any previous volume. The criticisms of Volume I by Malcolm Ellis and AGL Shaw that had crippled Clark in 1962 looked mild by comparison. Now the reviews laughed at his banal imagery, hackneyed phrases and cartoon characters. One of the most vicious came from Edward Kynaston in the *Australian*, who mocked his 'turgidity' and 'pseudo-heroics'. Clark's history was 'aesthetically painful', he said, and almost unbearable to read. He quoted Clark on Parkes: 'The eyes of Sir Henry Parkes that evening were suffused with light, as though some lamp inside him had been lit.' 'Perhaps it was Halloween,' mocked Kynaston. In the *Age*, Tony Griffiths described the book as 'tedious and predictable', a history written by a 'bitter and cynical' man and a 'committed servant of the left'. In *Quadrant*, only months earlier, AD Hope had published a satirical poem lampooning Clark and Patrick White as merchants of doom. 'Said Patrick to Manning: "let us take the warpath/God's prophets of doom in his Chariot of Wrath/With ABC backing we'll go on the air/With a message of Judgement and Despair"'. Clark was deeply cut by Hope's sarcasm. But worse was to come.

An Eye for Eternity

Under the title 'Bad History', *Quadrant* published a review of Volume V by the Chilean historian and sociologist Claudio Veliz, who accused Clark, among other things, 'of an anti-British obsession that could easily qualify as hatred'. In the *Age Literary Review*, another sociologist, John Carroll, wondered why Clark was not more grateful to the country that had treated him so well. Both Donald Horne and Clark, argued Carroll, had created the events of November 1975 as 'a myth of national fall'. The fact that Australians celebrated Clark, he said, actually showed their failure to recognise 'the crucial historical and moral truth that compared to most other human societies, and especially our own Western predecessors, Australia is a very good society'. Once again, the letters pages overflowed with correspondence from some of Clark's readers defending him and others condemning him.[55]

Six years after Whitlam's dismissal, with preparations already underway for the Bicentenary in 1988, Clark had become the central figure in the rising political and cultural war over the nation's past. In 1982, surveying all the reviews of Volumes I to V, historian Stuart Macintyre noticed how criticism of Volume V emanated from a new kind of conservatism—'sharper, non-apologetic, and more thorough going'—ideologues and partisan warriors irritated by Clark's elevated status, his denunciations of conservative politics and traditions, and his championing of the new politics—especially Aboriginal land rights, the anti-nuclear movement and a burgeoning environmental consciousness. Clark may not have devoted much of his historical writing to these issues, but in the early 1980s he was one of the most vocal proponents of Aboriginal rights and the campaign to stop the building of the Franklin Dam in Tasmania. The attacks on him were motivated by his politics more than his history. Confronted with the cultural nationalism of the Whitlam intellectuals, much of it built on a turning away from Australia's British heritage, as well as the wave of revisionist history that was feeding a more critical view of the country's colonial past and empowering a vocal Aboriginal protest movement, conservative intellectuals attempted to defend the traditional bases of Australian identity—particularly what they saw as the largely benign and progressive legacy of British settlement. By the early 1980s the political context in which Clark's work was received had shifted. History was increasingly being used as a barometer of patriotism. As the

Bicentenary approached, much of the criticism of *A History of Australia* pleaded for a more positive view of Australia's British inheritance, the very idea that would form the centrepiece of the conservative assault on 'black armband history' under Prime Minister John Howard at the end of the twentieth century.[56]

Peter Ryan's changing view of Clark's work and politics was another gauge of the shift in critical reception. Although he had doubted the quality of the *History* as early as 1968, and always enjoyed mocking Clark's sentimentality and vanity, Ryan became even more scornful in the aftermath of Whitlam's dismissal. As a man who had fought against the Japanese in Papua New Guinea, Ryan was appalled by the 'glaring and ghastly errors' in Clark's treatment of World War II in the *Illustrated Short History of Australia*, published by Macmillan in 1981. He resented Clark's frequent public appearances ('ubiquity is your middle name') and warned him on several occasions not to identify his work too closely with the ALP. It would risk being seen as too partial, Ryan told him. Whenever Clark praised and thanked him for his assistance over the years, Ryan demurred, declining to be publicly acknowledged. While he successfully fought off both Penguin and Macmillan from snatching the paperback rights to the six volumes, he was merely doing his job. As he put it: 'You can't look a milk cow in the back end.' Yet the acid tone of many of the notes he scribbled after phone conversations with Clark displayed his growing impatience with him. Although he wrote to Clark 'Just between us, it <u>has</u> been my amazing fortune to have been associated with such a project, and to have it span virtually my entire career at MUP', Ryan disagreed increasingly with Clark's politics. As his own political views began to shift more to the Right, he took an extraordinary step before the release of Volume V, writing to his friend Stuart Sayers at the *Age* in June 1981 as he sent him the proofs:

> You'll recall my thought (though whether it was a good one or not I don't know) that Hasluck might be interested to do, not a review in the conventional sense, but an article discussing Manning's highly idiosyncratic view of the basic ideas of the Founding Fathers of Federation. He seems to

believe that the Constitution's terms were dictated to make socialist legislation impossible. I've not found a constitutional lawyer who believes this, though they agree that some such tendency might have ensued in an incidental way.[57]

Ryan had done what a publisher would not normally do when seeking to advance an author's work. He had aired his personal criticisms of Clark's interpretation of history to a journalist and attempted to solicit a critical article on a book that he was apparently promoting. Rather than protecting the interests of the author, he appeared to be undermining him. While Ryan did not succeed in securing Hasluck to do his bidding, Sayers gave Ryan the impression that he had arranged to run a special article on Clark the constitutionalist in the *Age Monthly Review*. In the end, the only article that did run was Tony Griffiths' evisceration of Volume V.[58]

Underneath much of the invective directed at Clark's work was an unacknowledged truth. Conservative politics had no figure to equal him, either for the degree of public respect and affection he commanded, or for his ability to reach ordinary people through public speaking. Clark had a great gift. As with *Henry Lawson*, few critics seemed capable of appreciating just how appealing Volume V was to the non-professional reader. The narrative of Australia's journey from the centenary in 1888 through federation in 1901 to World War I (1914–18) was panoramic in its gaze, darting constantly from one scene to the next. It was never dull. The chapter on Gallipoli was one of Clark's finest pieces of writing since his work on Burke and Wills in Volume IV. Tragedy, as ever, was his preferred mode. Take the example of his description of Anzac Cove in 1915:

By the time the sun had risen the first Australians had reached the ridge, where they dug trenches to prepare for the fall of modern Constantinople. [When the fighting began] no one had ever before witnessed such an astonishing response to pain and danger. The wounded cheered the crew of the ship to which they returned. The dying cracked jokes. Australian voices echoed over the still waters of Gaba Tepe.

All the ingredients that had made his earlier volumes so successful were still there. Clark pushed the story along, telling the reader what happened without letting analysis get in the way, save for his own godly interventions. Readers who had little knowledge of Australian history could not know that he wrote his antipathy for Australia's British Constitution into his reading of the past; nor could they appreciate the historical oversights in the depiction of his characters. What they could see, and decided to endorse in their thousands, was a rollicking yarn. Clark was 'a good read'. He gave his audience what they wanted: the voice of a man who felt and thought for his characters. And in the 1980s, as historical mini-series on television were produced in quick succession, as Peter Weir's film *Gallipoli* played to packed houses in cinemas around the country, and as school curriculums turned to Australian history in a way unthinkable only two decades earlier, Australians were receptive to a historian–prophet in a way they had never been before and were unlikely to be again. Clark's work posed the burning question of the period: Who were Australians? At the same time his public pronouncements attempted to provide some of the answers: a godless, materialist, people whose hold on the continent was extremely tenuous. Each controversy that catapulted his name to the centre of public debate only added to his fame.

Manning Clark, the maker of myths, had himself become a mythological figure. As he did so, many of his colleagues left him stranded, refusing to review his work when asked by the literary editors of major newspapers. In this sense, Clark's detractors had a point. Some members of the historical profession chose not to speak their mind on his work. As the historian Allan Martin admitted in 1994, 'Most of us have kept quiet: I lost count of the times I turned down requests to review the volumes as they came out.' Frank Crowley was another historian who 'refused to write reviews of [Clark's] History for publication in periodicals and newspapers'.[59] Several of Clark's former colleagues declined to review his work in the press, particularly after his ascendance to the role of national prophet. They were embarrassed by his partisan interventions, which they saw as inappropriate for a scholar of his standing, and they thought less of his *History* with each successive volume. Their public silence was explained by a complex web of loyalty and anxiety; so many of them felt indebted to Clark, as either former students,

An Eye for Eternity

colleagues he had shepherded into university positions or simply fellow historians inspired by his role in establishing Australian history as a respectable sub-discipline. They felt they all owed Clark something of their daily bread. In the early 1970s, Geoffrey Serle offered a perfect example of an old student's loyalty, sending Clark his review of Volume III before publication. 'Forgive me for this,' he wrote Clark. 'It's not nearly as good as I hoped. Why are we such rotten reviewers in this country?' The remainder of Serle's letter partly answered his own question. 'Let me know quickly if there is anything to which you take exception or if I have made any silly blunder. I have a few days in which to revise it. You know it is well meant—and that I mean it. But does the gratitude I mean come through?'[60]

Because Clark was an academic historian who had been placed on a towering public pedestal, some historians feared that to bring him down would risk bringing the entire profession down with him. As historian Margaret Steven reflected, she felt torn: 'As an historian, I thought I should protect him in order to defend myself—that's professional loyalty—but on the other hand, my academic and intellectual credibility made me think I should be honest and say what I truly think about the work.' A similar tension could be glimpsed in some of the reviews of Volume V. Geoffrey Bolton admitted that many historians wished Clark would not make so many mistakes: 'Clark's inaccuracies are an old story … those of us who spend hours scoring red slashes across undergraduate essays because of factual errors must wish that Manning wouldn't do it … [but] we don't read Clark for the same purposes as we read a dictionary or an encyclopedia … the important thing is that he completes one of the major works of history undertaken anywhere in the English speaking world during the second half of the 20th century.' Like so many historians, Bolton was willing to forgive Clark because of the nature of his endeavour, the like of which Australia had never seen before. It was almost as if Australia needed Clark's epic canvas of the past more than it needed to hear the truth about the quality of his work.

Then there was the added problem of Clark's personal response to negative reviews.[61] None of his colleagues in Canberra relished the inevitable vilification they would receive if they looked upon his work unfavourably. After her husband's death, Anne Gollan explained that 'Bob chose not to review Manning's work when asked, because like everyone else, he knew he'd be punished badly if he dared to criticise him.' Clark's vindictiveness scared many of his potential critics from stating in public the views they offered freely to one another in university common rooms. On so many grounds— friendship, respect, gratitude, self-interest, and fear of vilification—the decision of Clark's colleagues to remain loyal to him in public was understandable. Yet it had deleterious consequences for both Clark and Australia. By choosing not to air their differences with Clark's *History*, a few historians handed the job of criticism to the conservatives, some of whom were little more than right-wing ideologues. One result was that at a crucial moment of historical awakening, the tenor of the country's intellectual debate became more intensely partisan, more polarised and more simplistic. Clark was portrayed either as a victim by his supporters or as the merchant of doom by his detractors. The public debate about his work often lacked nuance and subtlety, and Australia's intellectual culture was the poorer for it.[62]

THE WORDS OF THE PROPHET

In October 1983, Clark wrote to Lyndall Ryan: 'I have come to hate the person I presented to the world for most of my life—and am hoping in the few years remaining to show that the person in the written words is the person.' After so many years writing, Clark was painfully aware of the difference between his literary persona and the man who existed beyond the page. The person in his correspondence was the person he intended to be: the all-loving husband, father and friend who offered understanding and solace to others and dignified life through the music of his prose. This was the person he could compose and shape to his own liking. Now, as Clark struggled to come to terms with yet another dimension to his persona—the national prophet—he set out for the last time to convince Dymphna that the man she loved was indeed the person 'in the written words'.[63]

In September 1981, Dymphna found torn scraps of paper in the wastepaper basket in Clark's study. It was a letter from Lyndall Ryan. Piecing them together, she discovered that he had arranged to see Ryan in Brisbane. Enraged by his treachery, she threatened to leave him again. That she rummaged through Clark's discarded papers when he was out of the house showed the extent of her mistrust. Shortly afterwards, exasperated by his repeated claims that she did not want to hear what was troubling him, she lost her patience.

> Manning, I have pleaded with you to the point of humiliation for honesty between us. If there is not more of that, I fear this may be the end of the road as far as our personal relations are concerned. This is too stupid & silly to contemplate, but I see no alternative at the moment.[64]

Only ten days before Dymphna found his letter to Ryan in his study, Clark had promised his latest muse, the Canberra literary scholar Pat Dobrez, that he would use his talents in the years that remained to him 'in love and the writing of Volume Six'. Historian Roslyn Russell, who became Clark's research assistant in March 1982, described Dobrez as a woman who possessed 'an ethereal quality, that other worldly, romantic dreaminess' for which Clark had long hankered. Like her husband and fellow academic Livio Dobrez, she was a devout Catholic, and she listened sympathetically to Clark's spiritual questing, holding out the mysteries of faith as the answer to his inner loneliness. As Clark wrote in September 1981: 'I promised Pat Dobrez to read the order of the mass for the Feast of the Nativity of the Virgin ... I will dedicate [Volume VI] to her in gratitude for her faith and love. She calls it the gift I must still make to humanity in this part of the world. Very happy. Faith rushing back.' Over thirty years Clark's junior, Dobrez had become his amorous spiritual counsellor.[65]

The Dobrezes were also occasional visitors to Tasmania Circle. In the same month as she began working for Clark, Roslyn Russell attended his sixty-seventh birthday party. As soon as she arrived, she found herself in Clark's study, asked to type one of his short stories because 'Manning wanted to show Pat there and then'. While Russell sat typing at the study desk, Clark, dressed in a white shirt and cricket flannels from his days at Balliol, climbed the ladder with Dobrez to 'see how [Russell] was getting on'. 'They decamped to the study to have a bit of a cosy,' said Russell, 'standing in the corner behind me, giggling flirtatiously like young lovers, while Dymphna was downstairs attending to the guests, no doubt aware of their constant coming and going.' Two weeks before the party, Dymphna had left a note on Clark's desk: 'Manning—Please have pity on my attempt to save a mite of dignity and integrity for the last few years of my life D'. Underneath, Clark added the date: '14/2/82'.[66]

Later that year, Dymphna visited Sebastian and his family in Derbyshire, and Katerina in North America. It was one of several extended trips she made in the 1980s. Left alone at Tasmania Circle, Clark wondered if her departure was due to his 'abominable behaviour'. He wrote to her daily, numbering each of his letters, 'Day One', 'Day Ten', 'Day 22', as if measuring the depth of his loneliness in her absence. Occasionally, his letters managed to cast the old spell, especially when he wrote of his only companion, Tuppence, the family dog. 'So to bed, a read of Keats, a gospel, a think, drooling words of comfort to Tuppence, my bedroom mate, who replied with a soothing lick.' In Tuppence, 'the tail wagger of Tasmania Circle', Clark saw himself panting for Dymphna's affection. Writing in the middle of a Canberra drought, he found in the climate a metaphor for his state of mind: 'Dry weather, arid soil, arid soul'. Apart from one or two flashes of humour, his letters exuded a relentless, sentimental melancholy ('In a black mood', 'yesterday was a lonely, lonely day', 'still in a mood of melancholy and regrets for past follies'). He complained to her that his heart was no longer in the history. He wailed about the criticism of his work and, yet again, he pleaded for more demonstrative declarations of love. As always, when he did not receive a letter from her, he was forlorn: 'I was very, very disappointed not to get a letter from you so far this week.' Even when she did write he felt let down by her response. Unlike Clark's earlier swags of letters to Dymphna, there was little sign of levity. After so many years of grappling with his deluge of literary affection, only to find that his grand intentions were rarely carried out in practice, Dymphna had by now reached the point of exasperation, writing to Clark from Derbyshire in September: 'I am so sorry if my letters have been a disappointment to you. I have immensely appreciated the trouble you have taken to write to me so often … [but] I am afraid I cannot write

An Eye for Eternity

to you with the naïve conceit of my foolish youth—but believe me, I <u>am</u> warm, <u>very</u> warm in my feelings for you, <u>and</u> I believe I am yours forever. Is that enough?' She grew increasingly frustrated with his 'black letters' and despaired at his inability to be satisfied with the affection she offered him. 'I have spent hours on this letter, but I daresay it still isn't warm and personal enough. I hope one day something will make you content.' Clark seemed incapable of grasping her needs. He only wanted to convey his discontent, as if Dymphna's purpose in life was to keep his unhappiness at bay. At times she felt depressed by how little she had in common with Sebastian's teenage children. As she tried to explain to him, 'my time was filled in ministering to the needs of and spending time and concentration with Katerina &co. &

then Sebastian, which is what I came to do.' Knowing Clark was desperate for her letters, she rose at dawn to write to him, fearing all the while that the news of her domestic achievements as mother and grandmother would only disappoint him. Her last letter, written shortly before she returned home in October 1982, showed that she had become reconciled to the things she believed she could never change:

> And now for an attempt at personals … I too look forward to creeping back into my cocoon at Tasmania Circle. I dread making travel arrangements, dread failing with Sebastian's boys … dread losing things, hate wasting money … Manning you are the centre of my life. Will that do? It would be easier for me to write personally if I felt I had ever made you happy or well or content. But I accept [that is due to] my limitations, and to those of our situation. I can do nothing to affect what really concerns you—your reception as a historian, thinker, public figure, the fate of the children of your heart. I can only wish you well and look forward to seeing you rosy on October 15. Love Dymphna.[67]

Clark's deepest loves, she told him, were his own works, the books that he wept over and cradled like a child. For all Clark's protestations of love, she knew that he remained close to both Lyndall Ryan and Pat Dobrez. And the romantic bond with Dobrez was by now blatantly obvious to many of her friends and family. Sebastian's wife, Elizabeth Cham, recalled seeing Livio Dobrez 'incandescent with rage' over his wife's disloyalty, while Rosyln Russell saw that Dymphna too was incapable of hiding her jealousy. In his diary, Clark recorded his dreams of Dobrez: 'I dreamed I was dancing with P. We were happy. Happiness ruined by fear that those who could be pained by such happiness might notice the bond and the awareness.'

After every stream of reassuring correspondence to Dymphna came the inevitable let-down; when Dymphna returned home in late 1982, Clark continued his intimate friendship with Dobrez. By 1984, when Dymphna again travelled to England, Sweden and North America to visit family, the tone of her letters to Clark had hardened further. 'Your truth can never be the same as my truth, let us just accept that and do the best we can.' She had grown tired of being taken for a fool. Clark's infatuation with Dobrez, Ryan and so many other women had embarrassed her once too often. She told him that she would do anything for him except 'kid' herself. She had come to accept a bitter truth. He was only able to love her completely from a distance, in the pages of his letters; his actions told another story. In fact, she said:

[The letters] showed all too clearly how useless it would be to imagine that you felt for me anything like the 'love' you talk about, at least in the sense in which I understand 'love' from a husband to a wife. If you like, I will tell you about it when I get home, though it will cost me. But in spite of it all, if you could ever bring yourself to show that my presence brought you a quarter as much pleasure as you seem to feel pain in my absence, I think we would be very happy together. Enough.[68]

Throughout the 1980s, the couple were often apart. Not only because of Dymphna's visits to Sebastian and Katerina, who were living overseas, but also because of Clark's incessant travelling, to Europe, the United States, New Zealand and China, as well as weekly public engagements around Australia. Their children by now had all left home. His restlessness was matched by her determination to see her children and grandchildren and to engage in other pursuits now that she finally had the time and resources to devote to her own interests. In addition to her translation work, at the request of her friend Judith Wright she joined the Aboriginal Treaty Committee in 1980. It 'filled a gap' in her life and she was convinced constitutional redress for Aboriginal people was essential both for the health of the 'non-Aboriginal conscience' and 'as a matter of natural justice'. Heather Rusden saw how Clark envied Dymphna's friendships with both Judith Wright and Nugget Coombs. 'They were people Manning would have liked to have had friendships with,' said Rusden, 'and he was very much aware that they admired her.' As Clark busied himself building a relationship with the Australian public, Dymphna set about building a life independent of him. When she wrote to her friend Ninette Dutton in 1983, after Geoffrey Dutton had left her for a younger woman, her words of advice and support offered an insight into how she had survived the difficulties in her marriage.

> I do feel … for you because I am a wife too … I feel that you have much less to fear from the future than Geoff. You still have a large part of your sustaining <u>frame</u>, and with your own strength, and the work you have to do, your children and your friends, and the simple support of habits that require you to do-one-thing-after-the-last, you will gradually rebuild things to a harmonious whole (if harmony is ever really an attitude of human existence!).

While Clark lived preoccupied with his inner life, Dymphna lived occupied with those around her. And her 'sustaining frame' still had much to carry. In April 1985, Clark wrote to her from London, bombarding her with five letters that arrived in Canberra on the same day. In one, he outlined yet another program for the renewal of their love. Dymphna replied with a program of her own.

> I have just read all five letters that came today. This is a reply to them … YES, YES, I accept the program on your p.2 with a loving grateful heart, and in hopes of the miracle you believe in. We must try to prove that life is as good as we profess it to be—prove that one can drink at the fountain of youth at 70! … I will not say too much, for fear of lapsing into reservations, qualifications, objections, corrections, which I must banish—internally as well as externally—if the miracle is to happen. I have only one request: If you have not already done so, please do not write or say anything dramatic to Lyndall or Pat. It is your life—our life?—and we can be warm and appreciative to them both. If you want to change, you will change. If not, dramatic announcements will not help … there is nothing in [my program] incompatible with yours, if you really want to share my life; if it is to be a two-way stretch … No more personalia now for fear of lapses—just the best love I can give.[69]

The best love Dymphna could give was rarely enough for Clark. Before she signed off, she asked him again why his letters to her had been so full of misery. Whenever they spoke on the phone his chirpiness shone through. In his correspondence he only seemed able to show his melancholy and depression. Why could he not write to her in a way that reflected all his moods? If Dymphna could have read Clark's diary she would have asked the same question. Two weeks after arriving home he offered a summary of his predicament that might easily have been written any time in the previous ten years of his life:

> Confidence shattered by all those attackers, not just on my work, but attacks which called in question my ability, made me doubt my ability and hence, that it had been a mistake to write the history, the Lawson and the stories, that the rage of the critics was intended to draw my attention to my mediocrity, my poverty of thought and imagination. The thought of it is tormenting me, just as the memories of my past infamies torment me all the time. Am ending my life, broken in body, broken in spirit, lonely, lacking any inner confidence, wary of reaching out to anyone for sympathy, understanding and love because that only ends in resentments. Am so limited I only want sympathy for myself and rarely act for others, except the few I love. When do I love? save Benedict.[70]

Whenever the prophet picked up his pen, the emotions that flowed through his hand were almost always black. The more famous Clark became, the more he dramatised his fame in his diary, scripting his life as a tragic tale in pages that he knew full well would be used to tell the story of his life after his death. The formula was consistent. He admitted his hunger for admiration: 'Why do I do it? Is it because I cannot do without the daily clap?' He admitted his insecurity: 'People respect me, and are affectionate because I seem to help them to understand who they are. [I] speak to their heart. Perhaps, only meretricious speakers move listeners in that way.' And he saw the endgame of his public life through the teaching of Christ in Mark's gospel: 'For what shall it profit a man, if he shall gain the whole world and lose his own soul?' ('I spoke at St. Patrick's Hall, told again I was giving Australia a soul. But is that at the expense of my own soul? Am I embracing death by satisfying this pleasure in telling Australians who they are? The power in the flame which will snuff it—I give light—but I accelerate my own descent into the eternal darkness, the loneliness of it.') Clark was not making these emotions up, rather, he was writing them up—adding emphasis, sharpening contrast and shaping the dramatic arc of his final lead character's downfall: the prophet brought down by his most fatal flaw, the hankering for public adulation.[71]

Dymphna was well aware of the lie in 'the person in the written words'. She grew increasingly suspicious of Clark's literary outpourings not only because experience had taught her that his promises were not to be trusted but because she also knew that the maudlin man trapped in the pages of the letters was in large part fiction. She kept reminding him that his spoken voice was brighter (and more loveable) than his written voice. Clark asked his readers to believe that his loneliness increased in direct proportion to his fame. Yet for every mournful letter Dymphna received from him, as ever, she heard from friends and family that he was enjoying himself. Interviewed, Clark often spoke of how he felt more optimistic in his old age. He rarely allowed his readers to glimpse the sheer thrill he felt from being a public figure. When historian John Hirst watched Clark give a lecture on Henry Lawson in 1979, he saw a man 'half in thrall to his persona'. When historian Allan Martin attended a party at Tasmania Circle for the launch of Volume V, he arrived to find the book mounted on a lectern in the living room with a large candle burning nearby. 'It looked as though we were about to have a reading from St. Paul.' Clark was sending himself up, yet the scene seemed so bizarre that Martin wondered if he was serious after all. Whatever Clark's intentions, Martin thought 'he was having a ball'. In the early 1980s, during the campaign to stop the Franklin Dam, journalist Keith Dunstan accompanied Clark and Dymphna on a flight to Hobart. As they entered the departure hall at Canberra Airport, cameramen surrounded Clark. From a distance, watching him perform under the white glare of the television lights, Dymphna turned to Dunstan and said: 'Look at Manning, he just loves it.' Yet another benefit enjoyed by the boy from Phillip Island was being feted like royalty. Roslyn Russell remembered Clark returning from a public speaking engagement in the 1980s where his hosts had put him up in a five star hotel—'I like to think my parents would've been proud of me,' he told her. Clark was ever his parents' little boy. Historian Nicholas Brown, who lived for a time in the small flat in the backyard at Tasmania Circle, often heard Clark joking about 'the fame fuckers' who kept hammering at his door. Some sought personal guidance from him. Some wanted to tell him their life stories or learn how to write. Others wanted to convert him. For a time, it seemed that everyone wanted a piece of him.[72]

Clark's elevated status and his proximity to the centre of federal power in Canberra afforded him the opportunity to rub shoulders with the political elite. He enjoyed passing on advice to those in government. He wrote to ministers and shadow ministers whenever he felt inclined to offer praise or request a change in policy, assuming the mantle of wise counsel to prime ministers as if it were his natural destiny. And he expected his voice to be heard. After Labor came to power in March 1983, he wasted little time in marking down its leader Bob Hawke as shallow compared with the visionary Gough Whitlam. For his part, Hawke saw no reason to idolise Whitlam or Clark. As he later admitted, 'I was critical of Whitlam's mistakes, especially his ignorance of economics, and his lack of cabinet management, and to be honest, I'm not a fan of Manning's work. It's too overblown.' Hawke acknowledged that Clark had 'enlarged Australians' understanding of their past', but he found his work difficult to read, while Clark found Hawke's managerial style and rational, consensus-building politics too dry for his liking. Yet throughout the 1980s, many ministers in Hawke's government were drawn to Clark, none more so than Paul Keating, who as Treasurer met Clark in 1985.[73]

Keating first became interested in Clark after reading his articles in the press. He had read little of his work save the *Short History*. 'In 1985, I rang Manning up one day and asked him if he'd like to have lunch.' The two men met at the Ottoman restaurant in Manuka, then one of the favourite haunts of Canberra politicians and journalists. 'I went to listen and to learn,' Keating would recollect. 'Later, I went round to see him at his house. I can't remember how many times—quite a few. I'd ring and just go over. I lived close by in Red Hill.' Over the next five years, Treasurer Keating often made the twenty-minute walk to Tasmania Circle with a bundle of CDs under his arm. As he explained, their shared love of music was one of the reasons their friendship flowered. 'We'd both had brushes with greatness, but where we both saw true greatness was in music. Manning was happy to be a bit of a guinea pig so I went round with some of my music. I remember I took round Kathleen Ferrier's recording with Bruno Walter conducting Mahler's 'Song of the Earth'. You know the 'Abschied'. We listened to it together, just as we listened to Georg Solti's recording of Mahler's eighth symphony. Right through, in silence. What can you say?' Keating discovered that Clark could not be weaned off Bach. 'I wanted him to see the expanse of the Viennese symphonists but Manning couldn't quite get there. It wasn't his language. He liked Sibelius of course, especially the fifth symphony, that was the romantic in him.' After several visits to Clark's house in Tasmania Circle, which Keating found exuded an atmosphere akin to a manse, he slowly came to understand what made Clark tick—'the wellspring of the man'.

> Manning was almost like a man of the cloth. His brain was peppered with the history of his own life and of Australia and the world. This left him with a kind of vagueness, an interpretative uncertainty about everything. There was an introversion, a fragility about him. He wasn't confused, he was just trying to absorb it all—life—what does it all mean?

Over music and tea, they talked about Australia generally—not about the republic specifically, but 'more in condemnation of the Tories, and their small time, derivative, sold out view of the country'. Keating felt himself in the presence of a 'great figure', a man with 'a good heart and a deep humility'. 'He wasn't as mad as me, wasn't as wild as me, when I mentioned that I'd told Gough to arrest Kerr in 1975 he was very uncomfortable with that, "Oh no, no" Manning said'.

The day after Keating took him to lunch in 1987, Clark told Peter Ryan that Keating was 'one of the most impressive men' he had ever met in his life. He sensed that Keating felt the same about Australia as he did. Keating called this the 'kindred spirit feeling'. He thought that Clark got from him 'a clarity about power for high purpose'. Both men had a hunger to understand and learn from others in high places. For Clark, Keating was inspiring, a politician sustained by conviction and faith, someone who could make him feel that the visionary spirit he pined for was still alive within the Labor Party. From Keating's perspective, Clark was an older person from whom he could 'suck the life experience' and learn from his wisdom.

> What was I doing there with Manning? It was the romantic head, the love affair with humanity. I wanted to get a handle on Manning's personality, I wanted to understand how he had impacted on the country, what motivated him, what drove him. I was interested in the resonances of his personality.

To imagine the two men sitting together in the living room in Tasmania Circle, with Mahler, Bruckner and the 'reflective sorrow' of Richard Strauss's *Four Last Songs* pouring out of Clark's speakers, is to glimpse an Australian nationalism born of the insights gained from European high culture, particularly from the revelatory and transcendent power of music. For both Keating and Clark, this vision was associated with a religious sensibility, not in any doctrinal or denominational sense, but a religious feeling which recognised Australia as part of a greater whole, holding out the promise that life was not 'just now, just one whiff and then you're gone', as Keating put it. 'You hear this in music and Manning heard it too.'[74]

Under the surface of his undeniable passion for Australia, which Keating found so compelling, lay a contradiction that was harder to see—Clark's longing for recognition from the very Tory establishment he derided. In 1976, when Prime Minister Malcolm Fraser reintroduced knighthoods, making knights and dames the most senior levels of the Order of Australia, several 1975 recipients of the Companion of the Order decided to hand theirs back. Nugget Coombs and Patrick White led the way. Clark, the prominent republican, not only decided to keep his award but also, in March 1977, attended the formal investiture by Queen Elizabeth II at Yarralumla. Labor MP Barry Jones remembered White telling him that 'he was pissed off with Manning' for refusing to return his award. 'Coombs was also disappointed with Manning,' said Jones. Many of Clark's friends were surprised to find him eager to be honoured by the Queen after standing on so many public platforms and condemning the colonial mentality of Australia's conservative establishment. In March 1977, the *bête noire* of the left, Sir John Kerr, still presided as Governor-General. Clark declined to dine with Kerr after the ceremony, but he had no difficulty in accepting his award from the Queen. After the Dismissal, and the emergence of the republican movement in which Clark had played such a leading role, White found his hypocrisy galling. When Clark attended lunch at Government House three years later after he was invited by the new Governor-General, Sir Zelman Cowen, White made his feelings plain: 'I must say I am terribly disappointed in you. Where do we stand if everybody caves in, accepts gongs and honorary doctorates … and courtship from the Governor-General? … I'd be a rum puff indeed if I accepted, and you're a stuffed turkey to submit.'[75]

After the investiture, Clark invited a select group of friends to Tasmania Circle in the mid-afternoon for 'an unexplained purpose'. Ken Inglis watched as Clark cracked champagne and flashed his medal around the room. 'He was proud to have the ribbon put round his neck by Queen Elizabeth,' said Inglis, 'and simply delighted by her respectful murmur about his prowess as a historian.' Traces of that pride can be found in Clark's correspondence, where he was fond of noting that 'Her Majesty conferred on me the Companion of the Order of Australia.' He could not escape his origins or the values that had shaped his generation. Crowing over the honour bestowed by 'Her Majesty', he remained the Melbourne Grammar boy who pined for Yarraside's approval. The photograph taken at the investiture ceremony on 9 March 1977 captured Clark's longing for recognition; his head bowed, like a schoolboy he stood at assembly, awaiting the acclaim of his superiors.[76]

'Am I any good?' Clark would sometimes ask his friends. MUP's marketing manager, Dugald McLellan, who accompanied Clark around Australia as he promoted Volume V, saw his insecurity in his body language—'the continual darting of the eyes, the nervousness, the hesitancy of speech'. The need to be propped up, like an emperor carried aloft by his legion of admirers, was a need that Clark had felt since early adulthood, and it meant that he extracted pleasure from each successive shot of adulation. Interviewing Clark in the late 1980s, Phillip Adams saw a man revelling in his notoriety.

Manning was certainly enjoying his fame, although after interviewing him one night I suddenly realised he was enjoying it a bit too much. I think he was beginning to see himself as the public saw him—as a saint. In one way, it was touching, but in another way, it was demeaning. He'd become, by the 80s at least, a tribal elder. He'd crossed over from fame to celebrity—fame happens, but celebrity is pursued, it has to be worked on, and Manning was certainly working on his. I was concerned for him, mostly because I thought he was better than that. After the interview, I took him aside and very gently warned him that being a celebrity was a phantom and fugitive phenomenon and he'd be wise not to get caught up in it.[77]

By the late 1980s Clark occupied an unprecedented position on the national stage. The sixth and final volume of *A History of Australia* was launched by David Malouf in August 1987, only six months before the Bicentenary of British settlement on 26 January 1788 and the Melbourne premiere of *Manning Clark's History of Australia: The Musical*. These years represented the pinnacle of Clark's renown and the culmination of his life's work, both as a historian and as a public figure. At MUP, Peter Ryan tried to cash in on the fever for the *History* created by the Bicentenary. The promotional flyer for Volume VI showed a photograph of the entire six volumes accompanied by the caption: 'For *every* Australian home, library and school'. MUP published commemorative editions of the six volumes, some in hand-crafted scarlet leather, which were later offered for the price of 750 dollars to Australian Airlines frequent flyers as part of the airline's Bicentenary promotion strategy. Ryan marketed Clark's *History* as a national heritage item. In the press, reviewers assessed Volume VI in the context of its five predecessors, praising Clark for his 'magnificent ambition' in writing the six volumes, 'one of Australia's finest works of art'. The superlatives rained down: Manning Clark was 'the Hercules of history', his work was 'a heroic achievement' ('buy all six volumes!') while the man himself was 'a national treasure'. Editorials were devoted to his life and work. Clark, said the *Sydney Morning Herald*, had given Australians a sense of discovery and curiosity about their past; his *History* was 'a great achievement of Australian culture'.[78]

Although historians generally agreed that the complexity and grand themes of Clark's earlier volumes had given way to a more simplistic and narrower cultural nationalism, they were also generous in their praise. Only Clark's long-standing detractors, such as Colin Roderick, condemned the volume as history. Roderick had already forewarned Ryan that he would criticise Clark for his 'alarming errors of fact'. 'Of course, you'll be saying to yourself,' he told Ryan, 'there's nothing new in that.' At home, Clark received letter after letter from friends and admirers, none more gracious than the one from his former student, the economist Hugh Stretton:

You may not remember that I spent two terms in your first postwar Australian History class ... This feeble note is just to thank and congratulate and <u>praise</u> you for such a work for us all. Nobody that I can think of, political or intellectual, has done as much as you have done to dignify homo Australis, and suggest to us that we too have souls, can think high thoughts, know love and tragedy, and belong to the same species as (say) Donne and Beethoven.

Stretton's remark also revealed the depth of the isolation felt by many Australian intellectuals throughout the twentieth century. It was as if the country existed outside the realms of European civilisation. Clark had helped to end that feeling of isolation. In the letters he received from appreciative readers and listeners to his many radio interviews, it was possible to see how he touched people differently from other intellectuals and commentators. Some correspondents sent him verses from the psalms, others praised his passion for Australia, prayed for his soul or revealed stories of their own loss and grief. After hearing him talk about his parents in a lecture given in Melbourne in 1988, Peter Craven wrote to Clark, humbled by the experience: 'You spoke with such a sense of the dignity of ordinary people's lives.' Clark was the storyteller, the history man whose voice cut to the heart. He stirred metaphysical questions in his audience: How to live? How to be true to oneself and to one another? In what direction did Australians want to take their society? Was the future simply a question of managing the economy? Or could Australians be guided by principles and beliefs that went beyond the goal of material prosperity—Clark's 'Kingdom of Nothingness'?[79]

While he toyed with the idea of progressing to a seventh volume, Clark had neither the energy nor the will to do so; he had long said that he felt more comfortable writing the history of nineteenth-century Australia. Volume VI finished in 1935, with an epilogue bringing the story through to 1987. The closer he came to the present, the more uncomfortable Clark became. His stentorian tone worked best from a distance. Let loose on the living, it teetered on the edge of farce. Writing by hand, he also felt alienated by rapid technological change. 'Can anyone imagine the voice of a prophet emerging from a computer?' he asked. Exhausted by the effort of completing his last volume, he dramatised the struggle for the press, telling journalists that the writing had been 'a descent into hell'. By 1988, each of the six volumes had averaged 40 000 sales. Together with the sales of *A Short History of Australia*, which now stood at over 250 000, his short stories, *Henry Lawson*, *Occasional Writings and Speeches*, and the two volumes of historical documents, Clark had accrued sales of well over half a million. When he set out to write in the 1950s, such success had seemed unimaginable. Now, even his critics acknowledged that he had done more than anyone to awaken Australians to their own history.[80]

In the midst of the Bicentenary celebrations, Clark's solemn face gazed out from television screens and newspapers. On 26 January 1988, he appeared on 'Australia Live', the television program that broadcast the events at Sydney Cove around the nation. Seen against the blue-green backdrop of Sydney Harbour, Clark, with his bush hat and world-weary visage, appeared like a reincarnation of a nineteenth-century man, the prophet who had returned to earth to pass judgement on his people. Throughout the year, he shifted in and out of roles easily. One moment he was the activist, launching Wilderness Society calendars and speaking of the earth as 'our common mother'; the next moment he was the sports commentator, writing on the AFL grand final as if the result would decide the country's future. He seemed to be everywhere. When Patrick White rang Tasmania Circle to speak to Clark and found he was out on yet another speaking engagement, he quipped to Dymphna: 'I suppose he's opening a country dunny in Woop Woop.' White could not bear Clark's courting of celebrity. 'How can Manning be so old and so vain?' he asked Humphrey McQueen.

When a Gallup Poll commissioned by the *Sun* ranked 'the most admired Australians', White was listed at number 24, just below Clark (21) and John Howard (22). Clark and White were the only writers among a bevy of actors and sporting heroes, which included the Australian cricket captain Allan Border, the professional ocker Paul Hogan, entrepreneur Dick Smith and singer Olivia Newton-John. Clark had become a media 'face'. After he donated fifty dollars to the Balcatta Primary School's 'Magical Mystery Bus Tour' around Perth in 1988, student Christina Gulloto wrote to thank him, sending him a photograph of the bus festooned with the names of all the celebrities who had lent their support. The name 'Manning Clark' appeared on the lower deck of the school's double decker, directly above the fast bowler Dennis Lillee, and one to the right of the children's TV star Humphrey B Bear.[81]

Although he felt shunned by not being asked to contribute to the multi-volume bicentennial history, *Australia 1788–1988*, Clark's prominence in the Bicentenary celebrations was assured. He accepted a consultancy to advise the architects of the new Parliament House in Canberra (opened by the Queen in May 1988), while his summary of Australia's position at the end of the twentieth century went round the country with a Travelling Bicentennial Exhibition. One member of the public, Lyn Roger, who saw the exhibition in Traralgon, Victoria, was so moved by Clark's words that she wrote them out by hand and sent them to him in a letter as a tribute.

> We ... have a great challenge: the Aborigines and their descendants, the Europeans and their descendants have to learn to live together here. Part of the Australian dream is that human blood will never stain the wattle. Another part of the Australian dream is that all of us can create a way of life in which there is equality of opportunity without restraint on liberty, without conformism, mediocrity or spiritual bullying. I believe in the capacity of the Australian people to contribute to the quest of humanity for a society in which we can all enjoy the great banquet of life.

It was Clark's 'Song of the Republic', a testament of his hopes for the country's future. Asked to contribute ideas for the design of the new Parliament House, he searched for historical texts that would adorn the entrance hall in the form of wall hangings, explaining that he wanted something similar to the inspirational quotations on the walls of the Lincoln Memorial in Washington. With Dymphna's assistance on Aboriginal material, he decided on passages that would show:

> the attitude of the Aborigines to the land, the views of the Aborigines on government, the motives and hopes of the British in establishing settlement in Australia, the introduction of British political institutions in Australia, the creation of the Commonwealth of Australia ... and the debate on the society which should exist in Australia, the Australian-Britons and the Australian-Australians.

Clark rarely referred to multiculturalism, then such a common term in the national lexicon. Instead, he spoke of a shared Australian identity that could unify all groups in society.[82]

Soon after Clark took up the consultancy in 1983, the project's leading architect, Romaldo Giurgola, sought his guidance 'concerning [the] symbolism and character to be expressed by the new building', admitting that his firm had 'an acute awareness of [its limited] knowledge of Australian history and culture'. The discussions continued for a number of years, with Clark telling Giurgola that the design of the interior should be 'inspirational … in the old-fashioned sense … providing ideas which were capable of uniting people of disparate points of view in a sense of commonality'. The name Canberra, he said, meaning meeting place, should become 'the general theme of the building', with the Aboriginal concepts of 'coming together' and 'living in harmony' with the land forming a major presence. Clark's idea of hanging historical texts in the entrance hall was intended to steer the architects away from explicit references to British settlement and federation 'under the Crown' because he believed that these would be 'controversial' and 'politically disturbing' to a Labor government. He preferred to focus on the 'values' of the British colonists. As it turned out, due to funding shortages, few of Clark's ideas came to fruition. In 2010, only four of his suggested wall hangings graced the walkway between the marble foyer and the Great Hall: the Crown's instructions to Governor Arthur Phillip in 1787, William Wentworth's call for responsible government in 1853, James Cook's observations on the Aborigines, and Marcus Clarke's depiction of Australia's weird and grotesque land, 'the strange scribblings of nature learning how to write'. The Clarks' suggestions for Aboriginal voices to be heard were not realised. Perhaps the prospect of securing agreement on the emblematic history that would stand in the new parliament was too daunting, especially ones chosen by a controversial figure such as Clark.[83]

Building on the conservative backlash that had begun in the late 1970s, Clark's public comments during the Bicentenary stirred fierce hostility. After addressing the National Press Club in late 1987, he received mail critical of his pessimistic and anti-British stance, a response that echoed the growing conservative reaction to many of his public pronouncements. In January 1988, Opposition Spokesman on local government, Ian Cameron, offered a typical expression of the Coalition's frustration with Clark:

An Eye for Eternity

All we cop is day after day, hour after hour, interview after interview of Aborigines ... they've got that clapped out professor Manning Clark going on the wireless every hour [talking about how we've mistreated the Aborigines] ... the media's making us feel guilty ... it's media and Labor government propaganda, we hear nothing about the positive achievements of past Australians.[84]

Clark argued that 26 January 1788 marked not the beginning of British settlement but the invasion of Aboriginal Australia. In *A History of Australia*, Aborigines appeared as helpless or passive onlookers, a fact he regretted publicly in 1984 and lamented privately some years later—'my generation was told the Aborigines were silly children doomed to disappearance in the presence of a vastly superior power'. In 1988, he declined Prime Minister Bob Hawke's invitation to join the official celebrations at Sydney Cove on 26 January. Called upon to hand down judgement on two hundred years of 'British civilisation', his verdict was unflinching. On 25 January 1988, at the same time as his article appeared in the *Bulletin* warning yet again of 'a cleansing fire' that would 'sweep over the continent', Clark wrote a piece for *Time Australia*'s bicentennial issue which would be denounced in federal parliament and solidify conservative opposition to his legacy for decades to come.

Now we are ready to take the blinkers off our eyes. Now we are ready to face the truth about our past, to acknowledge that the coming of the British was the occasion of three great evils; the violence against the original inhabitants of the country, the Aborigines; the violence against the first European labour force in Australia, the convicts; and the violence done to the land itself. Recognition of those evils ... is one way to emancipate Australians from the dullness to which they committed themselves by not being prepared to face the truth. The Europeans in effect dispossessed something like half a million people of every square inch of the land of the whole continent; they brought about the extinction of the whole Tasmanian race; they killed thousands of the original inhabitants of the mainland; they all but destroyed their culture and brought hardship, degradation and humiliation to the survivors.[85]

With these words, in the eyes of conservatives Clark moved from being an apologist for the Labor Party to a traitor. He had denounced the British inheritance they believed had provided Australia with the scaffolding of civilisation—parliamentary democracy and the rule of law. For some of his critics, such as historian John Hirst, it was as if he doubted 'whether the word civilization was applicable to [Britain] anymore'. For Labor, a party that carried within its ranks a traditional streak of anti-British nationalism, Clark's words were manageable. But for the Liberal and National parties, for whom the British heritage was sacrosanct, both for their own history and their philosophy of individual and national progress, Clark's litany of evils was an outrage. He had cast doubt on the moral legitimacy of the colonial project and the nation that was founded in its wake. 'By what right are we living in this country?' he asked Australians. For a country in which history was more than ever a rallying point for national pride or shame, these comments struck a raw nerve. In 1988, Australia was not merely engaged in an argument over foundational history, its national character or the dark episodes in the country's past. Rather, the Bicentenary celebrations displayed a profound sense of unease over the nation's historical legitimacy. Clark was doing no more than he had done so effectively since Whitlam came to power. Refusing to espouse a simple celebratory line, he gave voice to views that were held by large sections of Australian society. So many of his public statements about Australia positioned the country at the moral and political crossroads. Either the nation faced the truth about Aboriginal dispossession and found the courage to declare its complete independence from Britain, or it lapsed into a self-satisfied inertia, believing in nothing other than the good life. This was Clark's mission as a prophet: to prick the nation's conscience, to speak to the country as if it had a soul, one that had been stained by the sin of violent dispossession and could only be redeemed through public acknowledgement and contrition.[86]

By the time Clark's article appeared in *Time Australia*, the first reviews of *History of Australia: The Musical* had already appeared. Conceived in 1983 by actor–playwright Tim Robertson, producer John Timlin and playwright John Romeril, all of whom had been associated with the Pram Factory Theatre collective in Carlton in the early 1970s, the production opened at

Postcard produced for The Musical

the Princess Theatre in Melbourne on 16 January 1988, directed by Sydney actor–director John Bell. Immediately its reception was coloured by the controversy over the Bicentenary. Interviewed in 1985, *The Musical*'s scriptwriter, historian Don Watson, envisaged the production as a 'radical antidote to … national self-congratulation'; it would be both 'a history of the country and a history of the historian', he told the press. Clark was flattered to think that his work might be adapted for the stage and willingly gave Timlin's Almost Managing Company permission to use his work. In so many ways, it seemed entirely appropriate that *A History of Australia* was made into a musical. The metre of Clark's prose and the structure of his work—exposition of theme; development and discussion of theme; return to theme; climax; and throughout, at the designated points, moments of heightened emotional intensity—combined with the endless parade of characters who walked onto the page to deliver spirited recitatives or melancholy arias, could not have been more tailor-made for the stage.[87]

From the outset, Peter Ryan was cynical: 'we seem now to have MC on TV and on the stage, and need him only on ice and tight highwire to complete our circus'. Discussing the idea with Tim Curnow, Clark's literary agent at Curtis Brown, Ryan saw the opportunity to sell more copies of the six volumes on the back of *The Musical*.

Curnow and I discussed Clark pretty frankly as 'a property'. (I got the impression that Curnow might be a bit fed up with him.) We both noted the increasing volume of hostile comment and review, but that this appeared to draw an equal or even greater volume of support. We agreed that there was a great deal of mileage left.

Ryan was insistent: the musical should not give Penguin the chance to promote the *Short History* in theatre foyers at the expense of MUP being able to sell the six volumes. Clark told him that he was not interested in money and never had been. He simply wanted the show to go on. If the selling of the *Short History* was creating a difficulty, he did not mind it being excluded. The standoff continued until shortly before the show opened. Finally, MUP's solicitors told Timlin that either the document guaranteeing the publisher's sole right to sell the *History* would be signed or they would seek an injunction to prevent the show opening. After many telephone calls, Ryan met Timlin in conference. He was extremely irritated with Clark. Mixing his metaphors, he told Timlin that Manning should not have his snout in so many troughs—'you can't suck two tits at the same time'. Timlin had little choice but to bow to MUP's pressure. When Ryan read the first draft of the script for the show he was aghast. 'It is such a vulgar, un-historic, tendentious, tasteless piece of rubbish that I doubt whether MUP should risk being identified with it … whether or not the stage play/musical will ever happen is open to doubt.' On this final point, Ryan's judgement was astute. The show had been beset by a chaotic leadup, with last-minute changes to the script and direction, as well as rushed publicity and a scramble for sponsors in the wake of the 1987 stock-market crash. Aside from this, as John Bell reflected in 1994, *The Musical* was 'doomed from the start'. 'To try and tell the whole story of Australia in three hours of musical theatre,' said Bell, 'leaving out nothing and no one, while satisfying everyone's ideas about that history and its vast array of characters, [was] clearly an absurdity.'[88]

Clark flew down to Melbourne on 14 January, reading Tolstoy's *My Confession* and lamenting that nobody was there to see him off from Canberra Airport. 'No one close to me' would be there on the opening night, he complained, 'save Dymphna, Don Baker, Sebastian, Benedict and

Andrew.' Katerina was in America and Axel was in hospital, awaiting an operation to remove his brain tumour. Two days later, when *The Musical* opened at Princess Theatre, the official program that accompanied the production included a full-page photo of Clark hauling in a fish at Wapengo, and statements of support from Prime Minster Bob Hawke, five of his ministers, and the Labor Premier of Victoria, John Cain. Of the eight politicians who appeared in the program, not one came from the conservative side of politics. Clark was praised as the nation's great storyteller, but this was a nation defined in Labor's image, one that seemed to invite the derision of conservatives. Clark wrote his own by-line for the program: 'He has been described by some as a "great master" and dismissed by others as a "bourgeois FALSIFIER". Most agree he has made a contribution to the debate in Australia on who we are and what we might be.'[89]

On the raising of the curtain at the Princess Theatre, Clark watched as Ivor Kants came on stage playing 'Manning Clark'. He 'started to shake'. Now he knew he had become more than an historian. The response of the audience was overwhelmingly enthusiastic. Afterwards, at a party given in Clark's honour at the Melbourne Town Hall, Hawke praised his contribution to Australian culture while Clark cut the cake iced in the shape of his hat. The following morning, when John Bell read the first reviews, he was devastated. Years later, he still believed that, despite the stunning quality of the visual production, performances and music, and 'houses that were enthusiastic to the point of being partisan', 'the conservative press tore into it'. Bell never forgot the condemnation of 'left-wing bilge spewing over the footlights'. 'Like Clark himself,' he said, 'the show had doughty champions and savage detractors.' Clark, equally despondent over the critical reviews, thought the same as Bell: 'as with everything I touch or write or say, the reaction is either hostile or enthusiastic … those who share my view hail me as a prophet and a hero. Those who feel threatened pour buckets of filth over my head.' He blamed 'the Protestant ascendancy and the New Right' for the failure of the production. Don Watson wrote to Clark hoping that, with 'faith', the show would ride out the controversy and go on. Within six weeks, *The Musical* was in crisis. Bell recalled how the entire stage crew at the Princess Theatre offered to work for nothing rather than see the show

Clark with Rolf Harris (right) on Michael Parkinson's show, May 1980

close—'but close, perforce, we did, with a loss of something like 1.5 million dollars and no way of recouping it.'[90]

Clark and Bell were understandably sensitive about critical reviews. But they both exaggerated the extent of the condemnation. Although it was true that reviewers pointed out the production's shortcomings as theatre, the majority of appraisals were positive. And as Bell himself admitted, *The Musical*'s demise was also due to the short-sightedness of the management, which failed to ensure sufficient time for rehearsals or promotion. What the reviews did reveal was the extreme sensitivity concerning public interpretations of Australian history—musical or otherwise. The same criticisms of the official bicentennial celebrations were levelled at *The Musical*. The Left argued that the role of women and Aborigines was given short shrift. The show 'perpetuated the myth of Australia's past as "white, male and British"'. Conservatives argued that the production was partisan, republican and jingoistic. Because *The Musical* was about Clark as much as Australia's past, the critical response reflected the political and cultural divisions that had been coalescing around his name since Whitlam's dismissal. Clark was no longer a mere participant in the nation's history and culture wars—he had become their subject.[91]

An Eye for Eternity

Laurie O'Brien, the widow of Clark's old friend John O'Brien from Melbourne University, saw *The Musical* on the opening night and thought it 'groaned'. Still on good terms with Manning and Dymphna, Laurie sensed after the show that they were both desperate to know what she thought of it. 'I couldn't bring myself to tell them,' she said. 'I could see that they were both living in this myth of themselves. Manning especially seemed to be caught up in this thing of his own creation and I liked that side of him less.' In some ways, fame had crippled Clark. He was incapable of seeing his shortcomings. In 2008, Pat Gray recalled a remark that Clark had made to her during their affair in 1955.

Speaking of Russel Ward, Manning said that by our age most of us had arrived at a realistic assessment of our own talents and achievements, whereas Ward had not. No doubt we all start out thinking we are world-shaking geniuses. I wonder now whether Manning had in fact achieved a modestly realistic self-assessment by 1955, and if so, whether he later lost it.

Throughout the 1970s and 1980s, whenever MUP's editors suggested significant changes to his manuscripts, Clark refused to accept them. Editing the six volumes down to a single edition in the early 1990s, Michael Cathcart found that their epic nature indulged his worst tendencies—'the grandiose, the winging phrase, the complete self-indulgence'. Cathcart also remembered Dymphna's revelation: 'the more the history took on a life of its own', he said, the more 'no one could rein Manning in'. 'Dymphna told me: "We all tried to persuade Manning to make cuts, but after volume one he became famous and then he wouldn't listen to anybody."' Editing Clark's last volumes, Wendy Sutherland found that he 'accepted minor changes, but baulked at anything further'. When changes were put to him, she said, 'he would turn slightly away, look over his shoulder, and say a little haughtily "You may change only *that* comma."' Elmer Zalums, Clark's indexer, tried on several occasions to amend errors of fact relating to Aboriginal history, but Clark refused to make corrections. Perhaps if he had listened to advice, even covertly as he was more prone to do in the 1960s, his work would have continued to benefit. As it was, his celebrity status resulted in his increasingly portentous voice overtaking Volumes V and VI to the point where his inter-pretations became so fictitious as to bear little resemblance to the historical events and people he described. In 1987, Clark received a letter from John Curtin's daughter, Elsie Macleod. She congratulated him on Volume VI but pointed out that her parents were not engaged in 1908 and in fact did not meet until 1912. 'My parents were never officially engaged, and my mother did not have an engagement ring—by her own choice.' Furthermore:

> [My father's name was John Curtin] as the names 'Joseph Ambrose' were baptismal names only and not included on his birth certificate ... I had not previously heard the story that my parents' marriage was delayed for years because my mother refused to marry my father until 'he promised to give up drinking'. This type of attitude sounds completely out of character for my mother, in spite of her Methodist upbringing—she was not the type of person ever to insist or demand that anyone do anything, she was quite the opposite ... My brother and I are rather puzzled by the description of our father having a 'sad' or mournful expression—but of course, he was always relaxed and happy at home, and so we saw him in a different light to other people, no doubt.[92]

Clark's *History* had grown closer and closer to autobiography, just as his grand themes had slowly been reduced to a nationalist crusade. Colonials, he said, did not make their own history. Only at the end of the twentieth cen-tury did Australians have that opportunity. The *History* had become the victim of Clark's success. When he began teaching and writing Australian history in the late 1940s and early 1950s, he could easily read all the relevant books and articles. Frank Crowley, defending his former supervisor, claimed that by the time Volume VI was published neither Clark nor any of his col-leagues could possibly absorb 'the avalanche of publications from a whole new, and larger, sub-profession of Australianists, including the opening up of numerous specialities—labour history, religious history, state histories, and women's studies'. This, of course, presumes that Clark was trying to keep up with new scholarship. By the 1980s, *A History of Australia* was writ-ten purely for a public audience. What began as a scholarly revolution ended as a popular marketing phenomenon. Convinced of his destiny as a prophet, Clark believed that he had a mystical relationship with the Australian people. Like his hero, Fyodor Dostoyevsky, he approached the end of his life besieged by requests. Reading the Russian's letters, Clark saw his own reflection. 'The entire literary world,' wrote Dostoyevsky, 'is hostile to me—only the readers of Russia love me'.[93]

For some of Clark's children, dealing with a prophet–father could be as demanding as it was rewarding. They all felt that his public appearances sapped his energy and put his health at risk. As the youngest child and the last to leave home, Benedict noticed that Clark was often unavailable. He was either away or writing. 'He became a bit of a loner,' says Benedict, 'and that was more than annoying.' 'Of course, I was not the only person who was denied his time. At dinner parties, when visitors had finished their dessert, he would stand up and start winding his watch, or wind the clock on the mantle piece, or simply invite them outside … would you like to see the chooks? But he was a very good father to me, great company and very witty, whenever any of us had a go at him, he'd say "you'll be sorry when I'm gone".'[94] It is no coincidence that Sebastian, Katerina and Axel all lived for extended periods in Europe and America. 'It helped to live overseas,' said Axel. Katerina told Clark in 1972 that it was 'only outside the family' that she could gain a sense of her 'own worth'. 'To live my life in the shadow of my parents (at 31) would be rather pathetic, a sort of ego-death. I have come to think that a major weakness in almost all Clark children stems from the fact that they are too tied to their family.'[95]

In 1988, when Axel, in his mid-forties, was facing a series of operations for a brain tumour, Clark struggled to come to terms with the fact that his son might die before him. Watching as Axel was wheeled from the operating theatre to intensive care, he was horrified by the sight of his swollen face. As often as he could, he visited and wrote to support him, his words straining to dissolve the pain of his son's cancer. As with Sebastian and Katerina, Axel's loyalty to his father was tinged with misgivings. Clark, aware of his son's potential as a literary scholar and writer, wasted no time in admonishing him if he thought he was not pushing himself hard enough. At times,

Axel felt 'reduced to some kind of lassitude' by his father's relentless drive for him to succeed. 'I feel as if I've spent the whole of my life being got out of bed,' he told his wife, Alison. Axel was an accomplished biographer and literary scholar. Yet when he weighed this against his father's achievements, his own work seemed slight. 'I feel I could never write anything so large or with such enormous impact on our society as he has done.' Axel—like Sebastian, Andrew, Roland and Benedict—had to learn how to deal with being Manning Clark's son. 'I was always pleased if people turned up in my room [and said] "I didn't know he was your father." It meant that at least to some people I existed as myself rather than [in] a shadow.'

In his diary, Clark frequently blamed himself for the faults of his children, seeing their lives through the prism of his own 'swinishness'. 'Was [Sebastian] the great failure of my life—the victim of my being ... possessed of devils ... he is the fruit of my mockery, my drinking, the dark side of my heart lives on in him, Axel never really tried. Is [Axel too] paying for the sins of the father?' Clark even saw his grandchildren's behaviour as his own fault. 'My sins are being visited on the children into the third and fourth generation. I corrupted them all.' As early as 1972, Katerina, who had long struggled to find her place in a male-dominated family, told Clark the truth about his tendency to see his offspring as the fruit of his transgressions. 'We have all been proud of you and looked to you for so long ... [but] I find it very vexing when you start one of your attacks of remorse for your "swinishness" of the past. In a sense, you are very egocentric when you think that you have done great damage to us all by your behaviour.'[96]

Despite every frustration they experienced with their famous father, pride and fierce love were the children's overwhelming response. Yet perhaps not all their pride and love combined equalled that of Dymphna. In September 1987, she apologised to Clark for spurning him after his flirtatious behaviour had hurt her yet again:

> I dare say that over the years I have become over-sensitised so that a trifle can flood me with negative feelings and memories which I normally try to keep at bay ... You are wrong about one thing: it is not anger, but emotional shock that makes me withdraw. I often think it would be better for all concerned

An Eye for Eternity

Manning and Dymphna, Canberra, 1987

if I could live alone. Then I could hurt no one by and not be oppressed by feeling inadequate or <u>de trop</u>. I might ramble on for pages, all about myself, but I know you would neither like nor remember a single word.

As Eirene Clark observed years later, Dymphna had much to forgive. Yet no matter how many times she felt let down by his failure to live up to his promises, her loyalty to him was unswerving.

On the night of 26 January 1988, David Malouf accompanied Clark and Dymphna to a house in Elizabeth Bay, Sydney. Like many others, they had come to the Harbour foreshores to watch the Bicentenary fireworks. During the display, Malouf went downstairs, where he noticed Dymphna, seated on a chaise next to a radio, her head tilted so that she could hear the broadcast of Clark's speech, recorded earlier that day. 'I remember wondering what she was thinking that night,' said Malouf, 'and what she thought of what Manning was saying. It was an image of devotion. She was sitting alone. Manning's speech was more important to her than the festivities.'[97]

and all very   to be teaching   a more disciplined

a unhappier   life so the   work well on

me for myself   conscious,   and have

made by my wife   ...   the

taken over me.

PART EIGHT

23: REMEMBERING KRISTALLNACHT

We live among feelings, to which
facts may or may not adhere
RICHARD ELLMAN, 1987

Kristallnacht: the aftermath

In 1987, after the publication of the final instalment in *A History of Australia*, Clark, aged seventy-one, turned his mind to writing his autobiography. Sensing his future closing in, he found more freedom in remembering his past. Whenever he tried to tell the story of why he became an historian and to explain the personal vision that drove him to write the *History*, he recited a series of personal epiphanies. In Clark's telling, these were moments of profound intellectual and spiritual revelation. They arrived like the words of an angel, shrouded in mystery, in a process that remained partially hidden, even from Clark himself. Through their telling, and in the contemplation of the morals they contained, Clark navigated his way through the story of his life. The imagined epiphanies provided inspiration and ultimately they served as his raison d'être, informing and guiding him in his final years.

Remembered in hindsight, the Clarkian epiphanies were plentiful. First, there were those of place: visiting Cologne Cathedral for the first time, awe-struck at the beauty created by man to praise God; standing on the South Head of Sydney Harbour, the sight of the turbulent sea making him want to write about what was inside the hearts and minds of the convicts; gazing at the ruins of Yorkshire's Whitby Abbey and dreaming of telling the story of how the Europeans had brought those two Great Expectations, Catholic

Christendom and the Enlightenment, to the ancient continent of Australia. Then there were the library epiphanies: discovering the Hindu fables about the world to the south of Java in a museum library in Jakarta; crying after reading that Magellan's 'black eyes wept' when he realised he had found a way through to the Pacific; seeing John Henry Newman's pencilled notes on truth in an 1864 article by Charles Kingsley, the genesis of Newman's *Apologia Pro Vita Sua*. And those that came through the meeting of fellow artists—James McAuley, Patrick White, David Campbell and many others—those bonds and friendships created by a spark of unspoken recognition and understanding rather than being earned slowly over time. Finally, there are those that relate to Clark's encounters with art, music and literature. Listening to Bach's *B Minor Mass* or the slow movement of Beethoven's *Piano Sonata Opus 111*; hearing Henry Handel Richardson read from *The Fortunes of Richard Mahony*; viewing Sidney Nolan's *Riverbend* or Rembrandt's *Return of the Prodigal Son*; visiting the Seamen's Bethel Chapel in New Bedford Massachusetts to view the plaque dedicated to the writer Herman Melville: 'Seaman extraordinary, whose voyages lured him across the stormiest of all seas, within the heart of man'; reading White, Chekhov, James or the usual suspect, Dostoyevsky: all of these encounters made Clark realise that history must always run second to art as a form of human expression.[1]

Of all Clark's epiphanies, though, there was one that stood out for its allegorical power. It was the one that he mentioned most often, the one he invested with the most significance, especially because it explained the genesis of his life as an historian. Clark alluded to the story for the first time in 1965 and again in an interview with Hazel de Berg, recorded for the National Library of Australia in 1967 but not publicly aired in any major way until 1978, when it was included in a profile of Clark written by Rob Pascoe for the *National Times*. Pascoe's article, 'The History of Manning Clark', led with the story, describing the 23-year-old Clark arriving in Bonn the morning after Kristallnacht, on 10 November 1938: 'Clark made his way amid the debris throughout Bonn in a state of disbelief.' Two years later, in 1980, the background article Clark had originally prepared for Pascoe was published under the title 'Themes in A History of Australia' in Clark's *Occasional Writings and Speeches*. Throughout the 1980s, Clark was invited to reminisce in the national media about his life and career, and he told the Kristallnacht story many times. In 1987, interviewed by John Tranter on Radio National, he offered a typically powerful telling:

What really got me going was that when I was about 22 or 23 I went to Germany to meet the woman I was going to marry, and I happened to arrive at the railway station at Bonn am Rhein on the morning of Kristallnacht. That was the morning after the storm-troopers had destroyed Jewish shops, Jewish businesses and the synagogues. Burned them and so on. And I came up out of the Bonn railway station, my head stuffed with these myths about progress and so on. And there I was confronted with these storm-troopers. Of course they didn't menace me, or threaten me. But I saw the fruits of evil, of human evil, before me there on the streets of Bonn.

Over the next three or four years, I gradually had to abandon all the myths I'd grown up with. That my world, my intellectual equipment, my spiritual equipment, couldn't cope with what I'd seen in Germany. And all the things that had meant a great deal to me and probably still do mean a great deal to me, like *Hymns Ancient and Modern*, the Old Testament, the King James Bible, the Dry Souls of the Enlightenment, as Carlyle called them, the hopes about things better, the belief in the British—all this had to go and I had to start on a new pilgrimage to see, was there anything which could replace these myths which I think I found then didn't correspond with the world as I'd come to know it.[2]

This telling of the Kristallnacht epiphany was similar to the version in *Occasional Writings and Speeches*, as are the lessons Clark drew from the encounter, except that in the published article Clark wrote about himself in the third person ('the author'), more consciously creating a figure of myth.

Two years before the Tranter interview, the story appeared in Max Crawford, Geoffrey Blainey and Stuart Macintyre's *Making History*, in Clark's brief address explaining his approach to the writing of history:

When I came up out of the Bonn railway station on the morning of 11 November I was confronted by men in military uniforms who had machine guns in their hands. They were wearing huge breeches. They would have made marvellous shepherd rucks for Carlton in the old days. That morning in the *Volkischer Beobachter* Dr Goebbels explained that the German people had taken their revenge on the Jews for the attempt by a Jew named Grunspan to assassinate a member of the German Embassy in Paris. Once again ... I found myself chewing over the question of human evil. There were at least two people inside me—the optimist and meliorist, and, dare one say it, the part-time messianic; and the other pessimistic, gloomy, the person who saw no answers to the problem of evil, or, as I liked to put it in those five volumes, 'the madness in men's hearts'.[3]

After the Kristallnacht story had been told by Clark on ABC TV and Radio on several more occasions in the 1980s, it appeared for the final time in the second volume of his autobiography, *The Quest for Grace*, published in 1990. At the last moment, in his ink scrawl, Clark had added the following words in the margins of the final manuscript draft: 'Dymphna was there on the platform at the Bonn railway station when I stepped off the train early in the morning of 8 [sic] November 1938 ... we were in for a rude shock, it was the morning after 'Kristallnacht' ... glass was everywhere on the footpath ... there were trucks with men in uniform standing in the tray.'[4]

If there is one personal experience that explains Clark's life and work, it is his experience of Kristallnacht, the point when the Nazi persecution of Jews turned towards the Holocaust. For Clark, the encounter in Bonn sent him on a journey to seek an understanding of the human condition. It was his Creation story, taking him back to the ancient classics, the Old Testament and Shakespeare. Witnessing the aftermath of Kristallnacht, the shards of glass still on the street, Clark confronted Conrad's heart of darkness, and he doubted the capacity of the Enlightenment to deliver human beings peace and happiness. It was the 'beginning of an awakening ... the moment when the author realised that he would have to start to think again about the whole human situation. He would have to base his beliefs on something more solid than those superficial, shallow ideas picked up in Melbourne.'[5]

In early 2006, I was reading correspondence from the 1930s between Clark and Dymphna. It was late and I was tired, struggling as usual with

Clark's handwriting. Reading one letter from Dymphna to Clark, dated 12 November 1938, I suddenly realised that Clark had not been in Bonn on the morning after Kristallnacht. At first, I thought I'd made a mistake. Like many others, I had taken Clark at his word. I re-read Dymphna's letter carefully, checked Clark's diary entries, and saw that it was impossible for Clark to have been in Bonn on the morning of 10 November. As his own diary confirmed, he did not arrive in Bonn until 26 November, more than two weeks after Kristallnacht. It was Dymphna, not Clark, who witnessed the immediate aftermath of Kristallnacht. She wrote to Clark on 12 November 1938, when he was still in Oxford, and she wrote again on 24 November, two days before Clark arrived in Bonn. In the letter of 12 November, she described the scene:

> The violence was over when I came—but the crowds were everywhere—following the smiling SS men, children shouting in excitement, grown-ups silent, except for children. We went along lots of streets, & saw about 15 smashed shops—mercers, frock shops, & laundry, a silk shop etc. Then we went down to the Rhein and saw the smoking ruins of the synagogue. Behind it the rabbi's house was burning ... Weitergehen! Weitergehen! [Keep moving!] from the police was the only sound to be heard except the shuffling feet of hundreds of curious sightseers, so we left the Rhein where the grey evening mist was just rising over the poplars & factory chimneys and the western sky was all rosy ... I went home but couldn't work ... on the way to the forest, I passed a second, smaller synagogue, gutted like the first ...[6]

Later, in the company of a friend, the Swiss student Hans Ehrenzeller, Dymphna walked the streets of Bonn to 'see the sights'. She enclosed the article by Joseph Goebbels that Clark referred to in one of his tellings of the Kristallnacht aftermath, describing it as 'a gem' before remarking that 'gentlemen in uniform were not very conspicuous during the actual venting of righteous wrath', although she did write that she had heard one girl say that 'gentlemen in black poured the oil on the synagogue here, & others set it on fire'. I felt a sense of disbelief and disappointment at having been misled, but this did not last long. When I told two of my friends, both historians, about my discovery, the response was the same: 'Oh, no!' they said, sighing. Like me, they wished that Clark had been there; they wished that the historian, of all people, would not play with the truth in such a way. When I told two other friends, both novelists who had known Clark, the response was different: 'Isn't that fantastic?' they said, 'typical Manning—theatrical, playful, pulling your leg. What a great subject for a biography!' It was as if they could imagine Clark laughing from beyond the grave. The novelists made me stop my rush to judgement. I began to see Clark's untruth as the most revealing parable of all.[7]

Clark not only placed himself in Bonn on the morning after Kristallnacht; he also used some of the material in Dymphna's letter, mixed it with his own recollections, and made it his own. In *The Quest for Grace*, for example, he described walking the streets of Bonn with Dymphna and Hans Ehrenzeller after Kristallnacht, as well as a later meal with two Irish students in a university *mensa*. These events seem to be taken directly from Dymphna's account. More importantly, Clark, by claiming the story as his own, denied Dymphna the voice of the narrator. Three years after Clark died, she wrote to Carl Bridge (the head of the Menzies Centre for Australian Studies at King's College, London), trying to dispel what she called 'the myth of Manning's rejection of Oxford'. But her letter revealed much more. She wrote, 'In December–January 1938–39 [Manning] certainly took an extended Christmas vacation to come to Bonn, but he returned willingly to Balliol and left only when the outbreak of war made it necessary for him to find a job.' 'December–January', not November. This letter alone demonstrated that Dymphna's memory was quite different from Clark's. But in a recorded conversation in 1995, she was even more explicit.

[Manning] says he arrived the morning after Kristallnacht. That's not true. What happened the morning after Kristallnacht, I knew nothing I was at home, studying, writing something and Hans Ehrenzeller this young Swiss came and knocked on the door, he'd never done that before, and I went down to see him and he said that I was to come with him and see "die Ausschreitungen" … (the outrages), and he took me and showed me a synagogue which I didn't even know existed all burned and I remember that the Rabbi's house was right next to the synagogue and it had an outside stairway ... and there were geraniums in pots on the steps and I remember he was a very sensitive chap Hans Ehrenzeller, and he said " Oh, da sind die Geranien von der frau Rabbine [the rabbi's wife's geraniums are still there] ... he couldn't get over it ... so that was how I saw it and then Manning must have arrived a few days later and there were still sort of vestiges of the sacked shops and the glass, maybe still glass, and these notices on windows 'Juden unerwunscht' [Jews unwelcome] and he would have seen that and then he would have seen the trucks with the Nazi youths, the storm troopers carousing round the city, but it was not the morning after, I would have told him all about that morning.[8]

Dymphna was not one to play with the facts. Her recollection of Kristallnacht, almost fifty years later, was entirely consistent with the letter she wrote to Clark in 1938. The fact that she insisted that Clark was *not* there, showed how much the issue of his absence mattered to her. She wanted her story recorded, exposing him on the one hand, yet covering for him on the other hand. When prompted about the glass on the streets, she suggested that he might have seen the glass ('maybe still glass'), before returning, emphatically, to the most important fact—'it was not the morning after'. Between 1978 and 1990, as Clark told the story of Kristallnacht repeatedly in public, she knew it to be untrue. Reading her blunt and occasionally caustic editorial comments on his manuscripts, it is difficult to imagine that she kept this knowledge to herself and that, some time between 1978 and Clark's death, in 1991, she did not question his recollection. Given her nature, it is possible that, one morning at Tasmania Circle, Dymphna climbed the ladder to Clark's study, confronted him and said, 'Manning, you weren't there, you know you weren't there. What do you think you're doing?' Exactly why she chose to remain publicly silent is an intriguing question. The most obvious answer is probably the right one: she was so loyal to him that she could never betray him. For their marriage, the Kristallnacht story raised many questions. If Dymphna did confront Clark, it had no impact. He continued to tell the story in the national media. If she did not confront him, her silence was yet another example of the sacrifice of her own life to the colossus Clark had become. Whatever Dymphna's response, she lived with the knowledge that Clark had claimed her experience as his own.

When Clark told the Kristallnacht tale, he did so in the context of telling his life story. He had retired and was already a significant national figure. Why could he not have told the story of Kristallnacht through Dymphna? Why did he need to reduce her to a woman who was simply waiting on the steps of the railway station to marry him? Why did he need so desperately to be the one who was there? Most likely, Clark, the great historian, needed to be there to make the parable of Kristallnacht more powerful, to draw from the events the great lessons he had undoubtedly drawn.[9]

In this sense, there was no fabrication. The impact of Kristallnacht on Clark was genuine and profound, somehow pushing aside the fact that he was not physically present. In the same way that Clark felt he could not write about events in the past without visiting the places where those events had occurred, he felt he could not speak of the significance of Kristallnacht for his intellectual and spiritual development without having been present. Clark needed to be *the* witness—the only way he could make meaning of the past was to inhabit it—and he willed himself to be there. Here, another question arises: how conscious was Clark's invention?

In a lifelong partnership, a couple's separate memories can sometimes become one, and through Dymphna, Clark no doubt felt he *was* there in Bonn on the morning after Kristallnacht. He had, after all, arrived in Bonn only two weeks later, on Saturday 26 November 1938. His diary entry for that day revealed a young man shocked by what he saw: 'I walked round the town, struggling against the oppressiveness, the sea of hostile, hard faces, and the strangeness of my surroundings ... uniforms, pictures of Hitler, notices in form of command, not of request. And yet life went on here very much the same as in England. It was very bewildering, almost frightening.'

Months later, he was certainly dwelling on the question of evil. He wrote in his diary on 15 February 1939: 'I have been worried lately by the problem of evil, the existence of which we are apt to ignore in our frantic search for the ideal.' When Clark arrived in Bonn, he saw the Nazi storm-troopers and was frightened by them; he also saw and heard evidence from several people of the Nazis' persecution of the Jews; and he was torn over the best means of resolving the political crisis between Germany and England—to appease or not to appease.[10]

His experience in Nazi Germany was a beginning. As he told an audience at Melbourne University in 1984, 'after the experience in Bonn in November 1938, followed by quite an epiphany in Cologne Cathedral in the same year, my mind was rather like a fugue in four voices.' For Clark, it was the beginning of his confrontation with the 'age of unbelief'. Kristallnacht, the portent of the Holocaust, was mankind's fall from grace. In this sense, there was considerable truth in Clark's account of it. The truth lay in the felt part—the emotional and moral truth—and the conclusions drawn. He did not see the glass on the street or the smoke rising from the burning synagogues on the morning of 10 November, but he certainly experienced its aftermath and the increasing terror of the Nazi dictatorship.[11]

At the same time, there is also something typically, comically Clarkian about the whole affair. Each time Clark told the story, he had himself arriving in Bonn on a different day. In *The Quest for Grace*, he arrived in Bonn on 8 November; in *Making History*, he arrived on 11 November. On other occasions, he arrived in 'early November' or on 'one of the mornings after Kristallnacht'. Many years later, after reading *The Quest for Grace*, a friend of Hans Ehrenzeller wrote to Dymphna, noting that Hans had lived for another four years after the date Clark had given as his death. The details of Clark's story shifted in each telling. Sometimes he claimed to have seen the synagogues burning (a sight he could not have seen arriving three weeks later). Sometimes he mentioned the glass on the street (the Nazis ordered the Jews to pay for the cleanup two weeks before Clark arrived). It is also highly unlikely that Dymphna met Clark at the *Hauptbahnhof* in Bonn, as he claimed. Clark's journey from London would have taken him through Belgium and across the border to Cologne. Here, Clark would have needed to change trains in order to get to Bonn, a journey of a little over half an hour on a regional train. Dymphna had written to him shortly before he left Oxford for Bonn, on 18 November, telling him that she would meet him in Cologne. Clark's details and dates, as usual, were unreliable.[12]

Clark seems to have streamlined the details in his telling of the story in order to dramatise his arrival. Typically, he described it in theatrical terms: coming up out of the darkness of the underground onto the streets of Bonn, meeting his waiting lover, confronting the portent of the twentieth century's greatest horror. The scene was operatic—both romantic and tragic—like Verdi doing Shakespeare. But it was also deeply existential. In late 1938, Clark was afraid of the onset of war. He feared for Dymphna's safety, and for his own. On a much larger scale, he feared for Europe and the future of civilisation. His Anglican upbringing and Enlightenment beliefs were no match for the Nazi terror. In this sense, the desolation Clark felt as he told the Kristallnacht story half a century later was for the sake of the future and not for the sake of understanding the past. The question he asked—Where to now?—he asked of himself and of human society. And even as he told the story, he did not believe he had found the answer.

In the late 1980s, Clark began to consult his diaries and letters as he worked on his autobiography. In the preface to *The Quest for Grace*, he explained that in writing the volume he had 'made use of diaries begun in April 1941'. This date suggests that in writing *The Quest for Grace*, Clark did not have access to the first volume of his diary, begun in Bonn in late November 1938 and proving that he arrived there two weeks after Kristallnacht. But the date he gave is also odd, given that the second volume of his diary began in May 1940, not in April 1941. Clark appeared to be plucking the date out of thin air. There is no volume of his diary that begins in April 1941.

It is possible, but unlikely, that he managed to find all of his diaries from the late 1930s and 1940s, bar one. Yet, even if it were true that Clark did not have access to his first diary while writing his autobiography, there is no doubt that he drew on Dymphna's correspondence from the same period. In *The Quest for Grace*, Clark's memory of Dymphna's visit to the home of the art historian Dr Busslei draws on a letter she wrote to him in October 1938. 'I had heard about him in letters from Dymphna,' Clark writes. At one point, recalling a belligerent outburst by Busslei, he quotes almost verbatim from her letter. That letter was kept together with others from Dymphna written in October and November 1938, including the one she wrote to him on 12 November 1938 that described her experience of Kristallnacht. Given that

Clark's account of Kristallnacht closely resembled Dymphna's, and that in writing *The Quest for Grace* he drew on her correspondence from the same period, it seems unlikely that he did not sight the letters she wrote to him in November 1938. Bundled up with Clark and Dymphna's correspondence was yet another letter Clark might easily have sighted: the one he wrote to Augustin Lodewyckx only five days after Kristallnacht, from Oxford: 'I suppose you were slightly anxious for [Dymphna's] personal safety during the recent pogroms in Germany, and so I hasten to reassure you. She is quite safe, though severely shaken & disturbed by the whole incident. She saw the debris in the streets of Bonn, and witnessed the burning of the synagogues.'[13]

If Clark chose to place himself on the streets of Bonn, knowing that he was not there, this was his inner lie. He had told the story in public and traded on his audience's trust in him as an historian. In 1997, Carl Bridge, another scholar who took Clark at his word on Kristallnacht, presciently summed up Clark as 'part mystic, part fraud'. 'He had to be', said Bridge. 'This was how he made us aware of his and our versions of the truth.' Referring to Clark's intellectual larrikinism and his penchant for preaching on the meaning of life, Bridge argued that this was part of his greatness; Clark revelled in the power of myth.[14]

I believe that the older Clark did have some awareness of the fact that he was not present on the morning after Kristallnacht. But to claim to know the *extent* to which he was conscious of it is to claim to know the inner depths of his mind. At times, I think I can see him lying, the details of his memories shifting with each telling; at others, his recollections are clear, the story told so powerfully that it seems he did believe he was there. I know I can never recover what he truly remembered, the memory of his inner voice, the voice that only he heard. But it is precisely this tension and uncertainty—fed by the shadowed, fallible nature of memory—that makes the story so fascinating.

One of the most interesting aspects of the Kristallnacht story is that Clark first alluded to it in fiction. In the 1960s, Clark began to write short stories 'for relaxation', as he told Beatrice Davis, his editor at Angus & Robertson. In 1966, he published 'Two Visits', a thinly veiled autobiographical story of the exploits of Charles Hogan in Bonn in 1938. The story's tone is oddly aggressive, occasionally misogynist and at times consumed by self-loathing. Like Clark in his twenties, Hogan is 'tormented by his own impotence' as a writer and frustrated by his time-wasting in Bonn. He seems incapable of producing the great work he believes himself destined to write. Hogan wanders Dostoyevsky-like through the streets of Bonn. He is 'never quiet': 'Some demon inside him drove him on the whole time he was there.' While Clark did not mention Kristallnacht, he drew conclusions from Hogan's experience in Germany that were similar to those he drew for himself when he first began to tell the Kristallnacht parable in the late 1970s. Of Hogan, he wrote:

> I think it likely that Hogan did discover things about himself in Germany; that first visit did confront him with the question: what is the source of human evil? Is the imagination of man's heart evil from the start, so that questions of social organisation, political systems, moral codes are but the scum on the pond of human life—not the well-spring?

Hogan struggles to come to terms with the brutality of Nazi Germany. He is a man without faith, an 'unbeliever' in 'Protestant Christianity', deeply sceptical of any utopian vision 'for the future of humanity'. Clark seemed to know himself better in fiction. He wrote of Hogan in Bonn that his 'flair for dramatising his life' was really 'one sustained effort to draw attention to himself'. And then this: 'His flair for the dramatic often caused his memory to play him tricks.' Indeed. Clark's experience in Germany, recounted first as fiction, was fleshed out and became autobiography a decade later. Finally, like much autobiography, it revealed itself as ultimately a strange and unavoidable amalgam of both fact and fiction. In Clark's case, however, this trajectory seemed entirely appropriate.[15]

Nevertheless, it is significant that Clark's memory of Kristallnacht is told in the context of autobiography, a notoriously imperfect and fraught enterprise at the best of times. Setting out to write her three-volume auto-biography, Doris Lessing was decidedly uncomfortable with the genre. Among novelists, she is not alone. JM Coetzee, for example, has preferred to fictionalise his autobiographical writings, believing that 'fiction has better resources for dealing with unconscious forces than discursive self-analysis'. In the process of writing her autobiography, Lessing found that it exposed 'the worst deceiver of all—we make up our pasts'. Well aware of the black holes and 'shifting perspectives' of memory, she remained adamant, like Coetzee, that 'fiction makes a better job of the truth'. But unlike Coetzee, she persisted with autobiography, largely out of her instinct for 'self-defence', given that at least four writers were then working on biographies of her.[16]

The unreliability of memory is the unreliability of autobiography, a necessarily apocryphal genre. Distanced by time, the self who is created by the narrator becomes a character, even a complete stranger to the person who writes. Details, dates and places are lost in the fog; the felt life is often a more abiding memory than the minutiae of the lived life. Work done by the US psychologist Jerome Bruner on autobiography and the self best expresses the fundamental strangeness of the genre. He writes:

> It is an account given by a narrator in the here and now about a protagonist bearing his name who existed in the there and then, the story terminating in the present when the protagonist fuses with the narrator … The self as narrator not only recounts but justifies. And the self as protagonist is always, as it were, pointing to the future.[17]

Clark showed no signs of discomfort with the genre of autobiography. Its potential for truthfulness seemed to him just as great, largely because, unlike Lessing, he rendered his life as narrative not out of necessity but willingly. As he told John Tranter in 1987, 'The only gift I had was to tell a story.' In the late 1980s, he turned to write autobiography at a time when the genre was experiencing extraordinary popularity. Writers such as Clive James, Barry Humphries, Geoffrey Dutton, Donald Horne, Jill Ker Conway and Bernard Smith had all turned their hand to memoir—often, as Bruce Bennett has pointed out, tracing their life 'as part of a national allegory'. Having told the nation's story, Clark was now being asked by his readers for his story, and he relished the opportunity to tell it.[18] Writing autobiography allowed him to do with his own life what he had already done with his historical actors: create himself as a character, and employ the same literary devices—particularly the epiphany as a moment of new consciousness—to reshape his life through literary reminiscence. Clark's memory was not his instrument of reference but his instrument of discovery. In the process of recollection, and in the creation of his life as story, he was able to find new meaning in past events. Many of the events from his past that the septuagenarian Clark saw as significant in the late 1980s were not invested with the same significance at the time when they occurred. Clark's diary entry after his visit to Cologne Cathedral on 9 December 1938 made no mention of the painting of the Madonna, or of the Heinrich Heine poem that allegedly moved him to tears:

> We saw the cathedral, beyond description … we walked round the town and saw the notices … 'Juden werden nicht bedient' [Jews will not be served] on shop windows. Everything looked very prosperous and very lovely in the soft glow of twilight, with the darkness of the buildings against the blue of the sky and the pink clouds. The … cathedral seemed to cast a spell on the whole town, and the darkness came down quietly, and one felt safe.[19]

This was a far cry from the memory of Cologne Cathedral recited by Clark in 1987. In other diary entries from the late 1930s, he was moved by a triptych of Rubens's paintings depicting the Immaculate Conception, the birth of Christ and his crucifixion ('Mary, in horror—that it should [come] to this'), and by Chartres Cathedral, 'which inspires that sense of awe and wonder'. 'I thought of the powers of inspiration of the Catholic Church,' wrote Clark, 'of the issues between Catholicism and Protestantism—authority & beauty against liberty of thought & dullness.' These entries revealed the traces of truth in his later recollections, and perhaps this is the best that the author and reader can hope for in autobiography. For Clark, and for every writer of autobiography, there are two competing truths: one's past life as it was perceived and lived (mostly lost from view), and one's past life as seen from the time of writing, a truth that leans on the paper-thin house of memory. Despite the fact that Clark had access to his diaries as he composed his autobiography, he was more concerned with the latter truth: making his life behave as literature. The older Clark shifted the time and

Stefan Lochner, Adoration of the Magi, *Cologne Cathedral, circa 1450*

place of many of his early encounters in Europe, then condensed and embellished his visions into one or two Earth-moving epiphanies as he reinvented his life before a public audience.[20]

In the last years of his life, on every occasion on which Clark told the Kristallnacht story, he recounted it together with the Cologne Cathedral epiphany. In 1987, two months before his interview with John Tranter, he appeared on ABC TV, interviewed by the arts presenter Peter Ross. Telling the story of the two epiphanies, Clark was very moved, as testified by the transcript.

> Clark: I went to Germany to see the girl, or the woman, I was going to marry—Dymphna—at the University of Bonn, and I happened to get there on the morning of the ninth or tenth of November ... I got there and came out of the Bonn Railway Station onto the footpath, the road, and it was one

of the mornings after Kristallnacht, when the SS in Germany had conducted this savage vendetta against the Jews for the murder, or the attempted murder, of a member of the German Embassy in Paris.

Ross: You saw the broken glass?

Clark: I saw the broken glass and I saw those troops with the their revolvers and their sub-machine guns and so on, on the back of trucks ... I was absolutely overwhelmed by it. I could scarcely speak, and in the long run—it's difficult to work it out, Peter, isn't it, when you're really ... But it was some time then, within the next few days or certainly within the next few weeks, that I realised that all the things I'd been brought up with ... *The Book of Common Prayer, Hymns Ancient and Modern*, and all the hopes and aspirations of those dry souls of the enlightenment ... all this was just pitiful equipment with which to face up to the phenomenon of human evil.

Ross: So the scales came from your eyes?

Clark: Yes the blinkers, the blinkers of being a member of British civilisation overseas, of being a simple boy from the Australian bush—all this had to go ... A few days after that, I went with Dymphna to Cologne, and remember I was a Church of England clergyman's son and a State school boy and a Melbourne Grammar boy, as it were, [and] I walked up those steps of Cologne Cathedral ... I went into the Cathedral ... and I ... yes ... I was overwhelmed.

Ross: You're overwhelmed now, as you recall it.

Clark: Yes, I am.

Ross: It must have been an extraordinary occurrence.

Clark: Yes, it was. I'd find it difficult to put into words.

[It was at this point that Professor Clark wept ...]

[Clark then tells the story of seeing, behind the high altar in the cathedral, Stefan Lochner's painting of the Madonna and Child (1450), which inspired Heinrich Heine's poem 'Painted on Golden Leather'. He translates the one line that had always remained with him: 'Inside the cathedral there stands a picture painted in golden leather and in the great wildness of my life it's always shone brightly.']

Clark: That episode in the cathedral in Cologne which had moved me so deeply—in fact, so deeply that I have never been able to speak about it since—it, I think, was germinal in writing the History, because then and subsequently I realised that I had to dispense with what had carried me through life so far, what I call my 'great expectations', either of Christian belief or the Enlightenment, and that I had to ... find another way. And that, really, in a sense the History became an account of how all we in Australia became citizens of the Kingdom of Nothingness—believing in nothing—but that doesn't mean nothing in one sense ... It's the opposite of nil. It's really giving up the great expectations and asking yourself, what then?[21]

Clark seemed to admit at one point that he was uncertain as to exactly when the encounter in Bonn revealed its mysteries to him ('It's difficult to work it out, Peter'). We see him in the act of fashioning memory anew, bringing himself to tears in the process.

He wrote to Kathleen Fitzpatrick shortly afterwards: 'I made an attempt to talk about what I had never talked about to anyone before ... [I] am still shaken by what happened during the interview.' Clark had never spoken before about the experience in Cologne. To some extent, he was discovering its significance as he told the story to Peter Ross. In 1978, he wrote of his visit to Cologne Cathedral but made no mention of the mystical experience he described to Ross in 1987. He seemed to create the emotionally shattering vision at Cologne in the telling, as if he could only reveal himself through the act of performance.[22]

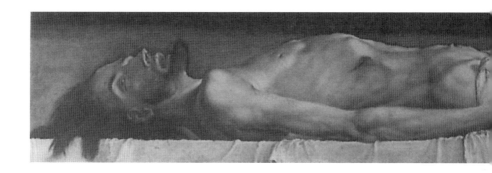

When Ross questioned him directly, Clark insisted that he *was* there in Bonn on the morning of 10 November ('I saw the broken glass'); then, at another point in the interview, he claimed that two days later, he was out cycling with Dymphna. 'It was Armistice Day,' he told Ross. In freezing cold weather, he and Dymphna came across a memorial to German soldiers. Clark claimed that this introduced him 'to the whole idea of *mittel-Europa* and German civilisation and what it had been like to be a German'. But Clark was no more in Germany on Armistice Day than he was in Bonn on the morning after Kristallnacht. Nor did he experience yet another epiphany on his return to Cologne Cathedral in 1956, on his way to England from Rome, as he claimed in 1978. As Dymphna remarked in 1995, 'I think Manning's memory of that has been shaped over the years ... it was added to in hindsight.' In 1956 Clark travelled from Rome to Oxford via Paris, bypassing Cologne completely. The closest he came to Cologne that year was late one September evening, driving south from Bonn to Basel on the autobahn, the lights of Cologne 'twinkling in the distance'. Driving the car through the night mist with the children asleep in the back seat and Dymphna sitting beside him, Clark thought of Lochner's *Madonna* behind the altar in the cathedral and of Heine's poem. 'Moved by the idea of being moved', he pressed on without stopping. Telling his life story in the media, Clark placed himself in Cologne in 1956 because it made his narrative more powerful. Cologne Cathedral followed tidily on from his epiphanies in Rome. He did return to Cologne in 1990, the aged pilgrim visiting his personal shrine, reciting Heine's verse to a Catholic attendant, his voice breaking as he sounded the words 'In my life's wildness'. Clark added layers of meaning to his experience in Cologne Cathedral over time, investing more

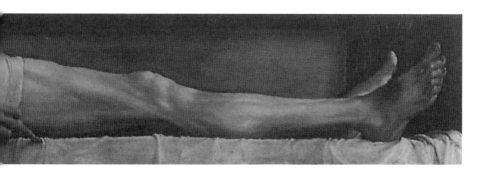

Hans Holbein, The Body of Dead Christ in the Tomb, *circa 1520*
'the wasted body, the wound in the side, the marks left by the nails in the hand and feet,
the fall blackened by death (as end of everything)—the bloodless lips, the mouth open,
the eyes vacant, expressionless, helpless, that blackness on the face which expresses
everything—the unstained linen—Christ is lying down—defeated—overcome by
death ... every feature of the body suggests defeat—the shoulder blade—the blackness of
death on the right hand—the fingers, flesh almost having wasted off the bones—one sees
already the skeleton behind the flesh, the protruding navel—the face of a man who had
just discovered he had lived for a lie, a cheated, disappointed—disenchanted man'.
Clark, Diary, Basel, 13 October 1973

and more significance in Lochner's painting as he saw his own death approaching. The dimmer his future appeared, the brighter his visions became.[23]

When he told the story of his first visit to Cologne Cathedral in 1938 in *The Quest for Grace*, it followed closely behind the Bonn epiphany: 'From the day I saw evil in Bonn am Rhein there would be no putting back to harbour: I launched further into the deep when I stood in front of the painting of the Madonna and Child behind the high altar in Cologne Cathedral.' Dymphna, aware of the 'tempests' raging within her lover, retired to the back of the building, apparently unable to partake in such a shattering moment: 'inside the cathedral I was strangely moved. Dymphna, noticing what was going on inside me, left me alone to feast on it all in my heart.' This epiphany in Cologne was, in fact, almost a reincarnation of Dostoyevsky's experience in Basel in the late 1860s, a fact of which Clark was well aware.[24]

In 1867, while travelling from Baden-Baden to Geneva, Dostoyevsky visited Basel and there saw Hans Holbein's *The Body of the Dead Christ in the*

Tomb, painted in the early 1520s. The painting depicted Christ's emaciated body in the tomb, the holes still visible on his blackened hands and feet, his gaunt and bearded face looking upwards in doubtful hope. Dostoyevsky remained haunted by the image for the rest of his life, just as he was by his memory of Raphael's *Madonna* in Dresden, a painting which he described in *Crime and Punishment* as bearing a kind of 'mournful religious ecstasy'. Dostoyevsky was moved and overwhelmed, unable to articulate the mystery he sensed within Holbein's work. Yet he was also plagued by the doubt that arose within him: what if Christ did not rise from the dead? Then man is truly alone.[25]

In the back pages of his copies of *Crime and Punishment*, *The Idiot* and *The Possessed*, Clark noted the page numbers of Dostoyevsky's writings about Holbein's and Raphael's paintings—'409–11 the Holbein painting'—marking the reaction of the narrator in *The Idiot*, who stood before Holbein's *Christ* and felt some 'dark, insolent, unreasoning and eternal power to which everything is in subjection'. Clark emulated the Russian's search for truth, cultivating (sometimes consciously) an artistic sensibility in which art, literature and metaphorical language were the one true source of spiritual revelation. Like Dostoyevsky, Clark was moved but did not fully understand the experience: it was mystical, forever hinting at profound truths destined never to be resolved.[26]

Clark visited Basel in 1956 and 1973 and viewed the Holbein. In 1961, during a lecture on Dostoyevsky, he told ANU students how Dostoyevsky's wife, Anya, had been present with the writer in Basel on the day when he first encountered Holbein's work. She watched as Dostoyevsky stood before the painting 'as if stunned'. 'His agitated face had a kind of dread in it', something she had noticed during the first moments of his epileptic seizures. As Clark told the story, Anya 'withdrew' from Dostoyevsky, retiring to another room in the gallery: 'she knew who he was, what came up from inside the man'. Thirty years later, when Clark told the story of his own epiphany before the painting of the Madonna in Cologne, he had Dymphna withdraw in the same manner as Anya, creating the memory of his own life in the image of Dostoyevsky's. Like Dostoyevsky, who, while travelling in Italy in 1869, stopped in Bologna on his way to Venice simply to see Raphael's

St Cecilia, Clark stood before the paintings of the masters transfixed as questions rose involuntarily in his mind, as if they were transmitted by an 'infinite power'.[27]

The two epiphanies, Kristallnacht and Cologne Cathedral, were spliced by Clark into an almost filmic scene of self-discovery, one representing the inadequacy of Protestant teachings and the Enlightenment to solve the problem of human evil, the other holding out the potential spiritual solace and compassion of the Catholic faith. Like the Spanish poet Federico García Lorca, with his notion of *duende*—which Lorca described in 1930 as 'a momentary burst of inspiration, the blush of all that is truly alive ... what Goethe called the 'demoniacal' [the 'dark force' that rises from within the poet] ... needing the trembling of the moment and then a long silence'— Clark was rendered speechless by the visions and inspirations that rose before his eyes. 'I could not speak of the experience then to anyone,' he wrote of the epiphany in Cologne Cathedral. 'Was there anyone who could understand? Many years later when I risked talking about the experience my whole body shook.'[28]

Clark sought and depended on *duende*, flashes of inspiration that brought the pain and suffering of a deeper awareness of the human situation but at the same time served as his intellectual and spiritual guiding lights. Writing was a whole-body experience. He had no alternative but to write from the gut, to feel the physical sensation of trembling and shaking, because his was a poetic imagination. The details of Clark's life, like Australia's past, were adapted to suit his dreams and mystical visions.

The true story of Kristallnacht revealed the true nature of Clark's voice: the voice of the heart and mind, the inner man seeking 'higher truths'. Voices spoke to Clark—from within him, from the past, from the present—and he struggled to play them back to us, mediated through his unique emotional intelligence and sensibility, so that we might hear them, too, as if for the first time.

In 1989, thinking on literature, music and art occupied many of Clark's waking hours, just as it had done all his adult life. Ahead of him lay the moment he had feared since the day he bought his first diary in Bonn in 1938.

We die without knowing
what we have lived
MILAN KUNDERA[1]

On 31 October 1990, Clark recorded an extraordinary event in his diary. Dubliner Samantha O'Donnell, a woman whom he had never met before, called on him in Canberra. Clark had been expecting her.

She explained to me why she had asked to speak to me. In the Ansett plane from Sydney to Coolangatta, she had read my article in *Panorama*, the Ansett in-flight magazine, on my favourite places. She decided she must speak to me. At the Gold Coast she saw the article on me in the *Weekend Australian*. So she asked the switchboard for my telephone number and rang up, hence her being in the house. She told me she knew I would understand what had happened to her—how one day in Dublin she was aware of Christ standing in front of her—though she could not see him or hear him. Yet he made her aware of his love and [of] his request [that] she should give her life to him. After that experience she examined her whole life and resolved to weed out all that was rotten. Some months later she went to Indonesia where, after drenching her body with water, Christ was again in front of her with his gift of love and understanding. Her whole life has been changed. She goes to Mass every day, twice on Saturday (late afternoon mass). She loves the tiny morsel of bread … partaking of the love of Christ. She knew I would understand. I took her back to the Hyatt hotel. We embraced body to body. I felt exalted by her, a warm-hearted fey-like fool in Christ. To whom can I speak about that?

In 2008, after hearing this story from Clark's former ANU colleague John Molony, I managed to track down Samantha O'Donnell in Dublin. The story she told me was remarkably different. 'In 1987, I suppose I was where Manning was. I felt this strong need for faith but had huge doubts about the whole church thing. But I had come to a point where I knew I had to do something. I just knew I had to follow the feeling inside me. I decided that I needed to leave my home, my husband and my four daughters, and travel to Indonesia. The whole experience was a life-changing event, a road to Damascus type event in my life. I handed my life over to Christ.' Three years later, in October 1990, together with her husband, O'Donnell left for a three-week holiday to Australia. Flying from Sydney to the Gold Coast, she read the profile on Clark in the in-flight magazine. 'I could see he was searching, looking for answers, searching through his memory of his father's life. When I gave the article to my husband to read and asked him what he thought he said: "He sounds like the grumpiest man I've ever heard." But I felt this huge aching for this man. I felt drawn very much to love him. It was not about me trying to help or rescue him, and the feeling didn't come from me, it came from another source. I was just the channel and it was so powerful that it floored me. I was fearful of it. But I just knew I had to let him know that God loved him.'

Having checked in to her hotel on the Gold Coast, O'Donnell was unable to settle. As she stood on the beach that afternoon, she couldn't stop thinking about Clark. 'It kept niggling me and I was quite disturbed by it. But I knew I had to follow it.' She went straight back to her hotel room and called a friend, Frank Carroll, the former Catholic Archbishop of Goulburn in New South Wales.

I remember saying to Frank that what I was about to tell him might seem strange and he said, 'Well, coming from you, nothing would surprise me!' I asked him if he knew who Manning Clark was and he explained that he was an historian, 'the wise old man of Australia' who lived in Canberra.

For O'Donnell, the news was like 'a door opening'. She had taken another step but couldn't let the matter rest.

I rang directory assistance and straight away they gave me his number in Canberra. I picked up the phone and called. He answered the phone. I couldn't believe it. I could hardly talk. He asked me why I was ringing, whether I was a journalist. I told him that I simply had to meet him.

On 31 October, O'Donnell arrived at Tasmania Circle at 11.30 am. Clark opened the door. They walked into the living room and sat down while Dymphna prepared morning tea. O'Donnell remembered feeling very nervous. 'I suppose I was worried he would think I was crazy. I just wanted this over with.' She tried to tell him the story from the beginning but found that she could not contain herself: 'Virtually straight away I told him, "I just had to come to tell you how much God loves you. I could not rest until I told you this message."' At first, Clark said nothing. 'He didn't really question me,' said O'Donnell, 'he just listened and kept staring intently. I still remember his eyes. They were piercing. He was shocked.' When Dymphna re-entered the room with the tea she noticed that something was wrong. She asked Clark 'if he was OK'. 'Yes, Yes I'm fine, just leave us alone,' he told her. O'Donnell didn't stay long.

I was going to call a taxi but Manning insisted on driving me back to the hotel. On the way, we spoke a little. I told him a bit about myself. Arriving at the hotel, we said goodbye, and I got out of the car and started to walk away. I'd gone no more than a few metres when I heard him call out. 'Wait, come back,' he cried. As we met, he embraced me. He gave me a long hug—like a baby almost—clinging on to me. And he clung to me for quite a while. Until that point, he'd given nothing away.

Remembering how she felt on leaving Clark that day, O'Donnell knew that she had fulfilled her mission. 'It is a hugely humbling thing to do,' she told me, 'to be taking a message from God. This is it. This is my life. This is my purpose, my true being. I knew that God was there for him, that God loved him. I just hope he took it.'

In Clark's telling, O'Donnell arrived like a pilgrim seeking counsel from the one who 'would understand'. She was the seeker. He was the wise old man. In O'Donnell's telling, the roles were reversed: Clark was the seeker, while O'Donnell was the messenger who had come to deliver him God's love and the promise of eternal life. Trust Clark to receive an angel; at first glance, the story seemed so fanciful that it would be hard to suspend disbelief even if it were fiction. But fiction it was not. If truth can be gleaned in the telling of a story, in O'Donnell's tone of voice, in her conviction, in her willingness to reveal more about herself than Clark, and in the fine detail of her memories, then Samantha O'Donnell spoke her truth about that day in October 1990. It was Clark who could not admit the truth—not to himself, nor to the readers who would come after him. Perhaps he feared that if he did write down everything that O'Donnell had told him, posterity might think him deluded. So he told a story that left him in control, with O'Donnell disappearing from his life as the 'fey-like fool in Christ', the fool he could never quite bring himself to be.[2]

All his life Clark had meditated on the meaning of death. But now, in the final two years of his life, meditation became an obsession. Some time in the late 1980s, he wrote out verse 12 from chapter nine of the Book of Ecclesiastes. It was the twelfth verse that spoke to him: 'For man also knoweth not his time: as the fishes that are taken in an evil net, and as the birds that are caught in the snare; so are the sons of men snared ... when it falleth suddenly upon them.' Annotations in many of the books in Clark's library revealed a similar preoccupation. Inside the jacket of a monograph on Goya, he wrote down a line from one of the last sonnets of Francisco de Quevedo (1580–1645), the Spanish poet who had made such a powerful impression on Goya. Death: 'since it is law and no punishment, why do I afflict myself?' In response to Goya's depiction of a dead woman surrounded by a halo of light, Clark asked: 'But will she rise again?' In public, he continued to repeat the mantra of his youth: 'Death should not exist. But it does, so what are you going to do about it? I've never been able to accept the idea of annihilation. The simplest answer is: soon we'll know.' Journalists noted his musings on the

afterlife and observed his physical frailty: 'a slight, middle-sized and elderly gentleman, left somewhat frail after two heart operations'. Accompanying photographs showed him propped up against the white-barked birches in the park opposite Tasmania Circle, his figure lean, bent gently like the trunks of the trees that surrounded him.[3]

In interviews, Clark spoke about the increasing importance of music as he grew older. 'Music helps me to understand Christ's remark that the Kingdom of God is within you.' Cocooned within the worlds of Bach or Sibelius, he felt ageless and free. Even hope was possible. Still searching for salvation, he replayed the scenes of his past searchings in his mind. Attending mass, he recalled the moment in his life when he had come closest to joining the Catholic Church. In the late 1970s, he had asked his friend and former student at the ANU, Father Frank Sheehan, to celebrate personal masses for him. Sheehan, a liberal Catholic priest who became a regular visitor to Tasmania Circle between 1977 and 1980, remembered the unusual nature of Clark's request. 'Manning would ring up and ask me if I would say a personal mass for him, so he would come over, and I would celebrate mass at Daramalan College, in Dickson. Dymphna would come along too but she never took communion. Manning would always bring his Book of Common Prayer with him. It was strange really. I never celebrated a personal mass for anyone else, but Manning and I were extremely close.' The masses took place in small rooms behind the college chapel. Sheehan was unperturbed by the fact that he was breaking Church doctrine by serving communion to a non-Catholic. 'In retrospect, not to give Manning communion would have hurt him. It would have been unkind.' Sheehan and Clark found in literature some of their most powerful expressions of faith. 'Faith was about probing a mystery,' said Sheehan, 'and that gelled with Manning—faith was about yearning.' In the poetry of James McAuley and Francis Webb, in the paintings of Arthur Boyd and Sidney Nolan and in the novels of Patrick White, the two men found images of Australian Christianity. 'We used to talk about an Australian theology, whatever that might be,' explained Sheehan. 'Something to do with literature and perceptions of God in a country where there is a desert at the centre.' The most obvious starting point was *Voss*. But there was one passage of White's in particular that resonated for both men, and it came from *The Twyborn Affair*: 'Love is an exhausted word and God has been expelled by those who know better, but I offer you one as proof that the other exists.' Clark gave Sheehan a copy of the novel, which he inscribed: 'In gratitude for Mass on the Feast of the Transfiguration'. It was this idea of transfiguration that so appealed to Clark's romantic imagination. Sheehan remembered how Clark's 'hands would shake and he would cry' as he gave him communion. In transfiguration, Clark imagined 'a glimpse into pure light' and the possibility of radical change. Said Sheehan: 'Manning always told me that Anglicanism could never be enough for him. He followed the Anglo-Catholic tradition, the same tradition that had attracted his father and John Henry Newman, who stepped off the tightrope of High Anglicanism and converted to Catholicism. But I always thought that he would never make the leap of faith.'[4]

When Sheehan moved away from Canberra, marrying, and leaving the Catholic Church to serve as an Anglican minister, his friendship with Clark continued but lost the intensity and closeness of earlier years. Attending mass between 1989 and 1990, Clark continued to weep when he heard the priest say the words 'the Body of Christ', just as he had wept before Sheehan ten years earlier. But now his tears were due to his failure to believe. Without a personal mediator to do his believing for him, he could not bring himself to

An Eye for Eternity

take communion. '[The priest] offered me the bread and I whispered "No", though a voice inside me whispered faintly "say yes, take the bread of life."' Trapped in the space between faith and doubt, Clark recited passages from literature to public audiences as if it were the novelists and poets who had inherited Christ's word. He grew fond of quoting Thomas Hardy's late poem, 'The Oxen', wherein Hardy wrote that if someone asked him to come and 'see the oxen kneel' on Christmas eve, as if in a child's world, 'I should go with him in the gloom, hoping it might be so'. At other times, Clark quoted Kirilov, the hero of Dostoyevsky's *Possessed*, who wondered what would happen to mankind if the story of Christ's resurrection was shown not to be true: if Christ lived a lie, said Kirilov, then all the planet was a lie and rested on a lie and on mockery. 'What is there to live for?' he proposed. 'Answer, if you are a man.' This was the question Clark had asked since the publication of Volume I of *A History of Australia* in 1962. In 1989, he told Humphrey McQueen that he still did not have the answer. Christ was a mirror in which people saw themselves, he said, 'or what they believe to be important in life'. Christ was not the miracle maker or the Son of God who rose from the dead. The claim was 'preposterous'. Dostoyevsky and Hans Holbein had taught him that much. Christ, he wrote to McQueen, was the man of the 'enigmatic remark' who had 'the sun of love in his heart', the one whose face the great painters had searched for, the ethereal vision of humility, innocence and love. It was this face that Clark saw in Stefan Lochner's *Adoration of the Magi*, which he returned to see for the last time in Cologne in July 1990. Standing before the painting behind the side altar, he gazed up at Lochner's *Madonna*— her cheeks flushed red, her eyes downcast, all the world at her feet.[5]

In the last two years of his life, Clark continued to erect a wall of words between himself and his own death. If, in the pages of his diary, it appeared that he no longer had the will to live, his correspondence with his closest friends showed that his love of life and restless curiosity burned as brightly as ever. To his former colleague at Melbourne, Kathleen Fitzpatrick, with whom he began a frequent correspondence after 1983, Clark wrote as the polite, sensitive and accomplished scholar ('so we live together, on the bookshelves of the university bookshops'). Yet compared with the letters he wrote to Humphrey McQueen in 1989–90, his correspondence with Fitzpatrick appeared stilted and guarded. While he respected Fitzpatrick, he loved McQueen. And while he romanticised his relations with women, his deepest friendships had always been with men. In 1983, shortly after McQueen returned from New York and Paris, he found himself invited to Clark's home for dinner. 'Manning sought me out—after nearly ten years without contact— he began to court me and I was open to suggestion. We would walk and "Tuppence" would come along.' By 1989, when McQueen left for Japan, Clark, whose relationship with Pat Dobrez had by then cooled, found in McQueen a man with whom he could show every side of himself.[6] McQueen had left university life and ploughed out a career as a freelance writer, so he was free of the taint of academia in Clark's eyes. And having acknowledged his homosexuality, he had also made the crossing that so intrigued Clark. Sensitive and sympathetic to Clark's loneliness in his old age, McQueen was the Renaissance man with whom Clark could parade his feverish appetite for literature, music and art. With McQueen, he could indulge in intellectual jousting, summing up Proust, Byron and Pushkin in throwaway lines, describing the disintegrating figures in Picasso's late drawings, or exchanging his thoughts on the music of Wagner. 'I have been playing the overture to Tristan & Isolde quite a lot lately. Dymphna dismisses Wagner as one never-ending act of self-indulgence. That is too simplistic. There are many Wagners—I like the Wagner of l'orgasme perpetuelle, and the tender, serene après l'orgasme.' As his reading ranged wider, Clark read biographies compulsively, writing to McQueen about the lives of writers and artists—Tolstoy, Modigliani, Strindberg, Plath, Jung, Dickens, Greene, Picasso and Goethe—which he consumed at the rate of almost one a week. As he read Gerhard Wehr's biography of Carl Jung, he noted Jung's remarks made in a lecture at Yale University in 1937.

> We can only follow Christ's example and live our lives as fully as possible, even if it is based on a mistake. No one has ever found the whole truth; but if we [could] only live with the same integrity and devotion as Christ ... we would all, like Christ, win through to a resurrected body.

Combing the lives of others, Clark appeared to be searching for answers; perhaps the story of someone else's life might hold the secret to the riddle of his existence. Tending his archive, he compiled the raw materials of his own biography in the shadow of the lives of his artist heroes, hoping that one day he would join them in the pantheon of literary gods.

As Clark's letters to McQueen gathered pace and intensity, McQueen found himself becoming 'the go-between' between Manning and Patrick White'. In 1989–90, Clark was constantly hoping for White's phone calls: 'Will Patrick ring?' 'Does he still love me?'[7] The turning point in Clark and White's friendship came in 1980 after the lunch Clark attended at Yarralumla with Governor-General Sir Zelman Cowen, whom Clark had known at Melbourne University in the 1930s. White was disgusted with him: 'You are unable to see what a very foxy number that Zelman Cowen is. If, as you say, he is a friend from Uni days, you could surely have gone and had a private cup of tea instead of confusing many people who are your admirers.' He offered to help Clark, but claimed that Clark was uninterested. 'I wish we could talk Manning. But you never will. You say repeatedly you are coming to see me. You never do, or if you do, you bring one of your children to act, I feel, as a shield.' A few days later the two men met in Centennial Park. White told Clark to his face: 'I don't give a fuck what they think of me. You still want them to think well of you.' From here on, White played on Clark's desperate need for his approval, teasing him with occasional displays of affection ('Patrick is again writing tender, loving letters'), before taunting him with savage denunciations, all of which were meticulously documented by Clark—'alas, my being received back by Patrick White did not last for long. I have again offended him. This hurts me, because I am still in love with him. I hope he will live long enough to receive me back.' The former Labor MP Barry Jones, a mutual friend, recalled how White 'talked a lot about Manning' in the 1980s, usually in a mixture of 'admiration and scorn'. Another mutual friend, David Malouf, thought that White was preoccupied with his status as a writer, and believed that 'Manning had let the team down with his frequent public appearances'. 'Patrick called him the Archbishop', said Malouf, and 'he hated Manning's sentimentality, partly because it reminded him of his own sentimentality, which he always tried to disguise'.[8]

Clark's moods swung dramatically according to the reception he received from the irascible monarch of Martin Road. There was no other Australian writer for whom he held more respect, no other writer with whom he wished to be mentioned in the same breath. It was not White's friendship that he hankered for; emotionally, he was much closer to McQueen. Rather, it was the companionship of great minds. Clark had sought similar if less intense friendships with writers such as Iris Murdoch and William Golding, both of whom had visited Tasmania Circle and (at least in Murdoch's case) through him had met Patrick White. Seeking intimacy with White, Clark was hankering for what Goethe called 'elective affinities', a spiritual communion between Australia's most acclaimed novelist and the country's most renowned historian. This is what White had denied him. And the spectre of his rejection even entered Clark's dreams. In 1984, Clark dreamt that he was in a room with White, who was dressed in drag. The only other person present was Katerina. The White figure asked him 'Have you been with your lover?' Clark stumbled over the reply, not knowing whether to admit that he had a lover 'albeit a very close friend'. He turned to see Katerina weeping, 'frozen in terror'. In Clark's unconscious mind, White appeared as 'the stern Jehovah', the punisher who maintained moral standards he could never possibly attain. Writing to McQueen, Clark vented his frustration. 'Patrick's personal vindictiveness is rather like the envy of Australian academics—bottomless and unfathomable ... he is a brilliant denouncer ... consumed with hatred and bitterness and crankiness.' Dymphna rarely accompanied Clark on his visits to Martin Road. As she explained later, 'Manning was drawn to visit Patrick a number of times. I never wanted to ... I always felt awkward in his company ... whereas Manning was amused & tolerant of White's emotional aberrations, Patrick was caustic and treacherous. On the phone, when I explained that Manning was absent on a speaking engagement, he said in his quavering voice: "But I thought he was at death's door."'[9]

As Clark's love affair with his public audience deepened, he recoiled from what he saw as White's hatred and contempt for ordinary Australians. In public, he held his tongue, refusing Peter Craven's request to review White's memoir *Flaws in the Glass*, because he did not want to damage his 'friendship' with the novelist. When White was severely ill, Clark put aside his differences and visited him in St Vincent's Hospital, crying at the sight of his shrunken body. For a short while, White's affection for Clark was rekindled, but every time he quickly reverted to condemnation. In February 1990, White refused to allow his photograph to be used in Clark's second volume of autobiography, *The Quest for Grace*. For Clark, this 'left a wound that only death could cure'. Shortly afterwards, White told him again that his vanity was the cause of the break in their relationship. He even felt sorry for Dymphna because she had to live with him. Only weeks before White died, Clark rang to find that White had cut him completely: '23 August 1990: Today Patrick White did not want to speak to me. Why? What have I done to deserve such treatment?' In order to win White's approval, Clark had been prepared to endure humiliation. In the end, not even this had saved him from being spurned.[10]

When White died on 30 September 1990, Clark was at Wapengo. The following morning, hungry for Clark's commentary, the ABC flew journalists and cameramen in helicopters from Sydney. Clark got up early, jotting down notes for his interview:

> Am to be interviewed for ABC television news & 7.30 report at Wapengo today. Points to make: There are very special people—Goethe's point—one great mystery is why the gods create such people who do their work and then are taken away. Maybe the gods sent him to condemn our greed and titillation culture ... Patrick as the judge of all of us—loyalty ... promiscuity ... Patrick the lover—he wanted something no one could give him. We were all inadequate. We all let him down.

A few hours later, the sound of the ABC choppers could be heard above the roar of the waves at Wapengo. Clark walked out onto the verandah, looking every bit the world-weary seer the ABC had travelled so far to interview.[11] Before the cameras, Clark eulogised White as one of Australia's greatest artists. Despite the fact that their relationship had soured, and the inspiration they once received from one another's work had ended in disappointment, it was Clark who performed the public rites for White's passing. The two men had fallen out over their different perceptions of the writer's responsibility to his country: how to speak, when to speak, what to speak about and which audience to speak to. Ironically, they had also fallen out over the issue Clark had fought for long before White took it up in

1975—Australian independence—and how the writer should live true to that ideal. With White gone, Clark felt the lofty view from his own perch even lonelier. While he occasionally saw friends such as Sidney Nolan when Nolan visited from London, he felt that he was slowly being deserted: 'My contemporaries, or, more accurately, near contemporaries all seem to be dying.' Kathleen Fitzpatrick had died four weeks before White. After Clark delivered the eulogy at her requiem mass on 31 August 1990, he stood outside the church talking with his friend, John Legge. Unexpectedly, a nun interrupted their conversation to compliment Clark on his eulogy: 'That was beautiful Professor Clark. You'll get a good eulogy too.' Clark was stunned. Legge saw how the reminder of his mortality had taken him aback. Accustomed as he was to entombing others, he was unprepared for his own death. When he visited John La Nauze on his deathbed five months earlier, Clark appeared to draw strength from La Nauze's imminent demise:

[I] visited John La Nauze in Woden Valley Hospital. He has shrunk more. He said: 'You've got to help me.' I sat in silence for twenty minutes. When I said good-bye he shook my hand and said in a blurred voice: 'I am extremely grateful to you for coming to see me.' For the first time in my life I felt sorry for him. The sight of a broken man nourishes the good things inside us, compassion for everyone, quietens the malice, the anger, the spite, the resentments.

Seeing a man whom he had often seen as his rival and nemesis 'broken' and waiting to die allowed him to feel compassion for him. When La Nauze died, Clark's feelings of rancour could die with him. Or so he thought. On 23 August 1990, he attended La Nauze's memorial service in Melbourne. 'A Terrible Day … Today John La Nauze was buried. He once did me great evil and I enviously let him & others know how much he had hurt me. In death many here in Melbourne only remember my retaliations—many professing love for me are this day weeping over his coffin in the Canberra crematorium. Such is life!' All too often, Clark was only capable of understanding others through the narrow prism of his own emotional needs. Yet in the deaths of La Nauze, White and Fitzpatrick, he saw his own death foreshadowed.[12]

After *The Quest for Grace* was launched in October 1990, he chastised himself for failing to tell the truth about his life, wondering if he should tell all in a third volume —'a book of reflections on life, like what Dostoevsky had in mind when he wrote of writing the confessions of a great sinner ... the story of a man who failed every test in life'. Within weeks, *Quest* was number one in the bestseller lists for non-fiction. But Clark already had his eyes on his next book. Afraid of hurting others, he decided to try first through fiction, resurrecting his alter ego, Charles Hogan, but the result was a familiar tirade of self-hatred broken by rare moments of self-awareness: 'tormented by lust but too cowardly to get down to business, too afraid of a rebuff, except when so drunk that he could do nothing even if his "partner" wanted it'. Unwilling to push ahead with the project, he turned to write a memoir for Allen & Unwin's publisher, John Iremonger, hoping to tell the story of his passion for historical writing. But the story was one he had told many times before. Complaining of exhaustion and breathlessness, and suffering from bouts of giddiness and nausea, he was beginning to feel that he had run out of subjects to think about. He no longer had the energy to write in long sittings.[13]

Circles in his life appeared to be closing. In October 1990, Pat Gray wrote to him from London, hoping that they might meet 'at least once more'. Since the end of the Bicentenary year in 1988, he had looked at the world around him and experienced a profound sense of alienation, as if preparing the path for his own exit. Delivering guest lectures at the ANU, he felt as if he were trying to communicate with 'people from another planet'. He no longer belonged in a society, he said, that had not heard of 'Job, Psalm 39, or the Sermon on the Mount'. The world he had known was slipping away from him. The images that haunted him from Hardy's late poems were of unrequited love or loneliness. In his darker moments, he wandered the country like Hardy in 'Wessex Heights', 'tracked by phantoms' and shut out from life, a man who could find liberty only in isolation. He was also beginning to lose faith in politics. When he attended a Labor Party dinner in Sydney in November 1990, he was bewildered by the display of wealth. BMWs and Jaguars were parked outside the hotel: the party of the working man courting the wealthy and the glitterati, the conversation around the dinner table vacuous and inane. 'I could see it was no longer my party,' he told his friend, the poet Mark O'Connor.

Events outside Australia were also increasing his sense of isolation.[14] When the Berlin Wall fell in November 1989, the ideological contest between capitalism and communism that had framed so much of Clark's intellectual life came to an abrupt end. Watching the events unfold on television, he seemed puzzled: 'I had hoped men & women with a vision of a socialist society would have raised their voices among the ruins of bureaucratised, party dominated socialism. But—alas—thousands are sprinting into the west … wanting their liquor and their women.' With the collapse of socialism, Clark experienced history as an external force, a relentless tide pushing aside many of the ideals that had governed his life's work. Would nothing but materialism be left in the wake of November 1989? A few months earlier, on his final trip to Europe, walking to the Colosseum in Rome, he was disgusted by modern technological society, with its 'spawning of tourism and consumerism'. Although he rekindled his 'love of all the "holy wonders of Europe"—the music, the theatre, the gardens, the melancholy, and the high seriousness'—he came to the conclusion that the forces of globalisation had destroyed the mystery of life in Europe. 'There can be no miasma,' he wrote in his diary, 'with half naked tourists filling the streets.' Dymphna travelled with him, but as ever she appeared in the diary primarily as a source of grievance. Looking at the Italian women on the streets of Rome, Clark summed up the country's entire sexual culture: 'Although women here show much flesh, they are not distracting or stirring. I suspect the men want something more than this apparent openness. I suspect here the cunts are dry, the tits not so spongy. Sex here is probably as shallow as the hedonism.' The observation was both ridiculous and appalling, and Clark knew it. The comment expressed his fear of women's sexuality and the envy of an old man who knew that the liberal sexual culture he saw before him was beyond his reach. But it also showed how he would stop at nothing to confound the future audience to whom he was now writing, leaving them with sharply conflicting literary images: the lover and believer and the iconoclastic sinner whose tortured heart overflowed with emotion. Some time in the last months of his life, Clark scratched a message on the underside of the brown paper lining in the desk drawer in his study: 'I hate my life.'[15]

After the publication of *The Quest for Grace*, Clark was without a major writing project for the first time since the 1940s. As ever, he feared the response of the critics, almost pleading for favourable treatment. 'I am sure now that the literary smart alecs will take over and cast their bucket of filth over my child.' The book was lauded in most reviews and won the Christina Stead Award in the Victorian Fellowship of Australian Writers' national literary awards. But prizes only offered Clark temporary relief. Retreating to Wapengo, he felt listless and bored. The only counter was to press ahead with more public appearances. Although he claimed that he would retire from public life after *Quest* ('I'm getting old. You've only got so much to say and when that is said you should shut up'), public speaking had become a way of life, the major source of his self-worth. Clark was incapable of shutting up. Swept up in the new wave of environmental consciousness, he warned that human beings had to exercise their power over the environment with 'great care'. He joined the fledgling Australian Republican Movement, adding his name to the list of notable Australians who called for an Australian republic by 1 January 2001. When there were public rites to be performed, such as the memorial dawn service held on 4 June 1990 outside the Chinese embassy in Canberra on the first anniversary of the Tiananmen Square massacre, Clark was often asked to preside over the ceremony. He continued to mix priestly duties with political activism. In late 1990, as the US invasion of Saddam Hussein's Iraq became more likely, he became one of the leading anti-war spokespersons, appearing on radio and television, demanding that Australia become the Sweden of the South Pacific by remaining neutral and brokering peace. 'The resurgence of Islam is a fact,' he declared. 'We have got to live with it. We have got to be very careful we do not provoke Islam. Australia has got Islam right on its doorstep with Indonesia.' When former Labor MPs suggested the idea of a special Australian envoy to Baghdad, Clark not only supported the idea, he volunteered to go, imagining for a moment that he might go down in history as the prophet who saved the world from war.[16]

The older he became, the more reporters found his public appearances strangely moving. He appeared to come from an Australia that was now lost, as the journalist, Sharon Webb, discovered when she reported on one of his last public appearances in Launceston, in April 1991.

Slowly and with dignity, the old, bearded man moved to the microphone; he was dressed in a dark suit with a university tie, and a gold watch chain swung from his waistcoat pocket. He spoke: 'Historians tell stories of the past by creating scenes. I want to tell my story by creating a scene in Russia in the 1880s' … At that point, close to 1000 people in the Albert Hall were silent, focussed on a man who was close to 80 years old and the universal truths he spoke. His powers of oratory, though perhaps unorthodox, were significant. He pulled us in. We wanted to listen … he spoke quietly. Whether he adopted the technique purposely is irrelevant: we leaned forward, we strained our ears so as not to miss a word.

Clark was seventy-six. There was no veneration like that preserved for the old historian. His sheer persistence in giving so much of himself to his country was capable of inspiring awe and reverence. The week after Clark delivered his public lecture in Launceston, the cartoonist Michael Leunig wrote to tell him of his response after hearing him interviewed on ABC Radio: 'It was a very personal and reflective piece … it moved me enormously. I carried it around within me for a long time … it had a strong, revelatory quality and gave me considerable inspiration and courage at a difficult turning point in my life.' By exalting 'the felt life', Clark helped others to tap their emotions, his voice unlocking the inner voices of his admirers. As he pushed on, committing himself to more and more public engagements, his behaviour with friends and family suggested that he was having premonitions of death. Determined to farewell friends, he sent postcards daily, like the one he sent to his old school-friend, Phil Harris, who bred greyhound racers: 'the great handicapper must be preparing to order both of us off the course of life'.[17]

In early May, he rang Benedict to tell him that Mark Faunce, his physician, had decided that he should go into hospital. At thirty-four, Benedict was a general practitioner in Victoria. He knew that Faunce was right but he also understood his father's reluctance to go back to hospital. Clark refused to go. He wanted no more 'indignities'. 'Goodnight Nurse,' he used to say to Benedict. 'Once you come into a hospital you might not come out.' He told Benedict that he felt he was going down rapidly. Fearful of telling Dymphna of his pain, lest she dismiss his fears as yet another bout of hypochondria, he left notes for her around the house. 'Dymphna: am at the point—am having constant mini-angina, and giddiness. Am again worried Manning.' Even when she was physically near, he preferred to communicate his deepest feelings through the written word, as if she were a woman who visited while he was out of the house. In Dymphna's editorial comments on the manuscript of *The Quest for Grace*, her frustration with Clark's self-important character was undeniable: 'Pitiful? Come on now! <u>She</u> needs to be identified—wife or flame? She has been doing it off and on for 140 pages! Do you think it tactful to talk about Russell's generosity to "those more gifted"? What about "to those with gifts different from his own"?' She had grown scornful of 'guru Clark'. When the couple appeared on ABC TV's *The Home Show* in May 1991, the tension between them was palpable, Dymphna's ice-like glances in Clark's direction suggesting much more than surface irritation. Meanwhile, in his study, under filing cabinets and bookshelves, Clark was stashing his last notes to her parents, Augustin and Anna: 'Fuck the Lodewyckxes.' After fifty-two years of marriage, the couple knew the lines of division that separated them all too well. As Clark resigned himself to accepting that she would never forgive him for his 'treacheries of the heart', Dymphna had given up hoping that Clark would change. He would always ask her for more than she could give. The notes Clark left for her in the weeks before he died were epigrammatic examples of the hundreds of letters he had written to her since their courtship began. He pleaded for her to rescue him. And he could not face his death alone.[18]

The last time David Malouf saw Clark, in May 1991, he found the experience 'really very strange'.

> I was due to get on the plane to Brisbane that day, before going overseas. Before I could get there, my agent rang, wanting me to sign a contract, and came over to get my signature. Shortly afterwards Manning and Axel arrived, and as we stood in the passageway between my kitchen and living room, Manning, with his usual warm embrace, and in an absolutely final way, said to me 'Goodbye Dear boy.' I'm sure he knew he was dying.

Only days earlier, Clark, ordered by his doctors to take complete rest, appeared to make a final gesture of his love for Dymphna, as she explained eight years later.

I was on my way back from Melbourne to Canberra by bus and it arrived at 6am. It was freezing cold when I got to the Canberra terminal at six o'clock in the morning. And when I arrived not only was Axel there, but in the background behind Axel there stood Manning wrapped up in his old navy blue velour coat. He must have got up at half past five to come out and meet me and I was absolutely overwhelmed. It was mad of him to do it and I couldn't understand. I still don't understand.[19]

On 23 May 1991, Clark was due to fly to Adelaide on yet another speaking engagement. Early that morning, he was so ill that he decided to abort the trip. Shortly afterwards, he rang Nicholas Brown, asking him to bring his mail over from the ANU. By late morning it became clear that Clark was in terrible pain. His heart was failing, his lungs filling slowly with fluid. Dymphna rang Mark Faunce, who told her that he would come as soon as he could. Then she called Clark's GP, Dr John Madden, at Manuka Medical Centre, but couldn't get through. By the time Brown arrived at Tasmania Circle, at 12.30, Clark was agitated. 'I walked into the bedroom and stood at the side of his bed. The first thing Manning said was "I need help."' Eva Manikis, who had lived in the Clarks' backyard flat the previous year was there with Dymphna. Within half an hour, Clark was shouting: 'For God's sake, I need help. Can't somebody do something?' Faunce and Madden were still busy with their patients. After hurried consultation with Dymphna, Manikis made the decision to ring the ambulance. 'Manning was struggling to breathe,' she remembered. 'He had a death rattle.' She felt alarmed and scared. Fifteen years later, she still felt 'traumatised' by the events of that day. 'It wasn't just that Manning died, she said, 'it was the way it happened'. When Brown walked into the bedroom to tell Clark that the ambulance had been rung, he sat with him for a while. 'He wasn't easy to be with,' he recalled. 'He kept asking me "When will someone come?" He was distressed and angry. Dymphna was working in the opposite room. She came in and out.'

While Manikis was out of the room ringing the ambulance, she could hear Clark gasping for breath, yelling 'death or release'. At that moment someone knocked at the door. 'Two unemployed people in their early twenties were asking for money to paint street numbers on the driveway. Dymphna gave them ten dollars and they started work immediately, painting the number 11 at the top of the drive.' Heather Rusden arrived at the same time as the ambulance. 'Some time that afternoon,' she later explained, 'Manning called me and said "Come now!" Stupidly, I wasted time buying flowers and chocolates and when I arrived the ambulance had just got there. I raced in and Dymphna grabbed me as I walked through the door and cried, "Help me, he's dying."' Nicholas Brown remembered that when the ambulance officers entered the bedroom, Dymphna remained in the kitchen. Brown, Manikis and Rusden stood at Clark's bedside. Rusden recalled the next moments vividly.

> I was touching his leg as the ambulance men walked in, they came in just behind me, and there was terror in Manning's face, there was no peace or tranquillity in his face, he was desperate to stay alive. The last things I remember him saying were 'Help me, I'm dying' and I can't remember if he said I don't want to die, but that was certainly the feeling I got, there was this overwhelming feeling of terror, of him not being ready. There was absolute fear in his face. It was just this chaotic minute and he was dead.

The ambulance officers walked out and told Dymphna 'There's nothing we can do.' She went briefly into the bedroom after they left. A few minutes later, she walked Rusden to the door of the bedroom and, holding her arm, said gently: 'You'll want to say goodbye, you spend as much time as you like.' Dymphna did not stay in the room. 'I found it odd,' Rusden reflected.

Eva Manikis shared a cup of tea later that afternoon with Dymphna. In a matter of fact way, Dymphna said to Manikis: 'I don't think I did the right thing by Manning this afternoon,' as if she could not explain her behaviour to herself. She had clung to her daily chores, the only source of order as the last chaotic moments of Clark's life unfolded around her. She had tried to ring the doctors. At times, she floundered and asked others for help and advice. And she kept the house running for everyone else, as she had always done. All her married life she had found it difficult to comfort Clark in his anguish. The last hours of her life with him were no different.[20]

AFTER LIFE

The universe is either chaos of involution and
dispersion, or a unity of order and providence.
My reason says the former, my heart the latter.
MANNING CLARK, DIARY, 4 DECEMBER 1982

Interior, St Christopher's
Cathedral, Manuka,
27 May 1991

It was Clark's final act: a set-piece performance to rival anything he had produced in life, and one that would confound many of his friends. He chose the celebrant and decided who would give the eulogy. He requested that 'one of [his] sons' be asked to speak. The service, scored for brass and strings, contained his favourite hymns and pieces of music. To begin, Henry Purcell's 'Trumpet Voluntary', a stately brass fanfare fit for the passing of royalty; followed by John Henry Newman's 'Lead Kindly Light', with its promise of salvation from 'the circling gloom', and 'Abide with Me'—'Hold thou the cross before my closing eyes; shine through the gloom and point me to the skies'—the same hymn sung for Henry Lawson's funeral at Waverley Cemetery in 1922. To close, Samuel Barber's *Adagio for Strings*—a slow swelling tide of melancholy, which, as Clark knew, was also heard at the funeral of Franklin D Roosevelt in April 1945 and often accompanied film of the destruction wrought by aerial bombing in World War II—a soundtrack for the end of the world.[1]

On the afternoon of Monday 27 May 1991, more than 600 people gathered in St Christopher's Catholic Cathedral in Canberra. Some stood in rows six to eight deep at the rear of the church, unable to find a seat, while others milled outside. On the streets nearby, several of Manuka's shopkeepers stood silently in front of their businesses. At Melbourne University, Clark's alma mater, the flag flew at half-mast. All the stars aligned to pay their respects. Like nearly everything else in Clark's life, grief at his passing was a public event. No other Australian intellectual had been given a send off quite like this. The front pews of St Christopher's were packed with Australia's political and cultural elite—Governor-General Bill Hayden, Chief Justice of the High Court Sir Gerard Brennan, Prime Minister Bob Hawke and most of the Labor Party Cabinet, including the man who walked from Parliament House to Tasmania Circle the day after Clark's death to offer his personal condolences to Dymphna and the family—Treasurer Paul Keating.[2]

Clark's coffin rested close by Dymphna and the family, at the foot of the altar where he had knelt on so many occasions, praying for the Virgin Mary to intercede in his life. St Christopher's was 'the closest you could get in Canberra to a Westminster Abbey type nave', a venue chosen not by Clark but by Father John Eddy SJ, Clark's former colleague at the ANU. Eddy greeted the crowd and offered the opening blessing; behind him, seated nearby, Clark's cousin, Justice Robert Hope and his brother, the Reverend Russell Clark, dressed in his clerical robes and 'slightly shaky' as he waited to give his reading. Russell was already showing the first signs of Alzheimer's. When Clark had left St Vincent's Hospital after his bypass operation in 1983, he wrote to Russell in an attempt to bridge their differences: 'I know we were often irritated with one another, but I treasure my underlying love for you, and your love for me … I am glad you and I did not end up as strangers to one another, but rather as brothers aware of a deep bond.' Clark was always the one who found words for his emotions, always the one who reached out. There were few people in the congregation who had not received his letters and postcards, and few who, like Russell, could not still feel his words resounding in their lives. Clark's postcards continued to arrive in friends' mailboxes for days after he died, as if he were writing from the grave. David Malouf received a Henry Lawson card when he returned home after the funeral. It read: 'I just wanted to say goodbye again.'[3]

When the atheist Don Baker stepped up to the podium to give the eulogy, he was overwhelmed by the size of the crowd. It fell to him to make sense of Clark's legacy. More than any of his friends, he understood Clark's humour and wit. The National Library recording of his interview with Clark in 1985 was laced with sardonic asides and mischievous laughter. Baker knew the jester in Clark. He saw the ruse behind the grave exterior. And he was not about to hand Clark over to Rome. His eulogy gave him his due, laying out the case for Clark's significance. 'One might almost say he invented Australian history,' he told the congregation, 'at least as an accepted and respectable subject.' He spoke of the importance of Clark's *Select Documents on Australian History* to a generation of school and university students. He stressed that Clark's *Short History of Australia* created an international audience for Australian history. And he praised his capacity for friendship and his enormous influence as a teacher, both in the nation's classrooms and in the public sphere. 'No one of his generation', said Baker, had 'done half as much to arouse in Australians an awareness of our past and a recognition of our national identity'. As for eternal life, Baker left Clark standing precisely where he had positioned himself for most of his life—uncommitted. 'Unlike most Australians,' he reflected, 'Manning talked a lot about death. He often brought to mind Dostoyevsky's words: "I want to be there when everyone suddenly understands what it has all been for"; whether Manning finally understood this we will never know.' For all Clark's talk of 'a shy hope' of an afterlife, as only a handful of people knew that day, he died racked by doubt, pleading for his life not to end.[4]

When Baker finished, each of Clark's five sons addressed the congregation. Katerina was the only one of his children not to speak. She travelled from the United States to attend the funeral to discover that her father had stipulated that his sons were to speak, 'and therefore', as she later explained, 'not me'. Dymphna chose not to speak, but she watched as Sebastian, Axel, Andrew, Rowland and Benedict each delivered their farewells. Yet it was Sebastian, Dymphna thought, who 'spoke as no one had heard him speak before'. In fact, he spoke like his father. He called on Australians to honour Clark's life by achieving three goals: a treaty with indigenous people, care for the environment, and the declaration of an Australian republic by 1 January 2001, the centenary of federation. One week later, the ALP passed the very same declaration at the Party's federal conference in Hobart. Unexpectedly, in the final moments of his speech, Sebastian gave the impression he could see his father standing before him. Pointing to the rear of the church, he called out at the top of his voice: 'Dad, Dad I see you!' Bob Reece remembered this as 'a moment of high gothic drama which Manning would have adored'. Like Reece, many people present believed that Sebastian had seen an apparition of his father. In fact, he was paraphrasing Emily Brontë's *Wuthering Heights*, in which Brontë's character Linton thinks that he hears his dead father's voice 'up on the nab', an allusion that Clark would have admired nonetheless. Regardless of the source of the quotation, for those like Iain McCalman, Sebastian's sudden cries and dramatic gesticulation were nothing more than an attempt 'to play Manning', the first stroke of myth-making in Clark's afterlife.[5]

With the family speeches over, Glen Tomasetti, Clark's former student and friend, sang 'Windy Gap', David Campbell's 'song of praise for travelling sheep and blowing days' on the Monaro plains, before John Eddy offered the final prayers and blessed the coffin, telling the congregation that one day they would all be united with Manning in paradise. As Clark's coffin was carried out of the church, Samuel Barber's dirge cast a pall of magnificent melancholy over the scene. Clark had always loved grand romantic statements. His vein of melancholy was boldly stated and sentimental. Not the restrained, hard melancholy of Samuel Beckett or Dimitri Shostakovich, but the soft, highly wrought melancholy of DH Lawrence's *Sons and Lovers* or Ralph Vaughan Williams' *Fantasia on a Theme by Thomas Tallis*. When Clark wept, the world wept with him.

As the dignitaries walked out behind the family and gathered in front of the cathedral steps, Helen Garner noticed the makeup on Bob Hawke's face. He was already prepared for the waiting television cameras. From now on, Clark's life was public property. Paul Keating, who would take Hawke's prime ministership from him seven months later, stood only a few metres away, convinced that few people there actually understood Clark. Arriving at Tasmania Circle for the wake, friends were already scoffing at the idea that he had made a deathbed conversion to Catholicism. The wake was Clark's second funeral, the catholic hour that followed the Catholic ceremony.[6]

Iain McCalman saw 'the two funerals' as the place 'where the numerous fantasies that Manning had unleashed in his life collided'. Walking from one

An Eye for Eternity

group to the next at the wake, McCalman heard snippets of conversation from different clusters of Clark's friends—former colleagues and students, writers, politicians and journalists. In every group, the funeral was the main subject of discussion: 'Manning will be turning in his grave,' they were saying. 'He must have lost it.' 'Perhaps he was conned.' 'How could he possibly have allowed Rome to snatch him at the last minute?' McCalman had his own doubts. He recalled one of Clark's soirees for his honours class held on Tuesday evenings twenty-five years earlier.

Invariably, as we walked in, Manning would be playing Bach on the piano. Then, he would point us up the ladder to his study. One night, he said to us: 'Everyone knows you can tell the spirit of a culture from its architecture, and the spirit of Catholicism in Manuka is St Christopher's.' He laughed and we laughed with him. It was Manning's joke about the building's mediocrity compared to the great cathedrals of Europe.

Like McCalman, Bob Reece was astonished to find that Clark had embraced Catholicism at the end of his life. Reece's Clark was the stirrer who lampooned the decrees of the Church hierarchy, the last person who would have converted to Rome. Yet like so many of Clark's friends, Reece and McCalman had little idea of the depth of Clark's yearning for salvation, of the personal masses he had requested from Frank Sheehan, or the many times he had visited St Christopher's alone to pray. Nor had Eddy presided over a full requiem mass. There was no communion, while the service mixed secular and religious ritual in a manner that faithfully reflected Clark's wishes. But it was precisely Clark's wishes that shocked and perplexed so many of his friends. They thought they knew him only to find that he had shifted ground. Where did he actually stand? What did he actually believe?

The answer was part of Clark's greatness. For everyone who tried to claim him on the day of his funeral—the Labor Party, the Catholic Church, his family, the men and women with whom he had been intimate, the friends who believed that Jesus Christ was the Son of God and those who did not— Clark gave them the man they wanted: Clark the mocker, Clark the humanist, Clark the spiritualist and Clark the believer; then he subverted them all. No one owned him. No one could pin him down. As his friends gathered at Tasmania Circle on 27 May 1991, reciting their different stories to one another as they drank to his memory, Clark's afterlife was just beginning.[7]

A few days after the funeral, on the morning of 5 June, Don Baker dropped round to Tasmania Circle to share morning tea with Dymphna and Katerina. That afternoon, he wrote to Ken Inglis with news of his visit. '[Dymphna] is in fine fettle and had her cleaning lady in fits of laughter as she explained how she would use her brand new second hand car to carry manure and seaweed. Katerina returns to [the] U. S. on Sunday; she wept as we embraced as I left—but not Dymphna'. To many of her friends, Dymphna appeared very much in control of her emotions in the weeks and months after Clark's

Treasurer Paul Keating, wife Annita Keating, with Prime Minister Bob Hawke and his then wife, Hazel Hawke, and Andrew Clark

death. But this was nothing unusual. Unlike her husband, she was not given to visible displays of mourning. Her grief was her own private possession. Less than two weeks after Baker's visit, she decided to escape the constant stream of visitors, telephone calls and sympathy cards and go to Wapengo alone. From there, she wrote to Ken and Amirah Inglis:

> Like you, I feel Manning will be with us forever. I am alone at Ness for 2 days, answering letters. This is a very still and healing place. Manning is everywhere here—fishing off the rocks, presiding at table, riding through the bush—but without the besetting physical weakness that dogged him for the past few years. But I must admit my eyes pricked with tears when I walked along the beach at the Clearing, the route to his favourite fishing hole a couple of rocky headlands further north. I thought of how he loved going there, of what a terrible effort that became, and how he finally gave up going.[8]

The letters she had taken with her were too numerous to answer in two days. Institutions, political movements and individuals wrote to honour Clark's life and work. The list was eclectic—the Australian Republican Movement, the Australian Conservation Movement, the Australian War Memorial, the Institute of Aboriginal and Torres Strait Islander Studies, the Painters and Dockers Union, the Archbishop of Melbourne (who praised Clark for having taken the history of Christianity in Australia seriously), and a long queue of admiring strangers. Even the nurse who tended Clark after his bypass operation at St Vincent's Hospital in 1983 wrote to offer her condolences. Everyone who had been moved by his writing or speeches, although they had not met Clark personally, felt that they knew him. Letters from writers and artists revealed the depth of their gratitude. Barry Humphries, who cherished his memory of Clark launching an anthology of his 'Sandy Stone monologues' in a Malvern thrift shop in 1990, wrote of his love for Clark, telling Dymphna: 'I think there is a child in us all who believes that all truly noble, generous, and loving people are immortal. Perhaps I thought Manning was immortal; certainly his memory is.' Alec Hope, who probably never allowed Clark to come as close to him as Clark had wanted, mourned his passing too: 'I miss Manning, very much. He had a curious habit of standing just in the doorway and rocking to and fro on his toes, [he'd] tell me a little story and disappear. I could hear his laughter echoing.' After the funeral, biographer Brenda Niall discovered a postcard Clark had sent her in 1974 after reading her small monograph on Martin Boyd. 'Manning wrote to tell me that he had liked it very much,' she told Dymphna. '"Write a long book," he said, and eventually, I did—and I am sure that these unexpected words on an equally unexpected postcard, from someone I admired but had never met, had their effect.' As Jill Waterhouse, Clark's former student, told Dymphna, 'one part of eternal life must be the extent to which one impinges for the good on the lives of others, and you and Manning have done this par excellence'.[9]

Death was a time for eulogies, not the unvarnished truth. Yet in the first days after Clark's death one undeniable truth emerged: his contribution to his country. In the second half of the twentieth century, across the whole spectrum of Australia's cultural, intellectual and political life, his work and public speaking had touched so many. Of the generation of Australians born at the time of World War I, he stood with Patrick White as the country's most significant cultural figure. And for the generation of writers who followed him—David Malouf, Geoffrey Blainey, Ken Inglis, Robert Hughes, Thomas Keneally, Alex Miller, Helen Garner and so many others, he erased the sense of unworthiness associated with Australian history and gave each of them the sense that their writing mattered. In the weeks following his death, a country that boasted few intellectual icons eagerly claimed Clark as one of Australia's greatest cultural monuments. Labor and conservative politicians delivered tributes in both federal and state parliaments. Journalists looked for, but failed to find, one historian who was clearly his successor. Newspaper editorials and obituaries at home and abroad praised his contribution not only to Australian history but to the nation's very formation. 'His life enlarged us all.' 'He taught us to see ourselves in a radically new and different way.' He was the voice of 'national morality', someone who gave his entire life to understanding his country, 'one of those writers who has changed the significance of what it means to be born in this country'. As Ian Hancock told the History department at the ANU, 'Manning helped to influence so many of us to abandon both the cultural cringe and the brash assertiveness of crude nationalism. His themes were the universal ones: his focus was the land he loved.' Amid the compliments, there were also signs of the contest to come. Only days after Clark died, Liberal MP David Kemp told the *Canberra Times*: 'What an infuriating man. He rejected the British heritage and unfortunately this led him to neglect the enormous achievements of institutions developed in Britain but recognised today around the world as central to protecting people against tyranny.'[10]

At Wapengo, Dymphna read all the obituaries, tributes and letters of sympathy. Her first weeks without Clark were spent trying to come to terms with the extent of private and public affection for him. When she posted the public notice of appreciation in the *Canberra Times* for 'the acts of friendship' the family received in the wake of Clark's death, she repeated Hamlet's well-worn epitaph for his dead father—'we shall not look upon his like again'—as if to reinforce the heroic myth of her husband that was beginning to emerge. Immersed in her unfolding grief, she saw that Clark had reached people in ways that even she had not appreciated. There was little time for her to separate the images of the man held in the public eye from the man she loved. Before she could think of a life independent from him, she was already managing Clark's legacy, replying to the mountain of correspondence, tending his archive and welcoming unexpected admirers who came to the house keen to catch a glimpse of the great man's study. But unlike some of her more star-struck visitors, she always retained her distance from the myth, as she wrote to Ken Inglis in August 1991:

> Being simple-minded myself I am often baffled by the massive impact he had on thousands of very disparate mortals, the high souls, the wits, the reformers, the sports, the fallen, the sceptics, the Old Australians—they all see themselves writ large in his life and work. One very troubling letter I had was from a young film maker who wants to make a film about him as the great apostle of <u>Reason</u>![11]

Nothing would prove harder for Dymphna than facing the prospect of reading Clark's diaries. Of all the papers and correspondence he had left behind in his study, the diaries were his most private thoughts, the last trace of his inner voice. She did not rush to read them. Perhaps she sensed their darkness. Perhaps there were times during their marriage when she stole upstairs to read them while Clark was out of the house. In 1993, she began to read them intensely. Initially, she decided that she did not want the diaries bequeathed to the National Library of Australia as Clark had set out in his will. There were too many entries that would only cause pain and embarrassment to friends and family. They belonged with her. But after polite pressure from Warren Horton, the Library's director-general, she gave way. Before they were handed over, she decided to photocopy every page to ensure that copies were held at Tasmania Circle, as if she could not bear the thought of separating from them. Graeme Powell, head manuscripts librarian at the National Library, watched as Dymphna visited the Manuscript Reading Room each morning to copy each page personally. The process was laborious and time consuming. Five decades of diaries, every page needing to be turned and copied individually before being checked and compiled. She not only read Clark's diaries; she became the keeper of every criticism, disappointment and grudge he had ever harboured towards her.[12]

As she read the diaries, Dymphna became increasingly distressed. The life Clark had recorded often bore little resemblance to the one she had lived and remembered. About her, there seemed to be little else but his complaints, usually expressed through the prism of his own self-pity:

[I have been] punished and whipped by Dymphna, who, when most needed, became punisher and avenger for my crimes against her ... why can't Dymphna be more generous after I have given what is inside me to the people? ... she wants me to suffer, she does not want reconciliation, renewal, forgiveness and togetherness. Perhaps, I am in her eyes never to be trusted.

When she read some of the entries written shortly before his death, she discovered that Clark had wondered if he should add her to the long list of people who had never loved him—Pat Gray, Patrick White, Pat Dobrez—'should I add Dymphna?' She also read Clark's recollection of a trip they made to Melbourne in April 1989:

This morning, at Surrey Hills, the train passed a park ... [and] Dymphna told me she remembered it as a place where she played with Sebastian & Katerina. I remembered it as the place where she told me about her sexual encounter with [another man] ('He touched me'). I cannot tell her that. I remain silent, morose and the moment passes. What could have been an occasion for drawing closer together, ended, as ever, in my conviction that I cannot speak to anyone who has judged me harshly. I know this is unfair to her. She probably wants to talk. But I do not dare risk more rejection.

The love Clark wanted from Dymphna was the love no woman could have given him: a love that never slighted him and never hurt him, a love that revered him, a love of total possession.[13]

As she continued reading, Dymphna encountered entry after entry where she was accused of being unloving and unforgiving. How could he have lived with her for so long harbouring such bitterness towards her? He had always depended on her. She was always the first up and the last to bed. At night, he would lie in bed and call for her to come to him. He pleaded that he was 'haunted by demons' that only her embrace could keep at bay. After all she had given to him, was this all that he could leave her? Had she failed him so completely? What of the joy and love they had shared? Occasionally, Dymphna's comments in the margins of Clark's diary betrayed her shock:

'March 24 1943, Mum's death, birth of Axel, but Axel's birth is never mentioned!' Katerina saw how the confrontation with Clark's diaries visibly affected her mother: 'Mum was upset about the level of negativity about her in the diaries, she had given so much to Dad and that he should resent her was deeply painful to her. Her sense of self-worth was intimately bound with his.'[14]

Dymphna found it difficult to accept Clark's wish that the diaries be made publicly available in the year 2000. He could easily have put an embargo on his diaries and personal correspondence until 2050 or later, by which time she and the children would be long dead. By handing his personal papers over for almost immediate public consumption, Clark placed a heavy burden on Dymphna and the children. When asked how she felt about the imminent public release of Clark's diaries, Dymphna's reply was unambiguous: 'I want to be gone by the year 2000.'[15]

In late August 1993, while Dymphna was still struggling to come to terms with the bile in Clark's diaries, she found herself asked to defend him. In *Quadrant*, the conservative monthly edited by Robert Manne, Geoffrey Blainey named Clark, his friend and former teacher, as the major architect of 'black armband history'—the overly gloomy view of Australia's past that had come to dominate the country's culture. Blainey was gracious in his criticism. He had great admiration for Clark and he had not forgotten how his former teacher had defended him when he was vilified for his views on Asian immigration in 1984. Other critics would not be so respectful. One month later, Manne, who believed that the time for reassessing Clark's work was now ripe, published Peter Ryan's scathing attack on Clark and his six-volume history of Australia. 'Of the many things in my life upon which I must look back with shame,' wrote Ryan, 'the chiefest is that of having been the publisher of Manning Clark's *A History of Australia*'. Clark's work, he argued, was little more than 'a vast cauldron of very thin verbal soup, in which swim morsels of nourishing meat, widely spaced'. As Ryan expected, a public controversy erupted immediately.

On Friday 27 August, the day *Quadrant* hit the newsstands, Dymphna appeared on the front page of the *Canberra Times*, sitting at the dining-room

An Eye for Eternity

table, underneath Arthur Boyd's portrait of Clark. She still had fond memories of the many lunches she and Clark had shared with Ryan over a period of more than twenty years. She was dismayed, seemingly at a loss to understand why Clark's former publisher had disowned him. She described Ryan generously: he was 'a most able and energetic midwife' to Manning and 'we continue to be grateful to him for his professional skill'. For Dymphna, the weekend ahead proved difficult. *Quadrant*'s print run of 7000 sold out in a few days. All the major newspapers covered the controversy. The *Australian* trumpeted Ryan's essay: 'Was Manning Clark a fraud? The publisher of Clark's History of Australia bares his soul'. Dymphna appeared on the *Australian*'s front page looking worn and tired. Close by, a photo of a chuffed Peter Ryan in three-piece suit and tie, clutching his vest and with a copy of *Quadrant* tucked under his arm. For weeks afterwards, Dymphna fielded phone calls and enquiries from the media, answered correspondence and hosted scores of friends and visitors who dropped by to offer her their support.[16]

The substance of Ryan's criticisms of Clark's work was hardly startling. Clark was too critical of the British, he said. He sneered at the bourgeoisie. He was too pessimistic. His depiction of historical figures was little more than crude caricature. His prose was inflated and repetitious and his history was factually unreliable. Nor were Ryan's remarks inconsistent with the reservations he had expressed privately since the late 1960s. Clark's historical writing, he argued, was 'a projection' of his personality. Ryan, however, went one step further than the conservative critics of Clark's final volumes. In contrast to the historians he quoted favourably, such as John Hirst, whose subtle critique painted Clark as a frustrated biographer, who 'in making Hamlets of all his tragic heroes went dangerously close to derision', Ryan used a sledgehammer. Clark's *History*, he trumpeted, was 'a fraud'. Unlike reputable literary critics such as Peter Craven, who acknowledged the excessive bathos and satirical impulse in Clark's writing yet also saw its vividness of colour and humour, Ryan appeared bent on destroying Clark's reputation. What created even more controversy and attracted condemnation, not only from Clark's defenders but also from many of those who agreed with Ryan's criticisms, was Ryan's flouting of his ethical obligations as Clark's former publisher. He had disowned his most prestigious and successful author, parading his embarrassment before the public in order to lay an axe 'to the stalk of a tall poppy'. But why did Ryan feel the need to condemn Clark publicly not only as an historian but as a man?[17]

In May 1978, shortly before Colin Roderick published his damning review of Clark's *In Search of Henry Lawson*, he wrote to George Ferguson, his former managing director at Angus & Robertson, to ask if Ferguson would publicly confirm that Clark's manuscripts of *Select Documents on Australian History* were riddled with errors and required major surgery before they were published in two volumes in 1950 and 1955. Like Ryan in 1993, Ferguson was then retired. His reply to Roderick was unequivocal:

> I have considered your idea that I might publicly recount the repair work that was necessary on *Select Documents*, but I decided against it because I have always felt that there should be a professional relationship between publisher and author similar to that between lawyer and client or doctor and patient. So that, no matter how much repair and reconstruction has had to be made on any manuscript the publisher should not talk about it publicly.

Ferguson's understanding of his professional obligations was the antithesis of Ryan's, who had no such scruples. After reading Ryan's demolition of Clark in *Quadrant*, Roderick wrote to him the next day and quoted Ferguson's remarks, but excused him from any sense of guilt. 'Do not be disturbed by the criticism that what you had to say had to wait until after Manning's death,' he told Ryan. 'How unreal of anyone to think otherwise!'[18]

Peter Ryan's motives in disowning Clark were a complex web of political difference and personal resentment. One week after Ryan's essay appeared in *Quadrant*, he received a phone call from Liberal Senator Rod Kemp, whose brother and fellow MP, David, had already accused Clark of propagating an anti-British view of Australian history in 1991. Ryan carried into his retirement his former habit of taking notes of telephone conversations, detailing Kemp's response: '7/9/93 Sen. Rod Kemp, congrat. re. M. Clark and Age column. His father greatly liked it. He will try to speak on Senate adj. tonight in support of my M. Clark stuff and also in support of Age column'. Kemp's father, Charles Kemp, founder of the free-market think tank, the Institute of Public Affairs, was another fierce critic of Clark's history and politics. Impatient to show Ryan his speech, Rod Kemp faxed it through to him from Parliament House. 'Clark is one of the few remaining icons of the Left,' he told the Senate, 'members of the chattering classes that surround Mr Keating have absorbed Manning Clark's vision of Australia.' Keating was now Prime Minister, having successfully challenged Bob Hawke in December 1991. In 1992 and 1993, Keating declared his intention to move Australia towards a republic. In parliament, he lambasted Britain for deserting Australia after the Fall of Singapore in 1942, claiming that the Opposition parties were still cringing to an Anglo-centric past. In other key policy areas, especially indigenous affairs, Keating aroused the ire of conservatives, who saw his public acknowledgement of Aboriginal dispossession as another damning of Australia's British heritage. What's more, Keating's speechwriter was none other than Don Watson, one of the authors behind the Clark *Musical* that had so repulsed Ryan in 1988. Within and outside parliament, Keating praised Clark's life and work. There was no doubt that he admired Clark's vision, as he told me in 2008: 'My greatest regret with Manning was that he didn't live long enough to see me challenge all those old Anglophile nostrums—the republic, native title, and my speech on the Fall of Singapore. Manning saw for us a unique Australian future.'[19]

By the time Keating led Labor to victory in the federal election of March 1993, many conservative intellectuals and politicians were convinced that Labor's 'anti-British' republican nationalism rested on Keating's channelling of Manning Clark. Peter Ryan was no different. In 1994, while reading the *Canberra Times*, he cut out a photograph of Keating opening the Manning Clark lecture theatre at the ANU and scribbled down the following note: 'It matters—because it affects things, e.g. Keating has been fed M. Clark & comes out with anti-British nonsense—on "Foreign Office" constitution.' Although Ryan had long had the intention of publicly disowning his association with Clark's work, Keating's brand of nationalism—which Ryan saw as Clark incarnate—sharpened his resolve to publish. Like other conservatives with whom he was in constant contact, Ryan realised that the way to undermine Labor's stranglehold on popular images of Australia's past and future was to undermine the intellectual who had given it succour. Manning Clark had to be cut down. Ryan's personal relations with Clark were entirely another matter.[20]

Dugald McLellan, who worked closely with Ryan in the early 1980s before being unceremoniously sacked, remembered Ryan as 'an urbane man and a great lunch person' with whom he got on well. At the same time, McLellan thought that Ryan 'envied Manning's success'. 'Ryan was a frustrated something or other,' he reflected. 'He always said Manning's work was bad history. But he tended to admire historians whom he could make some kind of part-claim over —"this has my image written over it"—the sort of thing he could never do with Manning.' Interviewing Ryan in 2007, I noticed how talking about Clark seemed to animate his whole being. 'I'll make sure I stay alive so that I can review your book,' he told me. His view of Clark lurched suddenly from affection—'Manning could be uproariously funny'— to outright contempt—'Manning was a hypocrite.' Ryan's scornful response rested on a long history. He was Clark's student at Melbourne University in 1947, shortly after he returned from fighting the Japanese in Papua New Guinea. He always felt that Clark had shown little interest in his wartime experience, as he admitted to Robert Manne in 1996. As publishing director at MUP from 1962 until his retirement in 1988, he gradually formed the view that Clark was vain, melodramatic, unreliable, miserly and sloppy in his historical writing. Ryan lost respect for Clark at the same time as he watched him become a hero of the Labor Left. His papers, held in the National Library in Canberra, betray an unusual preoccupation with Clark. Folders are titled 'Peter Ryan versus Manning Clark', as if the contest with Clark became a way of elevating his own status. He kept cuttings of reviews of Clark's work and every mention of his name in the press, noting down all phone conversations and writing over the top of his clippings, 'Manning'. Clark's work had defined Ryan's career as a publisher. In retirement, Clark's legacy came to define Ryan's identity as a writer, perhaps seen most graphically in the subtitle of Ryan's collection of essays published in 1997—*Lines of Fire: Manning Clark and other Writings*. Whenever Clark's name was found in the national media, Ryan's was not far behind. At no stage could Ryan let Clark go.[21]

At Tasmania Circle, Dymphna, assisted by Sebastian, Axel and Andrew, defended Clark as best she could. There were few weeks when she was not busy in some form or other tending Clark's posthumous reputation. Together with Sebastian, she had already prepared the manuscript of Clark's *An Historian's Apprenticeship*, published in 1992, as well as assisting Michael Cathcart in his abridgement of Clark's six volumes and the historian Carl Bridge with editing a collection of essays on Clark's legacy. There was already talk of publishing an edited volume of Clark's public speeches. The Ryan affair increased the number of hours she was already devoting to answering correspondence and photocopying Clark's diaries at the National Library. On top of these responsibilities, she was beginning to discuss the possibility of establishing her home as a future cultural institution. At times, she felt frustrated that she could not devote more time to her own work. When she translated and edited the journals of the Austrian diplomat and traveller Baron Charles von Hügel for publication in 1989, she completed most of the book in the kitchen. Her papers were kept where they had been kept for the duration of her life in Canberra—in the laundry. She had no room of her own. 'That was how it was,' she said. Now that she finally had a study of her own downstairs, she still found her time consumed by Clark's posthumous publications and the controversies surrounding his name. More were to come.[22]

Two weeks after Peter Ryan's essay was published in *Quadrant*, Ryan noted the details of a phone conversation he had with the journalist and anti-communist Peter Kelly:

12/10/93 that Peter Kelly rang, very pleased with Manning Clark affair … He was a friend of Geoffrey Fairbairn, and shortly before Fairbairn died he told Kelly of a drunken dinner attended by M. Clark, Fairbairn, Les Murray and David Campbell. Fairbairn and Campbell wore their medals, and Manning wore the Order of Lenin… Kelly said that, if he could get Les Murray to verify the story, he might write it up for publication in *Quadrant?*'

Kelly's gossip remained unpublished until late August 1996, when Brisbane's *Courier Mail*, edited by Chris Mitchell, turned the story into a national media event, alleging that Clark was an agent of the Soviet Union.[23]

The *Courier Mail*'s case against Clark rested on two allegations: first, poet Les Murray's claim to have seen Clark wearing the Soviet Union's most prestigious honour, the Order of Lenin, at the Canberra dinner party in the 1970s; and second, suspicions raised by Clark's visits to the Soviet Union in 1958, 1970 and 1973, in particular his friendship with the communist Ian Milner, his former colleague at Melbourne University who defected to Czechoslovakia in 1950. After the collapse of communism in Eastern Europe in the 1990s, the charge that Clark was a communist agent, if proven, would completely destroy his credibility and expose Labor's naïve idolisation of its cultural heroes. Convinced that he had a major spy scandal on his hands, Mitchell despatched reporters to Europe and the Soviet archives in Moscow to gather evidence against Clark. The one person with whom he failed to speak, at least not until the evening before the weekend edition of the *Courier Mail* appeared on 24 August, was Dymphna.

As literary editor of *Quadrant*, Les Murray was convinced that a clique of Left-leaning intellectuals dominated Australia's intellectual life. For him, the 'traitor Clark' was the hero of a 'solid leftist culture' in which *Quadrant* was the only refuge for Australian writers silenced by the 'totalitarianism' of the Left. Murray was also dismayed by Robert Manne's editorship of *Quadrant*. He believed that Manne had adopted 'the received leftist line on Aborigines' and taken the journal to the Left. Although Manne had contributed to the reappraisal of Clark's *History*, which he described as 'melodramatic and banal', he parted company with the *Courier Mail*, arguing that the allegations against Clark were groundless. When Manne refused to accept Murray's recommendation to publish an article by Hal Colebatch which accused Clark of being an anti-Semite, Murray was irate. The day after the *Courier Mail*'s exposé on Clark, he wrote to Manne: 'You're telling Hal Colebatch and me that some writers allegedly in sympathy with genocide can be pursued ad nauseam in *Quadrant*, while others in sympathy with even vaster mass murder—no "alleged" about Manning Clark: see yesterday's *Courier Mail*—are protected there.' Murray needed little extra incentive to stand as the first witness for the prosecution. His recollection of the Canberra dinner party was the crucial piece of evidence in the *Courier Mail*'s case against Clark. Under intense pressure after the story appeared, he admitted that he could not be completely certain that the medal Clark wore was, in fact, the Order of Lenin.[24]

Within weeks the *Courier Mail*'s charges had collapsed. The medal Clark had worn was shown to be nothing more than an everyday commemorative medal presented to him on the centenary of Lenin's birth in Moscow in 1970. The Russian Government confirmed that Clark had not received the Order of Lenin and was neither a spy nor an agent of influence. A Press Council complaint against the *Courier Mail* launched by former Governor-General Sir Zelman Cowen and journalist/diplomat Bruce Grant was upheld. By early November, every allegation against Clark was shown to be nothing more than malicious gossip. Yet the most crucial issue was the political motivations behind the allegations.

In death, Clark had become the symbol of the cultural ascendancy of Left intellectuals that had begun with the election of the Whitlam government in 1972. With the election of the Howard government in March 1996 after thirteen years of Labor rule under Hawke and Keating, conservative intellectuals and politicians were emboldened. The deep resentment that so many of them had long harboured over Clark's depiction of them as philistines and Paul Keating's republican nationalism could now be vented with the authority of power. Knowing that they had no popular intellectual hero of their own to equal Clark's standing on the Left, many of the conservatives attacking him were driven by base political envy as much as a desire to undermine the Left's cultural dominance.

Prime Minister John Howard wasted little time in condemning Clark, immediately endorsing the *Courier Mail*'s allegations as one sign of a new, more liberal climate of intellectual debate. 'Nauseated' by the 'rapture' of the cultural Left over Clark, Howard recited the same criticisms Geoffrey Blainey had made three years earlier, arguing that Clark's 'black armband' view of history was overly negative, pessimistic and anti-British. 'When you think of the way in which some on the right side of politics have been retrospectively demonised over the years,' Howard added, [the *Courier Mail*'s attack on Clark] is not unprecedented.' Now it was Clark's turn to be demonised. The historian who had been lauded by two Labor prime ministers—Whitlam and Keating—found himself denounced by a conservative prime minister.

This was but one indication of how important public stances on Australian history had become to defining party-political image by the 1990s. Clark's public life had helped to place Australian history at the centre of the nation's politics. Within five years of his death, he was the victim of the very forces he had helped to set in train. Each side of politics tried to assert its own version of the nation's past through his legacy—by either eulogising him or vilifying him. The accusation that he was a Soviet spy, ludicrous as it was, showed how Clark's name was again taking on 'the resonance of myth'.

An illustration that accompanied the *Courier Mail* story was a case in point. As journalist James Button noted, 'a bent line was drawn along Clark's mouth, his eyes acquired a more hooded shape, his beard was removed and replaced with stubble. The old bush hat central to his persona had disappeared and his grandfather shirt was gathered at the shoulder, like a Russian peasant blouse'. The image was a metaphor for nearly everything that had been written and said about him since his death five years earlier. Manning Clark had become one of the whetstones on which Australians, for good or ill, honed their sense of themselves. Where politicians, writers and intellectuals stood on Clark's work and politics had become a barometer of their position on Australian history and identity, even their political

An Eye for Eternity

allegiance; yet the more that was said and written about Clark, the more distant the man himself became. Exactly where did Clark stand in relation to communism in the last two decades of his life?[25]

Clark's diary entries during his visit to the Soviet Union in 1970 showed that he had little time for 'the spiritual arrogance' of governments in communist Europe. In Moscow, he was repulsed by the State's intrusion into the private lives of citizens and deeply suspicious of a government that insisted there was 'only one possible view' in human affairs. 'Why that long file of people to see Lenin? Do they know much of him has rotted away—as much, say, as his vision has rotted in the minds of his successors?' Speaking in public in Moscow, however, he played to his audience:

Lenin was convinced that [universal brotherhood] could only be attained when communism conquered the world. We are lucky to be living in a time when this tenet is being verified by life. Even those who don't share his belief feel that he was one of those mighty and great people, one of those giants, who are leading the world to creation and well being.

Clark's admiration for Lenin and the Bolshevik revolution of 1917 was driven by his conviction that the revolution 'contained the promise of better things for mankind'. It was for this reason that he often attended ceremonies held at the Soviet embassy in Canberra to commemorate the anniversary of the Russian Revolution—not because he was a communist but because he was an idealist. Clark's naïvety was much the same as when he first visited the Soviet Union in 1958: he failed to distance himself publicly from a Soviet regime that he knew had deserted the very ideals that inspired him. Five months before his death, he wrote to Ian Milner in Prague:

I wonder whether any crude secular position is conducive to poetry, music or painting ... I see us all as people who have lost their 'Great Expectations', either in any world to come, or in the here and now ... just because 1917 fell into the hands of spiritual bullies, that does not mean we should give up the hope of stealing fire from heaven—or that we should bow down to 5th Avenue.

Ever the iconoclast, Clark died dissatisfied with both communism and liberal capitalism.[26]

Coming so soon after the Ryan affair, the *Courier Mail* affair placed enormous strain on Dymphna. She was resolute in her response, doing exactly as she had done in 1993: defending Clark in public, writing letters of complaint and responding to the flood of enquiries and letters of support. One article in particular upset her more than any other. In May 1997, BA Santamaria wrote a column for the *Australian* in which he condemned Clark for the speech he delivered in Moscow during the celebrations for the centenary of Lenin's birth in 1970. Santamaria was not concerned with medals. Rather, he was offended by Clark's praise for Lenin's rejection of the 'Judeo-Christian view of the world', the 'one fixed point' of Santamaria's life. How was it possible, he asked, for a man who sided with Lenin rather than Christ, to have asked a Catholic priest to officiate at his funeral? One week later Dymphna decided to reply, writing to Santamaria personally:

> I am too sick at heart to face anyone from the media. Of all the distress caused by acres of vituperation about Manning appearing in print over the past ten months, nothing has saddened me as much as your piece in the Australian of 31.5.97 ... [I thought there was a bond of some affection between you and Manning] ... perhaps it never existed on your side but only on Manning's ... Would you deny that in the name of the Catholic Church, the Church of Divine Love, innocent blood has been spilt—in the Crusades, the Inquisition, in the Spanish Civil War? ... with hindsight, I daresay it would have been politic for Manning to refuse the invitation to attend the Lenin celebrations in Moscow in 1970, where he would inevitably have to make a speech. But he wanted to speak there on the Cook bicentenary, and above all he loved Russia and the Russians.

Santamaria apologised for hurting her, admitting that he had 'dreaded' receiving her letter since he wrote the column. He felt the bond with Clark too. It had been there since their days as students at Melbourne University in the 1930s. But when Clark appeared to be approving of those who sought the death of God, he had no alternative but to speak. 'Manning's life,' he replied, 'was a kind of striving upward from disbelief if not to a kind of certainty, then as a wish for it.'

> The road I have traversed has, in a sense, been downhill rather than uphill ... I have lived long enough to see the church into which many thousands of others than myself—in this as well as other countries—have invested so much effort, shattered into a thousand pieces ... In one of Dostoyevsky's letters which Manning quotes, the author says: 'If anyone could prove to me that Christ is outside the truth, and if the truth really did exclude Christ, I should prefer to stay with Christ and not with the truth.' A figure of speech of course. But I would make the opposite choice.[27]

The exchange between Santamaria and Dymphna said much about Clark's ability to unsettle his critics. His language was rarely direct. More often than not, it was oblique and figurative. He spoke through others, Lenin included. Even six years after his death, his public pronouncements provoked sharply contrasting reactions, leaving behind as much ammunition for his detractors as for his supporters. It was possible to find statements that suggested he was a communist, a social democrat, a social conservative, an atheist and a Catholic. Unlike Santamaria, Clark had no fixed point in his life, save Dostoyevsky.

For Dymphna, although she knew the *Courier Mail*'s charges were baseless, the ongoing fallout further sapped her energy. She felt as she did in 1992, when thieves broke into Tasmania Circle and stole a collection of Clark's medals: 'miserable and besmirched'. The only medal recovered was Clark's Order of Australia, which was found in a Manuka car park days later. She wondered if there was any connection between the theft and the *Courier Mail*'s investigations and feared that there would be no end to the Order of Lenin controversy. Would the scandal continue under other guises? A letter she wrote to MUP while she was editing *Speaking Out of Turn*, a collection of Clark's public speeches published in 1997, showed just how troubled she had become by the increasing volume of hostile publicity surrounding Clark's name:

My chief worry, and a very big worry, is the number of repetitions of Manning's favourite rhetorical phrases (often hidden quotations or variants from other writers and speakers, from Herodotus to the present day). This rhetorical style obviously said something & was very popular with Manning's large listening public, but when the phrases recur on page after page in a book—the great river of life, lovers and believers, mighty spirits, the values of the money-changers, the giant of British philistinism, a shy hope etc. etc, stealing fire from heaven—will they expose him to derision ... perhaps I am over-sensitive to the problem.

Dymphna had come to the point of thinking that every posthumous publication or activity associated with Clark would provoke further controversy.[28]

It was some time in 1997, not long after the *Courier Mail* allegations, that I first met Dymphna Clark. Then nearly eighty years of age, she still seemed to wear the scars of that battle, appearing both more determined to protect her husband's reputation and slightly jaded by the ferocity of the attacks against him. Despite this burden, which she always downplayed, she was a person of enormous warmth and generosity. Usually in the garden when I arrived, her hands black with soil, or serving tea to guests accompanied by sugared lemon peel, she managed to marry a European peasant-like earthiness with a commanding, clear-eyed intellect. In conversation, her voice was loud, even raucous at times. On windless days, her laughter could probably be heard down at Manuka Post Office, more than a kilometre away. When she spoke, words were not wasted. When she listened, she listened intently. Her memory was like a clear, still pool and there was little detail she could not call up when required.

In 1997, I had no idea that I would soon devote seven years to writing Manning Clark's biography. Now, it seems clear to me that I was slowly being led to that point through my friendship with Dymphna. We talked occasionally about Manning. But I was conscious of the fact that she often found herself under siege from a steady procession of people beating a path to her door to talk to her about her husband. When we had become friends, she joked that I was welcome to drop in any time because, she said, 'I had not come to worship at the feet of Saint Manning.'

Dymphna, August 1996

Two moments stay with me. Late one evening in the winter of 1999, I dropped by to return a book I had borrowed on the Aboriginal history of the south coast of New South Wales. From the outside, the house appeared almost completely dark, save for one light burning in the kitchen. Inside, it was cold. Despite the fact that the temperature was below freezing outside, the only active source of heating in the house was the old Rayburn wood-stove in the kitchen. Dymphna was sitting alone at the bench opposite the stove. Her dinner that evening consisted of a few gherkins and cheddar on dark German rye bread, washed down with a glass of sherry. The scene was Spartan, almost monastic, but also luminous in its image of the loneliness she must have felt at times in her final years. 'Would you like a glass?' she asked matter-of-factly. I accepted, and before long, the conversation turned to an essay I was writing on Clark's public life. When I mentioned that I sometimes had difficulty reading his work, she said in a wry, understated tone, 'Go on, I'm listening.' I explained that he often seemed to write his own feelings into his characters, and she nodded occasionally without comment, but I had the sense that she did not disagree. That evening, she was not herself. She looked tired and drawn. I left after little more than half an hour.

Later that same year, shortly before I left to live in London in 2000, I came to Tasmania Circle for a farewell lunch. Afterwards, when the other guests had left, we cleaned up, talking about the advantages of living and working in Europe. Standing directly underneath Arthur Boyd's portrait of

Clark, Dymphna picked up the tablecloth, shook it vigorously and asked, 'Mark, do you think he had something to say? Do you think he was as great as people say he was?' I was caught off guard. I sensed that she did not know the answer herself, and I felt she was looking for reassurance. 'Yes,' I said, 'I think he had something about him that set him apart.' Dymphna's question had come against the flow of the conversation. At the moment I looked towards her to give my reply, the late-afternoon light lit up the Boyd canvas behind her. The whole experience was dream-like. For years afterwards, I have retained the image of Dymphna, standing under Boyd's portrait of her husband, betraying a hint of uncertainty about the man to whom she had selflessly given so much of her life.[29]

In the last three years of Dymphna's life, I watched as she continued in her role as the keeper of the flame. She believed that 'Manning spoke to people from the heart rather than the head—of things that mattered both to him and to those who had asked him to speak.' She, as someone who found 'a lot of intellectual endeavour synthetic and perhaps even spurious and unnecessary', had been inspired by Clark's success in instigating public debate on 'consequential issues' to establish Manning Clark House. Working with Sebastian and a committee made up of historians and former friends of the family, she bequeathed $300 000 in her will from total assets of well over $1 million in order to get the project underway. Like Clark, she could not contemplate the sale of the house and its probable demolition to make way for yet another 'exclusive residential development'. Her vision for Manning Clark House was to establish it as 'a hub of industry and pleasure and exchange of mind'. It was not to become a shrine.[30]

Dymphna completed the final preparations for Manning Clark House in the shadow of terminal illness. In late 1998, during emergency surgery to remove a bowel blockage, doctors discovered a large abdominal tumour. It was an extremely rare but invasive soft-tissue cancer. In hospital, she experienced nightmares for the first time in her life. Back home, she found herself 'tormented by the demons' in Arthur Boyd's portrait of Clark. 'Nobody had seen the demons until I saw them,' she told Boyd's biographer, Darleen Bungey; 'it was as if something was springing out from the shadows.' Clark was everywhere in the house. His hat still hung from the peg in the kitchen;

Arthur Boyd, Professor Manning Clark at Wapengo NSW, *1972*

his books and study were barely disturbed; his bust remained on top of the chest of drawers, his portraits and photographs on the walls. She had changed little in the house since he died. Facing her own death, Dymphna felt Clark's presence more than at any point since his death in 1991.[31]

When she looked back on her life Dymphna's assessment was disarmingly frank:

> I feel that all my life I've been staggering from one blunder to the next and I feel that I have been inadequate on most fronts ... I spend many sleepless hours thinking of my inadequacies and failures because there are misfortunes in lives around me that I feel in part responsible for ... but this doesn't stop me from going on ... I don't feel at all satisfied or fulfilled ... I should have done more intellectually but then I think my aspirations were much more earthier than intellectual life ... although I've often been miserable and frustrated and felt impotent and perhaps angry, I've never been bored, not for a minute ... I've had a very interesting life.

For all the difficulty and turmoil she had experienced in her life with Clark, Dymphna had rarely wanted another life. Asked frequently about her role as

Clark's wife, editor and assistant, her reply was always self-deprecating. As she told Sebastian's wife, Elizabeth Cham:

I have a very old fashioned attitude to the role of the wife. If the husband has something important to do and say then it's part of the wife's role to help that along. I think it's very good if that can be mutual ... but primarily I think the wife and the mother is a nurturer ... and I think it's unfortunate if she has to sacrifice the nurturing role to be something else as well ... someone has to be the backstop ... I was no George Eliot, and no George Sand and nor was I an Emily Dickinson, so I don't think that anything of world moment was sacrificed because I took that role, I just felt that was what I was ordained to be and of course I chafed often, but there wasn't anything for it and I don't think that the world has lost all that much.[32]

In early 1998, Dymphna decided not to have chemotherapy. Cared for by Wilma Robb, her former household help who had also looked after Clark after his heart operation in 1983, she pressed on with life regardless. Robb recalled her indefatigable spirit:

Even when she began to feel the effects of the cancer, in summer and winter she would swim the channel at Wapengo, and when she got to the rocks at the end she'd haul herself back out and start all over again. At Tasmania Circle in winter she would take a hot water bottle to bed. The covers she had made for the bottles were knitted, one using the remains of Manning's old blue jumper and another, her old tartan skirt—'Do you want to sleep with Manning or with me?' she'd ask me.

The day before Dymphna died, she insisted on walking out into the garden to see the mushrooms that were sprouting under the birch trees. She saw them that day and they have never come up since. The following day, Robb lay with her in bed: 'I talked to her, I did her lips, and now and then, when I asked if she wanted anything, she just threw her hands out. She wanted her dignity.' Andrew walked in just before she died. Katerina and Sebastian were still asleep. Dymphna died in the early morning of 12 May

2000, lying on the same bed on which Clark had died in 1991; he calling out for help, she asking to be left in peace.[33]

In the last nine years of her life without Manning Clark she had lived virtually every day administering his literary estate and managing his legacy. She had never wanted the intimate details of her life with him made public. Yet in the end, she placed the historical importance of many of the documents she could easily have destroyed above her personal concerns. Dymphna understood that Clark's performance did not stop with his death. He had a habit of refusing to lie down, as I discovered too.

To write Clark's life was to wrestle with an irrepressible leviathan. There was rarely a moment when I could not feel him deploying all his wit, pathos and charm in order to direct this story. He refused to be silent, bobbing up incessantly despite my every effort to restrain him, a mercurial spirit who lived to be remembered. Whenever I picture him, there is always a playful glint in his eyes.

In the summer of 1989, Ann Moyal was driving up Hobart Avenue in Canberra's inner south. It was late in the afternoon, the sunlight flooding the interior of the car. Looking across the road she noticed Clark's car coming downhill. For a second, she felt as if it was sloping towards her. Unseen, she caught sight of Manning and Dymphna in the front seat. Their heads were tilted back, their faces cascading with laughter.

Acknowledgements

One of the privileges of writing Manning Clark's biography has been the opportunity to meet and talk with many of the people who knew him. Thanks to the openness and generosity of so many of Clark's family and friends, the seven years I have spent working on this biography have been among the most rewarding and stimulating of my life.

If one measure of our lives is the extent to which we make a positive contribution to others, the life of Manning Clark is surely one of Australia's most remarkable stories. From the moment I began in early 2005, I became aware of how deeply Clark had touched the lives of his students, colleagues, friends and the general public. He aroused their passions. He inspired fierce loyalty in some and he confounded or dismayed others. No one was neutral. Almost everyone with whom I spoke felt strongly about him.

I soon discovered that I was writing the life of a man about whom many people had a story to tell. In his vast collection of personal papers and the varied recollections of those who knew him, Clark seemed to have lived ten lives. I often marvelled at his ability to leave so many tracks behind; also at his capacity to record so much of his experience. I could not have wished for a richer subject.

In the years devoted to Clark's biography, I have incurred more debts than I could possibly acknowledge. To my family, Fiona, Siobhan and Claire, I owe more than anyone else. They have lived with Manning and me. To my agent Lyn Tranter, and Louise Adler, my publisher at Melbourne University Publishing, thank you both for the faith you showed in the book and your unfailing patience in waiting for delivery. Without the benefits of a research grant from the University of Sydney, I would still be writing today; my thanks both to the university and to all my colleagues in the History Department.

In some cases, the biographer has difficulty in reaching the private life of the subject, but with Clark, the inner life, or 'soul' as he called it, is archived along with everything else. Clark spent almost as much time documenting himself, as he did documenting Australia's past. He lays his private life bare in a way few people would do, especially historians. Thanks to the remarkable spirit of openness of Sebastian Clark, his eldest son and the executor of his literary estate, I was granted access to this material. How many families in this situation would adopt an open door policy? Most would surely keep the more private and sensitive material under restricted access. In Sebastian's approach, there is tacit acknowledgment that this was his parents' wish, and much like his mother, Dymphna, he has a commitment to truth telling, regardless of the cost to the family. I can only admire his courage. To Sebastian Clark, I owe a great debt. Thank you Sebastian.

To my friend John Blay, who has journeyed every step of the way with me, thanks for the music. Several friends and colleagues read the manuscript and made many helpful suggestions. My thanks to Alan Atkinson, Bain Attwood, Milton Cameron, Sebastian Clark and Stuart Macintyre; also to Sally Heath at MUP, whose close reading of the manuscript has made such a difference. To Foong Ling Kong at MUP, thank you for your understanding, patience and thoughtful suggestions. Special thanks to my copy editor, Sally Moss, and to my proofreader, Wendy Sutherland. My thanks also to friends and colleagues who read sections of the manuscript: Peter Read; Sheila Fitzpatrick; Emma Dortins; and Iain McCalman, whose passion for biography and Manning Clark helped to spur me on.

To Inga Clendinnen, my thanks for your interest and encouragement over the last seven years and to Humphrey McQueen, who offered valuable advice and assistance. To Catherine McGrath, Jan Nicholas and Roslyn Russell, many thanks for your research, knowledge and support over the years. Thanks too to Peter Read, whose enthusiasm helped to make the Biography seminars we co-taught at Sydney University so rewarding. To all our students: thank you for your insights on the writing of biography.

During the years spent moving between Sydney, Canberra and Melbourne, I have stayed with friends and family. To all of you who have listened to the stories of my life with Manning, thanks for the conversations, the bed and the wine. Especially to John Carrick and Geraldine McKenna, Christine Freudenstein, Ockert and Meiri Meyer, Martin Dwyer and Catherine McGrath, Rory Slater and Lyn Turner, Ross and Robin Gengos, Edwin and Sharon Ride, Ross and Belinda Ingram, Jan Bruck, Bain Attwood, Rudi Krausmann and Flis Andreasen, Jacqueline Medveca, Bernard McKenna, Chris McKenna and Deborah Hoffman, Adrian McKenna, Kieran and Carolyn McKenna, Virginia and Stephen Churchill, Ben Armstrong and Moya McKenna, James and Priscilla Curran, Robert Morrell, Ben Wellings and Shanti Sumartojo. Also in Europe, Stuart and Lill Ward, Ronald Kruger and Maria Jacoby, Odette Bereska and Dirk Neldner.

To the librarians at the National Library, especially the staff in Manuscripts and the Petherick Room, my sincere thanks. At the University of Melbourne Archives, I was assisted greatly by the late Tony Miller; also, in the Mitchell Library in Sydney, by the late Arthur Easton. To Brian Matthews, whose biography of Manning Clark I urge all those interested in Clark's life to read, my thanks for your advice and understanding. I am indebted to everyone who gave generously of their time in interviews, phone conversations and email. To everyone below, and to those who I have failed to mention, I am forever in your debt.

Phillip Adams, the late Bruce Anderson, Alan Atkinson, Don Baker, Geoffrey Blainey, Susan Boden, Frank Bongiorno, Shirley Bradley, Carl Bridge, Rosemary Brissenden, Ian Britain, Bill Brown, David Brown, Nicholas Brown, Darleen Bungey, the late Creighton Burns, Judy Campbell, Melissa Campbell, David Carment, Archbishop Frank Carroll, Noel Carroll, Mary Casolin, Michael Cathcart, Elizabeth Cham, Alison Clark, Anna Clark, Benedict Clark, the late Dymphna Clark, Eirene Clark, Katerina Clark, Tim Clark and Renate Wagner, Rowland Clark, Mads Clausen, Peter and Verna Coleman, Jill Ker Conway, Frank Crowley, James Curran, Ann Curthoys, Joseph Davis, Graeme Davison, the late Greg Dening, John Docker, Robert Drewe, Keith Dunstan, the late Arthur Easton, Father John Eddy, Ailsa Fabian, Anne Fairbairn, Peter Fay, Ross Fitzgerald, David Fitzpatrick, Sheila Fitzpatrick, Suzanne Foulkes, Bill Gammage, Alice Garner, Helen Garner, Anne Gollan, the late Bob Gollan, Alan Gould, Bruce Grant, Kate Grenville, Alastair Greig, Helga Griffin, the late James Griffin, Nick Gruen, Pamela Gutman, Rodney Hall, Ian Hancock, the late Phil Harris, Bob Hawke, Beryl Hill, David Hilliard, John Hirst, Stephen Holt, Alistair Hope, Deborah Hope, the late Donald Horne, Julia Horne, Barry Humphries, Philip Ingamells, Sid Ingham, John Ingleson, Ken Inglis, Barry Jones, Paul Keating, Bruce and Ann Kent, Tom Keneally, Rudi Krausmann, Marilyn Lake, John Legge, Ian Lodewyckx, Jamie Mackie, Susan Magarey, David Malouf, Eva Manikus, Robert Manne, David Marr, the late Allan Martin, George Martin, John Martin, Stuart Macintyre, Dugald McLellan, John Merritt, Donna Merwick, Alex Miller, Drusilla Modjeska, John Molony, Edmund Morgan, Ann Moyal, John Mulvaney, Doug Munro, Jan and Frank Nicholas, Laurie O'Brien, Mark O'Connor, Samantha O'Donnell, Rob Pascoe, Jonathan Persse, June Philipp, Graeme Powell, Cassandra Pybus, Penny Ramsay, Bob Reece, Henry Reynolds, Harry Rigby, Kate Rigby, Wilma Robb, Marian Robson, Jill Roe, Heather Rusden, Roslyn Russell, John Ryan, Lyndall Ryan, Peter Ryan, Susan Ryan, John Salmond, Moira Scollay, Jessie Serle, AGL Shaw, Father Frank Sheehan, Barry Smith, Bernard Smith, Margaret Steven, Hugh Stretton, Wendy Sutherland, Gwen Taylor, John Thompson, John Tranter, Nancy Underhill, Bob Wallace, Stuart Karl Ward, Jill Waterhouse, Suzanne Welbourne, Pat White, Gough Whitlam, Bid Williams, Ailsa Zainuddin and Elmer Zalums.

List of illustrations

17: A VIEW FROM THE STUDY

p. 416 View from Manning Clark's study at Tasmania Circle, Canberra 2010. Photo Mark McKenna

p. 419 Manning Clark in his study, Tasmania Circle, Canberra 1980s. MCH

p. 422 Manning Clark's annotations of Fyodor Dostoyevsky's *The Devils*. Photo John Blay, MCH

p. 425 Manning Clark at his study desk, Canberra, 1984, Photo The Estate of Rhonda Senbergs. MCH

pp. 426-427 Manning Clark's annotations of Leo Tolstoy's *Anna Karenina*. Photos John Blay, MCH

18: THE HISTORIAN

p. 428 Sidney Nolan, *Central Australia*, 1950. Ripolin on board, 91.5 x 12.4 cm. Courtesy of University of Sydney Art Collection

p. 433 Manning Clark, promotional flyer for volume one of *A History of Australia*. MCH

p. 439 Cover, *A Short History of Australia*, 1963. Photo John Blay

p. 453 Manning Clark in his living room, Tasmania Circle, Forrest, Canberra Circa 1980. MCH

p. 455 Peter Ryan, circa 1962. Courtesy Herald & Weekly Times Pty Ltd

p. 479 Sidney Nolan, *Riverbend* [panel 3], 1964-5. Oil on board (masonite) 1525mmx 1220mm. Australian National University Art Collection

p. 480 Arthur Boyd, *Portrait of Manning Clark*, 1972 oil on masonite, 90 x 121 cm. Arthur Boyd's work reproduced with the permission of Bundanon Trust

p. 482 Sidney Nolan, *Robert O'Hara Burke*, 16 May 1950. Oil and enamel paint on composition board, 122 x 91.5 cms. By permission Sidney Nolan Trust. Private collection.

p. 487 Sidney Nolan, *Burke and Wills at the Gulf*, 1961. Synthetic polymer paint on composition board. 122.2 x 152.6. National Gallery of Victoria. Presented for Claire Pitblado from Sunday Reed, 1972. Reproduced by the permission of the Sidney Nolan Trust.

p. 489 Manning Clark, Wapengo, circa 1985. MCH

19: THE TEACHER

p. 490 Manning Clark at his desk, ANU Canberra, mid 1960s. Photo Jeff Carter. MCH

p. 501 Manning Clark at Tasmania Circle, circa 1980, MCH

20: THE MUSES

p. 512 Lyndall Ryan, 1978. Photo courtesy Lyndall Ryan

p. 524 Susan Magarey, 1979 and Daphne Gollan 1971. Photos courtesy Susan Magarey

p. 535 Manning and Dymphna Clark, Cape Everard 1970. Courtesy MCH

21: WAPENGO

p. 540 Clarks' house Wapengo house,Wapengo 2008. Photo Mark McKenna

p. 543 Wapengo Lake, 2008. Photo Mark McKenna

p. 547 Clark catching salmon at Wapengo, late 1980s, Photo G. Chaloupka. MCH

22: The PROPHET

p. 552 Manning Clark in the film *Bliss*, 1985. MCH

p. 558 Manning Clark at Dunkeld, Victoria, 14 September 1980. By permission of the NLA and courtesy of *The Hamilton Spectator*

p. 582 Gough Whitlam and Manning Clark at the launch of volume five of *A History of Australia*, 1981. Courtesy MCH

p. 591 Sidney Nolan, sketch of Manning Clark on hotel paper, 1980. By permission NLA and the Sidney Nolan Trust

p. 603 Manning Clark at Tasmania Circle, Canberra, with his dog 'Tuppence', 1982, Photo The Estate of Rhonda Senbergs. MCH

p. 613 Manning Clark at investiture ceremony, Yarralaumla, Canberra, 1977. By permission NLA and courtesy *The Canberra Times*

p. 621 Postcard of Manning Clark's *History of Australia, the Musical*, January 1988. MCH

p. 624 Manning Clark on *Parkinson*, May 1980. MCH

p. 629 Manning and Dymphna Clark, Canberra 1987. MCH

23: REMEMBERING KRISTALLNACHT

p. 632 Kristallnacht: the aftermath. Copyright Bettmann/Corbis

p. 647 Altar Cologne Cathedral showing Stefan Lochner's, *Adoration of the Magi*, circa 1450. Photo Mark McKenna

pp. 650-651 Hans Holbein, *The Body of the Dead Christ in the Tomb*, circa 1521-22. 30.5 x 200 cms. Oil and tempera on limewood. Kunstmuseum Basel

24: MAY 23 1991

p. 654 Manning Clark at Wapengo, 1 October 1990. MCH

p. 659 Manning Clark, Canberra, July 1987. © Newspix/Simon Bullard

AFTER LIFE

p. 674 Interior, St Christopher's Catholic Cathedral, Manuka, Canberra, 27 May1991. Australian National University Archives, Canberra

p. 679 Manning Clark's coffin being carried from St. Christopher's Cathedral, 27 May 1991. MCH

p. 681 Prime Minister Bob Hawke and Treasurer Paul Keating outside St. Christopher's Cathedral, 27 May 1991. MCH

p. 694 Manning Clark's study, Tasmania Circle, Forrest, Canberra 2005. Photo Jan Nicholas

p. 699 Dymphna Clark in Manning Clark's study, August 1996. © Andrew Meares/Fairfax Photos

p. 701 Arthur Boyd, *Professor Manning Clark at Wapengo*, 1972 oil on canvas, 99.5 x 90.5. Arthur Boyd's work reproduced with the permission of Bundanon Trust

p. 703 Headstones of the graves of Manning and Dymphna Clark, Gungahlin Cemetery, Canberra. Photo Mark McKenna

Further Reading

Manuscript collections at the National Library of Australia
The Papers of Manning Clark, MS 7550
The Papers of Dymphna Clark, MS 9873
The Papers of Humphrey McQueen, MS 4809
The Papers of Peter Ryan, MS 9897
The Papers of John La Nauze, MS 5248

Audio material at the National Library of Australia
Manning Clark, interviewed by Hazel de Berg, 1967, ORAL TRC 1/253–54
Manning Clark, interviewed by Don Baker, 1985, ORAL TRC 1817
Manning Clark, interviewed by Neville Meaney, 1986–87, ORAL TRC 2053/13
Dymphna Clark, interviewed by Heather Rusden, 1997, ORAL TRC 3548
Dymphna Clark, interviewed by Heather Rusden and Elizabeth Cham, 1991, ORAL TRC 2597 (the National Library also holds sound recordings of interviews with Sebastian, Axel, Katerina, Andrew and Rowland Clark)

Other important collections
The Papers of RM Crawford, University of Melbourne Archives
Melbourne University Press Archives, University of Melbourne Archives
Manning Clark House, Tasmania Circle, Forrest, Canberra
Dymphna Clark, interviewed by Bill Bunbury, ABC Radio National, 7 June 1998

Select reading on Clark
Bridge, Carl (ed.), *Manning Clark: essays on his place in history*, Melbourne University Press, Carlton, Vic., 1994
Holt, Stephen, *Manning Clark and Australian History, 1915–1963*, St Lucia, University of Queensland Press, Queensland, 1982
——*A Short History of Manning Clark*, Allen & Unwin, St Leonards, New South Wales, 1999
Macintyre, Stuart, and Sheila Fitzpatrick (eds), *Against the Grain: Brian Fitzpatrick and Manning Clark in Australian history and politics*, Melbourne University Press, Carlton, Vic., 2007
Matthews, Brian, *Manning Clark: a life*, Allen & Unwin, Crows Nest, New South Wales, 2008
McQueen, Humphrey, *Suspect History: Manning Clark and the future of Australia's past*, Wakefield Press, Kent Town, South Australia, 1997
Russell, Roslyn (ed.), *Ever, Manning: selected letters of Manning Clark, 1938–1991*, Allen & Unwin, Crows Nest, New South Wales, 2008
The Young Tree Green: a film biography of Manning Clark, video recording written and directed by Bridget Goodwin & narrated by Paul Murphy, Bridie Films Pty Ltd in association with the Australian Film Finance Corporation, Lindfield, New South Wales, distributed by Film Australia, 1999

A Select Bibliography:
Published Works by Manning Clark

Note: This list is arranged in order of date of publication. Revised editions are included if there have been changes or additions. A first paperback reprint is also listed, as are any works reprinted after many years of being out of print. *A Short History of Australia* has been translated into Chinese, Korean, Japanese and Italian but these editions have not been listed. Bibliographical details courtesy of Jan Nicholas.

Select Documents in Australian History, 1788-1850, selected and edited by CMH Clark with the assistance of LJ Pryor, Angus & Robertson, Sydney, 1950; reprinted in paperback, 1977

Foreword by CMH Clark to *Settlers and Convicts, or, recollections of sixteen years' labour in the Australian backwoods* by an Emigrant Mechanic, Melbourne University Press, Carlton, Vic., May 1953. This is a reprint of the original edition published in England in 1847. CMH Clark was instrumental in the publication of the Australian edition. The Foreword is dated 3 March 1953. Reprinted with Postscript to Foreword by CMH Clark, 2nd Australian edn, Melbourne University Press, Carlton, Vic., May 1954. Postscript is dated 31 March 1954.

Select Documents in Australian History, 1851–1900, selected and edited by CMH Clark, Angus & Robertson, Sydney, 1955; reprinted in paperback, 1977

Sources of Australian History, selected and edited by M Clark, Oxford University Press, London, 1957 (The World's Classics, no. 558); reprinted in paperback, 1977 (M Clark is now Manning Clark.)

Abel Tasman, Manning Clark, Oxford University Press, Melbourne, 1959 (Australian Explorers), paperback; reprinted 1969 with an additional reading list, paperback

Meeting Soviet Man, Manning Clark, Angus & Robertson, Sydney, 1960.

A History of Australia, [Volume] I: from the earliest times to the age of Macquarie, CMH Clark, first published in Australia by Melbourne University Press, Parkville, Vic., 1962; first published in London & New York by Cambridge University Press, 1962; reprinted with corrections, November 1962; reprinted with alterations, 1963; reprinted in paperback as one of set of four, volumes I, II, III and IV, 1979

A Short History of Australia, Manning Clark, a Mentor Book published by The New American Library, New York, September 1963; published in paperback in Australia by Tudor Distributors, Balmain, New South Wales; Chapter 12: Between Two Worlds, 1941–1963. (See below for revised editions.)

A Short History of Australia, Manning Clark, Heinemann, London, 1964. The text of this first hardbound edition published in Great Britain differs slightly from that of the New American Library edition. (See below for revised edition.)

Revised Foreword by CMH Clark to *Settlers and Convicts, or, recollections of sixteen year's* [sic] *labour in the Australian backwoods* by an Emigrant Mechanic (Alexander Harris?), Melbourne University Press, Parkville, Vic., 1964. This is a reprint of the Australian edition with a substantially revised Foreword, dated March 1963; reprinted for the first time in paperback in 1969; reprinted in paperback with attractive cover, 1995

A History of Australia, [Volume] II: New South Wales and Van Diemen's Land, 1822–1838, CMH Clark, Melbourne University Press, Carlton, Vic., 1968; reprinted in paperback as one of set of four, vols I, II, III and IV, 1979

Disquiet and Other Stories, by Manning Clark, Angus & Robertson, Sydney, 1969; contents: 'Disquiet'; 'Discovery'; 'Learning to Bowl an Out-swinger'; 'Portrait of a Freethinker'; ''Twere Best Not Know Myself'; 'A Democrat on the Ganges'; 'Monologue by a Man in Black'; 'The Love of Christ'; 'A Moment of Illumination'; 'A Long Time Ago'; 'At The Exhibition'; 'Still Hope for God'. The stories were written between 1957 and 1968 and most appeared first in periodicals. 'Disquiet', 'Learning to Bowl an Out-swinger' and ''Twere Best Not Know Myself' had not been published previously.

Reprinted in paperback, 1982 (Sirius Quality Paperbacks/MUP). See below for *Manning Clark: collected short stories*, 1986.

A Short History of Australia, Manning Clark, 2nd edn, revised and updated, a Mentor Book, New American Library, New York, 1969, published in Australia by Tudor Distributors, Balmain, New South Wales; paperback; Chapter 12: Between Two Worlds, 1941–1969, with amendments, text update and additions to A Note on the Sources

A Short History of Australia, Manning Clark, rev. edn, Heinemann, London, 1969; Chapter 12: Between Two Worlds, 1941–1969, with amendments, text update and additions to A Note on the Sources

A History of Australia, [Volume] III: the beginning of an Australian civilization, 1824–1851, CMH Clark, Melbourne University Press, Carlton, Vic., 1973; reprinted in paperback as one of a set of four, vols I, II, III and IV, 1979

A Discovery of Australia: [the] 1976 Boyer Lectures, Manning Clark, Australian Broadcasting Commission, Sydney, 1976. CMH Clark was one of eight Boyer lecturers who contributed a postscript in the bicentennial year, 1988. These postscripts were published as a separate book by the Australian Broadcasting Corporation. A combined edition of lectures plus postscripts, published in 1991, is listed below.

In Search of Henry Lawson, Manning Clark, The Macmillan Company of Australia, South Melbourne, 1978; reprinted in paperback with amendments in 1985 as *Henry Lawson: the man and the legend* (listed below)

A History of Australia, [Volume] IV: the earth abideth for ever, 1851–1888, CMH Clark, Melbourne University Press, Carlton, Vic., 1978; reprinted in paperback as one of a set of four, vols I, II, III and IV, 1979

David Campbell, 1915–1979: words spoken at his funeral, by Manning Clark, St John's Church, Canberra, 1 August 1979, Brindabella Press, Deakin, ACT, September 1979; paperback

The Quest for an Australian Identity, Manning Clark, University of Queensland Press, St Lucia, Queensland, 1980 (James Duhig Memorial Lecture 1); paperback; text of the inaugural James Duhig Memorial Lecture sponsored by St Leo's College Students' Club and delivered on 6 August 1979 at the University of Queensland

A Short History of Australia, Manning Clark, 2nd rev. edn (3rd edn), a Mentor Book, New American Library, New York, June 1980; paperback; Chapter 13: An Age of Ruins, 1969–1980; with new Preface and additions to A Note on Sources

Occasional Writings and Speeches, Manning Clark, Fontana/Collins, Melbourne, 1980, paperback; writings from 1943 in three parts: Writings on History; Writings on Australia; Personal

A History of Australia [Volume] V: the people make laws, 1888–1915, CMH Clark, Melbourne University Press, Carlton, Vic., 1981; both hardbound and paperback

A Short History of Australia, Manning Clark, illustrated edn of 2nd rev. edn (3rd edn, 1980), The Macmillan Company of Australia, South Melbourne, 1981; designed and produced by Mead & Beckett Publishing, Sydney; paperback; Chapter 13: An Age of Ruins, 1969–1980

A Short History of Australia, Manning Clark, revised large-format paperbound edn (rev. 2nd illustrated edn), Mead & Beckett Publishing in association with William Collins, Sydney, 1983; paperback; Chapter 13: An Age of Ruins, 1969–1983

Making History: RM Crawford, Manning Clark & Geoffrey Blainey, with an Introduction by Stuart Macintyre, McPhee Gribble Publishers, Fitzroy, Vic./Penguin Books Australia, Ringwood, Vic, 1985; paperback; originated in The History Institute, Victoria's forum of 8 April 1984, *Historians on history: why do they do it?* chaired by Graeme Davison; the three speakers represented three generations of the Melbourne History School

Henry Lawson: the man and the legend, Manning Clark, Sun Books, The Macmillan Company of Australia, South Melbourne, 1985; with new Preface to this amended paperback edition of *In Search of Henry Lawson* (listed above); reprinted by Melbourne University Press in 1995 for their Australian Lives series (listed below)

Manning Clark: collected short stories. Penguin Books Australia, Ringwood, Vic., 1986, paperback; contents: same as for *Disquiet and Other Stories* with two additional stories, 'A Footnote to the Kokoda Story' (first appeared in *Australian Short Stories*, edited by Bruce Pascoe, 1982) and 'A Diet of

Bananas and Nietzsche'

A Short History of Australia, Manning Clark, rev. 3rd illustrated edn, Penguin Books Australia, Ringwood, Vic., 1986; paperback; Chapter 13: An Age of Ruins, 1969–1986, with some alterations and corrections to the 1980 text

A Short History of Australia, Manning Clark, 3rd rev. edn (4th edn), a Mentor Book, New American Library, New York, June 1987; paperback; Chapter 13: An Age of Ruins, 1969–1986, with alterations and corrections to 1980 text

A History of Australia [Volume] VI: 'the old dead tree and the young tree green', 1916–1935, with an Epilogue, CMH Clark, Melbourne University Press, Carlton, Vic., 1987; both hardbound and paperback

Manning Clark's History of Australia: the musical, written by Tim Robertson and Don Watson with John Romeril; composed by Martin Armiger, George Dreyfus and David King; directed by John Bell at the Princess Theatre, Melbourne, from 16 January 1988

The Ashton Scholastic History of Australia, Manning Clark and Meredith Hooper, with illustrations by Susanne Ferrier, Ashton Scholastic, Sydney, 1988, created and produced by Mead & Beckett Publishing, Sydney; paperback for children; from the publisher's note: 'The idea for this History of Australia, designed to appeal mainly to young readers, was developed by Meredith Hooper and Manning Clark. Meredith Hooper using Manning Clark's multi-volume *History of Australia*, as well as other sources, wrote chapters 1–23. Manning Clark wrote the final chapter ... which takes the story from 1945 to the present.' Title was changed to *The Scholastic History of Australia* when reprinted in 1995.

The Puzzles of Childhood, Manning Clark, Viking/Penguin Books Australia, Ringwood, Vic., 1989; reprinted in paperback, 1990 (Penguin Books)

The Quest for Grace, Manning Clark, Viking/Penguin Books Australia, Ringwood, Vic., 1990; reprinted in paperback, 1991 (Penguin Books)

A Discovery of Australia: the 1976 ABC Boyer Lectures and their 1988 Postscript, Manning Clark, Australian Broadcasting Corporation, Crows Nest, New South Wales, 1991, paperback (*A Discovery of Australia* was first published in 1976; *Postscript* was first published in 1989; this is a combined edition.)

A Historian's Apprenticeship, Manning Clark, with a Foreword by Sebastian Clark and two excerpts from *A History of Australia*, Melbourne University Press, Carlton, Vic., 1992; published posthumously; excerpts are: On William Charles Wentworth (from vol. II, 1968, pp. 41–52); On Robert O'Hara Burke (from vol. IV, 1978, pp. 146–59); reprinted in paperback, 1994

Manning Clark's History of Australia; abridged by Michael Cathcart, Melbourne University Press, Carlton, Vic., 1993

Manning Clark's History of Australia, abridged by Michael Cathcart, Chatto & Windus, London, 1994 (Text for this UK edition is the same as the Melbourne University Press edition.)

Manning Clark's History of Australia, abridged (and with a Coda) by Michael Cathcart, Penguin Books Australia, Ringwood, Vic., 1995, paperback

Manning Clark's History of Australia, abridged (and with a Coda) by Michael Cathcart Pimlico/Random House, London, 1995; paperback

A Short History of Australia, Manning Clark, with Addendum by Sebastian Clark, 4th rev. edn (5th edn), Penguin Books Australia, Ringwood, Vic., 1995; paperback; additional to Chapter 13: An Age of Ruins, 1969-1986 is Chapter 14: Addendum by Sebastian Clark, which brings the work into the 1990s

Henry Lawson: the man and the legend, Manning Clark, Melbourne University Press, Carlton, Vic., 1995 (Melbourne University Press Australian Lives); paperback (This is a reprint of the 1985 Macmillan paperback edition.)

Foreword by Manning Clark to *Settlers and Convicts, or, recollections of sixteen years' labour in the Australian backwoods* by an Emigrant Mechanic [Alexander Harris?], Melbourne University Press, Carlton, Vic., 1964; reprinted 1995 with an attractive new cover illustrated with Augustus Earle's *A bivouac of travellers in Australia in a cabbagetree forest, day break*

Dear Kathleen, Dear Manning: the correspondence of Manning Clark and Kathleen Fitzpatrick, 1949–1990, edited by Susan Davies, Melbourne University Press, Carlton, Vic., 1996

Speaking Out of Turn: lectures and speeches, 1940–1991, Manning Clark, with Foreword by Stuart Macintyre, Note on the Text by Dymphna Clark and Sebastian Clark, and Preface by Manning Clark, Melbourne University Press, Carlton South, Vic., 1997; paperback; published posthumously; Preface is dated 1991; Foreword and Note on the Text are both dated May 1997

Manning Clark's History of Australia; abridged (and with a Coda) by Michael Cathcart, Melbourne University Press, Carlton South, Vic., 1997 this edition, with minor corrections and alterations and the Coda, written originally for overseas readers, was published to coincide with both the 10th anniversary of the completion of the six-volume *A History of Australia* and the 75th birthday of Melbourne University Press

The Ideal of Alexis de Tocqueville, Manning Clark, edited by Dymphna Clark, David Headon and John Williams with an Introduction by Dymphna Clark, Melbourne University Press, Carlton South, Vic., in association with Manning Clark House, 2000; paperback; posthumous publication of CMH Clark's first-class honours thesis for which he was awarded Master of Arts from the University of Melbourne

Notes

1: Song of Himself

1   On voice: Letter from Jessie at Toorak, 15 November 1990, in Clark papers, box 173, folder
    'Correspondence 1988–1991', (iii) 'melodious timbre, tentative, even reluctant'; its musicality
    'made you want to listen', Bob Reece, in his 'Don't accept any lifts from Professors to Wagga': Some
    personal recollections of Manning Clark, *Australian Historical Association Bulletin*, no. 83, 1996,
    pp. 86–92. 'Manning's musical voice', Jill Ker Conway to me, phone conversation, May 2008.
    'Gusts of laughter', Ann Moyal to me, Canberra, March 2007; Manning's singing voice, Katerina
    Clark to me, Wapengo, March 2006. Manning was also fond of breaking into song, John Blay to
    me, Wapengo, September 2008. Pat White's comments to me, Canberra, May 2008. Also Jill
    Waterhouse to me, Canberra, September 2006 (Jill Waterhouse thought Clark loved nothing better
    than 'the joy of trouble, he would sometimes phone people at 3 am [...] if he wanted to talk some-
    thing over'). Helen Garner's comments to me, Melbourne, June 2008. On his tutorial voice, Ailsa
    Zainuddin (nee Thomson) to me, Melbourne, August 2005. The words 'gentle, wavering, at times
    cracking to falsetto' belong to Ken Inglis, as do the comments on Clark's public voice, taken from
    his personal notes for Clark's obituary. Also on voice, Barry Jones to me, Melbourne, February
    2008, 'Manning was a giggly drunk, he'd say something and laugh and his voice would drop sud-
    denly, so much so that you'd sometimes have the sense he was talking to himself'.
        On lightness: Bruce Grant to me, Melbourne, March 2007. Clark's speech at Alice Springs
    Folk Festival in 1987 is on cassette tape and held at Manning Clark House. Also listen to Clark
    speaking on tape to the Counterpoint Forum held in Perth in 1981, also held at Manning Clark
    House; on Clark's ability to hold an audience, John Ingleson to me, January 2008.

2   'Halting' and testing conversation, Nicholas Brown to me, Canberra, November 2007; Mark
    O'Connor to me, Canberra, November 2008; searching for the 'grand aphorism' and thinking 'he
    was great', Gwen Taylor to me, phone conversation, July 2007.

3   On Clark's 'island' of hair, Sebastian Clark to me, September 2008; Bob Reece, 'Don't accept any
    lifts from Professors to Wagga': Some personal recollections of Manning Clark, *Australian
    Historical Association Bulletin*, no. 83, 1996, pp. 86–92, (pp. 86–7); on his blue eyes, Roslyn Russell
    to me, Canberra, April 2008. On those 'darting eyes', Dugald McLellan to me, April 2008.

4   On Clark's appearance, Roslyn Russell to me, April 2008; on Clark in the garden, Sebastian Clark
    to me, September 2008.

5   Details drawn from Dymphna Clark to Jan Nicholas, 29 November 1995, tape courtesy of Jan
    Nicholas; in this interview, Dymphna also said that Clark 'did tell me once that he fell down at
    Civic. He obviously gradually outgrew it, totally, I mean on the surface.' On Franklin at Melbourne
    Grammar, see Clark, *Puzzles of Childhood*, 1990, p. 189; on getting up from the table, Eirene Clark
    to me, Canterbury, Melbourne, February 2008; on skipping, Sebastian Clark to me, September
    2008; on walking, John Legge to me, Melbourne, November 2006; regarding epilepsy, David
    Malouf to me, Sydney, April 2008.

6   'Hissing of the academic serpents', Clark to Dymphna, 16 September 1982, in Russell (ed.), *Ever,
    Manning*, p. 431; on his sensitivity, John Molony to me, Canberra, September 2006; on touching,
    Sebastian Clark to me, September 2008.

7   On his habit of kissing and touching, drawn from various interviews with women who knew him.
    On his being a tease, Laurie O'Brien to me, phone conversation, March 2008. Other information
    as attributed: Ann Moyal to me, Canberra, March 2007; Ailsa Fabian to me, London, August 2005;
    Alison Clark to me, Sydney, November 2006.

8   On wit and intelligence, Laurie O'Brien, ibid.; Bob Hawke to me, June 2008; Bruce Grant to me,
    Melbourne, March 2007.

9   On pitting Catholics against communists, Katerina Clark to me, Wapengo, March 2006; on
    Rimbaud, John Tranter to me, Sydney, September 2006; on having the world on, John Legge to me,
    Melbourne, November 2006; on posturing, Jessie Serle to me, phone conversation, September
    2007; Pat Gray's comments in letter to me (writing as Ailsa Fabian), February 2008.

10 Noel Carroll to me, Canberra, November 2005; June Philipp to me, Melbourne, November 2006; Creighton Burns to me, Melbourne, March 2007; Jesus under the shower, Anne Gollan to me, Canberra, June 2008; Verna and Peter Coleman to me, phone conversation, January 2008.

11 Article from *The Times* quoted in *Sydney Morning Herald*, 18 April 1964; Stetson hat in the *New Zealand Listener*, 26 April 1980; on people noticing the hat, Margaret Steven to me, phone conversation, April 2008. I am grateful to Jessie Serle for suggesting I look closely at the portrait of Carlyle; Anne Gollan to me, second interview, Canberra, June 2008; Helen Garner to me, Melbourne, June 2008.

12 Sheila Fitzpatrick to me, Sydney, August 2007; Heather Rusden to me, Canberra, November 2007. Hardy's poem 'The Voice' is in Claire Tomalin (ed.), *Poems of Thomas Hardy*, Penguin, London, 2006, p. 85.

13 Iain McCalman to me, Sydney, September 2008; also see Clark to Anne Gollan, 14 September 1973, in Russel (ed.), *Ever, Manning*, pp. 350–51, & Clark to Dymphna, 12 May 1969, pp. 288–9.

14 David Fitzpatrick to me, email February 2008; 'lack of spontaneous reality', Anne Fairbairn to me, Sydney, February 2008.

15 Gwen Taylor to me, phone conversation, August 2007.

16 Ailsa Fabian (Pat Gray) to me, London, June 2006.

17 Jessie Serle to me, phone conversation, September 2007.

18 Margaret Steven to me, phone conversation, April 2008.

19 John Molony to me, Canberra, September 2006.

20 Edmund Morgan to me, email attachment, dated 14 November 2007; on being open to all human experience, John Molony to me, Canberra, September 2006; on 'desperate need for certainty', Jessie Serle to me, phone conversation, September 2007; on 'absolute truth', David Malouf to me, Sydney, April 2008.

21 Dymphna's address book is held at Manning Clark House.

22 Johnson's comment quoted in Hermione Lee, *Biography: a short history*, Oxford University Press, Melbourne, 2009, p. 11; see also Johnson's 'On Biography', in *The Rambler*, no. 60, 13 October 1750. Margaret Steven to me, phone conversation, April 2008; Anne Gollan to me, Canberra June 2008; Alison Clark to me, Sydney, November 2006.

2: Manning Clark, MS7550

1 Gabriel Garcia Marquez, *Living to Tell the Tale*, Jonathan Cape, London, 2003, Epigraph.

2 Roslyn Russell to me, 1 August 2008.

3 Clark, diary, 7 January 1940.

4 Clark, diary, 7, 11, 15, 19 & 23 October 1988.

5 Graeme Powell, 'The Manning Clark archives', *Australian Book Review*, December 2004 – January 2005, p. 10, & Stuart Harris in *The Times*, 2 April 1964.

6 Philip Larkin in John Banville, 'Homage to Philip Larkin', *The New York Review of Books*, vol. 53, no. 3, 23 February 2006; Janet Malcolm, *The Silent Woman: Sylvia Plath and Ted Hughes*, Picador, London, 1994 (first published 1993), pp. 8–9.

7 Keith Dunstan's description of Clark's handwriting, *Sydney Morning Herald*, *Good Weekend*, most probably September 1987.

8 Richard Holmes, *Footsteps: adventures of a romantic biographer*, Hodder & Stoughton, London, 1985. Clark's papers were assigned to the NLA under the tax incentive scheme, which caused difficulties when it was discovered that the library had allowed a considerable amount of material to remain with the family.

9 Bill Gammage, '"Ros Russell, Ever Manning"', speech at launch held at Manning Clark House, 1 August 2008.

10 Manning Clark Papers, box 159, folder 29, letter 6/9/87, Ruth Perry, '(one of the abusers)'; box 166, folder 20, 'my great wound'. This related to the Bicentennial History Project, *Australia 1788-1988*, to which Clark was not invited to contribute largely because he had retired and the editors decided to seek other younger historians. Comment on Shaw's review ('New Explanations in Australian History', *Meanjin*, no. 2, 1967, pp. 216–21) in box 9, folder 68. 'Backstabber'

comment in box 19, folder 151, atop a letter from 'Glen', in Carlton, 14 July 1983; box 18, folder 145, below the invitation to John Molony's farewell (27 July 1990) and request for a donation towards, Clark writes 'Gave money—with a heavy heart because of past treacheries'; box 14, folder 108, atop a letter from Patricia White, registrar at the ANU, 12 September 1985, thanking him for his letter recommending John Molony for an honorary degree, he writes of Molony 'MEINE SCHANDE!' (sic) (my violator); then, atop a similar request to pen words in support of an honorary doctorate from the ANU for Dorothy Green, he places three exclamation marks above the comment that Green had had 'a long and distinguished career as a literary critic'. (Green had been critical of Clark's biography of Henry Lawson, published in 1978); Clark's comments relating to the *Labor History* editorial can be found in box 166, folder 20.

11 'See above' in Clark, diary, 9 July 1990, all others in Manning Clark's Papers; trip to Gulf in box 186 , folder 2; *Sydney Morning Herald* in box 164, folder 8; Counihan comment in box 16, folder 129. For further evidence of Clark instructing the biographer, see Clark quickly jotting down the sales figures for his *Select Documents in Australian History*, and dating when he 'first heard of them', in box 54, folder 25; also Clark dating cuttings of bookshops stocking his work in box 19, folder 151 & on a *Quadrant* flyer, dating when he received his cheque for the publication of a short story, 'Man in Black', in box 4, folder 25. On a preliminary manuscript of volume I of *A History of Australia*, Clark writes at a later date in brackets '(This was begun in Oxford England on 1 October 1956)', in box 58, folder 1.

12 Clark papers, Christmas menu in box 193, folder 60; Andrew's note in box 1, folder 5.

13 Roslyn Russell to me, 7 November 2007; crossword cutout in Clark papers, box 9, folder 68, Melbourne airport note in box 18, folder 149; *7.30 Report* in box 159, folder 29; ANU luncheon in box 20, folder 164.

14 Clark papers, box 175, folder 22.

15 Richard Ellman, *James Joyce*, Oxford University Press, London, 1983 (first published 1959), pp. 521–2.

16 Private correspondence held at Manning Clark House.

17 Louis Menand, 'The Lives of Others: the biography business', *New Yorker*, 6 August 2007; Regarding the failure of historians to speak of their relationship with the archive see the introduction to Antoinette Burton (ed.), *Archive Stories: Facts, fictions, and the writing of history*, Duke University Press, Durham, 2005, p. 8.

18 Clark's review of Donald Horne's *Education of Young Donald* in *Overland*, no. 38, March 1968, pp. 39–40.

19 Clark papers, box 157, folder 11.

20 Dymphna Clark to Manning Clark, 18 April 1985, private correspondence held at Manning Clark House.

21 Mark O'Connor to me, Canberra, November 2008; Philip Ingamells to me, 14 February 2008.

22 Doris Lessing, *Time Bites, Views and Reviews*, Fourth Estate, London, 2004. See the essay 'Writing Autobiography', pp. 90–103, especially pp. 91–2.

3: Boats Against the Current

1 This note is still held in Clark's study at Manning Clark House, Canberra. The photograph taken in 1987 can be found in Clark papers, box 172, folder 28, 'Correspondence 1983–1989'.

2 Clark to Ailsa Zainuddin, 8 February 1981, in Russell (ed.), *Ever, Manning*, p. 414.

3 Clark (from London) to Axel Clark, 26 March 1964, in *Ever, Manning*, p. 204. Also see Clark's letter to Axel regarding the anniversary of his father's death in same, p. 231. For letters that show Clark depicting himself as a 'boy', see the following letters in *Ever, Manning*: Clark to Dymphna Clark, 6 May 1969, p. 283; Clark to Dymphna, 18 May 1969, p. 294; and again 25 May 1969, p. 302; finally see Clark's speech on receiving the Australian of the Year Award, 26 January 1981, p. 415. On Clark's postcards to his parents, Benedict Clark to me, Phillip Island, April 2008.

4 Clark, diary, Box Hill Cemetery, 22 March 1987.

5 Clark, diary, Box Hill Cemetery, 19 April 1989; Renate's comments in joint interview with Tim Clark, Sydney, April 2008.

6   Clark, diary, Box Hill Cemetery, 22 March 1987.

7   McQueen to Clark, 31 August 1989; Anne Fairbairn to me, Sydney, February 2008, Helen Garner to me, Melbourne, June 2008.

8   For but one example, listen to the oral history interview Clark gave with Hazel de Berg in 1967, held at the NLA. Clark's commemoration of certain anniversaries extended to significant milestones in his life; see, for example, Clark's diary, 10 August 1980 & 10 December 1989.

9   Inga Clendinnen, National Biography Lecture, State Library of Victoria, 7 November 2007, unpublished document.

10 Clark, de Berg interview, May 1967.

11 My thanks to Jan Nicholas for her assistance with references concerning St Peters and the life of Charles Clark; Reverend Edward Madgwick (vicar at St Peter's in 1896), *An Historical Sketch of St. Peter's Church, Cook's River Sydney 1839–1896*, Newtown, New South Wales; *Chronicle*, 1896, p. 8; Parish Notes, St. Peter's Parish Church, vol. 1, no. 5, May 1928; according to Ruby Clark (daughter of Clark's grandfather Thomas Clark and sister of Charles), Thomas Clark's parents also came out to Australia and one of them was of Spanish descent. Copy of Charles Clark's birth certificate carries the following details: Charles Clark born 21 August 1881 at 86 Hudson Rd Plumstead, to Jane Ann Clark (formerly Logan) and Thomas William Benjamin Clark, Blacksmith. Dymphna Clark told Jan Nicholas on 22 February 1994 that family history reported Thomas Clark helped build one of the brickworks' chimneys. His mother came from Tipperary, Ireland. Charles Clark had three sisters according to Clark (*Puzzles of Childhood*, 1990, p. 2) but baptismal records exist only for two girls, Ruby (born 4 August 1886) and Annie (born 25 August 1889).

12 On music see St Andrew's Cathedral Reader for Lent 1911, notice of Coronation Day service in *Sydney Diocesan Magazine*, vol. 2, no. 5, 1 May 1911, p. 7. Details in *Sydney Morning Herald*, 23 June 1911, & *Sydney Diocesan Magazine*, vol. 2, no. 7, 1 July 1911, pp. 6–14; details of Titanic service in same, vol. 3, no. 5, 1 May 1912, pp. 18–20. Reverend James Napoleon Manning was Rector of St Peter's 1885–1892. On Sydney Anglicanism see Jill Roe, 'Manning Clark and the Church', in Macintyre & Fitzpatrick (eds), *Against the Grain*, pp. 232–9, especially p. 235.

13 Clark, diary, 25 April 1960.

14 Clark to Dymphna Lodewyckx, 16 January 1938, in Russell (ed.), *Ever, Manning*, pp. 3–4; Clark family tree courtesy Jan Nicholas; Sebastian Clark to me, April 2008; also see Clark, *Puzzles of Childhood*, 1990, chapter 2, and Holt, *Manning Clark and Australian History*, pp. 1–4.

15 *Sydney Morning Herald*, March/April 1915, details on Burwood drawn from Bernard Smith, *The Boy Adeodatus*, UQP, Brisbane, 2004 (first published 1984), pp. 17–20, 60–3, 76–7, 101–6.

16 Material on Charles Clark, enlistment and discharge on medical grounds, from Australian Archives, Series B2455 (regimental no. 18399 & AWM Embarkation Roll no. 26.104.3). Details of Charles Clark's failure to gain promotion in St Andrew's Cathedral records, private correspondence from Roslyn Russell to Jan Nicholas, 19 December 1993. On his father's departure from Sydney to Kempsey, see Clark's 1985 interview with Don Baker: 'It was not until after the second world war, indeed not until the 1950s that I found out from my cousins in Sydney the reasons why my father went from the diocese of Sydney up to Kempsey; he'd had a row with the Archbishop of Sydney'; Kempsey details, as told by Clark, *Quest for Grace*, 1990, p. 106; on Kempsey see Thomas Keneally, 'My Father's Australia', *Granta*, vol. 70, Summer 2000 (Australia the New World), pp. 331–50; also Tom Keneally to me, phone conversation, August 2007.

17 I visited Phillip Island, with Clark's youngest son, Benedict Clark, in April 2008. The impressions of the island are my own, assisted by Benedict's knowledge and memories. My thanks to Jan Nicholas for the following references: Recollections of Edith Jefferey, and Raymond Grayden's typescript manuscript, 'Memories of Manning Clark 1 September 1993'; Edith's memories are contained in correspondence to Jan Nicholas, 24 July 1993, 19 August 1993, 14 March 1994 and 19 April 1994; details of names and their Anglican heritage contained in letter from June Cutter to Jan Nicholas, 20 April 1994; also see V Thompson, *Island Church, 1870–1970: A History and Memoir of St. Phillip's Church of England*, [self-published], Cowes, 1970; on Clark's affection for Phillip Island see *The Advertiser* (Phillip Island), 13 June 1991, p. 5. The Phillip Island Historical Society attempted unsuccessfully to name 'the Springs' after Clark, see *Historical Society Advertiser*,

17 June 1993, p. 14; also Clark's various pieces on his love for the island, e.g. 'Phillip Island' in G Dutton (ed.), *The Book of Australian Islands*, Macmillan, South Melbourne, 1986, pp. 89–94; 'Phillip Island', in *Weekend Australian Literary Magazine*, 21–22 December 1985; 'A Place in the Heart', *Panorama*, no. 98, October 1990, pp. 4–8.

18 David Brown to me, phone conversation, February 2008. Clark's image of leaving the island behind, aged nine, is in his 1985 interview with Don Baker, held at the NLA.

19 Bob Wallace to me, March 2008; Sid Ingham, who met Charles Clark at a Test match at the MCG in 1950, was surprised by 'how working class he was'; Ingham to me, April 2005.

20 David Brown to me, February 2008; Clark, *Puzzles of Childhood*, 1990, pp. 8, 33–6, 48, 51, 62, 67.

21 Drawn from the following interviews: Eirene Clark to me, Melbourne, February 2008; Philip Ingamells to me, Melbourne, February 2008; David Brown to me, phone conversation, February 2008; Sebastian Clark to me, phone conversation, September 2008; Dymphna Clark's comments on *Puzzles* were made in a letter to Jan Nicholas, 22 July 1993 (my thanks to Jan Nicholas); obituary of Russell Clark (1912–1998) by Canon Evan L Burge, *Australian*, 7 August 1998.

22 Clark to Catherine Clark, 9 October 1938 & 27 November 1938, in Russell (ed.), *Ever, Manning*, pp. 9 & 36.

23 Clark to Catherine Clark, 27 November 1938, *Ever, Manning*, pp. 36–8.

24 Clark to Russell Clark, postcard from Oxford, 1939 (day and month obscured), courtesy of Eirene Clark, Clark to Gladys Hope, 16 October 1938, held at Manning Clark House.

25 David Brown to me, phone conversation, February 2008; Eirene Clark to me, Melbourne, February 2008; also J Ross (ed.), *Chronicle of Australia*, Penguin Books, Ringwood, Vic., 2000, p. 586.

26 Clark to Catherine Clark, 7 February 1939, unpublished, held at Manning Clark House; details of bushfires in *Sydney Morning Herald*, 14 & 16 January 1939; details of Hope's illness in Catherine Clark to Clark, 30 October 1938, unpublished, held at Manning Clark House.

27 Clark to Catherine Clark, 31 December 1939, in Russell (ed.), *Ever, Manning*, pp. 55–6, Catherine Clark to Clark, 30 October 1938, unpublished, held at Manning Clark House.

28 ibid., Eirene Clark to me, Melbourne, February 2008.

29 Details in this paragraph were drawn from the following interviews: Eirene Clark to me, Melbourne, February 2008; on Clark's reading as a child, Nicholas Brown to me, April 2008 (recalling a comment made to him by Russell Clark); Dymphna's memories are drawn from a taped interview she gave with Jan Nicholas, 29 November 1995, courtesy of Jan Nicholas; also see Clark, diary, 8 July 1989, which records his discovery that his Uncle Tom Hope also had epilepsy.

30 Dymphna Clark to Jan Nicholas, 29 November 1995.

31 Dymphna Clark interviewed by Bill Bunbury for ABC Radio National, *Hindsight*, June 1998; Sebastian Clark to me, Melbourne, March 2007.

32 Dymphna Clark interviewed by Heather Rusden, 13 February 1997, NLA transcript, p. 20.

33 JT to Clark, 2 February 1988, in Clark, Papers, box 172, folder 29, 'Puzzles of Childhood, Correspondence 1988–91'.

34 Clark, diary, 29 March 1943; also see entries 1 & 4 October 1942 & 10 August 1980; Clark's interview with Don Baker, 16 August 1985 (tape 1), is held at the NLA.

35 Clark, diary, 4 April 1943; also see 1 October 1942.

36 Clark, diary, 15 December 1942, 10 February 1942, 29 March 1943.

37 Clark, diary, 18 December 1949.

38 Clark, diary, 25 October 1949; story of the butterflies in the cupboard at Croydon, Sebastian Clark to me, Melbourne, March 2007.

39 Clark, diary, 18 December 1949; Clark's copy of Freud's *Outline of Psychoanalysis*, in his study library, is inscribed 'Canberra University College 16/11/49'.

40 Sebastian Clark to me, Melbourne, March 2007.

41 Obituary of Charles Clark, in *The Church of England Messenger*, vol. 85, no. 1982, 26 January 1951, p. 25; Dymphna's memories of Charles Clark in private correspondence to Jan Nicholas, 18 November 1993. The memory of the 'bluebird jar' comes from Katerina and Axel Clark, in their interview with Susan Marsden held at the NLA.

42 Clark, *Quest for Grace*, 1990, p. 200; details on Charles Clark courtesy of Eirene Clark.

43 Clark, diary, 2 May 1954; also see Clark's notebooks, 6 November 1954–'Dad could never endure the tension of watching a child put on a singlet–the tangle of sleeves soon wore out his patience– "Why can't you do it? I'll knock a bit of sense into you."'

44 Ibsen quote in the 1964 Penguin Classics edition held in Clark's study at Manning Clark House, Canberra; also see diary, 5 March 1962.

45 Clark to Axel Clark, 27 May 1964, in Russell (ed.), *Ever, Manning*, pp. 208–9. Jung reference in Clark's study, Frieda Fordham, *An Introduction to Jung's Psychology*, Penguin, Harmondsworth, 1966 (first published 1953), Clark's markings on p. 135.

46 Clark papers, box 172, folder 28–'Correspondence 1983–1989', undated letter from Marjorie Thompson to Clark.

47 Margaret Reynolds to Clark, undated, Clark papers, box 172, folder 30. Correspondence 1988–91 (ii); other details drawn from interviews; Eirene Clark to me, Melbourne, February 2008; Philip Ingamells to me, Melbourne, February 2008; also see Clark, diary, 23 October 1961.

48 Philip Ingamells to me, Melbourne, February 2008; also see Clark, diary, 23 October 1961.

49 Philip Ingamells to me, Melbourne, February 2008; also Clark, diary, 25 April 1960 & 22 June 1987; Clark to Russell Clark, 26 September 1983, private, courtesy Eirene Clark.

50 Clark, diary, 22 June 1987.

51 Hope to Dymphna, 17 July 1991, Dymphna Clark Papers, NLA, box 5 9873/1/37.

52 Eirene Clark to me, Melbourne, February 2008; Philip Ingamells to me, February 2008; Tim Clark to me, Sydney, April 2008; Clark's comments in *Quest for Grace*, 1990 (p. 106), is oblique: he fails to state clearly that his father was also Margaret's father, preferring to imply that this was the case. Little wonder Tim Clark was perplexed.

53 Margaret Reynolds to Dymphna Clark, 4 July 1991, Dymphna Clark papers, NLA, 9873/1/37, box 5.

54 Margaret Reynolds to Clark, undated, Clark papers, box 172, folder 30, Correspondence 1988–91 (ii); in same folder see another letter from Margaret Reynolds, 18 April (1987 or 8, difficult to make out) thanking Clark for his ' Easter gift' which she has used for 'tyres for my old bomb'. Clark's notes to himself regarding sympathy for his father are not in his diary but scribbled on A4 sheets of paper and can be found in Clark papers, box 172 folder 28– 'Correspondence 1983–1989'.

55 Clark, *Disquiet*, 1969; also see Clark sketching his ideas for the Tug Smith story in his diary, 10 January 1966; on childhood as creative source, Clark to Axel Clark, 27 May 1964, in Russell (ed.), *Ever, Manning*, pp. 208–9; Ibsen quote in jacket cover of Clark's copy of *Ghosts*, Manning Clark House; on Clark's quest to discover 'who we are' see his biographical entry in the programme for the Musical (1987), Clark papers, box 168, folder 8, 'A History of Australia; the Musical, Correspondence and Drafts 1987'.

56 Clark to Russell Clark, 10 February 1979, courtesy Eirene Clark, and Clark, diary, 21 May 1969; also see 'The Childhood of Manning Clark', published in 1979, held in Clark papers, Series 27, 'Manuscripts' 1979; Clark's interview with Hazel de Berg in 1967 shows the first signs of understanding his urge to write *A History of Australia* through his memory of the class differences between his parents.

57 Clark to Russell Clark, 26 September 1983 (courtesy Eirene Clark), Clark, diary, 2 October 1977.

58 Virginia Woolf, 'Sketch of the Past', in *Moments of Being: autobiographical writings*, edited by Hermione Lee, Pimlico, London 2002, p. 81; also see Hermione Lee, *Virginia Woolf*, Vintage, London, 1997, p. 20.

59 'The Childhood...' (see note 56 above); DH Lawrence's poem 'The Piano' (1913), in Harriet Harvey Wood & AS Byatt (eds), *Memory: an Anthology*, Chatto & Windus, London, 2008, p. 131; also see Clark's 1987 interview with Keith Dunstan and his diary, 27 January 1989.

4: Coming to History: the Melbourne Years, 1928–38

1 Memories of Melbourne Grammar: Phil Harris to me, August 2005; David Brown to me, February 2008; Sebastian Clark to me, April 2007; AGL Shaw to me, December 2008; also see Mervyn Austin, 'A Classical Education: a partial autobiography', unpublished manuscript held in NLA, pp. 36–47; Weston Bate & Helen Penrose, *Challenging Traditions: a history of Melbourne Grammar*,

Australian Scholarly Publishing, Melbourne, 2002, p. 168, & Clark, *Puzzles of Childhood*, 1990, pp. 194-6.

2   Headmaster's report in *The Melburnian*, vol. LVIII, no. 3, 12 December 1933, pp. 202-9; for the school prayer see JB Kiddle (ed.), *Liber Melburniensis, 1848-1936, Melbourne Church of England Grammar School Official History*, Robertson & Mullens, Melbourne, 1936, pp. 674-5: the second paragraph of the prayer begins 'And that there never may be wanting a sufficient supply of persons duly qualified to serve thee, whether in Church or State'; also see pp. 126-7 for details on Franklin—headmaster of Melbourne Grammar 1915-36 [MA Cambridge], served as Lieutenant in Australian army 5th divisional Artillery 1917-1919, died 1942.

3   For Clark's later memories of Melbourne Grammar, see Clark, *Puzzles of Childhood*, 1990, the last chapter ('The Ordeal'), especially p. 205; also his interviews with historians Neville Meaney and Don Baker (NLA); also Keith Dunstan, 'Boy Manning', *Age, Good Weekend*, 23 September 1989, pp. 70-9, Clark's review of Chester Eagle's *Play Together, Dark Blue Twenty*, in *Age, Saturday Extra*, 12 July 1986, p. 11; and Clark, 'Some People I have Known', in Andrew Rutherford & David Wilson (eds), The Ormond Papers, vol. V, 1988, pp. 188-99; Clark's piece on the school's centenary can be found in the *Age, Literary Supplement*, 12 April 1958; many of his memories of the school are reproduced in the short story 'Discovery', published initially in *Quadrant*, January-February 1966, vol. X, no. 1, pp. 49-69; the twelve-year-old Clark's letter to Franklin requesting entry to Melbourne Grammar, based on evidence from David Brown to me, February 2008—'Mrs Clark informed my mother that Manning had personally written to the Principal seeking enrolment as the son of a C of E Minister'. Clark's memories of the school contrasted sharply with others'. Russell Clark, who earned the nickname 'Pops Clark' at Melbourne Grammar, because he was continually shielding his younger brother from the brow-beaters of the long dorm, simply 'took the initiations and the bullying and wore it'. AGL Shaw ('AGL'), a day pupil, 'barely recognised' Clark's depiction of Melbourne Grammar. When he read *The Puzzles of Childhood*, he found Clark had completely 'distorted' the 'reality and culture' of the school, presenting a picture so far removed from his own memory that it read like fiction. While AGL found the education he received 'poor' ('the library was hopeless') and 'the quality of teaching sub-standard ('I first learnt about the Reformation at University'), the few teachers he had found inspiring Clark hardly mentioned— nor did he see the same brutality (Eirene Clark and AGL Shaw to me).

4   Clark's sense of freedom in essay writing can be found in Clark, *Puzzles of Childhood*, 1990, p. 175; Clark's memories of Franklin in his interviews with Don Baker and Neville Meaney held in the NLA, and Clark, *Puzzles*, pp. 182-90; also see Clark in the *Herald* [Melbourne], 23/4 March 1985, p. 7, 'When I was a boarder at Melbourne Grammar I was still thinking about being a doctor. When I came to do my matriculation, [Franklin] said, he thought I could do the "history stuff" as he called it'; for another historian coming to history, see Kathleen Fitzpatrick, 'The Role of Imagination in History', Presidential Address, History, ANZAAS conference, Hobart, January 1949, in 'Handbook for Tasmania: prepared for the members of ANZAAS, January 1949', Government Printer, Hobart, 1949 pp. 57-65; Clark's claim that he had first intended to study medicine appears in his interview with *Australian Playboy*, July 1981, pp. 31-44.

5   Franklin's note on the tragedy can be found in *The Melburnian*, vol. LIV, no. 3, 12 December 1929, p. 158; for Clark's recollections see the Baker and Meaney interviews, together with Clark's 'Some People I have known' (see Note 3) and Clark, *Puzzles of Childhood*, 1990, pp. 184-5; for Clark's role as a storyteller see his interview with *Australian Playboy*, July 1981, pp. 31-44; David Brown and Phil Harris both told me of Clark's talent for spinning 'a good yarn', as Harris put it.

6   Clark's memories of Unaipon appear in 'Some People I have Known' (see Note 3), as well as Clark, *Puzzles of Childhood*, 1990, pp. 149-50; Clark's juvenilia appears in *The Melburnian*, vol. LVI, no. 2, 26 August 1931, p. 121 ('The Australian Aborigine'), *The Melburnian*, vol. LVIII, no. 1, 10 May 1933, pp. 33-4, & *The Melburnian*, vol. LVIII, no. 1, 10 May 1933, p. 36; Clark claimed Franklin referred to his talent for 'this history stuff' in the *Herald* [Melbourne], 23/4 March 1985, p. 7; biographical details on Clark's time at Melbourne Grammar are scattered throughout *The Melburnian*; he entered the school in February 1928 and became a boarder in Creswick House when it opened in 1929; see *The Melburnian*, vol. LIII, no. 1, 17 May 1928, p. 19; Clark held the

Ronald Guy Larking Scholarship, see *The Melburnian*, vol. LIV, no. 3, 12 December 1929, p. 162; he was selected in the school's First XI in 1933, see *The Melburnian*, vol. LVIII, no. 1, 10 May 1933, p. 24; in 1934 he came first in Greek and Roman History and gained a first class honour in European History together with AGL Shaw, as well as second class in Latin, see *The Melburnian*, vol. L1X, no.1, 15 May 1934, pp. 9-10; the headmaster's report in *The Melburnian*, vol. LVIII, no. 3, 12 December 1933, p. 208, reports that both Clark and Shaw won scholarships to Trinity College; Clark's activities in Grammar's debating club appear in *The Melburnian*, vol. LVIII, no. 1, 10 May 1933; topics included 'that the present relationship between employer and employee is immoral' and 'that science by prostituting itself to capitalism had failed to serve its true end'.

7   For Clark's influences at Belgrave see his interview in the Melbourne *Herald*, 23/4 March 1985, p. 7; 'Some People I have Known' (see Note 3); & Clark, *Puzzles of Childhood*, 1990, p. 145, on his father's library; on Melbourne in the 1930s I have drawn on Stuart Macintyre, *The Oxford History of Australia, Volume 4, 1901-1942: the succeeding age*, Oxford University Press, Melbourne, 1997 (first published 1986), pp. 311-15; the quote from Macintyre is drawn from his *The Reds: The Communist Party of Australia*, Allen & Unwin, Sydney, 1998, p. 319; also see Janet McCalman, *Journeyings: the biography of a middle-class generation 1920-1990*, Melbourne University Press, Carlton, Vic., 1993, pp. 136-45 & 164, and Sheila Fitzpatrick's comments on the isolation of Melbourne, in Sheila Fitzpatrick, 'Brian Fitzpatrick and the World Outside Australia', in Macintyre & Fitzpatrick (eds), *Against the Grain*, pp. 39-41.

8   Dymphna's recollections come from her interview with Elizabeth Cham (NLA).

9   Mervyn Austin, 'A Classical Education: a partial autobiography', unpublished manuscript, NLA, p. 89; also see Zelman Cowen, *A Public Life: the memoirs of Zelman Cowen*, Miegunyah Press, Carlton, Vic., 2006, pp. 66-70.

10   On Clark and billiards, Noel Carroll to me, Canberra, November 2005; on Jessie Webb, see Max Crawford's obituary in *Farrago*, 15 March 1944, vol. xx, no. 2, p. 1, and Clark, *Quest for Grace*, 1990, pp. 2-3; on Clark's bookshop haunts, Clark, *Quest*, p. 15; in Clark's library there is a copy of 'Workers' Songs, old and new' an eight-page pamphlet, inscribed 'M. Clark, the Vicarage, Melbourne' and published by the Friends of the Soviet Union, Melbourne, which included the Marseillaise, Solidarity, the Red Army March and the Soviet Airman's Song; Joyce Manton, *The Centenary Prepares for War*, Melbourne University Council Against War, 1935, especially pp. 13, 23 & 30; on Kisch see *Farrago*, vol. 24, no. 7, 1938, p. 4, and the *Australian Dictionary of Biography* online entry by Carolyn Rasmussen; on Duke of Gloucester in Australia see Kate Cumming, *Royalty in Australia: records relating to the British Monarchy in Australia, held in Canberra*, National Archives, Canberra, 1998, p. 89; also see *Sydney Morning Herald*, Royal Visit Supplement, 22 November 1934, p. 14; Clark's subjects taken at Melbourne, from his academic record (enrolment number 340082), held at the University of Melbourne Archives; Dymphna Clark attested to the existence of Clark's 'Jottings of a Recluse', written in 1935, in her conversation with Jan Nicholas, 29 November 1995, but after searching the house she explained she was unable to find them.

11   All inscriptions and lists of books come from what I have found on the shelves of Manning Clark's study in Canberra, also with the help of Jan Nicholas. The report of Clark's address on Lawrence to the Literature Society appears in *Farrago*, vol. XIII, no. 10, 18 May, 1937, p. 3. In 1986, Clark told Neville Meaney: 'I was in the Literature Society at Melbourne University, in fact secretary of it for years. But I was never very at ease with the way they discussed literature'; in the *Trinity College Dialectic Society Minute Book 1915-1953*, pp. 262-3, Clark wrote the report on 1936 activities, noting that 'the society lacks the support of the college. Attendance at ordinary meetings is still very low.' It seems more students attended football matches than debating. Clark editorialised: 'the society does not exist purely for the purpose of cultivating perfection in public speaking. It has its cultural side. The society should be a forum for the dissemination of ideas.' On John Masefield, see Clark, *Quest for Grace*, 1990, pp. 13-14; in *Puzzles of Childhood*, 1990, p. 190, Clark described the Melbourne Public Library as his 'oasis'; on Clark's first readings of Dostoyevsky, see Clark's 'Some People I have Known' (see Note 3).

12   Clark's academic record states that Clark obtained first class honours in Modern Political Institutions in 1936, and in 1937 first class honours and first place in the final exam in the School

of History and Political Science; also see *The Mitre* [Trinity magazine], vol. xxx, no. 2, August 1938, p. 5, for anonymous recollection of Clark; at the end of 1937, he was awarded the MA Bartlett Research Scholarship in History (100 pounds) and the Dwight's prize in Political Science; on Ernest Scott, see Kathleen Fitzpatrick's entry in the *Australian Dictionary of Biography* online, and Stuart Macintyre, *A History for a Nation: Ernest Scott and the making of Australian History*, Melbourne University Press, Carlton, Vic., 1994, introduction, pp. 5 & 196; also Max Crawford's obituary in *Historical Studies*, vol. 1, no. 1, April 1940, p. 3; for Clark on Scott, see *Quest for Grace*, 1990, pp. 2–3, on Crawford, pp. 29–31, on Macmahon Ball, pp. 23–4; in his interview with Don Baker, Clark related how Macmahon Ball introduced him to Marxism and Leninism through the Communist Manifesto and chapter 21 of *Das Kapital*. Cowen's recollections in *A Public Life: the memoirs of Zelman Cowen*, Miegunyah Press, Carlton, Vic., 2006, p. 70; also see pp. 72–4, where Cowen remembers Macmahon Ball more favourably and Crawford less so than Clark.

13 On Crawford's train trip to Melbourne, see Fay Anderson, *An Historian's Life: Max Crawford and the politics of academic freedom*, Melbourne University Press, Carlton, Vic., 2005, p. 59; Priestley's comment is quoted in John Poynter, '"Wot Larks to be Aboard": The History Department 1937–71', in Fay Anderson & Stuart Macintyre (eds), *The Life of the Past: the discipline of history at the University of Melbourne, 1855–2005*, Department of History, University of Melbourne, Parkville, Vic., 2006, p. 41; also see Crawford's obituary in *Sydney Morning Herald*, 26 November 1991; further biographical details are in Geoffrey Serle, 'RM Crawford and his School', *Melbourne Historical Journal*, vol. 9, 1970, pp. 3–6, and Stuart Macintyre, 'Raymond Maxwell Crawford 1906–1991', *Australian Historical Studies*, vol. 25, no. 98, April 1992, pp. 123–5; & Stuart Macintyre & Peter McPhee (eds), *Max Crawford's School of History*, Department of History, University of Melbourne, Parkville, Vic., 2000, in which, on p. 41, Inga Clendinnen quotes Bob Dare on Crawford and adds some of her own reflections. The impression of Crawford's speech is my own, after listening to a recording of the paper he gave at the Victorian History Institute in April 1984, which was later published in RM Crawford, M Clark & G Blainey, *Making History*, McPhee Gribble/ Penguin, Ringwood, Vic., 1985.

14 Clark's memories of Crawford in *Quest for Grace*, 1990, pp. 29–31; also see Clark, 'RM Crawford: some Reminiscences', *Historical Studies*, vol. 15, no. 57, October 1971, pp. 5–7, & Clark, 'Melbourne an Intellectual Tradition', *Melbourne Historical Journal*, no. 2, 1962, pp. 17–23, especially p. 21, where in writing of Crawford he implicitly refers to himself: 'It is the divided ones, the ones who thirst to believe, and who are sceptical of all belief, who believe in the perfectibility of mankind, and yet perceive that the hearts of the sons of men are filled with evil, who become the great teachers.'

15 On the Spanish Civil War debate, see Clark, *Quest for Grace*, 1990, pp. 44–5; 'overwhelmingly on the side of the republic', 'no assumptions in common', 'the catholic tribe' and 'not an exercise in persuasion' in Zelman Cowen, *A Public Life: the memoirs of Zelman Cowen*, Miegunyah Press, Carlton, Vic., 2006, pp. 80–2 (Cowen also quotes Rivkah Mathews' memories: 'the war in Spain had become the symbol [of the march] ... to world war'); also *Farrago*, vol. xiii, no. 2, 17 March 1937, p. 1, and report of the debate in *Farrago*, vol. xiii, no. 4, 5 April 1937, p. 4, as well as *Age*, 23 March 1937, p. 11, *Argus*, 23 March 1937, p. 9; also BA Santamaria, *Santamaria: a memoir*, Oxford University Press, Melbourne, 1997, pp. 26–31; Stuart Macintyre, 'History in the headlines', in Anderson & Macintyre, *The Life of the Past*, pp. 355–76; Bruce Duncan, *Crusade or Conspiracy? Catholics and the anti-communist struggle in Australia*, UNSW Press, Sydney, 2001, p. 25; Fay Anderson & Stuart Macintyre, 'Crawford as Controversialist', in their collection *The Life of the Past*, pp. 89–112 (p. 96 on Crawford's protest); I am also grateful to Fay Anderson for sending me her paper 'Reviewing the 1937 Spanish Civil War Debate at the University of Melbourne 70 years on'; for Clark and debates at Trinity, see Trinity College Dialectic Society, Minute Book, 16 March 1915–13 September 1953, pp. 265, 274, 276, also Minute Book, 22 April 1936, pp. 248–9, and *Fleur-de-Lys*, vol. iv, no. 37, 1937, pp. 9–10; Clark also spoke on Dickens before the Literary Club— see *Farrago*, XII, no. 11, 23 June 1936, p. 1; the question 'whither Britain' was one Manning Clark expressed in reference to this period in his interview with Don Baker.

16 After taking up his appointment, see Crawford in *Farrago*, 5 March 1937, p. 4; Crawford on history

in *Farrago*, 22 June 1937, p. 1; also see Crawford's *The Study of History: a synoptic view*, Australian Medical Publishing, Sydney, 1939, pp. 117–26, and Crawford's 'History as Science', *Historical Studies*, vol. 3, no. 11, November 1947, pp. 153–75.

17 Thomas Carlyle, *The French Revolution, vols. 1–3*, Robson & Sons, London, 1837, pp. 265–6; on Carlyle also see Clark's interview with Neville Meaney: 'I read Carlyle because in 1937 we were doing the French Revolution and walking down to the train one night I saw in a second-hand bookshop the 3 volumes of the French Revolution by Carlyle and I bought them–I've still got them ... I didn't read every word of it, but I was bowled over by it!' Clark also read his mother's calf-bound copy of Macaulay's 'History of England' which she'd won as a prize–'I thought it was absolutely wonderful', he said.

18 For the original copy of Clark's BA thesis, see Clark papers, box 177, folders 1–2.

19 Letter from Crawford to AD Lindsay, Master of Balliol, 9 September 1938, Balliol Archives, Oxford, courtesy Jan Nicholas.

20 Bob Phillips to Jan Nicholas, February 95, Jan Nicholas, interview with Bill Brett, 9 February 1995, and Jim Lemaire, March and April 1938. Clark's Trinity College record card shows he enrolled as an 'ARTS/LAW' student. Clark is also listed as such in *Fleur-de-Lys*, vol. 3, no. 34, 1934, p. 7; he graduated in 1937 with honours from the School of History and Politics.

21 Crawford to Lindsay, Balliol, 9 September 1938; Sebastian Clark to me, Melbourne, 27 March 2007; for further details on Clark's cricketing feats, see team photographs in *Fleur-de-Lys*, vol. 3, no. 34, 1934, and *Fleur-de-Lys*, vol. 4, no. 38, 1934, p. 12; in his interview with me, Noel Caroll praised Clark's sporting prowess: 'I saw him make 150 one day on the main oval. He had to have a runner. If it were not for his epilepsy he would have been a test cricketer.' Clark played both cricket and football while at Trinity College, he was a forward in the first XVIII in 1934 and half forward in first XVIII in 1935 and in 1934–37 he played in the first XI–see *Fleur-de-Lys*, vol. 4, no. 38, 1938, Valete, p. 18; also see Mervyn Austin, 'A Classical Education: a partial autobiography', unpublished manuscript, NLA, p. 69; for letters of reference regarding Clark see W Macmahon Ball to AW Grieg, 26 October 1937; when Clark sailed for England he took with him the reference dated 9 August 1938 from Frank Shann, Headmaster of Trinity, whose English classes he had taken, describing him as 'a deep thinker and a lover of good things in literature, with the power of communicating his enthusiasm to others'; also see letter from Behan, warden at Trinity College, recommending Clark for Balliol, 3 February 1938; another from Crawford, 4 February 1938, describing Clark (compared to Shaw and Rivett), as 'the best and most promising' and 'of unusual calibre'; also see cable from Crawford to Balliol, 7 February 1938–'Strongly recommend Clark Melbourne admission Balliol, First place History Exceptionally Fine Mind Crawford', KH Bailey to Lindsay at Balliol, 9 August 1938–'he expresses himself with force and elegance'; also see note from Tutor for Admissions, 19 February 1938–'we have a lot of Australians, but this man does sound very good, and I suggest that we recommend taking him and definitely ditch Shaw', all of above in Balliol archives.

22 AGL Shaw to me, Melbourne, December 2008; regarding Clark's decision to go to Oxford, see his interview with Neville Meaney, held in NLA, 'by then I'd decided to go in for some sort of academic career ... it was just assumed at the University of Melbourne by then if you wanted to enter ... that you'd need to go overseas'.

5: Corresponding Loves: Melbourne, Oxford and Bonn, 1936–38

1 Dostoyevsky, *The Brothers Karamazov*, Everyman edition, 2003, p. 237.

2 Details of Eileen Martin's memories, based on the account given to me by her son, John Martin, linguist, scholar and friend of the Lodewyckx family, Melbourne, April 2008.

3 Dymphna explained she was in Latin 1 with Clark in 1934 but they didn't know one another until 1936. For Dymphna's memories of her school and university life, see her January 1991 interview with Elizabeth Cham (NLA); also, at NLA, her interview with Heather Rusden, and her interview with ABC's Bill Bunbury on Radio National's *Hindsight*, broadcast, June 1998. The first batch of correspondence between Clark and Dymphna is held at Manning Clark House. See in particular Dymphna Lodewyckx to Manning Clark, 27 November 1936, and several undated letters from

Clark to Dymphna, all of which predate their journey to Europe–for example, Clark to Dymphna, most probably April 1937, headed 'Conclusions': 'You have a yearning for the cosmopolitan–or rather the non-Australian element in life, and of course, you don't see it in me.' He claims he has the same yearning, understands she likes her life at 'the [German] club'; 'One final word about jealousy, you think I am suspicious, that is not quite the real position ... but I am deeply sorry that I have been unpleasant to you before ... especially about Ventar [a potential suitor] ... this is the crux: we are both uncertain. At this stage, I more than you–the wheel has gone full circle now'; he finishes with words of 'faith which will gather strength & momentum'; the remaining details are drawn from my interview with Noel Carroll, November 2005.

4 For Clark on Dostoyevsky, see his 1987 interview with Jill Kitson on ABC Radio's *First Edition*, held on audio cassette at Manning Clark House; other quotes from letters held at Manning Clark House, Dymphna Lodewyckx to Clark, 7 January & 9 February 1938, Clark to Dymphna, undated, early 1938.

5 All letters held at Manning Clark House; see undated letter from Clark to Dymphna, from Cronulla, early 1938, also Dymphna Lodewyckx to Clark, 4 & 7 January 1938.

6 Dymphna Lodewyckx to Clark, 9 February 1938 & 16 April 1938, both held at Manning Clark House; on her teaching Clark German at Tate's Coffee Lounge, this information is contained in a letter from Dymphna to Jan Nicholas, 29 November 1995; in another letter to Nicholas, 25 February 1995, Dymphna stated she had typed Clark's thesis, both letters courtesy of Jan Nicholas; Dymphna to Jan Nicholas, 29 November 1995.

7 Dymphna's memories are recorded in her interview with Elizabeth Cham, January 1991, NLA. Her academic results (1934–36) were outstanding: each year, she came first in both German and French, majoring in German, her strongest language, in 1936. See the *Calendar* of the University of Melbourne, 1935, 1936 and 1938, pp. (1202–1203), (1257, 1260, 1262), (1324, 1331, 1338) respectively; also see the Melbourne *Sun*, 19 April 1937, 'Girl Wins 230 pounds scholarship'; Dymphna graduated BA Hons on Saturday 10 April 1937–see *Farrago* vol. xiii, no. 5, 13 April 1937, p. 2; Clark graduated on Saturday 9 April 1938–see *Farrago*, vol. xiv, no. 3, 2 March 1938; for quote on engagement, see *Herald*, 29 July 1938, & *Fleur-de-Lys*, vol. 14, no. 38, p. 6 (AGL Shaw travelled on the same ship). On the couple first making love, Clark stated, in an undated letter from Oxford, held at Manning Clark House, that Dymphna had been subjected to the double fear of 'pregnancy and exposure' since June [1938].

8 For Clark's editorial comments on newspaper cuttings reporting their departure, see Clark papers, box 35, in which there is an album of clippings he compiled, headed 'M.Clark Trip to England beginning August 16 1938'; above the photo of Dymphna 'Engagement announced', from the *Herald*, 29 July 1938, he writes 'Before & the Complication' (the complication of impending war); above the clipping from the *Herald*, 1 August 1938, 'The Possibilities'; above the clipping from the *Sun*, 2 August 1938, 'A More Moderate Statement'; and above the cutting from the *Herald*, 15 August 1938 (which finishes with the statement 'Both [Clark] and his fiancée have completed brilliant arts courses at Melbourne University') he writes 'Is this True?' He also kept the report in the *Argus*, 9 April 1938, reporting on his graduation; the remainder comprises cuttings from German papers in 1938–39, British papers in 1940 and Melbourne papers through to 1944, all relating to the war.

9 Lodewyckx family photograph album courtesy of Dymphna's nephew, Ian Lodewyckx; Dymphna's memories of Durban can be found in her interview with Heather Rusden, held in the NLA, & KA [Axel] Lodewycks (sic), *The Funding of Wisdom: revelations of a library's quarter century*, Spectrum, Melbourne, 1982, p. 9. I have also drawn on my interview with Ian Lodewyckx, Melbourne, March 2007.

10 On the planting of the ash tree and cutting of firewood, Ian Lodewyckx to me, Melbourne, March 2007; details of languages spoken in the Lodewyckx home, John Martin to me, Melbourne, April 2008; Martin also told me of Lodewyckx's adaptation of wood-piling techniques in a twenty-page document he wrote on the Lodewyckx circle (11 March 2009), which I have deposited with the NLA. Ian Lodewyckx told me that for a period of time his grandfather had worked for the Censor's Department translating during World Wars I and II, and for the Immigration Department,

dispensing the notorious dictation test (he was proficient in eighteen languages). Memories of Lodewyckx family history, Sebastian Clark to me, Melbourne, March 2007; Dymphna Clark's interview with Elizabeth Cham, NLA; and Dymphna's interview with Bill Bunbury, ABC Radio National, June 1998.

11 Details of the Lodewyckx circle, John Martin to me, Melbourne, April 2008. His Tennyson analogy appears in his typed document, forwarded to me on 11 March 2009, now held in the NLA; for a sample of Augustin Lodewyckx's articles in the press, see *Argus*, *Weekend Magazine*, 20 November 1937, p. 8; *Herald*, 1 October 1938, p. 38; his views on immigration can be seen in his opinion pieces in the *Argus*, 23 September 1948, and 18 & 20 January 1949; see the positive reaction to his *People for Australia*, published in 1957, in *News-Weekly*, 20 February 1957, p. 5, & 'Populate our Empty Continent', in the Adelaide *News*, 5 December 1956; also see 'The Name of Australia: Its Origin and Early Use', in *Victorian Historical Magazine*, June 1929, pp. 1–17, and KA [Axel] Lodewycks (sic), *The Funding of Wisdom: revelations of a library's quarter century*, Spectrum, Melbourne, 1982, first chapter. Dymphna's memories are taken from her NLA interviews with Heather Rusden and Elizabeth Cham. In *Manning Clark: a Life*, 2008, Brian Matthews describes Lodewyckx as an 'unreconstructed Europhile who could find little of value in Australia' (see p. 241).

12 The story of Dymphna telling her father of her exam results, Ian Lodewyckx to me, Melbourne, March 2007; also see Dymphna's NLA interviews with Heather Rusden and Elizabeth Cham, as well as details of the Lodewyckx circle, John Martin to me, Melbourne, April 2008; for the story of Augustin Lodewyckx's first interest in German, see KA [Axel] Lodewycks (sic), *The Funding of Wisdom: revelations of a library's quarter century*, Spectrum, Melbourne, 1982, p. 8.

13 My description of Augustin Lodewyckx and the story of his deathbed are based on information given to me by Ian Lodewyckx and on Sebastian Clark to me, Melbourne, March 2007; Katerina Clark, in her interview with Susan Marsden held at the NLA, described the Lodewyckx family as 'pathologically parsimonious and puritanical'; also see Dymphna's interview with Elizabeth Cham, which also tells the story of the dances at Beatty St; KA [Axel] Lodewycks (sic), *The Funding of Wisdom: revelations of a library's quarter century*, Spectrum, Melbourne, 1982, p. 23.

14 For Dymphna's memory of reading *Little Women* to Anna, and of her loneliness as a child, see her interview with Elizabeth Cham, together with the Heather Rusden interview, 13 February 1997, NLA; Clark to Catherine Clark, 10 September 1938, held at Manning Clark House.

15 Clark to Catherine Clark, 10 & 13 September 1938, from SS *Orama*, and same, undated, but early October 1938, just before leaving London for Oxford, all held at Manning Clark House.

16 Dymphna's recollections are recorded in her correspondence with Jan Nicholas, 29 November 1995; on Naples also see Clark to Hope Clark (date difficult to determine but most likely September or October 1938) held at Manning Clark House, and Clark to Catherine Clark, 9 October 1938, in *Ever, Manning*, pp. 8–10.

17 Dymphna's memories in her correspondence with Jan Nicholas, 29 November 1995, and in her interviews with Heather Rusden, 13 February 1997, NLA, and Bill Bunbury, ABC Radio National, June 1998; for Clark's arrival in London, see Clark to Hope, 9 October 1938, held at Manning Clark House; for Clark weeping in Sweden, see his diary, 15 December 1942.

18 For Dymphna's later recollections, see her typed manuscript 'Memories of Germany 1933–1995' held in her papers at the NLA; all other references are drawn from her 1933 journal, held at Manning Clark House. Gullett quoted in John Passmore, *Memoirs of a Semi-detached Australian*, p. 178; on Anna Lodewyckx see the ASIO security file on Augustin Lodewyckx, press interview with Mrs AS Lodewyckx, 28 February 1934, extract from D/745, Professor Augustin Lodewyckx, Folio 6.

19 Augustin Lodewyckx to Dymphna Lodewyckx, Melbourne, 27 September 1938–my thanks to Ockert Meyer, for translating this letter; also see Dymphna's first letter to Clark, from Lloyd Hotel, Invalidenstrasse 124, Berlin.

20 Thanks again to Ockert Meyer, who translated the letters written by Augustin and Anna to Dymphna, held at Manning Clark House.

21 Clark to Anna Lodewyckx, 15 October & 13 November 1938, in the former Clark also writing 'what a pity' it was that 'people in Australia are so indifferent & so materialist in their outlook?'–both

held at Manning Clark House; also see Clark to Anna Lodewyckx, 18 & 24 November 1938; 'those barren leaves' is the title of Aldous Huxley's satirical novel, published in 1925.

22 Busslei's comments and Dymphna's reaction, in undated letter from Dymphna to Clark, most probably early October 1938, held at Manning Clark House (my translation of the German); also see Dymphna's later recollections, in 'Memories of Germany 1933–1995', in her papers, NLA; I have also drawn on Dymphna's interview with Jan Nicholas, 29 November 1995, and two letters from Dymphna to Clark, 6 & 9 October 1938, and one from Clark to Dymphna, undated, but shortly after arriving in London from Sweden, early October 1938; also see undated letter from Dymphna to Clark, early October 1938, where she writes of going alone to the Frauenklinik in Berlin, two weeks late with her period, the letter's first lines: 'forgive it this time—we have been let off again— in all probability'; all unpublished and held at Manning Clark House; on the Oxford political climate in 1938, see Paul Addison, 'Oxford and the Second World War', in Brian Harrison (ed.); *The History of the University of Oxford, Vol. VIII, The Twentieth Century*, Clarendon Press, Oxford, 1994, pp. 167–88 (p. 167), and Adam Sisman, *AJP Taylor: a biography*, Mandarin, London, 1995 (1994), p. 120.

23 Clark's copy of *The Idiot* (dated 1938 Stockholm) is still in his study in Canberra. I have drawn on the following letters: Clark to Dymphna, 8 October 1938, in *Ever, Manning*, pp. 6–8; Clark to Catherine Clark, 9 October 1938, *Ever, Manning*, pp. 8–10, and 16 October 1938, unpublished, held at Manning Clark House; Clark to Gladys Hope, 16 October 1938, *Ever, Manning*, p. 13; Clark to Catherine Clark, 7 November 1938 & 14 November 1938, *Ever, Manning*, pp. 20 & 27; Clark to Hope Clark, 15 October 1938, unpublished, held at Manning Clark House.

24 AGL Shaw to me, Melbourne, June 2005 & December 2008; Clark's comments on his allegiance to Australia appear in his letter to Hope, 15 October 1938, unpublished, held at Manning Clark House.

25 The Dr Livingstone anecdote comes from Dymphna Clark, in her interview with Jan Nicholas, 29 November 1995; percentages of foreign students in JG Darwin, 'A World University', in Brian Harrison (ed.), *The History of the University of Oxford, Vol. VIII, The Twentieth Century*, Clarendon Press, Oxford, 1994, pp. 607–36 (p. 627); also in Harrison, see Jose Harris, 'The Arts and Social Sciences, 1939–1970', pp. 217–49 (pp. 217–19); on Bowen, see John Jones, *Balliol College: a History, 1263–1939*, Oxford University Press, Oxford, 1988, p. 169.

26 For historical background on Oxford I have drawn on the following chapters in Harrison's edited history of Oxford; Brian Harrison, 'College Life', 1918–1939, pp. 81–108 (pp. 92–6); Jose Harris, 'The Arts and Social Sciences, 1939–1970', pp. 217–49 (pp. 217–19), and JG Darwin, 'A World University', pp. 607–36; on Graham Greene's time at Balliol, see Norman Sherry, *The Life of Graham Greene, Vol. One 1904–1939*, Penguin, Harmondsworth, 1989, p. 129.

27 Clark to Dymphna, undated, but early October 1938, unpublished, held at Manning Clark House. For Oxford apparel see Brian Harrison's chapter–'College Life, 1918–1939', p. 94, which is in his edited volume on Oxford; and other chapters listed in previous note.

28 Max Crawford to AD Lindsay, 9 September 1938, Balliol Archives; Crawford supported Clark's application for 'advanced status' and noted that he had 'little money'. 'We have awarded him a scholarship of 100 pounds this year and I hope that that may be renewed next year. But this money can be granted only to a student carrying on graduate research. With it he has enough, just enough, to spend two years in Oxford, but not without it'. On Clark's lack of funds see Dymphna Clark's introduction to D Clark, D Headon & J Williams (eds), *The Ideal of Alexis de Tocqueville: Manning Clark*, Melbourne University Press, Carlton, Vic., 2000, p. 2; also Clark to Crawford, 16 October 1938 & 2 November 1938, Crawford Papers, University of Melbourne Archives. It is also in this letter that Clark tells Crawford 'I would like to get some small post in Melbourne if that is at all possible'; Dymphna's standard response to questions regarding their marriage and her time in Germany can be seen in her interviews with Heather Rusden, 13 February 1997, NLA ('I had to fulfil my promise and just abandon everything in Germany'), and with Bill Bunbury, ABC Radio National, June 1998; also see *Canberra Times*, Books Supplement, 21 March 1993, in which Dymphna is quoted: 'In comparison with Manning I had very little to contribute.' In *Manning Clark, a Life*, p. 40, Brian Matthews quotes Dymphna to similar effect, but does not refer to her letters to Clark.

29 Dymphna Lodewyckx to Clark, Bonn, 6 October 1938, and Clark to Dymphna, undated, but early October 1938, both unpublished and held at Manning Clark House; on Bonn, Dymphna Clark to Jan Nicholas, 29 November 1995; also see Dymphna's letter to Clark, 19 October 1938, in which she writes that she is 'hurt' by his complaint that she wrote 'too dispassionately'.

30 Clark to Dymphna, early October 1938, undated, but he refers to the fact that his grandfather died 'last week' (27 September 1938), even if he did not hear by telegram, but by mail, one week later, the date of the letter is most probably early in the second week of October 1938, unpublished and held at Manning Clark House. In 1995, Dymphna Clark told Jan Nicholas that she was asked out by other men in Bonn.

31 Dymphna Lodewyckx to Clark, 20 October 1938; for Dymphna wishing she could write more passionately, see her letter to Clark, 26 October 1938; on her response to Clark's letter, see her undated letter to Clark, October 1938—all held at Manning Clark House. Also see her letter of October 20 in which she can be seen trying to write more romantically—'The Rhineland is undoubtedly beautiful—if only not another leaf would fall, not another flower die, till you come'; in this letter, Dymphna also refers to Clark's request for her to read *Love Among the Haystacks*.

32 Dymphna Lodewyckx to Clark, 1 November 1938; Dymphna's comments on propaganda in Bonn in her letter to Clark, 20 October 1938; both letters held at Manning Clark House.

33 Clark to Dymphna Lodewyckx, 4 November 1938; also see Clark to Dymphna, and Dymphna to Clark, both written on 3 November 1938; all letters held at Manning Clark House.

34 Dymphna Lodewyckx to Clark, 6 November 1938, held at Manning Clark House.

35 ibid.

36 Dymphna Lodewyckx to Clark, 6 November 1938.

37 Dymphna Lodewyckx to Clark, 5 & 6 November 1938, and Clark, writing on the evening of November 7, in *Ever, Manning*, pp. 23–4, in which he also speaks of his insomnia and reliance on 'drugs'; 'one can rely on you', Clark to Dymphna, 15 November 1938, *Ever, Manning*, p. 31; Dymphna writes of Clark's visit to a 'psychiatrist' in her letter to Clark, 3 November 1938, held at Manning Clark House. Also see Clark to Catherine Clark, 13 November 1938, *Ever, Manning*, pp. 26–7; Clark to Dymphna, 7 November 1938, *Ever, Manning*, pp. 20–3; and Dymphna to Clark from Bonn, 16 November 1938, worried because she has not had a letter from him in the last few days: 'It's like the nightmares I had when I first came to Germany—every night I dreamt that you were furious with me.'

38 Dymphna Lodewyckx to Clark, 12 November 1938, unpublished, held at Manning Clark House; AGL Shaw to me, Melbourne, December 2008; Clark to Hope Clark, 17 November 1938, *Ever, Manning*, p. 33 (similar sentiments expressed in Clark's letter to Anna Lodewyckx, also written on 17 November 1938); Clark to Dymphna, 14 November 1938, *Ever, Manning*, pp. 28–30; Clark asking if Dostoyevsky was any help in his letter to Dymphna, 15 November 1938, *Ever, Manning*, p. 31.

39 Dymphna Lodewyckx to Clark, undated, Bonn, but likely 23 November 1938, held at Manning Clark House; also there, are the letters written in Dutch from her parents—see, for example, the letters from Anna to Dymphna, 2, 9 & 18 November 1938; her mother's letter on 18 November states that Clark had been writing frequently, which both she and Augustin appreciated, my thanks to Ockert Meyer for these translations; also see Clark to Dymphna, 18 November 1938, and Dymphna to Clark, 18 November 1938, both held at Manning Clark House; for Dymphna's later recollections, see Gia Metherell, 'A Modest Scholar Unearths a Triumph', *Canberra Times* (Books Supplement), 21 March 1995, p. 4; Dymphna: 'in comparison with Manning I had very little to contribute, so I contributed what I had in the way I could ... I think (my father) probably misread my character a bit'; on 15 January 1939, Clark wrote to Anna Lodewyckx, 'I think the 10th of November was rude shock to her over-sentimentalised views of life in Germany.'

40 Clark's quip about the best dressed man was made in his letter to Dymphna on 14 November 1938, *Ever, Manning*, pp. 28–30; also Clark to Anna Lodewyckx, 24 November 1938, held at Manning Clark House.

1 For Clark's idealised image of Dymphna, see his letters to her, 7 & 14 November, in *Ever, Manning*, p. 24 & pp. 28-30, in which he imagined their future life together as a response to his 'vague yearning for immortality'; also Dymphna to Clark, 16 November 1938.

2 Dymphna Clark, journal, 1933-1934, held at Manning Clark House.

3 Clark, diary, November 1938-May 1940, Clark papers, box 28.

4 On the aftermath of Kristallnacht, see Richard Grunberger, *The 12-Year Reich: a social history of Nazi Germany 1933-1945*, Holt, Rinehart & Winston, New York, 1971, pp. 454 & 460; Ian Kershaw, *Hitler: 1936-1945 Nemesis*, Penguin, London, 2000, pp. 131-48; Richard J Evans, *The Third Reich in Power 1933-1939*, Penguin, Harmondsworth, 2006 (first published 2005), pp. 580-602; and Martin Gilbert, *Kristallnacht; Prelude to Disaster*, HarperCollins London 2006, pp. 139-52 (Goebbels' quote on p. 141).

5 Victor Klemperer, *I Shall Bear Witness: the diaries of Victor Klemperer 1933-1941*, Weidenfeld & Nicolson, London, 1998, pp. 264-6, 268 & 273.

6 Clark, diary, 2, 3, 11, 23, 25, 27 & 28 December 1938; also see his entries on 31 December and 1 & 3 January 1939; on the latter date, Clark wrote that as they said their goodbyes to Frau Dr Diddmar, she kept repeating: 'Wir leben unter einem Terror (we live under terror)'.

7 Letters from Anna and Augustin Lodewyckx to Dymphna Lodewyckx, 20 November 1938, 29 November 1938 ('Kapo spoke to Crawford last week'), 1 December 1938, 4 December 1938 ('With the five o'clock post came a letter from Manning from Oxford. He still seems to be feeling out of place/uncomfortable there. According to him, Australians are regarded as strangers in a strange country.') In her letter of 9 November 1938, Anna sent Dymphna a book of photographs of the Victorian countryside, hardly the act of a woman uninterested in Australia. In her letter of 4 December 1938, she also told Dymphna that she never expected the [German] population to 'have allowed themselves to become so excited about the Jewish issue'; my thanks to Ockert Meyer for his translation of these letters from the Dutch originals.

8 Dymphna Clark interview with Heather Rusden, 13 February 1997, NLA: 'I was always aware right from the very start, that he was a very, very gifted person, there was absolutely no question of that. I suppose that was a great part of the attraction that he was far more gifted than anyone else I knew'; also Dymphna Clark to Jan Nicholas, 29 November 1995, Dymphna Clark, *Memories of Germany 1933-1995*, held in Dymphna Clark Papers, NLA; Deborah Hope, 'Life after Manning', *The Weekend Australian*, 6-7 June 1998, pp. 5-6 (it is in this interview that Dymphna states that her father thought Clark would make a 'serviceable librarian'); also see *Canberra Times* Books Supplement, p. 4, 21 March 1995, for Gia Metherell's article on Dymphna Clark, 'A Modest Scholar Unearths a Triumph', in which Dymphna is quoted: 'in comparison with Manning I had very little to contribute, so I contributed what I had in the way I could ... I think (my father) probably misread my character a bit'; also Clark to Anna Lodewyckx, 18 & 24 November 1938, Manning Clark House.

9 I have drawn on Dymphna's letters to Clark, 14 & 18 January 1939, two undated (January 1939), in one of which she remarks to Clark on the 'greatness' of *The Brothers Karamazov*, also 22 January 1939 & 24 January 1939, all unpublished and held at Manning Clark House; Dymphna told Jan Nicholas that, when she arrived in Oxford, she found that Clark had still not delivered the coat, watches and jewellery to the address in Hampstead, so she took them down from Oxford herself.

10 Clark to Anna Lodewyckx, 15 January 1939; see Clark's diary entries for the following dates in 1939: 16 January ('We saw 6 bombers to-day, like beasts of prey') 21, 22, & 25 January; also Dymphna to Clark, 22 & 24 January 1939, Clark's description of his sad letters is in his letter to Dymphna, 14 November 1939, *Ever, Manning*, p. 29; on the mood in Britain, see Martin Gilbert, *Kristallnacht; Prelude to Disaster*, HarperCollins London, 2006, p. 164, and Norman Davies, *Europe: a History*, Pimlico, London 1997 (first published 1996), pp. 990-3.

11 Clark, diary, 30 January 1939 (most probably 28 January); the rest of this paragraph is built on Dymphna's memories of her wedding in her conversation with Jan Nicholas, 29 November 1995; also see *Age*, 22 February 1939, for a report of the wedding; in Clark papers, MS 7550/1, 'Correspondence 1939-49', there is a letter from Humphrey Sumner, 30 January 1939,

apologising that he could not be at the wedding due to teaching commitments; Graham Greene's recollections of Bell in Graham Greene, *A Sort of Life*, Simon & Schuster, New York, 1971, p. 135; also see Norman Sherry, *The Life of Graham Greene, Vol. One 1904–1939*, Penguin, Harmondsworth, 1989, p. 222, and Anthony Powell, *To Keep the Ball Rolling: The Memoirs of Anthony Powell, Vol.1: Infants of the Spring*, Heinemann, London, 1976, p. 150, where he describes Bell as a 'wartime gunner major with an MC, military moustached, bluff in demeanour ... full of unexpected powers of discrimination'.

12 Dymphna to Jan Nicholas, 29 November 1995; Clark, diary, 31 January 1939; also Clark to Catherine Clark, 1 February 1939, in *Ever, Manning*, p. 43.

13 Honeymoon recollections, Dymphna Clark to Jan Nicholas, 12 May 1993; Clark to Catherine Clark, 7 February 1939, unpublished, held at Manning Clark House, and Clark to Catherine Clark, 1 February 1939, *Ever, Manning*, pp. 43–4; on helping Clark in libraries, Dymphna's interview with Heather Rusden, 13 February 1997; for Clark's anxiety concerning the response of Dymphna's parents, see his diary, 16 February 1939, and Clark to Anna Lodewyckx, 1 February, 2 April, 31 May 1939, *Ever, Manning*, pp. 44–52; Dymphna was also distancing herself from her father: in her letter to Clark, 18 January 1939, she is annoyed by an article, written by Augustin and published in the Australian press, 'surely that is not the best the Australian press will publish'.

14 Clark, diary, 29 August 1939.

15 Dymphna to Jan Nicholas, 29 November 1995, also see *Oxford* (magazine of the Oxford Society founded in 1932), Summer 1939, pp. 40–3; Clark's 'wounded pride', diary, 24 May 1939; also see *The Times*, 28 April 1939, report of Freshmen's match at Oxford–'Clark, an Australian, came in to make himself almost a certainty for trial in the eleven. On Wednesday his wicket keeping was first-rate, and yesterday his batting was in the same category. He is very quick on his feet, has a wide range of strokes and is older than the average undergraduate.'

16 Dymphna Clark to Jan Nicholas, 1 September 1995; also see Bell's obituary in the *Times Literary Supplement*, 2 January 1953, p. 11.

17 On Bell and Sumner, Dymphna Clark to Jan Nicholas, K Bell & WP Morrell, *Select Documents on British Colonial Policy 1830–1860*, Oxford at the Clarendon Press, 1925; K Bell & GM Morgan, *The Great Historians: an Anthology of British history arranged in chronological order*, Macmillan, New York, 1935, and Anthony Powell, *To Keep the Ball Rolling: the memoirs of Anthony Powell, Vol.1 Infants of the Spring*, Heinemann, London, 1976, p. 152; Clark on Sumner in his diary, 2 February 1939; on Seton-Watson, diary, 18 January 1939; on AJP Taylor see Clark's comments to Neville Meaney, NLA; Clark, diary, 18 & 26 January & 15 February 1939; also Adam Sisman, *AJP Taylor: a biography*, Mandarin, London, 1995 (1994), pp. 127, 132, 136; on Trevelyan see David Cannadine, *GM Trevelyan: a life in History*, Fontana, 1993 (first published 1992).

18 Hermann Rauschning, *Germany's Revolution of Destruction*, Heinemann, London, 1939, trans. EW Dickes, first published in Germany in 1938 as *Die Revolution des Nihilismus*, pp. ix–xii; Guido de Ruggiero, *The History of European Liberalism*, Oxford University Press, London, 1927, trans. RG Collingwood; Clark claims in his interview with Neville Meaney (NLA), that he was 'very, very influenced' by Rauschning and also mentions the position of Christopher Hill's room in Balliol; also see Macmahon Ball, Papers (NLA), box 1, folder 4, letter from Clark (Devon) to Ball, March 1940, on verso of letter from AGL Shaw (who was staying with them at Tiverton that weekend) in which Clark mentions how impressed he is by Rauschning; in his diary, 13 February 1939, Clark toys with the idea of testing the validity of Marx's interpretation of the 1848 revolutions but is daunted by his lack of knowledge; Clark's conversation with Fin Crisp, see his diary, 19 January 1939; Clark's reflections on Australia in diary, 24 February 1939.

19 On general trends in historical writing in the twentieth century, see John Burrow, *A History of Histories: epics, chronicles, romances and inquiries from Herodotus and Thucydides to the twentieth century*, Allen Lane, London, 2007, pp. 467–519; Clark's intention to write a thesis is first expressed in his diary, 23 April 1939, also Clark to Crawford, 16 March & 19 June 1939; on Tocqueville see Harvey C Mansfield's & Delba Winthrop's introduction to Alexis de Tocqueville, *Democracy in America*, University of Chicago Press, Chicago, 2002, especially pp. xix–xxiii, & Hugh Brogan, *Alexis de Tocqueville: democracy in the age of revolution, a biography*, Profile, London, 2006; for

Clark on Tocqueville see his diary, 2 February & 1 May 1939, and his interview with Neville Meaney, NLA transcript.

20 See Clark to Crawford, 24 January 1939, in which he stresses his gratitude, and tells Crawford: 'Sumner is licking me into shape'; also 16 March 1939 & 19 June 1939 (all held in the Crawford papers at the University of Melbourne archives); also see Dymphna Lodewyckx to Clark, 14 January 1939, in which she tells him she is reading Toynbee, and Clark to Anna Lodewyckx, 15 January 1939, both held at Manning Clark House.

21 See Dymphna Clark's introduction to Dymphna Clark, David Headon & John Williams (eds), *The Ideal of Alexis de Tocqueville*, Melbourne University Press, Carlton, Vic., 2000; also Clark, diary, 21, 23, 27, 31 July & 6 August 1939.

22 ibid. & Clark, diary, 6, 21, 23, 29 August 1939.

23 Dymphna Clark to Augustin and Anna Lodewyckx, 6 September 1939, held at Manning Clark House, also Clark, diary, 4, 6, 13, 20, 21, 26 September & 5, 17 October 1939.

24 Dymphna to Augustin & Anna Lodewyckx, 6 September 1939, held at Manning Clark House; Clark, diary, 26 September, 15 November 1939, Dymphna to Clark, 4, 12, 13, 19 November 1939, Clark's comments on young girls appear in a letter he wrote to Dymphna from Tiverton, undated but November 1939, before Sebastian's birth, held at Manning Clark House.

25 Quote from Clark to Dymphna, from Tiverton before the birth, mention of Sebastian's name in another letter, undated from Tiverton, again before birth, held at Manning Clark House.

26 Clark to Dymphna, undated, but November 1939, held at Manning Clark House. For Clark musing on the effect of his letters, see another letter from Clark to Dymphna, also written in November; also Clark, diary, 7 December 1939.

27 Dymphna to Clark, from Radcliffe Infirmary, undated, but early December 1939, held at Manning Clark House, in this letter she finishes by writing in Sebastian's voice: 'I am getting more and more angelic looking every day—I can tell that from the gooey way Mummy looks at me, she got so silly, that I thought I would try it on with her—this sucking business—I mean, So I squawked & tossed my head about and made tantalising windmill movements with my tongue & went to sleep till she was nearly frantic. Then an awful old bully named Nurse Creech came along & rammed my head onto the breast & held it there for what seemed like days, so that now I find it more profitable to drink in the first place & not wait for her to come along ... it gets a bit dull, cooped up with these silly babies ... Good night Daddy, or since you insist that I shall be bi-lingual—Grüss dich Gott, Vati, John Sebastian.'

28 Dymphna to Clark, 11 December 1939; also see Dymphna to Clark, 10 December 1939, and Clark to Dymphna, undated, but mid-December 1939, all held at Manning Clark House.

29 Clark to Dymphna, undated, December 1939, and Dymphna to Clark, from 9 Museum Rd Oxford, 'Friday afternoon', December 1939; 'house of the long knives', John Martin to me, phone conversation, 6 April 2009.

30 Dymphna to Clark from 9 Museum Rd Oxford, 'Friday afternoon', December 1939, Dymphna to Clark, 11 December 1939, and Clark to Dymphna, undated, either late December 1939 or early January 1940; also see Dymphna to Clark, December 10 1939, 'What will you do with your incorrigible wife? Not content with the story about the kick in the balls, today, to entertain Mrs Layng, I showed your card addressed to John Sebastian. She indiscreetly turned it over and read it. I trembled & when she had gone I read it in agitation—you say my nipples are your inspiration. Heaven knows what else!' All letters held at Manning Clark House.

31 Dymphna to Clark, undated, from 9 Museum Rd, Oxford, late December 1939 or early January 1940, and Clark, diary, 18 January 1939.

32 Dymphna Clark interview with Heather Rusden, 13 February 1997, NLA; Dymphna's other memories are drawn from her conversations with Jan Nicholas, 20 January 1993 & 12 May 1994, courtesy Jan Nicholas, also *The Blundellian*, vol. 1, no. 21, June 1940, p. 2.

33 Clark to Catherine Clark, 10 September 1938, unpublished, held at Manning Clark House; for Dymphna's recollections to both Rusden and Nicholas (see ibid.) and Virginia Woolf, *Diaries*, 15, 20 & 30 May 1940, Vintage Classics, London, 2008 (first published 1977); also Clark, diary, 21 May 1940, Clark Papers, Series 27, folder 2, 'Manuscripts 1940–45', draft–'Written in England June

1940'—'Moods in Wartime'.

34 Sumner's correspondence, 26 June 1940, in Clark's papers, MS 7550/1, 'Correspondence 1939–49'; in the same folder see Sumner's letter of 30 July 1940, assuring Clark the decision to move was the right one and encouraging him with Tocqueville: 'your MA thesis plan sounds a good one, and I hope you win first prize'. Other details drawn from Dymphna's recollections to Jan Nicholas, her introduction to *The Ideal of Alexis de Tocqueville*, pp. 5–6, also AGL Shaw to me, Melbourne, May 2009, and Adam Sisman, *AJP Taylor: a biography*, pp. 138–9.

35 Dymphna to Rusden, Dymphna Clark Papers, NLA; and Clark, diary, 28 April & 25 May 1940.

36 For Clark's memories of Tiverton, see his interview with Neville Meaney, NLA, and Clark, *Quest for Grace*, 1990, pp. 106–12; also *The Blundellian*, vol. 1, no. 22, July 1940, p. 4. (Blundell Archives, courtesy of Jan Nicholas); and Clark, diary, 7 December 1939 & 27 February 1940.

37 For the difficulty of Clark's decision, see Clark, notebooks, 4 July 1940, in which he also admits his main reason for leaving: 'I think my determinant was fear.''

7: What a Life: Geelong Grammar 1940–44

1 Clark, diary, 5 August 1940.

2 Arthur Miller, 'On Home Ground', 1979 documentary film on his life and work.

3 Clark's reference to a split in consciousness is in his letter to Crawford, 19 June 1939; all other quotes from Clark's diary, 13 September & 19 November 1939, 5 & 7 May 1940.

4 Dymphna Lodewyckx, Journal 1933–1934; Clark, diary, 4 July 1940 and 5 August 1940. (I found this diary in the pages of Clark's notebooks, at which time it was not catalogued as a diary in his papers at the NLA.)

5 Dymphna's recollections regarding their arrival home can be found in her introduction to the *Ideal of Alexis de Tocqueville*, p. 6; Clark wanting to sing 'dirty' songs, in his letter to Dymphna from Tiverton, undated, but December 1939; all other references from Clark, diary, 5 & 7 May 1940.

6 Clark, diary, 19 November 1939 & 7 May 1940.

7 Clark, *Quest for Grace*, 1990, pp. 114–15.

8 Bruce Anderson to me, telephone conversation, August 2005; Sidney Webb (Lord Passfield) to Clark, 22 July 1943; Clark, papers, Series 1, 'Correspondence 1939–49'; another from Lord Passfield; Clark's memory of Curtin in Clark, *Quest for Grace*, 1990, p. 135.

9 Clark, diary, 14 August 1980.

10 This paragraph is based on Clark's recollections in his interview with friend and historian Don Baker (NLA); also see Clark in *Australian Playboy*, July 1981, pp. 31–44, his interview with the historian Neville Meaney (NLA), and Clark, *Quest for Grace*, 1990, chapter 5; in his interview with Meaney, Clark admitted his disappointment at not being offered a tutoring job at Melbourne: 'I found it rather painful that they didn't seem to want to give me a job ... I tried to get jobs and it just didn't happen'; I am also indebted to Melissa Campbell, archivist at Geelong Grammar, for retrieving Clark's file, filed under M! It is in this file, held in the school archives, that the correspondence between Darling and Clark, and Darling and Crawford, can be found; see in particular Clark to Darling, 15 August 1940, Crawford to Darling, 19 August 1940, Darling to Crawford, 22 August 1940, Darling to Clark, 22 August 1940 (offering Clark the position), Clark to Darling, 11 September 1940 (accepting the position), and Darling to Clark, 30 August 1940 (on his timetable). The file also contains Clark's application for the Mastership, 'Religious persuasion: Communicant member of the church', and references, including the one by Neville Gordon.

11 Darling in *The Corian*, December 1944, pp. 137–8; for a potted history of Geelong Grammar see the school's website http://www.ggs.vic.edu.au/index.asp?menuid=060.060; also Weston Bate, *Light Blue Down Under, The History of Geelong Grammar School*, Oxford University Press, South Melbourne, 1990, pp. 1 & 177, and Peter Gronn, 'Schooling for Ruling: the Social Composition of Admissions to Geelong Grammar, 1930–1939', *Australian Historical Studies*, vol. 25, April 1992, pp. 72–89; Bate's obituary of Clark appears in *The Corian*, July 1991, pp. 227–9; Clark's arrival at Geelong Grammar is noted in *The Corian*, August 1940, p. 130 ('he is an old Melburnian, and a very good cricketer'); Clark's role as cricket coach can be seen, together with photographs, in *The Australasian*, 21 March 1942 & 25 April 1942, p. 15.

12 Bruce Anderson, from notes sent to me, August, 2005; Bate, *Light Blue Down Under*, p. 177–80; Russel Ward, *A Radical Life*, Macmillan, South Melbourne, 1988, pp. 93 & 100; Jamie Mackie to me, Melbourne, May 2009; Prince Charles, 26 January 1988, Sydney Opera House; and Holt, *Manning Clark and Australian History*, pp. 62–3; the memory of Darling's comments at chapel, Keith Dunstan to me, phone conversation, June 2009.

13 Clark, notebooks, April 1943. The remainder of this paragraph is based on interviews with former students Jamie Mackie, Don Baker, Keith Dunstan, Bruce Anderson & Syd Crawcour. In John Monks, *Elisabeth Murdoch: two lives*, Sun Books, Melbourne, 1994, pp. 314–15, Rupert Murdoch is quoted as saying that he never met Clark at Geelong but remembered Dymphna. Collecting for the Red Cross, he recalled 'knocking on [Clark's] door and being met by a nude Mrs. Clark who said "Go away". That is the only memory I have of the Manning Clarks at all. I was twelve years old at the time.' Although this story has circulated with much mirth in the Clark family for a number of years, it is almost certainly the result of a typographical error. The word 'nude' should read 'rude'.

14 Jamie Mackie to me, phone conversation, December 2007, and in person, Melbourne, May 2009; also see Mackie's recollections of Clark in *The Corian*, July 1991, pp. 229–31; Bruce Anderson to me, December 2005, and his memoir of Clark, 'One Memory of Manning', *Overland*, 125, 1991 pp. 48–51 (p. 48); the Führer's skirt anecdote, Syd Crawcour to me, Melbourne, May 2009; on Clark's 'throaty warble' etc., Weston Bate, *Light Blue Down Under*, p. 213; also Keith Dunstan, 'Defending a Literary Hero', *Herald Sun Weekend Magazine*, 4 September 1993, p. 56, and Keith Dunstan, *No Brains at All*, Viking, Ringwood, Vic., 1990, pp. 60–1; letter to *The Australian*, 15 September 1993, from David Chipp in London; and the letter from Geoffrey Fairbairn, 29 March 1978, in Clark papers, box 157, folder 16, 'Vol IV, Correspondence and Reviews'; also see Clark's obituary of Fairbairn, *Australian*, 14 September 1980, and Richard Woolcott's memories of Clark as cricket coach in Bill Bunbury's documentary on Clark, ABC Radio National, June 1998; the description of McAuley (actually playing the piano in Dorothy Wilson's house in Biddlecombe Avenue) is Dymphna's, in her letter to Jan Nicholas, 7 August 1993.

15 Darling in *The Corian*, December 1940, principal's report, pp. 220–21; Clark's editorial (anonymous) appears in *The Corian*, December 1942, pp. 135–6; also Clark, interviewed by Don Baker in 1985, NLA; Richard Woolcott to Bill Bunbury's documentary on Clark, ABC Radio National, June 1998; see the report of Clark's address to the Public Affairs Society in *The Corian*, December 1940, p. 258; other reports of his speeches can be found in *The Corian*, August 1942, pp. 93 & 95, May 1943, p. 8, August 1943, p. 92, December 1943, pp. 164 & 166; also Stephen Holt, *Manning Clark & Australian History*, pp. 66–7; Clark on Germany in 1941, see the first speech in Clark, *Speaking Out of Turn*, pp. 3–5; for an example of Clark's questioning, see his address to the Literary Society in *The Corian*, May 1941, p. 19: he spoke on Lawrence and discussed Copernicus's discovery that the earth was not the centre of the universe, pointing out that it 'completely upset the catholic viewpoint that man and the earth were the centre of things'. As for Lawrence, he claimed his writing tried to put an end to the accepted equation 'material well-being equals happiness'; Clark also spoke on behalf of the University of Melbourne Extension Board, in co-operation with the Adult Education committee, in a series of Geelong Tutorial Classes in 1941 on the subject of International Affairs; his 'talks' were given at Bostock Memorial Hall, Gordon Institute of Technology, commencing 6 May 1941 at 8 p.m.; he delivered ten lectures on French history, and wrote his bio, which was to be used for the advertisement: 'the lecturer has recently returned from a period of study abroad. He has a wide knowledge of French literature and social conditions, and spent a considerable time in France as a student of French politics and thought'; memory of Clark as 'the voice of Moscow', Jamie Mackie to me, phone conversation, December 2007; in *Light Blue Down Under*, p. 213, Weston Bate claims that Darling wasn't sorry to lose Clark in 1944, especially because of the controversy he aroused, his 'forthrightness about the futility of war ... was seen as defeatism if not subversion'. Bate writes that complaints 'echoed around the western district and flew back to council' because of Clark's description of chapel as 'that Jesus business'. In *Quest for Grace*, 1990, p. 122, Clark claims letters of complaint and protest were addressed to Darling because of his political views. In his autobiography, *Richly Rewarding*, Hill of Content, Melbourne, 1978, pp.

34–5, Darling denies that he received 'any official protests', pinning most of the complaint on the shoulders of an inarticulate old boy, Frank Austin, who lost two sons in the war and was allegedly upset by Clark's editorial in *The Corian*.

16 On the communist 'brush', see Russel Ward, *A Radical Life*, p. 103: 'all pacifists were [seen as] the dupes of communist agents'; memory of Clark and short-wave radio, Jamie Mackie to me, December 2007; on the home-front climate at Geelong in the early 1940s, see *The Corian*, August 1940, editorial, p. 118, and December 1940, editorial, quoting Kipling, p. 209; Dymphna on Clark's guilt in her interview with Bill Bunbury, ABC Radio National, June 1998 (Dymphna's brother, Axel, enlisted in 1940) and Clark on Barber in his interview with Don Baker; also see Clark's obituary of Barber, 'My Friend John Barber', in *The Corian*, June 1977, pp. 242–3, and his obituary of KC Masterman, in *The Corian*, September 1981, pp. 18–19. Clark's visit to the school is reported in *The Corian*, March 1977, pp. 204–5.

17 The best expression of Clark's belief in the creative process serving as a means of purging anxiety is in his diary, 18 October 1942; also see Clark, diary, 11 & 30 September 1942, and his notebook, 25 April 1943.

18 Clark, diary, 13 August 1942. Clark's various job applications are referred to in his diary, 18 October 1942, 3 January 1944; Clark wrote to Crawford, 10 March 1941, after talking with Crawford and frustrated by his inability to devote sufficient time to his thesis: 'I feel at a dead-end, bitter, but not down'; he told Crawford he was not interested in the public service and wanted instead to hold out for 'some opening at a University'; also Clark to Crawford, undated, but late 1941, Crawford papers, University of Melbourne Archives; for Clark's hatred of Geelong Grammar, see his diary, 13 August & 10 September 1942; his determination to be a writer, diary, 26 September & 2 November 1942; Clark on Freud, diary, 2 November and 16 November 1942; for religion see Clark papers, Series 19, 'Manuscripts', folder 1 (i), First sketches for 'Confessions of a Schoolteacher'. At a later date Clark has dated this as 1943, and his comments on virtue and temptation are written in the margin, while his comments on religion are written on a separate piece of paper and can be found in the same folder. Finally, see Sigmund Freud, *Civilisation and its Discontents*, Penguin, 2004 (first published 1930), on the dulling effects of 'intoxicants', pp. 14–15; on sublimation, p. 21; on religion as mass delusion, p. 23; on institutions regulating individual behaviour, p. 29; on repressing sexual drives, pp. 44, 52; on monogamy, p. 53; on guilt, p. 91.

19 From notes sent to me by Bruce Anderson, December 2005; also Clark, *Quest for Grace*, 1990, p. 127.

20 Bruce Anderson to me, notes, December 2005; Russel Ward, *A Radical Life*, Macmillan, South Melbourne, 1988, p. 98; Clark, notebook, 16 July 1943; also see Keith Dunstan, *No Brains at All*, pp. 50–1. Dunstan, who had been 'dobbed in for mutual masturbation', found himself the catalyst of a mini crisis in the school; dorm heads were demoted and replaced with new prefects with 'unmasturbatory records'.

21 Clark, notebook, 18 April 1943; the first quote from Clark's diary, 29 March 1943.

22 Clark, notebook, 12 April 1943, and diary, 7 March 1943.

23 On the culture of bullying and attitudes to sex and homosexuality, see Bate, *Light Blue Down Under*, pp. 144–5; Dunstan, *No Brains at All*, pp. 38–42, 51, & 60–1; also Clark, notebook, 12 April & 16 July 1943.

24 This episode is based on material from Clark's file in the Geelong Grammar archives; for Darling's attempts to stall Browne, see Darling to Browne, 29 January 1941, 6 November 1941, 2 March 1942, and particularly 10 November 1941: 'I do not mean to be offensive about Manning Clark, and agree with you that he has an unfortunate manner. I think really that it is more manner than intention, however, and am of the opinion that he is worth persevering with. He has been very much better here during the last month since the mirage of university employment has faded'; also 6 November 1941: 'as you know he is a good historian and perhaps more suited to university work than school work. Under those circumstances, he is obviously more likely to do his best work with the top forms and finds difficulty in getting down to the level of the lower middle school 'he has done very good work ... I know that he is endeavouring to write a book at the moment, and this may have taken some of his time which ought to have possibly been spent on the Diploma'. For Browne's

frustration see Browne to Darling (quoted), 8 November 1941 & 30 April 1942 (quoted); also see 30 October 1941; on Clark's permission to teach withdrawn, see Browne to Darling, 28 February 1942, and Registrar to Clark, 23 April 1942; Clark's certificate of registration to teach, dated 29 November 1943, can be found in Clark Papers, box 193, folder 60.

25 Clark, notebook, undated, but most likely early 1943; Clark's article on 'History', in Rev. P St J Wilson (ed.), *The Open Eye: a series of essays for senior boys and girls*, Ramsay Ware Publishing, Melbourne, 1941, pp. 37–50; his letters to Crawford–10 March 1941 and undated, but most likely mid-1942–in the papers of Max Crawford, University of Melbourne Archives; also see Dymphna Clark's introduction to Clark, *The Ideal of Alexis de Tocqueville*, pp. 6–7; Clark's remarks on the progress of the thesis, Clark, diary, 20 & 26 September 1942, 6, 7, 15, 16, 24 & 29 December 1942, 6 December 1943 & 10 February 1943; Clark's comments on his reading were made in his interview with Don Baker (NLA).

26 Clark's reflections on history can be found in his notebooks, undated, but most probably mid-1943; his thoughts on the artistic nature of his vision in his diary, 22 February 1943; William Prescott, Notebooks, IX, quoted in David Levin, *History as Romantic Art: Bancroft, Prescott, Motley, and Parkman*, Stanford University Press, California, 1959, p. 3.

27 Clark, *The Ideal of Alexis de Tocqueville*, pp. 144–5, also pp. 1, 52–3, 106.

28 Dymphna's recollections of life at Corio in her correspondence to Jan Nicholas, 7 August 1993, 1 September 1994 and 25 February 1995; Kay Masterman later became Professor of Classics at the ANU in Canberra; Dymphna also commented on Darling: 'I will not forgive JR Darling for spending ca. 10 pages in his memoirs on CMHC. (and his own heroic role in defeating him) because CMHC. became a celebrity and hardly a sentence on the Mastermans who kept the school together intellectually for a whole generation'; Dymphna's reflections on her role in the Tocqueville work, in her introduction to Clark, *The Ideal of Alexis de Tocqueville*, pp. 5 & 11–12; for Clark's disappointments in their marriage see his diary, 11 March 1943, notebooks, 4 May 1943, and also in his notebooks, the margins of 'First sketches for "Confessions of a Schoolteacher"', which at a later date Clark dated as 1943; also, on the argument at Corio, Clark to Dymphna, 17 June 1956, held at Manning Clark House; other information from my various interviews with Sebastian Clark, 2005–2009; Clark's note to Dymphna on the draft of his 'Letter to Tom Collins', which also contains his advice to her regarding Augustin, can be found in Clark papers, box 186, folder 1, 'Lectures 1940–1949'; Clark's confession of feeling 'like a little child', in his diary, 15 December 1942.

29 Clark to Don Baker (NLA). His first attempts to write newspaper articles can be found in his papers, box 177, 'Manuscripts, 1931–1933' & 'Manuscripts 1940–1945'; Clark, 'France and Germany', *Australian Quarterly*, June 1941, pp. 14–21; Clark to Clem Christesen, 26 January 1943, Meanjin Archives, University of Melbourne; Clark's first article in *Historical Studies* was a review of JP Mayer's *Study of Alexis de Tocqueville, Historical Studies, Australia and New Zealand*, vol. 1, no. 3, 1940, p. 211; on Clark and James McAuley, see Clark, *Quest for Grace*, 1990, pp. 129–30, and Holt, *Manning Clark and Australian History*, pp. 102–3.

30 Stuart Macintyre, 'The Radical and the Mystic', in Macintyre & Fitzpatrick (eds), *Against the Grain*, pp. 12–36 (p. 20); Lynne Strahan, *Just City and the Mirrors: Meanjin Quarterly and the Intellectual Front 1940–1965*, Oxford University Press, Melbourne, 1984, pp. 5, 39, 42, 46–7; Richard Haese, *Rebels and Precursors: the revolutionary years of Australian art*, Penguin, Ringwood, Vic., 1988 (1981), pp. 103–4, 157; Stuart Macintyre, *The Oxford history of Australia, Volume 4: the Succeeding Age, 1901–42*, Oxford University Press, Melbourne, 1997 (first published 1986), pp. 314–15; Craig Munro, *ADB* entry on PR Stephensen (available online), and Munro's *Wild Man of Letters: the story of PR Stephensen*, Melbourne University Press, Carlton, Vic., 1984, pp. 151–5, and finally, John Dally's *ADB* entry on Rex Ingamells.

31 Christesen quoted in Lynne Strahan, *Just City and the Mirrors*, p. 36; *The Publicist*, 1 July 1941, pp. 3–7; also found in Clark Papers, box 193, folder 60; the words 'cultural watershed' were used by Richard Haese to describe the years 1940–43, in *Rebels and Precursors: the revolutionary years of Australian art*, p. 100; the distance between Corio and Geelong, in Keith Dunstan, *No Brains at All*, Penguin, Ringwood, Vic., 1990, p. 46.

32 Geoffrey Serle, 'Recreating an Era', in D Duffy et al., *Historians at Work: investigating and recreating the past*, Hicks Smith, Sydney, 1973, pp. 51–2; on Australia 1942, see the final chapter, 'Free of any Pangs', in Stuart Macintyre, *The Oxford History of Australia, Volume 4, 1901–1942: The Succeeding Age*, Oxford University Press, Melbourne, 1997 (first published 1986); in Darling's talk of evacuation in *The Corian*, December 1941, p. 172; Gwen Taylor to me, phone conversation December 2007.

33 Clark papers, notebooks, box 34, undated but 1942; on postwar attraction of CPA see Stuart Macintyre, *The Reds: The Communist Party of Australia*, Allen & Unwin, Sydney, 1998, p. 412; the characterisation of Hancock is Clark's–see *Quest for Grace*, 1990, p. 136.

34 Clark, notebook, 25 April & 3 June 1943; Clark, 'A Letter to Tom Collins', in *Occasional Writings and Speeches*, Fontana, Sydney, 1980, pp. 91–3; also Holt, *Manning Clark and Australian History*, p. 106.

35 Clark, diary, 29 November 1942; Nolan to Hester, 1943, in Nancy Underhill (ed.); *Nolan on Nolan: Sidney Nolan in his own words*, Viking, Ringwood, Vic., 2007, pp. 147–8; Clark on Australian history, diary, 15 February 1943; Eleanor Dark, *The Timeless Land*, Angus & Robertson 2002 (1941), p. 13 (also see Humphrey McQueen's introduction to the 1990 edition, reprinted in the 2002 edition); Clark's description of the Aborigines as 'these strange members of human society' is in his 'Letter to Tom Collins', p. 93.

36 Clark to Darling, 16 March 1944, Geelong Grammar Archives; Clark's references can be found in the University of Melbourne Archives–see the folder pertaining to his application for the Political Science Lectureship, 1944; the folder also includes the following references. Sorry to see him leave, KC Masterman, the Classics Master at Geelong, and who later became Professor of Classics at the ANU, pointed out that university was 'his proper sphere of activities'. While Darling thought his talents entitled him to seek a university appointment, Neville Gorton stressed his ability in the classroom at Tiverton: 'he does not regard education as pouring matter through pipes into a cistern but elicits the interests and personality of the individual boy ... he is a born teacher.' Milner's letter in Macmahon Ball, Papers (NLA), box 1: folder 8, I; Milner to Ball, 28 July 1944, with copy of Milner's letter to Vice-Chancellor; Clark's departure from Geelong Grammar is noted in *The Corian*, May 1944, p. 7; evidence of Clark's and Dymphna's attitude to Geelong can be seen in Clark's letter to Dymphna, 19 October 1949, in *Ever, Manning*, p. 62, in which Clark refers to their life at Corio.

37 All of the following material can be found in Clark's file, held in the Geelong Grammar Archives: Clark's brief letter of resignation, Clark to Darling, 17 March 1944; Darling's reply, Darling to Clark, 20 March 1944; Darling's reply to Clark's missing letter, Darling to Clark, 3 May 1944, in which Darling refers to a prize Clark had presumably proposed to endow, no doubt in memory of his time at Grammar. There is no evidence that the prize was established. As a farewell gift, Clark sent Darling a copy of a book by Sidney Dark. Darling does not mention the title.

38 DH Lawrence, 'The Spirit of Place', in DH Lawrence, *Studies in Classic American Literature*, Penguin, London, 1971, chapter 1, p. 12; references I've drawn from *Kangaroo* are in the 1980 Penguin edition, pp. 18, 32, 33, 38, 43 & 365; Clark's notes on Australian literature in his papers, box 34, see the notebook titled 'University of Melbourne 1944: Australian Literature'; *Kangaroo* was written in 1922 when Lawrence and his wife Frieda visited Australia for three months and lived at 'Wyewurk', 3 Craig Street, Thirroul. It was published in 1923. When Clark left for England, Tampion Daglish, a friend from Trinity College, gave him a copy of *Phoenix: the posthumous papers of D.H. Lawrence* (1936). In a letter to Kathleen Fitzpatrick (9 November 1986) Clark writes: 'Am rereading *Kangaroo*. After all the work on 1919–22 I find myself now overwhelmed by the genius of the man. How did he find out so much about us in six weeks? Most of us need a life-time to find out enough for a small picture. Lawrence has written our Bayeux Tapestry–and like that work, he is often close to caricature, and the methods of the cartoonists' (Davies (ed.), *Dear Kathleen, Dear Manning*, p. 96). When asked about Manning's interest in Lawrence, Dymphna told Jan Nicholas, 'M. and Lawrence–A very confused but passionate relationship. M's volumes of *Sons and Lovers* & *The Rainbow* were almost in tatters from use' (Dymphna Clark to Jan Nicholas, 27 March 1995). In 1988, when there was a plan to put a second storey onto 'Wyewurk', a committee was formed

to stop the development, Clark offered to be its chairman (*Sydney Morning Herald*, 25 April 1988, p. 5); also see Holt on Lawrence in *Manning Clark and Australian History*, p. 97.

39 Clark Papers, box 177, folder 2, 'Ideals in Australian Literature', 28 October 1945, piece written for 'Army Education'.

40 Dark quote from the second volume of her trilogy, *Storm of Time*, published in 1947, and quoted by Barbara Brooks in her introduction to Eleanor Dark, *The Timeless Land*, Angus & Robertson, Sydney, 2002 (1941), p. 15; Clark asking do we belong here in diary, 15 February 1943; and the need for prophets–Clark, 28 October 1945, in Clark papers, box 177, folder 2, 'Ideals in Australian Literature', also in the form of notes by Stephen Holt, sent to Jan Nicholas, and forwarded to me, ABC Radio talk for 'Army Education', Clark: 'We do not want "talent" to be one of our main articles of export, and we do not want a gulf between the people and the intellectuals.'

8: Journey without Maps

1 I am indebted to Clark's former students and others who remembered Clark from these years for their helpful comments: Jamie Mackie to me, Melbourne, May 2009; Hugh Anderson to me, Canberra, August 2008; Sid Ingham to me, phone conversation, August 2005; John Legge to me, Melbourne, November 2006; Bid Williams (Althea Stretton) to me, phone conversation, October 2007; Jessie Serle to me, phone conversation, September 2007; June Philipp to me, Melbourne, August 2005, & phone conversation, March 2008; Gwen Taylor to me, phone conversation, July 2007; Bruce Grant to me, Melbourne, March 2007; Don Baker to me, Canberra, January 2005; Laurie O'Brien to me, phone conversation, March 2008; Creighton Burns to me, Melbourne, March 2007; Peter Ryan to me, phone conversation, May 2007; Ailsa Zainuddin (nee Thomson) to me, Melbourne, August 2005; I have also drawn on the memories published in *Manning Clark, By Some of His Students*, Manning Clark House, 2002–in particular, Gordon Fisher (pp. 3–5), Lucy Meo (pp. 26–8), Jamie Mackie (pp. 16–19, 'a man with whom a boy could talk', Mackie quoting Baker, p. 18), Ken Inglis (pp. 12–15), Hugh Stretton (pp. 30–2), Sid Ingham (pp. 8–11, 'his eye was ever on eternity', p. 11), Pauline Grutzner (pp. 6–7) and John Mulvaney (pp. 22–5); John Poynter, '"Wot Larks to be Aboard": The History Department 1937–71', in Fay Anderson & Stuart Macintyre (eds), *The Life of the Past: the discipline of history at the University of Melbourne, 1855–2005*, Department of History, University of Melbourne, Parkville, Vic., 2006, p. 53, describes Clark's teaching at Melbourne as 'unforgettable'.

2 Bob Phillips, who served in the Middle East, recalled the mood among his fellow soldiers: 'It was a fairly common opinion among those who had returned that we owed our freedom to Hitler's ill-fated invasion of Russia. Thus, on the way home, the catch-cry developed among us–'Joe for King'. Phillips to Jan Nicholas, 24 February 1995, courtesy Jan Nicholas; Vincent Buckley, in his memoir, *Cutting Green Hay*, Penguin, Ringwood, Vic., 1983, p. 58, rejects the notion of ex-servicemen being mostly left as a myth. When Buckley started at Melbourne in 1946 on a veteran's grant 'the teaching in the arts faculty was amateurish and remote. Tutorials were too big ... contrary to nostalgic rumour [ex-servicemen and women] ranged from revolutionary to arch-conservative, and there were far more on the latter part of the spectrum.'

3 Clark's speech in July 1948 can be found in Clark papers, box 186, folder 1, 'Lectures 1940–1949'; his comments on socialism in his notebook, 27 April 1943; and his recollection of the dropping of the atomic bomb in Clark, *Quest for Grace*, 1990, p. 158; on the strength of history at Melbourne, see John Poynter, '"Wot Larks to be Aboard": The History Department 1937–71', in Anderson & Macintyre (eds), *The Life of the Past*, p. 51.

4 Herbert Burton to Macmahon Ball, Papers of W Macmahon Ball, NLA, MS7851, box 2, folder 11; Bob Phillips to Jan Nicholas, 24 February 1995 & 7 April 1995; for Clark on his first lectures in Politics, listen to his interview with Don Baker, NLA.

5 Cairns to Clark, 7 August 1974, Clark Papers, box 20, folder 163; also Clark to Don Baker, NLA.

6 Ian Milner to Clark, 12 February 1985, in Clark papers, box 1, folder 1, 'Correspondence 1939–49'; for Clark's plan to write a textbook in his diary 1940–1949, see the undated entry 'Events 1944'.

7 On virginal state of many undergraduates in their mid-twenties, see Janet McCalman, *Journeyings: the biography of a middle-class generation 1920–1990*, Melbourne University Press, Carlton, Vic.,

1993, p. 177; Stephen Murrray-Smith in Hume Dow (ed.), *Memories of Melbourne University*, Hutchinson, Melbourne, 1983, p. 120; for conditions in the first weeks of teaching, 1946, see John Thompson, *The Patrician and the Bloke: Geoffrey Serle and the making of Australian history*, Pandanus Books, Canberra, 2006, p. 117 & 122; also John Poynter, '"Wot Larks to be Aboard", pp. 39–91; also see Fay Anderson, *An Historian's Life: Max Crawford and the politics of academic freedom*, Melbourne University Press, Carlton, Vic., 2005, pp. 162–3, & on the control of information during wartime, see Lynne Strahan, *Just City and the Mirrors: Meanjin Quarterly and the Intellectual Front 1940–1965*, Oxford University Press, Melbourne, 1984, p. 41.

8   See Smith in Dow (ed.), *Memories of Melbourne University*, p. 124, and quoted in John McLaren, *Free Radicals of the Left in Postwar Melbourne*, Australian Scholarly Publishing, Melbourne, 2003, pp. 48–55; Bob Phillips to Jan Nicholas, 24 February 1995 & 7 April 1995; Sid Ingham to me, August 2005; and Clark to Eleanor Dark, 16 September 1946, in *Ever, Manning*, p. 59.

9   Jamie Mackie in *Manning Clark, By Some of His Students*, Manning Clark House, 2002, p. 16; John Mulvaney in same, pp. 22–5; Clark's 'journey without maps' in Clark, *Quest for Grace*, 1990, p. 159.

10 Portus quoted in John Poynter, '"Wot Larks to be Aboard", p. 40; on Crawford see Jack Gregory 'Max Crawford and Ourselves and the Pacific', in Stuart Macintyre & Peter McPhee (eds), *Max Crawford's School of History*, History Department, University of Melbourne, Parkville, Vic., 2000, pp. 63–8; also see Crawford's opening remarks in the first issue of *Historical Studies: Australia and New Zealand*, vol. 1, April 1940–October 1941, p. 1, and Brian Fletcher, Australian History, *History at Sydney: centenary reflections*, Highland Press, Canberra, 1992, pp. 159–69; see, for example, p. 160: in the early twentieth century, Wood did encourage postgraduate research in Australian History and, by the time Roberts came to Wood's chair in 1929 (staying till 1947), 'Australian history', argues Fletcher, 'was more firmly established at Sydney University than is generally appreciated'; also Graeme Davison, 'Discovering Australian History', in Anderson & Macintyre (eds), *The Life of the Past*, p. 256, argues that Clark exaggerated 'the image of Australian history as terra incognita'. The Fitzpatrick/Clark anecdote can be found in Ian Mair to Clark, 26 June 1975 (held at Manning Clark House).

11 Geoffrey Serle, RM Crawford and his School, *Melbourne Historical Journal*, vol. 9, 1970, pp. 3–6; also see Graeme Davison, 'Discovering Australian History', in Anderson & Macintyre (eds), *The Life of the Past*, p. 258. (By the late 1940s 32 students at Melbourne were enrolled in MAs and PhDs on Australian topics.)

12 Ann Moyal, *Breakfast with Beaverbrook: Memoirs of an Independent Woman*, Hale & Iremonger, Sydney, 1995, pp. 34–5; other recollections drawn from the following interviews: Hugh Anderson to me, Canberra, August 2008; John Mulvaney to me, Canberra, February 2008; Ailsa Zainuddin to me, Melbourne, August 2005; Sid Ingham to me, phone conversation, August 2005; Jamie Mackie to me, Melbourne, May 2009; Hugh Stretton to me, phone conversation, March 2007; Gwen Taylor to me, phone conversation, July 2007.

13 Clark to Smith, 19 July 1946, Murray-Smith Papers, [VSL] box 265/1–9, General papers 1945–1947; Clark's thoughts on teaching methods can be found in Clark, *Speaking Out of Turn*, pp. 51–6; on this see also, Kathleen Fitzpatrick Papers, University of Melbourne Archives, box 5, 'Seminar and Discussion Notes', which contains Fitzpatrick's notes for her Staff Seminar Talk on Lecturing, in 1948: 'If nature has given you a resonant voice, clear articulation & some range of tone you are lucky: otherwise they must be acquired; and I would ruthlessly sack any lecturer who did not acquire them'. 'Posture. Posture is important. You must stand up and face your audience—if you don't look them in the face you will be unable to tell whether they grasped that point, whether it needs repetition or clarification. If you have a large class, keep still as possible without stiffness ... as far as possible, don't fiddle: we all have eccentric little habits, get candid friends to tell you about them.' Also Ken Inglis to me, Canberra, March 2005, & Jamie Mackie to me, Melbourne, May 2009.

14 Clark, diary, 13 April 1944; on 'moral sensitivity', see Inga Clendinnen in Stuart Macintyre & Peter McPhee (eds), *Max Crawford's School of History*, History Department, University of Melbourne, Parkville, Vic., 2000, pp. 41–4; 'the deeper problems of human existence', John Mulvaney in

Manning Clark, By Some of His Students, Manning Clark House, p. 25; John Poynter quotes Crawford in 1952 in Poynter, 'Max Crawford as Head of Department', in Macintyre & McPhee (eds), *Max Crawford's School of History*, p. 125. Graeme Davison is especially good on the 'religious' intellectual culture fostered by Crawford, in same; pp. 70–1.

15 Ken Inglis, from preparatory notes for his obituary of Clark, courtesy Ken Inglis; see also Ken Inglis, 'Remembering Manning Clark', in *Observing Australia, 1959 to 1999*, Melbourne University Press, Carlton, Vic., 1999, pp. 219–30, originally published in *Overland*, Spring 1991, pp. 219–20. Clark's lecture notes at Melbourne University can be found in his papers, box 35, folders 2–5, 'Lectures in Australian History, 1946–49' (most of the lectures are from 1948).

16 John Mulvaney to me, Canberra, February 2007.

17 Clark, Periods and Themes in Australian history, July 1948, in Clark papers, box 35, folder 2.

18 Clark on his reasons for choosing O'Dowd's poem: see http://www.centennialparklands.com.au/about_us/history_and_heritage/heritage_buildings_and_structures/federation

19 For the radio series organised by Macmahon Ball see *The ABC Weekly*, vol. 8, no. 6, 23 February 1946, p. 28; in 1945, Clark took part in a Listening Group series 'International Co-operation or Conflict? Twenty Five Years 1920–1945', heard on 3AR on Mondays at 8.40 pm, 1 October–5 November 1945; see also *Radio Times News Pictorial*, vol. 1, no. 42, 14–20 October; edited transcripts of some radio programs can be found in Manning Clark Papers, NLA, box 177, folder 1, 'Manuscripts 1931–33', and the folder 'Manuscripts 1940–45'; Clark's talk on anti-Semitism is reported in *Farrago*, XXII, no. 16, 10 July 1946 p. 5; see also Clark, 'History's Persecuted Race', in the Melbourne *Herald*, 28 July 1945, p. 9; for the topics of Clark's radio broadcasts in 1946 see Clark papers, box 177, 'folder 3, 'Manuscripts 1947–48'; this folder also contains notes from another broadcast for 3AR on 31 May 1946, 'Recent Elections in Europe', in which Clark speaks of the need for peaceful resolution of conflict; Clark's comments on Evatt's nationalism can be found in Political Nationalism, *Austral–Asiatic Bulletin*, vol. VI, no. 4, April 1946, pp. 47–51 ('period piece nationalism' is at p. 51); also see Clark delivering an interesting piece of 'News Commentary' for the ABC on 'The Choice of a Governor-General', 17 October 1946, found in box 177, folder 3, 'Manuscripts 1947–48'; the non-Labor parties, he said, wanted 'the pageantry of monarchy transplanted to Australia ... And they want a way of life for him represented by the British leisured classes'. There was a danger of a governor-general, Clark argued, who would allow his own political views to influence his decisions. In the same folder, he can be found debating GS Wood, on 9 February 1948, who contended that the Commonwealth should provide 'enlightened guidance towards self-government ... based on its long experience in dealing with backward peoples'. Clark argued in reply: 'you believe that a new, enlightened capitalism can create this better world. I don't'.

20 Fairbairn's correspondence can be found in Clark papers, box 22, folders 180–1, 'Geoffrey Fairbairn, 1945–80', Fairbairn to Clark, undated, 1945, 9 March 1948 & 6 July 1948; for Clark's comments, see Note 19, especially 31 May 1946.

21 My thanks to Ian Lodewyckx for passing on the security files on his parents; on Augustin and Dymphna, see D/745, folio 74, Copy of Memorandum from Major Weale to the Deputy Director dated 4 January 1943; also Axel Lodewyckx, Security file, 10 April 1944.

22 Stuart Macintyre and Fay Anderson, 'Crawford as Controversialist', in Macintyre & McPhee (eds), *Max Crawford's School of History*, pp. 89–112, see especially pp. 97–9; on Clark and Edmunds, three sources are indispensable: Humphrey McQueen's *Suspect History* (chapter three), Fay Anderson's *An Historian's Life* (chapter four), and Holt, *Manning Clark and Australian History*, pp. 110–14.

23 Clark's relevant radio broadcasts can be found in his papers, box 175, folder 21, which includes details of the security checks carried out by the Commonwealth Investigation Branch. The first report, dated 10 June 1947, contains details of Clark's debate with Edmunds on Radio 3DB, 31 May 1947, 8.30 p.m.; Edmunds' attacks on Clark in *Victorian Parliamentary Debates*, vol. 224, 13 May 1947, p. 4984; vol. 226, 9 December 1947, p. 173; vol. 226, 6 May 1948, p. 986; also for similar attacks on Ian Turner, see vol. 226, 30 May 1948, p. 1444; on the *Courier-Mail* relying on Edmunds, see Humphrey McQueen, *Suspect History*, pp. 43–4; Clark defended academic freedom on campus,

see *University Gazette*, August 1948, p. 68; for student rallies to defend Crawford and Clark, see Fay Anderson, *An Historian's Life*, p. 181, and *Age*, 24 March 1948; the public letter, also signed by Jim Cairns, Vance Palmer and Walter Murdoch, can be found in the *Jewish Herald*, 16 July 1948. Evatt was chair of the UN Committee responsible for advancing a similar argument; on the university's concern, see Stuart Macintyre, 'History in the headlines', in Anderson & Macintyre (eds) *The Life of the Past*, pp. 355–76, especially pp. 360–6. Macintyre points out that, at face value, Clark's appearance on 'The Heckle Hour' breached the new university guidelines on staff involvement in politics. Medley, however, stated that the university had 'complete confidence' in Clark as a teacher.

24 AGL Shaw remarked on Crawford's fear of public embarrassment for the department, in Macintyre & McPhee (eds), *Max Crawford's School of History*, pp. 76–7; for Crawford's retreat and resignation from Australia–Soviet House, see Anderson, *An Historian's Life*, pp. 183–5.

25 Regarding Clark's application for the position in Adelaide, see Clark papers, box 1, folder 1, 'Correspondence 1939–49', Sumner to Clark, 28 September 1948, writing from Oxford to let Clark know he has sent his reference in support of Clark's application for the chair at Adelaide; also see Sumner to Clark, 16 August 1949, congratulating him on his appointment to Canberra; the description of the Croydon house on a 'broad hillside' belongs to Hugh Stretton, in his piece in *Manning Clark, By Some of His Students*, Manning Clark House, p. 32; Dymphna's recollections in her interview with Bill Bunbury, ABC Radio National, June 1998, and her NLA interview with Elizabeth Cham; otherwise, in private correspondence, specifically Dymphna to Jan Nicholas, 29 November 1991 ('intimidating hush' in the tea room); on this, also see John Poynter, '"Wot Larks to be Aboard": The History Department 1937–71', in Anderson & Macintyre (eds), *The Life of the Past*, p. 56; and Dymphna to Jan Nicholas, 29 November 1995. Clark to Humphrey McQueen, 20 May 1988, Arthur Boyd introduced him to Vermeer in the early 1940s; the architect of the Croydon house, Arthur Berry, had proposed to Dymphna before Clark; details of austerity measures in *The Australian Encyclopedia*, vol. IX, Grolier Society, Sydney 1977, p. 502; on Martin Boyd, see Kerryn Goldsworthy's remarks in Nicholas Jose (general editor), *Macquarie Pen Anthology of Australian Literature*, Allen & Unwin, Sydney, 2009, p. 400.

Clark's letters to Roderick are held in Manuscripts, Mitchell Library, MSS 3265, Angus & Robertson Papers, second series, vol. 186, 'Charles Manning Hope Clark 1946–1969'; see Clark to Mr. Roderick, 8 August 1948 & 12 October 1948. In the same year Clark had successfully applied for a research grant of 50 pounds from Melbourne University, in order to continue working on the documents, and to write his Tocqueville-like work 'Democracy in Australia'; 'I ... want to examine the reception of democratic ideas in Australia, noting the emphasis placed on social equality and mateship ... is there political democracy in Australia? ... Is there a social democracy? ... what part do workers play in the control of state and private enterprise? Is there a career open to talent in Australia? Is their civil liberty in Australia, or liberty for "groups"?' ANU Archives, 103/1/21; also see Clark papers, box 51, folder 1, 'Select Documents in Australian History: Plans 1948 Index to Vol 1'. Ailsa Zainuddin told me in August 2005 that she had been willingly 'roped in' to proofreading the documents; AGL Shaw recalled Joe Burke (first Professor of Fine Arts at Melbourne University) saying to him that 'when Clark was at Melbourne he worked so hard on the documents', AGL Shaw to me, Melbourne, December 2008; the remainder of this section is built on my many discussions with Sebastian Clark and Eirene Clark, and my own conversations with Dymphna Clark between 1997 and 2000; also Sid Ingham to me, August 2005, and Ken Inglis to me, Canberra, February 2005.

26 Clark describes Herbert Burton's phone call in his interview with Don Baker, NLA; for more on Burton see Bob Brissenden's obituary in the *ANU Reporter*, vol. 14, no. 12, 12 August 1983, p. 2, and Clark, *Quest for Grace*, 1990, p. 182; for Clark's comments on the lure of a Canberra salary, see his interview with Daniel Connell, ANU Oral History Project, 13 November 1990, ANU archives; security reports were contained in Clark's ASIO file, kindly copied for me by Dymphna Clark, see TM Owen, Registrar, Canberra University College, to the Director, Commonwealth Investigation Service, Canberra, 26 April 1949, requesting a report on Clark. The security report, dated 16 May 1949, included a full CV, a copy of the *Who's Who in Australia* entry on Clark for 1950, and a

summary of the ABC 'Heckle Hour' program from 1947; in the summary report on Clark from the director of the CIB dated 16 May 1949, he refers to 'a contact who knows Mr. Clark intimately', yet this same contact, in his letter to the CIB, spelt Clark's name incorrectly; Don Baker recalled hearing across the corridors at the ANU, 'you can't appoint Clark; he's a communist' (Baker to me, Canberra, January 2005); Fairbairn to Clark, 9 October 1949, in Clark papers, box 22, folders 180–1, 'Geoffrey Fairbairn, 1945–80'; also see Fairbairn to Clark, 10 February 1948, on his love for Australia: 'perhaps the smell of the eucalypt will bring back the fresh spirit which should permeate our people down under. God how I love Australia.'

27 Clark's letters to Dymphna, written in Canberra in late 1949, can be found in *Ever, Manning*; see especially pp. 62–72, Clark to Dymphna, 19, 20, 29 & 31 October, 1, 2, 3, 4, 7, 11 & 13 November and 1 December 1949; also see Clark to Crawford, 16 October 1949, and other letters to Crawford, pp. 59–61; and Crawford Papers, University of Melbourne Archives, series 6, box 18, 'Outgoing correspondence 1943–1970', Crawford to T Truman (Department of History, University of Queensland), 9 September 1949, 'I shall be sorry to lose Manning'. Crawford praised Clark for his teaching of Australian history: 'I shall take over Australian history with a good deal of pleasure'; similar sentiments expressed in Crawford to Clark, 13 March 1950.

28 The final paragraphs of this chapter are based on my many conversations with Sebastian Clark.

9: The Crossing

1 Clark, notebook, 19 April 1943, and diary, 18 December 1949.

2 Sebastian Clark to me, Melbourne, March 2007.

3 Clark, interviewed in the Melbourne *Herald*, 23–24 March 1985, p. 7; Sebastian Clark to me, Melbourne, March 2007.

4 The memory of Clark cursing Dymphna's parents, Sebastian Clark to me, Melbourne, March 2007; the description of the Bible as a confused novel belongs to Lawrence, 'Why the Novel Matters', in *Phoenix: the Posthumous Papers of DH Lawrence*, Heinemann, London, 1967 (1936), p. 535.

5 The phrase 'prayer-like communion', belongs to Thomas Mann, *Thomas Mann, Diaries 1918–1939*, Harry N Abrams, New York, 1982, p. vi; Clark explained the importance of Dostoyevsky to him in his 1988 ABC Radio National interview with Jill Kitson, cassette held at Manning Clark House.

6 *Nation*, 12 March 1960, pp. 23–4; Bruce Anderson to me, phone conversation, August 2005; Katerina Clark to me, Wapengo, March 2005; there was also talk of naming Roland Dimitri, see Clark papers, box 1, folder 7, 'Correspondence 1955', Axel Lodewyckx to Clark and Dymphna, 24 October 1955, advising them against naming their new baby 'Dmitri': 'I don't favour foreign names' he told them; also Katerina Clark, 'Manning Clark and Russia: a Memoir', in Macintyre & Fitzpatrick (eds), *Against the Grain*, p. 259; Humphrey McQueen told me in Canberra, May 2009, of Clark's remarks to tutors at the ANU regarding Dostoyevsky.

7 Clark's comment regarding Father Sergius, notebook, 26 April 1943; Benedict Clark to me, Phillip Island, April 2008.

8 Lawrence 'Why the Novel Matters', p. 535; Clark to Dymphna, 14 August 1950, *Ever, Manning*, p. 78; David Malouf to me, Sydney, April 2009.

9 I own two copies of *The Brothers Karamazov*: the Everyman's Library edition, translated by Richard Pevear and Larissa Volokhonsky, New York, 1992; and the 2003 Penguin Classics edition, translated by David McDuff. The relevant passage from Father Zossima appears on p. 320 of the Everyman edition and pp. 414–15 of the Penguin edition. Neither of these two translations, in my opinion, betters the one by David Magarshak, in the 1979 Penguin edition, which I found quoted by John Hughes, in *Someone Else: Fictional Essays*, Giramondo, 2007, p. 166; David I Goldstein (ed.), *Selected Letters of Fyodor Dostoevsky*, Rutgers University Press, New Brunswick, 1987; Dostoyevsky to VA Alekseyev from St Petersburg, June 7/1876 pp. 420–2; also Dostoyevsky, in St Petersburg, February 1878, to NL Ozmidov, p. 447; the first Russian translation of *The Communist Manifesto* appeared in 1863, and it is likely Dostoyevsky had read Marx and Engels' pamphlet.

10 Clark, notebook, 26 April 1943; Clark on McAuley at Corio Bay, in his interview with Don Baker (NLA); Dostoyevsky, *The Brothers Karamazov*, Everyman, New York, 2003, pp. 246–64 (chapter 5,

'The Grand Inquisitor'); Clark to Dymphna, 15 November 1938, in *Ever, Manning*, p. 31; Clark's pessimism concerning human beings' capacity to organise a just and equitable political system can be seen early on, in his diary, 7 January 1940: 'My profoundest conviction is that mankind will always hope for life beyond the grave, and that the possibility of harmony or the kingdom of God in this world will be embraced but feebly, as though they were being cheated out of their inheritance.' It is interesting to compare this with Dostoyevsky's comment in *The Brothers Karamazov* (p. 257 of the 2003 Everyman edition): 'Mankind in its entirety has always yearned to arrange things so that they must be universal. There have been a great many nations with great histories, but the higher these nations stood, the unhappier they were.' Clark and Dostoyevsky both felt the desire for universal brotherhood, at the same time as they felt it was doomed.

11 Clark, speaking on Dostoyevsky, with Jill Kitson, ABC Radio National, 1988, cassette held at Manning Clark House; Clark notebook, 26 April 1943; also see Clark's review of G Steiner's book on Tolstoy or Dostoyevsky sent to *Nation*, 28 October 1960, held in Clark papers, box 40, folder 24, 'Articles and Reviews 1960-68', and Clark's review of Xavier Pons's psychoanalytic biography of Lawson in *Sydney Morning Herald*, 18 August 1984.

12 *The Letters of D.H. Lawrence* edited by Aldous Huxley, William Heinemann, London, 1932, p. 547; to Curtis Brown, 15 May 1922, p. 547; to Mrs. AL Jenkins from Thirroul, 28 May 1922 & pp. 549–50', to Catherine Carswell from Thirroul 22 June 22; details on Clark and Tampion Daglish, drawn from Dymphna Clark to Jan Nicholas, 27 March 1995; Clark to Bruce and Joan Anderson, who were then staying at Croydon, 1 December 1949, *Ever, Manning*, p. 75.

13 On White, see David Marr, *Patrick White: a life*, Vintage, Sydney, 1992 (1991), p. 316; for Nolan's paintings of central Australia in 1949–50, see Geoffrey Smith (ed.), *Sidney Nolan: Desert and Drought*, National Gallery of Victoria, Melbourne, 2003, pp. 26–67–Nolan's comments can be found on p. 36 & p. 38; on Boyd, I have drawn on Janet McKenzie, *Arthur Boyd: Art & Life*, Thames & Hudson, London, 2000, especially chapter three, which, at pp. 64 & 67, includes reproductions of 'The Mockers' (1945), and 'The Mourners' (1945); on the 1946 exhibition at Melbourne University, see Richard Haese, *Rebels and Precursors: the Revolutionary Years of Australian art*, Penguin, Ringwood, Vic., 1988 (1981), pp. 172–3 (the Boyd quote is on p. 173) and finally, for Clark on Boyd, see Clark, *Quest for Grace*, 1990, p. 162.

14 Marr, *Patrick White*, p. 316, the Nolan quotes can be found in Geoffrey Smith (ed.), *Sidney Nolan: Desert and Drought*, p. 27 & 36; the Reed letter appears in Richard Haese, *Rebels and Precursors*, p. 254.

15 Nolan's portrait of Lawrence is discussed in Richard Haese, *Rebels and Precursors*, p. 175; for Nolan's comments on the first Kelly paintings and Dostoyevsky, see Nancy Underhill (ed.), *Nolan on Nolan: Sidney Nolan in his own words*, Penguin, Camberwell, Vic., 2007, p. 351–also see p. 245; on Boyd and Dostoyevsky, see Brenda Niall, *The Boyds*, Melbourne University Press, Carlton, Vic., 2007 (2002), p. 195, & Janet McKenzie, *Arthur Boyd, Art & Life*, pp. 36–7 & 49–50.

16 Ian Lodewyckx to me, Mont Albert, March 2007.

17 Clark to Dymphna, 6 October 1949 (Manning Clark House); Lawrence's 'unwritten land' comes from the 1980 Penguin edition of *Kangaroo* (with an introduction by Richard Aldington), p. 365.

10: Canberra

1 I am grateful to Sebastian Clark and Katerina Clark for their memories of the family's journey from Melbourne to Canberra; descriptions of the coast and Monaro are my own.

2 Dymphna's memories can be found online at http://thetocumwalarchive.photoaccess.org.au/003_japonica.htm and in her interview with Elizabeth Cham (NLA); also see oral history interviews given by Katerina and Axel Clark (NLA); aerial photographs of Canberra in the late 1940s and early 1950s can be found on the NLA website and in Mary Machen, *Pictorial History: Canberra*, Kingsclear Books, Sydney, 2000; surveyor Charles Scrivener first used the term 'an amphitheatre of hills' to describe the site and this was picked up by Walter Burley Griffin in his design; other details on Canberra's population and housing shortage in *Canberra Times*, 30 December 1949, p. 4.

3 Brissenden's impressions of Canberra in his introduction to RF Brissenden, *Gough & Johnny Were Lovers*, Penguin, 1984; other recollections, Rob Wetselaar to me, Canberra, July 2009; Gwen Taylor

to me, phone conversation, May 2007, Anne Gollan to me, Canberra, August 2007, Bob Hawke to me, Sydney, June 2008 [Hawke: 'our wives got pregnant at the same time—I always tell Peter Costello that I kissed his wife long before he did']; Verna Coleman to me, Sydney, October 2008; 'isolated from the world beyond', Ann Moyal to me, Canberra, November 2008; also *Canberra Times*, 30 December 1949 & Crocker in SG Foster & Margaret M Varghese, *The Making of the Australian National University 1946–1996*, Allen & Unwin, Sydney, 1996, p. 61.

4   For Clark on the beauty of Canberra's natural setting, see Clark to Dymphna, 29 October 1949, in *Ever, Manning*, p. 66, and Clark to Dymphna, 7 November 1949, p. 71; also Clark on Canberra in his oral history interview with Daniel Connell, ANU Archives; on Clark's love–hate relationship with Melbourne, the letters reproduced in *Ever, Manning*, pp. 59–111, provide many examples.

5   Clark to Crawford, on diplomatic cadets and ANU, in Clark to Dymphna, 3 November 1949, in *Ever, Manning*, p. 70; also Clark with Daniel Connell, ANU archives, & Dymphna Clark, interviewed by Elizabeth Cham (NLA); Bob Hawke to me, Sydney, June 2008; Clark's comments on the direction of the ANU, Clark to Crawford, 5 March 1950, 20 April 1951, *Ever, Manning*, pp. 76 & 80; showering Crawford with flattery, Clark to Crawford, 11 May 1951 (p. 81), 1 March 1953 (p. 95); anxious to return to Melbourne, Clark to Crawford, 5 March 1952 (p. 89).

6   Clark's letters to Crawford, Dymphna and family from Tumbarumba in March 1952, *Ever, Manning*, pp. 83–92; also see Clark to Dymphna, 29 September 1953, held at Manning Clark House ('those hard cruel people ... I doubt whether I will reappear at that History School'); also Sebastian Clark to me, Melbourne, May 2009.

7   Sebastian Clark to me, Melbourne, May 2009.

8   Clark to Dymphna, 15, 16 & 18 March 1952, in *Ever, Manning*, pp. 88–9, 90–1; Clark told Daniel Connell: 'if any visitor came to Canberra, because it was so small, you got asked, e.g. Bertrand Russell, it was a great experience at close range to listen to and hear one of the great minds of the 20th century ... there were only about 20 of us in the blue room'. Clark said he was too shy to speak to Russell; also on Clark leaving the 'centre of things', Jessie Serle to me, phone conversation, March 2007.

11: Tasmania Circle, Forrest

1   Clark's first intentions on building in Canberra in Clark to Dymphna, 19, 20 October & 1 November 1949, in *Ever, Manning*, pp. 62–3 & 68; on Eccles see Dymphna's recollections regarding the house, in an interview posted on the Manning Clark House website; the description of Robin Boyd comes from Axel Clark on p. 20 of the transcript of his NLA interview, held at the NLA's oral history unit.

2   Clark papers, box 27, folder 223, 'Houses 1949–53'; see Boyd to Dymphna, 19 April 1952 (taking on the job), 2 July 1953 (discussing colour schemes); also see Dymphna interviewed in *Australian Home Journal*, September 1973, 'A House of History'; and Geoffrey Serle, *Robin Boyd: a life*, Melbourne University Press, Carlton, Vic., 1996 (first published 1995), pp. 132–3. Boyd was also engaged by Frank Fenner to build on a much larger site at Red Hill shortly after agreeing to design Clark's house; on Boyd and Breuer, my thanks to Milton Cameron.

3   Clark to Russell Clark, undated but probably April/May 1953, courtesy Eirene Clark. In early 1954, Clark was still chasing any money left to his mother's estate after the death of his father, turning up the promise of 500 pounds to be split between Clark and Russell; also see Clark papers, box 27, folder 223, 'Houses 1949–53'. On 18 February 1953, they had news from their Melbourne solicitor, Dick Hamer, that the Croydon house had sold; Boyd was paid 273 pounds (3.75 per cent of the total outlay of 7302 pounds); in the same folder there is a receipt from him dated 1 March 1953; also see Robin Boyd to Dymphna, 21 August 1955, regarding the final bill, 'we are square, though, as you've been nice enough to bring up the subject, I must say I've never been able to afford a copy of Manning's Select Documents. If you happened to have a spare copy I would cherish it.'

4   Dymphna's recollections on the Manning Clark House website & *Australian Home Journal*, September 1973; also see Axel & Katerina's NLA interview, NLA Oral history unit; on Rene McGuire, my thanks to her nephew, John Carrick, Sydney, October 2009; on Canberra see Roderick

Campbell on Canberra in the 1950s in *Canberra Times*, Panorama, 30 June 2001. In 1959, Douglas Copland, ANU vice-chancellor, lived in Tasmania Circle; Clark was fortunate to have found accommodation so quickly. Even as late as the early 1960s, when families from Sydney and Melbourne moved to Canberra as the public service expanded, some of the hostels in which they were housed were 'run down wooden buildings on the western side of Capital Hill ... a mere stone's throw from the Prime Minister's Lodge'. In the 1959 census, no one claimed to be unemployed in Canberra; also see Mary Machen, *Pictorial History Canberra*, Kingsclear Books, Alexandria, NSW, 2000, pp. 110–12.

5 'An Ivory Tower for a Professor', *Sydney Morning Herald*, undated clipping given to me by Dymphna Clark, probably late 1953 or early 1954.

12: Five Bells

1 Dymphna's recollections are drawn from her interview with Elizabeth Cham, held in the Oral History unit at the NLA; also see Clark papers, box 1, 'Correspondence 1953–54 (ii)'; on the back of Clark's draft letter of application for the Rockefeller Grant are Dymphna's editing comments on his short stories, as usual quite abrupt, questioning consistency, grammatical corrections, and plot.

2 ibid.; also see Susan Marsden's interviews with Axel and Katerina Clark held in the same collection.

3 Clark 'no sap', diary, 21 March 1954; on Dymphna's illness, Clark to Crawford, 12 March 1954, in *Ever, Manning*, p. 97; also Dymphna's interview with Elizabeth Cham.

4 Clark and the old man, diary, 6 July 1954; ideas of free love, diary, 3 September & 8 December 1954; also see Clark's review in *Age*, 1 May 1954.

5 An 'Ivory Tower' for a Professor, *The Sydney Morning Herald*, Women's Section, 10 February, 1955, p. 3.

6 Diary, 26 November, 8 December 1954, 27 January & 8 February 1955.

7 Clark's correspondence with Ferguson is held in the Angus & Robertson papers in the Mitchell Library, see Clark to Ferguson, 6 February 1955, 9 November 1954, 4 May 1955 (in which Clark mentions he has written to JM Pringle, literary editor of the *Sydney Morning Herald*), Ferguson to Clark, 17 February 1955; Dymphna on the trip to Sydney to collect *Select Documents*, in her letter to Ailsa Thomson, 24 December 1954, courtesy Ailsa Zainuddin.

8 I am indebted to Ailsa Fabian (formerly Pat Gray), whom I have had the pleasure of knowing over the last few years. Ailsa has been of enormous assistance to me. The narrative draws extensively on her recollections, given to me both in person and by mail between 2005 and 2009. The correspondence, with Ailsa's permission, will be included in the papers I have left with the NLA; for Clark's comments, see his diary, 3, 8 & 13 March 1955, also the letters of Pat Gray to Dymphna, 24 & 28 March 1955, and to Clark and Dymphna, 25 March 1955, and Creighton Burns to Clark, undated but March 1955, all of which are held in Clark papers, box 1, folder 6; my thanks also to Katerina Clark, who remembered overhearing Dymphna tell a friend that she had discovered she was pregnant when she was in Sydney, and had returned home shortly afterwards. Telegrams as follows: Clark to Dymphna, 15 March 1955, 'Souviens tu de la premiere ligne de High Noon et reviens le jeudi Marmeladov' (*High Noon* (1952), American western starring Gary Cooper); Clark to Dymphna, 17 March 1955, sent from Manuka to her in Sydney (c/YWCA Liverpool St Sydney), 'Vergiß Mir für alles, ich brauche dich, melde mich an um elf uhr heute abend, dein Manning'; another sent 18 March 1955: 'Heudi est la grande Esperance ma Kleinie Ton Manning' (all telegrams held at Manning Clark House).

9 Clark, diary, 19 June 1955; see also 4 & 24 July 1955.

10 Drawn from correspondence and interviews with Ailsa Fabian, 2005–2009.

11 These notes were found in Clark's study, among material originally withheld from the NLA. Also in Clark's study are several letters to Dymphna written by Clark in the early 1950s (mostly 1952/3, some undated), while he was away from home. The correspondence is usually about family matters but is always warm and affectionate, Clark ending each letter by saying how much he misses her; see, for example, Clark to Dymphna, 19 October 1952, May 1953, 30 June 1953, 28 July 1953, 1 October 1953, 25 & 29 September 1953.

12 Again, my thanks to Ailsa Fabian; Clark's copy of Slessor's *One Hundred Poems*, published in 1944, which contains 'Five Bells' written by Slessor in 1939, is still in her possession.

13: An Uncharted Sea: Rewriting Australian History 1954–55

1 Clark, notebook, on family relations, 15 November 1954.

2 Clark's review of AJP Taylor's *Bismarck, the Man and the Statesman*, *Age*, 5 November 1955; see also his glowing review of Malcolm Ellis's *John Macarthur*, *Age*, 1 October 1955; his review of Greenwood's collection, *Sydney Morning Herald*, 9 July 1955 (on the top of a photocopy of this Clark wrote 'MY first review for the *SMH*'); other reviews, *Age*, 14 March, 20 June & 5 December 1953, 9 January 1954, 9 April, 21 May & 19, 20 August 1955; *Bulletin*, 7 December 1955, p. 19; more reviews collected in Clark Papers, box 178, folder 8. Also see Clark's notes for his paper on Wood & Scott in his papers, box 186, folder 1, 'Lectures 1940–59'.

3 'Rewriting Australian History', in Clark, *Occasional Writings and Speeches*, 1980, pp. 3–19; also see *Canberra Times*, 24 June 1954; in the same, see Clark's 'The origins of the Convicts Transported to Eastern Australia 1787–1852', pp. 94–144; on the negligible contribution of academic historians to Australian history, see Clark's 'The Teaching of History in Australia 1955', Clark papers, box 185, folder 69; also see box 185, folder 67, 'The Rewriting of Australian History 1953', which contains rough notes for the lecture: 'The only worthwhile history is that which says something which contemporaries find significant ... Our great problem is that no one is saying anything significant about our day and age ... we have no History because no one has attempted to enlighten us ... I am interested in that view of history which helps to make the world bearable, explains the world, our comforter, myths, legends, stories.' Clark went to Melbourne University on 6 and 7 September 1954 to talk to students and give his 'Rewriting Australian History' paper. Clark, at least, was able to find employment, unlike Brian Fitzpatrick, whom he had criticised in his lecture as a 'disappointed radical'. On 6 October 1954, Fitzpatrick wrote to Clark, thanking him for his support for his unsuccessful application for a Rockefeller Grant. Fitzpatrick was rightly convinced that his political activities virtually precluded him from university positions, as he told Clark: 'Being notorious for these activities and views ... and carrying some weight in the worlds of books and politics, are impediments to earning a living. Having existed for some years by a sort of miracle, I am now driven to a humble task for 40 hours per week, starting at the PMG's mail branch next Monday. The honorary public service will have to be done in the remaining 128 hours.' In another letter (17 October 1954) Fitzpatrick referred to his work as a mail sorter as 'my labour for the Queen'; see Clark Papers, box 1, folder 4, 'Correspondence 53–54 (ii)'.

4 On Ward, Clark Papers, box 1, folder 7, 'Correspondence 1955'; Clark, introduction to *Select Documents in Australian History 1851–1900*, pp. xi–xviii; Kathleen Fitzpatrick to Max Crawford, 19 July 1948, Crawford Papers, box 15, University of Melbourne Archives.

5 Crawford to Margaret Kiddle, 3 March 1955, Crawford Papers, University of Melbourne Archives, box 18; Clark to Crawford, 1 & 2 March 1955, in *Ever, Manning*, pp. 104–5; Clark's florid style, Clark to Crawford, 7 March 1955, in *Ever, Manning*, pp. 105–6; Clark's 'Olympian attitude', Duncan MacCallum's review in *The Australian Quarterly*, June 1955, pp. 107–10; Clark wrote to MacCallum (History Sydney), annoyed at his criticisms; MacCallum defended himself in his reply, 8 July 1955; see Clark Papers, box 1, folder 5, 'Correspondence 54–55 (i)'; in same see Malcolm Ellis to Clark, 8 March 1955, to let him know he has reviewed vol. 2: 'I have been able to be kind', Ellis review, *Bulletin*, 13 April 1955; also see Clive Turnbull review in *Tasmanian Historical Research Association Papers and Proceedings*, vol. 4, no. 2, July 1955: Turnbull criticised the 'dull title' and castigated Clark for his statement in the introduction that 'academic history is little more than hasty selections of what is available in the main libraries'; Robin Gollan, in *The University Gazette*, May 1955, pp. 68–9, despite reservations, was enthusiastic: 'one of the most important books published on Australian History in the last 15 years'; the *Age* review of 12 March 1955 was also positive, as was that in the *Herald Sun*, 5 March 1955.

6 June Philipp to Clark, 10 March 1955, Clark papers, box 1, folder 6; Philipp did not like Clark's introduction to *Settlers & Convicts* (1954), 'In your introduction to *Settlers & Convicts* I felt that you

gave [Alexander] "Harris" later religious conversion & experience, his moral struggle, undue might & space.'

7   On the expansion of the university sector, see Stuart Macintyre, 'Always a Pace or Two Apart', in Bridge (ed.), *Manning Clark*, pp. 22–3; and Fay Anderson, *An Historian's Life: Max Crawford and the politics of academic freedom*, Melbourne University Press, Carlton, Vic., 2005, pp. 250 & 286; on Dymphna wishing to remain in Canberra, Sebastian Clark to me, phone conversation, November 2009; Clark to Crawford, 17 April 1955, in *Ever, Manning*, pp. 107–8; Crawford to Clark, 'March 1955', Crawford Papers, box 15, University of Melbourne Archives; Crawford had also attempted to reassure Clark that Geoffrey Serle's teaching of Australian history would not preclude his possible return to Melbourne; see Crawford to Clark, undated but replying to Clark's letter of 5 March 1952 (*Ever, Manning*, p. 83), 'No, Geoff Serle's appointment does not prevent your possible return', Crawford Papers, box 15.

8   Clark to La Nauze, 4 April 1955, La Nauze Papers, box 24; also see Clark to La Nauze (1955), & Snippets, La Nauze to Clark, 25 July 1952, all in La Nauze, Papers (NLA), box 24; La Nauze to Clark, 27 March 1955 & 6 April 1955 in Clark Papers, box 1, folder 6, 'Correspondence 1954–55 (ii)'; Creighton Burns to Clark, undated but March 1955, in which he told Clark La Nauze was the hot candidate, Clark Papers, box 1, folder 6, 'Correspondence 1954–55 (ii)'; also see Barry Smith's obituary of La Nauze, http://www.humanities.org.au/Resources/Downloads/Fellows/Obituaries/ JohnAndrewLa%20Nauze.pdf

9   Clark to La Nauze, 14 April 1955, La Nauze Papers, box 24; Crawford to Margaret Kiddle, 1955 (undated), Crawford Papers, box 15, and Margaret Kiddle to Crawford, 1 June 1955: 'To-day I had a letter from Manning telling me he had withdrawn his application, a face saved in the nick of time; now I suppose he'll say "but if I hadn't withdrawn"', Crawford Papers, box 16; in same, see Norman Harper to Max Crawford, 3 June 1955: 'Manning has announced to a number of people that he has withdrawn his application. I think this was rather foolish of him under the circumstances'. On 29 April 1955, Clark wrote to La Nauze telling him he would apply for the Scott chair; La Nauze replied cagily on 2 May: 'I shall be taking no part in the selection, and will not even be seeing the applications', La Nauze Papers (NLA), box 24; Herbert Burton to Crawford, 27 April 1955, Crawford Papers, box 20; verification of Clark's letter of application, Manning Clark Papers, NLA, box 1, folder 6, 'Correspondence 1954–55 (ii)', which contains a letter from the Registrar, 2 May 1955, noting that his application was received.

10 Ian Mair to Clark, 14 March 1955, in which he also quotes Clark's telegram, Clark papers, box 1, folder 6, 'Correspondence 1954–55 (ii)'; re *Sydney Morning Herald* review, Clark to G Ferguson, 4 May 1955, and Ferguson to Clark, 10 May 1955, Angus & Robertson Papers, Mitchell Library, MSS 3265, second series, vol. 186, 'Charles Manning Hope Clark 1946–1969'; Clark to Christesen, 28 August 1952 ('Would you please remove my name forthwith from the list of subscribers to "Meanjin"'); Clark to Christesen, 25 October 1955, 'if you do not like it, don't hesitate to throw it in the waste-paper basket'; another 12 August 1958, 'don't hesitate to say its awful or hopeless'; all in Meanjin Archives University of Melbourne, box 7.

11 Clark at Kiddle's funeral; Barry Smith to me, Canberra, October 2007; Crawford on Clark, Crawford to Claude Bissell, 25 February 1955, Crawford Papers, University of Melbourne Archives, box 18; Clark, telegram to La Nauze, 6 December 1955. La Nauze's review can be found in Clark Papers, box 54, folder 25, 'Select Documents in Australian History: Reviews of Vol. 2 1955–56'; Kathleen Fitzpatrick to Crawford, 1 April 1955; on 'sustaining' a visit from Clark, Crawford Papers, box 15; Crawford on the mellow La Nauze and driving him to work, Crawford to Margaret Kiddle, undated, 1955 (probably June); Crawford Papers, box 16; the drama of the Ernest Scott chair is covered at length by Fay Anderson, in *An Historian's Life*, pp. 278–89; also see Holt, *A Short History of Manning Clark*, pp. 101–6.

12 Details of Clark's application to the Rockefeller Foundation, including references from Burton (30 June 1955) and Crawford (2 March 1955) can be found in the Rockefeller Archive Centre, New York; my thanks to Jan Nicholas for both these letters. Clark's letter of application to Roger Evans (22 December 1954), his letter to Crawford requesting support (15 December 1954) and another thanking him for his support (3 August 1955) and several to Ailsa Zainuddin regarding contacts

in Djakarta are most easily found in *Ever, Manning*, pp. 101–3 & 108–11; also see Clark Papers, box 1, folder 5, 'Correspondence 54–55 (i)'. ASIO were asked to clear Clark's application; see following chapter.

13 Sebastian Clark to me, November 2009; Katerina Clark to me, November 2009; Dymphna's memories in her interview with Elizabeth Cham (NLA) and also in her conversations with Jan Nicholas.

14: To South-East Asia 1955–56

1 Oxford University Press wrote to Clark on 4 March 1952 offering him editorship of what would become *Sources in Australian History*, published in the 'World's Classics' series in 1957; all correspondence in Clark, papers, box 54, folder 26. For reports on Clark, see *Argus*, 5 March 1955; *Age*, 10 December 1955, p. 17; *Sydney Morning Herald*, 29 October 1955. In 1954, at the request of Gwyn James, then at Angus & Robertson, Clark had edited and introduced the republication of *Settlers and Convicts* by Alexander Harris, which was critically reviewed by Colin Roderick in *Biblionews*, vol. 7, no. 3, March 1954. Clark had recently failed Roderick's doctoral thesis and this was the beginning of the friction between the two men that would resurface in the 1970s; also see Brian Fletcher, *Australian History, History at Sydney: Centenary Reflections*, Highland Press, Canberra, 1992, pp. 159–69. Australian History had been offered at Sydney (almost always as part of a degree majoring in British or American History)—first, in the early twentieth century, by GA Wood; later, in the 1930s, by Stephen Roberts; and after the war by Eris O'Brien and John Manning Ward. Roberts and Ward both encouraged empirical history rather than the more literary history fostered by Wood. After the publication of the *Herald* editorial in 1955, Ward wrote on 29 October 1955 calling for a professor to be appointed whose interests lay in both Australian and British history.

2 On Australian intellectuals and Asia in the 1950s, see Nicholas Brown, *Governing Prosperity*, Cambridge University Press, New York, 1995, pp. 22–49; also Brown's article, 'Australian Intellectuals and the Image of Asia: 1920–1960', *Australian Cultural History*, no. 9, 1990, pp. 80–92, and John Legge, 'Asian Studies from Reconstruction to Deconstruction', in same, pp. 93–102. The Colombo Plan (1951) of which Australia was a member, was an attempt to aid development in South-East Asia. Clark on Asia and the White Australia Policy, in *Argus*, 4 December 1954. Clark's views on immigration paid no heed to the advice he received from PR 'Inky' Stephensen, who wrote to him on 19 August 1952, warning: 'If Australia is to be mongrelised, like the USA, by the admission of Asians, Jews, Italians, the prospects of National Unity and of a distinctive Australian culture will soon disappear.' (Clark papers, box 1, folder 2.)

3 Humphrey McQueen, *Social Sketches of Australia*, Penguin, Ringwood, Vic., 1986 (first published 1978), pp. 195–8; AD Hope's 'Australia' can be found in his *Collected Poems*, Angus & Robertson, Sydney, 1972 (first published 1966), p. 13.

4 Clark, diary, 26 December 1955. I have compressed Clark's impressions from his South-East Asian diary, December 1955–end January 1956.

5 Ailsa Zainuddin to me, Melbourne, August 2005 ('we were not attempting to represent Western civilisation or Christianity to anybody but simply enjoying ourselves'); Clark on Christmas celebrations in Jakarta, Clark, diary, 26 December 1955; my thanks to Ailsa, who became Clark's research assistant in July 1952, for her correspondence with Clark; for information on Herbert Feith, who in the 1960s formed the Overseas Service Bureau, which grew out of the Volunteer Graduate Scheme and of which Clark was a patron, see Feith's online biographical details at www.herbert-feithfoundation.org; on Clark's depression, see especially diary, 4 January 1956.

6 Clark, diary, Delhi, 14 February 1956; also see diary, Singapore, 18 January 1956 & 31 January 1956; on the sky melting, diary, 18 January 1956.

7 Clark, diary, 27 January 1956; on Australia's reputation in Asia, Clark, diary, 5 March 1956; on Cyril Parkinson, see Clark, diary, 15 January 1956.

8 Sarvepalli Gopal, *Jawaharlal Nehru: a biography*, Volume 2: 1947–1956, Jonathan Cape, London, 1979; also Clark, History notebook, 5 September 1954–September 1956—see especially entries for 19 February 1956 & 10 March 1956. Clark wrote later on the inside cover of this notebook, 'some

of the ideas for volume one'; Clark's reflections on India, in his diary, 18 March 1956, 'The pacifi-cation of India–which was not finished till after the Indian war of Independence, and in a sense was never completed the pacification was maintained by force, not by consent. (See Gandhi's point that western civilisation is based on force.) ... Rule of law–but c/f Indian comments on British justice. Could. an Indian win a case against a European? ... bribing of jurors, of witnesses, and pressures on judges by the English community to bring in the right verdict.'

9   Clark, diary, 11 February–1 March 1956; Dymphna's recollections of her trip to India, in her 1997 interviews with Jan Nicholas and her correspondence with Jan Nicholas (7 November 1995).

10 Clark, diary, 4 February & 1 March 1956.

11 ibid., 2 March 1956; Dymphna's recollections, 1 September 1997, courtesy Jan Nicholas. Varanasi was also known as Banares or Benares.

12 Clark, diary, 26 December 1955; 3, 4, 6 & 19 February & 9 March 1956. Of Buddhism, Clark also remarked, 'Where is the art of the Buddhist religion, where its scholarship, and where its monu-ments other than the pagodas?' (8 February)

13 Clark, diary: on Hinduism, 9 March 1956; on visits to Catholic churches–in Rangoon, 6 February 1956, in Malacca, 30 January 1956, in Calcutta, 4 March 1956.

15: To England and Ireland, 1956

1   Bruce Grant to me, Melbourne, March 2007. There are in fact twelve steps at the entry of the British Museum. Presumably, Grant was standing on the eleventh step. On Suez, Eden and decolo-nisation, see Norman Davies, *The Isles: a History*, Macmillan, London, 1999, pp. 909–10. Grant also mentioned that, at this time, Clark was thinking of becoming a Catholic. He was also still in touch with Pat Gray. Grant recalled going to a party with Clark after they had been to see *The Seagull*, and Gray was there. Clark's comments on his love life, said Grant, were 'often very elliptical'. 'Sometimes he would say to me, "Of course you know Dymphna's from peasant stock."' Grant claims that, in London, 'he certainly behaved as if the affair with Gray was still continuing'. After he began to write the history, he would often quote from Uncle Vanya (Dr Arstrov): 'And now we must work.' When he arrived in the United Kingdom, Clark wrote to the BBC suggesting he give a talk on the foundation of Australia for broadcast; see PH Newby (BBC) to Clark, 9 November 1956, in Clark's papers, box 1, folder 7, 'Correspondence 1955'.

2   Dymphna Clark to Jan Nicholas, 1 September 1997.

3   Clark to Canberra University College, early 1957, in Russell, *Ever, Manning*, pp. 124–5.

4   Clark, diary, 11 April 1956; on Lawrence and Clark, Dymphna Clark to Jan Nicholas, 27 March 1995; Clark on history as a play, notebooks, 8 February 1956.

5   Clark, notebooks, 9 January 1956; also see Clark on Whitby, 12 April 1956; on spring, 6 May 1956; on Wales, 16 August 1956; on Edinburgh, 15 April 1956; on Cork, 19 June 1956. On visions enter-ing Clark, see Clark to Ailsa Zainuddin, 28 December 1956, in Russell, *Ever, Manning*, pp. 122–3.

6   Nolan on sacramental feeling, 1956, in Nancy Underhill, *Nolan on Nolan: Sidney Nolan in His Own Words*, Penguin, Camberwell, Vic., 2007, p. 270; White's statement on Voss, in 'The Prodigal Son', *Macquarie Pen Anthology of Australian Literature*, Allen & Unwin, Crows Nest, NSW, 2009, pp. 557–60; Clark on Beethoven and Mozart, notebooks, 19 June 1956; on jeerers and mockers, diary, 1 December 1956; Nolan on cannibalism etc., Nolan to Albert Tucker, 28 May 1964, in *Nolan on Nolan*, pp. 178–9.

7   Clark, diary, 14–19 March 1956.

8   For Clark's complaints about the children, see diary, 14, 16 & 19 March 1956 (Katerina); also 5 April, 25 August & 6 September 1956; for financial concerns, see diary, 25 & 27 August 1956; also Clark papers, box 1, folder 8, 'Correspondence 1956', which contains a letter from Angus & Robertson, 15 May 1956, replying to Clark's letter asking for his royalty cheque (he received 223 pounds); on their arrival in Bonn and conversations with the Ungers, diary, 4 September 1956; Clark on *Look Back in Anger* and *The Seagull*, diary, 16 June and 4–5 August 1956; in his diary, 25 June 1956, Clark reports on a dinner he shared with AL Rowse, the historian of Elizabethan England: 'At night went to dinner at All Souls with A.L. Rowse. I first saw him at the top of the

stairs in a dressing gown looking like Charley's Aunt, and then with the exaggerated gestures of the effeminate exhibitionist, swinging the arm in a circle before shaking hands, and saying rather loudly: "Hullo, Professor." While he dressed ('It will only take me three minutes.') ... There will be the stories—but they, like his books and conversation will die. I wonder whether he could live outside All Souls—a tender exotic, who does not draw strength from his day & age, but from the Elizabethans!' On 25 September, in conversation with Jan Nicholas, Dymphna recalled Rowse: 'There they all were at high table at All Souls. I don't know how Manning scored the invite but he was there. And I remember we were really on hard rations then because we had just paid for our tickets back to Australia and we were really broke. And as I tell the story there I was at home with the three children, you know sharing a hard-boiled egg so to speak or on herrings for the fourth time that week ... And Manning would come home from these high table dinners ... with strawberries and cream coming out of his ears ... Anyway he was there and there was a bit of a silence ... round the high table and A.L. Rowse just dropped it like that: I had a letter from Kim Philby this morning. They were apparently old mates of some kind.'

9 Dymphna's recollections to Jan Nicholas, 1 September 1997; on staying with Ehrenzeller, Clark, diary, 6 September 1956; on the visit to Baden Baden, see Clark, *A Historian's Apprenticeship*, 1992, p. 17, and diary, 4 September 1956; also Clark marked the letter from Dostoyevsky to his wife Anya, 16–28 April 1871, in his copy of Joseph Frank and David I Goldstein (eds), *Selected Letters of Fyodor Dostoevsky*, Rutgers University Press, New Brunswick, 1987, pp. 353–7.

10 Dymphna to Clark, 15 September 1996; Clark to Dymphna, 7 & 10 September 1956 (all held at Manning Clark House); also Dymphna's recollections to Jan Nicholas, 1 September 1997, and Clark, *A Historian's Apprenticeship*, 1992, pp. 18–19.

11 Clark to Dymphna, 5 October 1956; also Dymphna to Jan Nicholas, 1 September 1997.

12 Clark in Rome, diary, 6–16 September 1956.

13 Dymphna to Jan Nicholas, 1 September 1997; Clark in Ireland, diary, 16 June–21 June 1956; also see letter dated 1 May 1956 from Reverend Michael O'Connor to Clark regarding his enquiry for 'leaflets' on the catholic faith, in Clark, papers, box 1, folder 8, 'Correspondence 1956'; also Matthew 25: 31–46; for Clark on Catholicism and Ireland, see his 'Themes in "A History of Australia"', in Clark, *Occasional Writings*, 1980, pp. 80–2, and Clark's 1967 interview with Hazel de Berg (NLA), 'I was lucky enough to discover Catholicism in Ireland ... I suppose it was in Ireland that I first became consciously aware of the great gap between what I would loosely call the Protestant upright man and the catholic view of the world ... I saw the importance of having compassion on everyone. I think probably that it was during that stay in Ireland that I saw very clearly that the Catholic Church had done something or achieved something which really astonished me as a simple boy from Australia ... this image of Christ alive. Perhaps I should say quite simply that it wasn't given to me then to become a believer.'

14 Clark, diary, 1 October 1956; the first manuscripts of *A History, Volume I*, including Dymphna's editorial comments, can be found in Clark, papers, box 58, folder 1, 'Volume One Preliminary Manuscript'. At a later date, Clark wrote on the manuscript '(This was begun in Oxford England on 1 October 1956)'. These drafts also contain signs of his frustration—for example, on Monday 31 December 1956, 'And very unhappy with it. It has not satisfied me.' Another note at the end of the first draft: 'Today, Friday 4th October 1957, Hancock told me he thought my first volume should end with the shape of the society after [the colonies were] clearly established. This means it should run to at least 1840 when Port Phillip, Western Australia, South Australia were well established, when the British government had announced the end of transportation to New South Wales, when the colonists had debated the future of the colony...value of this is the artistic unity of the volume ... The history of Australia is a story of the break up of traditions—withering away of evangelical Christianity, Catholic Christendom, humanism, even the enlightenment'; also Dymphna Clark to Jan Nicholas, 15 December 1993, 'We could see Tom Tower in the back of the house in Raleigh Park Road—across the field which was Raleigh Park.'

During his stay in England, Clark wrote frequently to librarians at the Mitchell Library requesting assistance. On 1 June 1956, a librarian notes, 'A friend of mine who is research assistant to Manning Clark has received an agitated letter ... from the Professor (who is at Oxford at the moment) asking her to go to the Mitchell as soon as possible to consult some of the MSS there.' The reply from the Mitchell Librarian, 13 August 1956, noted: 'It has taken a number of weeks to complete the research and the order and I should not like the films and account to go chasing the Professor around the world.' Sometimes Clark's enquiries were exasperating; for example, he wrote to the Mitchell, 19 September 1958, 'In one of the issues of the *Sydney Gazette* of May 1807 is a description of Laycock's arrival in Hobart. Could you please arrange for a Photostat of this article.' GD Richardson, Mitchell Librarian, replied on 30 September that he needed 'further information', pointing out to Clark that 'the Sydney Gazette was not issued in May 1807'. All these letters held in Mitchell Library, Manuscripts, Library correspondence files.

15 On White's *Tree of Man*, see Clark, *A Historian's Apprenticeship*, 1992, p. 19; also David Marr, *Patrick White: a life*, Random House, Milsons Point, NSW, 1991, pp. 288–90.

16 Virginia Woolf, 'Sketch of the Past', in Hermione Lee (ed.), *Moments of Being: autobiographical writings*, Pimlico, London, 2002, pp. 78, 81 & 83.

16: To Russia, 1958

1 Clark, diary, 11 December 1956.

2 Clark, diary, 10 January 1957; also based on the recollections of Dymphna Clark; Dymphna to Jan Nicholas, 7 November 1995, and her recorded interview with Nicholas, 10 March 1994, courtesy Jan Nicholas (Clark attended the 32nd ANZAAS conference in Dunedin); in Clark's papers, box 2, folder 9, 'Correspondence 1956'. Barbara Atkins, Clark's research assistant in Canberra, wrote to him on 15 November 1956, quoting his remarks on Canberra and the ANU back to him: 'How petty and "bloated in its own conceit" it will seem to you when you come back: the sheer mediocrity of it all will revolt you I'm sure.'

3 Clark, diary, 19 June & 23 August 1956.

4 Clark to the manager, Shaw Savill Line, undated, late 1956, in Russell, *Ever, Manning*, p. 123; 'twilight of colonialism', diary (Trinidad), 20 December 1956. For reports of Clark's travels and research findings see Patricia Ryan writing in early 1957 for the Commonwealth News and Information Bureau, 'Australia in the Legends of Asia'; 'he discovered [in Jakarta] there was a tremendous amount of work to be done by researchers in studying the old palm leaf manuscripts and the oral traditions of the Indonesian people, before exact statements could be made about their ideas of early Australia', held in Clark's papers, box 2, folder 9, 'Correspondence 1956'; also Stephen Holt, 'Manning Clark and Australia's Asian Past', *ANU Reporter*, 4 October 1995 p. 7; Clark on eastern transcendentalism, after attending a lunch in Canberra for visiting Indian and Pakistani philosophers, diary, 11 December 1957.

5 Vincent Buckley to Clark, 15 May 1957, Clark, papers, box 2, folder 13 ('Correspondence 1957'); on New Zealand, diary, 18 January 1957; Clark's public lecture was reported in the *Canberra Times*, 9 May 1957, p. 5 ('Asia entitled to determine its own destination').

6 Dymphna Clark, interviewed by Elizabeth Cham ((NLA), and Dymphna Clark to Jan Nicholas, 7 November 1995; Clark's royalty statement from Angus & Robertson (15 May 1956), 223 pounds, in Clark, papers, box 1, folder 8; on Benedict, Katerina Clark to me, Wapengo, March 2007.

7 All letters written in 1958 in Russell, *Ever, Manning*, pp. 129, 131, 134 & 136.

8 Clark on the publication of *Democrat in the Ganges*, diary, 24 March 1957, and *Bulletin*, 1 May 1957, pp. 11, 36, 56–7; Clark's dissatisfaction with chapter one, diary, 31 December 1956; his thoughts on a textbook, in Clark, *A Discovery of Australia*, 1976, p. 46.

9 Clark's reaction to the publication of *Sources of Australian History*, diary, 2 October 1957; his introduction to *Sources* is less idiosyncratic than his introduction to the second volume of *Select Documents*. OUP Australia wrote to Clark on 10 October 1958 asking him to sign a contract to write a new history of Australia (single volume, 80 000 words, by March 1960). On 'Roman Catholicism' OUP suggested they didn't want him to suppress anything but 'on the other hand, we should not want to give offence needlessly'; another note from OUP, 4 November 1959: *Sources of Australian History* had sold 6117 to that point; in the same folder (Clark, papers, box 2, folder 13) another note from Angus & Robertson, royalty statement, in the first six months of 1958: they sold over 300 copies of each volume of *Select Documents*.

10 On McAuley and *Captain Quiros*, see Peter Coleman, *The Heart of James McAuley: life and work of the Australian poet*, Connorcourt, Bacchus Marsh, Vic., 2006 (first published 1980), pp. 81–9; and Cassandra Pybus, *The Devil and James McAuley*, University of Queensland Press, 1999, pp. 152 &177–82; Clark's article, 'Quiros', in *Prometheus* (Journal of ANU Students Association), 1958, pp. 15–16; his later comments on Quiros in Clark, *A Discovery of Australia*, 1988, pp. 46–7, and Clark, *A Historian's Apprenticeship*, 1992, p. 41; Clark's meeting with McAuley, diary, 13 October 1957.

11 Clark's description of Mannix and his record of the journey to Sorrento with James Murtagh can be found in his papers, box 160, folder 1, 'Manuscripts (i)'. He continued, 'We talked of W.M. Hughes. During the conscription controversy he had always called Mannix–liar or a traitor or a rebel–But I always called him Mr. Morris Hughes [said Mannix] ... once when he called me a liar, I said you needed to do more than spend a night or two at Buckingham Palace to become a gentleman ... On the Anglicans and conscription: [Mannix said], 'If an Anglican archbishop can talk in favour of the Yes case on a pulpit, surely, I said, I can talk about the No case in a paddock.' Mannix then told Clark how Hughes had reconciled with him at the end of his life, coming to visit him after Mannix wrote to console him after the death of his daughter. In the same folder, contrast Clark's sympathetic reading of Mannix with his reflections 'on meeting M. Teichman, Thursday 12 July 1956'; 'am writing this in the British Museum on the next afternoon. Well, what infernal, uncouth bullies these university educated, rationalist, secular, socialists are, what shocking moral bullies, moral prigs. Last night, as soon as I met Teichman & his wife, I felt ill at ease, on the defensive, exposed, naked'; on McAuley, see Clark, diary, 13 October 1957, and on the 'intellectual turmoil', see McAuley to Clark, 27 February 1958, Clark, papers, box 23, folder 190.

12 Undated, but late 1950s, Clark, papers, box 161, folder 'Short Stories: 'Manuscripts 4 (iii)'.

13 Clark marked this passage in his copy of Dostoyevsky's *The Double: a poem of St. Petersburg*, Harvill Press, London, 1957, pp. 167–9. Clark inscribed on the title page, 'Manning Clark Canberra April 1958'. Clark admonishing himself for his sinful behaviour, in his papers, box 160, folder 2, 'Short Stories: Manuscripts 1 (ii)'; see, in particular, the note headed 'Written on Monday 29 July 1957', 'On the night of Wednesday and Thursday 24 and 25 July I became drunk. On Friday 26 July I vowed in St. Christopher's Church before the altar that I would not drink again till I am 50, and lit a candle in the Church to confirm the vow. Today I realise the evil of my behaviour on the Wednesday night. I was excited by the meeting of the committee of the Fellowship of Australian Writers, by my election as President, by Sarah Fitzgerald (her face and her bosom). Was excited still further by drinks with Kurt Baier who told me Pat Gray had been married to Erwin Fabian (the choice of the active [sic] is deliberate.) After the concert by the Sydney Sinfonietta I went to Graham Hughes' room, and it was there that my sins were committed. First, by playing up to Graham Hughes' fascination with vice, with drink, with sex, all Dionysian talk and behaviour. This is not corrupting the innocent, not taking pleasure in their fall or degradation. I do not know what it is but have always done it as a teacher ... Think for one moment of how I poured the drink into Don, encouraged him in his infidelities, encouraged him to leave home–all those things I would not dare do to myself'; Clark on St John's Gospel in his diary, 13 October 1957.

14 Clark's comments on Goldyakin can be found in his markings on his copy of *The Double*, held in his study; his fear of 'self destruction' is not in his diary, but forms part of the note written on Monday 29 July 1957, see previous note; Clark's comments on the unbearable nature of unbelief were made shortly after his meeting with McAuley in Sydney–see diary, 13 October 1957; his remarks about the mystery and wonder of life being drained away can be found in a letter to Bruce Grant, 6 November 1957, written from Canberra Hospital, where Clark was recovering from an 'operation for rupture', held in Clark, papers, box 160, folder 2, 'Manuscripts 1 (ii)'; 'IT possessed me', Clark, diary, 25 January 1960.

15 Figures on deaths under Stalin drawn from Norman Davies, *Europe: a History*, Pimlico, London, 1997, p. 1329; Eric Hobsbawm, *Interesting Times: a twentieth-century life*, Abacus, London, 2003 (first published 2002), pp. 204–5; on Khrushchev, I have drawn on two main sources–David Priestland, *The Red Flag: communism and the making of the modern world*, Allen Lane / Penguin, London, 2009, pp. 328–36, and Orlando Figes, *The Whisperers: private life in Stalin's Russia*, Penguin, London, 2007, pp. 538 & 594–5.

16 Clark to June Philipp, 22 July 1954, in Russell, *Ever, Manning*, pp. 98–9; on Hungary, see Priestland, *The Red Flag*, pp. 334–6; Clark's reaction to the invasion, diary, 11 November 1956; I am grateful to Bruce Grant, who worked as a journalist in London in 1956, for his recollections of the reaction to the Soviet Union's invasion of Europe; Clark's doubts about Marxism can be found in his diary, 26 February 1956, and in his papers, box 160, folder 1, 'Manuscripts (i)', see 'on meeting M. Teichman et al. Thursday 12 July 1956'.

17 On the Cold War climate in Australia, see Geoffrey Bolton, *The Oxford History of Australia, vol. 5: the middle way*, OUP, South Melbourne, 1996 (first published 1990), pp. 139–43; Clark on the Petrov Commission and Evatt, diary, 20 April 1954 & 3 October 1955; Clark wrote to Evatt often, donating money towards ALP election campaigns, see telegram from Arthur Calwell to Clark, 29 May 1954, 'Many thanks for your good wishes', and Calwell to Clark, 14 April 1954, thanking him on behalf of Evatt for his donation of 5 pounds 5 pence to the ALP for the coming election, in Clark, papers, box 1, folder 6; for ASIO's comments on Clark see his ASIO file, memorandum from ACT regional director, 10 September 1953, after Clark was nominated as president of Peace and War Convention Committee for Canberra: 'External Affairs have asked for urgent consideration of Manning Clark's appointment re selection of diplomatic cadets'; also p./doc folio 49, 18 September 1953, and later, in 1955, ASIO's full security check included Clark's CV and personal details– 'Motor Vehicle: 1948 Austin Saloon–black. Registered No. ACT 137'–and noted that Clark 'contributed to the finances of Canberra Peace Group, a Communist controlled organisation'. This report includes a photocopy of the press report from *Argus*, 18 November 1955, on Clark and Dymphna winning the 800 pound Rockefeller Foundation Fellowship 'to travel in South and South East Asia to study relations of those areas with Australia'. Clark wrote to CUC Principal, Herbert Burton, protesting against the selection committee's decision not to interview the communist Ian Turner for a lectureship in history. On 17 September 1958, Burton wrote to Clark defending his decision; see Clark, papers, box 3, folder 21. Through his contact with the Soviet embassy, Clark (and Dymphna through her teaching there) knew Petrov and his wife; see Vladimir Petrov to Clark, 8 December 1954, 'I'm beginning to understand what a difficult time the Lord is going to have on judgement day. And I'm more than ever sure that it's better to be judged than to judge'; he agreed to meet Clark in Melbourne on 20 December, in Clark, papers, box 1, folder 4, 'Correspondence 53–54 (ii)'.

18 Fairbairn to Clark, 29 April 1954 & 4 April 1955, in Clark, papers, box 22, folder 181 (also see folder 180); in the same folder, Fairbairn to Clark, 8 December 1954, 'I am tired of writing at length explaining what I think about an issue only to receive in reply a fricassee of inverted self-righteousness ... Friendship cannot be based on histrionics. You're no Marmeladov Manning. You're on board, as the sailors say'; on Clark and Indo-China, see *Canberra Times*, 8 April 1954 (letter); also *Commonwealth of Australia, Parliamentary Debates*, House of Representatives, 8 April 1954, pp. 239–40 (Wentworth) and 7 April 1954, pp. 124–5 (Casey).

19 Clark to La Nauze, 28 November 1957, papers of John La Nauze, MS 5248 (NLA), box 24; also Clark, diary, 28 November 1958. Clark's comments to Fairbairn regarding John Burton are quoted in Fairbairn to Clark, 29 April 1954; on literary journals and the Cold War, see Lynne Strahan, *Just City and the Mirrors: Meanjin Quarterly and the Intellectual Front 1940–1965*, OUP, South Melbourne, 1984, pp. 161–74, 182–3, 197–207; Clark defending McAuley, see Clark to Stephen Murray-Smith, 19 August 1957, in Russell, *Ever, Manning*, p. 126.

20 Arthur Phillips to Clark, undated but late 1958, held at Manning Clark House; on the delegation, see Clark's Preface to *Meeting Soviet Man*, 1960, and McQueen, *Suspect History*, 1997, pp. 72–3; on the Fellowship of Australian Writers and the response of writers to the Cold War, see Patrick Buckridge, 'Clearing a space for Australian Literature 1940–1965', in Bruce Bennett & Jennifer Strauss, *The Oxford Literary History of Australia*, OUP, South Melbourne, 1998, pp. 169–92, especially pp. 180–6. By opening up contact, the FAW also hoped to increase the sale of Australian literature in the Soviet Union; Dymphna began teaching at the Soviet Embassy in 1958 and continued until 1962, receiving $2 per hour. This also aroused ASIO'S suspicion, mistakenly. ASIO 'thought her to be the daughter of her brother, Axel Lodewyckx, the Librarian at Victorian State Library': see Dymphna's interview with Elizabeth Cham (NLA); for an example of other visits to

the Soviet Union in 1958, see H Myles Wright, 'A Visit to Russia', *The Town Planning Review*, vol. XXIX, 1958–59, pp. 163–78.

21 Clark to Bruce Grant (draft letter), 6 November 1957, in Clark, papers, box 160, folder 2, 'Manuscripts 1 (ii)'; also Katerina Clark, 'Manning Clark and Russia: a memoir, in Macintyre & Fitzpatrick (eds), *Against the Grain*, pp. 258–70; on Kruschev's Russia and modernisation, see Priestland, *The Red Flag*, pp. 344–5.

22 Orlando Figes, *The Whisperers: Private Lives in Stalin's Russia*, Penguin, London, 2007, p. 599; and McQueen, *Suspect History*, 1997, pp. 71–2. On Pasternak, Orlando Figes, *Natasha's Dance: a cultural history of Russia*, Penguin, London, 2002, pp. 509–10.

23 Clark in Delhi, diary, 4 November 1958; on the British embassy, I have drawn on the unpublished memoir of Harry Rigby (my thanks to Harry's daughter, Kate Rigby).

24 On Krushchev's slums, see Priestland, *The Red Flag*, p. 343; also see Clark to Dymphna, 6 November 1958, in Russell, *Ever, Manning*, p. 144; Judah Waten's impressions quoted in McQueen, *Suspect History*, 1997, pp. 73–4; undated, unidentified note on *Age* letterhead in Clark, papers, box 3, folder 18; on Waten & Devaney, see Clark, diary, 31 October & 4 November 1958.

25 Clark's letters to Dymphna from India and the Soviet Union, written in November and December 1958, are collected in Russell, *Ever, Manning*, pp. 139–61; Dymphna to Clark, 19 November 1958 & 14 December 1958, held at Manning Clark House.

26 Clark, diary, 8 November 1958.

27 I have drawn on two sources—Harry Rigby's unpublished memoir, and his letter to Dymphna Clark, 6 November 1996—both courtesy of Kate Rigby.

28 Clark, diary, 7 December 1958, on Dostoyevsky, Tolstoy, and Chekhov see diary, 10, 11, 12 & 14 November 1958; also Clark to family, 15 November 1958, in Russell, *Ever, Manning*, pp. 151–2.

29 Clark in *Nation*, 28 March 1959, also see *Nation*, 14 February 1959; Clark's articles in *Age Literary Supplement* 3 & 10 January 1959; for the letter published in the *Moscow News*, see McQueen, *Suspect History*, 1997, p. 76.

30 Buckley's letter is in Clark's papers, box 55, folder 3, Buckley suffered from his own delusions, wondering if Clark's articles were written of his own volition; see also John McLaren, *Journey Without Arrival: the life and writing of Vincent Buckley*, Australian Scholarly Publishing, North Melbourne, Vic., 2009, p. 174; Clark's articles in *Bulletin*, 1 April 1959, also see McQueen, *Suspect History*, pp. 74–5; Ian Turner to Clark, 15 January 1959, in Clark, papers, box 55, folder 3; also see 'Brian Fitzpatrick's *Labor Newsletter*, May 1959, p. 8. Fitzpatrick praised Clark for his courage in speaking up for the Soviet Union; for further press reports on Clark's visit to Russia see *Age*, 11 December 1958, *Canberra Times*, 19 February 1959 & *Herald Sun*, 26 January 1959. My thanks to Doug Munro for sending through the Milner correspondence; papers of Ian Milner, Alexander Turnbull Library, Wellington, New Zealand, MS papers 4567–003, Correspondence 1959. Clark to Milner, 14 April 1959, thanks him for his hospitality, sends him the articles on Russia and his foreword to a memorial for Noel Ebbels, '[I] am tremendously glad to have seen Russia because it showed me the strength, the possibilities in the dreams of the Enlightenment & point where they clash with older faiths.'

31 Waten's letters to Clark, in his papers, box 25, folder 206, see Waten to Clark, 13 & 30 January 1960, 10 February 1960, also his undated letter to Clark, written after he reads the manuscript of *Meeting Soviet Man*, in which he accuses Clark of anti-communism, in box 4, folder 25; Clark's replies in Judah Waten, papers, NLA MSS 4536/2/230-478, 1958–61; see especially Clark to Waten, 5 February 1960; also Clark to Waten, 28 May 1959 & 19 July 1959, in Russell, *Ever, Manning*, pp. 168–70; Angus & Robertson accepting *Meeting Soviet Man*, Beatrice Davis to Clark, 26 June 1959, in Clark, papers, box 4, folder 25, 'Correspondence 1959 (ii)'. Reviews of *Meeting Soviet Man*, Donald Horne, *Observer*, 5 March 1960, pp. 21–3; Tom Fitzgerald, *Nation*, 12 March 1960, pp. 23–4; Douglas Stewart, *Bulletin*, 16 March 1960 (letters); James McAuley, *Quadrant*, vol. IV, no. 3, Winter 1960, pp. 91–2; Judah Waten, *Tribune*, 2 March 1960, p. 6; Clark's letters to Oksana Krugerskaya, in Russian State Archive of Literature and Art, Moscow, my thanks to Katerina Clark, see especially Clark to Krugerskaya, 9 February 1960. For more reviews and correspondence relating to *Meeting Soviet Man*, also see Clark's papers, box 55, folders 3, 6 & 7, in

folder 7; for example, Geoffrey Fairbairn to Clark, 12 January 1961, in which he tells Clark that he finally understands what the book is about and Geoff Serle to Clark, 3 March 1960 (Donald Horne, said Serle, was a 'prize bastard')–this folder also contains Dymphna's telegram to Clark, 25 February 1960; also see box 2, folder 15, which contains a scrap of paper bearing Dymphna's notes made while editing *Meeting Soviet Man*: 'confused, but must be fixed, too important not to do the idea full justice'.

32 Clark, *Meeting Soviet Man*, 1960: on the price of the revolution, p. 2; on taking them seriously, p.6; on Lenin as Christ-like, p. 12; Tiflis, p. 13; Pasternak, pp. 27–32; ripping out the past, p. 69; Lenin, the great teacher, p.78; muddying the waters, p. 84; conclusion, pp. 115–17. Clark claimed that the Soviet Union, 'with more charity towards those who do not share its faith', 'could become the first to create equality and brotherhood', adding 'I believe they will', p. 68. In his conclusion he also lumped together completely different historical events, describing them simply as 'ordeals'; for example, the Russians were 'the people who had endured great ordeals–the First World War, the Revolution of 1917, the civil war, the collectivization of agriculture, the purges, the Second-World War and the Cold War crisis of 1948–53'. Waten on Menzies: see Waten to Clark, 30 January 1960, in Clark, papers, box 25, folder 206. My thanks to Robin Gollan, who made the point about Clark and Marx in a letter to me, 3 April 2005.

33 I am grateful to Peter Coleman for passing on the correspondence of McAuley to Eris O'Brien, which he kindly copied for me. At the time of publication, the letters were still in Coleman's possession; see Eris O'Brien to McAuley, 13 April 1959. O'Brien praised Clark's short story: 'At midnight, last night, I looked into your most recent issue of *Quadrant* (which, by the way, is an excellent number). Manning Clark's extraordinary essay dispelled sleep, however. It is brilliantly written, I think: pelting along with such impetuous speed. One scarcely sees such monologues in modern Australia ... In a few places it is a little crude; but it is graphic; fearless; and, if I read it right, it reveals a situation of the recent past, which was nastier than I had believed it was. So, that monologue leaves me wondering: I should not like to ask Manning to elucidate it; but, one of these days, you might do that for me'; and McAuley's reply, 16 April 1959. Also of interest, McAuley to Clark, 24 July 1959: 'I would be interested in anything further you produced about "The Man in Black" ... various people have both praised and blamed the previous one. Some complained of the over-simplified plague-on-both-your houses stance and lectured me on publishing it. Of course that is to make the elementary mistake of assuming that I endorse everything I publish. Actually, I would criticise you on that score myself, but the point is to me that it seemed to be a document worth peoples' attention', in Clark, papers, box 55, folder 3; later, on a small *Quadrant* flyer, Clark wrote: 'when they sent the cheque for Man in Black'; also see Peter Coleman in *Weekend Australian Review*, 16–17 January 1999, p. 10.

34 Clark's copy of *Meeting Soviet Man*, in his study, Manning Clark House.

17: A View from the Study

1 Dymphna Clark's memories of Clark's writing routine, including her remark about 'frivolous visitors' can be found at www.manningclark.org.au; also see her interview in *Canberra Times*, 2 June 1997; the council objected to some aspects of Robin Boyd's design, including the stairs, and in Boyd's letter to the ACT Planning & Development Branch, 14 February 1953, he explained that 'Professor Manning Clark requested such steps because he requires isolation in his work in the study and deliberately does not wish to encourage much use of the access to it'; in Clark, papers, box 27, folder 223, 'Houses 1949–53'; also see 'A House of History' in *Australian Home Journal*, September 1973; I have also drawn on my many conversations with Sebastian Clark and Wilma Robb ('Clarkie's corner'), as well as my own visits to the study.

2 Clark on his 'abandoned loves', 'Transcending time and place', *Vogue Australia*, June 1988, p. 38; on his inability to face reality and using literature like a 'pyschedelic drug', see Clark on ABC Radio National's *Reading Books*, 21 October 1979 (cassette tape courtesy Manning Clark House).

3 Clark's comments on railways and his markings in his copies of *The Devils* (Penguin Classics 1960) and *The Idiot* (Penguin, Harmondsworth, 1970). Almost any edition of Dostoyevsky's novels in his study will yield similar remarks.

4 Dymphna's 1958 inscription can be found in Clark's copy of *The Autobiography of Charles Darwin 1809–1882*, Collins, London, 1958; the full inscription reads: 'Dem Umwälzen des 20sten Jahrhunderts, Für die Russische Reise Oktober 1958 Dymphna' ('For the revolution of the 20th century. For the Russian journey October 1958 – Dymphna'). Clark's inscription to Dymphna can be found in the paperback edition of his *Sources of Australian History* (1957).

5 Sebastian Clark to me, Canberra, March 2009; Axel Clark, interviewed by Susan Marsden (NLA), and Benedict Clark to me, Phillip Island, April 2008; the figures on Clark's library are drawn from a three-page typed document in the papers of Dymphna Clark, MS 9873, box 28, 'Personal Documents and papers, 1979–2000'.

6 For *Volume V*, Clark re-read *Crime and Punishment* (trans. & ed. David Magarshack, Penguin, Harmondsworth, 1972).

7 I found these typed notes in a yellow folder labelled 'Sources of ideas' in Clark's study; interview with Tennessee Williams, published in *Theatre Arts*, January 1962, quote from Albert Schweitzer's biography of Bach (Harper, New York, 1947), p. 145; Ibsen quote in the Penguin edition of three plays (*Hedda Gabler, The Pillars of the Community* and *The Wild Duck*) 1972, p. 156; Chekhov quote in the Penguin edition of Chekhov's Plays 1971, p. 181, all in Clark's study.

8 See Clark's copies of *Crime and Punishment* (Penguin, 1972) and *The Idiot* (Stockholm, 1938).

9 In August 1990, Katerina gave Clark *Selected Letters of Fyodor Dostoevsky* (edited by Joseph Frank & David I Goldstein and published by Rutgers University Press, New Brunswick, 1987); although Clark did not mark this passage until the last year of his life, he had already read several editions of Dostoyevsky's letters beforehand; earlier editions were published in English in 1914, 1917, 1923 and 1962; for Dostoyevsky's plans for epic legends see Dostoyevsky (in Florence) to AN Maikov, 1869 (pp. 306–15), Dostoyevsky to Anya, 24 July 1876 & Anya's reply, quoted by Frank (pp. 439–42); in Clark's copy of *The Possessed*, Modern Library, New York, 1963, is a folded piece of A4 paper on which Clark (or his research assistant) typed the quote from Dostoyevsky on the central question of faith.

10 Dostoyevsky to MN Katrov from Dresden, 8 October 1870, in Frank & Goldstein (eds), *Selected Letters of Fyodor Dostoevsky*, pp. 340–2, and Dostoyevsky to AN Maikov, 1869, p. 310.

11 Dostoyevsky to Maikov, 1869; Frank & Goldstein (eds), pp. 307–8.

18: The Historian

1 DH Lawrence, 'Spirit of Place', *Studies in Classic American Literature*, Penguin, 2007 (first published 1923), p. 7.

2 Pierre Loti, *Constantinople in 1890*, trans. David Ball, Unlem, Istanbul, 2005, pp. 25 & 45; for 'historical melancholy', also see Frederico Garcia Lorca, *Selected Letters*, New Directions, New York, 1983, especially Lorca to Ana Maria Dali, from Huerta de San Vicente, his family's house on the outskirts of Granada, August 1927, p. 113 (also see p. 90, 'Granada, definitely, is not pictorial, not even for an impressionist ... everything runs, plays and escapes. Poetic and musical. A city of grays without a skeleton. A vertebrate melancholy').

3 There are many descriptions of Australia as a country 'without history'. I have drawn on the official souvenir of the visit of Princes Albert Victor and George to Queensland in 1881 (Manuscripts, State Library of Victoria), which emphasised that the Princes were visiting a country 'just emerging from Aboriginal savagery', where 'all was waste and barbarous ... these colonies have no history'.

4 On the extra terror of death in the Australian outback, see the journals of Ernest Giles, April 1874, in Kathleen Fitzpatrick (ed.) *Australian Explorers: a selection from their writings*, Oxford World's Classics, London, 1959 (first published 1958), pp. 466 & 474.

5 In his poem 'Ascent into Hell' (1955), in which Hope reflected on his childhood in Tasmania, he asked: 'Who are we, stranger? What are we doing here?' Judith Wright, in her poem 'At Cooloolah' (1955), saw herself as a stranger: 'but I'm a stranger, come of a conquering people'; Patrick White, in a short article, 'The Prodigal Son' (1958), tried to explain his motivation for writing in Australia: 'I wanted to discover the extraordinary behind the ordinary, the mystery and the poetry which alone could make bearable the lives of [ordinary people]'; all these can be found in Nicholas Jose

(general editor), *Macquarie PEN Anthology of Australian Literature*, Allen & Unwin, Sydney, 2009, pp. 526, 596 & 559 respectively; Clark's question can be found in his 1967 interview with Hazel de Berg, NLA.

6 Clark's comment on Australia's lack of history, diary, 7 May 1961; his description of Australia can be found in Clark, *A History, Volume IV*, p. 2; Thomas Keneally to me, September 2007.

7 Clark, interviewed on Darwin's 8TOPFM 1987, cassette courtesy of Manning Clark House; Dymphna Clark to me, October 1999.

8 Clark, diary, 24 January 1962 ('union with God'); on Clark's depression, diary, 15 & 18 July 1962, May 1963; on playing Bach, diary, 13 April 1965; on despair, diary, 9 July 1961, & Clark to Christesen, 11 March 1963, Meanjin Archives, Archives Melbourne University, box 7.

9 On blood not ink, Clark, notes for a graduation ceremony talk, University of Melbourne, 21 December 1974, in his papers, box 40, folder 27; on the times suiting him, see his interview with Don Baker, NLA; Clark's views on history were similar to those of Thomas Carlyle, 'A man lives by believing something; not by debating and arguing about many things' (Carlyle, *Selected Writings*, edited by Alan Shelston, Penguin, Harmondsworth, 1986, p. 253). In his essay 'On History', first published 1830, pp. 55–8, he distinguished between the artist historian and the artisan historian: the artisan had no 'eye for the Whole ... not feeling that there is a Whole', whereas the artist historian could see 'the Infinite in man's Life' and the rest were merely 'instructive gazetteers'.

10 On the pubescence of Australian culture, see Ian Mair, reviewing *Australian Civilization*, in *Age*, 7 July 1962; comments by US academic Norman Mackenzie in *Pacific Historical Review*, vol. XXXIII, no. 2, May 1964, p. 250, below Norman Harper's review of Clark's *A History, Volume I*; VS Naipul, 'The Long Way Round', *Guardian*, 10 March 2007; *AA Phillips on the Cultural Cringe*, MUP, Carlton, Vic., 2006 (essay first published in *Meanjin*, 1950).

11 Pringle to Clark, 25 January 1963, Clark, papers, box 5, folder 36; Donald Horne, *The Lucky Country*, Penguin, Ringwood, Vic., 1986 (1964), pp. 22–4 & 216; Geoff Serle, 'Some Stirrers and Shakers of the 1950s and 1960s', *Overland*, no. 128, Spring 1992, pp. 16–21; Dutton to Clark, 7 November 1961 & 16 May 1962, Clark, papers, box 22, folder 1; details of television series in box 4, folder 32 (Russel Ward and Michael Roe also worked on the series).

12 Clark's article appeared in *The Observer*, 4 April 1963; also in his papers, box 5, folder 36.

13 Dymphna's pressed flower is in Clark, papers, box 156, folder 4; on event publications, see Stuart Sayers' review of Volume I, *Age Literary Supplement*, 8 September 1962, p. 17; on Clark's desire for a party, see Peter Ryan to William Macmahon Ball, 10 July 1962, MUP editorial files, box 20, Melbourne University Archives; also CB Schedvin, 'Manning Clark's Image of Man', in Peter Munz et al., *Australia 1888*, Bulletin No. 3, December 1979, p. 28.

14 Peter Coleman to me, Sydney, October, 2008; Hancock to Clark, Clark, papers, box 156, folder 'Vol. One Correspondence 1960–1967 (i)'; in the same folder, see Ryan to Clark, telegram 13 September 1962, 'Congratulations virtually sold out'; also Gwyn James to Clark, 20 August 1962, private letter, refers to MUP's 'damned stupidity' in doing an initial print run of only 2000; see the review of Volume I in *The Economist*, 8 June 1963; also John Arnold, *Australian History in Print: a bibliographical survey of influential twentieth century texts*, available at www.dest.gov.au. Clark chose to publish with MUP largely on sentimental grounds, Clark to George Ferguson, 13 January 1961, 'it is a work which is appropriate for a University press, and partly on the sentimental ground that Melbourne was the place where the passion for these things was first conceived'; the point about 'interpretative essays, first made by Bede Nairn, 'Writing Australian History', *Manna*, no. 6, 1963, pp. 107–31.

15 Peter Coleman to me, Sydney, October 2008; also Peter Coleman, *Australian Civilization: a symposium*, FW Cheshire, Sydney, 1962, especially Coleman's introduction and Clark's essay 'Faith'.

16 Clark, notebook, 9 January 1956; Menzies statement told to Clark by Richard Woolcott, see Clark, diary, 26 July 1955.

17 Gwyn James to Clark, 30 May 1962, & James McAuley to Clark, 28 October 1960, Clark, papers, box 156, folder 1; Bruce Grant to me, Melbourne, March 2007; on Manly ferry and assassins, Clark, diary, 23 August & 7 September 1962; on amendments, Clark to Gwyn James, 16 December 1960, MUP editorial files, box 20, 'Clark History of Australia Vol.1', Melbourne University Archives.

18 On undermining his deepest self, Clark to Dymphna, undated, but 1967, held at Manning Clark House; John Manning Ward to Keith Hancock, 25 August 1963, in Ward's papers, box 13, General Correspondence, Sydney University Archives; also Alan McBriar to Clark, 4 October 1955, in Clark, papers, box 54, folder 25; Lyndall Ryan to me, Canberra, August 2009; Gwyn James to Clark, 27 January 1961, Clark papers, box 156, folder 2; Australian historian, John Mulvaney, explained to me in Canberra, in January 2008, that Clark's interpretation of Australia's 'prehistory' in the first chapter of Volume I relied heavily on the work of anthropologist J Birdsell (nearly two decades old by the time Volume I was published), which was already out of date in 1962. Clark later acknowledged the fact; see Clark to Ryan, 21 July 1969, asking Ryan to let him change the first two or three pages of Volume I: 'research on the pre-history of Australia has now established pretty clearly that the view held when I wrote Volume I is wrong', Clark, papers, box 156, folder 9 (he had made allowance already for these changes in the *Short History*); Clark's *A History of Australia, Volume I* shared the Ernest Scott Prize with Geoff Serle's *The Golden Age*; all other references are to Volume I of Clark's *A History of Australia*.

19 Ann Moyal on Ellis in her unpublished paper, The Establishment Era, ANU, 2 December 2009; also Moyal's *Breakfast with Beaverbrook: memoirs of an independent woman*, Hale & Iremonger, Sydney, 1995, pp. 137–49; Ellis review, 'History Without Facts' (a headline devised by Associate Editor Peter Coleman), in *Bulletin*, 22 September 1962; also see Andrew Moore, '"History Without Facts": MH Ellis, Manning Clark and the Origins of the Australian Dictionary of Biography', *Journal of the Royal Historical Society*, vol. 85, part 2, December 1999, pp. 71–84; Stuart Sayers' review in *Age*, 8 September 1962; Clark's response, diary, 7 September 1962; and on Ellis, diary, 23 September 1962; Ryan tried to buoy Clark (Ryan to Clark, 18 April 1963) after Clark told him of his depression at the reviews: 'It upsets me that you should be so affected by a few reviews which so patently have sour grapes festooned all over them. Vol.1 is the first installment of a work which none of those who talk so big have had the spirit even to attempt. You ought to feel great satisfaction that so many thousands of people are reading your work with such interest and pleasure', Clark, papers, box 156, folder 3.

20 Crawford to Clark, 25 September 1962, in Clark, papers, box 156, folder 2; Dymphna's memories to Elizabeth Cham (NLA); also Ellis to Hancock, 7 June 1963 (Ellis resigned the previous day), Clark, papers, box 156, folder 3; and Ellis, 'Why I have resigned', *Bulletin*, 15 June 1963, p. 25. Clark's support for Ellis pre-1962 can be found in his letters to Ellis, 9 April 1953 (inviting him to deliver a paper at ANZAAS), 10 August 1955 (praising his biography of John Macarthur) and 12 February 1956 (congratulating him on his CMG), all in Malcolm Ellis papers, Mitchell Library, MLMSS 1712; see also Clark's review of Ellis's Macarthur, in *Age*, 1 October 1955. Ellis reviewed Clark's *Select Documents* favourably too: *Bulletin*, 13 April 1955, p. 2; predictably, Ellis looked on Clark's early work on documents as the right kind of history; his own approach to biography, for example, contrasted sharply with Clark's ideas of character portrayal; 'biography', said Ellis, is basically factual—facts, more facts and again facts are the secret of ... the truth about your man'; see Ellis, 'the Writing of Australian Biographies', *Historical Studies* (Australia and New Zealand), vol. 26, no. 24, May 1955, pp. 432–46 (p. 444); on Ellis and Clark not being in the same room together, Margaret Steven to me, phone conversation, April 2008; for Clark's response, see his diary, 23 September 1962.

Clark on Hancock and Ellis and his disappointment with the *ADB*, diary, 11 July 1960. Clark lamented that 'after six years of work' he had been asked to write only one entry for the *ADB*. 'Ellis got what he wanted by a tantrum—not by explaining what he wanted—the innocent were rejected—men of no account—the wicked rewarded; also Clark, papers, box 5, folder 35, 'Correspondence 1962 (i)', general editor of the *ADB*, Douglas Pike, to Clark, 26 March 1962, letting him know that the editorial board of the *ADB* accepted his resignation as editor of Volume 2 on 14 March 1962; also Clark, papers, box 156, folder 3. Ellis had formally resigned as section editor of volumes 1 and 2 of the *ADB* in 1962, and from the National Committee on 6 June 1963. Pike, in June 1963, wrote to Ellis saying that the editorial board of the *ADB* 'does not accept your account of the circumstances leading to your resignation. It considers that your letter of 7th June [i.e. the allegations Ellis had made against Clark] is defamatory'. AGL Shaw was appointed as Section editor for the period 1788–1825, although in the editorial board minutes of the meeting held on 14 March 1962 item 7, regarding Clark's resignation. It was decided that 'Professor Clark will retain his seat as a foundation member of the Editorial Board' and 'It was noted that in view of the stage already reached the volume already carried the imprint of Professor Clark's editorship, and this should be born[e] in mind in considering a new appointment. It was also suggested that Professor Clark's share in the volume should be appropriately recorded on the title page.' For Clark's view, see Clark, *A Historian's Apprenticeship*, 1992, pp. 8–9.

21 Geoff Serle to Clark, 24 September 1962, Clark, papers, box 156, folder 2.

22 Clark's efforts to persuade Fitzgerald to drop the review draw on a conversation between Fitzgerald and Ken Inglis, Inglis to me, Canberra, March 2005; McManners to Clark, 3, 8 & 15 October 1962, Clark, papers, box 156, folder 2 (McManners occasionally quotes Clark's words back to him); Clark's stereotyping of Catholic and Protestant traditions was already evident in his essay, 'Melbourne an Historical Tradition', *Melbourne Historical Journal*, no. 2, 1962, pp. 17–23, see especially p. 18.

23 McManners to Clark, 15 October 1962, Clark, papers, box 156, folder 2; originally, Clark wrote to Fitzgerald, suggesting *Nation* review Volume I; see, in same folder, Tom Fitzgerald to Clark, 1 August 1962, 'I have heard about you lately from Ken Inglis ... I will certainly be looking forward eagerly to reading it but as you know I am no historian and I think it would be pretty presumptuous of me to try to tackle it'; the review and letter appear in *Nation*, 20 October 1962.

24 Ryan to Clark, 21 December 1962, Clark, papers, box 156, folder 2; Michael Roe's review appeared in the Summer edition of *Quadrant*, 1962.

25 Shaw to Ward, 10 September 1963, John Manning Ward papers, box 4, University of Sydney Archives. I am grateful to Peter Coleman for his colourful descriptions of the seminar; Forsyth's criticisms of Volume I were listed in the *Bulletin*, 3 November 1962 (letters); also see Forsyth's papers, held in the Mitchell Library, which contain one folder devoted to Clark's errors and related correspondence; the transcript of the seminar appears in *Speaking Out of Turn*, pp. 57–63; Shaw's review of Volume I in *Meanjin*, vol. 22, no. 1, 1963, pp. 117–19; another seminar on Volume I was held at the ANU; Margaret Steven to me April 2008: 'After the Ellis attack, Hancock organised a seminar in Seminar room D, in the History Department corridor, in order for Manning to defend himself. Manning sat and spoke, while Hancock said a few words. Hancock was concerned about the Ellis attack, and its wider impact beyond Manning. He'd worked hard to bring the two history departments together and to reinforce the stability of Australian history. As for the seminar it was stiff with embarrassment, Manning was very earnest, and there was an obvious discomfort and tension in his voice. He didn't quite pull it off, he wasn't very convincing although he did speak for a long time and there were not many questions.'

26 Clark on Mann, diary, 9 February 1964; Clark's unending grievance over critical reviews in Clark to Ryan, 9 April 1963, in Russell, *Ever, Manning*, p. 190; to Dymphna & Axel, 1 & 5 July 1964, pp. 214–15; on Clark's journey to the USA in late 1963, see his diary (1960–1967), September–December 1963; I am grateful to Jan Nicholas, who passed on Dymphna's recollections of the trip which were drawn from an interview she recorded with Dymphna on 29 November 1995 and correspondence from Dymphna to Jan Nicholas, 22 August 1998; Jan alerted me to Faulkner's car, which she sourced in Jay Parini, *One Matchless life: a life of William Faulkner*, HarperCollins, New York, 2004, p. 418. AGL Shaw, 'Manning Clark's History of Australia', *Meanjin*, 1968, pp. 74–81, on p. 81, Shaw, quoting from the dust jacket of Volume II, 'I would doubt if it will become "the standard and definitive treatment of the subject for it is too much tied to a philosophy of life" which many readers will reject'. For reviews of Volume I, see the following: Russel Ward in *Sydney Morning Herald*, 20 October 1962; Bede Nairn, 'Writing Australian History', *Manna*, no. 6, 1963, pp. 107–31 (defends Clark); Lloyd Churchward, in *Guardian*, 18 October 1962, p. 4, points out that Clark views Australian history 'in the context of world history' and, as a Marxist, he is disappointed in Clark's lack of social and class analysis; Robin Winks in *American Historical Review*, July 1964, 'one of the truly major contributions to Australian historiography'; George Rude in *Historical Studies, Australia and New Zealand*, vol. 10, no. 40, May 1963, pp. 525–7, 'the book opens up new fields of vision and perception in Australian history'; Patrick O'Farrell in *Irish*

Historical Studies, March 1966, praises it as a 'major achievement' giving Australian history 'a new dimension and stature'; Ian Turner, *Overland*, no. 24, September 1962, 'a history rich with passion and compassion', new focus on ideology, 'this book is an action which demands a response'; *Canadian Historical Review*, June 1965, 'added a new dimension to Australian historiography'; widely and positively reviewed in American academic journals, *Virginia Quarterly Review*, Winter 1963–64, and the *American Academy of Political and Social Science*, The Annals, Jan. 1964, *Yale Review*, Winter 64; OHK Spate in *Australian Journal of Politics and History*, November 1963, 'elements of greatness ... for the first time we have a full-scale history of Australia lifted above the level of the annals. Clark pictures all his people, all the time, as wrought up to a state of moral hypertension ... [and] this gloomy, almost masochistic, sense of strain, expressed now and then in rhetorical over-writing, is a serious weakness ... But above all we have here a book which combines amplitude of treatment with a philosophy of life.'

27 On 'alterations', Clark to Ryan, 1 May 1963 (MUP archives, Melbourne University); for Clark taking notice of his critics see same: 'You will notice there are twenty alterations. They come from checking the points made by Ellis & Forsyth, and from points made in letters to me by people such as Michael Roe'; Clark on the pleasure of peer recognition, diary, 11 February 1964; also Clark to Crawford, 14 June 1963, in Russell (ed.), *Ever, Manning*, pp. 191–2; Clark to Dymphna, 1 July 1964, in Russell (ed.), *Ever, Manning*, pp. 214–15; Clark's caricatures, see Clark to Ryan, 9 April 1963, in Russell (ed.), *Ever, Manning*, p. 190.

28 Clark's visit to Ellis on his deathbed, Ann Moyal to Jan Nicholas, 28 October 1995; also see Clark's generous obituary in *Australian*, 20 January 1969, p. 3; John Legge to me, Melbourne, November 2006; Bob Reece to me; Manning Clark House, Canberra, August 2005.

29 Clark's comments on history as entertainment from his speech at the NSW Premier's Literary Awards Dinner, 3 September 1984. Clark had won the first award, given in 1979. Clark, papers, box 39, folder 16, 'Correspondence Jan–Dec 72'.

30 Ryan to Clark, 22 August 1968; also see Clark to Ryan, 5 September 1968: to this letter, Ryan attached an internal memo regarding Cassells, MUP Archives, University of Melbourne (Folder, 'Clark, Volume II').

31 'Tidy little earner', Peter Ryan to me, phone conversation, May 2007; on other historians and Clark, see the chapters by John Hirst, Stuart Macintyre and Alan Atkinson in Bridge, *Manning Clark*; 'lonely furrow', Geoffrey Blainey, reviewing Clark's *A Historian's Apprenticeship* (1992), *Weekend Australian*, 17–18 October 1992; also see Humphrey McQueen, 'The Old Dead Tree and the young tree green', review of Volume VI, in *Continuum: The Australian Journal of Media & Culture*, vol. 1, no. 2, 1987; trendies, comment made by Clark, in his 1990 interview with Mark O'Connor, courtesy Mark O'Connor; Russel Ward's review in *Sydney Morning Herald*, 20 October 1962; also see Clark, papers, box 38, folder 7. On 25 June 1969, Clark received a letter from FD McCarthy, principal of the Australian Institute of Aboriginal Studies, ACT, asking him to supply a list of any work being undertaken in his department on Aboriginal Studies. He replied on 27 June 1969, 'the only work which has been done in this department at the moment is the work done by myself as part of 'A History of Australia 1838–1854'.

32 AGL Shaw to me, Melbourne, June 2005; Robin Gollan to me, 3 April 2005; Katerina Clark to me, Wapengo, March 2006; the La Nauze comment, Carl Bridge to me, Canberra, April 2009 (this comment has become part of academic folklore in the historical profession). John Molony did not read Clark's volumes, and after reading the *Short History* as part of his preparation for the course he taught with Clark in 1971, he found so many mistakes, especially in New South Wales history, that he was not encouraged to pick up Clark again. John Molony to me, Canberra, September 2006.

33 Reviews, see Max Crawford in *Australian Book Review*, November 1962, p. 7; also reviews of Volume II in *News Weekly*, 12 June 1968; *Sydney Morning Herald*, 15 May 1968; and Geoffrey Serle's review of Volume III in *Meanjin*, vol. 38, no. 1, Autumn 1974, pp. 86–8; Helen Garner to me, Melbourne, June 2008; Philip Ingamells to me, Melbourne, February 2008.

34 Clark, *A History, Volume II*, p. 111; 'big with Arthur', Clark, diary, 19 December 1965; history in his veins, Clark, Boyer Lectures 1976, reprinted in Clark, *Occasional Writings and Speeches*, 1980, p. 36.

35 Clark on Hargraves, *A History, Volume IV*, p. 3; on Bligh, Volume I, p. 210; on the Derwent, Volume II, p. 149; on Thomson, Lyndall Ryan to me, Canberra, August 2008.

36 Clark, *A History*: golden Sunday, Volume I, p. 81; Macquarie, Volume I, p. 379; tiger tiger, Volume II, p. 148; all creatures, p. 160; heart dampeners, Volume III, p. 17; bitch goddess, p. 19, Parkes, Volume IV, p. 97; and for Messiah-like conclusions see the epilogue of Volume I and every volume thereafter; reviews of Volume I, see note 26; 'passion packed pages', Clark to Ryan, 3 August 1968, University of Melbourne archives, MUP file, Clark, *History*, Vol. II.

37 EM Forster, *Aspects of the Novel*, Penguin, Ringwood, Vic., 1974 (first published 1927), p. 122; Clark on women in the bush, *Volume IV*, pp. 178–9; on Sarah Cox, *Volume II*, p. 93; 'you mark my words boy', Clark, *Puzzles*, p. 145; Michael Cathcart to me, Melbourne, June 2008.

38 Clark on his own method, in his 1967 interview with Hazel de Berg, NLA; on the historian staying out of the way, see his interview with David Fitzpatrick, *Melbourne University Magazine*, 69, 1969.

39 'My lord Bathurst', Clark, *A History, Volume I*, p. 376; Hancock to Clark, 4 May 1968, Clark, papers, box 156, folder 9; Ken Inglis, notes on Clark's obituary.

40 On Clark's polyvocal writing, see Peter Craven, 'A Man of Contradictions', *Australian Book Review*, August 1999, available online at htpp://home.vicnet.au/abr. Edmund Campion was probably the first to compare Clark's work to an oratorio; see his 'Manning Clark', *Scripsi*, vol. 5, no. 2, 1989, pp. 183–7; also see Clark on the voices in his mind, in his contribution to Clark et al., *Making History*, 1985, pp. 60–1.

41 AGL Shaw to me; Melbourne, December 2008; Bram's memo to Ryan, 13 November 1974, MUP Archives.

42 Clark, diary, 30 June 1963.

43 *Pix*, 25 January 1964, p. 1, and 1 February 1964, p. 29; for reviews of the *Short History*, see Kenneth Slessor's glowing review in *Daily Telegraph*, 30 May 1970, p. 15; Bede Nairn's review in *Bulletin*, 8 February 1964, and Malcolm Ellis in same; praised in the *Times Literary Supplement*, 24 December 1964, p. 1157; Clark on the writing of *A Short History of Australia* in his interview with Don Baker, NLA; Clark received $1000 from the New American Library, see letter from NAL to Clark in his papers, box 56, folder 7, which also includes a wonderful letter from Edgar Walters of Glebe, whose grandfather was a pioneer in the Richmond district and told him stories as a child. After reading the *Short History*, Walters told Clark 'you're the only Australian historian who writes about Australia's past as well as my grandfather talked about it'. In Clark's papers, box 195, folder 1, is a letter from Clark to Dymphna, 12 December 1975, 'since 1963 the gross sales of *A Short History of Australia* are 204,515'.

44 Ryan to Clark, 3 January 1966, Clark, papers, box 156, folder 2; Dymphna's recollections to Heather Rusden, NLA interview; 'my mistake to begin', Clark to Ryan, 10 March 1967, MUP Archives; Ryan on setting his watch, Ryan to me, phone conversation, May 2007; Clark on his inability to transcribe accurately, diary, 30 March 1967.

45 Dymphna on the details of her editing to Bill Bunbury, ABC RN interview and to Heather Rusden, NLA interview, Clark complaining about Dymphna's indifference to his work, diary, 21 February & 3 April 1966.

46 Clark arguing there is little difference between history and fiction, in his 1967 NLA interview with Hazel de Berg; also see Clark's Boyer lectures (Clark, *A Discovery of Australia*, 1976, p. 45): '[The historian] cannot invent facts, or put into the mouths of characters words which they never used. If he does, he slides into fiction or imaginative biography'; Shaw on Clark's mistakes, see his letter to John Manning Ward, 7 November 1962, also see Ward's comments in his letter to AGL Shaw, 15 September 1963, both Sydney University Archives, papers of JM Ward, box 4; Humphrey McQueen to me, Canberra, June 2005. Barry Jones alerted me to the errors in Volume VI, pp. 448–9: re trial of Tiger and 7 Aborigines in May 1934 in Darwin, Clark writes 'the Australian Board of Missions, philanthropists and humanitarians asked that the lives of the eight Aborigines be spared. Vain hope' but Jones checked and found that they were not executed–the sentence was commuted days afterwards–Jones to me, Melbourne, March 2008. Frank Crowley informed me of the errors in relation to Forrest (April 2005). On Marsden, see KJ Cable's review of Volume II in *Australian Economic History Review*, September 1968, pp. 165–6; for an example of Clark's mistakes being

forgiven because of his narrative drive, see the review of Volume II in *Times Literary Supplement*, 2 January 1969, p. 11; for a good example of reviewers focusing on Clark's narrative verve, see *Advertiser*, 16 March 1968, review of Volume II by Brian Dickey.

47 Clark, diary, 23 December 1975 (which includes his later interpolations); Suzanne Welborn to me, phone conversation, July 2010.

48 Clark, notebook, 10 March 1956, Fort George at Madras; Clark, writing ahead to historical societies, see papers, box 37, folder 1, letter to R Kearns, Broken Hill Historical Society, 8 August 1967; also folder 6, Clark to RB Joyce, History UQ, October 1968 & same to Miss M Lukis, State Archives Perth, 17 October 1968, enlisting her services for Perth and surrounds.

49 Lyndall Ryan to me, Canberra, August 2008; Clark to Andrew and Axel, 27 May 1964 & to Dymphna, 1 May 1964; Russell, *Ever, Manning*, pp. 207–9; Bill Gammage to me, Queanbeyan, March 2008; Benedict Clark to me, Phillip Island, April 2008.

50 Clark, *A History, Volume II*, p.1; on Clark's visit to Portsmouth, Clark to Allan Martin, 14 May 1964, Allan Martin papers, box 3, Correspondence from Clark 1954–84, NLA, Clark on Adelphi House and the Thames, diary, no specific date but March 1964.

51 Clark's comments on 'backdrop' in his speech to the NSW Premier's Literary Awards Dinner, 3 September 1984, papers, box 58, folder 7; on Wentworth, diary, 19 February 1964; *Volume II*, p. 45; Joseph Conrad, Author's Note to *Heart of Darkness*, Penguin, Harmondsworth, 1978 (first published 1899), p. 122.

52 Clark on his method with Wentworth, in *A Historian's Apprenticeship*, 1992, p. 65; also see his diary, 24 April 1964 & 27 March 1967; *A History, Volume II*, p. 92; *A History, Volume III*, p. 317; James McAuley introduced Peter Coleman to Clark and Coleman vividly recalls McAuley telling him how much he admired Clark's ability in *Volume I* to write in the style of the characters he was sketching, so engrossed was he that he would take on the personality of the historical actor–Peter Coleman to me, phone conversation, January 2008; McAuley was also attuned to the dangers of Clark's method–see his letter to Clark, 28 October 1960, after reading the draft of *Volume I*: 'The danger of sinking yourself into the style of the period is that you can slide over into pastiche, rhetorical inflation, etc', Clark, papers, box 23, folder 190.

53 Clark driving across the United States, diary, September–December 1963.

54 Clark on Brahms, Bach, Mozart, Handel, diary, 9 February, March (no day), 14 April & 1 July 1964; Clark writing to London regarding recordings of *The Well-Tempered Klavier*, see the letter from Bert York, 21 August 1960, advising Clark to have Tureck's recordings imported to Rowe's of Melbourne or J Stanley Johnstone of Sydney; in Clark, papers, box 5, folder 34, Venice, in Clark, diary, 1964.

55 John Henry Newman, *Apologia*, OUP, Oxford, 1964 (first published 1886), p. 251. Clark later inserted the relevant page numbers: 'p. 251 for vol. 2 (25/11/66) /see pp. 105–6 for Vol. 1)'; on visits to the Prado, see Clark to Geoff Serle, 25 January 1968, papers, box 37, folder 11. The exhibition at the Royal Academy was *Goya and His Times*, Winter, 1963–64. Clark's comments in his diary, 28 February & 6 March 1964, the latter containing his notes for the lecture at the Institute of Commonwealth Studies.

56 Clark, *A History, Volume II*, p. 1.

57 Barry Humphries, *More Please*, Penguin, Ringwood, Vic., 1992, pp. 218–27.

58 I am grateful to Darleen Bungey for passing on Dymphna's recollections; Clark on Humphries, to Axel, 6 April 1964, in Russell, *Ever, Manning*, pp. 205–6, and Clark to Humphries, 5 April 1964, courtesy of Barry Humphries; Clark, diary, 3 March 1964; on Dymphna's reaction, diary, 22 March 1964.

59 Clark on his meeting with Nolan, diary, 8 August 1964; re Nolan at Qantas Building, also see 15 August (Clark was initially puzzled by the Kelly paintings) and his letter to Dymphna, 9 August 1964, in Russell, *Ever, Manning*, pp. 232–3; Nolan, reflecting on Clark's work in 1969, in Nancy Underhill, *Nolan on Nolan: Sidney Nolan in His Own Words*, Penguin, Camberwell, Vic., 2007, p. 314.

60 Clark to White, 8 November 1961 (drafted several times), White's reply, 12 April 1961, also 28 June 1961 & 6 July 1961, White's praise for Volume I, in his letter to Clark, 13 August 1964, all in Clark,

papers, box 25, folder 209; Nolan to Clark, 17 December 1964, Clark, papers, box 24, folder 197; Campbell to Clark, 8 July 1966, Clark, papers, box 6, folder 44; also see Clark's description of his epiphany on meeting White in Sydney in 1959, Clark, *Quest*, 1990, p. 220.

61 Clark, A talk to Victorian Historical Society, 29 September 1967, in *Speaking Out of Turn*, pp. 64–6; Clark to Nolan, 11 September 1967, Clark, papers, box 156, folder 2; Clark on his beloved Burke and Wills, diary, 19 October 1967.

62 Clark at the Nolan exhibition in Sydney, diary, 12 October 1967; Clark to Nolan, 17 October 1967, papers, box 24, folder 197; 'primeval landscape', Nolan interviewed by *The Listener*, 8 October 1964, in *Nolan on Nolan*, p. 290; Clark's comments on Nolan's Gallipoli paintings in a hastily scribbled note, 'Nolan–Gallipoli Yet the spirit of man had prevailed, And in this sublime triumph– were both the dead and the living, those to go, and those to stay eternally on the ravaged coast, all were one and the same–flesh and spirit fused into one unity w. Olympian gods and ancient heroes', papers, box 156, folder 2; on the snake in paradise see Clark, diary, 9 March 1974.

63 Clark in Ireland, visiting Burke's home, diary, 12 November 1973; at Nolan exhibition in Melbourne, Clark, diary, 21 December 1974; Nolan on Burke and Wills, to Dutton, 1967, quoted in TG Rosenthal, *Sidney Nolan*, Thames & Hudson, London, 2002, p. 122.

64 Clark on his budget, diary, 3 August 1975.

65 Drawn from Clark's 1975 diary, dates as shown.

66 Drawn from Clark's chapter on Burke and Wills in *A History, Volume IV*, pp. 144–64.

67 ibid; Ryan to Clark, 15 June 1977, Clark, papers, box 157, folder 16.

68 ibid; Clark, *A History, Volume IV*, 1978.

69 Patrick White, *Voss*, Vintage, Sydney, 1994, first published 1957: p. 33 (Voss: 'I will cross the continent from one end to the other'); p. 35 (Voss: 'in this disturbing country, so far as I have become acquainted with it already, it is possible more easily to discard the inessential and attempt the infinite'.); p. 124 (Voss, heading out from Newcastle remembering his earlier trips inland–'the volcanic silence of solitary travel through infinity'); p. 267 ('an environment so harsh that men's souls were more woundable than flesh'); p. 342 (Voss and the party exhausted, waterless, without hope, 'almost all members of the expedition were so contorted by apprehension, longing, love or disgust, they had become human again'. 'All remembered the face of Christ that they had seen at some point in their lives, either in churches or visions, before retreating from what they had not understood, the paradox of man in Christ, and Christ in man. All were obsessed by what could be the last scene for some of them. They could not advance farther.'); p. 446 (White saw in the land '[release] Of rock and scrub. Of winds curled invisibly in wombs of air. Of thin rivers struggling towards seas of eternity. All flowing and uniting. Over a bed of upturned faces.')

70 Michael Cathcart to me, Melbourne, June 2008; Blainey, 'The Manning Clark School of History', *Scripsi*, vol. 6, no. 2, 1990, p. 65.

19: The Teacher

1 Bill Brown (a student in the class), to me, April 2010.

2 Clark's teaching philosophy in 1940, espoused in a letter to Dymphna, undated, but shortly before Sebastian's birth, held at Manning Clark House; comparing teaching to music, and 'log of wood' in his interview with Daniel Connell, 13 November 1990, ANU Oral History Project, ANU Archives; Clark to staff on teaching, Humphrey McQueen to me, Canberra, March 2009; also see Clark, 'The Teaching of History', in *Speaking Out of Turn*, 1997, pp. 51–7; on teaching as a noble calling, Iain McCalman to me, Sydney, March 2010; other quotes from Clark's address to the NSW Teachers Union on history teaching in schools in Sydney in late 1979, Clark, papers, box 181, folder 33.

3 Ken Inglis, notes on Clark's obituary; Iain McCalman to me, Sydney, March 2010; Bob Reece to me, Canberra, August 2005, and Bob Reece, '"Don't accept any lifts from Professors to Wagga": Some personal recollections of Manning Clark', *AHA Bulletin*, no. 83, 1996, pp. 86–92.

4 Humphrey McQueen to me, phone conversation, June 2008; Jill Waterhouse to me, document, 23 August 2006.

5 Jill Ker Conway to me, phone conversation, May 2008; many historians felt a sense of indebtedness to Clark–Jill Roe, for example, who came to Canberra from Adelaide in the early 1960s to take

up an MA scholarship at the ANU, felt that she owed her opportunity to Clark, Jill Roe to me, phone conversation, April 2010.

6 John Thompson to me, email correspondence, April 2010, Iain McCalman to me, Sydney, March 2010. Russel Ward (in *A Radical life: the autobiography of Russel Ward*, Macmillan, South Melbourne, Vic., 1988, p. 228) describes Clark, on meeting him at ANU in the late 1950s: an 'intensely alive, ruddy-faced man, his scalp balding naturally in the manner of a friar's tonsure ... the first genius I ever met. That is to say that everyone he ever met either admired or hated him. It seemed impossible to dismiss him as boring or irrelevant.'

7 ibid.; also Peter Read to me, Sydney, March 2010, and Ian Britain to me, phone conversation, April 2010.

8 I am grateful to Moira Scollay for sending me her eulogy for Bob Gollan, October 2007; also Jill Waterhouse to me, document, 23 August 2008; Clark's comments on the foetus, Drusilla Modjeska to me, Sydney, June 2007; on women's liberation, Jill Waterhouse; on his support for Women's Studies, Humphrey McQueen to me, Canberra, March 2008.

9 Ann Moyal to me, Canberra, September 2006, and Ann Moyal, *Breakfast with Beaverbrook: memoirs of an independent woman*, Hale & Iremonger, Sydney, 1995, p. 121. Moyal also related to me the story of her mandatory health check in late 1958 before taking up a job at the ANU: 'I was asked by Dr Faunce to take all my clothes off and then hop up on the table, where I lay totally naked for my physical examination. The Doctor's first point of conversation was to ask me about Lord Beaverbrook's sex life'; also David Malouf to me, Sydney, April 2008; Anne Gollan to me, Canberra, August 2007; Verna Coleman to me, Sydney, October 2008; Joan Lemaire's recollections courtesy Jan Nicholas; on women staff at ANU, see Stephen Foster & Margaret Varghese, *The Making of the Australian National University 1946–1996*, Allen & Unwin, Sydney, 1996, p. 325.

10 Clark, diary, 15 December 1954.

11 Clark on flesh off the bone, undated, in his notebook, 18 March 1953–22 June 1954; Clark in seminars, Ken Inglis, notes for Clark's obituary; Clark mocking the divinity of Australian professors, in his correspondence with John Legge; Legge to Clark, 2 April 1963, 'there is only one God Professor, who modesty forbids me to name ... Professor Manning Clark has all the appearances of divinity, and a photograph of him might certainly enhance the quality of your thesis if it were interesting as a frontispiece'. Clark had written to Legge as 'York Harding III', a Fullbright scholar working on a thesis on 'the naming of Australian professors' and their 'divinity'; courtesy John Legge.

12 For an example of theses making news in Canberra, see the *Canberra Times* report of Clark's first MA graduate, Laurie Gardiner, 24 April 1952; Joan Lemaire's memories courtesy Jan Nicholas; also see Foster & Varghese and Clark's interview with Daniel Connell, 13 November 1990, ANU Archives.

13 ibid.; on Clark's initial allergy to Hancock, Bob Gollan to me, document, 3 April 2005; LaNauze's comment was made in 1977 to Paul Turnbull, Turnbull to me, Sydney, December 2009; Clark and LaNauze, Bob Gollan to me, 3 April 2005.

14 Robin Gollan to me, document, 3 April 2005, and phone conversation, April 2005; also Clark with Daniel Connell, 13 November 1990, and Clark, 'Reminiscences', in *ANU Reporter*, 23 May 1980, p. 5; also John Eddy to me, Canberra, September 2006; 'advanced fuckers', Peter Ryan to me, phone conversation, May 2007.

15 On Menzies and the ANU, see Jill Waterhouse, *University House as they Experienced It: a history*, ANU Press, Canberra, 2004, pp. 72–3; on Canberra, Humphrey McQueen to Stephen Foster, 21 February 1994, ANU Archives.

16 On expansion at the ANU, see Foster & Varghese, pp. 197–200; John Molony, 'History Lesson on gifts and legacies lost', *Canberra Times*, 29 November 2008 (op.ed); also Judy Campbell to me, Canberra, March 2008.

17 Humphrey McQueen to me, Canberra, March 2008; also see McQueen's interview with Stephen Foster, 21 February 1994, ANU Oral History Project, ANU Archives; on Crawford and Melbourne, John Eddy to me, Canberra, September 2006. Eddy also stressed the importance of personal tuition cultivated within Crawford's department, which Clark carried on in Canberra, a feature

made possible (until the mid-1960s at least) by the relatively small number of students.

18 ibid.; on Inglis, see Clark to Hancock, undated but 1962, Clark, papers, box 5, folder 32; also John Molony to me, Canberra, September 2006, and Iain McCalman to me, Sydney, March 2009; also James Griffin to me, Canberra, November 2007 (Griffin was Senior History Master at Xavier College in Melbourne in the 1960s): 'I get a note from Manning saying he'd like to talk to me. He was interested in employing me in Canberra as a first year lecturer and tutor ... Over lunch, I explained that with 5 children and a house in Melbourne which Xavier had bought for me, I was reluctant to move the family to Canberra and look for rental accommodation. I had no money at all. "Don't worry," said Manning, "we'll make you a senior lecturer." But I only had one degree and I had no publications, and the last thing I wanted was to cause hostility in Canberra because Manning had favoured me over others. I thought that he only really wanted me because I was a Catholic. I'd written some fiery editorials for the *Catholic Worker* and he no doubt thought my presence would counter that of the communists like Gollan.'

19 Shirley Bradley to me, Canberra, May 2008, and Pat White to me, Canberra, May 2008.

20 Bid Williams to me, phone conversation, September 2007. Bid came with her husband Mick Williams from Armidale in 1967, 'after Manning talked him into accepting the appointment as chair of history at the ANU, promising Mick, who had carried the administration at Armidale and was now keen to do some research and writing, that he would not be burdened with administration at the ANU'. 'When they arrived in January 67, Canberra, with its customary summer atmosphere, was a ghost town, everyone it seemed, including Manning, was down at the coast, and Mick was immediately saddled with the administrational duties, delegated by force and it never changed in all the years he was there. Manning did little of it.' Clark also clashed with Eric Fry, who arrived in the department in the late 1960s, largely over his unorthodox approach to administration; see McQueen's interview with Foster, p. 9, details in note 21.

21 Frank Crowley to me, document, 14 April 2005; David Carment to me, email correspondence, November 2007; Ken Inglis, notes for Clark's obituary; also Humphrey McQueen's interview with Stephen Foster, 21 February 1994, ANU Oral History Project, ANU Archive.

22 This paragraph is built on the recollections of all those I have spoken to about social gatherings at Tasmania Circle. I have heard so much about them that I feel I must have been there myself.

23 Helen Garner to me, Melbourne, June 2008; Tom Keneally to me, phone conversation, October 2009; Alex Miller to me, Canberra, October 2009; also see Christopher Koch to Clark, 18 May 1965, 'I was surprised and moved to receive your letter; no one has ever written me such a letter before. It happens that praise from you is particularly gratifying for me—I recently finished your history of Australia, and I was filled with admiration for the quality of your writing ... Certainly I need responses like yours at the moment, having been butchered in last Saturday's "Herald"!'

24 Bob Reece, 'Don't accept any lifts from Professors to Wagga', p. 92; Iain McCalman to me, Sydney, March 2010; on the child in Clark, Ian Hancock to me, Canberra, December 2007; letter from George Virtue, 3 March 1991, can be found in Clark, papers, box 176, folder 26; Clark's letter to Jill Roe, 24 December 1968, in his papers, box 38, folder 8; to Susan Magarey (Eade), 13 December 1968, box 38, folder 6; in a similar vein, see Clark to Allan Martin, 10 February 1954, 'This is to tell you how much I have enjoyed and learnt from your thesis. It is one of the few genuine contributions to the understanding of Australian history I have read in recent years', Allan Martin papers NLA, MS 9802, box 3, Correspondence from Clark 1954–84. Peter Corris was another writer who was encouraged and inspired by Clark; see Clark's letters to Corris in Corris, papers, box 18, 1972–1990, Mitchell Library; also see Clark, papers, box 156, folder 2, Geoffrey Fairbairn to Clark, 30 August 1962. Fairbairn, an ex-student of Clark's at Geelong, was employed in Politics at the ANU. 'I first became interested in history as a way of understanding the human condition under your guidance at Geelong. Since then we have had serious disagreements about the significance of modern historical developments; in some ways we still do, I suppose, though nothing like the extent you sometimes pretend to believe—I reckon we loathe the society in which we live with equal intensity... It is a result of your teaching, your friendship, your encouragement, in part even as a result of your deep-felt & movingly expressed pain, that I am at Canberra now...'

1   Clark to Axel Clark, 5 July 1964, in Russell (ed.), *Ever, Manning*, p. 215, and Clark on women, 7 April 1972; the typescript is held in his papers, box 40, folder 27.
2   On whipping boys, see Clark to Axel Clark, 5 July 1964, in Russell (ed.), *Ever, Manning*, p. 216.
3   See Clark's letters to Dymphna from Norway in early July 1964, in Russell (ed.), *Ever, Manning*, pp. 216–24.
4   Clark to Dymphna, 12 July 1964, held at Manning Clark House; also see Clark to Dymphna, circa 12–14 July 1964, in Russell (ed.), *Ever, Manning*, p. 224, and all the letters in Note 3.
5   Clark to Dymphna, 21 July 1964, held at Manning Clark House; for Dymphna's 'poignant gratitude' see her aerogram letter to Clark, 15 September 1965, held in Clark, papers, box 195, folder 1.
6   On reading *Brothers*, Clark to Axel, 21 July 1964; also Clark to Dymphna, 27 July & 13 August 1964, Russell (ed.), *Ever, Manning*, pp. 227–8 & 235.
7   Dymphna to Clark, 21 August 1964, in Clark, papers, box 5, folder 39; also Clark to Dymphna, 16, 17 & 18 August 1964, in Russell (ed.), *Ever, Manning*, pp. 237–41.
8   Clark to Dymphna, 20 & 24 August 1964, in Russell (ed.), *Ever, Manning*, pp. 242–4.
9   Dymphna to Clark, 15 September 1965, held in Clark, papers, box 195, folder 1.
10 Clark to Dymphna, undated, 'Wednesday' [1960s], held at Manning Clark House; Helen Garner to me, Melbourne, June 2008; for more examples of Clark's humour see his papers, box 195, folder 1, 'Family correspondence 1958–75', 'A Valedictory address on the Occasion of the Lamentable Departure of D. Clark'.

There once was a lady named Clark,
Whose dwelling resembled the ark,
She had children galore
And friends by the score.
For life, so she said, was a lark.

She's been working for many a day
On Morobe, Madang and Milne Bay
She hunts and she seeks
For Islands and creeks
For remarkably miniscule pay.

When we gather together for tea,
We are always delighted to see
The ale and the cakes
Which she busily bakes.
In phenomenally large quantitee.

We're sorry she feels she must go
We're plunged in an abyss of woe,
We hope and we pray
She'll come back some day
When she's feeling the "knead" of the dough.

11 On *Sehnsucht*, Clark to Dymphna, undated, July 1964, in Russell (ed.), *Ever, Manning*, pp. 217–18; 'in love with the idea of being in love'—a phrase Clark used to describe Geoffrey Fairbairn, in his letter to Dymphna, 17–18 August 1964, in Russell (ed.), *Ever, Manning*, p. 239; Clark's separation of self can be seen best in his letter to Dymphna, 7 July 1964, in Russell, *Ever, Manning*, pp. 216–17; on the wider connotations of *Sehnsucht* and German romanticism, see Maynard Solomon, *Late Beethoven: Music, Thought, Imagination*, University of California Press, 2003, pp. 45–6.
12 Bob Brissenden, *Gough and Johnny Were Lovers*, Penguin, Ringwood, Vic., 1984, p. xii; Roger McDonald on Canberra, *Sydney Morning Herald*, 30 January 1982; Susan Magarey to me, Canberra,

November 2008; Anne Gollan to me, Canberra; Jill Waterhouse to me, Canberra, September 2006.

13 Drusilla Modjeska to me, Sydney, March 2007; Lyndall Ryan to me, Canberra, August 2008; Anne Gollan to me, Canberra, June 2008; Ann Moyal to me, Canberra, November 2008; Eirene Clark, fourth born in her family, recalled a strange comment from Clark in relation to women. Eirene's mother, who had six girls, gave birth to her seventh, a boy, who died shortly after childbirth. It was a breach birth and the child lived for only six hours. When she related this story to Clark, he replied, 'Yes, there are some women who can't produce live boys.'

14 On Dymphna and Canberra society, Jill Waterhouse to me, Canberra, September 2006; Dymphna's unhappiness at parties, Clark, diary, 31 July 1960. Deirdre Morris, who was Clark's research assistant before Susan Magarey, was rumoured to be another of Clark's infatuations. Of Morris, Benedict Clark commented that she was 'very, very friendly with Dad. She was a very attractive girl. When she finished working as Dad's research assistant she gave him her bikini and my Dad used to keep it in the drawer'; Benedict Clark to me, Phillip Island, April 2008.

15 Clark, asking himself if Dymphna really liked him, diary, 19 December 1965; comparing Dymphna's dislike of him to that of her parents, diary, 30 March 1969; for similar comments see diary, 18 November 1968.

16 Bruce Kent's obituary of Daphne Gollan is in *Australian Feminist Studies*, vol. 15, no. 31; letters from Daphne Gollan to Clark are held in the Mitchell Library, Manuscripts, in Gollan's papers (my thanks to the late Arthur Easton for allowing me access to this collection); the letters range over more than a decade, from 1962 to 1973, with some undated. The peak period of contact was from 1967 to 1969; the letters I have drawn on are Clark to Gollan, 27 May 1969, 4 March 1968, 29 August 1967 and undated notes, most on ANU letterhead; otherwise, I have drawn on my conversations with Lyndall Ryan, Canberra, August 2008.

17 Clark's letters to Dymphna and Gollan, in May 1969, appear in Russell (ed.), *Ever, Manning*, conveniently set side by side, pp. 282–305; also see Clark to Dymphna, 17 February 1971, from Hobart, held at Manning Clark House.

18 Clark to Gollan, 12 February 1968, 27 May 1969; Lyndall Ryan to me, Canberra, August 2008.

19 Lyndall Ryan to me, Canberra, August 2008; Clark's note to Susan Magarey, 3 December 1971, and others, especially 1 September 1971 ('for Susan on a strange day'), and his touching thank you letter, 13 March 1972, all courtesy Susan Magarey; on Katerina, see Clark, diary, 27 October 1988; on Benedict, see diary, 12 October 1984.

20 See Clark's letter to Dymphna, 3 & 4 November 1971, in Russell (ed.), *Ever, Manning*, pp. 317–18, where Clark apologises for his behaviour with both Jill Waterhouse and Magarey; also Susan Magarey to me, Canberra, November 2008.

21 For the copy of Clark's newspaper article on women (undated and source unidentified, most likely *Sydney Morning Herald*), and his flippant comment, 9 April 1972, courtesy Susan Magarey; Lyndall Ryan to me, Canberra, August 2008; Clark's letters to Ryan, late 1971 until late 1972, in Russell (ed.), *Ever, Manning*, pp. 320–39.

22 Lyndall Ryan to me, Canberra, August 2008; on Ryan and Clark, see, for example, *Canberra Times*, 15 November 2008; Ryan told the *Canberra Times* on 22 November 2008: 'Let me set the record straight. I did not have an affair with Manning Clark' (these comments were in response to Brian Matthews' reading of the relationship in *Manning Clark: a life*). On Campbell and Clark, Judy Campbell to me, Canberra, March 2008, and Clark to Dymphna, undated, most likely early 1970s, held at Manning Clark House; on Baker and Clark, Pat White to me, Canberra, May 2008.

23 Dymphna's letter to Clark, undated, 'Brisbane', December 1972, held at Manning Clark House; also Lyndall Ryan to me, Canberra, August 2008; and Clark to Ryan, 26 December 1972, in which he tells Ryan of Dymphna's departure and refers to Ryan's phone call to him, and to the fact that she spoke to Dymphna, in Russell (ed.), *Ever, Manning*, p. 339.

24 Dymphna to Clark, undated, 'Brisbane, Thursday', also see 'Brisbane, Wednesday', held at Manning Clark House.

25 Dymphna to Clark, 'Brisbane, Christmas Eve', held at Manning Clark House; John Molony to me, Canberra, September 2006; Benedict Clark to me, Phillip Island, April 2008.

26 On Dymphna's bag being packed, Wilma Robb to me, October 2007; the folder in which Clark placed the letters was held in his study; also Benedict Clark to me, Phillip Island, April 2008.

21: Wapengo

1 Dymphna, interviewed by Elizabeth Cham, NLA; and John Blay to me, Canberra, March 2008.
2 Clark to Axel and Alison Clark, 9 October 1969, in Russell (ed.), *Ever, Manning*, p. 307; also Clark on smoke, in *Bega District News*, 4 September 1981; and Clark on Aboriginal settlement, to Stephen Murray Smith, 5 January 1968, in Russell (ed.), *Ever, Manning*, p. 264.
3 Philip Ingamells to me, Melbourne, February 2008; Ingamells' evidence concurs with the archive—for example, see internal memo from Ryan, 4 August 1982: 'Manning rang to say that he feels Volume 1 rather "short-changes the Aboriginals". He doesn't "want to be thought a trendy", or one of those "penitent white men". But he'd like volume 1 to reflect some of the considerable new knowledge not widely available when vol. 1 appeared. Then he rather backtracked and said that maybe it ought to remain "as is"–a definitive statement of things as he saw them at the time. So his position is not decided ... my own view is that it should stand unaltered, and I will urge him to accept that opinion.' (MUP files, Melbourne University Archives.)
4 Suzanne Foulkes to me, phone conversation, January 2008.
5 Bob Gollan to me, Canberra, August 2007; John Blay to me, Canberra, March 2008.
6 ibid.
7 John Blay to me, Canberra, August 2008.
8 John Blay to me, Canberra, March 2008; Clark to Ryan, 20 February 1987, Clark, papers, box 159, folder 29.
9 Mark O'Connor to me, Canberra, November 2008.
10 Both this unsent letter and Clark's comments on the silence at Wapengo (1 January 1976) can be found in his papers in box 162, 'Short Stories Manuscripts and Typescripts (iii)'; on Clark's idea of the sea as healing, see Melbourne *Herald*, 6 June 1989. For more on Ness, see Matthews, *Manning Clark*, pp. 295–9.

22: The Prophet

1 Francis Bacon, 'Of Praise', *Essays*, Everyman, London, 1994, p. 135.
2 Clark to David Campbell, 18 November 1963, in Russell (ed.), *Ever, Manning*, p. 197; my thanks to Roslyn Russell for alerting me to I Corinthians 13:12.
3 On Clark's health see his papers, box 39, folder 34, 'Yale University Oct 1988 (ii)'. When Clark travelled he carried a letter with him from Marcus Faunce, this one dated 15.9.88: 'Professor Manning Clark has coronary artery disease with stable angina pectoris. He had coronary artery bypass surgery in September 1983'; on Clark's hyper-tension and Dymphna's reaction, Dymphna to Jan Nicholas, 14 August 1993 & 4 November 1995.
4 Ross Fitzgerald to me, Sydney, May 2010; on Clark's old bag of tricks, see Clark to Daphne Gollan, 13 December 1963, in Russell (ed.), *Ever, Manning*, pp. 198–9; Clark pleading for forgiveness, diary, 2 March 1980.
5 Clark on Yeobright to Humphrey McQueen, 16 December 1987, Humphrey McQueen, papers Volume VI NLA (courtesy Humphrey McQueen); Clark's letter was in response to McQueen's review, in which he quoted the passage on Yeobright; see Humphrey McQueen, 'The Old Dead Tree and the Young Tree Green', *Continuum: The Australian Journal of Media & Culture*, vol. 1, no. 2, 1987; for Dostoyevsky's speech see his letter to Anya, Moscow, 8 June 1880, in Clark's papers, box 36, folder 5, 'lectures on Russia'; also Joseph Frank, *Dostoyevsky: a writer in his time* (single volume), Princeton University Press, 2010, p. 760; on Clark's fame also see both *Bulletin* and *Time Australia*, 26 January 1988.
6 Bitch goddess, Clark, diary, 12 October 1984; Thomas Carlyle, 'On History', *Selected Writings*, Alan Shelston (ed.), Penguin, Harmondsworth, 1986, pp. 56–7. There is nothing particularly unusual about historians being active as public figures, most often as a combination of political activist, social commentator and historical authority. In late twentieth-century Australia, Geoffrey Blainey and Henry Reynolds have both played this role, albeit in markedly different

ways. In mid-twentieth-century England, AJP Taylor (1906–1990) was probably Clark's closest equivalent, largely because of his talent as a polemicist and his readiness to embrace the media in order to reach a broad audience. As well as from AJ Toynbeee (1889–1975), Clark also drew inspiration from the likes of GM Trevelyan (1876–1962) who, in the tradition of the great nineteenth-century historians such as Trevelyan's great-uncle, Thomas Babington Macaulay (1800–1859) and Thomas Carlyle (1795–1881), believed that it was the duty of the historian to communicate with the public and to demonstrate history's civic and educational roles. In the United States, the life of the historian Henry Steele Commager (1902–1998) roughly paralleled Clark's; Commager was a prominent critic of McCarthyism and the Vietnam War and–like Toynbee, Trevelyan, and Taylor in England–he appeared frequently in the media, firmly convinced that the historian, perhaps more than any other intellectual, carried a special responsibility to reach the general public. In New Zealand, poet and historian Keith Sinclair (1922–1993) was reminiscent of Clark in his literary aspirations and his staunch nationalism. A friend and correspondent of Clark's, his one-volume history of New Zealand, published in 1957, made a profound impact in New Zealand, similar to that of Clark's *A Short History of Australia*, published in 1963.

7 Heather Rusden to me, Canberra, November 2007; cards from Clark still in her possession.

8 Clark to Barbara Todd, Sandy Bay, Hobart, undated but 1961, in papers, box 5, folder 34, 'Correspondence 1961'; McQueen and Clark, Humphrey McQueen to me, Canberra, June 2005.

9 Clark to Gwen Ellis, 1 March 1969, papers, box 15, folder 122, 'My Great Friends (vi)'; Bid Williams to me, phone conversation, September 2007.

10 Clark to Daphne Gollan, undated note, late 1960s, in Gollan's papers, Mitchell Library (courtesy of the late Arthur Easton); 'trumpeter', Helen Garner to me, Melbourne, June 2008; on Manuka postmaster, Bill Gammage to me, Canberra, March 2008; on Clark and recognising vulnerability in others, Iain McCalman to me, Sydney, March 2010; Clark to Margaret Coen on the death of Douglas Stewart, 19 February 1985, in Douglas Stewart, papers, NLA, MSS5147 Add-on 2077; 'in memory of so much', Sheila Fitzpatrick found this inscription in both her gifted copy of Volume IV, and later in her brother David's copy as well; Shelia Fitzpatrick to me, July 2009; also see La Nauze to Clark, 4 May 1980, in Clark, papers, box 15, folder 122.

11 Edmund Morgan to me, November 2007.

12 John Salmond to me, February 2010.

13 *Times*, 2 April 1964, p. 15; Larkin on Clark, diary, 25 April 1964.

14 On new nationalism, see James Curran & Stuart Ward, *Unknown Nation: Australia after Empire*, MUP, Carlton, Vic., 2010; on *Meanjin* and the new national idea, see for example C Badger, 'In Search of a National Idea', *Meanjin*, vol. 3, no. 3, Summer 1943; in *Australian*, 23 August 1968, he writes an appraisal of the significance of Cook's voyages.

15 Clark, 'Hope from the Bomb', *Nation*, 27 February 1960; on holocausts, Clark to Kenneth Bailey, 16 November 1965, in his papers, box 19, folder 154; on Vietnam, *Australian*, 24 November 1966, p. 10.

16 Clark, draft for speech in his papers, box 40, folder 28, and *The Times*, 23 January 1968.

17 On 'whittling away', see Clark on the new nationalism, interviewed by Kenneth Randall and Alan Rams, *New Accent*, 22 March 1974, pp. 11–14, 23; Clark, 'The Quality of Life in Australia', November 1971, Wagga Wagga Teachers College, Paper No. 10; on Aborigines, *Age*, 5 June 1970, Clark speaks to Melbourne Rotary Club; also Clark in *Sunday Australian*, 29 August 1971.

18 Clark, re Austerlitz and sending Whitlam a donation, Clark to Whitlam, undated but late 1972, in his papers, box 39, folder 16; also Clark to Whitlam, 13 October 1969, box 38, folder 8; also see Clark to Axel Clark, 8 August 1968, in Russell, *Ever, Manning*, p. 277, in which Clark states that he is uninspired by Whitlam Labor and that Jim Cairns might well take over as leader. Clark's special relationship with Whitlam did not develop until after 1972.

19 Whitlam to Clark, 17 January 1974, in Clark, papers, box 157, folder 13; letter, *Sydney Morning Herald*, 23 November 1972.

20 Clark to Jim Cairns, undated but December 1972, in his papers, box 7, folder 52; in the same folder see Clark's letters to Frank Crean and Gordon Bryant; also Clark to Whitlam, 16 July 1973, Clark, papers, box 39, folder 18.

21 Robert Drewe to me, email correspondence, May 2009.

22 Clark, 'Laying the Ghosts', *Australian*, 14 May 1973, p. 2.

23 Coombs to Clark, 22 June 1972, Clark, papers, box 40, folder 27; Clark to Coombs, 5 September 1973, box 20, folder 162; also see Clark to Geoff Serle, 28 March 1973 (box 39, folder 18), in which he lists his associations with government, '1. Consulted by Victorian, New South Wales and Commonwealth governments on National Trust matters. 2. Asked written questions about men governments were thinking of honouring (advice always ignored!) 3. Asked by Dr Coombs to prepare material for McMahon government when the Prime Minister spoke on general Australian questions. Declined to provide material which could be used for political purposes, but provided material for non-party political occasions. (e.g speeches on trips abroad) 4. Member of Australian Literature Board since March 73. 5. Member of National Anthem Committee. All the items above except number four are confidential. I do not mind you saying historians have done that sort of thing, but do not want to be mentioned by name in those contexts. I should add that my contact with Whitlam is close, but that comes from a long association, and a common interest in some things in our past.'

24 Evan Williams to Clark, 23 April 1974, Clark, papers, box 20, folder 162; on the new chapter in Australian history, Whitlam to Clark, 9 April 1974, and Clark's 'Why I will vote', box 20, folder 162; on the decisive moment, Clark, *Sunday Telegraph*, 12 May 1974, p. 17.

25 Clark, interviewed by Douglas Aiton, *Age Saturday Review*, 2 February 1974, p. 9; on Easter, Melbourne *Herald*, 29 April 1974; on Carlton, see Clark in *Age*, 26 September 1981, and his letter to the Carlton Football Club, 16 May 1972, in his papers, box 39, folder 14.

26 Opera House rally, *Sydney Morning Herald*, 14 May 1974, p. 1; Clark, diary, 13 May 1974.

27 White to Clark, undated postcard, probably 1968, Clark, papers, box 25, folder 29; White, accepting his Australia Day award, *Australian*, 26 January 1974; 'go it alone', Clark in *Sunday Telegraph*, 12 May 1974, p. 17; also see Clark to Barry Humphries, 16 October 1972, 'Wake in Fright and Bazza Mackenzie are two things we have to accept as being a mirror of what we are—as what is part of us all. So I hope you will give us some more.'

28 White to Cynthia and Sid Nolan, 3 January 1971, in David Marr (ed.), *Patrick White: letters*, Jonathan Cape, London, 1994, p. 372; also in same, White to Dutton, 20 January 1974, p. 432; Clark to White, 30 October 1970, in papers, box 38, folder 9; on their readings of one another's work, see same and White to Clark, 7 April 1968, in papers, box 25, folder 209; White on Volume III, White to Clark, 3 January 1974, box 157, folder 12; in the same folder, White's teeth falling out and using Clark's work as a pivot in White to Clark, 3 January 1974 (thanking him for the gift of tickets to see *The Magic Flute*).

29 Christesen to Clark, 11 April 1973, Clark, papers, box 19, folder 153; Clark on Humphries, 'The Quest for an Australian National Identity', James Duhig Memorial Lecture, University of Queensland, 6 August 1979; Clark on politicians needing help, *Sunday Australian*, 29 August 1971, p. 11; Freudenberg to Clark, 2 September 1974, copy given to me by Dymphna Clark.

30 Clark's 'The Years of Unleavened Bread' in Clark, *Occasional Writings and Speeches*, 1980, pp. 194–202; see Whitlam to Clark, 12 April 1973 and Clark's reply, 16 April 1973, Clark, papers, box 157, folder 12.

31 Robert Drewe to me, email, May 2009; letters from Bail, Drewe, Bernard Smith, Ruth Park in Clark's papers, box 20, folder 161; letter from Christopher Koch to Clark, 18 May 1965, in box 6, folder 43; Keneally to Clark, 18 May 1968, box 156, folder 9; Clark's correspondence with Peter Craven can be found in the Melbourne University Archives, 'Scripsi', box 7; on Literature Board, David Malouf to me, Sydney, April 2008. In January 1973, Clark was appointed to the Literature Board, see *Launceston Examiner*, 7 May 1973, and *Canberra Times*, 17 February 1973. Clark one also of the judges for the new national anthem (*Australian*, 7 July 1973), was Chair of the USA Bicentenary Advisory Committee (*Canberra Times*, 11 April 1975) and was voted the first president of the National Book Council, in December 1974.

32 Clark to Whitlam, 28 April & 26 June 1975, Clark, papers, box 26, folder 219; Whitlam to Clark, 2 September 1975, box 20, folder 161.

33 Ken Inglis, notes for his obituary of Clark, courtesy Ken Inglis; Clark on revolutionary students, to

Notes

Bruce Hodgins, 9 April 1975, in Clarks, papers, box 40, folder 23; Robert Drewe to me, email, May 2010.

34 Whitlam to Clark, undated, but late December 1975, Clark, papers, box 20, folder 161; Clark, 'Violent Change the next step', *Australian*, 12 November 1975; after the election, Clark in Derby, diary, 13 December 1975; on Old Left v new Left, see Clark to John Molony, 7 November 1984, in Russell (ed.), *Ever, Manning*, p. 444.

35 Clark, *Australian*, 7 January 1976, p. 7; White to Clark, 15 November 1975, in Marr (ed.), *Patrick White: Letters*, Random House, Milsons Point, 1994, p. 465.

36 Clark, 'the Cleansing Fire Speech, 1978', in Clark, *Speaking Out of Turn*, 1997, pp. 30–3 (the draft of his speech, from which he extemporised); also see the report of the speech in *Age*, 10 June 1978, in which he is quoted as predicting a civil war.

37 Clark, *Four Corners*, ABC TV, July 1978; also 'Who Cares? Australians at Risk in the Eighties', Counterpoint Forum speech delivered at Murdoch University, 18 May 1981; White to Dutton, 22 December 1975, in Marr (ed.), *Patrick White: letters*, p. 466.

38 Dostoyevsky to SA Ivanova, from Dresden, 17 August 1870, in Joseph Frank and David I Goldstein (eds), *Selected Letters of Fyodor Dostoevsky*, Rutgers University Press, New Brunswick, 1987, p. 338; on downfall of European civilisation, see Joseph Frank's *Dostoyevsky: a writer in his time*, p. 960; also Glen Mitchell, 'An interview with Professor Manning Clark', *University of Wollongong Historical Journal*, vol. 1, no. 1, March 1975, pp. 65–75, and Clark to Kathleen Fitzpatrick, 17 December 1976, in Davies (ed.), *Dear Kathleen, Dear Manning*, p. 30.

39 Gough Whitlam in *Canberra Times*, 14 October 1981; 'we want Gough', *Age*, 31 January 1978, 'Hellenica', *Sun*, 21 April 1978, p. 19, and Clark, diary, 4 August 1981.

40 Katerina Clark to me, Wapengo, March 2006; Clark, diary, 2 May 1975; letters to Clark can be found in his papers, box 20, folder 164.

41 Clark to Dymphna, 23 April 1976, and Dymphna to Clark, 20 September 1982 (held at Manning Clark House); for Dymphna's recollections, see her interview with Elizabeth Cham (NLA) and with Bill Bunbury (ABC Radio National, June 1998).

42 Max Harris, *Australian*, 25 May 1978, p. 7; 'Sayings of the Year', *Sydney Morning Herald*, 31 December 1977, Clark's cutting in papers, box 20, folder 164; also see folders 165 & 166, and box 181, folders 32–5, the latter containing Clark's undated article for the *Australian* in 1979 on the possible explosion in the Moslem world.

43 Clark's 1976 speech in Clark, *Speaking Out of Turn*, 1997, pp. 27–9; also see Clark's Australia Day speech, reported in the Townsville *Daily Bulletin*, 27 January 1983, and Clark in *Australian*, 13 April 1984; also Clark, 'Are We a Nation of Bastards?', in Clark, *Occasional Writings and Speeches*, 1980, pp. 209–14, first published in *Meanjin* in 1976.

44 *Commonwealth of Australia, Parliamentary Debates*, Senate Daily Hansard, 22 September 1976, p. 808, 23 September, pp. 948–56; the relevant correspondence from Ashbolt and Mackriell, late September and early October 1976, can be found in Clark's papers, box 163, folder 7, and box 164, folders 8 and 9; also see *Sydney Morning Herald*, 6 October 1976, *Australian*, 7 & 13 October 1976; the episode is also covered extensively in Ken Inglis, *This Is the ABC: Australian Broadcasting Commission 1932–1983*, Black Inc, 2006 (first published 2003), pp. 397–9.

45 Clark, *A Discovery of Australia*, 1976, and his comments in *Australian*, 7 October 1976, Melbourne *Herald*, 13 October 1976, p. 3; comments on radio coverage from my memory of the broadcast.

46 White to Ryan, 16 January 1978, and Ryan, memo, 27 March 1975; also Ryan to Sayers, 13 January 1978, and Sayers' reply, 16 January 1978; see the internal memo from Ryan to other MUP staff, undated but late 1976 or early 1977, which reads: 'should be able to get Vol. 4 out by March 78 ... I am assuming that MUP will want to retain this prestigious author in our list, and not sell off paperback rights to another publisher. Macmillan are frantic to get their hands on the paperback, and there is no doubt that we could command a good price from Penguin, as an alternative. But my feeling is that the appeal of our list would be weakened overall if we let this go.' Held in MUP Archives, [Clark's A History of Australia] University of Melbourne.

47 Beverley Kingston's review is in *Weekend Australian Magazine*, p. 3, 25–26 March 1978; best

books in *National Times*, 14–19 February 1977, pp. 18–19; Clark's comments on republican v British Australia, see his Australia Day comments in *Canberra Times*, 26 January 1977, p. 4.

48 For reviews of Volume IV, see Bill Mandle in *Australian Book Review*, June 1978, Weston Bate in *Age*, 4 March 1978, Maurice Dunlevy in *Canberra Times*, 4 March 1978, Stewart Firth, in *Sydney Morning Herald*, 11 March 1978, and Edmund Campion in *Bulletin*, 28 March 1978; also Alan Marshall to Clark, 22 March 1978 and Kathleen Fitzpatrick to Clark, 14 May 1978, both in Clark, papers, box 157, folder 16.

49 Clark on Lawson, diary, 2 October 1973, 21 March 1974, 18 April 1977; also see Brian Matthews on Lawson, in Matthews, *Manning Clark: a life*, chapter 11.

50 *Age*, 20 May 1978 (quoting Roderick's comments) and *Townsville Bulletin*, 20 May 1978; Dorothy Green's review in *Nation Review*, 15–21 June 1978.

51 Dorothy Green to Clark, 21 & 27 February 1980. Clark's replies are undated, see Clark, papers, box 11, folder 87; see the reference to Green's letter to Carrick, 23 September 1976, in box 20, folder 163; White to Clark, 21 May 1978, box 172, folder 23 (includes White's comments on Roderick); Clark's postcard to Campbell, 16 July 1978, box 4, folder 22; Ryan's notes on the phone conversation with Clark, Memo, 17 May 1978, MUP Archives, University of Melbourne.

52 Christesen to Clark, 12 May 1978, Clark, papers, box 157, folder 16; Clark, *In Search of Henry Lawson*, p. 44, sales figures in Ryan's memo to Clark, 17 May 1978, MUP Archives, University of Melbourne, sales figures on *A History of Australia*, Ryan to Stuart Sayers, 16 October 1973, MUP Archives.

53 Clark in Harvard, diary, 14 December 1978, 9 January & 26 February 1979; on the public controversies, see *Sydney Morning Herald* editorial, 22 May 1978, cartoons in *Australian*, 22 May 1978; in same see the article by Bob Ryan, 18 May 1978.

54 Clark, diary, 18 September 1981; also the *Bulletin* quoted in *Australian Playboy*, July 1981, pp. 31–44; also *Sydney Morning Herald* and *Age*, 26 & 27 January 1981.

55 Reviews of Volume V, see Stuart Macintyre, *Age*, 10 October 1981, Donald Horne, *Sydney Morning Herald*, 10 October 1981, Don Watson, *National Times*, 11–17 October 1981, Edmund Campion in *Bulletin*, 20 October 1981, Gough Whitlam, *Canberra Times*, 14 October 1981, Edward Kynaston, *Weekend Australian*, 24–25 October 1981, Samuel McCulloch, *American Journal of Political Science*, vol. 28, no. 3, 1982; Tony Griffiths in *Age Monthly Review*, December 1981/January 1982 (Carroll's response in following issue), Claudio Veliz, 'Bad History', *Quadrant*, May 1982, pp. 21–6; letters in *Australian*, 6–7 & 8 March 1982.

56 Stuart Macintyre, 'Manning Clark and His Critics', *Meanjin*, December 1982, pp. 442–52 (the best overview of reviews of Clark's work).

57 Ryan to Stuart Sayers, 19 June 1981 (MUP Archives); also see Ryan to Clark, 13 January 1987 (box 160, folders 37–9); Clark's gratitude to Ryan, see Clark to Ryan, 8 April 1981 (MUP archives); Ryan on 'the milk cow', Wendy Sutherland to me, phone conversation, January 2008; Ryan on Clark's ubiquity, see Ryan to Clark, 12 February 1978 (Clark, papers, box 157, folders 16–17); on Clark's 'ghastly errors', Ryan to Tim Curnow, 27 April 1983 (MUP Archives).

58 Stuart Sayers to Ryan, 27 July 1981 (MUP Archives); Tony Griffiths' review of Volume V, *Age Literary Review* (monthly), December 1981, p. 21.

59 On Gallipoli, see Clark, *A History of Australia, Volume V*, p. 404; Allan Martin to Peter Ryan, 7 October 1994; Frank Crowley, memo to Brigid Goodwin, 15 July 1997, and sent on to Ryan, both letters in Ryan's papers, NLA, box 12, 'Manning Clark' folders 1994 and 1997.

60 Serle to Clark, undated but 1973, in Clark, papers, box 157, folder 14.

61 Geoffrey Bolton's review appeared in *Australian Book Review*, December 1981, pp. 3–4 ; Margaret Steven to me, phone conversation, April 2008.

62 Anne Gollan to me, Canberra, June 2008.

63 Clark to Lyndall Ryan, in Russell (ed.), *Ever, Manning*, 30 October 1983, p. 439.

64 Clark, diary, 18 September 1981; Dymphna to Clark, 1 November 1981 (Manning Clark House).

65 Clark on Dobrez, diary, 8 & 18 September 1981; Roslyn Russell to me, Canberra, March 2008.

66 Dymphna's note held at Manning Clark House; Roslyn Russell to me, Canberra, March 2008.

67 Dymphna to Clark, undated but late September 1982 (Manning Clark House), also see Dymphna to Clark, 20 September 1982; a selection of Clark's letters to Dymphna in 1982 appear in Russell, *Ever, Manning*, pp. 423–36, others are held at Manning Clark House; also see Clark on Dymphna's departure, diary, 29 August 1982.

68 Dymphna to Clark, 30 October 1984; also 7 October 1984; Clark's dreams of Dobrez, diary, 4 April 1982; Roslyn Russell to me, Canberra, March 2008.

69 Dymphna to Clark, 18 April 1985 (Manning Clark House); Dymphna to Nin Dutton, 20 October 1983, in the uncatalogued papers of Nin Dutton (NLA); Heather Rusden to me, Canberra, November 2007; on Aboriginal Treaty Committee, see Dymphna's interview with Elizabeth Cham, and Dymphna's papers, NLA, MS9873, Series 4.

70 Clark, diary, 14 May 1985.

71 Clark on his own fame, diary, 5, 20 & 25 April 1987.

72 Nicholas Brown to me, Canberra, October 2009; Roslyn Russell to me, Canberra, March 2008; Keith Dunstan to me, phone conversation, June 2009; Allan Martin to me, Canberra 1997; John Hirst to me, Sydney, March 2009; Dymphna on Clark's chirpiness over the phone, her letter to Clark, 17 September 1982 (Manning Clark House).

73 Bob Hawke to me, Sydney, June 2008.

74 Paul Keating to me, Sydney, September 2007; also see Clark to Peter Ryan, 30 January 1987, in Russell (ed.), *Ever, Manning*, p. 451.

75 White to Clark, 16 June 1980, Clark, papers, box 25, folder 209; Barry Jones to me, Melbourne, February 2008.

76 Ken Inglis, notes for Clark's obituary, courtesy Ken Inglis.

77 Phillip Adams to me, Sydney, May 2008; Dugald McLellan to me, Sydney, April 2008.

78 Reviews of Volume VI: James McLelland, *Sydney Morning Herald*, 22 August 1987; Stuart Macintyre, *Weekend Australian*, 22–23 August 1987; John Rickard, *Times on Sunday*, 23 August 1987; Brian Dickey, Adelaide *Advertiser*, 22 August 1987, Geoffrey Blainey in *Herald*, 24 August 1987; also see *Canberra Times*, 22 August 1987, and *Sydney Morning Herald* editorial, 22 August 1987; on Volume VI, Clark, papers, box 160, folders 36–40.

79 Peter Craven to Clark, 28 June 1988, *Scripsi* papers, Melbourne University Archives, box 7; see the correspondence to Clark after Volume VI in his papers, box 159, folders 27–35; Stretton to Clark, 7 August 1987, box 158, folder 27; Roderick to Ryan, 20 August 1987, papers of Peter Ryan, NLA.

80 Clark on computer, *Sydney Morning Herald*, 21 November 1984, p. 11; sales figures, *Bulletin*, 3 May 1988; Ryan to Stuart Sayers, *Age*, 16 October 73 (MUP Archives); Volume VI sold 22 000 in the first six months alone: see the article by Edmund Campion, 'Manning Clark', *Scripsi*, vol. 5, no. 2, 1989, pp. 183–7.

81 Christina Gulloto to Clark, 8 December 1988, Clark, papers, box 159, folder 9; *Sun*, 27 February 1987, p. 3; Dymphna Clark to me, Canberra 1997; 'our common mother', Alan Tate, 'Manning Clark overcomes Australia', *Sydney Morning Herald Good Weekend*, 1 August 1987.

82 Lyn Roger's letter, undated, in Clark, papers, box 8, folder 58.

83 For the correspondence relating to Clark's consultancy, see Clark, papers, box 13, folder 102.

84 Cameron in *Sydney Morning Herald*, 29 January 1988.

85 Clark, 'The Beginning of Wisdom', *Time Australia*, 25 January 1988, also see *Bulletin*, 26 January 1988; on Clark declining Hawke's invitation, Dymphna to me, Canberra 1997; among many examples of Clark's regrets on Aborigines, see *Border Mail*, 4 November 1986, p. 33.

86 John Hirst in Robert Dessaix, *Speaking Their Minds: intellectuals and the public culture in Australia*, ABC Books, Sydney, 1998, p. 198.

87 Watson in *Age*, 8 March 1985.

88 John Bell, foreword to *History of Australia: the musical*, Yackandandah Playscripts, 1994; John Timlin, 'A Little Footnote to a History of Australia', *Australian Book Review*, March 1988, pp. 46–8; Ryan on Clark, and the musical, file note on phone conversation with Tim Curnow, 25 May 1982; file note on *The Musical*, 22 January 1984 (MUP Archives).

89 Clark's notes in his papers, box 168, folder 8; *A History of Australia: the musical*, official program (held in Clark's papers (Series 23)); Clark flying to Melbourne, diary, 14 January 1988.

90 John Bell, foreword to *History of Australia: the musical*; Clark on the musical in his diary, 18 December 1987, 16 January, 8 February 1988; also see Clark in *Age*, 16 January 1988, p. 11; Watson to Clark, undated but 1988 and misfiled by Clark, papers, box 167, folder 3.

91 ibid. Bell for reviews of the musical, see Clark, papers, box 169, folder 15, where they are collected.

92 Laurie O'Brien to me, phone conversation, March 2008; Pat Gray to me, Sydney, August 2005; Michael Cathcart to me, Melbourne, June 2008; Elmer Zalums to me, phone conversation, March 2006; Elsie Macleod to Clark, undated, papers, box 159, folder 36.

93 Dostoyevsky to P Ye. Guseva, 15 October 1880, in Joseph Frank and David I Goldstein (eds) *Selected Letters of Fyodor Dostoevsky*, Rutgers University Press, New Brunswick, 1987, pp. 511–13; Frank Crowley to me, 14 April 2005.

94 Benedict Clark to me, Phillip Island, April 2008.

95 Katerina and Axel Clark, NLA interviews.

96 ibid; Katerina to Clark, 1 February 1972 (Manning Clark House); Clark on Sebastian etc., diary, 16 July 1978, 29 July 1989 (in a similar vein on Axel and his children, 16 July 1989); Clark on Axel, diary, 10 & 31 January 1980, 18 January 1988; also see Clark's letters to Axel in Russell, *Ever, Manning*—a mixture of affection and admonition.

97 David Malouf to me, Sydney, April 2008; Eirene Clark to me, Melbourne, February 2008; Dymphna to Clark, 11 September 1987 (Manning Clark House).

23: Remembering Kristallnacht

1 Richard Ellmann, 'Freud and Literary Biography', 1987, available online at http://dio.sagepub.com/cgi/reprint/35/139/70; for Clark's various epiphanies see *A Historian's Apprenticeship*, especially chapter 1; although the first three chapters contain a succession of them, his list of musical works appears on p. 50.

2 Clark interviewed by John Tranter, ABC Radio National, 17 June 1987. Rob Pascoe, 'A History of Manning Clark', *National Times*, 2 June 1978; also Clark, *Occasional Writings and Speeches*, p. 84; his interview with Hazel de Berg, NLA, 1967, and Clark, 'R.M. Crawford: some Reminiscences', *Historical Studies*, vol. 15, no. 57, October 1971, pp. 5–7, 'until that day in November 1938 at Bonn am Rhein when I looked into the heart of a great darkness'; and Clark, 'Melbourne Views', *Cultural Freedom*, Saturday 5 June 1965, 'I remember that in November 1938 I had the great good fortune to go to Germany—arriving the day after the Grunspan [sic]'. Although this earlier telling contains none of the baggage Clark would load onto the story in the late 1970s and the 1980s, it is the first recorded example of his arriving on 10 November 1938; significantly made before the death of Anna Lodewyckx in 1967 (Brian Matthews argues that Clark would not have told the story before the death of both Augustin and Anna Lodewyckx; see Matthews, *Manning Clark: a life*, p. 431).

3 Clark in Clark et al., *Making History*, pp. 57–8.

4 Clark, *Quest*, 1990, pp. 68–9, & Clark, papers, box 175, folder 16.

5 Clark, *Occasional Writings and Speeches*, 1980, p. 84.

6 Dymphna to Clark, 12 November 1938, held at Manning Clark House.

7 ibid.

8 I am grateful to Jan Nicholas for letting me listen to her taped conversation with Dymphna, recorded on 29 November 1995; also Dymphna to Carl Bridge, 14 November 1993, with kind permission of Carl Bridge; also see Dymphna Clark, papers, NLA MS9873, Series 7, box 28, "Personal Documents and papers 1941, 1979–2000, in particular, the seven-page typewritten undated manuscript, 'Memories of Germany 1933–1995', in which she writes of Clark's arrival in Bonn, 'Manning Clark soon visited me for the Oxford Christmas break', and Clark in *Quest*, 1990, p. 69. It is interesting to see how Dymphna, in her interview with Heather Rusden, dodged answering questions about her time in Germany: 'two people must always have very different memories of the same events. Manning has told parts of that story ... and they may not always be the same as the story I would tell ... I don't think I will be telling very much of the story [laughing].'

9 Brian Matthews argues that Clark's appropriation of Dymphna's story was 'his answer to the Lodewyckxs and their teutonic rage'; his full reading of the Kristallnacht episode can be found in

Manning Clark: a life, Chapter 13; for a rebuttal see John Stanley Martin, 'Augustin Lodewyckx (1876–1964) Teacher and Scholar', University of Melbourne, 2007, available online at http://www. huu.unimelb.edu.au/pdf/Martin,%20Augustin%20Lodewyckx.pdf; the first public airing of the Kristallnacht episode was my essay, 'Being There: the Strange History of Manning Clark', cover story in the *Monthly*, March 2007.

10 Clark, diary, 26 November 1938 & 15 February 1939.

11 Clark in Clark et al., *Making History*, 1985, p. 60.

12 Clark, *Quest*, 1990, p. 68; Clark, *Occasional Writings and Speeches*, 1980, p. 84; interview with Peter Ross, *The Arts on Sunday*, ABC TV, 12 April 1987; also Clark on *Talking History*, ABC Radio National, just after the release of *The Quest for Grace* in early 1990, in which Clark claims he saw the synagogues burning, recording (undated held at Manning Clark House); for the letter regarding Ehrenzeller's death, see the letter written to Clark from Basel (author unclear) in January 1991, in Clark, papers, box 176, 'Correspondence relating to Quest for Grace'.

13 Clark, *Quest*, 1990, Preface & p. 68; Dymphna to Clark, 18 November 1938, and Clark to Augustin Lodewyckx, 17 November 1938, both held at Manning Clark House.

14 Carl Bridge, 'Manning Clark and the Ratbag Tradition' (1997), available on line from the API network, http://www.api-network.com/cgi-bin/page?archives/jas55_bridge

15 Note from Beatrice Davis, 18 October 1967, regarding a phone conversation with Clark on 12 October 1967; Angus & Robertson papers, second series, Mitchell Library, MSS 3265, vol. 186, 'Charles Manning Hope Clark 1946–1969'. See also Manning Clark, 'Two Visits', in John Iggulden (ed.), *Summer's Tales 3*, Macmillan / St Martin's Press, New York, 1966, pp. 90–113.

16 Doris Lessing, *Under My Skin*, Flamingo, London, 1995 (first published 1994), pp. 12–13; JM Coetzee, 'Doris Lessing', in his *Stranger Shores: Essays 1986–1999*, Secker & Warburg, London, 2001, p. 295. Examples of Coetzee's autobiographical fiction include *Boyhood* (1997) and *Youth* (2002).

17 Jerome Bruner, *Acts of Meaning*, Harvard University Press, Cambridge, Mass., 1990, p. 121; my thanks to Inga Clendinnen for this reference.

18 Manning Clark interviewed by Tranter, ABC Radio National, 17 June 1987; Bruce Bennett, 'Literary Culture Since Vietnam', in Bennett and Jennifer Strauss (eds), *Oxford Literary History of Australia*, Oxford University Press, South Melbourne, 1998, p. 255.

19 Clark, diary, 9 December 1938; Samuel Beckett made the distinction between memory as an instrument of reference and an instrument of discovery in his *Proust and Three Dialogues* (with Georges Duthuit), John Calder, London, 1999 (first published 1965), p. 29.

20 ibid; 21 July & 1 August 1939.

21 Transcript from interview by Peter Ross with Manning Clark, *The Arts on Sunday*, 12 April 1987, reproduced by permission of the Australian Broadcasting Corporation © 1987 ABC. All rights reserved..

22 ibid; Davies (ed.), *Dear Kathleen, Dear Manning*, pp. 107–8; Clark, *Occasional Writings and Speeches*, 1980, pp. 79–88.

23 Clark with Ross; the story of visiting Cologne in 1956 appears in 'Themes in Australian History' (originally published in the *National Times* in 1978), in *Occasional Writings and Speeches*, 1980, p. 82; Clark driving along the autobahn, diary, 4 September 1956; Clark's 1990 pilgrimage in his diary, 16 July 1990; Dymphna to Jan Nicholas, 29 November 1995, recorded conversation. Remembering their first visit to Cologne in 1938, Dymphna pointed out that Clark, familiar with the Robert Schumann song that drew on the words of Heine's poem, already knew that the painting was inside the cathedral. Even in 1938, he did not discover Lochner's *painting* so much as go 'looking for it'; there is also doubt about Clark's translation of Heine's *wildniss*; as Helga Griffin argued to me in Canberra, January 2008, the word *wildniss* in German 'does not mean wildness, but is closer to wilderness as in organic or primitive or full of creativity, its meaning is more external to Heine, but Manning has translated it as "in all the wildness of my life", which is very different.' Also see Clark, diary, 15 May 1987; watching rehearsals for *The Musical*, 'When man playing me began to speak of my feelings on arriving in Bonn in November 1938 I shook & wept.'

24 Clark, *Quest*, 1991, p. 75. In his interview with Don Baker, Clark linked the Cologne Cathedral epiphany with Kristallnacht; the two dovetail. 'Not long after the episode at the Bonn railway

station I went to the cathedral at Cologne and I suppose, and I went behind the high altar ... [where] there was a painting in gold of the Virgin and it's a painting which has influenced lots of people. And I knew—I went, by the way, I went to have a look at it because I was familiar by then with a poem by Heine that in the cathedral ... there's a painting painted out of gold and leather ... and in all the wildness of my life ... it's always shone a light inside me. And I thought a lot then ... about the whole question ... about what happened at the Bonn railway station.'

25 On Dostoyevsky, see John Rowlands, *Holbein: The paintings of Hans Holbein the younger*, Phaidon, New York, 1985, pp. 52–3; Fyodor Dostoyevsky, *Crime and Punishment* (1972 reprint, Penguin Classics, London) p. 492. See also Clark, 'Fyodor Dostoyevsky', in Clark, *Speaking Out of Turn*, 1997, pp. 151–65, especially pp. 158–9, and 'Melbourne: An Intellectual Tradition', *Melbourne Historical Journal*, no. 2, 1962, pp. 17–21. In this article (p. 19) Clark mistakenly places Holbein's painting in Baden Baden instead of Basel.

26 See Clark's copy of *The Idiot*, William Heinemann, London, 1927, p. 410, bought in Stockholm, October 1938, and read at Balliol.

27 The words 'infinite power' belong to Dostoyevsky, *The Idiot*, p. 410; Clark, 'Fyodor Dostoyevsky', in *Speaking Out of Turn*, 1997, pp. 151–65, especially pp. 158–9; on Dostoyevsky and Anya, see Anya Dostoevsky, *Dostoevsky: Reminiscences*, Liveright, New York, 1975 (first published in Russian as *Vospominaniya*, by AG Dostoevskaya, Mezhkniga, Moscow 1971) and translated into English by Beatrice Stillman, pp. 133–4, 119 (where Anya lists Dostoyevsky's favourite works of art) & 153 (on Dostoyevsky in Italy in 1869).

28 Federico Garcia Lorca, *In Search of Duende*, New Directions, New York, 1998 (first published 1955), p. vii; Clark, *Quest*, 1991, p. 75.

24: 23 May 1991

1 Milan Kundera, *Testaments Betrayed*, Harper, New York, 1996, p. 129.

2 Samantha O'Donnell to me, phone conversation, November 2007; Clark, diary, 31 October 1990.

3 Clark in *Weekend Australian*, 18–19 July 1987; see Clark's annotations in DB Wyndham Lewis, *The World of Goya*, Michael Joseph, London, 1968; the passage from Ecclesiastes was among Clark's papers held at Manning Clark House.

4 Frank Sheehan to me, phone conversation, August 2010; Clark's comments on music can be found in many sources, one of the most revealing being his appearance on Radio 2CN Canberra, 31 October 1984, tape courtesy of Manning Clark House.

5 Clark's visit to Cologne, diary, 16 July 1990; Clark to McQueen, 5 September 1989; papers of Humphrey McQueen, National Library, Clark quoted the passage from Dostoyevsky's *The Possessed* on many occasions. For what was possibly the first time, see his 'Melbourne: an Intellectual Tradition', *Melbourne Historical Journal*, no. 2, 1962, pp. 17–23; Clark referring to Hardy's 'The Oxen', *Herald*, 6 June 1989; Clark on refusing to take communion, diary, 15 December 1988.

6 Humphrey McQueen to me, Canberra, June 2009; Clark to Fitzpatrick, 18 March 1987, in Davies (ed.), *Dear Kathleen, Dear Manning*, 1996, p. 101.

7 On White and Clark, McQueen to me, Canberra, June 2009; also see Clark's correspondence to McQueen, held at NLA, especially 6 & 22 October 1989; also see Clark's annotations in his copy of Gerhard Weber, *Jung: a biography*, Shambhala, Boston, 1987, held at Manning Clark House.

8 David Malouf to me, Sydney, April 2008; Barry Jones to me, Melbourne, February 2008; Clark on White, diary, 24 August 1980; Clark to McQueen, 5 September 1989, and White to Clark, 10 August 1980, Clark, papers, box 25, folder 209.

9 Dymphna to Jan Nicholas, 20 September 1993; Clark to McQueen, 29 June 1989; Clark's dream in his diary, 22 June 1984; see Clark to Patrick White, 22 February 1967, regarding a meeting with Iris Murdoch and John Bayley, in Clark, papers, box 37, folder 4; also Clark to Iris Murdoch, 31 May 1972, box 39, folder 16; Ken Inglis told me of dinner parties at Tasmania Circle attended by William Golding. Clark also continued to see Sidney Nolan when the painter visited Australia. The last time the two men saw one another was in March 1988. On 8 March, Clark wrote in his diary, 'I met Sidney Nolan ... he was charming, flirtatious, looked as though he wanted or needed some-one to take charge of him.'

10 Clark, diary, 23 August 1990; also 7 February 1990 for the wound that only death could cure and 21 September 1989 for White's shrunken appearance; also Clark to Craven, 5 October 1981, box 7, *Scripsi* papers, Melbourne University Archives.

11 Clark, diary, 30 September 1990.

12 Clark on La Nauze, diary, 13 March 1990 and 23 August 1990; John Legge to me, Melbourne, November 2006; Clark on contemporaries, diary, 15 August 1988.

13 Clark complaining of nausea, lack of energy and of fictional sketch, see his diary, 29 December 1990.

14 Clark on ALP, Mark O'Connor to me, Canberra, November 2008; Hardy's 'Wessex Heights' is in Claire Tomalin, *The Poems of Thomas Hardy*, Penguin, Harmondsworth, 2006, pp. 128−30; re Job and Sermon on the Mount, Clark to Kathleen Fitzpatrick, 2 February 1985, in Davies (ed.), *Dear Kathleen, Dear Manning*, p. 66; 'people from another planet', Clark to McQueen, 5 September 1989; Pat Gray to Clark, 17 September 1990, in Clark, papers, box 172, folder 29.

15 I saw the scratching in Clark's desk drawer in 2005. The paper has since been removed. Clark in Italy, diary, 28 July 1992; also see 11 July 1990, 'I find the young & middle-aged women have small, hard looking, coarse grained bosoms, not stirring to an old man, or even a reminder. I notice the fondling does not include touching breasts and cunts−a surface titillation. Do they experience the peace, the grace that can come after making love or is it all frenetic sex ... rather than the awareness, the recognition and the embrace' (Clark was also in Italy to launch the Italian translation of *A Short History of Australia*); Clark on the fall of the Wall, in *The Catholic Leader*, 24 December 1989.

16 Clark on the Gulf War, *Sunday Age*, 19 August 1990; as possible envoy, *Sunday Telegraph*, 28 October 1990; on ARM, see Franca Arena to Clark, 1 November 1990, in Clark, papers, box 18, folder 143; on Tiananmen Square, see Clark in *Speaking Out of Turn*, 1997; on shutting up and bucket of filth, see Clark in *Canberra Times*, 5 October 1989.

17 Clark to Harris, 23 March 1991, in Russell (ed.), *Ever, Manning*, pp. 476−7; Leunig to Clark, 12 April 1991, in Clark, papers, box 160, folder 41; also see *Examiner*, 30 April 1991.

18 On Clark's notes to Dymphna's parents (found after his death), Wilma Robb to me, October 2007, Manning Clark House; Dymphna's notes on the manuscripts of *The Quest for Grace* in Clark, papers, box 173, folders 1−4. Clark's note to Dymphna regarding angina I found in a yellow folder labelled 'sources of ideas', at the back of the filing cabinet in his study, Manning Clark House. Wilma Robb also told me that Clark left similar notes around the house for Dymphna in his last months; also Benedict Clark to me, Phillip Island, April 2008.

19 Dymphna on Clark to Bill Bunbury, Radio National interview; David Malouf to me, Sydney, April 2008.

20 I am grateful to Nicholas Brown, Heather Rusden and Eva Manikus, all of whom shared their recollections of Clark's death with me.

After Life

1 See Clark's will (1989) in his papers, box 193, folder 60; also Order of Service for his funeral, 27 May 1991, Manning Clark House.

2 Keating's visit, Sebastian Clark to me, Canberra, March 2007; also see *Canberra Times*, 28 May 1991.

3 David Malouf to me, Sydney, April 2008; Clark to Russell Clark, 26 September 1983, courtesy Eirene Clark; on the funeral, Allan Martin to Ken Inglis, undated but shortly after the funeral, courtesy Ken Inglis.

4 Recording of Clark's funeral, courtesy Sebastian Clark; also Don Baker to Ken Inglis, 5 June 1991; courtesy Ken Inglis.

5 ibid; Sebastian Clark to me, Canberra, September 2008; Bob Reece to me, Canberra, August 2005; Katerina Clark to me, September 2010; Iain McCalman to me, Sydney, September 2010; Dymphna on Sebastian in her undated letter to Ken & Amirah Inglis (probably June 1991), courtesy Ken Inglis.

6 Paul Keating to me, Sydney, September 2007; Helen Garner to me, Melbourne, June 2008.

7   Iain McCalman to me, Sydney, September 2010; Bob Reece to me, Canberra, August 2005; John Eddy to me, Canberra, September 2006.

8   Dymphna to Amirah and Ken Inglis, undated but June 1991, and Don Baker to Ken Inglis, 5 June 1991, both letters courtesy Ken Inglis.

9   All the letters of condolence can be found in the papers of Dymphna Clark, MS9873/9/7, box 33; I am grateful to Barry Humphries for his recollections of Manning, email correspondence, November 2010.

10 Kemp, *Canberra Times*, 2 June 1991; Ian Hancock's notes for the speech he delivered to the ANU History Department in May 1991, courtesy Ian Hancock; also see 'The Parliament of the Commonwealth of Australia; A Tribute to the Memory of Emeritus Professor Manning Clark, AC, containing the condolence motion speeches of various members of the House of Representatives of 28 May 1991', including Prime Minister Bob Hawke, Opposition Leader John Hewson and several others; for newspaper editorials see *Age*, 25 May 1991, *Launceston Examiner*, 25 May 1991; also see obituary in *The Times*, 25 May 1991, *Independent*, 27 May 1991, *Canberra Times*, 24 May 1991, Max Harris, *Australian*, 25 May 1991, and Barry Oakley, *Australian*, 24 May 1991.

11 Dymphna to Ken Inglis, 27 August 1991, courtesy Ken Inglis; for Dymphna's thank you, see the Return Thanks Column, *Canberra Times*, 6 July 1991.

12 Graeme Powell to me, Canberra, April 2008.

13 Clark, diary, 3–7 December 1973, 23 April 1985, 15 July 1987, 19 April 1989, 11 July 1990.

14 Katerina Clark to me, Wapengo, March 2006; Dymphna's remark is entered in the margin of Clark's diary, 24 March 1943.

15 Dymphna to Wilma Robb, Robb to me, Canberra, October 2007.

16 Ryan affair reported in *Australian*, *Age* and *Sydney Morning Herald*, 27 August 1993; also see *Canberra Times*, 27 August 1993; Ryan's *Quadrant* article, 'Manning Clark', is collected in his *Lines of Fire: Manning Clark & Other Writings*, Clarion, Sydney, 1997, pp. 179–213; Robert Manne's critique of Clark's *History* appeared in *The Australian's Review of Books*, October 1996, pp. 81–91; also see his comments in *The Weekend Australian*, 28–29 August 1993, p. 4; Geoffrey Blainey, 'Drawing up a Balance Sheet of Our History', *Quadrant*, vol. 37, nos 7–8, July–August 1993, pp. 10–15.

17 Peter Ryan, 'Manning Clark', in *Lines of Fire*, pp. 179–213; Ryan also claimed that Clark had misrepresented his former teacher, Macmahon Ball; also see John Hirst 'Australian History and European Civilisation' *Quadrant*, May 1993, pp. 28–38, and Peter Craven's review of the Cathcart abridgement in the *Age*, 23 June 1994.

18 Colin Roderick to Peter Ryan, 28 August 1993 (which includes Ferguson's comments in 1978), papers of Peter Ryan, box 10, folder 4.

19 Paul Keating to me, Sydney, September 2007; details of Kemp's contact with Ryan in Ryan's papers, box 10, folder 3.

20 Ryan's note regarding Keating in his papers, box 10, folder 4; the perception that Keating was channeling Clark can also be found in international coverage such as the British conservative intellectual Paul Johnson's review of Michael Cathcart's abridgement of Clark's six volumes in *Times Literary Supplement*, 13 May 1994; it is also important to remember that Clark's work was not as political as that of other historians. Consider the bold statements of position by some of Clark's contemporaries: history is 'the struggle between the organised rich and the organised poor' (Brian Fitzpatrick, in *A Short History of the Australian Labor Movement*, Melbourne, Rawson's Bookshop 1940); 'I am for the weak not the strong, the poor not the rich, the exploited many not the select few' (Russel Ward, in the preface to the 1987 edition of his *Concise History of Australia*, University of Queensland Press, St. Lucia 1992); 'This book is deliberately biased' (Humphrey McQueen in his introduction to *Aborigines, Race and Racism*, Penguin, Ringwood, Vic., 1974); 'This history is critical not celebratory. It rejects myths of national progress and unity. It starts from a recognition that Australian settler society was built on invasion and dispossession' (Verity Burgmann and Jenny Lee's introduction to *Making a Life: A People's History of Australia*, Penguin, Ringwood, Vic., 1988). Nowhere in Clark's histories did he seek to reveal his political sympathies so openly.

21 Peter Ryan to me, phone conversation, 31 May 2007; Robert Manne to me, Melbourne, March 2007; Dugald McLellan to me, Sydney, April 2008.

22 Roslyn Russell to me, Canberra, March 2008.

23 Ryan's note is in his papers, box 10, folder 4; the story broke in the *Courier Mail*, weekend edition, 24 August 1996.

24 ibid; I am grateful to Robert Manne for his summary of the correspondence he received from Les Murray in June 1997.

25 James Button, 'Man versus Myth', *Age Saturday Extra*, 23 November 1996; the words 'resonance of myth' belong to Button, whose article was by far the best piece of journalism on the affair. Howard's remarks quoted in *Courier Mail*, 31 August 1996; on the Press Council complaint, Bruce Grant to me, Melbourne, March 2007; on the Russian government confirming that Clark was not a spy, *Canberra Times*, 7 November 1996; essential references for the *Courier Mail* affair include McQueen's *Suspect History* (1997), Holt's *A Short History of Manning Clark* (1999) and Stuart Macintyre & Anna Clark, *The History Wars*, MUP, Carlton, Vic., 2003 (Chapter four). For ongoing evidence of conservatives failing to understand Clark, see John Howard's speech, reported in *Australian*, 4 October 2006; celebrating the fiftieth anniversary of *Quadrant*, Howard reminded dinner guests that Manning Clark was one of many intellectuals in postwar Australia who had championed 'the collectivist ideology' of communism. In the eyes of many Australian conservatives, said Howard, Clark was much more than a communist sympathiser; he was also responsible for casting Australian history as 'a litany of sexism, racism and class warfare'. Howard seemed unaware, as did so many commentators after the speech was reported, that Clark sat on the editorial board of *Quadrant* in the early 1960s.

26 Clark to Ian Milner, 25 November 1990, papers of Ian Milner, Alexander Turnbull Library, Wellington, New Zealand, MS4567012; also see Clark's letter to the Soviet Ambassador in Canberra, 11 November 1974, in which he apologises for missing 'the ceremony on 7 November to mark the anniversary of the great October Revolution ... I find it reassuring to go to your ceremony each year because it is a reminder of an event which contained the promise of better things for mankind', in Clark's papers, box 39, folder 21; Clark's speech in Moscow, 1970, reprinted in the *Australian*, 16 June 1997; also see his diary entries, 15-27 June 1970.

27 Dymphna to Santamaria, 8 June 1997, and his reply, 17 June 1997 (both letters courtesy of Dymphna, who copied them for me in 1998); Santamaria's article, *Australian*, 31 May 1997.

28 Dymphna to Jean Dunn, 27 January 1997, MUP Archives, University of Melbourne; also Dymphna quoted in Mark Metherell, 'An Agent of Controversy', *Canberra Times*, 28 August 1996, p. 11; and my own conversations with Dymphna Clark in 1998.

29 These paragraphs are based on entries in my own diary, 1997-99.

30 See Dymphna's 1997 typed document on Manning Clark House in her papers, MS 9873/7/2 3, in which she notes 'Manning could not contemplate the sale of the house and its probable demolition to make way for yet another exclusive residential development. Nor could I.' Dymphna also noted that the house and grounds were placed on the Interim Heritage Places Register of the Australian Capital Territory in 1994. I am grateful to John Thompson, who sat on the committee for Manning Clark House, for passing on his recollections to me, Sydney, August 2010; 'above all', said Thompson, 'Dymphna wanted Manning Clark House to be a place where ideas were discussed and shared and where various kinds of creative and intellectual enterprise might be supported and encouraged'; on Dymphna's bequest, Sebastian Clark to me, Canberra, September 2010; also see Dymphna's 'Note on the Text', in Clark, *Speaking Out of Turn*, 1997, pp. xv-xvi.

31 My thanks to Darleen Bungey, who sent me her notes from her interview with Dymphna, conducted in November 1999; on Dymphna's illness, Katerina Clark to me, September 2010.

32 Dymphna's memories are drawn from her interview with Elizabeth Cham for the National Library.

33 Wilma Robb to me, Canberra, October 2007. Katerina recalled Dymphna's death: 'Wilma kept a vigil beside Mum and Andrew was writing something in Dad's study. He came down to see how Mum was and Wilma said Mum's breathing was getting shallower and she thought Mum was going, so Andrew stayed in the room and was there when she died. He then immediately woke up Sebastian and me'. Katerina Clark to me, email, January 2011.

Index

Note: page numbers in bold face indicate illustrations.

as older man, 22, 26–9, 31–2, **35**, **38**, 85, 551, 583, **629**, 671–2; alienation, 667, 668; frailty, **659**; reminiscence of childhood and past, 45, 47, 48–9, 58, 81, 82, 93, 192, 202, 301; reflections on his parents' lives, 44–8, 69, 71, 78, 80, 83, 202, 280

on *Quadrant*'s editorial advisory board, 387, 397, 412, 779 n. 25

relationship with Dymphna, 30, 64, 168–9; and affairs/infidelities, 30, 321–4, 325, 329, 331, 338, 376, 389, 391, 424, 514, 524, 525, 535, 601–2, 671; courtship, 8, 115–21, 144, 150, 319, criticism and judgement of her, 35, 159, 224, 515, 523, 668; doubts, 181, 322; expectations, 150–1, 183–4, 685; estrangement, 69, 530–4; as important to his career and state of mind, 145–6, 167, 174, 183, 186, 188, 225, 276, 324, 386, 424, 465, 514–15, 516, 584; jealousy, 144; love, 61, 63, 116, 136, 158, 180, 185, 271, 516, 517, 671; married life (earlier years) 170, 187, 191, 224, 275, 318 (later years), 550, 622, 670–1 (middle years), 344, 345, 372, 375, 384, 513–14, **535**; meeting, 116–17; tensions and conflict, 224, 225, 303, 320, 464–5, 518–19, 520; unhappiness, 319, 323, 328, 460

relationship with in-laws, 171, 187, 202, 266, 280, 281, 288, 344, 523, 671

relationship with parents, 67, 69; father, 56, 71–2, 279, 280; mother, 45, 61, 63, 64, 65–6, 69, 170, 279

and relations with women other than Dymphna, 9–10, 12, 16, 184, 216, 252, 371, 522, 533, 662; affairs and infidelities, 30, 321–4, 325, 326–8, 329, 331, 506, 524, 525, 526–8, 532, 601–2, 604, 628; friendships, 3, 10, 16, 18, 229, 299, 337, 394, 407, 466, 522, 523, 527, 529, 554, 678; sexism, 9, 496–8

schooling: Melbourne Grammar (as boarder), 8, 60, 81, 89–90, **91**, 92, 94–6, 184, 206

and siblings, 60, 63, 78, 79, 116, 170, 281, 310; rivalry with Russell, 60

social life, 153, 172–3, 288, 301–2, 510–11, 519, 542, 544, 583, 601, 608, 664, 691; and students and colleagues, 12, 269, 508–9, 527, 541, 679–80

spirituality and religion, 18, 22, 57, 82, 117, 281, 284, 329, 359–60, 361–2, 388, 403, 404, 412, 472, 517, 546, 579, 601; anguish, 320, 391–2; and Catholicism, 22, 26–7, 361,

376–7, 388, 389, 390–1, 394, 406, 515, 646, 653, 659–60, 676; and (lack of) faith, 100, 101, 182, 214, 282, 376, 660–1, 677, 680; and figure of Christ, 22, 25, 101, 179–80, 246, 283, 319, 376, 377, 418, 424, 434, 607, 659, 661; and mysticism, 284, 642, 649, 652

student at Trinity College, University of Melbourne, 8, 11, 98–101, 111, 184; drawn into debates, 98, 105, 106; inspired about history, 104, 106; reads for a Bachelor of Education, 119 (incomplete), 218, 219; skips lectures, 98, 100; subjects, 98, 100, 101, 104, 109

studies at Balliol College, Oxford, 61, 134, 135–6, 139–41, 145–6, 149, 152, 167, 168–70, 174–5, 184; reading on the nineteenth century, 153, 174, 175–8, 186, 187

under suspicion, 263, 264, 273, 274, 394, 396; as communist, 264, 395

travel in Australia, 4, 118, 294–6, 385, 423, 466–7, 468, 477, 479, 481–4, 584, 605, 608, 612

travel overseas: Asia (South-East), 15, 349, 352–5, **356**, 357–63, 371, 467 (China), 605; England, 15, 36, 61, 82, 327, 365–9, 372, 376, 381, 469, 470–1, 472–3, 475–6, 513, 517, 576; Europe (in 1938), 61, 64, 65, 69, 120, 129–30, 157–8, 161–3, 637, 640–2 (later), 467, 468, 471, 513–14, 516–17, 590, 605, 650, 652, 668; France, 179–80; Germany, 372, 373, 661; Holland, 367, 372–3; Ireland, 15, 36, 73, 367, 369, 376, 478; Italy, 374, 376–7, 777 n. 15; New Zealand, 15, 383–4, 467, 605; Russia/ Soviet Union, 13, 394, 399, 400–1, **402**, 403–5, 692, 695; Scotland, 15, 369; Spain, 473; United States, 15, 16, 25, 26, 83, 450, 467, 471, 559, 576

tussle between love for Australia and pull of Europe, 129, 137, 138, 177, 197–9, 201, 381, 382, 546, 571

visits to Melbourne from Canberra, 12, 45, 277, 282, 293, 304, 321, 322, 337, 343

wins scholarships and prizes, 92–3, 94, 96, 98, 101, 120

as young man: attachment to his childhood, 69, 70; delivers sermon, 66; holidays, 118; intellectual formation, 96–7, 98, 99, 100, 117, 640; offers to do voluntary work, 247; reading, 70, 98, 99, 100, 230, 232–3, 235 (history), 219–20, 230; separation from parents, 61–3,

64, 68, 69, 70, 224

materialism, 563; politics, 529, 564–5, 567–70, 572–3, 576, 577, 578–9, 585–6, 595, 598, 611–12, 669

radio broadcasts and debates, 259–60, 263–4, 552, 562–3, 739 n. 19; presents Boyer Lectures, 587

television programs and appearances, 437, 541, 552–3, 578, 616, 671

WRITING AND PUBLICATIONS

and Aboriginal people, 95–6, 295, 455, 481, 485–6

as adolescent, 94, 95–6, 106

as angst-ridden process, search, 37, 40, 80–1, 212–13, 214, 219, 653

articles, letters to the editor, essays, 93, 220, 225, 226, 228, 232, 350, 386, 388, 437, 440 (on Soviet Russia), 406–7; as public figure, 528–9, 550, 553, 555, 560, 561, 566, 567, 568, 569, 572–3, 577, 585, 592, 619; rejected, 226, 231

autobiography, 426, 633, 645–6; and accuracy, 646–7, 652, 667; *A Historian's Apprenticeship*, 374, 691; *The Puzzles of Childhood*, 27, 47, 75 (portrait of parents), 58–9, 60, 61, 65; *The Quest for Grace*, 27, 33–4, 120, 172, 192, 214, 636, 638, 641, 642, 643, 644, 651, 666–7, 668 (portrait of parents), 67, 79

compulsion and motivation to write, 160, 213, 413, 520; as aid to thought, 180–1, 319, 514; for an audience and posterity, 30, 31–2, 34, 37, 39, 217, 254, 259, 279, 420, 607; recording his experience and inner life, 8, 27, 68, 93–4, 100, 159, 162, 181, 199, 217–18, 221, 279–80, 282, 323, 403, 515, 570; record keeping, 28, 29, 32–3, 421

correspondence, 18, 27, 29, 31, 34, 40, 167, 218, 233–4, 261–2, 325, 338–9, 386, 398–9, 407–8, 476, 477, 549, 553, 555, 556, 571, 583, 591–2, 600, 612, 661–2, 663, 670, 695; as deep form of communication, 47, 62–3, 525–6, 671, 676; with Dymphna, 114, 117, 118–19, 122, 374–5, 376, 671 (early years), 134, 135, 137, 140, 141–7, 148–51, 155, 159, 164, 165, 166, 167, 182, 183–4, 185, 186, 636–7, 638, 642–3 (later years), 532, 565, 576, 584, 602–3, 604–5, 606–7 (middle years), 275–6, 282, 286, 325, 385, 386, 401–2, 403, 513–19, 520, 523, 524–5, 527; *Ever, Manning* (posthumous collection), 30; to family, 61, 62–3, 64, 70, 78, 128, 129, 135–6, 137, 137, 153, 163, 164, 167,

170, 171, 178, 310–11, 385–6, 400, 451, 468, 643, 676; to his 'muses', 520, 524, 525, 528, 529–30, 535; with politicians, 564, 565, 576, 609, 752 n. 17

diaries and notebooks, 27, 29, 31, 33, 36, 39, 61, 68, 71, 76, 77, 100, 157, **158**, 159, 169, 171, 181, 191, 212, 217, 224, 235, 325–6, 345, 371–2, 384, 386, 523, 550, 553, 583, 684–5; as catharsis, 37, 221; experimenting with ideas, 225–6, 230–1, 245, 355, 362, 366–7, 368, 590–1; and his literary persona, 193, 220, 272, 367, 434–5; reflections and impressions, 243, 353, 357, 362, 400, 401, 403, 406, 411, 481–4, 499, 576, 607, 628, 640, 646, 651, 655–6, 668, 695; and women, 459, 604

creative imagination, 19, 94, 146, 653; ability to tell a story, 95; and history writing, 220, 221–2, 333, 367, 368, 370, 379, 435, 470

handwriting, 29, **254**, 379, 462, 506, 565, 637

A History of Australia, 420, 426, 434, 455, 467; bases and development, 386, 388, 389, 453–4, 457, 474–5; impact, 22, 440; influences, 220, 284–5, 424, 474, 478, 488, 578; nationalist bent in last three volumes, 93, 560, 589, 626; sales and popularity, 438, 454, 456, 458, 461, 569, 589, 592, 596, 597, 598, 614, 615, 627, 756 n. 14; as serialised public drama, 82, 437–8; Volume I, 13, 28, 81, 362, 431, **433**, 455, 456, 465, 757 n. 18 (impact), 438, 440–1 (launch), 438, 441 (writing and rewriting), 225, 312, 367, 368, 377–9, 382, 386, 442, 443, 571; Volume II, 81, 420, 433, 451, 453, 459, 460, 465, 469, 470, 474, 477, 478, 524, 564 (writing), 457, 463, 469, 473, 571; Volume III, 433, 458, 461, 477, 545 (prize), 569 (writing), 463, 464, 471, 477, 478, 528; Volume IV, 460, 477, 589, 593 (launch), 588 (writing), 477, 478, 484–8; Volume V, 420, 578, 581, 594, 596–8, 612, 626 (launch), 594, 608; Volume VI, 43–4, 466, 614, 615, 626 (launch), 424, 613

history-writing style and technique, 191–2, 335, 369, 438, 441, 461, 470, 488, 589; and Aborigines, 619, 767 n. 3 (ch. 21); characterisation, 389–90, 456, 457–8, 459, 460, 484–5, 486, 578, 621, 645; language, 455, 458–9, 465, 474; and myth, 478, 486, 598; narrative history, 220, 432, 438, 460, 466, 478, 598; and place and atmosphere, 146, 235, 237, 286, 369, 467, 468, 469–71, 484, 485, 486,

Pringle, John Douglas, 341, 437

Quiros, Pedro Fernandez de, 388, 389, 442

Ramsay, John, 215–16, 217, 218
Raphael
  Madonna, 652
  St Cecilia, 653
Reece, Bob, 7, 452, 492, 511, 678, 680
Reed, John, 227, 287
Rembrandt, 571
  Return of the Prodigal Son, 418
Reynolds, Margaret (MC's half-sister), 75–6,
  77, 78, 79, 80
Richardson, Henry Handel, 70, 235
  The Fortunes of Richard Mahony, 272, 634
Rigby, Harry, 403–5
Roberts, Stephen, 99, 250
Roderick, Colin, 272, 591, 592, 614, 688
Roe, Michael, 251, 448
Romanova, Helena, 407, 408
Ross, Peter, 647–8, 649, 650
royal commissions
  on Communism (Vic), 273, 394
  on Espionage, 337, 351, 394, 395, 396, 397
Ruggiero, Guido de: *History of European
  Liberation*, 175
Rusden, Heather, 18, 67, 164, 554, 605, 673
Russell, Roslyn, 32, 601–2, 604, 608
Russia, 285, 399, 403
  Russian Revolution, 96, 228, 400, 695
Ryan, Lyndall, 443, 468, **512**, 522, 524, 525,
  526, 527–8, 529–30, 535, 600–1, 604, 606
Ryan, Peter, 241, 243, 248, 438, 451, 454, **455**,
  459, 464, 485, 502, 542, 545, 588, 591, 610,
  614, 689–90, 770 n. 46
  cynicism of, 621–2
  Lines of Fire, 690
  views on MC's work, 448, 463, 596–7, 690;
  attacks *H of A*, 686–9, 691

Santamaria, BA, 105–6, 351, 394, 696–7
Sayers, Stuart, 444, 588, 596, 597
Scollay, Moira, 496–7
Scott, Ernest, 99, 101–2, 109, 250, 263
  A Short History of Australia, 440
Serle, Geoffrey, 230, 240, 251, 445–6, 599
Shaw, AGL, 31, 111, 191, 209, 449, 450, 451,
  455–6, 462, 465, 594, 721 n. 3
  at Balliol with MC, 138, 145, 154, 168, 170,

  172, 185
  at Melbourne, 321
  The Story of Australia, 440
Shead, Garry: *DH Lawrence at Thirroul*, **236**
Sheehan, Frank, 659–60, 680
Slessor, Kenneth
  'Five Bells', 305, 329, 334
  One Hundred Poems, 329
Soviet Union, 99, 228, 411
  and culture, 399–400, 405; Soviet Writers'
  Union, 399, 402, 406
  MC's thoughts and impressions, 398, 400,
  401–2, 405, 406–8, 695; blinded to realities,
  403, 410
  postwar, 261, 262, 394, 398, 399; Gulag, 392
  in World War II, 230, 245
Spanish Civil War, 104–5, 166
Stalin, Joseph, 99, 262, 392–3
Stephensen, PR, 260, 287
  Foundations of Australian Culture, 146, 227
Steven, Margaret, 23, 496, 599
Stewart, Douglas, 410, 556
Stretton, Hugh, 239, 614–15
Sumner, Humphrey, 141, 170, 174, 177, 178,
  181, 190
Sutherland, Wendy, 47, 625
Sydney, 50, 53
  Mitchell Library, 10, 252, 279
  St Peters, 49–50
  MC's impression, 118–19

Taylor, AJP, 174–5, 333
  The Hapsburg Monarchy 1848–1914, 174
Taylor, Gwen, 5, 229, 241, 243, 299
Thompson, John, 494, 495, 496, 779 n. 30
Thompson, Marjorie, 74–5, 76, 78, 80
Timlin, John, 620, 622
Tocqueville, Alexis de, 177–8, 179, 186, 187,
  199, 219
  Democracy in America, 177
Tolstoy, Leo, 5, 37, 282, 405, 420
  Anna Karenina, 117, **426, 427**, 554
  My Confession, 622
  The Resurrection, 100
Toynbee, Arnold, 139, 175, 178, 553
Tranter, John, 11, 635, 645
Trevelyan, GM, 175, 176
Tucker, Albert, 227, 286
Turner, Ian, 249, 251, 252, 273, 399, 408

United States, 197, 229, 285, 358, 395–6, 559
universities in Australia, 97, 105, 227
  expansion, 436, 499, 503
University of Melbourne, 97–8, 233, 239, 244,
  247–8, 676
  academic independence, 107, 273; and public
  debate, 264–5
  history department, 99, 101–2, 104, 107, 109,
  245, 250, 253, 263, 275, 282, 338, 341, 456,
  496
  MC's love–hate attitude, 302, 303
  political debate, 104, 105–6, 263; student
  politics, 248–9
  Trinity College, 98, 99, 106
University of Sydney, 97, 250, 251

Victoria
  Black Friday bushfires, 64
  censorship in, 97
  centenary, 98, 100
  'infantile paralysis' epidemic, 63–4

Wagner, Richard
  Lohengrin, 424
  Tristan and Isolde, 662
Ward, John Manning, 442, 466
Ward, Russel, 205–6, 215, 318, 335–6, 455, 589,
  625
  The Australian Legend, 335, 440
Waten, Judah, 398, 400, 401, **402**, 409, 411, 573
Waterhouse, Jill, 496, 498, 521, 523, 682
Watson, Don, 621, 623, 689
Webb, Jessie, 98, 102
Webb, Sharon, 669–70
Welborn, Suzanne, 466, 467
Wentworth, William Charles, 396, 458, 459,
  460, 470–1

White, Pat, 3–4
White, Patrick, 564, 569, 574, 580, 585, 594,
  611, 682
  and Australia, 288, 431, 557, 570, 577, 579
  The Eye of the Storm, 571
  Flaws in the Glass, 664
  and MC, 475, 476, 477, 588, 592, 612, 616,
  634, 660, 663–5
  Riders in the Chariot, 476, 571
  The Solid Mandala, 571
  The Tree of Man, 370, 379, 476
  The Twyborn Affair, 660
  The Vivisector, 571
  Voss, 286, 287, 370, 432, 476, 477, 485, 488,
  660
Whitlam, Gough, 396, 528, 530, 561, 566, 570,
  580
  and MC, 564, 565, 567, 568, 569, 572, 573,
  574–5, 576–7, 580–1, **582**, 586, 587, 588, 594,
  609, 693, 769 n. 23
Whitlam government, 557, 567, 571, 575, 576,
  577, 693
  dismissal of, 576, 578, 584, 595, 612
Williams, Bid, 241–2, 243, 555–6
Williams, Mick, 555–6
Williams, Tennessee, 422–3
Wills, William, 477, 478, 480–1, 483, 484, 485,
  486
Woolf, Virginia, 83, 190, 379
World War I, 123
World War II, 65, 173, 244, 245
  in Europe, 180, 181, 190–1, 209
  in the Pacific, 229, 245
Wright, Judith, 29, 431, 565, 580, 605

Zainuddin, Ailsa (nee Thomson), 45, 323, 353

THIS BOOK WAS DESIGNED BY PFISTERER+FREEMAN

THIS BOOK WAS TYPESET BY J&M TYPESETTING

THE TEXT WAS SET IN 11 POINT CASLON

WITH 15½ POINTS OF LEADING

THE TEXT WAS PRINTED ON 100 GSM WOODFREE

THIS BOOK WAS EDITED BY SALLY MOSS

Tuesday 28th November.

...of it. they were not even in possession,
...be justified Italian & German
Claim by the analogy ...
...ily & Italy – in the interests of the
...tion. this is a dangerous principle

...day 29th November.

...with the Dutch ...ländisch
...first they sang songs, mainly military
...German play. boys clapped, joyfully
...ing. We bought a bottle of beer each,
...good dancing. We met a young Englishman
...Wilkes, a man with a bitter, red face,
...the pride & arrogance of the German
...men. They asked us to ...